THE WRITINGS
of JOHN

THE WRITINGS
of JOHN

A Survey of the Gospel, Epistles, and Apocalypse

C. MARVIN PATE

ZONDERVAN

ZONDERVAN

The Writings of John
Copyright © 2011 by C. Marvin Pate

This title is also available as a Zondervan ebook. Visit www.zondervan.com/ebooks.

Requests for information should be addressed to:

Zondervan, 3900 *Sparks Dr. SE, Grand Rapids, Michigan 49546*

This edition: ISBN 978-0-310-53067-1

Library of Congress cataloged the previous edition as follows:

Pate, C. Marvin, 1952-.
    The writings of John : a survey of his Gospel, Epistles, and Apocalypse / C. Marvin Pate.
       p. cm.
    Includes index.
    ISBN 978-0-310-26737-9 (hardcover)
    1. Bible. N.T. John — Criticism, interpretation, etc. 2. Bible. N.T. Epistles of John — Criticism,
interpretation, etc. 3. Bible. N.T. Revelation — Criticism, interpretation, etc. I. Title.
    BS2601.P38 2011
    226.5'061 — dc22
                                                      2009046395

Cover design: www.wdesigncompany.com
Cover photography: Bridgeman Art Library
Interior design: Ben Fetterley

Printed in the United States of America

Contents

PART 3: REVELATION

List of Abbreviations

AnBib	Analecta biblica
Ant.	*Jewish Antiquities*
AUSS	*Andrews University Seminary Studies*
CBQ	*Catholic Biblical Quarterly*
CD	Cairo Genizah copy of the *Damascus Document*
HTR	*Harvard Theological Review*
ICC	International Critical Commentary
JBL	*Journal of Biblical Literature*
JSNT	*Journal for the Study of the New Testament*
JSOT	*Journal for the Study of the Old Testament*
JSOTSup	Journal for the Study of the Old Testament: Supplement Series
J.W.	*Jewish War*
LCL	Loeb Classical Library
LXX	Septuagint
Neot	*Neotestamentica*
NICNT	New International Commentary on the New Testament
NIGTC	New International Greek Testament Commentary
NovTSup	Novum Testamentum Supplements
NTS	*New Testament Studies*
SBLDS	Society of Biblical Literature Dissertation Series
SNTSMS	Society for New Testament Studies Monograph Series
STB	Hermann L. Strack and Paul Billerbeck, *Kommentar zum Neuen Testament aus Talmud und Midrash*
TOTP	The Old Testament Pseudepigrapha
TV	*Teología y vida*
WBC	Word Biblical Commentary
WUNT	Wissenschaftliche Untersuchungen zum Neuen Testament
ZNW	*Zeitschrift für die neutestamentliche Wissenschaft und die Kunde der älteren Kirche*

For the abbreviations of the Dead Sea Scrolls, see the list of Extrabiblical Writings.

Extrabiblical Writings

DEAD SEA SCROLLS FROM QUMRAN

Thanksgiving Hymns	1QH
Isaiah, copies a and b	1QIsa[a,b]
War Scroll	1QM
Commentary on Habakkuk	1QpHab
Rule of the Community	1QS
Rule of the Congregation	1QSa
Florilegium	4QFlor
Eschatological Midrashim	4QMidrEschat
Miqsat Ma'aseh Ha-Torah	4QMMT
Prayer of Nabonidus	4QPrNab
Pseudo-Daniel	4QpsDan ar[a,b,c]
Songs of the Sabbath	4QŠirŠabb[a-h]
Testimonia	4QTest
Geniza Damascus Document	6QD
Melchizedek Text	11QMelch
Psalms Scroll	11QPs[a]
Temple Scroll	11QT[a,b]

OLD TESTAMENT APOCRYPHA

1 Esdras
2 Esdras
Tobit
Judith
The Additions to the Book of Esther
Wisdom of Solomon
Ecclesiasticus, or the Wisdom of Jesus Son of Sirach
Baruch
Letter of Jeremiah
Prayer of Azariah
Song of the Three Young Men
Susanna
Bel and the Dragon
Prayer of Manasseh

1 Maccabees
2 Maccabees
Psalm 151

OLD TESTAMENT PSEUDEPIGRAPHA

This list includes the most significant works and is not exhaustive.

2 Baruch
1 Enoch
4 Ezra (= 2 Esdras 3–14)
Book of Jubilees
Letter of Aristeas
Life of Adam and Eve
Psalms of Solomon
Sibylline Oracles
Testaments of the Twelve Patriarchs
3 Maccabees
4 Maccabees
Ascension of Isaiah

NEW TESTAMENT APOCRYPHA

This list includes well-known apocrypha apart from Nag Hammadi.

I. Gospels and Related Forms
    A. Narrative Gospels and Acts
        1. *Gospel of the Hebrews*
        2. *Gospel of Peter*
        3. *Infancy Gospel of Thomas*
        4. *Protevangelium of James*
        5. *Acts of Paul (and Thecla)*
II. Letters
    A. Correspondence between Paul and Seneca
    B. Paul's Letter to the Laodiceans
III. Liturgical Materials
    A. *Odes of Solomon*

Introduction

Welcome to the wonderful world of the writings of the apostle John! As we will soon see, evidence strongly indicates that John, the beloved disciple of Jesus Christ, wrote the fourth gospel, the epistles of John, and Revelation—books scholars label the "Johannine literature." Many interpreters of the Bible regard these works of John as the apex of divine revelation, and for good reason. The Christology (doctrine of Christ) of the Johannine literature is more exalted than that of any other biblical author. For John, Jesus Christ is God from eternity past (John 1:1–18), yet he is fully human in the present (so 1, 2, and 3 John). For the Beloved Disciple, Jesus is both the Lamb of Calvary (John 1:29, 36; 19) and the conquering Lion-Lamb of history (Rev. 6). Little wonder then that the later church councils drew heavily on John's portrait of Jesus to craft their christological creeds, confessions that set in place the parameters of orthodoxy.

John's eschatology is breathtaking, catapulting the blessings of the end times back into the present: the indwelling of the Holy Spirit, the new birth, eternal life, and much, much more. John's soteriology (the doctrine of salvation) complements the preceding "realized eschatology" and is based on the substitutionary death of Christ on the cross. Such salvation is received by simple but genuine faith (John 20:30–31). Finally, we might also mention John's ecclesiology, his doctrine of the church. For the Beloved Disciple, the followers of Jesus are both united with the story of Israel in the Old Testament and with the Trinity in the New Testament and beyond. Indeed, the spiritual union of the Christian with the triune God and his people is a Johannine teaching rivaled in the Bible only by Paul's "in-Christ" mysticism. And on and on it goes with the magnificent themes John's literature addresses, themes this textbook will discuss in some depth.

Introducing the work of any biblical author is a bit of a juggling act, balancing general, commonly accepted statements on the one hand with specific, analytical comments on the other hand. To emphasize only the former of these runs the risk of saying little more than nothing, while overemphasizing the latter will restrict the message of the biblical author to ivory-tower theologians. In this textbook, I have tried to strike the balance between the general and the technical by offering a thorough summary of the paragraphs comprising each of the three writings of John. User-friendly features, such as objectives, callouts, sidebars, photos, charts, review questions, and key terms, should make the more intense material engaging to the audience. This textbook divides naturally into three parts, each with its respective chapters: part 1: the Gospel of John; part 2: the Epistles of John; part 3: Revelation. This sequence reflects the generally accepted chronological order of the writing of John's works.

Writing a book, especially a lengthy one like this one, is a collaborative effort. It is, therefore, with a deep sense of gratitude that I offer my appreciation to the following people for their role in this process:

First, regarding its content, this textbook on Johannine literature stands on the shoulders of others. From commentator to colleague; in text and endnote; before conference attendees and church congregations, much of the material in this volume owes its origin and inspiration to many others, and I am profoundly indebted to them.

Second, it continues to be a joy and a privilege to publish with Zondervan. To Stan Gundry, Katya Covrett, Jim Ruark, Laura Weller, Kim Tanner, and all those at Zondervan who had a role in this work go my sincere thanks for their excellence in the industry, their commitment to evangelicalism, and their enduring friendship. Thank you for including this work in your repertoire of publications.

Next, it is a continual sense of joy to teach at Ouachita Baptist University. The love and support of its administration, students, and faculty assure one that Jesus' hope for the unity of his children is alive and well today.

And, then, there are four individuals without whom this book would never have seen the light of day. The superb typing and computer skills and the encouraging spirit of Cora-Fay Nykolaishen, Marla Rigsby, and Adam Kirby turned the mere dream of a manuscript into a reality. For these three, therefore, I am sincerely grateful. Above all, I thank my wife, Sherry, for the soul mate that she is. She helped me start, continue, and finish this project. I have no doubt that if Scripture were still being written today, her insight, integrity, and Christlike love would qualify her to be one of its authors.

Finally, I dedicate this work to our grandson—Ethan Andrew. Years ago, when I wrote my first book for Zondervan—a book on Paul's theology—I expressed in its preface my longing that our daughter Heather Lee might one day grow up to love the writings of the apostle Paul as much as her father does. Thankfully, that prayer has come true. Now my newest wish and hope is that her son might grow up to one day love the writings of the apostle John as much as his grandfather has come to love them.

PART 1

The Gospel of John

CHAPTER 1

Introduction to the Gospel of John

Objectives

After reading this chapter, you should be able to:

- Evaluate the evidence regarding the authorship of the fourth gospel.

- Explain the concept of the "Johannine school."

- Discuss the possible backgrounds of the thought world of the fourth gospel.

- Discuss the eschatology of John.

- Describe the relationship between John, the epistles of John, and Revelation.

- Explain the genre of gospel.

- Delineate the twofold historical setting of the gospel of John.

- Point out the similarities between the Dead Sea Scrolls and the fourth gospel.

- Assess the Greek manuscript evidence for the gospel of John.

- Compare/contrast John with the Synoptic Gospels.

INTRODUCTION

I first studied the gospel of John seriously as a Bible college student in the fall semester of 1971. It was then that I was introduced to the distinctives of the fourth gospel. It is simple but profound in thought. Regarding this, Augustine supposedly said of John's gospel, "John's gospel is deep enough for an elephant to swim and shallow enough for a child not to drown."

John's language is dualistic (light versus darkness, above versus below, believers versus unbelievers, etc.). The fourth gospel records seven sign miracles and seven "I am" statements. It contains discourses rather than parables. Following a majestic prologue (John 1:1–18), the fourth gospel delineates certain stages of belief one proceeds through to achieve discipleship. Its polemical usage of the title "the Jews" is famous, and it is filled with realized eschatology (see below). These are but some of John's unique features.

Yet John, like Matthew, Mark, and Luke, is obviously a gospel, a presentation of the life, death, and resurrection of Jesus Christ. And it has been beloved by both believers and heretics (see my later discussion of second-century Gnosticism's affinity with the fourth gospel). From the end of the second century AD on, there was no doubt in the church's mind that John belonged to the New Testament canon. It was, as Clement of Alexandria labeled it, a "spiritual gospel,"[1] one to be mined for its depth of meaning. Even today new believers are encouraged to first read the gospel of John, so beautiful and edifying is its message. Indeed, John 20:31 supports such advice: "These are written that you may believe that Jesus is the Christ, the Son of God, and that by believing you may have life in his name."

Scholars, too, since Origen's third-century AD commentary on John, have been preoccupied with interpreting the fourth gospel. It is likely that it claims the attention of more scholars at the present time than any other book of the Bible. For example, from 1920 to 1965 alone, over three thousand academic works were written on the gospel of John,[2] and interest in it has not waned since then. Obviously, therefore, in an introductory work like this one, we can only scratch the surface of the meaning of the fourth gospel.

Palestine at the Time of Christ, A.D. 6-44

---

1. Eusebius, *Eccl. Hist.* 6.14.
2. Eduard Malatesta, *St. John's Gospel*, Analecta Biblica 32 (Rome: Pontifical Biblical Institute, 1967).

But wrestle with the meaning of John we will! After touching upon the key issues surrounding the fourth gospel, we will then move our way through the book chapter by chapter. So fasten your seat belt and hold on to your hat as we enter the wonderful world of the gospel of John.

We proceed now to discuss the following introductory issues associated with the fourth gospel: its authorship, its canonicity, the conceptual background of John, its historical setting, John as gospel, its structure, the Greek manuscript evidence for John, John and the Synoptic Gospels, and the theology of the fourth gospel.

> "These are written that you may believe that Jesus is the Christ, the Son of God, and that by believing you may have life in his name."

I. THE AUTHORSHIP OF THE GOSPEL OF JOHN

Up until modern times, the traditional view of the authorship of the fourth gospel has been that John, "the beloved disciple," wrote said book. I now summarize the evidence for that perspective, after which I consider alternative views of the authorship of the fourth gospel.

A. The Traditional View

The traditional view appeals to both internal evidence and external evidence in support of its claim that the apostle John wrote the fourth gospel.[3] The former has to do with the contents of John, while the latter deals with the testimony of the church fathers.

---

3. For a classic defense of the Johannine authorship of the fourth gospel, see Donald Guthrie, *New Testament Introduction*, 3rd ed. (Downers Grove, Ill.: InterVarsity, 1970), 241–71, and, before him, B. F. Westcott, *The Gospel according to John* (London: Murray, 1881), v–xxviii.

The Hebrew Bible: Its Divisions and Contents	
Torah (Law)	**Minor Prophets**
Genesis	**Kethubim (Writings)**
Exodus	Psalms
Leviticus	Job
Numbers	Proverbs
Deuteronomy	Ruth
	Canticles
Nevi'im (Prophets)	Ecclesiastes
Joshua	Lamentations
Judges	Esther
Samuel	Daniel
Kings	Ezra-Nehemiah
Isaiah	Chronicles
Jeremiah	
Ezekiel	

1. Internal Evidence

B. F. Westcott's classic commentary on John presents the internal evidence regarding the authorship of the fourth gospel in narrowing concentric circles, leading to the conclusion that the apostle John authored the fourth gospel. I now summarize this line of thinking.[4]

1. The author of John was a Jew. Thus he, like most Jews, awaited the Messiah promised in the Old Testament (John 1:21; 4:25; 6:14–15; 7:40–42; 12:34; et al.). He quotes the Old Testament (6:45; 13:18; 19:37). The author knows about Jewish traditions (2:6; 5:1; 10:22).

2. The author of John has a knowledge of Palestine (John 1:44; 2:1; 4:46; 5:2; 9:7; 10:22; 11:1; et al.).

3. The author presents himself as an eyewitness of the events he recorded (John 1:29, 35, 43; 2:6; 4:40, 43; 5:5; 12:1, 6, 12; 19:35; et al.).

4. The author was an apostle. He was "the Beloved Disciple" (cf. John 21:20, 24) who leaned on Jesus' breast at the Passover supper (cf. 13:23; 19:26; 20:2; 21:7). The Synoptic Gospels (Matthew, Mark, and Luke) restrict the attendants at the Last Supper to the twelve apostles. Moreover, the author knows the disciples' thoughts (2:11, 17, 22; 4:27; 6:19, 60; 12:16; 13:22, 28; 21:12) and Jesus' private feelings (6:6, 61, 64; 13:1, 3, 11; 18:4; 19:28).

5. The author was the apostle John. The author was one of the inner circle of the disciples: Peter, James, and John (the latter two being the sons of Zebedee [John 13:23, 24; 20:2–10; 21:2, 7, 20]). Because James had long since been martyred before the writing of the fourth gospel (Acts 12:1–5) and Peter appears as a different person from the Beloved Disciple therein (John 21:7), only John is left to be the author.

---

4. Westcott, *Gospel according to John*, v–xxviii.

A scriptorium (a room for writing or copying scrolls) at Qumran.

©Joseph Calev/www.istockphoto.com

Left: The Dead Sea. Middle: The caves of Qumran adjacent to the Dead Sea. Home of the Dead Sea Scrolls. Right: The entrance to cave 4, the treasure trove of the Dead Sea Scrolls' find.

Since Westcott's arguments, only the first two points have been confirmed. The Dead Sea Scrolls reveal the uncanny similarity of thought between the fourth gospel and their writings,[5] confirming that the author was a Palestinian Jew. Not even the fact that John was written in Koine Greek detracts from its Jewish background, for more and more scholars recognize that, at the very least, Galilean Jews spoke Greek.[6] But the other three of Westcott's points are hotly contested, as we will see later.

2. External Evidence

External evidence from the time of the church fathers reflects an early belief that the apostle John wrote the fourth gospel. Irenaeus (AD 120–202) wrote, "Afterwards, John, the disciple of the Lord, who also had leaned upon

A portion of the Isaiah Scroll from Qumran (ca. 100 B.C.)

His breast, did himself publish a gospel during his residence at Ephesus in Asia" (*Against Heresies* 3.1.1.). As for the reliability of Irenaeus, Eusebius says his authority was Polycarp (AD 70–155/60), who had personally heard the apostles (*Eccl. Hist.* 4.14).

Theophilus of Antioch (AD 115–88), Clement of Alexandria (AD 190), Origen (c. AD 220), Hippolytus (AD 225), Tertullian (c. AD 200), and the Muratorian Fragment (AD 170) agree in attributing the fourth gospel to John, the son of Zebedee.

---

5. See the discussion below under "Conceptual Background of John."
6. See the discussion by D. A. Carson and Douglas J. Moo, *An Introduction to the New Testament*, 2nd ed. (Grand Rapids: Zondervan, 2005), 240.

One possible exception to the testimony of the church fathers is Papias's statement (early second century AD) recorded by Eusebius (early fourth century AD), referring to two Johns:

> And if anyone chanced to come who had actually been a follower of the elders, I would enquire as to the discourses of the elders, what Andrew or what Peter said, or what Philip, or what Thomas or James, or what John or Matthew or any other of the Lord's disciples; and things which Aristion and John the elder, disciples of the Lord, say.

Eusebius then comments:

> Here it is worth noting that twice in his enumeration he mentions the name of John: the former of these Johns he puts in the same list with Peter and James and Matthew and the other Apostles, clearly indicating the evangelist; but the latter he places with the others, in a separate clause, outside the number of the Apostles, placing Aristion before him; and he clearly calls him "elder." (*Eccl. Hist.* 3.39.45)

The tradition of the early church fathers is consistent: John the apostle, the Beloved Disciple, wrote the fourth gospel.

Some have inferred from this comment that it was the second John, a disciple of John the son of Zebedee, who wrote the fourth gospel. But this interpretation is refuted by four considerations. First, for Papias, "apostle" and "elder" are the same—one of the twelve disciples. Second, Papias therefore refers to John the elder with reference to one of the apostles (cf. 1 Peter 5:1, where Peter the apostle designates himself as an elder). Third, it is likely that the distinction Papias is making in his two lists is not between apostles and elders of the next generation but between first-generation witnesses who have died (Andrew, Peter, Philip, Thomas, James, Matthew) and first-generation witnesses who were still alive (Aristion and John). In other words, the same John is mentioned twice—the first time because he is grouped with the apostles and the second time because he alone of the apostles is alive.[7] Fourth, D. A. Carson observes of Eusebius: "In any case, Eusebius had his own agenda. He so disliked the apocalyptic language of Revelation that he was only too glad to find it possible to assign its authorship to a John other than the Apostle, and he seizes on 'John the elder' as he has retrieved him from Papias."[8]

---

7. For support of this view, see ibid., 142 – 43; and Guthrie, *New Testament Introduction*, 167 – 68.
8. Carson and Moo, *Introduction to the New Testament*, 142 – 43.

All of this to say that the tradition of the early church fathers is consistent: John the apostle, the Beloved Disciple, wrote the fourth gospel.

B. Nontraditional Views of the Authorship of the Fourth Gospel

For about a century now, scholars have decried the preceding traditional view, arguing instead that John the apostle did not write the gospel attributed to him. This approach divides into two categories: John was written by an individual other than the apostle or the fourth gospel was written by a group.

1. An Individual Other Than John the Apostle

Non-Johannine theories of authorship of the fourth gospel center on one of three individuals: John the Elder, Lazarus, or an ideal figure. The first of these was suggested by Eusebius's interpretation of Papias's aforementioned statement. But I already registered my disagreement with that argument.

Another individual thought to be the author of the fourth gospel is Lazarus, whom Jesus loved (John 11:3).[9] Yet the Synoptics, and presumably John, record only the twelve apostles as attending the Last Supper. So how could Lazarus lean on Jesus' breast as the Beloved Disciple did (13:23)? And why is Lazarus mentioned by name in John 11 and 12 and then referred to as the anonymous "Beloved Disciple" later? Contrast this to the apostle John who is nowhere mentioned in the fourth gospel (but at least twenty times in the Synoptics). It looks very much as if John wanted to keep his name anonymous as the author of his gospel. Such anonymity also detracts from any criticism that, in calling himself the "Beloved Disciple," John is being boastful. Therefore Lazarus does not seem to be the author of our gospel.

> Many interpreters today argue that a group of authors, or a school of writers, produced the Johannine literature: the gospel of John, the epistles of John, and Revelation.

Still others regard the Beloved Disciple as an ideal figure; that is, the church's testimony to Christ.[10] But, as Donald Guthrie ably responds, this view renders the Beloved Disciple as unhistorical, which undermines the very claim of the fourth gospel to be an eyewitness account of the life and times of Jesus.[11] In light of the above considerations, therefore, we are led to the conclusion that John the apostle was the Beloved Disciple, the author of the fourth gospel. This, however, does not solve the whole problem; hence the next point.

2. Group Authorship

Many interpreters today, however, argue that a group of authors, or a school of writers, produced the Johannine literature: the gospel of John, the epistles of John, and Revelation.

R. Alan Culpepper examined ancient literary schools approximately contemporaneous with the New Testament and identified nine characteristics that they and the Johannine corpus share:

---

9. See Guthrie's discussion, *New Testament Introduction*, 248.
10. Ibid., 249.
11. Ibid.

(1) The school gathers around a founding figure; (2) the founder is a teacher and exemplar of wisdom or goodness; (3) members of the school are disciples (pupils) of the teacher and loyal to his teaching; (4) teaching and learning are the focal activities of the school; (5) common means commemorate the role of the founder; (6) there is an emphasis on *philia* [friendship] and *koinōnia* [fellowship]; (7) rules define the life of members; (8) the school is distanced from wider society; (9) institutional structures (routinization) provide a basis for the perpetuation of the school.[12]

These characteristics are thought to be applicable to the apostle John and his followers. As one of the twelve apostles, John was an eyewitness of the historical Jesus who passed on his knowledge of him (Jesus) (numbers 1–2 above). John had pupils, too—the editor of John (chap. 21), Gaius (3 John 1, 4), Demetrius (3 John 12), and undoubtedly unnamed protégés. These, then, formed the nucleus of the Johannine school (numbers 3–4 above). We may gather that John continued to celebrate the memory of Jesus with his devotees through the observance of meals (cf. John 13 with John 21). Indeed, the very word "fellowship" (*koinōnia*) in 1 John 1:3 (twice), 6, 7 may well imply the celebration of meals together by the Johannine community in the name of Christ (numbers 5 and 6 above) patterned perhaps after the Last Supper (John 13–17). It is clear that the Johannine community maintained theological parameters of belief and behavior (number 7 above); hence John's opposition to the "Jews" in his gospel and later his consternation at the secessionists' exit from his churches (1, 2, and 3 John focus on these disgruntled members of John's churches who departed from that apostle's teaching that Jesus Christ is fully God and fully human). In a later section, I will discuss the sociology, or the social dynamics, of the Johannine community, suggesting that it was sectarian in nature (number 8 above). That the Johannine school was perpetuated is clear from the editing that went on after John's death; thus John 21 (see number 9 above).

The possibility that there was a Johannine school is all the more plausible since there were other known literary schools roughly at the time of John. In the Greek world, there were the schools of the Pythagoreans and the Stoics. In the Jewish world, there were the schools of the Essenes, Philo, and Rabbi Hillel. In the Christian era, the Antiochene and Alexandrian schools prevailed in the fourth century AD. Within the New Testament itself, there may have been a school of Matthew[13] and a school of Paul.[14]

In subscribing to the theory that there was a Johannine school, one caveat, however, should be issued: the central role of John the apostle must not be downplayed in the overall literary process, as indeed the Johannine school proponents tend to do.[15]

---

12. R. Alan Culpepper, *The Johannine School.* Society of Biblical Literature Dissertation Series 26 (Missoula, Mont.: Scholars, 1975), 258–59.

13. Krister Stendahl, *The School of St. Matthew and Its Use of the Old Testament*, Acta Seminarii Neotestamentici Upsaliensis 20 (Uppsala: Uppsala Universitet, 1954).

14. Hans Conzelmann, "Paulus und die Weisheit" (Paul and Wisdom), *New Testament Studies* (1965–66): 231–44.

15. See, e.g., Raymond E. Brown, *The Epistles of John*, Anchor Bible 30 (Garden City, N.Y.: Doubleday, 1982), 14–35; Georg Strecker, *The Johannine Letters*, trans. Linda M. Maloney, Hermeneia (Minneapolis: Fortress, 1996), xxxv–xliii; John Painter, *1, 2, and 3 John*, Sacra Pagina (Collegeville, Minn.: Liturgical, 2002); cf. 44–51 with 75–77. It should be noted that the "Johannine school" theory has not convinced all scholars. Thus, e.g., D. A. Carson finds three flaws in Culpepper's argument. First, the characteristics of "schools" identified in Johannine tradition could also fit a church. Second, parallels between the Beloved Disciple and the

Yet I see no reason why John could not be the author of all three writings associated with his name—the gospel, the epistles, and Revelation (I will discuss the authorship of the epistles and Revelation separately). So, even if he did use colleagues and followers in the writing process, they wrote under his authority, or at least with his blessing. And no doubt this process continued after his death, as was the case with John 21.

II. CANONICITY

"Canon" literally means "rule or measure." It is used by theologians figuratively with reference to the books included in the Bible; thus, for a book to be admitted into the "canon" was to confirm its divinely inspired contents.

Virtually no one in the second-century church doubted that the gospel of John was sacred Scripture.[16] In fact, it was revered by orthodox and heretic alike. Regarding the latter, Gnostics (from Gk., *gnōsis*, "knowledge"; see my later discussion under the conceptual background of John) appealed to the fourth gospel's emphasis on "knowledge" and "revelation" from God in support of their own theological system.

Actually, the earliest known commentary on the gospel of John was by the Gnostic Heracleon, a student of Valentinus (AD 180), one of the leaders of the Gnostic movement. If John's gospel took a little longer in the second century to be accepted as canonical compared to the Synoptic Gospels, it was because of this Gnostic attraction to the work.[17]

Paraclete do not make them equivalent. Third, Culpepper's argument assumes what is to be proved; could not the Johannine literature testify to the personality of the author, rather than to that of a Johannine "community" as a whole? D. A. Carson, "Historical Tradition in the Fourth Gospel: After Dodd, What?" in *Studies of History and Tradition in the Four Gospels*, ed. R. T. France and David Wenham, Gospel Perspectives 2 (Sheffield: JSOT, 1981), 83–145.

16. The only exceptions were the heretics Marcion and the Alogoi.

17. Charles Hill has recently challenged this commonly accepted notion by arguing that the fourth gospel was accepted early as canonical, even prior to Irenaeus, and that the Gnostics were not in fact all that drawn to John. Charles Hill, *The Johannine Corpus in the Early Church* (New York/Oxford: Oxford University Press, 2006). There are three planks in Hill's argumentation: First, the gospel of John was already read widely as Scripture in the early second century. Second, the fourth gospel was not "rehabilitated" from the Gnostics but, rather, was from the start intended to refute Docetic/Gnostic-like teaching, much like 1 John does. Third, the Johannine corpus was early on considered to be a unity, because the apostle John was thought to have written it all. Related to this last point, Hill suggests that theories of redactional/later editorial additions to the gospel

Alexander the Great as divine hero: The conquests of Alexander spread Greek culture throughout the eastern Mediterranean world.

Irenaeus of Lyons, however, masterfully used the fourth gospel itself to dispel any notion that that gospel was tainted by Gnostic thought.

On the side of orthodoxy, Clement of Alexandria, Tertullian, and later Origen all bore witness to the canonical status of John. Indeed, by AD 180 Tatian had composed his *Diatessaron* (Greek for "through four"), the first harmony of the four Gospels. And he used John's gospel as a chronological framework for the other three gospels. Clement of Alexandria (AD 180s) well summarized the church's view of John's gospel at that time: "Last of all, John, perceiving that the external facts had been made plain in the Gospel, being urged by his friends and inspired by the Spirit, composed a spiritual gospel" (in Eusebius, *Eccl. Hist.* 6.14.7).

III. CONCEPTUAL BACKGROUND

In all New Testament books, the conceptual background is important for interpreting those writings, and none more so than for the gospel of John. For over a century now, debate has raged over where John fits in terms of ancient philosophy and religious thought. We may organize that discussion into three categories: Hellenism, Hellenistic Judaism, and Palestinian Judaism.

A. Hellenism

Hellenism is a term that captures Greek influence on the ancient world, beginning with the conquests of Alexander the Great (330 BC) and continuing until AD 300. The importance of the city (*polis*), rule by democracy, philosophy and religion, not to mention Koine (common) Greek — the language of the Septuagint (Greek translation of the Hebrew Bible, ca. 250 BC), the New Testament, and the early church fathers — were all bequeathed to the world by Hellenism. Three religious-philosophical belief systems emerged out of Hellenism that possibly influenced the gospel of John, according to some: Gnosticism, the Hermetic corpus, and Mandaeism.

1. Gnosticism

Gnosticism, traditionally understood, was a second- to third-century AD interpretation of early Christianity. It taught that in the beginning there was God, the perfect one, the Spirit, who created an original primal man, who was a figure composed of light. Unfortunately, this man fell into sin, causing his body to disintegrate into myriads of particles of light, which were then seeded in the souls of humans in this dark world. The plight of humanity, therefore, is the struggle for individuals to remember the heavenly origin of their souls. God solved this problem by sending his Son, Jesus Christ the Redeemer, whose task

of John are thereby rendered suspect. There is much in Hill's work that provides a healthy corrective to previously assumed constructs regarding the origin of the Johannine corpus. I, however, remain convinced that John 6:35–59; 13:31–16:33; 21 (esp. vv. 24–25); and Revelation contain duplicates and perhaps even later additions to John's writings. See the pertinent discussions to follow.

was to bring this knowledge (*gnōsis*) to people. On recollecting their true nature, those souls are led back to their heavenly home, no longer encumbered by their sinful bodies.

Thus Gnosticism refers to the *gnōsis,* or knowledge, that one is ultimately spiritual, not physical, in origin. The goal, therefore, is for one to rid the soul of the prison house of the body and return to the Spirit-being. The Platonic dualism of soul and body is apparent in all of this.

While some Gnostic works were known before 1945 (*The Arabic Infancy Gospel, The Infancy Gospel of Thomas,* et al.), the discovery of the Nag Hammadi Library in Upper Egypt in that year introduced the modern world to a cache of Gnostic texts, the most famous of which is the *Gospel of Thomas.* The emphasis on "knowledge" in the gospel of John was thought to be due to such Gnostic influence, along with the fourth gospel's dualism between below and above and a descending/ascending redeemer, not to mention the fact that Gnostics were drawn to the gospel of John.[18]

Nag Hammadi: Site of Discovery of the Nag Hammadi Manuscripts

But today most New Testament scholars discard any supposed Gnostic influence on the gospel of John for a number of reasons. First, John doesn't even use the noun *gnōsis*, probably because he wants to avoid being confused with Gnostic thought. Second, Gnosticism wasn't alone in its usage of dualism; Jewish apocalypticism, the Dead Sea Scrolls, and rabbinic literature also used dualism. And it is the Jewish flavor of dualism, especially the Dead Sea Scrolls, that impacts the fourth gospel (as I will show later), not Gnosticism. Third, the descending/ascending redeemer motif in John is not Gnostic; rather, it is rooted in Daniel 7 and the portrait there of the heavenly Son of Man. Moreover, John's emphasis on Jesus' incarnation (John 1:14) was diametrically opposed to the Docetic[19] message of Gnosticism. Fourth, most biblical scholars since the 1970s have concluded that Gnosticism did not develop as a full-blown system until the second century AD, and that as a reinterpretation of orthodox Christianity. What Gnosticism did exist at the time of the gospel of John was an incipient stage.[20]

2. Hermetic Literature

The Hermetic corpus is attributed to *Hermes Trismegistus* and illustrates how Egyptian cults sought to incorporate Hellenism into their writings, especially Platonic and Stoic thinking. Therefore, some biblical scholars have sought to root John's gospel in that

---

18. Gary M. Burge provides a list of the supposed parallels between the fourth gospel and Gnosticism in *The Anointed Community: The Holy Spirit in the Johannine Tradition* (Grand Rapids: Eerdmanns, 1987), 9–10.

19. "Docetics" (Gk., *dokeō*, "to appear") believed that Jesus was only God and only appeared to be human. This heresy will be explored more fully in our later treatment of the epistles of John.

20. This rules out the thesis of Elaine Pagels, who argued in her very popular book *Beyond Belief: The Secret Gospel of Thomas* (New York: Random House, 2003) that the Gnostic *Gospel of Thomas* was known by the author of the fourth gospel. For a critique of Pagel's work, see C. Marvin Pate and Sheryl L. Pate, *Crucified in the Media: Finding the Real Jesus Amidst Today's Headlines* (Grand Rapids: Baker, 2005), 31–49.

Plato was the greatest of Socrates' pupils and has had a major influence on Western intellectual history

Marie-Lan Nguyen/Wikimedia Commons

background.[21] But key terms in the *Hermetica*, such as *gnōsis* and *mystery*, are missing in the fourth gospel. Moreover, the *Hermetica* most likely betrays dependence on John rather than the reverse.[22] Furthermore, the Hermetic literature dates no earlier than the second century AD, after the writing of the gospel of John.

3. Mandaean Texts

Others have attempted to connect the fourth gospel to the Mandaean texts because of their adherence to John the Baptist traditions.[23] But two problems prevent such a connection. First, the Mandaean literature was written hundreds of years after John (fourth to fifth centuries AD). Second, the dualistic themes in the Mandaean religion stem from Iranian, not Jewish, influence.[24]

B. Hellenistic Judaism

The most famous illustration of the merger of Hellenistic philosophy with Jewish faith can be found in the writings of Philo (ca. 40 BC). Philo used the former to commend the latter to Greco-Roman audiences in Alexandria, Egypt.

One of Philo's favorite concepts was the logos. Philo borrowed his understanding of the logos from Stoicism, which equated logos with universal reason, the spark of divinity residing in humanity. More specifically, Philo and Stoicism shared some seven

---

21. C. H. Dodd explores the possible parallels between John and the Hermetic literature in *The Interpretation of the Fourth Gospel* (Cambridge: Cambridge University Press, 1953), 10–53.

22. Craig S. Keener makes these points in *The Gospel of John: A Commentary*, vol. 1 (Peabody, Mass.: Hendrickson, 2003), 165.

23. So Rudolph Bultmann, "Die Bedeutung der neuerschlossenen mandäischen und manichäischen Quellen für das Verständnis des Johannes-evangeliums," *Zeitschrift für die Neutestamentliche Wissenschaft* ("The Meaning of Newly Discovered Mandaean and Manichean Sources for the Understanding of John's Gospel," *Journal for New Testament Scholarship*) 24 (1925): 100–146.

24. See Keener, *Gospel of John*, 165; and Guthrie's critiques, *New Testament Introduction*, 323.

comparisons regarding the logos. The logos is (1) eternal, (2) divine, (3) natural law governing the universe, (4) expressed in terms of light, (5) the mediating role in creation, (6) the universal presence, (7) to be followed in life. The major differences between Philo and Stoicism's logos is that the former emphasized the personal dimension of the logos and separated it from God, whereas the latter did neither.[25]

Interestingly enough, John's Logos in 1:1–18 shares the preceding parallels while agreeing with Philo's differences with Stoicism. Older commentaries, therefore, rooted the fourth gospel's conceptual background directly in Philo and indirectly in Stoicism,[26] based on John's prologue.

Yet modern interpreters doubt any direct contact between Philo and John. While the latter probably was aware of Hellenistic Jewish conceptions of logos, there are three critical differences between the two. (1) John's Logos is a historical person (Jesus Christ); Philo's is not. (2) Philo's interest in the logos is metaphysical, while John's is salvation-historical. (3) Philo emphasizes the "reason" nuance of the logos, whereas John focuses on the "word" aspect.[27]

> The most famous illustration of the merger of Hellenistic philosophy with Jewish faith can be found in the writings of Philo (ca. 40 BC).

C. Palestinian Judaism

1. The Dead Sea Scrolls

I noted in the discussion of the authorship issue that the fourth gospel is thoroughly Jewish in its orientation.[28] Since the discovery of the Dead Sea Scrolls in 1947, that literature has become the most viable candidate for influence on the gospel of John in particular and the rest of the Johannine literature in general. More than sixty years have elapsed since the discovery of the Dead Sea Scrolls in 1947, the most celebrated, if not fortuitous, archaeological discovery of the last century. In the spring of that year, three Bedouin shepherds were in the area called Qumran, which is adjacent to the Dead Sea, apparently tending their flock. The shepherds were cousins and members of the Ta'amireh tribe, one of whom, Jum'a Muhammad Khalil, amused himself by throwing rocks at a cave opening in the cliffs nearby the plateau at Qumran. One of the stones went into the cave and made a shattering noise.

---

25. See Keener, *Gospel of John*, 343n111.
26. Thus Ed. L. Miller, "The Logos of Heraclitus: Updating the Report," *HTR* 74 (1981): 161–76, esp. 174–75. See Keener's discussion and bibliography, *Gospel of John*, 343nn111, 117, 118.
27. Ibid., 346–47.
28. Recall Westcott's observations, *Gospel according to John*, v–x.

Some Important Works of Philo
De Opificio Mundi (On the Creation of the World)
De Confusione Linguarum (On the Confusion of the Languages)
De Vita Mosis (On the Life of Moses)
De Vita Contemplativa (On the Contemplative Life)
De Legatione ad Gaium (On the Embassy to Gaius)

Since the discovery of the Dead Sea Scrolls in 1947, that literature has become the most viable candidate for influence on the gospel of John in particular and the rest of the Johannine literature in general.

The Bedouin did not enter the cave that day, but two days later one of them, Muhammad ed-Dhib, went back to it and, venturing in, found ten jars. One of those jars held three ancient manuscripts. The rest of the containers were empty, but later four additional scrolls were found hidden in that cave. The discovery of those ancient documents and the hundreds more that nearby caves would later yield is regarded by many as the most significant archaeological finding in the twentieth century and as nothing short of providential.[29]

Now that supposed Gnostic, Hermetic, and Philonic parallels with John have fallen on hard times in scholarly discussions regarding the background of the fourth gospel, Palestinian Judaism in general and the Dead Sea Scrolls in particular have emerged as the most likely influence on that writing and, indeed, as well on the remainder of the Johannine corpus. This is the case in terms of the eschatologies of the two groups, particularly the idea that the age to come has been or is about to be inaugurated. According to early Judaism, time is divided into two consecutive periods: *this age* and *the age to come. This age* is characterized by sin and suffering as a result of Adam's fall. *The age to come* will be inaugurated when the Messiah comes and with him righteousness and peace. In effect, the age to come is synonymous with the kingdom of God.

But according to the Gospels, the life, death, and resurrection of Jesus Christ marked a paradigmatic shift resulting in the overlapping of the two ages. The age to come, or the

---

Characteristics of Jewish and Christian Apocalyptic Literature

(ca. 200 BC — AD 100)

1. The writer tends to choose some great man of the past (e.g., Enoch or Moses) and make him the hero of the book.
2. This hero often takes a journey, accompanied by a celestial guide who shows him interesting sights and comments on them.
3. Information is often communicated through visions.
4. The visions often make use of strange, even enigmatic, symbolism.
5. The visions often are pessimistic with regard to the possibility that human intervention will ameliorate the present situation.
6. The visions usually end with God's bringing the present state of affairs to a cataclysmic end and establishing a better situation.
7. The apocalyptic writer often uses a pseudonym, claiming to write in the name of his chosen hero.
8. The writer often takes past history and rewrites it as if it were prophecy.
9. The focus of apocalyptic is on comforting and sustaining the "righteous remnant."

---

29. For further discussion, consult C. Marvin Pate, *Communities of the Last Days: The Dead Sea Scrolls, the New Testament and the Story of Israel* (Downers Grove, Ill.: InterVarsity, 2000), chap. 1.

kingdom of God, was inaugurated within this age. In other words, the two ages are coterminous, and Christians live in the intersection of the two. This idea is commonly referred to as the *already–not yet* eschatological tension. That is, the age to come has already dawned because of the first coming of Christ but is not yet complete; that awaits his second coming. A similar concept seems to have informed the Qumran community (see 1QH; 1QM; et al.), minus the Christian interpretation.

Related to the preceding is the concept of the *signs of the times*, events associated in Judaism with the transition of this age to the age to come: the messianic woes (wars, earthquakes, famines, etc.), the rise of the Antichrist and apostasy, the arrival of the kingdom of God, judgment of the wicked and the resurrection of the righteous, and the new creation. These events were subsumed under the category of the "day of the Lord," or the last days. I do not wish to give the impression that all of these attendant circumstances were treated with equal interest in the pertinent Jewish writings; in actuality, some were of more concern to certain authors than others. But in general these happenings were equated with the signs of the times; hence their occurrence in a number of Jewish works. For the current purpose, I wish to point out that the Dead Sea Scrolls and the Johannine literature both attest to the dawning of the signs of the times, the overlapping of the two ages. The accompanying chart encapsulates the eschatological similarities between the two bodies of materials in this matter.

Similarities of the Eschatologies of the Johannine Literature and the Dead Sea Scrolls[30]		
Signs	**Johannine Literature**	**Dead Sea Scrolls**
Messianic woes	John 15:18–16:11 (cf. 1 John 2:18); Rev. 6–18	1QH 3:7–10; 5:30; 7:20–21; CD 1:5–11
Antichrist, apostasy	John 6:70; 13:2; 17:12; Rev. 6:2; 13:1–18; 17:8–13 (cf. 1 John 2:18, 22; 4:3)	CD 1:5–11; 20:13–15; 1QS 3:17–4:22; 1QM
Resurrection	John 5:24–30; Rev. 7; 14 (20:1–6)	1QH 3:5–6; 7
The two spirits	John 3:3–8; 14:16–17; 15:26; 16:13; 1 John 4:1–6; et al.	1QS 4:2–26; et al.
Sons of light, sons of darkness	John 8:12; 12:36, 46; 1 John 1:5–7; 2:8–11; Rev. 21:23–25; 22:5	1QM 1:1; 13:1–18; 14:12–18; 1QS 1:9–10; 3:1–4:26
New creation	Rev. 21–22	The New Jerusalem texts; 1QH

30. Ibid., chap. 9 and the bibliography identifying scholars who find Johannine literature rooted in the Dead Sea Scrolls. Below I offer a more nuanced perspective on John's eschatology.

2. Rabbinic Judaism

After the fall of Jerusalem to the Romans in AD 70, rabbinic, or Pharisaic, Judaism became the dominant form of Judaism. For two key reasons, some New Testament

After the fall of Jerusalem to the Romans in AD 70, rabbinic, or Pharisaic, Judaism became the dominant form of Judaism.

scholars have seen rabbinic Judaism as an important Palestinian influence on the fourth gospel. (1) As I will discuss shortly, the historical background of the fourth gospel may well be that of rabbinic opposition to Johannine Christians in the AD 90s, particularly the expulsion of Jewish believers from the synagogue. To put it another way, Johannine Christianity was forced to define itself vis-à-vis rabbinic Judaism. (2) The discourses in John resemble rabbinic sermons (most notably John 6:32 – 51).[31] How these two backgrounds — the Dead Sea Scrolls and rabbinic literature — relate to John's purpose will be explored as this introduction progresses.

IV. HISTORICAL SETTING, PURPOSE, AND DATE

Uncovering the historical setting of any ancient document is a critical part of the process of accurately interpreting that text, the Bible included. And so we must here raise the question: What is the historical setting of the gospel of John? Since the groundbreaking work of Louis Martyn,[32] Johannine scholars have applauded his theory that the fourth gospel reflects two historical settings. The first was that of the life of Jesus (AD 30), especially his conflict with the Jewish leaders over his messiahship (John 1:19 – 28; 2:12 – 23; 6:25 – 70; 7:11 – 52; 8:12 – 59; 9:13 – 41; 10:1 – 42; 11:45 – 57; 12:37 – 49; 15:18 – 16:4; 18:1 – 19:42). Certainly the key verse of John — 20:31 — seeks to clarify the fact that Jesus is the Christ, the Son of God in the face of Jewish opposition to him during his ministry on earth.

The second setting was the AD 90s. By then John had moved from Palestine to Ephesus, probably during the Jewish revolt against Rome (AD

Rabbinic Literature: The Mishnah

The Mishnah is divided up into six parts with tractates (or divisions) for each of the parts. The six tractates are:

1. *Zeraim* ("Seeds")
2. *Moed* ("Feast")
3. *Nashim* ("Women")
4. *Nezikin* ("Damages")
5. *Kodashim* ("Holy Things")
6. *Taharoth* ("Cleannesses")

---

31. Rabbinic material essentially refers to the Talmud, which consists of the Mishnah (commentary on the Torah) and the Gemara (commentary on the Mishnah) and is comprised of sixty-three tractates. These tractates attempt to apply the law of Moses to every aspect of life. There is a problem, however, with comparing the Talmud (which dates in written form to no earlier than the second century AD) with the New Testament. Yet many scholars think, correctly I believe, that the oral traditions later codified in the Talmud were in circulation at the time of the New Testament period. Jacob Neusner has championed the view that the Talmud should not be viewed in comparison with the New Testament (*The Rabbinic Traditions about the Pharisees before 70*, 3 vols. [Leiden: Brill, 1971]), while E. P. Sanders has argued that the Talmud can be used in connection with the New Testament if done so judiciously (*Jewish Law from Jesus to the Mishnah: Five Studies* [London: SCM, 1990], 166 – 254, 309 – 31).

32. J. L. Martyn, *History and Theology in the Fourth Gospel*, 2nd ed. (Nashville: Abingdon, 1979).

Arcadian Way, Ephesus. Ephesus was the probable home of John in his later years and the place of origin of the fourth gospel and the Epistles of John.

66–70). Martyn argued that in Asia Minor non-Christian Jews were expelling Christian Jews from the synagogues, thus exposing them to the Roman demand to worship Caesar. Since Julius Caesar (d. 44 BC), Jews had been exempt from emperor worship, and as long as Jewish Christians were perceived as Jews who worshiped in synagogues, so were they. But when the synagogue leaders dismissed Christian Jews, the latter ceased being Jewish to the mind of Rome and hence were obligated to submit to the cult of Caesar.

According to Martyn, rabbinic Judaism became the leading contender for redefining Judaism in the aftermath of the destruction of Jerusalem by the Romans (AD 70). And so it was that, at the coastal city of Jamnia in Palestine, the Pharisees conducted a series of meetings to reconstitute Judaism. All other branches of Judaism had been wiped out in the Jewish revolt — Sadducees, Herodians, Zealots, Essenes — except for rabbinic/Pharisaic Judaism and Jewish Christianity. Thus rabbinic Judaism made a concerted effort to suppress and defeat Jewish Christianity.

Martyn argued that the synagogue therefore constructed the *Birkath Ha-Minim* (the curse of the heretics). This was the twelfth benediction of the eighteen benedictions that was repeated by Jews in the synagogue worship service throughout the ancient world in the late first century AD. It read: "For the renegades let there be no hope, and may the arrogant kingdom soon be rooted out in our days, and the Nazarenes and the *minim* perish as in a moment and be blotted out from the book of life and with the righteous may they not be inscribed. Blessed art Thou, O Lord, who humblest the arrogant."

Synagogues in Capernaum and Sardis. Jewish Christians were probably expelled from Jewish synagogues like these because they believed in Jesus Christ.

Martyn hypothesized the following scenario based on a number of rabbinic texts:

1. A member of the synagogue does something to arouse suspicion regarding his orthodoxy (cf. John 3:2; 7:50a).
2. The president instructs the overseer to appoint this man to be the delegate of the congregation, that is, to lead in the praying of the Eighteen Benedictions.
3. Unless the man has a means of avoiding the appointment, he must go before the ark (*Torah Nitch*) and recite aloud all of the Eighteen Benedictions, pausing after each to await the congregation's "Amen." All listen carefully to his recitation of Benediction number 12.
4. If he falters on number 12, the Benediction against Heretics, he is removed from his praying (cf. *b. Ber.* 28b – 29a). He is then, presumably, drummed out of the synagogue fellowship.[33]

According to Martyn, the expulsion of Christian Jews from the synagogue accounts for the following data in the gospel of John:

---

33. Ibid., 58 – 60.

1. The negative, almost hostile, way the fourth gospel speaks of Jesus' opponents as "the Jews" (though Jesus himself was a Jew!).
2. The references to the Jews putting followers of Jesus "out of the synagogue" (9:22; 16:2), something not referred to in the Synoptics and not known to have occurred in Jesus' ministry.
3. The dualism of John's gospel—that is, the "us-against-them" mentality.
4. The emphasis on loving one another rather than loving everyone, a sign of a sectarian perspective (see my later discussion).
5. The high Christology in John, which presents Jesus the Son of God as misunderstood by the Jews because he is "from above" and they are "from below."

In the years that have passed since Martyn's groundbreaking study, Johannine scholars have come to doubt the precise method of how Jews expelled Christian Jews from the synagogue, that is, the twelfth benediction. But there is still some sentiment today that the expulsion of Jewish believers from the synagogue remains a viable theory about the second-level historical setting of John.[34]

Before proceeding any further, I must take a moment to attempt to answer the thorny question of whether the fourth gospel is anti-Semitic. In times past, John's mostly negative portrayal of "the Jews" (e.g., 1:19; 2:18, 20; 3:25; 5:10, 15, 16, 18; 6:41, 52) was appealed to in support of anti-Semitism from medieval to modern times, culminating in Nazi propaganda that brought about the Holocaust.[35] But recent New Testament scholars have exonerated John of any such accusation. Rather, John's gospel was written by a Jew to Jews. Particularly, John opposes especially the Jewish leadership in his day for their rejection of God's Word (in Christ) much like the Old Testament prophets thundered forth against Israel for failure to obey God. A near-contemporary Jewish group to John's day did the same, namely, the Essenes of the Dead Sea Scrolls. Moreover, as Craig S. Keener has argued, the fourth gospel uses the term *Jews* ironically. Even though they claim to be Jewish, in fact, the synagogue leaders have forfeited the right to be called Jews precisely because they rejected their Jewish Messiah—Jesus (cf. Rev. 2:9; 3:9)! Rather, the Johannine community constitutes true Israel.[36] In other words, John is not against all Jews, but those Jews in Jesus' day, especially the leaders, and John's own day who were persecuting his faith community. Furthermore, I, like most modern Christians, believe that the fourth gospel in no way countenances anti-Semitism. To do so is to undermine the very heritage of the Christian faith.

I conclude this section by observing that the gospel of John reflects two historical situations: the time of Jesus' conflict with the Jewish leaders in his day who rejected his

> I, like most modern Christians, believe that the fourth gospel in no way countenances anti-Semitism. To do so is to undermine the very heritage of the Christian faith.

---

34. See Keener's careful assessment of the topic in *Gospel of John*, 194–214.
35. George R. Beasley-Murray provides a helpful discussion of this, reaching a conclusion similar to mine, in *John*, Word Biblical Commentary, vol. 36, 2nd ed. (Nashville: Nelson, 1999), 362–64.
36. Keener is helpful on this point. See *Gospel of John*, 214–28.

messiahship (AD 30s) and the time of the Johannine community's conflict with synagogue leaders in Asia Minor, probably Ephesus (AD 90s). The fourth gospel was therefore written to establish the fact that Jesus is the Christ, the Son of God, who offers eternal life to all who believe in him.[37]

V. JOHN AS "GOSPEL": GOSPEL AS LITERARY GENRE

In this section we will tackle the subject of the literary genre of "gospel."

Matthew, Mark, Luke, and John were the first books to be called "gospels." But what does *gospel* mean? More specifically, what is the genre of gospel? Determining the genre of a piece of literature—whether a poem, history, narrative, op-ed, joke, cartoon, obituary, apocalyptic, or something else—is vital to properly interpreting that piece of literature. The genre provides the reader with the rules of the interpretive game. For example, to read poetry and apocalyptic literature is to engage in figurative interpretation, while history and narrative ask to be read literally, at face value.

Matthew, Mark, Luke, and John were the first books to be called "gospels."

So what is the genre of gospel, and how is it to be read? The Greek word for *gospel* is *euangelion*, which means "good news." It translates the Hebrew *basar* ("bear [good] tidings"), which is found frequently in the Old Testament (e.g., Ps. 95:1; Isa. 40:9; 41:27; 52:7; 61:1). Jesus brought these two ideas—*euangelion* and *basar*—together when he announced the good news that the kingdom of God was near (e.g., Matt. 4:23; Mark 1:15; Luke 2:10; "kingdom of God" does not occur in John, but the idea is clearly there). Because of Jesus' proclamation of the gospel of the kingdom of God in the first four books of the New Testament, the respective titles of "The Gospel according to Matthew (Mark, Luke, John)" were attached to those writings early on.

Inscription to Augustus

Providence ... created ... the most perfect good for our lives ... filling him [Augustus] with virtue for the benefit of mankind, sending us and those after us a saviour who put an end to war and established all things ... and whereas the birthday of the god [i.e. Augustus] marked for the world the beginning of good tidings through his coming.

Inscription from 9 BC; translation from *Roman Civilization II*, ed. N. Lewis and M. Reinhold (New York: Harper & Row, 1955), 64.

Emperor Caesar Augustus

---

37. I will discuss the nature of faith in the fourth gospel later.

I n writing for this book the [life] of Alexander the king ... I have before me such an abundance of materials that I shall make no other preface but to beg my readers not to complain of me if I do not relate all [his] celebrated exploits or even any one in full detail, but in most instances abridge the story. I am writing not histories but lives, and a man's most conspicuous achievements do not always reveal best his strength or his weakness. Often a trifling incident, a word or a jest, shows more of his character than the battles where he slays thousands, his grandest mustering of armies, and his sieges of cities. Therefore as portrait painters work to get their likenesses from the face and the look of the eyes, in which the character appears, and pay little attention to other parts of the body, so I must be allowed to dwell especially on things that express the souls of these men, and through them portray their lives, leaving it to others to describe their mighty deeds and battles. (Plutarch, *Alexander*, chap. 1)

I should also mention that the term *gospel* was applied in Greco-Roman literature to the accession of a new emperor. The usage of that term occurs in a famous inscription to the Roman Emperor Augustus (see sidebar "Inscription to Augustus").

But closer to home, the four Gospels use *euangelion* with the thought in mind of God's saving acts on behalf of his people in the Old Testament (especially so in Isaiah; see, e.g., 40:9; 52:7; cf. Joel 2:32; Nah. 1:15). We will explore this aspect more in the next point (the theological message of *gospel*).

For the last generation or so, New Testament scholars have been suggesting that the genre of gospel is related to ancient Greco-Roman literature. Three possible types of that literature have surfaced that might be parallel to our four Gospels: "acts," "memoirs," and "lives."[38] We now look at these possibilities, focusing on the last one.

First, the "acts" (Gk., *praxeis*) were books giving accounts of great historical figures and their deeds. For example, Arrian (second century AD) wrote his *Anabasis* about the military campaigns of Alexander the Great. Related to this, Luke wrote his Acts of the Apostles, highlighting the mighty works of God through the apostles of the early church.

However, the four Gospels contain more than Jesus' miraculous acts; they record his teachings. Furthermore, Jesus' exploits were not political and military in nature. Not only that, his trial and execution would make him suspect to ancient leaders accustomed to reading Acts.

Second, others have suggested that the Gospels fit the category of "memoirs" (Gk., *apomnēmoneumata*), which were collections of individual stories about, or sayings of, a famous person. For example, Xenophon wrote his *Memoirs* about the philosopher Socrates (ca. 380 BC), and Plato (ca. 350 BC) wrote his *Dialogues* also about Socrates. Similarly, the church father Justin Martyr (AD 150) described an early Christian meeting: "And on the day called Sunday there is a meeting in one place of those who live in cities or the country, and *the memoirs of the apostles* or the writings of the prophets are read as long as time per-

---

38. I follow here the remarks of David Wenham and Steve Walton, *Exploring the New Testament: A Guide to the Gospels and Acts* (Downers Grove, Ill.: InterVarsity, 2001), 47 – 51.

mits" (*Apology* 67.3, italics mine). Justin also wrote, "The memoirs of the Apostles are called Gospels" (*Apology* 66). However, the four Gospels do not fit the memoir genre either. The former contain much action, whereas the latter does not.

Third, the Gospels better match the ancient Greek and Roman "lives" (Gk., *bioi*), or historical biographies. Plutarch (AD 46–120) is one of the most widely cited authors of the ancient world. Well known for his essays on moral philosophy and religion, he also composed fifty biographies of prominent Greek and Roman men. These biographies, which Plutarch calls "Lives," were written not to provide an exhaustive accounting of the major events of an individual's public career, but to reveal the person's character as it became manifest in the various situations that he confronted. Plutarch summarized his approach in his introduction to his *Life of Alexander the Great* (see sidebar "Plutarch's *Life of Alexander*"). For Plutarch, a "life" was written to reveal a famous person's character.[39]

In the past, New Testament interpreters did not view the four Gospels as biographies, because they are so different from modern biographies. Unlike most modern biographies, the Gospels do not cover the whole life of Jesus, but rather jump from his birth to his public ministry. Neither are the Gospels arranged chronologically, but topically. Nor do they provide any psychological analysis of Jesus like modern biographies often provide.[40]

Yet Richard Burridge has mounted a strong argument for considering the Gospels as ancient "lives." He studied a wide range of ancient lives and established a set of features of this literary genre:

- *Opening features:* there is usually a title and an opening formula.
- The *subject* of the biography tends to be the subject of a large proportion of the main verbs in the book and is given the lion's share of the space, providing the focus on the subject Plutarch describes.
- *External features* include the structure of the book, its style, and so on, which enhance the focus on the subject.
- *Internal features* include the settings, the topics and content included, the values and attitudes espoused or promoted by the work, and the author's intention and purpose (whether stated explicitly or not).[41]

Burridge's arguments have convinced many New Testament scholars to consider the Gospels as ancient lives.

VI. THE STRUCTURE OF THE GOSPEL OF JOHN

The gospel of John is divided into four distinct parts:

---

39. See Bart D. Ehrman's discussion in *The New Testament: A Historical Introduction to the Early Christian Writings*, 3rd ed. (New York and Oxford: Oxford University Press, 2004), 61–66.

40. For a helpful comparison of modern biography and ancient biography in terms of the four gospels, see J. Scott Duvall and J. Daniel Hays, *Grasping God's Word: A Hands-On Approach to Reading, Interpreting, and Applying the Bible* (Grand Rapids: Zondervan, 2001), 236.

41. Richard A Burridge, *What Are the Gospels? A Comparison with Graeco-Roman Biography.* SNTSMS 70 (Cambridge: Cambridge University Press, 1992).

Prologue	1:1–18
The Book of Signs	1:19–12:50
The Book of Glory	13:1–20:31
Epilogue	21:1–25

The prologue ("before word") of John (1:1–18) identifies Jesus as the Christ, the eternal Son of God. It does so, as we will see, using the familiar Jewish category of wisdom. The Book of Signs (1:19–12:50) is called such because that section largely concerns Jesus' signs/miracles and discourses interpreting those signs, demonstrating that he is the Christ. The overall purpose of this section is to encourage John's readers to *believe* in Jesus, the light of God. The Book of Glory (13:1–20:31) narrates what happened in Jesus' life from the Last Supper to his postresurrection appearances to his disciples. Intertwined with these narratives is the theme of Jesus' return to his heavenly Father (13:1; 14:2, 28; 15:26; 16:7, 28; 17:5, 11; 20:7). This return means the glorification of Jesus (13:31; 16:14; 17:1, 5, 24), which was manifested through the resurrected Jesus as he appears to his disciples as Lord and God (20:25, 28; cf. 1:14). The purpose of the Book of Glory is to motivate Jesus' followers to love their brethren. The epilogue (21:1–25) records Peter's recommissioning as a disciple of Jesus.[42]

VII. THE MANUSCRIPT EVIDENCE FOR THE GOSPEL OF JOHN

Now we briefly turn to the question of the manuscript evidence for the gospel of John. We will consider the Greek manuscript tradition for the epistles of John and Revelation when we cover those works. Most likely, the gospel of John was originally written in Greek, not Aramaic, as an earlier generation of scholars argued.[43] D. A. Carson nicely summarizes the Greek manuscripts of John:

> The earliest New Testament fragment known to us is the fragment of John, p^{52}, dating from about A.D. 130 and containing a few words from John 18. Two other papyrus witnesses, both codices, spring from the end of the second century: p^{66} includes most of John 1–14 and parts of the remaining chapters, while p^{75} contains most of Luke, followed by John 1–11 and parts of chapters 12–15. From the beginning of the third century comes p^{45}, which contains parts of all four Gospels plus Acts, though the mutilated state of the manuscript ensures that no book is complete. Thereafter the manuscript evidence becomes richer, capped by the great fourth-century uncials (manuscripts written in capital letters) and followed by the many minuscules in succeeding centuries.[44]

A papyrus fragment from the Gospel of John 18:31-33, dated to the early second century, possibly only about fifty years after it was written. This fragment was acquired in 1920 in Egypt and is located in the John Rylands Library in Manchester, England.

---

42. Typical of this outline is Raymond E. Brown's *The Gospel according to John I–XII*, Anchor Bible 29A (Garden City, N.Y.: Doubleday, 1966), cxxxviii–cxxxix.

43. C. C. Torrey, "The Aramaic Origin of the Gospel of St. John," *HTR* 16 (1923): 305–44, championed this view.

44. Carson and Moo, *Introduction to the New Testament*, 172. Three types of New Testament Greek manuscripts factor into this discussion: papyrus (fragmentary texts that date to the second century), uncials (texts in capital letters, more complete than the papyri manuscripts and dating back to the fourth century), and minuscules (small letters comprising the Greek texts; much more numerous than the papyri and uncials but dating back only to the ninth century).

What emerges from this summary is the observation that the fourth gospel falls under the Alexandrian family of manuscripts (Vaticanus, Sinaiticus, p^{52}, p^{66}, p^{75}). Only John 7:53–8:11, a text derived from the Byzantine family, poses a challenge to this statement. We will postpone discussion of that passage until my later analysis.

VIII. JOHN ON THE SYNOPTIC GOSPELS

The careful reader of the fourth gospel will note significant differences between it and the Synoptic Gospels. Following are three of these dissimilarities:

1. Additional material in John: five of seven miracles (except feeding of multitudes and walking on water), early Galilean ministry (Cana), journey through Samaria (woman at well), washing of disciples' feet, Farewell Discourse, three trips to Jerusalem, and more.
2. Missing in John: no virgin birth, baptism of Jesus, temptation of Jesus, transfiguration, parables, explicit institution of Lord's Supper, cure of demoniacs and lepers, and more.
3. Different chronology:

John	Synoptics
Temple cleansing early	Later
Three years ministry	One year
Last Supper = Passover	Last Supper = Passover

Contrast the above differences with the few similarities between John and the Synoptics. They both record the feeding of the five thousand, the anointing of Jesus for burial, and the passion narrative. There may also be some "interlocking traditions" between John and the Synoptics (e.g., John's report of an extensive Judean ministry helps to explain the assumption in Mark 14:49 that Jesus had constantly taught in the temple precincts; the charge reported in the Synoptics that Jesus had threatened the destruction of the temple [Mark 14:58; 15:29] finds its only adequate explanation in John 2:19).[45]

> I suspect that John shaped the story of Jesus based on his affinity with the thinking of the Dead Sea Scrolls as well as on his interaction with rabbinic-style discourses.

Scholars have long debated what we are to conclude from these major differences between John and the Synoptics: does it mean that John did not know the other Gospels or that he did but chose to supplement them with his own material? Regardless of the answer to this question, it is clear that John did not make extensive use of the Synoptics in composing his own "life" of Christ. I suspect that John shaped the story of Jesus based on his affinity with eschatological thought similar to that of the Dead Sea Scrolls as well as on his interaction with rabbinic-style discourses.

---

45. Carson supplies some of these interlocking traditions (ibid., 161). A recent work that might confirm that the gospel authors were aware of each other's writings is that by Richard Bauckham, ed., *The Gospels for All Christians* (Grand Rapids: Eerdmans, 1998).

IX. THE THEOLOGY OF JOHN

I include here an overview of the major theological themes developed in the fourth gospel. Doing so now will provide the reader with a bird's-eye view that will better facilitate my analysis later. The most significant themes occurring in the gospel of John are: theology (the view of God), Christology, pneumatology (the Holy Spirit), soteriology (salvation), ecclesiology (the church), and eschatology (the end-times). We will now survey each of these themes.

A. Theology

The general view of God recorded in the Old Testament is affirmed in the fourth gospel. God is eternal (John 1:1), the creator (1:3–4), invisible (1:18; 6:46), Spirit (4:24), served by angels (1:51), and manifested in the temple, which is now replaced by Jesus (4:22; cf. 2:16–19). God raises the dead (2:22; 5:21; 11:24; 20:1–9). He has a kingdom (3:3, 5). God loves the world (3:16). God superintends his creation (5:17). God judges humanity, but through his Son, resulting in life for some and death for others, depending on their response to Christ (5:22–30). God performs miracles through his Son (5:26–47; et al.). God nurtured Israel in the wilderness with manna, but now he sustains his people through Christ (6:32–33). God inspired the law of Moses (1:17; 7:22–24; 9:29; et al.) and the prophets (6:45). God required Jews to observe the feasts of the Old Testament: Passover (2:13, 23; 6:4; 11:55; 12:12); Tabernacles (7:2, 37; cf. dedication, 10:22). God predicted in the Old Testament the coming Messiah (7:42). God made a covenant with Abraham (8:37–41, 52–58). He is glorified even through sickness (9:1–3). God is holy (9:31). He is sovereign (10:29) and is one and unrivaled (10:33). God is opposed by the Devil, the prince of the world, but the Devil will be defeated (cf. 8:44 with 12:31–32; 16:11).

> The general view of God recorded in the Old Testament is affirmed in the fourth gospel.

All of this is pretty much standard Old Testament theology. But what is striking in John is that nearly all of the preceding attributes and actions of God are shared by Jesus Christ, because he is God! In fact, Jesus makes the invisible God visible (1:18). This no doubt unsettled many ancient Jews, for to place Jesus on par with God was to compromise their monotheistic faith. Yet the fourth gospel implicitly answers this criticism by emphasizing more than any other gospel that Jesus as God's Son is subordinate to the Father.

B. Christology

The Christology of the fourth gospel is as exalted as any other New Testament work, if not more so. Unlike the Synoptic Gospels and comparable only to Paul (Phil. 2:5–11; Col. 1:15–20), John begins with a prologue (John 1:1–18) that equates Jesus with God from eternity past, which is reaffirmed in John 8:58 and 17:5. Moreover, as commentators have long noted, throughout the gospel of John Jesus' deity is emphasized seemingly over his humanity. This is especially clear in John's passion narrative, where the Jewish and Roman guards do not capture Jesus, but he surrenders to them (18:1–11), and on the cross Jesus gives up his spirit to death, rather than death overtaking him (19:30).

We may divide John's Christology into two major features: Jesus' person and his work. It is clear that John presents Jesus as on par with God: he is eternal (1:1–2, 14) and the creator (1:3). Other titles of deity applied to Jesus in the fourth gospel are "Son of God" (e.g., 1:49; 3:16–18; 5:16–27, 36–47; 6:32–33; 17:1, 21, 25; 19:7; 20:28, 31); "Messiah/Christ" (1:17, 41; 4:25–26; 7:41; et al.); "Son of Man" (1:51; 6:27, 53, 61; 12:23; et al.); and the seven "I Ams" (6:35; 8:12; 10:9; 10:11; 11:25; 14:6; 15:1), which are allusions to God as the great "I AM." Other honorific titles for Jesus in John include "the Word [Wisdom] of God" (1:1–18); "King of Israel/the Jews" (12:13; 19:19); "revealer" of God (1:18; 17:6; et al.).

> The Christology of the fourth gospel is as exalted as any other New Testament work, if not more so.

Concerning Jesus' work, the fourth gospel portrays Jesus' death as his crowning achievement. His was an atoning death, the sacrifice of the Lamb of God for the sins of the world (1:29, 35; 19:34b–35).

C. Pneumatology

John's teaching on the Holy Spirit can be summarized in three words: *eschatological, christological,* and *personal.*

1. *Eschatological.* Like the rest of the New Testament, the fourth gospel presumes that the presence of the Holy Spirit in the church is the sign that the age to come (the end of history) is here. John 3:5–6; 7:37–39; and 20:17–23 draw on the new covenant prophetic texts of Jeremiah 31:31–34; Ezekiel 36:26–29; and Joel 2:28–32 to make that point.

2. *Christological.* The Holy Spirit in John is Jesus' representative — the Paraclete (John 14:16–18). As such, he rehearses Jesus' truth (14:26), imparts Jesus' peace (14:27), bears witness to Jesus (15:26; 16:13–14), and convicts the world because of their rejection of Jesus (16:7–11).

3. *Personal.* Jesus lives in union with his followers by the indwelling presence of the Spirit (cf. John 20:22–23 with 14:17; 17:21, 23).

D. Soteriology

> John's teaching on the Holy Spirit can be summarized in three words: *eschatological, christological,* and *personal.*

Four words can be used to characterize John's understanding of salvation: its *basis, means, scope,* and *permanence.*

1. *Basis.* While some have argued that John, in good Gnostic style, teaches that salvation is by revelation,[46] it is clear, rather, that the nature of salvation is that of forgiveness of sins based on the atoning death of Jesus (John 1:29, 36; 11:49–52; et al.).

2. *Means.* The means for receiving salvation is faith in Christ (John 1:12–13; 3:1–16; et al.). Though, as my later analysis will show, faith is a slippery concept in the fourth gospel that involves different levels of belief.

3. *Scope.* According to John 3:16 and 4:42, salvation is universal; it is for the whole world.

---

46. See J. Terence Forestell, *The Word of the Cross: Salvation as Revelation in the Fourth Gospel,* AnBib 57 (Rome: Biblical Institute Press, 1974).

4. *Permanence.* Those who accept the eternal security of the believer appeal to John 6:37 and 10:29. However, those who think Christians can lose their salvation appeal to John 15:6 and the apostasy of Judas (13:21–30).

E. Ecclesiology

In contrast to the rest of the New Testament, the fourth gospel does not use key terms for the Christian community of faith, such as "church" (*ekklēsia*), "people of God," "body of Christ," "bride of Christ," and "kingdom of God" (rarely). This is sometimes said to be the case, because John emphasizes individual salvation over against the corporate dimension of the church. And, along with such individualism, so it is argued, goes a de-emphasis on the sacraments of baptism and the Lord's Supper, for these are not discussed in John.

However, the above picture is overstated, for three reasons. First, there are ecclesial images in John. The church is the vineyard of God (cf. John 15 with Ps. 80:9–16; Isa. 5:1–7; 27:2–6; Jer. 2:21; Ezek. 15; 19:10–14; Hos. 10:1), the replacement of Israel. It is the flock of God (John 10; 17; 21:15–23; cf. Ps. 23; Isa. 40:11; Jer. 23:1; Ezek. 34:11). The church is also the new covenant community (cf. John 20:17 with Ex. 6:7; Lev. 26:12). Second, there is a corporate dimension to faith in the fourth gospel alongside the emphasis on individual salvation—namely, followers of Jesus are called upon to love one another and pursue unity with one another (John 13:34–35; 15:12–13; 17:20–26). Third, John is familiar with baptism and the Eucharist. He alludes to the former in John 7:37–39, the latter in John 6:51–52, and perhaps both in John 19:34b–35.

F. Eschatology

The doctrine of the end times receives an unusual twist in the fourth gospel in two ways. First, John's eschatology is more realized than futurist in perspective. In other words, those blessings that early Christianity expected would occur at the second coming of Christ actually transpired at the first coming of Christ. Note the following: (1) Eternal life, or entrance into the kingdom of God, can be a present possession according to the gospel of John (6:47; cf. 3:15–16, 36; 6:51, 58; 8:51–52; 10:28; 11:24–26). (2) The eschatological promise of sonship is granted to the believer in Jesus now (1:12–13; 3:3–8; 4:14). (3) The general resurrection has already begun (5:25). (4) The Spirit, the gift of the end times, currently indwells believers (7:37–39; 14:15–31; 15:26–27; 16:5–16; 20:22–23). (5) The presence of the new creation is an important theme to John (1:1–5). (6) Last day judgment is determined by one's present response to Jesus (3:19; 5:22–24, 27, 30–38; 9:38; 12:31–33). (7) The spirit of antichrist has already entered the world scene to oppose Christ (6:70; 13:2, 27; 14:13; et al.). (8) I have argued elsewhere that John understands Jesus' death on the cross as absorbing the messianic woes, or the Great Tribulation. In other words, Jesus' passion was where the end-time holy war was raged, and his death and resurrection signaled the defeat of the forces of evil.[47]

But this is not to deny that a strand of futurist eschatology also occurs in the fourth gospel. Note the following: the kingdom of God is both present and future (John 3:3, 5); the future resurrection is still expected (5:26–30), and that juxtaposed to the present

---

47. Pate, *Communities of the Last Days*, chap. 9.

resurrection (5:19–25); the second coming of Christ is alluded to (14:1–6) because it is delayed (21:22–23).

Second, John's eschatology is more spatial/vertical than historical/horizontal. Raymond Brown summarizes the first of these types of eschatology in John:

> In many ways this Gospel betrays a vertical approach to salvation. The Son of Man has come down from heaven (iii 13), the Word has become flesh (I 14), with the purpose of offering salvation to men. The culmination of his career is when he is lifted up toward heaven in death and resurrection to draw all men to himself (xii 32). There is a constant contrast in John between two worlds: one above, the other below (iii 3, 31, viii 23); a sphere that belongs to Spirit, and a sphere that belongs to flesh (iii 6, vi 63). Jesus brings the life of the other world, "eternal life," to the men of this world; and death has no power over this life (xi 25). His gifts are "real" gifts, that is, heavenly gifts: the real water of life, as contrasted with ordinary water (iv 10–14); the real bread of life, as contrasted with perishable bread (vi 27); he is the real light that has come into the world (iii 19). These characteristics betraying an atemporal and vertical approach to salvation have constituted one of Bultmann's main arguments for advancing the hypothesis of Gnostic influence on John.[48]

But as Brown goes on to point out, the historical/horizontal aspect of salvation is not missing in John. Thus the prologue (1:1–18) proclaims the incarnation to be God's climactic intervention in history. At the other end of the spectrum, the "hour" appointed for Jesus' death (2:4; 8:20; 12:23; et al.) represents the culmination of God's plan of salvation history. And this end of history is accompanied by the time of the church, whose persecution (15:18–16:4) and evangelistic mission (4:35–38; 20:21) hasten the return of Christ.[49]

The combination in John of realized and futurist eschatologies and of vertical and horizontal dualism is not new. Earlier the Dead Sea Scrolls had made the same connections (see 1QM; 1QH; et al.).[50]

With the preceding introductory matters in mind, we now proceed to an analysis of the gospel of John.

---

48. Brown, *Gospel according to John I–XII*, cxv.
49. Ibid., cxv–cxvi.
50. See Pate, *Communities of the Last Days*, chap. 9.

1. What is the internal evidence for the traditional view of the authorship of the fourth gospel?

2. What are the three divisions of the Hebrew Bible?

3. Did Papias distinguish the author of the fourth gospel from John the apostle? Why or why not?

4. What other individuals beside the apostle John have been thought to have written the fourth gospel?

5. How would you evaluate the theory that the fourth gospel was produced by a "Johannine school"?

6. Why was the gospel of John not considered canonical until the late second century AD?

7. Discuss whether Hellenistic systems like Gnosticism, the Hermetic corpus, and Mandaeism provided the conceptual background of the gospel of John.

8. How do the writings of Philo and the thought world of Stoicism compare and differ from the fourth gospel?

9. What are some of the similarities in eschatology between the Dead Sea Scrolls and Johannine literature?

10. Was there a relationship between rabbinic Judaism and the gospel of John?

11. What may have been the twofold historical setting of the gospel of John?

12. Is the fourth gospel anti-Semitic?

13. Of the three types of literature — "acts," "memoirs," "lives," — which most probably shaped the "gospel" genre?

14. What are some of the differences between John and the Synoptic Gospels?

15. How does John both equate and distinguish Jesus and God?

16. How would you describe the eschatology of the fourth gospel?

KEY TERMS

apocalyptic literature

Athanasius

canon

Dead Sea Scrolls

eschatology

Essenes

Eusebius

Gnostics/*gnōsis*

gospel genre

Gospel of Thomas

Hellenism

Hellenistic Judaism

Hermetic literature

Johannine literature

Johannine school

John Rylands p^{52}

Josephus

logos/Logos

Mandaean literature

Mishnah

Nag Hammadi manuscripts

Palestinian Judaism

Papias

Paraclete

Philo

Plato

Platonic dualism

rabbinic Judaism

realized eschatology

Sadducees

Septuagint

Stoicism

Synoptic Gospels

Tatian's *Diatessaron*

twelfth "benediction"

CHAPTER 2

The Prologue of John

JOHN 1:1-18

Objectives

After reading this chapter, you should be able to:

- Identify the main purpose for John's usage of *logos* in his prologue.

- Describe the points of contact between Wisdom and John 1:1-18.

- Provide an outline of John's prologue.

- Discuss the relationship between Jesus and John the Baptist.

- Contrast the grace of Christ with the law of Moses.

INTRODUCTION

John's prologue (John 1:1–18) functions like an overture to an opera. Most notably, the theme of Logos that pervades John 1:1–18 also deeply impacts the gospel of John as a whole, portraying as it does that Jesus is the embodiment and replacement of the Torah (see my discussion below). I will overview John's prologue by covering two points: its background and purposes, and its structure. After that, I will summarize the content of John 1:1–18.

I. THE BACKGROUND AND PURPOSES OF JOHN'S PROLOGUE

Observers have long noted that virtually everything John says about the Logos/Word in his prologue is paralleled in Palestinian Jewish discussions about Wisdom, texts that clearly predate the New Testament period. Note the accompanying comparisons.

John's Prologue and Wisdom[1]	
John	**Wisdom**
The Word was in the beginning (John 1:1).	Wisdom was in the beginning (Prov. 8:22–23; Wisd. Sol. 9:9; Sir. 1:4).
The Word was with God (John 1:1).	Wisdom was with God (Prov. 8:30; Wisd. Sol. 9:4; Sir. 1:1).
The Word was cocreator (John 1:1–3).	Wisdom was cocreator (Prov. 3:19; 8:25; Wisd. Sol. 7:22; 9:1–2).
The Word provides light (John 1:4, 9).	Wisdom provides light (Prov. 8:22; Wisd. Sol. 7:26; Sir. 4:12; Bar. 4:2).
The Word as light is in contrast to darkness (John 1:5).	Wisdom as light is in contrast to darkness (Wisd. Sol. 7:29–30).
The Word was in the world (John 1:10).	Wisdom was in the world (Wisd. Sol. 8:1; Sir. 24:6).
The Word was rejected by its own (John 1:11).	Wisdom was rejected by its own (Sir. 15:7; Bar. 3:12; cf. *1 Enoch* 42:1–2).
The Word was received by the faithful (John 1:12).	Wisdom was received by the faithful (Wisd. Sol. 7:27; Bar. 3:37).
The Word became flesh (John 1:14).	Wisdom indwelled Israel (Sir. 24:8, 23; Bar. 3:37–4:2).

---

1. The Wisdom background to John's prologue is to be preferred as the main influence on "logos," rather than the logos of Hellenistic philosophy, Philo's logos, and the logos of Gnosticism. Recall my similar conclusion in the introduction. The following is from C. Marvin Pate, *Communities of the Last Days: The Dead Sea Scrolls, the New Testament and the Story of Israel* (Downers Grove, Ill.: InterVarsity, 2000), 227–28, and the bibliography. Wisdom Christology also informs 1 Corinthians 1:24, 30; 8:6; 2 Corinthians 4:4; and Colossians 1:15–20.

This particular wisdom background seems to best identify the conceptual framework of John's prologue, although other alternatives have been suggested.[2]

I conclude this discussion of the background of John's prologue by identifying three purposes it served. First, John's prologue refuted the rabbinic notion that the law of Moses is the Wisdom of God by equating Jesus Christ with Wisdom who replaces the Torah. Second, verses like John 1:14 (the Word became flesh "and made his dwelling among us") may be a polemic against the beginnings of Gnostic thinking that denied the humanity of Christ (cf. 1, 2, 3 John). Third, the parenthetical statements about John the Baptist in the prologue (John 1:6–9, 15) may be directed against those who continued to follow the teachings of John the Baptist rather than Jesus (see Acts 19:1–7).

II. THE STRUCTURE OF JOHN'S PROLOGUE

Although there is at the present no consensus on what the precise structure of John 1:1–18 is,[3] more and more scholars recognize that the prologue's overarching outline parallels ancient Jewish Wisdom hymns found in texts like Proverbs 8:22–25; Wisdom of Solomon 9:9–12; and Sirach 24:5–27.

M. E. Boismard has identified that structure as follows: Wisdom's relation with God, her preexistence, her role in creation, her being sent to dwell among God's people on earth, and finally, her benefits to those who seek her.[4] John 1:1–18 fits this pattern: Wisdom's/Christ's relation to God (1:1), his preexistence (1a, 2b), his role in creation (1:3–5), his being sent to dwell among God's people (1:10–14), and his benefits to those who seek him (1:12, 16–18).

> More and more scholars recognize that the prologue's overarching outline parallels ancient Jewish Wisdom hymns.

When it comes to outlining the hymn, Raymond Brown's delineation is as good as anyone's, and we will follow it, but include part E:

A. First Strophe: 1:1–2

B. Second Strophe: 1:3–5

C. Parenthetical Statement about John the Baptist: 1:6–9

D. Third Strophe: 1:10–13

E. Fourth Strophe: 1:14–18[5]

With these introductory remarks in mind, let us now survey John 1:1–18, following Brown's outline as a guide.

---

2. See Andreas J. Köstenberger's discussion in *John*, Baker Exegetical Commentary on the New Testament (Grand Rapids: Baker, 2004), 26–27. Those possibilities include Stoic usage of logos and the Old Testament's depiction of the Word of God.

3. See Craig S. Keener's overview of the numerous possibilities, *The Gospel of John: A Commentary*, vol. 1 (Peabody, Mass.: Hendrickson, 2003), 334–37.

4. Marie-Émile Boismard, *St. John's Prologue*, trans. Carisbrooke Dominicans (London: Blackfriars, 1957), 74–76.

5. Raymond E. Brown, *The Gospel according to John I–XII*, Anchor Bible 29A (Garden City, N.Y.: Doubleday, 1966), 3–4. Other authors propose a chiastic structure for John's prologue; see Köstenberger's discussion in *John*, 19–23.

John's Prologue as a Chiasm

A   in the beginning
 B   was
  C   the Word
   D   and the Word
    E   was
     F   with God
     F'   and God
    E'   was
   D'   the Word
  C'   this one
 B'   was
A'   in the beginning with God

III. ANALYSIS OF JOHN 1:1–18

A. First Strophe (1:1–2): The Word and God

We know from 1:14 that the "Word" is Jesus Christ. The first strophe, or verse, of John's prologue forms a chiasm, as numerous commentators recognize (see sidebar "John's Prologue as a Chiasm").

Two truths about Jesus Christ the Word surface from this arrangement. First, the Word was with God in the beginning, attesting to Christ's preexistence. In other words, before Jesus Christ came to earth, he existed in eternity past as the Son of God, the second member of the Trinity. The idea that Wisdom was with God in the past would have made this claim more palatable to the Jewish monotheistic faith. Second, more than that, the Word was God; that is, Jesus is equal to God.

B. Second Strophe (1:3–5): The Word and Creation

Wisdom/Torah was thought in ancient Judaism to be God's cocreator, who caused light to shine in the darkness and who granted life to humans. John says as much of Jesus, the Wisdom of God, in 1:3–5. He states it positively in verse 3a and then negatively in 3b.[6] The term "came into being" (Gk., *egeneto*) is used in the LXX of Genesis 1 for God's acts of creation. And the terms "life" and "light" take the reader back to the creation account in Genesis 1. John seems to be saying, then, that Jesus, the Wisdom of God, not the Torah, was God's agent in creation: he brought the world into being, caused God's light to shine, and gave life to creation.

C. Parenthetical Statement about John the Baptist (1:6–9)

Verses 6–9 interrupt the hymn regarding the Word. Two facts about John the Baptist emerge in John 1:6–9. First, John was sent by God to be a witness to Christ the true Light. As such, John is the first witness of Jesus in the fourth gospel (1:6–9, 15, 19, 32–34; 3:26; 5:33–36), who is followed by other witnesses to Jesus: Jesus' miracles (3:11, 32; 5:36; 8:14, 18; 10:25, 32, 37–38; 15:24; 18:37), Moses and the Scriptures (5:39, 46), the Father (5:32, 36–37; 8:18), the Spirit (chaps. 14–16; esp. 15:26), the disciples (e.g., 15:27), and the fourth evangelist himself (19:35; 21:24).

Second, John's role as a witness to Jesus was intended to bring people to believe in Jesus. As the commentators regularly point out, the fourth gospel consistently uses the verb *pisteuō* (nearly 100 times), not the noun *pistis*, to indicate that

> Wisdom/Torah was thought in ancient Judaism to be God's cocreator, who caused light to shine in the darkness and who granted life to humans. John says as much of Jesus, the Wisdom of God, in 1:3–5.

---

6. *Ho gegona* ("that has come into being") goes with the end of v. 3 ("apart from him nothing came into being that *has come into being*") rather than with v. 4 (v. 3: "apart from him nothing came into being; v. 4: what *has come into being* through him was life").

faith in Christ involves a personal relationship with him, not just intellectual assent to a creed.

Note that John 1:6–9 might be combating a John the Baptist sect. According to Acts 19:1–7, long after John the Baptist's death, he was apparently exalted by his followers. For some time now, scholars have maintained that the gospel of John seeks to demonstrate in the face of the Baptist sect that Jesus is superior to John the Baptist; the former is the Messiah and true Light, while the latter is only the forerunner of the Messiah and merely witness to Jesus the true Light (cf. 1:6–9 with 1:15, 24–27, 29–34; 4:1; 5:36; 10:41).

John 1:9 is a transitional verse. The reference to Jesus the "true light" refers back to verse 8, while his "coming into the world" anticipates verse 10.[7] "The coming one" (*erchomenos*) is a messianic title applied to Jesus in the fourth gospel and elsewhere in the New Testament (1:15, 27; 3:31; 6:14; 11:27; 12:13; cf. Heb. 10:37; 2 John 7; Rev. 1:4).[8] But what does it mean that Jesus "lights [enlightens] every man"? Most commentators rightly rule out the possibility that John is advocating "universalism"—that is, that all people are saved because the light of Christ resides within them. Rather, the statement speaks of a historical moment, namely, the incarnation of Christ. At that time, the light of the gospel of Christ began to shine for all to see. Regrettably, however, many chose not to receive that light (John 1:10–11). As Craig Keener notes, it may be that John's assertion counters the rabbinic notion that God made available to the world the light of his law when he revealed it to Moses at Mount Sinai.[9]

D. Third Strophe (1:10–13): The Word and the World

Undoubtedly John 1:10–11 records the greatest irony in the gospel of John: Jesus the Jewish Messiah was rejected by his own people. Like God's Wisdom of old who offered life to men but was rejected (*1 Enoch* 42:1–3), so Jesus the Wisdom of God was rejected by the world. The word "world" (*kosmos*) occurs three times in verse 10. In the fourth gospel, the term has three different meanings. First, "world" means the natural creation of God through Christ (cf. v. 10a with 1:3–5). Second, "world" is humanity, which God loved enough to send his Son to save (3:16, 17; 10:36; 12:47). Third, the "world" can also refer to the satanic evil system that dominates humanity and sets its heart against Christ (cf. 1:10b with 9:39; 12:31; cf. 1 John 2:15–17).

Verse 10 is a general statement about humanity's rejection of Jesus while verse 11 is a specific statement about Israel's rejection of Jesus. The irony and tragedy is that God's covenant people rejected their long-awaited Messiah.

In contrast, those who did receive Christ, those who believed in him, became the children of God; that is, the new covenant people. "Received" and "believed" are synonymous. John's usage of "believed" calls for two comments. First, as I just mentioned, the fourth gospel always uses the verb,

> Undoubtedly John 1:10–11 records the greatest irony in the gospel of John: Jesus the Jewish Messiah was rejected by his own people.

---

7. See Brown, *Gospel according to John I–XII*, 28.

8. "Coming into the world" refers to Jesus the Light, not the light coming to every man. This is so because the relative pronoun is neuter—*ho*—and thus modifies *phōs* ("light," which is neuter) and not man ("*anthrōpon*," which is masculine).

9. Keener, *Gospel of John*, 394.

pisteuō, never the noun form. This is so because, for John, belief is a dynamic personal relationship with God through Jesus, not a static, intellectual assent to a creed.

Second, the fourth gospel combines *pisteuein* with *eis* ("believe into") to indicate true faith in Jesus Christ (this construction occurs 36 times therein). The "name" (v. 12) probably alludes to the name of God, thus equating Jesus with God (see 8:24, 28, 58; 13:19). So belief in Jesus is not without doctrinal content. Those who demonstrate true belief in Jesus become the children of God. In Johannine literature the author reserves the title "Son" for Jesus. The term used for believers is "children" of God. This is so because Jesus is the "one and only Son" (see 1:14, 18; 3:16).

Israel is also referred to as the children of God in the Old Testament (see esp. Deut. 14:1; 32:18; cf. Ex. 4:22). Yet since the advent of Jesus the Messiah, the criterion for becoming a child of God is faith in Christ. Natural procreation (John 1:13)—that is, just being born Jewish—no longer qualifies one as a child of God. One must be born of God—that is, born spiritually (see 3:3, 5).[10]

> The fourth gospel always uses the verb, *pisteuō*, never the noun form. This is so because, for John, belief is a dynamic personal relationship with God through Jesus, not a static, intellectual assent to a creed.

E. Fourth Strophe (1:14–18)

John 1:14–18 is the fourth strophe of the hymn[11] comprising the prologue. Verse 15 contains another testimony of Jesus' superiority to John the Baptist. But the overriding concern of John 1:14–18, like the rest of the prologue, is to contrast Christ and Moses and, thereby, to discredit rabbinic Judaism. Four points of discontinuity therefore emerge in verses 14–18 between Christ and Moses.

1. *The glory of the old covenant was temporary, but the glory of the new covenant in Christ is permanent.* God's glory left the temple in Jerusalem because of ancient Israel's sin (Ezek. 11:23), and they were then carted away into Babylonian exile. But Ezekiel prophesied of the coming day of restoration when God's glory would once again indwell his people (Ezek. 44:4). John 1:14 draws on that background, equating Christ with such restored glory. He is the true tabernacle and the new temple (2:19–22). God's glory has permanently become incarnate in Jesus and through him in his followers.

The word "flesh" here is not used with the connotation of evil but rather of humanity. As such, it is a polemic against the beginning stages of Gnosticism (cf. John 1:14 with 6:51–59; 19:34–35; 1 John 4:2–3; 2 John 7). This also rules out any gnostic nuance to the words "full" (John 1:14) and "fullness" (v. 16).

Another key word describing Jesus in verse 14 is "*monogenēs.*" While some translations render this word "only-begotten," it is better translated "one of a kind."[12]

Verse 15, like verses 6–9, have to do with John the Baptist's testimony to the superiority of Christ over him. Verses 6–9 claim that Jesus was superior to John in ministry, while

---

10. Verse 13 seems to be a commentary on the third strophe (1:10–12) and not a part of the hymn itself.

11. The two telltale signs that the prologue contains a hymn are (1) the recurrent usage of *kai* ("and") and (2) coordinating clauses.

12. For a thorough treatment of the term *monogenēs*, see Dale Moody, "God's Only Son: The Translation of John 3:16 in the Revised Standard Version," *JBL* 72 (1953): 213–19.

verse 15 asserts that Jesus is superior to John in that the former was preexistent while the latter was not.

2. John 1:16 resumes the hymn to Jesus. The phrase that could literally be translated "grace in place of grace" most likely refers to the grace of Christ's new covenant as replacing the grace of Moses' covenant.

3. John 1:17 contrasts Moses' law, which was based on works, with Christ's covenant, which is based on grace.

4. Verse 18 alludes to the fact that Moses was not permitted to see God's face (Ex. 33:20), while Jesus was at God's side in eternity past, viewing his glory face-to-face and now revealing that glory to his followers.

These contrasts herald John's belief in Christ's superiority over the Mosaic law and rabbinic Judaism.

> The phrase that could literally be translated "grace in place of grace" most likely refers to the grace of Christ's new covenant as replacing the grace of Moses' covenant.

REVIEW QUESTIONS

1. What is the main purpose of John's usage of *logos* in his prologue?

2. What are some of the comparisons between John 1:1 – 18 and the Wisdom background?

3. What is the structure of John's prologue (1:1 – 18)?

4. What do we learn about the relationship between John the Baptist and Jesus, according to John 1:6 – 9?

5. What is the great irony of John 1:10 – 11?

6. How does faith in Christ contrast with the law of Moses, according to John 1:14 – 18?

KEY TERMS

believer	Logos	prologue
faith	Monogenes	Wisdom

CHAPTER 3

The Witnesses of John to Jesus

JOHN 1:19–51

Objectives

After reading this chapter, you should be able to:

- Describe the affirmations John the Baptist made about Jesus.
- List the titles of Jesus expressed by his disciples.

INTRODUCTION

John 1:19–2:11 seems to depict the first seven days of Jesus' public ministry like this:

Day 1: John's testimony regarding Jesus (1:19–28)

Day 2: John's encounter with Jesus (1:29–34; "the next day")

Day 3: John's referral of two disciples to Jesus (1:35–39; "the next day")

Day 4: Andrew's introduction of his brother Peter to Jesus (1:40–42)

Day 5: Philip and Nathanael follow Jesus (1:43–51; "the next day")

Day 6: Not explicitly mentioned

Day 7: Wedding at Cana (2:1–11; "on the third day")[1]

The purpose of this schema evidently is to craft Jesus' first week of ministry as an analogy to the seven days of creation. That is, Jesus' first week of ministry was the beginning of the new creation.

The overall theme of John 1:19–51 is the witness of John the Baptist to Jesus. John made three points: he denied that he is God's end-time (eschatological) figure (1:19–28); he then affirmed that Jesus is that person (1:29–34); and finally, he referred some of his disciples to Jesus (1:35–51). I now summarize these three points.

---

1. The chart is from Andreas J. Köstenberger, *John*, Baker Exegetical Commentary on the New Testament (Grand Rapids: Baker, 2004), 57.

The Jordan River, where baptisms are still conducted today.

Pharisees and Sadducees

Josephus refers to the Pharisees, Sadducees, and Essenes as "schools of thought,"[2] something of a mix between a religious faction and a political affiliation.

1. The name *Pharisee* is probably derived from the Hebrew/Aramaic *perušim*, the separated ones, alluding to both their origin and their characteristic practices. They tended to be politically conservative and religiously liberal and held the minority membership on the Sanhedrin:[3]

   - They held to the supreme place of Torah, with a rigorous scribal interpretation of it.
   - Their most pronounced characteristic was their adherence to the oral tradition, which they obeyed rigorously as an attempt to make the written law relevant to daily life.
   - They had a well-developed belief in angelic beings.
   - They had concrete messianic hopes, as they looked for the coming Davidic messianic kingdom. The Messiah would overthrow the Gentiles and restore the fortunes of Israel with Jerusalem as capital.
   - They believed in the resurrection of the righteous when the messianic kingdom arrived, with the accompanying punishment of the wicked.
   - They viewed Rome as an illegitimate force that was preventing Israel from experiencing its divinely ordained role in the outworking of the covenants.
   - They held strongly to divine providence, yet viewed humans as having freedom of choice, which ensures their responsibility.
   - As a lay fellowship or brotherhood connected with local synagogues, the Pharisees were popular with the common people.

2. The *Sadducees* were a small group with aristocratic and priestly influence, who derived their authority from the activities of the temple. They tended to be politically liberal and religiously conservative and held the majority membership on the Sanhedrin:

   - They held a conservative attitude toward the Scriptures, accepting nothing as authoritative except the written word, literally interpreted.
   - They accepted only Torah (the five books of Moses) as authoritative, rejecting any beliefs not found there.
   - For that reason they denied the resurrection from the dead, the reality of angels, and spirit life.
   - They produced no literature of which we are aware.
   - They had no expressed messianic expectation, which tended to make them satisfied with their wealth and political power.
   - They were open to aspects of Hellenism and often collaborated with the Romans.
   - They tended to be removed from the common people by economic and political status.

---

2. Josephus, *Ant.* 13.5.9 §171.

3. The composition of the "Sanhedrin" is debated by modern scholars because the ancient sources (e.g., Josephus, New Testament, and the rabbinic literature) demonstrate a changing nature of this body. See comments on 26:59; cf. Anthony J. Saldarini, *Pharisees, Scribes, and Sadducees* (Wilmington, Del.: Michael Glazier, 1988).

I. JOHN'S DENIALS (1:19–28)

Because John was promoting a baptism of repentance—a type of purification ritual—the priests and Levites, possibly at the instigation of the Pharisees, came to John to investigate his activity (1:19, 24). Baptism in the Jordan River in the Judean desert suggested to the Jewish leadership that John was staging a new exodus or a new conquest designed to overthrow the yoke of the Roman enslavement of Israel; hence their questions to John about his eschatological message. Was he the Messiah/Christ (1:19–20, 24)? In other words, was John the anointed Son of David predicted in the Old Testament who would defeat Israel's enemies and establish God's kingdom (see e.g., 2 Sam. 7:11b–16; Hos. 3:5; cf. *Pss. Sol.* 17:72; 4QFlor.; 1QS 9:16; 10:11)? The Baptist denied the identification. Next, the Baptist was asked if he was Elijah (1:21, 25). The resemblances between the two were striking. John dressed like Elijah the prophet (cf. 17aff. 3:4 with 2 Kings 1:8) and preached like him as well (cf. Matt. 3:7–12; Luke 3:7–17). Elijah, who never died (2 Kings 2:11), was expected by Jews to be the forerunner of the Messiah (Mal. 4:5; cf. Mal. 3:1; *4 Ezra* 6:26–27). John, however, denied being literally Elijah, even though Jesus connected the two (Matt. 11:14; 17:12; Mark 9:13).

The miqveh pools were used for Jewish ritual purity washings.

John also denied being the "Prophet." According to Jewish interpretation of Deuteronomy 18:15, 18, a prophet like Moses was expected to appear at the end of history to call

Mount Sinai, where the law was given to Moses.

Israel back to God's law and thereby inaugurate the restoration of the nation (1 Macc. 4:41–50; 14:41; 1QS 9:11; 4QTest).[4]

Rather than being the eschatological Savior of Israel, John was only a voice crying in the wilderness to prepare the way of the Lord (John 1:23; cf. Isa. 40:3). In the original setting of this statement, Isaiah refers figuratively to preparing the roads to allow Israel to return home from the Babylonian exile. Accordingly, John saw himself as one whose ministry was to prepare the way for God's chosen one to come and effect the true restoration of Israel, namely, to turn their hearts to God.

II. JOHN'S AFFIRMATIONS (1:29–34)

On the second day, John the Baptist saw Jesus and made a number of affirmations about him. First, he addressed Jesus as "the Lamb (*amnos*) of God, who takes away the sin of the world" (1:29; cf. v. 36). The title Lamb of God could have stemmed from one of three backgrounds.

1. It could have been an allusion to Jewish expectations of an apocalyptic lamb who would slay Israel's enemies and establish God's kingdom at the end of time (*1 Enoch* 90:38; *T. Jos.* 19:8; cf. Rev. 7:17; 17:14). But the problem with this possibility is that the word for "lamb" in John 1:29 is *amnos*, while the term in the texts heralding the apocalyptic lamb is *arnion*.

2. "Lamb of God" in John 1:29 more probably draws on the Suffering Servant of Isaiah (Isa. 42:1–9; 49:1–13; 50:4–11; 52:13–53).

3. It may also be that the title Lamb of God in John 1:29 includes the concept of the paschal lamb, the lamb slain yearly on Passover to commemorate Israel's exodus (Ex. 12:1–13). Later John's passion narrative makes this connection explicit (see John 19:14, 29, 35; cf. Rev. 5:6; 15:3).

© Dr. James C. Martin (bibleworldseminars@gmail.com). Istanbul Archaeological Museum.

John the Baptist points to Jesus as the Lamb of God.

Second, John the Baptist testified that Jesus was preexistent with God in the past (1:30). The Baptist had already confessed that Jesus was before him in ministry (1:27). Now he asserts that Jesus was before him in existence (v. 30; cf. 1:1–5; 8:58; 17:5).

Third, John the Baptist acknowledged that Jesus possessed the end-time Holy Spirit and will baptize his followers with that Spirit (cf. Joel 2:28–30 with John 1:31–34; 3:5, 34; 7:38–39; 14–16).

Fourth, it may be that the Baptist applied one more title to Jesus, namely, the "hidden Messiah." In John 1:31, 33 the Baptist says that he did not recognize Jesus to be the Messiah.[5] While the dominant Jewish messianic expectation seemed to be that the Messiah would be the Son of David who would emerge from Bethlehem, the house of David (Mic. 5:2; John 7:42), another strand of Jewish messianism thought the origins of the Messiah would be unknown (see the Son of Man figure in *1 Enoch* especially).

In all of this, John the Baptist's testimony is clear: Jesus is the Messiah, not him.

---

4. It is clear from these eschatological figures that there was no uniform messianic expectation in Second Temple Judaism.

5. How this is to be reconciled with Luke 1 and the report that John was Jesus' cousin is difficult to know. Perhaps John the Baptist was not privy to that information while growing up.

III. JOHN'S REFERRALS (1:35–51)

On day three of Jesus' opening week of ministry, John the Baptist referred two of his disciples to Jesus—Andrew and an unnamed disciple (1:35–39).[6] Those two disciples went to Jesus' lodging about 4:00 p.m. and apparently stayed there for the rest of the evening. On Day 4 Andrew brought his brother Peter to Jesus (1:40–42). And, then, on Day 5 Jesus found Philip in Galilee, who then brought Nathanael to Jesus (1:43–51).

So what emerges in John 1:35–51 is a spiritual chain reaction: John the Baptist sent two of his disciples to follow Jesus, one of whom—Andrew—brought Peter to Jesus.[7] Philip then brought Nathanael to Christ. Thus, John the Baptist had performed his mission—his testimony to Jesus set in motion a chain of witnesses to the Savior. Along the way in this narrative, the disciples of Jesus confirmed the titles that the Baptist applied to Jesus, and more.[8]

John is the only gospel to address Jesus as "Messiah."

A. Rabbi (vv. 35–39)

The two disciples of John the Baptist who followed Jesus addressed him as "Rabbi" (v. 38). "Rabbi" literally means "my great one/master," that is, "teacher" (cf. 1:38, 49; 3:2; 4:31; 6:25; 9:2; 11:8).[9]

B. Messiah (vv. 40–42)

I touched upon this title earlier. Here we observe that John is the only gospel to address Jesus as "Messiah" (Hebrew for "anointed"; cf. 4:25). All the other gospels call Jesus "Christ" (Greek for "anointed").

C. Moses and the Prophets (v. 45)

The reference in verse 45 to "the one Moses wrote about in the Law, and about whom the prophets also wrote" probably reinforces the title Messiah/Christ applied to Jesus earlier. That is, Moses predicted the coming Messiah—Jesus (Deut. 18:15, 18)—as did the prophets (e.g., Isa. 9:1–7; 11:1–5, 10–12; 52:13–53:12; cf. John 5:39, 46; 6:45). Nathanael

---

6. It may be that the unnamed disciple was John, the author of the fourth gospel. This would be in keeping with his practice of referring to himself only anonymously therein. If so, we would have an explanation as to how Essene thought dominates Johannine literature: John the Baptist, a one-time Essene, introduced John to it. Also, if as some commentators suspect, Jesus was initially a disciple of John the Baptist, that, too, would account for the influence of the thinking of the writers of the Dead Sea Scrolls on early Christianity.

7. The changing of Simon's name to "Cephas" (Aramaic for "Rock") or "Peter" (Greek for "Rock") is reminiscent of Peter's confession as recorded in Matthew 16:16–18.

8. The commentators call attention to two significant differences between the calling of the disciples as found in John and in the Synoptics. First, in the Synoptic Gospels the disciples do not immediately follow Jesus at his invitation to follow him; rather, an interval of time transpires. John, however, has the disciples instantaneously following Jesus. Second, in the Synoptics the disciples' understanding of Jesus' nature takes time to develop. But in John 1 the disciples manifest a clear perspective regarding Jesus' deity, as is evidenced in the numerous christological titles in John 1:35–51. But perhaps these two viewpoints can be harmonized. First, John does not necessarily rule out an interval between the call and following of the disciples. Second, the Synoptics allow for an exalted view of Jesus on the part of the disciples early on. Otherwise, why would they have left all to follow him in the first place?

9. See Köstenberger, *John*, 74.

Left: Nazareth, Jesus' boyhood town. *Right:* Excavations at Sepphoris, a bustling Hellenistic town at the time of Christ. It was near Nazareth, but no mention of it is made in the Gospels.

found it hard to believe that Jesus was the Messiah because he thought Jesus was from Nazareth, an insignificant town compared to Bethlehem, the true birthplace of the Messiah (John 1:46). Nathanael was unaware that Jesus was actually born in Bethlehem.

D. Son of God (v. 49)

"Son of God," Nathanael's term for Jesus, again takes us to the messianic significance of Jesus. "Son of God" in the Old Testament was applied to angels (Gen. 6:1–4; Job 1:6; 38:7), Davidic kings (2 Sam. 7:14; Pss. 2:7; 89:27), and Israel itself (Deut. 14:1; Hos. 11:1; et al.). "Son of God" was also a name for the Davidic Messiah in current Jewish circles (1QSa 2:11–12; 4QFlor 1:6–7; *1 Enoch* 105:2; *4 Ezra* 7:28–29; 13:52). Moreover, "Son of God" was applied in pagan sources to the pharaoh, Roman emperors, and divine men miracle workers.[10]

E. King of Israel (v. 49)

Nathanael also called Jesus "the King of Israel," a militaristic title (see Ps. 2:6–7; cf. John 12:13). Jesus, however, had other ideas (John 6:15; 12:15; 18:36).

F. Son of Man (vv. 50–51)

"Son of Man" was Jesus' favorite self-designation as recorded in the Gospels. I make three comments here about the title: its background, its classification in the Gospels, and the connection of the title to its context in John 1:50–51.

1. The Background of the Son of Man

"Son of Man" is a frequent phrase in Ezekiel, but there it is a synonym for mortal man. However, Daniel 7:13 attributes divinity to the heavenly Son of Man, which is probably a reference to Israel as the inheritor of the kingdom of God. In *1 Enoch* the heavenly Son of Man is a messianic-like individual who delivers Israel at the end of history (46:2–4; 48:2;

---

10. See the references in Joseph A. Fitzmyer, *The Gospel according to Luke I–IX*, Anchor Bible 28 (New York: Doubleday, 1979), 205–6.

62:5–7, 13–14; 69:27–29). This figure is presently hidden in heaven but will be revealed at the end of days. Jesus' use of the title seems to presume the background of Daniel 7 and *1 Enoch*. If so, then "Son of Man" was a title by which Jesus conveyed his divinity but without the political connotation of the title Messiah/Christ.

2. The Classification of Son of Man

In the Synoptic Gospels, Jesus' application of "Son of Man" to himself falls into three categories: references to the earthly activity of the Son of Man (eating, dwelling, saving the lost, etc.), references to the suffering of the Son of Man, and references to the future glory at the parousia (second coming) of the Son of Man. In John's gospel, the first Son of Man classification does not occur.

3. Son of Man in the Context of John 1:50–51

The background of John 1:47–51 seems to be Genesis 27–28 and Jacob's vision of angels ascending and descending a heavenly ladder. But Nathanael realized that Jesus the Son of Man is that ladder and therefore believed in him.

REVIEW QUESTIONS

1. What did the first seven days of Jesus' public ministry correspond to?

2. What roles did John the Baptist deny, according to John 1:19–28?

3. What three backgrounds might have informed John the Baptist's confession that Jesus is the Lamb of God (John 1:29)?

4. What four affirmations did John the Baptist make about Jesus in John 1:19–34?

5. What titles did the disciples apply to Jesus in John 1:35–51?

6. What is the Old Testament background of Jesus' title Son of Man?

7. What are the three classifications of the Son of Man in the New Testament?

KEY TERMS

King of Israel	Messiah/Christ	Son of God
Lamb of God	Moses and the Prophets	Son of Man
	rabbi	

CHAPTER 4

The Miracle at Cana and the Cleansing of the Temple

JOHN 2

Objectives

After reading this chapter, you should be able to:

- Discuss the two sign miracles in John 2.
- Discuss the messianic significance of those two signs.
- Explain why Jesus cleansed the temple at Jerusalem.

INTRODUCTION

John 2 records the first two sign miracles that initiated Jesus' public ministry: the changing of water into wine at Cana (2:1–12) and the cleansing of the temple in Jerusalem (2:14–25). The common bond between these two signs—the one positive and the other negative—is that Jesus thereby inaugurated the messianic age, the kingdom of God.

The Seven Signs/Miracles of Jesus in John

1. The changing of water into wine (2:1–11)
2. The temple cleansing (2:13–22)
3. The healing of the nobleman's son (4:46–54)
4. The healing of the lame man (5:1–15)
5. The feeding of the multitude (6:1–15)
6. The healing of the blind man (9:1–41)
7. The raising of Lazarus (11:1–44)

I. THE MIRACLE AT CANA (2:1–12)

John 1:51 promised that the Son of Man was about to perform the mighty works of God. That promise began to be realized with the miracle at Cana. It would be concluded in John 11–12, when Jesus performed the seventh sign, namely, the resurrection of Lazarus. These miracles were performed by Jesus to bring his audience to faith in himself (John 20:31). The miracle at Cana can be summarized in three points: its setting (vv. 1–2); the miracle itself (vv. 3–10); the significance of the miracle (vv. 11–12).

A. The Setting (vv. 1–2)

"On the third day" probably refers back to the events of John 1:19–51, in particular Jesus' encounter with Nathanael (1:43–51). Most contemporary scholars identify Cana with Khirbet-Qanah, which is located about eight miles northeast of Nazareth. This site fits Josephus's description of the ancient town (*Life* 16/86).[1]

Modern Cana, the town where Jesus performed his first miracle.

Weddings in ancient Judaism were festive occasions. They consisted of a procession in which the bridegroom's friends brought the bride to the groom's house, and then a wedding supper. That celebration lasted for seven days (Judg. 14:12; Tobit 11:18). The Mishnah (*Ketuboth* 1) states that Jewish virgins were married on Wednesday; this may suggest, then, that the miracle at Cana took place on that day.

B. The Miracle (vv. 3–10)

Shortage of wine at a wedding in ancient Judaism was a social disgrace.

---

1. Keener's discussion and bibliography amplifies this point, Craig S. Keener makes these points in *The Gospel of John: A Commentary*, vol. 1 (Peabody, Mass.: Hendrickson, 2003), 495–96.

The presence of Jesus and his disciples may have contributed to the shortage, prompting Mary's suggestion that Jesus do something about the problem. Verses 3–5 are difficult to interpret, but the general sense seems to be that Jesus was accountable to his heavenly Father's plan as to when he should perform his first miracle, not to his earthly mother's wishes.

The six stone water pots were used by Jews for purification — that is, for washing eating utensils and the guests' hands (see Mark 7:2–5). The amount of 120 gallons of water indicates that the jars were filled to the brim. The quality of the wine, even to the "bottom of the barrel," was not lost on the master of ceremonies.

Large jars like these were used by ancient Jews for, among other purposes, ceremonial washing.

C. The Significance of the Miracle (vv. 11–12)

Verse 11 states that the miracle at Cana was Jesus' first sign, and that by it he revealed his glory. "Sign" in John essentially means a miracle with a message; that is, the miracle is literal, but also symbolic.

As the commentators rightly note, the sign at Cana symbolized the presence of the messianic age in Jesus. Three points confirm this interpretation. First, the wedding was a symbol in ancient Ju-

"Sign" in John essentially means a miracle with a message; that is, the miracle is literal, but also symbolic.

Model of Jerusalem temple. According to the Jewish historian Josephus, Herod the Great began extensive remodeling of the temple in 20–19 BC.

daism and early Christianity of the arrival of the messianic age, or the kingdom of God (Isa. 54:4–8; 62:4–5; Matt. 8:11; 22:1–14; Luke 22:16–18; Rev. 19:9). Second, the abundance of wine was another symbol of the dawning of the messianic age (Jer. 31:12; Hos. 14:7; Amos 9:13–14; *1 Enoch* 10:19; *1 Bar.* 25:5). Third, at the arrival of the messianic age, God was expected to display his glory (Ps. 102:16; *1 Enoch* 49:2; *Pss. Sol.* 17:32; cf. John 2:11).

II. THE CLEANSING OF THE TEMPLE (2:13–25)

> The setting of Jesus' cleansing of the Jerusalem temple was Passover.

Though it is debated, it does seem that Jesus' cleansing of the Jerusalem temple was the second of the seven sign miracles recorded in John's Gospel.[2] This will become clear from my comments on verses 18–22. The cleansing of the temple episode can be summarized in five points: its setting (v. 13), the act of cleansing (vv. 14–17), its significance (vv. 18–22), the number of cleansings, and the conclusion to the narrative (vv. 23–25).

A. The Setting (v. 13)

The setting of Jesus' cleansing of the Jerusalem temple was Passover, which was the most important of Jewish feasts, celebrating God's deliverance of Israel from ancient Egypt. It

---

2. The alternative is that the cleansing of the temple was not a sign performed by Jesus and that his death and resurrection were the seventh sign of the fourth gospel. However, in light of the discussion to follow, probably both were signs: the destruction and rebuilding of the Jerusalem temple were a preview of the death and resurrection of Jesus, respectively. Andreas J. Köstenberger carefully defends the view that the temple cleansing was indeed a sign in "The Seventh Johannine Sign: A Study in John's Christology," *Bulletin of Biblical Research* 5 (1995): 87–103.

constituted the official beginning of that nation and has been celebrated annually ever since (Ex. 12). Passover was one of three feasts Jewish males were required to attend in Jerusalem (Tabernacles and Pentecost were the other two; see Deut. 16:16). John mentions three Passovers during Jesus' public ministry (2:13; 6:4; 11:55). This is the basis for calculating Jesus' public ministry to have been three years,[3] which is different from the only mention of the Passover in the Synoptics, Jesus' passion week in Jerusalem.

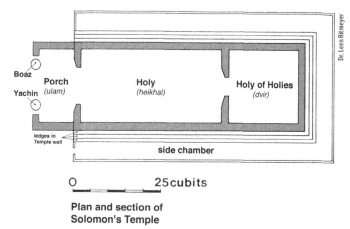

Plan and section of Solomon's Temple

B. The Cleansing (vv. 14–17)

The temple of Jerusalem had a storied history. It was built by Solomon in 966 BC, destroyed by the Babylonians in 587 BC, rebuilt by Zerubbabel in 516 BC, remodeled by Herod (beginning in 20–19 BC), and destroyed again by the Romans in AD 70.

Floor plan of Jerusalem temple.

John 2:14 and 19–21 refer to the two major areas of the temple: the outer court, the Court of the Gentiles (*hieron*, v. 14), and the inner court, consisting of the Court of the Women, the Court of the Men (Jews), the Holy Place, and the Holy of Holies (*naos*, vv. 19–21).

The presence of the animals and money changers in the Court of the Gentiles served two purposes. Because Passover pilgrims preferred not to bring their sacrificial animals with them on an arduous trip to Jerusalem, Caiaphas the high priest provided sacrificial animals for them (oxen, sheep, and, for the poor, doves). But to pay for these animals, only Tyrian coinage was permitted. Roman denarii and Attic drachmas were not allowed in the temple because they bore imperial and pagan imagery.[4]

The presence of the merchants in the temple with their sacrificial animals and currency exchange operation infuriated Jesus. With a whip, he drove out the animals and the merchants and overturned the tables of the money changers. Holy zeal consumed Jesus (cf. John 2:17 with Ps. 69:9) at the thought that the merchants had commercialized God's house of worship (cf. John 2:16 with Zech. 14:21; Mal. 3:1, 3). Thus, Jesus' clearing of

---

3. Scholars debate whether Jesus' three-year public ministry stretched from AD 27–30 or AD 30–33. It depends on how we are to understand Luke 3:1: Do we count from the year when Tiberius became coruler with Caesar Augustus (AD 12) or from when he became sole emperor of Rome (AD 15)? If the former, fifteen years later places us at AD 27 for the beginning of Jesus' ministry. If the latter, we arrive at AD 30 for the beginning of Jesus' ministry. Most scholars side with the former. Thus Jesus' ministry lasted from AD 27 to 30.

4. See Raymond E. Brown's discussion in *The Gospel according to John I–XII*, Anchor Bible 29A (Garden City, N.Y.: Doubleday, 1966), 115. V. Eppstein discusses the possibility that Caiaphas, the high priest of Israel at the time of Jesus, set up merchants in the outer temple precinct to rival the animal markets in the Kidron Valley or on the slopes of the Mount of Olives. "The Historicity of the Cleansing of the Temple," *Zeitschrift für die Neutestamentliche Wissenschaft* (*Journal for New Testament Scholarship*) 55 (1964): 42–58.

the temple was prophetic action like that of the Old Testament prophets who condemned Jerusalem's temple for becoming spiritually barren (Isa. 56:7; Jer. 7:11; Zech. 14:21; Mal. 3:1; et al.). In addition, we learn from John 2:19–21 that Jesus' body had become the new temple. This last idea fits in with Jewish expectation that the Messiah would rebuild God's temple (cf. John 2:19–21; Rev. 21:22 with Ezek. 40–46; Tobit 13:10; 14:5; 11QT[a,b]; and Mark 14:47–61).

C. Significance of the Cleansing (vv. 18–22)

Johannine irony is at work in verse 18: the Jewish leaders demand of Jesus a sign of his authority in clearing the temple. On the one hand, this is a reasonable request given the

Old Testament Feasts and Other Sacred Days			
Name	**Old Testament References**	**OT Time**	**Modern Equivalent**
Sabbath	Ex 20:8-11; 31:12-17; Lev 23:3; Dt 5:12-15	7th day	Same
Sabbath Year	Ex 23:10-11; Lev 25:1-7	7th year	Same
Year of Jubilee	Lev 25:8-55; 27:17-24; Nu 36:4	50th year	Same
Passover	Ex 12:1-14; Lev 23:5; Nu 9:1-14; 28:16; Dt 16:1-3a,4b-7	1st month (Abib) 14	Mar.–Apr.
Unleavened Bread	Ex 12:15-20; 13:3-10; 23:15; 34:18; Lev 23:6-8; Nu 28:17-25; Dt 16:3b,4a,8	1st month (Abib) 15-21	Mar.–Apr.
Firstfruits	Lev 23:9-14	1st month (Abib) 16	Mar.–Apr.
Weeks (Pentecost) (Harvest)	Ex 23:16a; 34:22a; Lev 23:15-21; Nu 28:26-31; Dt 16:9-12	3rd month (Sivan) 6	May–June
Trumpets (Later: Rosh Hashanah–New Year's Day)	Lev 23:23-25; Nu 29:1-6	7th month (Tishri) 1	Sept.–Oct.
Day of Atonement (Yom Kippur)	Lev 16; 23:26-32; Nu 29:7-11	7th month (Tishri) 10	Sept.–Oct.
Tabernacles (Booths) (Ingathering)	Ex 23:16b; 34:22b; Lev 23:33-36a,39-43; Nu 29:12-34; Dt 16:13-15; Zec 14:16-19	7th month (Tishri) 15-21	Sept.–Oct.
Sacred Assembly	Lev 23:36b; Nu 29:35-38	7th month (Tishri) 22	Sept.–Oct.
Purim	Est 9:18-32	12th month (Adar) 14,15	Feb.–Mar.

On Kislev 25 (mid-December) Hanukkah, the feast of dedication or festival of lights, commemorated the purification of the temple and altar in the Maccabean period (165/4 B.C.). This feast is mentioned in Jn 10:22 (see note there).

fact that Jewish authorities regularly investigated any would-be prophets among them (see Matt. 12:38; 16:1) and the Messiah was expected to perform certain signs (John 7:31).[5] But, on the other hand, the sad fact is that Jesus' cleansing of the temple was a divine sign in and of itself, and the religious leadership failed to realize such.

Jesus' response in verses 19–21 connects the sign of the cleansing of the temple with his coming death and resurrection: Jesus called for the demise of the temple, which ultimately cost him his life, but by his resurrection he became the eschatological, true locus of God's presence.

---

5. See Leon Morris, *The Gospel according to John*, rev. ed., New International Commentary on the New Testament (Grand Rapids: Eerdmans, 1995), 173–74.

Description	Purpose	New Testament References
Day of rest; no work	Rest for people and animals	Mt 12:1-14; 28:1; Lk 4:16; Jn 5:9–10; Ac 13:42; Col 2:16; Heb 4:1-11
Year of rest; fallow fields	Rest for land	
Canceled debts; liberation of slaves and indentured servants; land returned to original family owners	Help for poor; stabilize society	
Slaying and eating a lamb, together with bitter herbs and bread made without yeast, in every household	Remember Israel's deliverance from Egypt	Mt 26:17; Mk 14:12-26; Jn 2:13; 11:55; 1Co 5:7; Heb 11:28
Eating bread made without yeast; holding several assemblies; making designated offerings	Remember how the Lord brought the Israelites out of Egypt in haste	Mk 14:1; Ac 12:3; 1Co 5:6-8
Presenting a sheaf of the first of the barley harvest as a wave offering; making a burnt offering and a grain offering	Recognize the Lord's bounty in the land	Ro 8:23; 1Co 15:20-23
A festival of joy; mandatory and voluntary offerings, including the firstfruits of the wheat harvest	Show joy and thankfulness for the Lord's blessing of harvest	Ac 2:1-4; 20:16; 1Co 16:8
An assembly on a day of rest commemorated with trumpet blasts and sacrifices	Present Israel before the Lord for his favor	
A day of rest, fasting and sacrifices of atonement for priests and people and atonement for the tabernacle and altar	Atone for the sins of priests and people and purify the Holy Place	Ro 3:24-26; Heb 9:7; 10:3,19-22
A week of celebration for the harvest; living in booths and offering sacrifices	Memorialize the journey from Egypt to Canaan; give thanks for the productivity of Canaan	Jn 7:2,37
A day of convocation, rest and offering sacrifices	Commemorate the closing of the cycle of feasts	
A day of joy and feasting and giving presents	Remind the Israelites of their national deliverance in the time of Esther	

In addition, new moons were often special feast days (Nu 10:10; 1Ch 23:31; Ezr 3:5; Ne 10:33; Ps 81:3; Isa 1:13-14; 66:23; Hos 5:7; Am 8:5; Col 2:16).

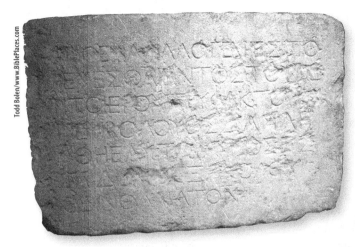

A warning sign prohibiting foreigners from entering the Jerusalem temple area. The sign was discovered in 1871. The translation of the Greek inscription reads, "No foreigner is to enter within the balustrade and enclosure around the temple area. Whoever is caught doing so will have himself to blame for his death which will follow."

The Jewish leadership persisted in its spiritual imperception by confusing the physical temple with God's house. They failed to see how a temple that had been remodeled by Herod beginning in 20–19 BC and continuing into their lifetimes could be rebuilt in three days (v. 20).[6]

D. The Number of Temple Cleansings

A debate has raged among scholars about the number of times Jesus cleansed the Jerusalem temple: One or two? And when? (1) A minority of interpreters think Jesus cleansed the temple twice: early on in his ministry (John 2:13–25) and at the end of his ministry (Matt. 21:12–16; Mark 11:15–18; Luke 19:45–47).[7] (2) An even smaller group of scholars think Jesus cleansed the temple once and it happened early on in his ministry (John 2:13–25), not at the end of his life (the Synoptics). (3) Most scholars today, however, believe Jesus cleansed the temple only once, and it was at the end of his ministry (the Synoptics). On this reading, John has taken the liberty to transpose the temple cleansing from the end to the beginning of Jesus' ministry.

E. Conclusion (vv. 23–25)

Verses 23–25 conclude the episode of the temple cleansing by recording the reaction of the multitudes to Jesus during Passover. At that time Jesus performed various signs or miracles,[8] and the crowds "believed in him" for doing so. Even though *pisteuō* with the accusative in John indicates true faith in Jesus, John 2:23 is the exception to that grammatical rule. For in John's gospel, belief in Jesus based merely on signs is not genuine faith (cf. v. 18). Consequently, in a play on words, the text says that Jesus did *not believe* in the crowds because he knew their hearts were fickle (vv. 24–25).

In John's gospel, belief in Jesus based merely on signs is not genuine faith.

---

6. Josephus says in his *Antiquities* (15.11.1/380) that the reconstruction of the temple proper (*naos*) was begun in the eighteenth year of Herod the Great (20/19 BC). Adding forty-six years to this, we arrive at AD 27 (recall Luke 3:1). The restoration of the entire temple area was not completed until AD 63/64 under Herod Agrippa II and Governor Albinus (Josephus, *Ant.* 20.9.7/219), just a few years before the Romans destroyed it in AD 70.

7. Andreas J. Köstenberger provides a list of those who dissent from the majority view (view 3 above), arguing for two temple cleansings (view 1 above) in *John*, Baker Exegetical Commentary on the New Testament (Grand Rapids: Baker, 2004), 111, no. 36.

8. This is in keeping with John 20:30, the theme of John, which says that Jesus performed far more miracles than the seven specifically recorded in the fourth gospel. The seven described there conveyed in their own ways the fact that Jesus was the Messiah who came to offer Israel true restoration.

REVIEW QUESTIONS

1. What two signs or miracles occur in John 2?

2. What three points suggest that the miracle at Cana symbolized the arrival of the messianic age?

3. What three reasons did Jesus have for cleansing the temple?

4. What did Jesus' cleansing of the temple signify?

KEY TERMS

Court of the Gentiles

Herod's temple

Josephus

messianic age/kingdom of God

sign miracle

Solomon's temple

Zerubbabel's temple

CHAPTER 5

"Born from Above"

JOHN 3

Objectives

After reading this chapter, you should be able to:

- Discuss the background and meaning of the new birth.
- Explain the phrase "of water and the Spirit."
- Explain what Jesus meant by saying that he would "be lifted up."

INTRODUCTION

Commentators note that John 2:23–3:36 divides into two sections: 2:23–3:21 and 3:22–36. Both sections follow the same threefold structure: prologue (2:23–25/3:22–24); dialogue (3:1–12/3:25–30); and monologue (3:13–21/3:31–36).[1] We now survey the preceding two sections, which deal with Jesus and Nicodemus (2:23–3:21) and with John the Baptist and Jesus (3:22–36).

I. JESUS AND NICODEMUS (2:23–3:21)

The above three components—prologue, dialogue, and monologue—will serve as our guide through this first section.

A. Prologue: Introducing Nicodemus (2:23–25)

John 2:23–25 is a transitional passage, concluding John 2 and introducing John 3, in particular verses 1–21. As the introduction to John 3:1–21, 2:23–25 sets the stage for Jesus' conversation with Nicodemus, (3:1–21). Jesus was still in Jerusalem at Passover time (cf. 2:13–22), and there he did not entrust himself to those who believed in his miracles, because he knew what was in the heart of "man" (v. 25). Similarly, John 3:1 introduces Nicodemus as just such a "man," suggesting that Jesus knew the heart of Nicodemus, and that he did not possess true faith—that despite Nicodemus's initial praise for Jesus (v. 2).

B. Dialogue: Jesus' Conversation with Nicodemus (3:1–12)

> Nicodemus was a Pharisee and a member of the Sanhedrin, the ruling political body of ancient Israel.

"Nicodemus" occurs only in the gospel of John (here in 3:1–21; and in 7:50–51; 19:39–42).[2] Nicodemus was a Pharisee and a member of the Sanhedrin, the ruling political body of ancient Israel. He came to Jesus at night, perhaps to avoid the embarrassment of a trained rabbinic scholar like himself meeting in broad daylight an untrained teacher like Jesus (v. 2). Raymond Brown's suggestion does seem to be right that the night is a metaphor for spiritual darkness (cf. 9:4; 11:10; 13:30) and that Nicodemus's approaching Jesus is symbolic of Nicodemus's coming out of darkness (v. 2) to light (vv. 19–21).[3]

Nicodemus acknowledged that Jesus was a teacher and that his miracles were a sign that he had been sent to Israel by God (v. 2). But Jesus cast aside such flattery with a word that cut to the heart of Nicodemus, "I tell you the truth, no one can see the kingdom of God unless he is born again (*anōthen)*" (v. 3). For John, "seeing," or "entering" the kingdom of God is to experience the life of the age to come (cf. vv. 3, 5, 36, respectively).

---

1. See George R. Beasley-Murray's discussion and bibliography in *John,* Word Biblical Commentary 36 (Nashville: Thomas Nelson, 1999), 46. His first title is "Report," whereas I have opted for the term *prologue.* The latter term means "before word" and introduces the main theme of the following sections. Some interpreters see vv. 16–21 as being the words of the evangelist John himself.

2. Not to be confused with Nakdimon ben Gurion, one of the wealthiest and most powerful Jewish aristocrats at the time of the Judean-Roman War. As far as we know, Nakdimon remained a pious Jew and did not embrace Christianity as Nicodemus apparently did; see Craig S. Keener's discussion in *The Gospel of John: A Commentary,* vol. 1 (Peabody, Mass.: Hendrickson, 2003), 535.

3. So Raymond E. Brown's *The Gospel according to John I–XII,* Anchor Bible 29A (Garden City, N.Y.: Doubleday, 1966), 130.

The word *Sanhedrin* represents the Hebrew transliteration of the Greek word *synedrion* ("council," "meeting"). The Sanhedrin in Jerusalem during New Testament times was composed of the chief priests, elders of the people (lay aristocracy around Jerusalem), and scribes (sages learned in the law). It tried cases dealing with a whole tribe, a false prophet, and the high priest (*Sanh.* 1.5). According to *Tos. Sanhedrin* 7.1, it also had appellate jurisdiction over a court of twenty-three in interpreting the law.

To see the kingdom of God, one must be *gennēthē anōthen*—born, or begotten, from above/again. The word, *anōthen*, can mean either "again" or "above." In the course of the dialogue to follow, Nicodemus assumed the former meaning while Jesus intended the latter. This is so because Jesus himself is from above (see 3:13–21, 31–36).

The immediate background of the idea of being "born again" is the Old Testament concept that Israel was God's son (Ex. 4:22; Deut. 32:6; Hos. 11:1). This idea is also used of the Davidic king (2 Sam. 7:14; Pss. 2:7; 89:27). Later, in Jewish intertestamental literature, especially pious believers in God were labeled God's son (Wisd. Sol. 5:5; *Pss. Sol.* 17:30; Sir. 4:10; et al.)[4] And approximately contemporaneous with John, rabbinic writings spoke of Gentiles who became Jewish proselytes through baptism as "like a new-born child" (*T. Pisha* 7:14).[5] This background fits well John 3:3, 5 (though some deny any baptismal connotation for vv. 3, 5).

Nicodemus misunderstood Jesus' statement, thinking that he must be born "again" a second time from his mother's womb. Such misunderstanding on the part of Jesus' dialogue partners in John serves as a foil to Jesus' true and fuller teaching (see, e.g., John 4, 6, 7, 8, 9, 11, 18–19).

In verse 5 Jesus reiterated the need to be born from above, this time describing it as being born "of water and the Spirit." Being "born/begotten of water and the Spirit" means to experience rebirth of the heart based on repentance and faith in Jesus and accomplished by the transformation brought about by the long-awaited Spirit of the new covenant (see Ezek. 36:25–27). Undergirding the new birth is the contrast between flesh and Spirit (vv. 6–8). The dualism here is spiritual in nature: spiritual birth (Spirit) is categorically different from natural birth (flesh). The former provides entrance into the kingdom of God while the latter is insufficient to do so.

Verses 9–12 conclude Jesus' dialogue with Nicodemus. Once again Nicodemus failed to comprehend Jesus' message: how can one be born above of the Spirit? Jesus responded using a minor-to-major argument. If Nicodemus did not understand earthly things—the foundational truth of the new birth (the minor argument), how then could he understand spiritual realities—the advanced teachings of the kingdom (the major argument)?

C. Monologue: The Testimony of Jesus (3:13–21)

Verses 13–21 record Jesus' testimony about his mission, which was to descend to earth in his incarnation, present himself as the Messiah, be crucified for sin, and then be resurrected.

---

4. See ibid., 139.
5. Keener is helpful on this point in *Gospel of John*, 542–44.

In verses 14–15, John draws on Numbers 21:8 and Moses' lifting up of the bronze serpent as the means to forgive Israel's disobedience and restore her to life. Isaiah 52:13 is also in the background: just as the Servant suffered for Israel and was lifted up to glory, so will Jesus suffer on the cross and be exalted. In fact, in the fourth gospel Jesus' moment of exaltation coincides with his crucifixion (John 3:14; 8:28; 12:32). His death on the cross is his glory!

The death of God's one and only Son (*monogenēs*) demonstrates the depth of divine love for the world (v. 16). One hears here an echo of Genesis 22:2, 12 and Abraham's willingness to give up his son, his only son, Isaac. Jesus' mission to die for the sins of the world becomes an invitation to salvation for all (John 2:17–21).

> The death of God's one and only Son (*monogenēs*) demonstrates the depth of divine love for the world (v. 16).

We may conclude John 2:23–3:21 with the observation often made of Nicodemus by the commentaries in terms of his progression of faith in Christ: he moved out of darkness into the light (3:1–21), went public with his faith before the Sanhedrin (7:50–52), and became a full disciple after Jesus' death (19:39–42).[6]

II. JOHN THE BAPTIST AND JESUS (3:22–36)

The above threefold structure—prologue, dialogue, and monologue—also informs John 3:22–36, which we now survey.

A. Prologue: John the Baptist and Jesus (3:22–24)[7]

Verses 22–24 signal to the reader that controversy was in the air between the disciples of John the Baptist and Jesus. John was baptizing in Aenon near Salim. Aenon ("spring"), Salim ("peace") is probably to be equated with Salim, a town four miles east-southeast of Shechem, Samaria (v. 23).[8] Not far away, Jesus and his disciples were also baptizing.[9]

---

6. Keener expresses this perspective well in ibid., 533. Andreas J. Köstenberger is among the minority view in claiming that Nicodemus never became a believer in Jesus. See Köstenberger's discussion in his *John*, Baker Exegetical Commentary on the New Testament (Grand Rapids: Baker, 2004), 118–19.

7. For a couple of reasons, some scholars believe John 3:22–30 originally followed John 1:19–34 in chronological order. First, the baptismal context of John 3:22–30 fits John 1:19–34. Second, it is odd that the Baptist's disciples do not know who Jesus is in John 3:22–30 when they were already told who he was in John 1:29–42.

8. See Brown, *Gospel according to John I–XII*, 151.

9. John 4:2 clarifies this statement by stating that it was Jesus' disciples who were actually doing the baptizing, not Jesus himself.

B. Dialogue: John the Baptist's Last Testimony (3:25–30)

An argument broke out between some of John the Baptist's disciples and a "certain Jew" over a matter of purification (v. 25), probably relative to the meaning of John's baptism.

According to verse 26, John's disciples were perturbed that Jesus was drawing larger crowds for baptism than their mentor. But John set the record straight, declaring that Jesus was superior to himself. Two images are used. First, in verses 27–28 John the Baptist reminded his followers that he was called of God to be the forerunner of the Messiah but that Jesus was the Messiah. Second, in verses 29–30 John compared himself to the best man and Jesus to the groom. In all of this John the Baptist's ministry had to wane while Jesus' ministry had to be on the rise. This was the divine plan.

C. Monologue: The Voice of Jesus through the Evangelist (3:31–36)

One need not decide if it is Jesus or John the evangelist speaking in 3:31–36. It is probably both; John is reflecting on Jesus' words. Again we meet with the contrast between earth and heaven. The immediate context of this antithesis is the contrast between John the Baptist and Jesus: the former, though sent by God, was nevertheless of this earth while Jesus is from heaven and therefore above all (v. 31). But verses 3–36 also summarize the entirety of John 3. Jesus is the true testimony from God (vv. 31–34a), who gives the Holy Spirit to those who believe in him (v. 34b). And whoever believes in Jesus has eternal life, but God's wrath abides on those who reject him.

REVIEW QUESTIONS

1. Why did Nicodemus come to Jesus by night?

2. What is the background for the "new birth" Jesus refers to?

3. What does the phrase in John 3:5 "of water and spirit" most likely refer to?

4. Does the reference in John 3:14–15 to Jesus being lifted up refer only to his death?

5. What two images did John the Baptist use, according to John 3:27–28, to contrast himself with Jesus the Messiah?

KEY TERMS

born again/born from above	Nicodemus	water and Spirit
bronze serpent	Sanhedrin	

CHAPTER 6

The Woman at the Well and the Nobleman's Son

JOHN 4

Objectives

After reading this chapter, you should be able to:

- Identify the various barriers Jesus overcame in speaking to the woman at the well.

- Explain what Jesus meant by "living water."

- Discuss the titles the Samaritan woman applied to Jesus.

- Compare and contrast Nicodemus and the woman at the well.

- Explain Jesus' healing of the official's son.

INTRODUCTION

John 4 records two familiar, endearing episodes in Jesus' early ministry: the conversion of the Samaritan woman and the healing of the official's son. The last episode is labeled the "second sign" Jesus performed in Cana, Galilee (4:53), which ties the narrative with the wedding at Cana, Galilee (2:1–11). Thus John 2:1–4:54 comprises the first circuit of Jesus' public ministry as recorded in the fourth gospel. We now examine the preceding two episodes.

> John 4 records two familiar, endearing episodes in Jesus' early ministry: the conversion of the Samaritan woman and the healing of the official's son.

I. THE SAMARITAN WOMAN (4:1–42)

John 4:1–3 is transitional in nature, providing the background for Jesus' departure from Judea (3:22–36) and subsequent entrance into Galilee (4:3). The change of venue was occasioned because the Pharisees purposed to investigate Jesus' baptismal activities, as they did for John the Baptist (1:19–27). The fact that more people were being baptized (*ebaptizen*) by Jesus than John the Baptist attracted the Pharisees to the situation.[1]

A. Jesus' Conversation with the Woman at the Well (vv. 4–26)

Jesus' conversation with the Samaritan woman unfolds in two scenes: Jesus' discussion with the woman at the well (vv. 4–26) and Jesus' discussion with his disciples (vv. 27–38). The first scene focuses on two topics of conversation: the living water (vv. 4–15) and true worship (vv. 16–25).

---

1. John 4:2 clarifies 3:26—it was Jesus' disciples, not Jesus, who were actually performing the baptisms. A couple of other points call for comment here. First, it is unclear whether John the Baptist was imprisoned by this time. John 3:24 seems to indicate that he was not, while the Synoptics uniformly have John in prison by this point in Jesus' ministry. But perhaps John 3:24 alludes to the Baptist's imprisonment. Second, John 4:2 may be an anti-Baptist polemic or, more precisely, a polemic against the followers of the Baptist who continued to exalt him over Jesus. They may have done so by claiming that Jesus' baptizing activities were copycatting John, but our author disallows that by not including Jesus in the actual acts of baptism.

The Samaritans

The Samaritans are the descendants of two groups: the remnant of the native Israelites who were not deported at the fall of the northern kingdom in 722 BC, and foreign colonists brought in from Babylonia and Media by the Assyrian conquerors of Samaria (2 Kings 17:24–34 gives an anti-Samaritan account of this). There was theological opposition between these northerners and the Jews of the South because of the Samaritan refusal to worship at Jerusalem. This was aggravated by the fact that after the Babylonia exile the Samaritans had put obstacles in the way of the Jewish restoration of Jerusalem, and that in the second century BC the Samaritans had helped the Syrian monarchs in their wars against the Jews. In 128 BC the Jewish high priest burned the Samaritan temple on Gerizim.

Today the Samaritans are an endangered race, living in Israel in Nablus (Shechem) and along the coast of the Mediterranean Sea in northern Israel. They number only about one thousand and are neither Israeli or Palestinian. They still celebrate Passover in Shechem.

1. The Living Water (vv. 4–15)

Verse 4 makes a theological, not geographical, statement: Jesus "had" (*edei*) to go through Samaria because it was divinely appointed that he do so (cf. 9:4; 10:16; 12:34; 20:9). So, even though Jews and Samaritans were hostile to each other, Jesus, a Jew, felt compelled to go to Samaria.

Jesus came to the town Sychar in Samaria and stopped at Jacob's well (vv. 4–6). Sychar was near the land Jacob gave his son Joseph (cf. Gen. 33:18–19; 48:21–22; Josh. 24:32). Jacob's well is not mentioned in the Old Testament. Many scholars, however, are confident that the 100-feet-deep well at the foot of Mount Gerizim is Jacob's well.[2] Jesus arrived there at noon, the hottest part of the day in Israel. And at that very time, a Samaritan woman came to Jacob's well to draw water (v. 7). The ensuing narrative implies that the Samaritan woman wanted to avoid contact with other women in the village because of her moral shame (vv. 16–18).

Jacob's well, one of the deepest wells in Palestine (over a hundred feet deep), was the setting of Jesus' conversation with the Samaritan woman.

The disciples had gone into Sychar to buy food for Jesus and the group, so Jesus was alone at the well (v. 8). Jesus engaged the Samaritan woman in conversation, asking her to draw a drink of water for him. Already Jesus had broken two social taboos: he had spoken with a woman in public (cf. vv. 7–9 with v. 27 and rabbinic works like *Pirke Aboth* 2[10] and *Qidd.* 70a that forbade men to speak with women in public), and to a *Samaritan* woman no less! The conversation that followed centered on the exchange between the woman giving Jesus well water and Jesus giving to her living water (John 4:10–15). Living water was flowing, fresh water unlike the water stored in wells or cisterns. As most commentators remark, by "living water" Jesus meant his gift of the Holy Spirit and the revelation the Spirit provides.

2. True Worship (vv. 16–25)

The first part of Jesus' conversation with the Samaritan woman at the well piqued her interest and desire in the living water he had to offer. The second part of that conversation brought the woman to an awareness of her need—forgiveness and fellowship with God (vv. 16–25). Jesus' question about the woman's husband exposed her immorality (vv. 16–18). Jesus revealed that she had been married five times before and was now living with a man. The woman then tried a diversionary tactic to get Jesus off the topic of her sin—she tried to embroil him in religious controversy! The Samaritans worshiped on Mount Gerizim as opposed to the Jews who worshiped in Jerusalem (v. 20).

---

2. Raymond E. Brown's discussion is helpful here. See *The Gospel according to John I–XII*, Anchor Bible 29A (Garden City, N.Y.: Doubleday, 1966), 169.

Nicodemus and the Samaritan Woman	
Contrasts:	
Nicodemus	**Samaritan Woman**
Religious	Not religious
Jew	Samaritan
Moral	Immoral
Similarities:	
Both were spiritually lost and converted to Christ.	

In verses 21–24 Jesus offered a twofold response to the woman. First, from the historical perspective, "salvation is from the Jews" (v. 22)—that is, God's salvation came through the Jews and not through the Samaritans. But, second, Jesus had now come to change all that with a new theological principle, namely, true worship is not restricted to Jerusalem, Gerizim, or any other physical or national locale. Rather, because God is Spirit (v. 24), he desires to be worshiped in Spirit and truth—in the heart (vv. 21–24).

> By the end of the scene at the well, the Samaritan woman had undergone a notable progression in her understanding of Jesus, suggesting she became a follower of him.

By the end of the scene at the well, the Samaritan woman had undergone a notable progression in her understanding of Jesus, suggesting she became a follower of him. First, she began by thinking Jesus was only a Jewish man who broke with custom in addressing her (v. 9). Next, she recognized Jesus to be a prophet; probably the prophet like Moses that both Jew and Samaritan expected to come at the end of history (cf. v. 19 with Deut. 18:15–18). Third, the woman at the well expressed conviction about the coming Messiah, who, in Samaritan theology, was equated with the *Taheb* ("the one who returns") who would settle all legal matters and restore all things (see v. 25).[3] Jesus equated himself with that personage and more. Finally, the Samaritan folk in town, no doubt including the woman at the well, proclaimed Jesus to be the Savior of the world (v. 42).

B. Jesus' Conversation with His Disciples (vv. 27–42)

The disciples returned from buying food in the town and were surprised to find Jesus talking to the Samaritan woman. With that, the woman returned to her village (v. 27). In her excitement at receiving living water from Jesus, she forgot to draw water from the cistern! The Samaritan became a witness to Christ back in her town (vv. 28–30). Meanwhile the disciples showed their spiritual misunderstanding of Jesus' mission to do God's will, thinking the "food" he ate was physical (vv. 31–33). Jesus responded to them with two agricultural parables that illustrated that the Samaritans were a part of the end-time harvest (vv. 34–42).

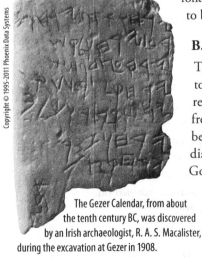

The Gezer Calendar, from about the tenth century BC, was discovered by an Irish archaeologist, R. A. S. Macalister, during the excavation at Gezer in 1908.

---

3. John Bowman discusses this background in his "Samaritan Studies," *Bulletin of the John Rylands Library* 40 (1957–58): 298–329; cited from p. 299.

An aerial view of the remains of the synagogue at Capernaum.

"House of Peter" excavations— the remains of this first-century home (above and below) are located adjacent to the synagogue.

II. THE HEALING OF THE OFFICIAL'S SON (4:43–54)

John 4 concludes with the account of Jesus' healing of the official's son (4:43–54). Verses 43–45 introduce the episode. After spending two days with the Samaritans, Jesus left for Galilee, Cana in particular (vv. 43–45). While in Cana, an official (*basilikos*), probably a Gentile aristocrat who served in Herod Antipas's court,[4] traveled from his residence in Capernaum to Cana for the purpose of seeking Jesus' healing for his dying son (cf. v. 47 with v. 52). After Jesus rebuked the Galileans for believing in him based only

on miracles (recall vv. 44–45), no doubt the official included, Jesus assured the father that his son would live. The official believed Jesus' word, and as he traveled back to Capernaum,[5] his servants reported to him that his son's fever had broken and he was now well. They determined that the boy was healed at 1:00 p.m., the exact hour Jesus pronounced the son to be healed (vv. 50–54)! Consequently, the father and his household believed in Jesus. This, now, was presumably genuine faith.

We conclude John 4:43–54 by noting that the healing of the official's son is the second sign miracle Jesus performed in Cana (cf. 4:54 with 2:11).

---

4. Craig S. Keener, *The Gospel of John: A Commentary*, vol. 1 (Peabody, Mass.: Hendrickson, 2003), 630.

5. Capernaum is about fourteen miles from Cana. The latter is in the Galilean hills, and Capernaum is below sea level. The text is quite correct to say that the official went down to Capernaum (v. 51). The official began his return trip from Cana to Capernaum in the afternoon and therefore probably stayed overnight along the way before completing his journey home on the following day (vv. 51–53).

REVIEW QUESTIONS

1. What was unusual about the Samaritan woman going to the well?

2. What was the "living water" Jesus offered to the Samaritan woman?

3. Discuss the four titles the Samaritan woman applied to Jesus.

4. Did the disciples understand Jesus' mission to the Samaritan woman?

5. Compare and contrast Nicodemus and the Samaritan woman.

KEY TERMS

God	Messiah	Samaritans
Jacob's well	Mount Gerizim	Savior
"living water"	prophet	*Taheb*

CHAPTER 7

The Healing of the Paralytic on the Sabbath

JOHN 5

Objectives

After reading this chapter, you should be able to:

- Identify the twofold prerogatives Jesus shared with God.

- Discuss the realized eschatology of John 5:19–25 and the consistent eschatology of John 5:26–30.

- List the five witnesses to Jesus recorded in John 5:31–47.

INTRODUCTION

John 5–10 constitutes the next major unit of the gospel of John.[1] It is devoted to showing that Jesus is the replacement of some major Jewish feasts/holy days: the Sabbath (John 5), Passover (John 6), Tabernacles (John 7–9), and Dedication (John 10).

John 5 contains another sign miracle of Jesus—this time the healing of a paralytic (vv. 1–15), followed by Jesus' discourse on the Sabbath. The theme of the discourse is occasioned by Jesus' healing of the paralytic on the Sabbath. The discourse is divided into two parts: (1) Jesus' twofold work on the Sabbath: giving life and exercising judgment (vv. 16–30) and (2) Jesus' divine witnesses (vv. 31–47). We now survey these sections.

> John 5 contains another sign miracle of Jesus— this time the healing of a paralytic (vv. 1–15), followed by Jesus' discourse on the Sabbath.

I. THE HEALING OF THE PARALYTIC ON THE SABBATH (5:1–15)

Sometime after the healing of the official's son, Jesus departed Cana for Jerusalem in order to celebrate an unnamed feast.[2] Northeast of the temple, at the Sheep Pool, called Bethesda, Jesus came across a man who

---

1. The first unit of John we studied was John 1. Then came 2:1–4:54 and the episodes of two signs: the turning of water into wine and the healing of the nobleman's son.

2. Andreas J. Köstenberger observes that the phrase "the festival of the Jews" was a technical way of referring to the Feast of Tabernacles (*John*, Baker Exegetical Commentary on the New Testament [Grand Rapids: Baker, 2004], 177). But whatever the referent of the phrase, the main focus of the healing of the paralytic is on the Sabbath.

The twin pools of Bethesda, surrounded by five covered colonnades, witnessed Jesus' startling healing of an invalid.

had been an invalid for thirty-eight years. Most commentators locate the site today under St. Anne's Church.

Healing came to the man in response to Jesus' command to take up his mat and walk (vv. 6–9a). Because the man was carrying his mat on the Sabbath, "the Jews"—the religious leaders in Jerusalem—complained that he was breaking the Sabbath. The Mishnah (ca. second century AD) lists thirty-nine categories of prohibitions on the Sabbath, and carrying one's mat was one of them. After the man's encounter with Jesus, he informed the religious authorities that it was Jesus who healed him on the Sabbath (v. 15)—not much of a thank you for Jesus' mercy.

II. DISCOURSE ON THE SABBATH (5:16–47)

Introduction (vv. 16–18)

The healing of the lame man on the Sabbath became the occasion for Jesus' ensuing discourse on the Sabbath. In effect, he proclaimed himself Lord of the Sabbath (cf. Mark 2:23–28; cf. Matt. 12:8; Luke 6:5).

The Sabbath

The Sabbath was fundamental to Judaism as a sign of Israel's sanctification among all the nations. (1) It marked a joyful entry into sacred time (the time of the beginning before human work) and divine repose. Josephus claimed that "the word Sabbath in the Jew's language denotes cessation from all work."[3] (2) It allowed the people to honor God's holiness, who sanctified this day.[4] (3) It set Israel apart from the nations and served as a bulwark against assimilation to pagan culture. Keeping the Sabbath became a profession of faith. (4) Desecrating the Sabbath was akin to dishonoring the covenant (Isa. 56:4–6) and was worthy of death.[5] It was believed to unleash God's judgment on Israel (Neh. 13:18). This last concern may have motivated the Pharisees' consternation over perceived Sabbath violations.

Pietist groups in Israel multiplied the strict rules related to Sabbath observance. The earliest list of restrictions is found in *Jubilees* 2:17–33; 50:6–13 and CD 10:14–11:18. The Mishna, the collection of the oral tradition compiled sometime before AD 220, contains three tractates specifically addressing Sabbath issues: *Šabbat* (prohibitions of work and what objects may or may not be carried), *'Erubin* (rules about extending the limits for movement on the Sabbath), and *Bes.a* (work permitted and prohibited on festivals). A rabbinic commentary on Exodus goes so far as to prohibit activities that merely detract from the restfulness of the day.[6] The rabbis recognized that the manifold Sabbath rules were only tenuously connected to scriptural law: "The rules about the sabbath, festal offerings and sacrilege are as mountains hanging by a hair, for Scripture is scanty and the rules many."[7]

---

3. Josephus, *Ag. Ap.* 2:27 §3.
4. Gen. 2:3; Ex. 20:8–11; 31:14; Deut. 5:12–15.
5. Ex. 31:14–15; 35:2; Num. 15:32–36.
6. *Mekilta Kaspa* 4 to Ex. 23:13.
7. *m.* Hag. 1:8.

John 5:16 records the first hostile action toward Jesus by the Jewish leadership in the fourth gospel. Jesus' statement in verse 17 only exacerbated the situation: "My Father is always at his work to this very day, and I, too, am working." The saying was tantamount to Jesus equating himself with God. The Old Testament was clear that God rested on the Sabbath after creating the universe (Gen. 2:2; Ex. 20:11). Yet Jewish theologians believed God's providence continued to govern the world. This was confirmed by the fact that people continued to be born and die on the Sabbath. Consequently, the belief developed that God exercised two prerogatives on the Sabbath: He gave life and he executed judgment (2 Kings 5:7; 2 Macc. 7:22–23; *Tal. Bab. Taanith* 2a). So only God could "work" on the Sabbath, and Jesus' claim in verse 17 to also work on the Sabbath (by healing the paralytic) made him equal to God. With this "blasphemous" assertion, Jesus' critics began to harbor the notion to kill him (v. 18).

Beggar in Jerusalem.

A. The Twofold Work of Christ on the Sabbath: Life and Judgment (vv. 19–30)

Not flinching at his accusers, Jesus proceeded to point out his twofold divine prerogatives regarding the Sabbath: like God, he gives life and exercises judgment. This is first stated in terms of realized eschatology (vv. 19–25) and then repeated in terms of final or consistent eschatology (vv. 26–30).

1. Life and Judgment Now (vv. 19–25)

Verses 19–25 present two truths: Jesus is subordinate to God his Father (vv. 19–20), and Jesus is equal to God (vv. 21–25). These two statements combine, on the one hand, to protect the doctrine of monotheism while, on the other hand, affirming Jesus' deity.

Verses 21–22 spell out the two sole prerogatives of God that Jesus exercised. Only God can raise the dead (Deut. 32:39; 1 Sam. 2:6; 2 Kings 5:7; Tobit 13:2; Wisd. Sol. 16:13), and only God executes eternal judgment (Gen. 18:25; Judg. 11:27), and those two tasks also belong to Jesus. The purpose of Jesus' performance of these divine prerogatives is to be glorified by men (John 5:23). But whoever does not honor Jesus, God's agent, does not honor God (cf. Matt. 10:40; Luke 10:16).

Verses 24–25 are a prime example of John's realized eschatology: he who believes in Jesus has eternal life now and is already delivered from divine judgment. Jesus thus exercised God's prerogatives of giving life and executing judgment now.

2. Life and Judgment Later (vv. 26–30)

Verses 26–30 delineate the same two divine prerogatives: Jesus gives life and executes judgment—except that these two tasks will be conducted in the future. Verse 28 reads, "A time is coming," but does not have "and has now come" as verse 25 does. Also, verse 28 refers to the future general resurrection of the dead first made explicit in Daniel 12:2. In other words, John 5:28–30 predict the future physical resurrection, while verses 24–25 project that resurrection—a spiritual one—back into the present.

Various theories can be proposed to account for this differing perspective in eschatology, but most commentaries root it in the already (vv. 19–25)–not yet (vv. 26–30) message of Jesus.

B. Witnesses to Jesus (vv. 31–47)

Jesus now invokes the first person singular in verses 31–47, identifying divine witnesses to his equal status with God: John the Baptist (vv. 33–35); Jesus' works (v. 36); God the Father (vv. 37–38); the Old Testament Scripture, Moses in particular (vv. 39–47). And in verse 31 Jesus recognizes that more than two witnesses are required to establish one's testimony (see Deut. 19:15; John 8:17). "Another" (v. 32) is God, in whom the following witnesses are rooted (cf. 8:18).

Witnesses to Jesus in John 5
• John the Baptist (vv. 33–35)
• Jesus' miracles (v. 36)
• God the Father (vv. 37–38)
• The Old Testament (vv. 39–44)
• Moses (vv. 44–47)

The first witness to Jesus mentioned is John the Baptist (vv. 33–35), as eloquently stated earlier (1:19–34; 3:22–30). The second witness to Jesus' deity is his miraculous works (v. 26; cf. 20:30–31). The third testimony to Jesus is God the Father (vv. 37–38). Although the precise nature of God's witness is debated, the context seems to indicate the internal witness of the Father. Those who receive Christ have that witness, which those who reject Christ do not.

The fourth witness to Jesus is the Old Scripture (vv. 39–44). We can detect two aspects to this testimony. The Old Testament in general points toward Jesus Christ.[8] It was commonplace for ancient Judaism to view the study of the Law as generating obedience to God and, therefore, life. Yet Israel's study of the Old Testament did not benefit them, for they failed to grasp who Jesus was.

More particularly, Moses himself testified to the coming of Jesus the Christ (vv. 44–47). Probably Deuteronomy 18:18–19 is the passage by Moses Jesus had in mind here. But Israel also failed to receive that message. Consequently, though Moses was considered to be Israel's intercessor (Ex. 32:11–14, 30–32; Num. 12:13; et al.), he would actually become their accuser for rejecting their Messiah.

---

8. Verse 39 is a statement of fact—"You diligently study the Scriptures," rather than an imperative.

1. What twofold prerogatives of God did Jesus appropriate for himself, according to John 5:19 – 30?

2. How can we account for the realized eschatology in John 5:19 – 25 and consistent eschatology in John 5:26 – 30?

3. What are the five witnesses to Jesus recorded in John 5:31 – 47?

KEY TERMS

consistent eschatology

divine witnesses

realized eschatology

Sabbath

twofold work of God's providence

CHAPTER 8

Jesus the Bread of Life

JOHN 6

Objectives

After reading this chapter, you should be able to:

- Identify the three Old Testament topics informing John 6.

- Compare the structure of Jesus' discourse on the manna from heaven with rabbinic sermons.

- Compare and contrast the duplicate Bread of Life Discourses in John 6:35 – 50 and 6:51 – 59.

INTRODUCTION

John 6 has it all: miracles, discourses, and controversies! The following outline will help us sort it out: verses 1–15: the feeding of the multitudes—the new Passover; verses 16–21: Jesus walking on the water—the new exodus; verses 22–59: Bread of Life Discourse(s)—the new covenant; verses 60–71: reactions to Jesus.

I. THE FEEDING OF THE MULTITUDES: THE NEW PASSOVER (6:1–15)

John 6 picks up the story of Jesus approximately a year after the events of John 5. We find that Jesus had just crossed the Sea of Galilee (v. 1). There, a large crowd followed Jesus to an unnamed mountain because of the miracles he performed earlier. This happened on

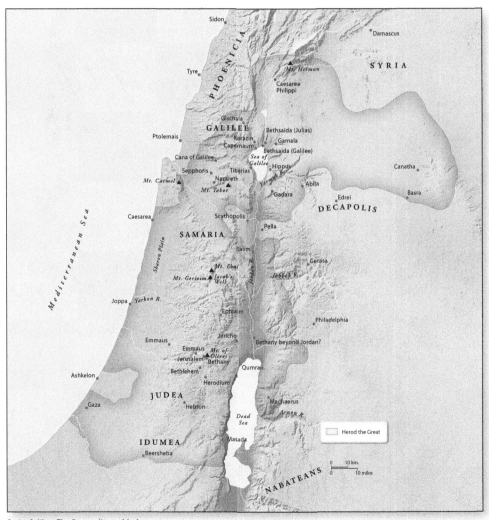

Syria, Galilee, The Decapolis, and Judea.

Modern fisherman on the Sea of Galilee.

The northern shore of the Sea of Galilee near Capernaum.

Passover (v. 4), the second such reference in John thus far (see 2:13). Philip demonstrated his lack of faith in Jesus' ability to feed the multitude. Andrew agreed, mentioning that a little boy's lunch (five barley loaves and two fish) was all that was available (vv. 8–9).

Jesus then told his disciples to have the men and their families sit down. The total was about five thousand men,[1] which along with their household of wives and children, could have numbered twenty thousand (v. 10). Verse 11 records without detail or fanfare the miracle of the multiplication of the bread and fish. Its wording, however, is noteworthy in that the institution of the Lord's Supper (which the fourth gospel does not narrate) is alluded to: "Jesus then took the loaves, gave thanks [*eucharistēsas*], and distributed to those who were seated," just as he did with the fish (see Matt. 26:26–28; Mark 14:22–24; Luke 22:19–20; 1 Cor. 11:23–25; cf. my comments on John 6:35–59).

The whole episode of the multiplication of the food reminds the reader of God's provision of manna in the wilderness (vv. 14–15 cf. vv. 31–32, the latter of which makes that explicit connection). That reality, combined with the setting of the Passover, created a messianic expectation among the crowd, as verses 14–15 make clear.

The miracle of the feeding signaled to the crowd that Jesus was the new Moses (v. 14; cf. Deut. 18:15–18) who had come to offer new manna and a new exodus (see Ex. 12).

The miracle of the feeding signaled to the crowd that Jesus was the new Moses (v. 14; cf. Deut. 18:15–18) who had come to offer new manna and a new exodus (see Ex. 12). Indeed, Jewish tradition equated Moses with a king (Deut. 33:5; Josephus, *Ant.* 4.327).[2] This connection explains why the crowds wanted to make Jesus their king; one who would expel the Romans out of their land (John 6:14). Jesus, however, wanted no

---

1. Ancient Jewish culture was patriarchal; hence the emphasis on men.
2. See the discussion by Wayne A. Meeks, *The Prophet-King: Moses Traditions and the Johannine Christology*, NovTSup 14 (Leiden: Brill, 1967): 125–29, 137–38, 147–50, 173, 198–200, 220–26.

part of that type of a Messiah (cf. v. 15 with John 18:36), and so he slipped away from the crowd.[3]

II. JESUS WALKS ON THE WATER: THE NEW EXODUS (6:16–21)

By now darkness had come and the disciples attempted to row their boat back to Capernaum, some six or seven miles across the lake from Bethsaida. Jesus did not accompany them (vv. 16–17). That was the scene for two more miracles performed by Jesus. First, he walked upon the sea[4] to the disciples (v. 19). Jesus' self-identification "*egō eimi* (I am)" seems to draw on the epiphany of Yahweh to Israel during the exodus (Ps. 77:16, 19). Second, as soon as Jesus came to the boat, it arrived at shore (John 6:21). This reminds us of the Synoptics' rendition of Jesus walking on the sea and calming the storm.[5] Interestingly enough, neither of these miracles recorded in John 6:19, 21 is called a "sign." The theological message of this scene is that Jesus was inaugurating a new exodus, which nicely fits with the theme of Passover present in verses 1–15.[6]

III. THE BREAD OF LIFE DISCOURSE: JESUS AND THE NEW COVENANT (JOHN 6:22–59)

John 6:22–59 records the Bread of Life Discourse(s) by Jesus. Verses 22–30 introduce the discourse(s) by calling attention to some key contrasts between the miracle of the food and the sign behind it. Then comes the discourse proper, which most likely is presented to us in two versions: verses 35–50 and verses 51–59.

The crowd's response in verse 31 sets the stage for the discourse on the Bread of Life proper: "Our forefathers ate the manna in the desert; as it is written: 'He gave them bread from heaven to eat.'" In discussing Jesus' response in verses 31–50, I draw on the insightful comments by Peder Borgen, postponing for later the debate over whether verses 51–59 are a duplicate passage of verses 31–50. Borgen has convinced many scholars that John 6:31–50

A Galilee boat from the time of Jesus.

Z. Radovan/www.BibleLandPictures.com

---

3. For a thorough discussion of the relation of the feeding of the five thousand in John 6 to the feeding of the four thousand and five thousand in the Synoptics, see Raymond E. Brown, *The Gospel according to John I–XII*, Anchor Bible 29A (Garden City, N.Y.: Doubleday, 1966), 236–50. He concludes that John's account probably reflects a combination of the two feedings.

4. Some take the phrase "upon the sea" as meaning "by the seashore" in order to downplay the miraculous element in the story. But this interpretation is clearly at odds with the intent of the episode, namely, to record the supernatural event of Jesus walking on the water.

5. Brown provides a helpful discussion of the relationship between the walking on the water episode in John 6 as compared to the account of the Synoptics. See *Gospel according to John I–XII*, 252–54.

6. Aileen Guilding made famous the idea that John 6 follows the readings in the Passover *Haggadah* (story), which included the combination of Psalm 77:19 (the exodus) and Isaiah 51:6–16 (an allusion to the exodus). This combination of Passover and exodus themes, argued Guilding, explains the connection in John 6:1–15 (manna/Passover) and 6:16–20 (exodus). *The Fourth Gospel and Jewish Worship* (Oxford: Clarendon, 1960), 62, 63, 67, et al.

is a homily crafted after the style of ancient synagogue preaching: a midrash, or commentary, on Old Testament passages. The homily consists of four parts: a Pentateuchal citation and correction (vv. 31–33); the homily itself, which explains the key words of the Pentateuchal citation (vv. 34–50); a subordinate citation from an Old Testament prophet (vv. 45–47); and a concluding remark that returns the reader/hearer to the theme of the homily (cf. v. 48 with v. 35).[7] We will now survey this homily.

A. Pentateuchal Citation and Correction (cf. vv. 31–33)

In requesting of Jesus a sign (which, ironically, he had just performed [vv. 1–15]), the crowd quoted Exodus 16:4 (cf. v. 15) in John 6:31: "I will rain down bread from heaven." Jesus then corrected their statement to the effect that God, not Moses, gave the true bread from heaven that brings eternal life, namely, Jesus Christ.

Five loaves and two fish. A mosaic in the church at Tabgha (Heptapegon).

B. Homily Proper (vv. 35–50)

The Pentateuchal quotation by the crowd was divided by Jesus into its three key statements, each of which he then comments on: "bread" (vv. 34–37); "from heaven" (vv. 38–44); "to eat" (vv. 49–50). Regarding the first statement—"bread"—Jesus identified himself as the Bread of Life; the first of seven "I am" statements in John. Bread in ancient Near Eastern culture was more than a staple food; it was perhaps the most commonly eaten food and thus was associated with life. It was bread, or manna, that sustained Israel in the desert (Ex. 16:31; Deut. 8:16). In like manner, Jesus equated himself with the source of spiritual life (John 6:35–37a).

Verses 37b–44 expand upon the words "from heaven," equating Jesus with the bread from heaven. In other words, Jesus had been sent by God to offer eternal life through faith

---

7. Peder Borgen, *Bread from Heaven: An Exegetical Study of the Concept of Manna in the Gospel of John and the Writings of Philo*, NovTSup 10 (Leiden: Brill, 1965).

The Seven "I Am" Sayings
1. "I am the bread of life" (6:35, 48, 51).
2. "I am the light of the world" (8:12; 9:5).
3. "I am the gate" (10:7, 9).
4. "I am the good shepherd" (10:11, 14).
5. "I am the resurrection and the life" (11:25).
6. "I am the way and the truth and the life" (14:6).
7. "I am the true vine" (15:1).

in him (Jesus); see verses 37b–40. But the crowd balked at Jesus' assertion by protesting that Jesus was only from earth—born of human parents (vv. 41–43). Such disbelief Jesus labeled "grumbling," an insulting description given the fact that the same term was used of Israel in the wilderness wanderings (*egongyzon*, cf. vv. 41, 43 with LXX Ex. 16:2, 7, 8; see also 1 Cor. 10:10).

Verses 49–50 expand upon the words "to eat," contrasting Israel in the wilderness and Jesus' present audience with those who follow him. The former have died or will die because they ate only physical food—the manna in the wilderness and the bread Jesus provided. The latter will live because they saw beyond the miracle to its sign—Jesus is the true Bread of Life. These remarks repeat verses 31–33.

C. The Subordinate Quote from the Prophets (vv. 45–47)

In between verses 37b–44 and 49–50 comes a subordinate statement freely drawing on Isaiah 54:13, which says, "All your sons will be taught by the LORD" (cf. John 6:45–47). The Old Testament setting of the prophet's remark is the future restoration of Israel and the new covenant. At that time Israel would finally be taught by God and obey him. Jesus contemporized the statement: he is the only one who can teach Israel to obey God, because he is the only one from God (vv. 45b–47).

> It may well be that John adds verses 51–58 because the Eucharist theme emphasizes the reality of Jesus' incarnation and death against the Docetic claim that Jesus only appeared to be human.

D. The Conclusion (v. 48)

Verse 48—"I am the bread of life"—is an inclusion, returning us to verse 35.

IV. DUPLICATE BREAD OF LIFE DISCOURSE (6:51–59)

Many commentators believe verses 51–59 duplicate the Bread of Life Discourse. Accordingly, they posit that the original discourse, verses 35–50, presents the miraculous bread in sapiential (Wisdom/Torah) language—that is, receiving God's audible Word inwardly; while verses 51–59 interpret the bread sacramentally—that is, receiving God's visible Word outwardly, as in the Eucharist. These two themes comprise the new covenant: obeying God's Word from the heart, which is based on the sacrificial death of Christ.

If this theory is true, then it would explain both the similarities and differences between verses 35–50 and 51–59. The similarities occur because the latter is a later duplicate of the former.[8] The differences proceed from John's desire to add verses 51–58 to his nar-

---

8. The similarities between the two are as follows:

John 6:35–50	John 6:51–58
"I am the bread of life."v. 35	"I am the living bread."v. 51a
"I have come down from heaven."v. 38	"that came down from heaven"v. 51b
Jews grumble against Jesus.v. 41	Jews argue sharply among themselves.v. 52
"I tell you the truth"v. 47	"I tell you the truth"v. 53
"Your forefathers ate manna and died."v. 49	"Your forefathers ate manna and died."v. 58
"eat and never die"v. 50	"eat and live forever"v. 58

rative to accentuate the sacramental theme. This is logical, because the fourth gospel does not contain the narrative of the Lord's Supper. It may well be that John adds verses 51–58 because the Eucharist theme emphasizes the reality of Jesus' incarnation and death against the Docetic claim that Jesus only appeared to be human.

V. REACTIONS TO JESUS THE BREAD OF LIFE (6:60–71)

Verses 60–71 seem to pick up the flow of thought from verse 50, suggesting that we are correct to view verses 51–59 as a duplicate of the Bread of Life Discourse. In other words, verse 50 flows into verses 60–71. Verse 60 registers Jewish negative reaction to Jesus' statement in verse 50—he is the Bread of Heaven. Furthermore, verses 60–71 contain only references to the crowd's hearing and not believing Jesus. No mention is made therein to eating Jesus' body and drinking his blood.

Two reactions to Jesus are mentioned in verses 60–71. The first was the rejection of Jesus by the multitude of one-time followers of Jesus. They could not believe in Jesus as the true Bread from heaven. The second reaction was that of Peter and the twelve disciples. Peter spoke for that group when he confessed that Jesus, as God's Holy One, was the only source of eternal life. The commentators rightly observe that this is the fourth gospel's rendition of Peter's confession that Jesus is the Christ found in the Synoptics (Matt. 16:16; Mark 8:29; Luke 9:20).

REVIEW QUESTIONS

1. What three significant Old Testament events form the background to John 6?

2. How does the Passover shed light on Jesus' feeding of the multitudes as recorded in John 6:1–13?

3. What Old Testament story lies behind Jesus' walking on the water, as discussed in John 6:16–21?

4. What three components of ancient rabbinic sermons surface in the Bread of Life Discourse in John 6:22–50?

5. How do the duplicate accounts of the Bread of Life Discourse (John 6:35–50 and 6:51–59) compare and contrast?

6. What two reactions to Jesus are highlighted in John 6:60–71?

Bread of Life Discourse(s)

new covenant

new exodus

new Passover

Pentateuchal citation and correction

sacramental

sapiential

seven "I am" sayings

subordinate citation from the Old Testament

synagogue preaching/ rabbinic sermon

CHAPTER 9

Jesus and the Feast of Tabernacles

JOHN 7:1–52

Objectives

After reading this chapter, you should be able to:

- Discuss whether or not Jesus contradicted himself by "going up" to Jerusalem when he told his brothers that he would not (John 7:6–10).

- Describe the significance of the water-drawing ceremony, as practiced at the Feast of Tabernacles, for John 7:37–39.

- Define the "living water" to which Jesus refers.

INTRODUCTION

John 7 – 10 gives witness to two interlocking themes: Jesus is the replacement of two popular feasts of Israel—Tabernacles (7:1 – 10:21) and Dedication (10:22 – 39)—and the Jewish leadership manifests escalating hostility to Jesus. The two seem to be related, the former leading to the latter. It will be helpful for our discussion of these chapters to provide the outline of John 7 – 10 in advance:

    I.   Prelude to the Feast of Tabernacles (7:1 – 13)

    II.   Jesus' Discourse at Tabernacles: Scene 1 (7:14 – 36)

    III. Jesus' Discourse at Tabernacles: Scene 2 (7:37 – 52)

    IV. Interruption in the Story: The Woman Caught in Adultery (7:53 – 8:11)

    V.   Jesus' Discourse at Tabernacles: Scene 3 (8:12 – 59)

    VI. Aftermath of Tabernacles: The Healing of a Blind Man (9:1 – 41)

    VII. Aftermath of Tabernacles: Jesus the Good Shepherd (10:1 – 21)

    VIII. Jesus and the Feast of Dedication (10:22 – 39)

    IX. The Conclusion to Jesus' Public Ministry (10:40 – 42)[1]

In this chapter we will cover the first three points of the above outline.

I. PRELUDE TO THE FEAST OF TABERNACLES (7:1 – 13)

It was decidedly safer for Jesus to be in Galilee because that province was governed not by the Jerusalem authorities but by Herod Antipas (v. 1). Despite the danger that lurked in Jerusalem for Jesus, his brothers advised him to celebrate the Feast of Tabernacles there (v. 2). Tabernacles (*sukkôt*—huts or booths) is the harvest (September – October) feast still celebrated by Jews in Israel. It commemorates, among other things, Israel's wanderings in the wilderness; hence the reason Jews build temporary shelters of branches to be occupied for eight days. Deuteronomy 16:13 mentions a seven-day celebration of Tabernacles, though Leviticus 23:26 – 32 speaks of an additional, eighth day of solemn rest.

On the surface, Jesus' brothers' request that he go to the feast in Jerusalem in order to win over disciples seemed well intentioned (vv. 3 – 4). In reality, however, verse 5 makes it clear that the suggestion of the brothers was born out of unbelief. They wanted Jesus to show off his miraculous power in Jerusalem.

John 7:6 – 10 illustrates the Johannine propensity for double entendre, centered on the words "time" (vv. 6, 8) and "go up" (vv. 8, 10). The word for "time" here is *kairos*, which connotes the idea of the in-breaking of God's kingdom and salvation into history. Thus what Jesus implied in verses 6, 8 is that it is not yet "time" for him to go to Jerusalem and die. "Go up" (*anabainō*, vv. 8, 10), as applied to Jesus in John 20:17, refers to his ascent to God the Father by way of his death in Jerusalem. These considerations resolve the apparent contradiction in verses 8 – 10: Jesus would "go up" to the Feast of Tabernacles, but that would not be the "time" at which he would "go up" to the Father.

---

1. I supplement here Raymond E. Brown's outline in *The Gospel according to John I–XII*, Anchor Bible 29A (Garden City, N.Y.: Doubleday, 1966), 305 – 412.

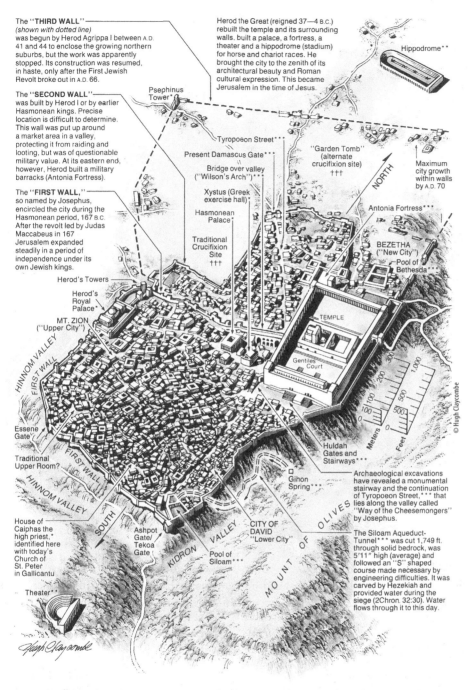

The "THIRD WALL"
(shown with dotted line)
was begun by Herod Agrippa I between A.D. 41 and 44 to enclose the growing northern suburbs, but the work was apparently stopped. Its construction was resumed, in haste, only after the First Jewish Revolt broke out in A.D. 66.

The "SECOND WALL"
was built by Herod I or by earlier Hasmonean kings. Precise location is difficult to determine. This wall was put up around a market area in a valley, protecting it from raiding and looting, but was of questionable military value. At its eastern end, however, Herod built a military barracks (Antonia Fortress).

The "FIRST WALL,"
so named by Josephus, encircled the city during the Hasmonean period, 167 B.C. After the revolt led by Judas Maccabeus in 167 Jerusalem expanded steadily in a period of independence under its own Jewish kings.

Herod the Great (reigned 37—4 B.C.) rebuilt the temple and its surrounding walls, built a palace, a fortress, a theater and a hippodrome (stadium) for horse and chariot races. He brought the city to the zenith of its architectural beauty and Roman cultural expression. This became Jerusalem in the time of Jesus.

Hippodrome**

Psephinus Tower*

Tyropoeon Street***

Present Damascus Gate***

Bridge over valley ("Wilson's Arch")***

Xystus (Greek exercise hall)*

Hasmonean Palace*

Traditional Crucifixion Site †††

"Garden Tomb" (alternate crucifixion site) †††

NORTH

Maximum city growth within walls by A.D. 70

Antonia Fortress***

BEZETHA ("New City")

Pool of Bethesda***

Herod's Towers

Herod's Royal Palace*

MT. ZION ("Upper City")

HINNOM VALLEY

FIRST WALL

TEMPLE

Gentiles Court

© Hugh Claycombe

Essene Gate*

Traditional Upper Room?

FIRST WALL

HINNOM VALLEY

SOUTH

Huldah Gates and Stairways***

Gihon Spring***

Archaeological excavations have revealed a monumental stairway and the continuation of Tyropoeon Street,*** that lies along the valley called "Way of the Cheesemongers" by Josephus.

House of Caiphas the high priest,* identified here with today's Church of St. Peter in Gallicantu

Theater**

Ashpot Gate/ Tekoa Gate*

CITY OF DAVID "Lower City"

KIDRON VALLEY

Pool of Siloam***

MOUNT OF OLIVES

The Siloam Aqueduct-Tunnel*** was cut 1,749 ft. through solid bedrock, was 5'11" high (average) and followed an "S" shaped course made necessary by engineering difficulties. It was carved by Hezekiah and provided water during the siege (2Chron. 32:30). Water flows through it to this day.

100 200 500 1,000

100 500

Meters Feet

* Location generally known, but style of architecture is unknown; artist's concept only, and Roman architecture is assumed.

** Location and architecture unknown, but referred to in written history; shown here for illustrative purposes.

*** Ancient feature has remained, or appearance has been determined from evidence.

Buildings, streets and roads shown here are artist's concept only unless otherwise named and located. Wall heights remain generally unknown, except for those surrounding the Temple Mount.

Jerusalem at the time of Christ.

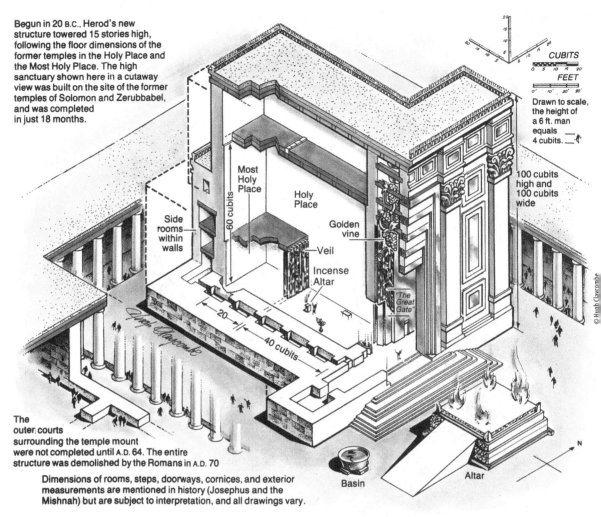

Begun in 20 B.C., Herod's new structure towered 15 stories high, following the floor dimensions of the former temples in the Holy Place and the Most Holy Place. The high sanctuary shown here in a cutaway view was built on the site of the former temples of Solomon and Zerubbabel, and was completed in just 18 months.

CUBITS

FEET

Drawn to scale, the height of a 6 ft. man equals 4 cubits.

Most Holy Place

Holy Place

Golden vine

100 cubits high and 100 cubits wide

Side rooms within walls

60 cubits

Veil

Incense Altar

"The Great Gate"

20

40 cubits

© Hugh Claycombe

The outer courts surrounding the temple mount were not completed until A.D. 64. The entire structure was demolished by the Romans in A.D. 70

Basin

Altar

N

Dimensions of rooms, steps, doorways, cornices, and exterior measurements are mentioned in history (Josephus and the Mishnah) but are subject to interpretation, and all drawings vary.

Herod's temple.

When Jesus shortly thereafter went to Jerusalem to celebrate Tabernacles, he did so alone and secretly (v. 10). But that did not stop the Jerusalem crowds from quietly seeking him out (vv. 11–12). Their opinion of him was mixed—some thought he was "good" while others thought he was a deceiver (v. 12).

II. JESUS' DISCOURSE AT TABERNACLES: SCENE 1 (7:14–36)

Jesus arrived in Jerusalem halfway through the Feast of Tabernacles (about the fourth day, v. 14). Judging from verses 21–23, Jesus might have reached there on the Sabbath. John 7:14–36 comprises scene 1 of Jesus' discourse at Tabernacles. It divides into two parts: Jesus the teacher and the Sabbath (vv. 14–24) and Jesus and the crowd's ineptness (vv. 25–36). The first part further divides into two topics: Jesus the teacher (vv. 14–20) and Jesus and the Sabbath (vv. 21–24).

A. Jesus the Teacher and the Sabbath (vv. 14–24)

1. Jesus the Teacher (vv. 14–20)

According to verses 14–15, upon arriving at Jerusalem, Jesus began to teach in the temple precincts. The audience was amazed at how well Jesus taught without having been trained by a rabbi; nor did he appeal to other rabbis for his authority. Rather, his teaching authority came directly from God.

2. Jesus and the Sabbath (vv. 21–24)

Apparently Jesus' healing of the lame man on the Sabbath (John 5:1–15) continued to disturb his compatriots (7:21–23).

Verse 24 records Jesus' indictment of the crowd: they should stop judging by outward appearance and rather evaluate matters by the reality of truth. This is a fitting summary of verses 14–24. Jesus should not be judged because he had no rabbi mentor; instead, his authority came from God (vv. 14–20). Furthermore, the Jerusalem audience should not conclude that Jesus was breaking the true spirit of the Sabbath when he healed the sick (vv. 21–23).

B. Jesus and the Crowd's Ineptness (vv. 25–36)

These verses highlight the Jewish crowd's ineptness in their understandings and dealings with Jesus. The section unfolds in three points: (1) verses 25–29: the crowd's ineptness in comprehending the origin of Jesus; (2) verses 30–32: the crowd's bungling attempt to arrest Jesus; (3) verses 33–36: the crowd's misunderstanding of Jesus' mission.

1. The Crowd's Ineptness in Comprehending the Origin of Jesus (vv. 25–29)

The Jerusalem crowd's response to Jesus' teaching was marked by ambiguity. On the one hand, it entertained the possibility that Jesus was the Messiah (vv. 25–26). But, on

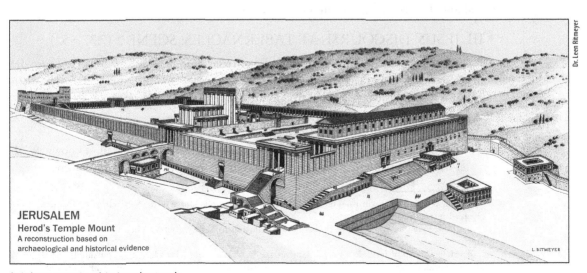

JERUSALEM
Herod's Temple Mount
A reconstruction based on
archaeological and historical evidence

L. RITMEYER

Dr. Leen Ritmeyer

Artist's reconstruction of the Jerusalem temple.

the other hand, the crowd labored under the assumption that the origin of the Messiah would be unknown (cf. *1 Enoch* 48:6; *4 Ezra* 13:42; Justin, *Dialogues* 8.5; 110.1) but that Jesus was from Nazareth (v. 27). Apparently the crowd was not aware that Jesus was born in Bethlehem (Matt. 2:5–8; Luke 2:4–7; cf. Mic. 5:2). More seriously, the crowd was not cognizant of the fact that Jesus was from God (vv. 28–29). This was so because they did not know God (v. 28b).

2. *The Crowd's Bungling Attempt at Arresting Jesus (vv. 30–32)*

Taking offense at Jesus' rejoinder, the crowd attempted a citizens' arrest of Jesus but to no avail. At the human level, Jesus may have slipped away in the throng of people. At the divine level, however, it was not yet God's timing for Jesus to be apprehended (v. 30).

Yet others in the crowd wondered if Jesus' miracles might not prove he was the Messiah (cf. Isa. 35:5–6). The debate over Jesus among the masses attracted the attention of the Jerusalem authorities, namely, the Pharisees and the high-ranking priests. So they sent the temple guard to arrest Jesus (v. 32), but as verses 45–52 later report, that official effort at apprehending Jesus also failed.[2]

> Jesus announced that his mission would soon be accomplished and then he would return to God his Father.

3. *The Crowd's Misunderstanding of Jesus' Mission (vv. 33–36)*

Addressing the crowd again, Jesus announced that his mission would soon be accomplished—that is, he would die for the sins of the world—and then he would return to God his Father. And should the crowd continue in its unbelief, they would not be permitted to join Jesus in the afterlife (vv. 33–34).[3] The crowd promptly misunderstood Jesus' pronouncement, thinking that he was referring to his going outside of Israel to Diaspora Judaism and teaching Gentiles (vv. 35–36).[4] Ironically, even though the crowd was wrong for the moment, by the time of the writing of the fourth gospel, the gospel of Jesus indeed had found a ready reception among the Gentiles.

III. JESUS' DISCOURSE AT TABERNACLES: SCENE 2 (7:37–52)

Round two of the debates over Jesus at Tabernacles unfolds in John 7:37–52. Three dramatic scenes emerge therein: the invitation of Jesus (vv. 37–39), the deliberation of the crowd (vv. 40–44), and the consternation of the Jerusalem authorities (vv. 45–52).

A. The Invitation of Jesus (vv. 37–39)

The last day of the Feast of Tabernacles climaxed with a solemn procession known as "the water-drawing ceremony." On each of the seven mornings, a procession went down to the

---

2. The temple police consisted of temple Levites and the police force of the Sanhedrin. The Sanhedrin was the Jewish ruling body over Israel.

3. Jesus' usage here of *egō eimi* probably is an allusion to Yahweh, which once again in the fourth gospel equates Jesus with God.

4. Since the fall of Jerusalem to the Babylonians in 587 BC, most Jews have lived outside Palestine. In the ancient world, Diaspora (dispersed) Jews clustered in three major cities: Rome; Alexandria, Egypt; and Antioch, Syria.

The modern Temple Mount.

fountain of Gihon on the southeast side of the temple, the fountain that supplied the waters to the Pool of Siloam. There a priest filled a golden pitcher with water and, after proceeding to the altar in front of the temple, poured the water into a silver funnel from which it flowed into the ground. On the seventh day there was a sevenfold circling of the altar. At that time Jesus stood and invited all to come and believe in him, the Living Water (cf. vv. 37–39 with 4:10–15). The source of that living water — the Spirit — is Christ, something the Old Testament predicted (see Ezek. 47:1–12; Zech. 14:8), but which is now applied to Jesus, not to the eschatological temple. On this reading, Jesus is the New Temple prophesied by Ezekiel and Zechariah from whom living water flowed to quench the spiritual thirst of all who come to him.

B. The Deliberation of the Crowd (vv. 40–44)

Verses 40–44 register the deliberation of the crowd concerning Jesus. Some believed him to be the prophet like Moses (cf. v. 40 with Deut. 18:15–18). Others thought Jesus was the Messiah, but they stumbled over the fact that he was not born in Bethlehem, as the Old Testament prophesied (John 7:41–42; cf. Mic. 5:2). But in reality Jesus *was* born in Bethlehem. Here we meet with a messianic expectation different than the one earlier mentioned in John 7:27. Jewish expectations about the Messiah were not uniform in the first century. Still others in the Jerusalem crowd were hostile to Jesus, wanting to arrest him (v. 44).

C. Consternation of the Jerusalem Authorities (vv. 45–52)

Ironically, the temple police were so awestruck with Jesus that they could not arrest him (vv. 45–46). The Pharisees' response revealed their misinformed judgment about Christ.

First, their sarcastic response that no one in the Sanhedrin believed in Jesus overlooked the fact that Nicodemus did believe in Jesus (cf. also Joseph of Arimathea, Mark 15:43; Luke 23:50). It took courage for that Pharisee to stand up for Christ by protesting the Sanhedrin's unjust treatment of Jesus (vv. 47–51).[5] Second, the Pharisees further taunted the temple police by reminding them that no prophet ever came from Galilee, which was not true. Jonah, for example, was from Galilee (2 Kings 14:25).

CONCLUSION

The Feast of Tabernacles, particularly its water-drawing ceremony, reminded ancient Israel of the covenantal blessings (Lev. 26:4; Deut. 28:12), as well as the eschatological blessings of the age of the Messiah (Ezek. 47:1–12; Zech 14:8–9). But now those blessings merged in the person of Jesus. His life, death, resurrection, and subsequent sending of the Spirit brought about the end-time restoration of the heart. Moreover, the Old Testament associated the end-time restoration of Israel with the conversion of the Gentiles to Yahweh (Isa. 45:15; 60:15–17; Mic. 4:13; et al.). That, too, had begun to happen in Jesus' day and continued in John's time (John 7:35–36) and beyond.

---

5. The derogatory reference to the masses as being unlearned (v. 49) was characteristic of the Pharisees' attitude to the "people of the land" ('am hā'āres). For more discussion, see *Pirke Aboth* 2.6; STB 2:494.

REVIEW QUESTIONS

1. What do "time" and "go up" mean in John 7:6–10?

2. What was different about Jesus' teaching that made it authoritative, according to John 7:14–20?

3. Please describe the "water-drawing" ceremony as performed by Jesus in John 7:37–39.

4. According to John 7:37–38, what is the "living water" to which Jesus referred, and from whom did it flow?

5. How did the Feast of Tabernacles speak to ancient Jews of the covenant and the Messiah?

KEY TERMS

Feast of Dedication

Feast of Tabernacles

Living Water

water-drawing ceremony

CHAPTER 10

Jesus and the Feast of Tabernacles (Part 2)

JOHN 7:53–8:59

Objectives

After reading this chapter, you should be able to:

- Explain whether the episode of the woman caught in adultery was a part of John's original text.

- Summarize the four interchanges between Jesus and his audience at the Feast of Tabernacles.

- Identify the meaning of the three fathers Jesus referred to in John 8.

INTRODUCTION

After briefly examining the story of the woman caught in adultery (John 7:53 – 8:11), we will focus in this chapter on scene 3 of Jesus' discourse at the Feast of Tabernacles (8:12 – 59).

I. THE WOMAN CAUGHT IN ADULTERY (7:53 – 8:11)

The vast majority of commentaries (and modern translations) seriously doubt that this passage is original to the fourth gospel.[1] After summarizing the evidence against its inclusion in John, we will, however, mention its theological importance for those who think it is still historical.

A. The Evidence against the Inclusion of John 7:53 – 8:11 in the Fourth Gospel

Three pieces of evidence strongly indicate that the pericope of the woman caught in adultery was not a part of the gospel of John and hence is not canonical and inspired.

First, textually these verses do not appear in any Greek manuscript of the fourth gospel before the fifth century AD.

Second, stylistically, virtually every verse from 7:53 – 8:11 contains words not occurring elsewhere in the gospel of John (i.e., "scribes," "Olives," "adultery," "condemn").

Third, logically, 7:53 – 8:11 interrupts the flow of thought of 7:52 – 8:12. Thus Tabernacles motifs in 8:12 – 9:7, especially Siloam, continue the discussion from 7:52, whereas

---

1. The exceptions are the King James Version and the New King James Version.

The northern part of the Mount of Olives where Gethsemane is located.

7:53–8:11 situates the episode of the adulterous woman in the temple precincts. As the commentators suggest, 7:53–8:11 fits better the week before Jesus' passion.[2]

Where did the pericope originate if not in the gospel of John? It may well be that this episode was first recorded in the second-century noncanonical *Gospel of the Hebrews* and from there made its way into the gospel of John thanks to some creative scribe.

B. The Theological Message of John 7:53–8:11

Even though the evidence against the canonicity of John 7:53–8:11 is overwhelming, many commentators believe the incident is historical.[3] Its message of Jesus' love and mercy for sinners is consistent with the four Gospels.

Some Well-Known New Testament Apocrypha (Apart from Nag Hammadi)

I. Gospels and Related Forms
  A. Narrative Gospels and Acts
    1. *Gospel of the Hebrews*
    2. *Gospel of Peter*
    3. *Infancy Gospel of Thomas*
    4. *Protevangelium of James*
    5. *Acts of Paul (and Thecla)*
II. Letters
  A. Correspondence between Paul and Seneca
  B. Paul's Letter to the Laodiceans
III. Liturgical Materials
  A. *Odes of Solomon*

II. JESUS' DISCOURSE AT TABERNACLES: SCENE 3 (8:12–59)

John 8:12 resumes the narrative of 7:52, pitting Jesus against the Jerusalem religious leadership. Scene 3 divides into three sections: Jesus the Light of the World (vv. 12–20), Jesus' origin and nature (vv. 21–30); Jesus and Abraham (vv. 31–59).

A. Jesus the Light of the World (vv. 12–20)

Jesus' discourse at Tabernacles continued in 8:12 with his proclamation, "I am the light of the world." This, along with the topics of Jesus as witness (vv. 13, 14ab, 17–19) and Jesus as judge (vv. 14cd, 15–16), comprise the outline of verses 12–20.

1. Jesus the Light of the World (v. 12)

"I am the light of the world" (8:12) is Jesus' second "I am" statement in the gospel of John (see "I am the bread of life," 6:35). It no doubt conjured up various images. Most immediately, Jesus' statement no doubt coincided with the light ceremony celebrated at the Feast of Tabernacles, which, along with the water-drawing ritual, was wildly popular with ancient Jews. The rabbinic writing *Sukkah* 5:1–4 describes the light ceremony:

> Towards the end of the first day of the feast of Tabernacles, people went down into the court of the women. Golden lamps were there, and four golden bowls were on each of them, and four ladders were by each; four young men from the priestly group of youths had jugs of

---

2. See Andreas J. Köstenberger's discussion in *John*, Baker Exegetical Commentary on the New Testament (Grand Rapids: Baker, 2004), 247.

3. Refer to Craig S. Keener's bibliography in his *The Gospel of John: A Commentary*, vol. 1 (Peabody, Mass.: Hendrickson, 2003), 737nn312–13.

oil in their hands containing about 120 logs and poured oil from them into the individual bowls. There was no court in Jerusalem that was not bright from the light of the place of drawing water.

2. Jesus the Witness (vv. 13, 14ab, 17–19)

The Pharisees took exception to Jesus' self-claim to be light, accusing him of providing insufficient testimony. He must have two witnesses to confirm his claim (v. 13; cf. Deut. 19:15; cf. *Kethubah* 2.9). But the Pharisees had a short memory, for earlier Jesus supplied a string of witnesses to his deity (John 5:31–39). Here Jesus focused on God the Father as his witness.

3. Jesus the Judge (vv. 14cd, 15–16)

As the commentators recognize, this "trial" scene, along with others in the gospel of John, turned the tables on Jesus' opponents. Whereas the Synoptic Gospels emphasize the trial of Jesus by the Jewish and Roman authorities, John does the reverse: he shows the authorities on trial before Jesus the judge.

> Whereas the Synoptic Gospels emphasize the trial of Jesus by the Jewish and Roman authorities, John does the reverse: he shows the authorities on trial before Jesus the judge.

The current controversy centered on the ignorance of the authorities as to Jesus' origin (vv. 14cd). Accordingly, they passed judgment on Jesus according to appearance (v. 15; cf. 7:24). But Jesus will judge them and the world according to truth (v. 16). The spiritual ignorance of the Pharisees was further revealed in their request that Jesus' Father come and give testimony to them! They still believed that Jesus was only human.

According to verse 20, Jesus' discourse took place near the temple treasury, which was adjacent to the Court of the Women, the site of the light ceremony. Jesus' words stung the authorities, but they could not arrest him because his hour had not yet come.

B. Jesus' Origin and Nature (vv. 21–30)

John 8:21–30 is like 7:33–34 but more serious in tone—Jesus warned that his audience would die in their sin if they refused to believe in him. Four verbal interchanges between Jesus and his audience at the Feast of Tabernacles transpired in those verses. In each case, Jesus made a statement about his origin or nature that his hearers misunderstood.

1. First Interchange (vv. 21–22)

Jesus' first statement was that he was going away (to heaven) but his audience would not be able to follow him and would consequently die in their sin (vv. 21–22).

2. Second Interchange (vv. 23–25a)

In verse 23 Jesus counteracted his audience's response with a second statement, namely, he was from above (heaven) and his listeners were from below (earth). Further, Jesus identified himself as God—"I am" (*egō eimi*). And unless the crowd believed that, they would die

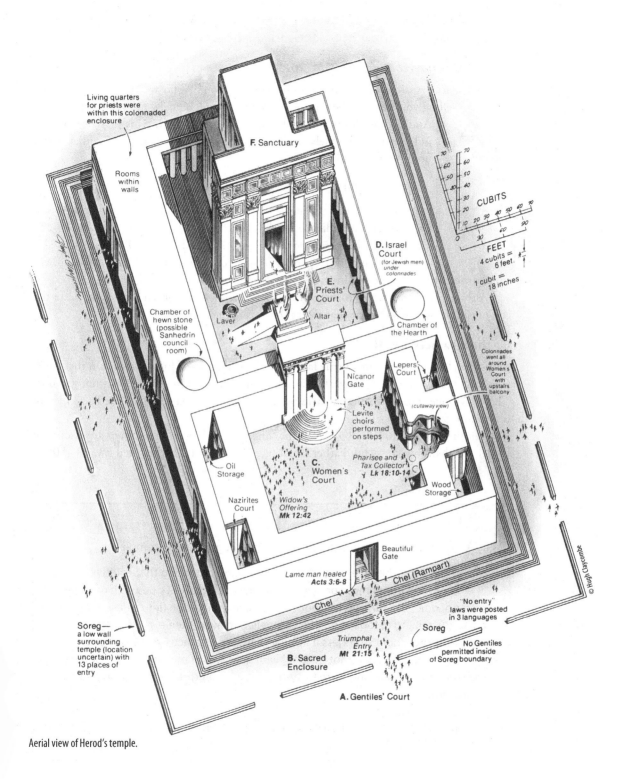

Living quarters for priests were within this colonnaded enclosure

Rooms within walls

F. Sanctuary

Chamber of hewn stone (possible Sanhedrin council room)

Laver

Altar

E. Priests' Court

D. Israel Court (for Jewish men) *under colonnades*

Chamber of the Hearth

CUBITS

FEET

4 cubits = 6 feet.

1 cubit = 18 inches

Nicanor Gate

Lepers Court

Levite choirs performed on steps

(cutaway view)

Colonnades went all around Women's Court with upstairs balcony

Oil Storage

Pharisee and Tax Collector ☩ *Lk 18:10-14*

C. Women's Court

Wood Storage

Nazirites Court

Widow's Offering **Mk 12:42**

Beautiful Gate

Lame man healed **Acts 3:6-8**

Chel (Rampart)

Chel

"No entry" laws were posted in 3 languages

Soreg — a low wall surrounding temple (location uncertain) with 13 places of entry

Triumphal Entry **Mt 21:15**

Soreg

No Gentiles permitted inside of Soreg boundary

B. Sacred Enclosure

A. Gentiles' Court

© Hugh Claycombe

Aerial view of Herod's temple.

in sin (v. 24). The crowd incredulously asked Jesus who he was (v. 25), showing no sign of spiritual comprehension that Jesus was God and therefore was from heaven.

3. Third Interchange (vv. 25b–26)

In essence Jesus responded to the audience's question, "Who are you?" with "What I have been telling you from the beginning [of my ministry], namely, I am God incarnate!"

And because Jesus is from God, his words, including his present words of judgment, are divinely inspired (v. 26). Still, however, Jesus' audience did not understand him.

> Jesus' being lifted up will simultaneously be his crucifixion and exaltation/resurrection.

4. Fourth Interchange (vv. 28–30)

Jesus' final statement in this part of his discourse at Tabernacles was to predict that his audience would lift him, the Son of Man, up (vv. 28–29). Comparing this assertion with John 3:14 and 12:32 ("lifted up"), 12:23; 13:31–32; and 17:1 ("glorify") make clear that Jesus' being lifted up will simultaneously be his crucifixion and exaltation/resurrection.

Although verse 30 seems to suggest that Jesus' audience believed him, verse 32 to the end of the chapter makes clear that their faith was not genuine.

C. Three Fathers (vv. 31–59)

John 8:31 clarifies the nature of true faith: true faith abides in Christ's word. On that basis, what occurs in verses 31–59 reveals that the faith referred to in verse 30 was not genuine. The crowd one moment believed in Jesus (v. 30) but the next moment tried to kill him (vv. 37, 40, 59).

The thematic key to John 8:31–59 is the concept of "father." Three fathers are discussed: Father Abraham (vv. 31–41a); Father Devil (vv. 41b–47); and Father God (vv. 48–50).

Josephus on the Magnificence of the Temple

With pride Josephus describes the former glory of the temple:

> Now the exterior of the building wanted nothing that could astound either mind or eye. For, being covered on all sides with massive plates of gold, the sun was no sooner up than it radiated so fiery a flash that persons straining to look at it were compelled to avert their eyes as from solar rays. To approaching strangers it appeared from a distance like a snow-clad mountain; for all that was not overlaid with gold was of purest white.... Some of the stones in the building were forty-five cubits in length, five in height and six in breadth.[4]

---

4. Josephus, *J.W.* 5.5.6 §§ 222–24. On the whole description of the temple, see *J.W.* 5.5.1–6 §§ 184–226; and *Ant.* 15.11.3 §§ 391–402.

1. Father Abraham (vv. 31–41a)

Like the other two sections in verses 31–59, verses 31–41a record a heated debate between the unbelieving Jews and Jesus. The debate was sparked when Jesus told the crowd that the true test of faith was to abide in (or obey) his word (see 5:38; 2 John 9; cf. John 15:4–10). This would set them free.

The crowd took offense at Jesus' statement, exclaiming that they were Abraham's "seed" (*sperma*) and therefore, were not enslaved (v. 33). By this the crowd meant that their descendancy from Abraham automatically made them the people of God, and that therefore they were free spiritually. Jesus fired back at his opponents in verses 34–41a, arguing that while they might be the physical descendants (sperma) of Abraham, their intent to kill him revealed they were not true children of Abraham. This showed that they were after all imprisoned to sin and not free.

2. Father Devil (vv. 41b–47)

The debate intensified to a boiling point in verses 41b–47. The crowd denied Jesus' accusation. Jesus responded with a twofold answer. First, in verses 42–43 he said to

Western Wall.

the crowd that God was *not* their father, as evidenced by the violent way they were treating him, the true representative of God. Second, in verses 44–47 Jesus told the audience that the Devil was their father! The following chart illustrates the nature of Jesus' response here in verses 44–47 in associating the crowd with the Devil:

	Devil[5]	Unbelieving Jews
Murderer	Cain was inspired by the Devil to murder Abel (Gen. 4:8; cf. 1 John 3:12–15).	The crowd is inspired by the Devil to murder Jesus (v. 44a).
Liar	The Devil lied to Eve in the beginning (Gen. 3:4–5).	The Devil inspired the unbelieving Jews to believe a lie about Jesus — that he is not from God (vv. 42–43; 44b–47).

---

5. References to "Satan"/"Devil"/"prince" of this world occur in John 12:31; 13:27; 14:30; 16:11; 17:15. Lying versus truth reminds one of the same dualism in the Dead Sea Scrolls (1QS 3–4).

3. Father God (vv. 48–59)

The verbal volleys between the Jews and Jesus continue in verses 48–59. The former accused Jesus of being a Samaritan and demon-possessed (v. 48). Jesus responded that he was not a demoniac (cf. Matt. 12:25–32; Mark 3:20–29; Luke 11:14–23) but rather sought to honor and glorify God, which God in turn bestowed on him (vv. 49–55). Furthermore, since Jews appealed to Abraham as their father, Jesus appealed to Abraham as a witness to himself. Indeed, Jesus existed long before Abraham was even heard of, because Jesus is "I Am"—God (vv. 56–58; cf. vv. 24, 28). Jesus' discourse at Tabernacles ended abruptly with that comment, for the crowd tried to stone him to death for blasphemy (v. 59; cf. Lev. 24:16).[6] But Jesus escaped such a fate by slipping away into the crowds.

---

6. According to Josephus there were plenty of stones lying around before Herod's temple was completed in AD 66 (*Ant.* 17.9.3/216).

REVIEW QUESTIONS

1. What three considerations indicate that the story of the woman caught in adultery (John 7:53 – 8:11) was probably not a part of John's original text?

2. Please summarize the four interchanges between Jesus and his audience at the Feast of Tabernacles recorded in John 8:21 – 30.

3. What does Jesus say about the three "fathers" in John 8:31 – 59?

KEY TERMS

Father Abraham   Father God   New Testament Apocrypha

Father Devil   light ceremony

CHAPTER 11

Jesus the Light of the World

Heals a Blind Man

JOHN 9

Objectives

After reading this chapter, you should be able to:

- Describe the Pool of Siloam as well as its source of water.
- Identify the infraction Jesus committed when he healed the sightless man.
- Explain the significance of the words "expelled from the synagogues."
- Contrast the sightless man with the Pharisees.

INTRODUCTION

Hailed as one of the most artistic passages in all of the Gospels, John 9 illustrates that Jesus is the Light of the World by his healing of a blind man. The narrative unfolds in five circumstances pertaining to Jesus' healing of the man born blind:

    I. The healing: physical sight (vv. 1–12).
    II. The Pharisees' first interrogation of the formerly blind man (vv. 13–17).
    III. The Pharisees' interrogation of the man's parents (vv. 18–23).
    IV. The Pharisees' second interrogation of the healed man (vv. 24–34).
    V. The judgment: the Pharisees' spiritual blindness (vv. 35–41).

I. THE HEALING (9:1–12)

Upon leaving the temple area, Jesus saw a man, blind from birth, begging for his livelihood (v. 1; cf. v. 8). The disciples (whom we have not heard from since John 6) raised the question as to who was at fault for the man's sightlessness—he or his parents (v. 2). Ancient Israel looked upon sickness as the direct effect of sin (see Job 4:7; *b. Sabbath* 55a), this despite the overall message of the book of Job. Jesus dismissed both possibilities (Jer. 31:29–30; Ezek. 18; cf. Tobit 3:3), explaining instead that the man's blindness was not due to sin but rather had happened to serve God's higher purpose (John 9:3).

> John 9 illustrates that Jesus is the Light of the World by his healing of a blind man.

In verses 4–5 Jesus conveyed the urgency of the situation (*dei*, "must"; see 3:14; 4:4; 10:16; 12:34). He was the Light of the World (cf. 8:12), and soon darkness (the Pharisees)

The Pool of Siloam.

Todd Bolen/www.BiblePlaces.com

Written in paleo-Hebrew, this inscription at the end of Hezekiah's tunnel was discovered in 1880 by a schoolboy going to the tunnel to bathe. Translation: [See] the boring. And this was the manner of the boring. While [the stonemasons were] still [strinking with] the pick-axe, each man towards his comrade, and when there were still three ells (1.35 m.) to bore thro[ugh, there was hear]d the voice of a man shouting to his comrade, as there was a resonance in the rock, in the south and i[n the nor]th. And on the day of the boring the stonemasons had struck, each towards his own comrade, pick-axe against [pick]axe. Then the water ran from the spring to the pool for 1200 ells (540 m.). And 100 ells was the height of the rock over the heads of the stonemasons. (K. A. D. Smelik, *Writings from Ancient Israel: An Handbook of Historical and Religions Documents*, trans. G. I. Davies [Louisville:Westminster/John Knox, 1991], 70) The above text describes the excitement that Hezekiah's workers felt as they chiseled their way toward each other — from the Gihon Spring to the Pool of Siloam.

would try to snuff out the Light. In other words, it was time now for Jesus to show he was the Light by healing the sightless man.

Verses 6–7 briefly record the miracle. Jesus applied his spittle and mud to the man's eyes as if it were an ointment (v. 6; cf. vv. 11, 14–15; see also Mark 8:23). Jesus then sent the man to wash in the Pool of Siloam (v. 7). The Pool of Siloam (mentioned in the New Testament only here) was a part of the water system built by King Hezekiah (ca. 700 BC). It was a rock-cut pool located southwest of the city of David whose supply of water flowed from the Gihon Spring in the Kidron Valley (cf. 2 Chron. 32:30).

The man did what Jesus commanded, and he was healed (v. 7). When the man's friends asked how his sight was restored,[1] he related his encounter with Jesus (vv. 8–12). This miracle constituted the sixth sign miracle performed by Jesus.

II. THE PHARISEES' FIRST INTERROGATION OF THE FORMERLY BLIND MAN (9:13–17)

The man's friends took him to the Pharisees, perhaps because the religious authorities were responsible for investigating whether a purported miracle was bona fide (v. 13). Because Jesus performed the miracle on a Sabbath (v. 14), the Pharisees were divided in their response to him. Some accused him of breaking the Sabbath (vv. 15–16a). According to rabbinic tradition, Jesus committed an act of kneading by mixing the spittle and mud. The

---

1. The verb *anablepō* (vv. 13, 15, 18 [2x]) literally means "see again" but was an idiom for "receive sight."

Mishnaic tractate *Shabbat* 7:2 counts kneading as one of thirty-nine categories of work forbidden on the Sabbath. Therefore these Pharisees judged that Jesus was not from God, but rather was a false prophet (Deut. 13:1–5). Other Pharisees disagreed, wondering how Jesus could perform such miracles and not be from God. When pressed further by the Pharisees, the man exclaimed that Jesus was a prophet. He may have associated Jesus with the prophets Elijah and Elisha, who were noted for their amazing miracles.

III. THE PHARISEES' INTERROGATION OF THE MAN'S PARENTS (9:18–23)

The "Jews" (Pharisees) did not believe the man's testimony, so they called in his parents (v. 18). It may be that the formerly blind man had lived under their roof. The parents responded to the Pharisees' interrogation of them by agreeing that he was indeed their son and that he was born blind, but they did not know how he came to receive his sight. The Pharisees would have to ask him about that; he was an adult and able to speak for himself (vv. 19–21). Actually, however, the parents were hedging in their answer. They apparently knew that it was Jesus who healed their son, but they were afraid the "Jews"/Pharisees (cf. 7:13; 19:38; 20:19) would expel them from the synagogue (v. 22).

Being expelled from the synagogue (*aposynagōgos*; cf. 9:34–35; 12:42; 16:2)[2] was a disciplinary practice going back at least to Ezra 10:8. The Jerusalem religious authorities had already determined (*sunetetheinto*—a pluperfect, v. 22) that anyone who confessed Jesus to be the Christ would be excluded from Jewish worship (cf. Luke 6:22). Emil Schürer identifies three levels of excommunication from the synagogue at the time of Jesus. First, there was the minor ban of about a week's duration. Second, there was the more formal banishment lasting about thirty days. Third, there was the solemn curse imposed by the Jewish authorities, permanently cutting off contact between the offender and the synagogue. This is no doubt the type of excommunication referred to in John 9:22; 12:42; 16:2.[3] It seems to resemble the twelfth benediction crafted in the synagogue for the purpose of excommunicating Jewish Christians in the last years of the first century AD (*birkat ha-minim* [curse of the heretics]; *b. Berakhot* 28b–29a).

IV. THE PHARISEES' SECOND INTERROGATION OF THE HEALED MAN (9:24–34)

The Pharisees called the healed man in for a second round of interrogation. Verses 24–34 contain the verbal volleys exchanged between the two:

Pharisees:	Give glory to God and confess that the man[4] (Jesus) is a sinner (v. 24).
Man:	I do not know whether or not Jesus is a sinner. But I do know that he healed my blindness (v. 25).

---

2. This term occurs in the New Testament only in these places in John.

3. E. Schürer, *The History of the Jewish People in the Age of Jesus*, rev. and ed. G. Vermes et al., 4 vols. (Edinburgh: Clark, 1973–79), II, 2:59–62.

4. "Give glory to God" is an oath formula uttered before confession of one's sin (see Josh. 7:19; 1 Esd. 9:8). It may be, however, that here we meet with Johannine irony: the man will indeed give glory to God by confessing the reality of Jesus' miracle on his behalf.

Pharisees:	How did he open your eyes? (v. 26).
Man:	I told you before, but you will not listen. Are you investigating me so that you might decide to become Jesus' disciples?[5] (v. 27).
Pharisees:	You are his disciple, and we have no idea about his origin. But we are disciples of Moses, God's appointed messenger[6] (vv. 28–29; cf. Ex. 33:11; Num. 12:2).
Man:	You do not know Jesus' origin, yet God has empowered him to heal my blindness; something only God can do[7] (vv. 30–33).
Pharisees:	Your blindness stems from the fact that you were a sinner from birth! And a sinner has no business lecturing us.

They then threw the man out of the synagogue (v. 34).[8]

V. THE JUDGMENT: THE PHARISEES' SPIRITUAL BLINDNESS (9:35–41)

The final scene of John 9 contrasts the spiritual status of the formerly blind man (vv. 35–38) with that of the Pharisees (vv. 39–41). After the healed man was expelled from the synagogue, Jesus sought him out and asked him if he believed in the Son of Man (v. 35). The reason Jesus used that title here was probably because the heavenly Son of Man was expected to establish God's kingdom on earth after judging unbelievers (cf. Dan. 7:13–14 with Matt. 24:27//Mark 13:26–27//Luke 21:27–28). As John 9:39–41 will show, that judgment was unleashed in part on the Pharisees. The healed man then believed in and worshiped Jesus as the Son of Man and as the Lord[9] (vv. 36–38).

But things were very much different with the Pharisees. While the blind man received his sight both physically and spiritually, the Pharisees, who thought they were spiritually perceptive, were in reality blind in their understanding of God and Jesus (vv. 39–41).[10] Both giving sight to the blind and the blinding of those who see are common Old Testament themes (for the former, see Ps. 146:8; Isa. 29:18; 35:5; 42:7, 18; for the latter see Isa. 6:10; 42:19; Jer. 5:21; cf. Matt. 13:13–15; John 12:40).[11] The first theme characterized the

---

5. The man is obviously being sarcastic.

6. Herein lies the crux of the matter between John's churches and the synagogue: the latter followed the law of Moses while the former preached the grace of Christ (cf. John 1:17). Yet, as the fourth gospel has pointed out, Moses was himself a witness to Christ (6:45–46; 7:19).

7. Giving sight to the blind was considered to be a rare miracle (2 Kings 6:8–23; Tobit 11:10–14; cf. 2:10).

8. Though some think this disciplining act was not the same in severity as that in v. 22, I see no reason not to equate the two, especially since the decision was made by the Jerusalem authorities, not just the local synagogue ruler.

9. "Lord" (*kurios*) in v. 36 is merely a title of respect, but in v. 38 "Lord" (*kurios*) is obviously a title of deity, especially since the healed man worshiped Jesus. We should note that two very reliable Greek manuscripts do not contain the words "'I do believe, Lord,' he said, 'and worshiped him'" (Sinaiticus and p[75]). However, the longer reading, which is attested to by the majority of ancient manuscripts, is probably original, so Bruce M. Metzger, *A Textual Commentary on the Greek New Testament* (Reading, Eng.: United Bible Societies, 1971), 195.

10. Verse 41 is a second-class conditional sentence, making a contrary-to-fact statement. The Pharisees are indeed guilty of sin, for they are not blind. The logic of this verse seems to parallel Matthew 9:12–13, where Jesus says that the "well" do not need a physician; only the sick do. That is, those who consider themselves to be well (when in fact they are not) are not candidates for Christ's healing (forgiveness). The Pharisees in John 9 think they are sighted and therefore need no healing, when, in fact, the opposite is the case.

11. See C. K. Barrett, *The Gospel according to John*, 2nd ed. (Philadelphia: Westminster, 1978), 365–66.

healed man, while the second theme applied to the Pharisees. Indeed, the following outline highlights the contrasting spiritual developments of the blind man and the Pharisees:

A. The Man: Started Out Physically Blind but Ended Up Spiritually Sighted

Note the spiritual progression of the formerly blind man:

1. He called Jesus a prophet (9:17).
2. He defended Jesus against the Pharisees' charges (9:25).
3. He invited the Pharisees to become followers of Jesus (9:27).
4. He confessed Jesus as Lord and worshiped him (9:38).

B. The Pharisees: Started Out Physically Sighted but Ended Up Spiritually Blind

Note the spiritual decline of the Pharisees:

1. They began by accepting the fact of Jesus' healing of the blind man (9:16–17).
2. They doubted the miracle; hence their reason for calling in the man's parents for interrogation (9:18–23).
3. They tried to bully the man into confessing that Jesus was a sinner (9:24–34).
4. Their spiritual blindness brought them under the judgment of Christ (9:40–41).

CONCLUSION

John 9 is a masterful chapter that accentuates Jesus as both the source of light (illustrated in his healing of the sightless man) and judgment (illustrated in his judgment on the Pharisees and their subsequent plunge into spiritual darkness).

REVIEW QUESTIONS

1. What was the source of the Pool of Siloam?

2. What infraction did Jesus commit by healing the blind man, according to John 9:13–17?

3. What was the historical background of John's phrase, "expelled from the synagogues"?

4. What were the developing contrasts between the healed blind man and his Pharisee interrogators as John 9 unfolds?

5. What were the three levels of excommunication from the synagogue?

KEY TERMS

expulsion from the synagogue	Hezekiah's tunnel	Pool of Siloam
	kneading	synagogue bans

CHAPTER 12

Jesus' Discourses at the Feasts of Tabernacles and Dedication

JOHN 10

Objectives

After reading this chapter, you should be able to:

- Understand what Jesus meant when he said, "I am the gate."
- Understand what Jesus meant when he said, "I am the good shepherd."

INTRODUCTION

John 10 transitions from the Feast of Tabernacles to the Feast of Dedication. Verses 1–21 record a discourse Jesus uttered in the aftermath of Tabernacles, while verses 22–39 record Jesus' discourse at the Feast of Dedication.

> John 10 transitions from the Feast of Tabernacles to the Feast of Dedication.

I. JESUS' DISCOURSE IN THE AFTERMATH OF TABERNACLES (10:1–21)

John 10:1–21 provides two more of Jesus' "I am" statements—"I am the gate" (v. 7) and "I am the good shepherd" (v. 11). Verses 1–21 serve as a transition from the Feast of Tabernacles to the Feast of Dedication. Thus, on the one hand, John 10:1–21 relates to John 9 (note that v. 21 refers back to the healing of the blind man reported in John 9). But, on the other hand, 10:26–27 refers to Jesus as the Shepherd (cf. 10:1–21); now, however, the setting is the Feast of Dedication (10:22).[1] So it seems that John 10:1–21 is a discourse spoken by Jesus after Tabernacles but before Dedication.

John 10:1–21 can be outlined as follows:

A. Two Parables (vv. 1–5)

    1. The Gate (vv. 1–3a)

    2. The Shepherd (vv. 3b–5)

B. The Pharisees' Initial Reaction (v. 6)

C. Jesus' Explanations (vv. 7–18)

    1. Jesus is the Gate (vv. 7–10)

    2. Jesus is the True Shepherd (vv. 11–18)

D. The Pharisees' Divided Response (vv. 19–21)

A. Two Parables (vv. 1–5)

Jesus spoke two parables in vv. 1–5. The first little parable (vv. 1–3a) illustrated the fact that there was only one legitimate way into the sheep pen: through the gate. Jesus' description here matches Near Eastern shepherding practices whereby the sheep are kept at night in a pen, either one erected in the open country or in a yard surrounded by a wall adjacent to a house. The walls were made of stone topped with briars, a design intended to keep robbers and thieves from scaling the walls and stealing the sheep. Quite often several flocks shared the same fold. The shepherd arrived in the morning, gathered his sheep by calling to them individually, then led them out to pasture.

The second parable (vv. 3b–5) also rings true with Near Eastern shepherding practices. To this day, Palestinian shepherds assign names to their sheep based on distinguishing

---

1. The Feast of Tabernacles was and is celebrated in September/October while the Feast of Dedication/Hanukkah was and is celebrated in December. For a different view of the relationship between John 9 and 10, see Andreas J. Köstenberger, *John*, Baker Exegetical Commentary on the New Testament (Grand Rapids: Baker, 2004), 297, who argues that there is no transition between the two, with the audiences likely being the same.

Sheep pen in Israel.

Sheep resting in the shade of a tree near Jotapata, Galilee.

characteristics, "long ears," "white nose," and the like. When the shepherd has separated his sheep from the other flocks in the pen, he leads them out into pasture.

B. The Pharisees' Initial Reaction (v. 6)

The Pharisees did not understand what Jesus was getting at in the parables. Their incomprehension reminds one of the crowd's failure to understand Jesus' parables as recorded in the Synoptics (see, e.g., Mark 4:13).

C. Jesus' Explanations (vv. 7 – 18)

Jesus accommodated his audience by explaining the meanings of the two parables.

1. Jesus Is the Gate (vv. 7 – 10)

Verses 7 – 10 are characterized by contrasting parallels:

I.   A   Jesus is the true gate (v. 7).

      B   The Jewish leaders are thieves (v. 8).

II.   A′   Jesus is the true gate (v. 9).

      B′   The Jewish leaders are thieves (v. 10).

Twice Jesus equated himself with the gate of the sheep (vv. 7, 9), which means theologically that he is the true way to salvation. On the other hand, the Pharisees, along with the Jerusalem leadership, were no more than thieves and bandits who steal and slaughter the sheep (vv. 8, 10).

It may be that the term *lēstis* (vv. 1, 8) connoted the false messiahs that Josephus spoke of, who falsely raised the hopes of Israel's deliverance from Rome (*Ant.* 20.5.1/97 – 98; 20.8.5/169 – 72; 20.8.10/188; *J.W.* 7.11.1/437 – 40; cf. Acts 5:36 – 37; 21:38).

2. Jesus is the True Shepherd (vv. 11 – 18)

Just as verses 7 – 10 explain the parable of the gate (vv. 1 – 3a), applying it to Jesus, so verses 11 – 18 explain the parable of the shepherd (vv. 3b – 5), applying it to Jesus. Indeed,

> The Pharisees, along with the Jerusalem leadership, were no more than thieves and bandits who steal and slaughter the sheep.

A shepherd tends his sheep near Bethlehem.

Jesus is the good, noble, or model (*kalos*) Shepherd (v. 11a), because he lays down his life to protect his sheep.

The Good Shepherd stands in contrast to the hired hand who is more interested in being paid than protecting the sheep from marauding predators (vv. 12–13). The metaphor of "hired hand," like the metaphors of "robbers and thieves" (vv. 1, 8), no doubt refers to the Jerusalem leaders whose concern was for their own welfare, not for the well-being of Israel. The contrast here between Jesus the Good Shepherd and the Jerusalem leaders as, in effect, "false shepherds" is rooted in the Old Testament, especially Ezekiel 34. There Israel's leaders (false shepherds) are the foil to God (the True Shepherd). The preceding contrast informs John 10:11–18: Jesus is the Good Shepherd; the Jerusalem leaders are the evil shepherds.

> Jesus is the good, noble, or model (*kalos*) Shepherd (v. 11a), because he lays down his life to protect his sheep.

Jesus knows his sheep and they know him (v. 14), just as God knows Jesus (v. 15a). The "knowledge" referred to here is rooted in the Old Testament—it is intimate knowledge that God the Shepherd has for his sheep (Ezek. 34:14; cf. Isa. 40:11).[2]

But Jesus is the Good Shepherd not only of Israel but also of Gentiles (v. 16).[3] Although Jesus' earthly ministry to the Gentiles was minimal, his death was for the whole world (John 3:16; cf. 1 John 2:2; Isa. 56:8), the proclamation of which was well-known in John's

---

2. This background is closer to hand for John 10 than Bultmann's proposed Gnostic, Mandean background; see Raymond E. Brown's discussion in *The Gospel according to John I–XII*, Anchor Bible 29A (Garden City, N.Y.: Doubleday, 1966), 399–400; and Craig S. Keener's statement in his *The Gospel of John: A Commentary*, vol. 1 (Peabody, Mass.: Hendrickson, 2003), 799.

3. That the "other sheep" referred to Gentiles rather than Diaspora Jews is preferred by the majority of commentaries; see Keener's discussion in *Gospel of John*, 810. 19.

day. Together, believing Jew and believing Gentile form the one flock of God (cf. John 17:20–21; see also Isa. 56:6–8; Ezek. 34:23; 37:15–28; Mic. 2:12).

The reason Jesus is the good shepherd is the same reason God loves him, namely, he laid down his life for others (vv. 17b–18).[4] Here again the sacrificial nature of Christ's death surfaces.

D. The Pharisees' Divided Response (vv. 19–21)

"The Jews" (Jerusalem authorities in general and the Pharisees in particular; see 9:16) were divided in their response to Jesus' most recent discourse (v. 19). Many thought he was demonically possessed (v. 20; cf. 7:20; 8:48, 52), but others believed his healing of the blind man refuted the supposition that he was influenced by demons (v. 21; cf. 9:16b).[5] In other words, Jesus was from God.

II. JESUS' DISCOURSE AT THE FEAST OF DEDICATION (10:22–42)

The Feast of Dedication was the occasion of Jesus' words in verses 22–42. The following outline will guide our discussion:

- A. The Setting (vv. 22–23).
- B. Jesus the Messiah and Son of God (vv. 24–39).
- C. Conclusion to Jesus' Public Ministry (vv. 40–42).

A. The Setting (vv. 22–23)

Jesus' teaching in this episode occurred at the Feast of Dedication (v. 22), a feast that commemorates Judas Maccabaeus's rededication of the Jerusalem temple in 164 BC (1 Macc. 4:36–59; 2 Macc. 10:1–18; Josephus, *Ant.* 12.7.6/320–21), after its desecration in 167 BC by the Seleucid ruler Antiochus Epiphanes (Dan. 11:3; 1 Macc. 1:59). Antiochus IV (Epiphanes) had forbidden Jews to continue to practice their religion and had tried to force them to worship Zeus, the supreme Greek god. Antiochus had an altar set up in the temple of Jerusalem and ordered that a pig be sacrificed on it. This abomination of desolation sparked the Maccabean revolt against Antiochus and culminated in Jewish independence until 63 BC. Remarkably, the temple was profaned on the 25th of Chislev (December) in 167 BC and restored to Yahweh on the same date in 164 BC. An eight-day feast was held to commemorate that event, and that tradition has continued until this day, known as Hanukkah or the Feast of Lights. Hallmarks of the festival are the lighting of lamps and a sense of joy.

At that time Jesus was teaching in Solomon's colonnade (v. 23), which was an open, roofed 45-foot walkway with double columns that were 38 feet tall. It was not in the temple area itself but was situated along the east side of the Court of the Gentiles.

---

4. The phrase "to lay down one's life" (vv. 11, 15, 18) is rare in Greek and may reflect the Hebrew idiom "to hand over one's life" (cf. Judg. 12:3; 1 Sam. 19:5; 28:21; Job 13:14; Ps. 119:109); for more detail see Köstenberger, *John*, 305n38.

5. *Mē* with the question in v. 21 expects a negative answer. Thus, "Can a demon open the eyes of the blind?" Implied answer: "No."

B. Jesus the Messiah and Son of God (vv. 24–39)

Two concerns dominated Jesus' discourse at the Feast of Dedication: Jesus is the Messiah (vv. 24–31) and the Son of God (vv. 32–39). The two paragraphs addressing these respective themes are balanced:

Messiah (vv. 24–31)	Son of God (vv. 32–39)[6]
1. Theme: Jesus the Messiah (v. 24)	1. Theme: Jesus the Son of God (vv. 32–33)
2. Jesus' discourse (vv. 25–29)	2. Jesus' discourse (vv. 34–38a)
3. Jesus' unity with God the Father (v. 30)	3. Jesus' unity with God the Father (v. 38b)
4. The Jews' reaction (v. 31)	4. The Jews' reaction (v. 39)

1. Jesus the Messiah (vv. 24–31)

The Jews (the Pharisees) could stand it no longer: "Was Jesus the Messiah or not?" they asked (cf. v. 24). Jesus replied that he had already answered his opponents' question, but they did not believe him (v. 25). Without exactly claiming to be the Messiah (probably to avoid the political, nationalistic associations of that title), Jesus pointed to his miraculous works as indicating who he was (v. 25). Furthermore, the reason the Pharisees did not believe him was because they were not his sheep (v. 26). On the contrary, Jesus' sheep hear his voice and believe in him, and he and the Father eternally keep them (vv. 27–28).[7] The Jews got Jesus' message that he the Messiah was equal to God, thus explaining their attempt to stone Jesus (v. 31; cf. 5:17–18; 8:58–59).

2. Jesus the Son of God (vv. 32–39)

Jesus responded to his opponents with irony by asking them which miracle they were stoning him for (v. 32). The Pharisees countered with the accusation that Jesus was a blasphemer (v. 33). Though the Pharisees had earlier implied that Jesus was such (8:59; cf. Mark 14:64/Matt. 26:65), this was now an official charge.[8]

Verses 34–36 record Jesus' quotation and interpretation of Psalm 82:6 in response to the Jews' accusation. That text reads, "I said, 'You are "gods"; you are all sons of the Most High.'" That passage speaks of Israel's leaders in terms of being gods. Jesus interpreted the

---

6. I adapt here Brown's outline from *Gospel according to John I–XII*, 404–5.

7. The words *ou mē* plus the aorist subjunctive (*apolōntai*) express emphatic negation. Jesus will "never ever" lose one of his followers. For many interpreters, this is an expression of the eternal security of the believer.

8. This scene is reminiscent of Jesus' trial scene in the Synoptics. There Jesus is accused of blasphemy (Matt. 26:65//Mark 14:64), which follows on the heels of the combined two questions asked of him by the authorities: Is he the Messiah and is he the Son of God (Matt. 26:63//Mark 14:61)? Luke, like John, separates the two questions: Is Jesus the Messiah (Luke 22:67; cf. John 10:22–31), and is Jesus the Son of God (Luke 22:70; cf. John 10:32–39)? According to Brown, the episode in John 10 is confirmed historically by the Synoptic parallels, with which I agree. See *Gospel according to John I–XII*, 408–9.

Old Testament passage using the rabbinic technique of *qal wahomer*—the lesser to the greater argument.

Lesser Statement:	Greater Statement:
God called humans (Israel's judges) gods.	How much more so should Jesus be called God since he was sent from God and therefore is not a mere human!

Jesus concluded his discourse at the Feast of Dedication by once again grounding his ministry and claims in his unity with God (vv. 37–38). The Jews responded in unbelief yet again by trying to arrest Jesus, but Jesus escaped their grasp (v. 39).

C. Conclusion to Jesus' Public Ministry (vv. 40–42)

Jesus then left Jerusalem and traveled back to Bethany beyond the Jordan River, which was outside of the jurisdiction of the Jerusalem authorities (vv. 40–42; cf. 1:28). It was there that John the Baptist had ministered and where Jesus' ministry had its roots. In stark contrast to the Pharisees, Jews on the east side of the Jordan flocked to Jesus en masse and believed in him ("believe" plus the accusative case indicates that their faith was genuine). Thus Jesus' ministry received the public's stamp of approval (10:40–42). Thereafter, he would conduct his divine affairs in private.

---

9. See Andreas J. Köstenberger's discussion in "John," in *Commentary on the New Testament Use of the Old Testament*, ed. G. K. Beale and D. A. Carson (Grand Rapids: Baker, 2007), 415–512; cited from p. 465.

REVIEW QUESTIONS

1. What is the historical background of the *"lēstis"* alluded to in John 10:8, 10?

2. What is the historical background of the Feast of Dedication?

3. What two truths about Jesus are developed in John 10:24–39?

4. What is the *qal wahomer* argument at work in John 10:34–36?

| abomination of desolation | *lēstis* | *Qal wahomer* |
| Feast of Dedication | *Maccabees* | Shepherd/Messiah |

CHAPTER 13

The Raising of Lazarus

JOHN 11

Objectives

After reading this chapter, you should be able to:

- Discuss John's usage of irony therein.
- Explain the relationship of future and realized eschatology in Jesus' dialogue with Martha and Mary.
- Compare Lazarus's resurrection with Jesus' future resurrection.

INTRODUCTION

John 11 records the spectacular feat of Jesus' raising of Lazarus from the dead. As such, it constitutes the seventh sign miracle of Jesus selected for discussion by the fourth evangelist.[1] John 11 also provides the fifth "I am" — "I am the resurrection and the life" (v. 25).

John 11 is an excellent example of Johannine irony: Jesus' raising of Lazarus to life (vv. 1–44) becomes the point of no return for the Jews to plan Jesus' death (vv. 45–57). Yet such irony is a part of the message of the seventh sign. Lazarus's death and resurrection form a picture of the upcoming death and resurrection of Jesus.

I. THE RAISING OF LAZARUS (11:1–44)

Four main characters are highlighted in the drama of John 11:1–44: Lazarus, his sisters Martha and Mary, and Jesus.

A. Lazarus's Death (vv. 1–16)

Verses 1–16 record Lazarus's sickness and death and how all that would display the glory of God. Lazarus lived in Bethany (not to be confused with Bethany beyond the Jordan; 1:28; 10:40–42), a village situated east of the Mount of Olives, about two miles from Jerusalem on the Jericho road. Jesus stayed in Bethany as well as Bethphage when he traveled to Jerusalem (Matt. 21:17; 26:6; see also Neh. 11:32). Mary and Martha, Lazarus's sisters, lived in Bethany, possibly with him. Lazarus fell sick, and his sisters sent word to Jesus for his help (v. 3).[2]

A paradox emerges from verses 5–6, which is already solved in verse 4. On the one hand, Jesus loved the three siblings (v. 5), but on the other hand, he did not immediately respond to the sisters' request to

Four main characters are highlighted in the drama of John 11:1–44: Lazarus, his sisters, Martha and Mary, and Jesus.

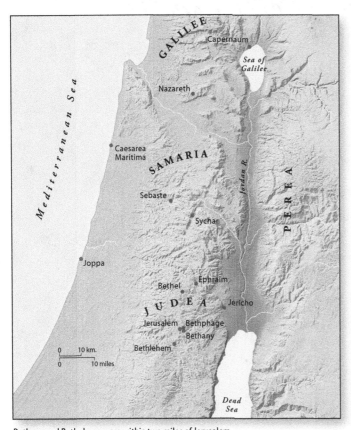

Bethany and Bethphage were within two miles of Jerusalem.

---

1. M. W. G. Stibbe proposes the following connections between the sign miracles in John: 2:1–11 with 4:46–54 (the two Cana miracles); 5:1–15 and chap. 9 (by way of contrast between the paralytic and the blind man); 6:1–15 with 6:16–21 (both are nature miracles), leaving chap. 11 to stand alone as the supreme sign miracle ("A Tomb with a View: John 11:1–44 in Narrative-Critical Perspective," *NTS* 40 1994. : 38–54; 41.)

2. The theory that "The one you love" points to Lazarus as "the disciple Jesus loved," and thus the author of John, is based on 11:3. Most scholars, however, have not been convinced by this view.

Modern Bethany.

come aid Lazarus (v. 6). But verse 4 anticipates the resolution to the paradox: Jesus allowed Lazarus to die in order that he might be raised from the dead, resulting in glory to God and his Son (v. 4; cf. 9:3).

After two days, Jesus announced his intention to go back to Jerusalem (v. 7; implied) to help Lazarus. Jesus' disciples questioned their rabbi's decision, since the Jerusalem authorities had tried to kill him earlier (v. 8). Jesus offered a little story in verses 9–10 that assured his disciples that he would be protected by God until his time to die came.

Jesus then announced that Lazarus had fallen asleep (v. 11), a euphemism in ancient Judaism for death (cf. Job 14:11–12; Dan. 12:2; Matt. 9:24//Mark 4:38//Luke 8:23; Matt. 27:52; *4 Ezra* 7:31–32). With typical Johannine irony, the disciples misunderstood Jesus' remark, thinking he meant Lazarus was sleeping because he had recovered from his illness (vv. 12–13). Jesus then spoke plainly of Lazarus' death (v. 14). Furthermore, Jesus upbraided the disciples for their misunderstanding, declaring that it was good that he was not with Lazarus before he died so that his raising of Lazarus would instill some much needed faith in the disciples (vv. 15–16).

B. The Sisters' Grief (vv. 17–32)

By the time Jesus arrived at Bethany, four days had passed since Lazarus's death. Later Jewish sources than John attest to the rabbinic belief that death was irrevocable three days after a person's demise (*Lev. Rab.* 18.1 on Lev. 15:1; *Eccles. Rab.* 12.6; *Yebam.* 16.3; *Sem.* 8, rule 1). Apparently the rabbis thought the soul of the deceased hovered over the body for three days and then departed. Jews from Jerusalem, a short two miles[3] to the west of Bethany, came to pay their respects to Martha and Mary (vv. 18–19). Comforting the bereaved was considered a religious duty, which included loud mourning and dramatic displays of grief.

---

3. Verse 18 literally reads "fifteen stadia." A stadion is about 200 yards; 15 stadia is thus about two miles.

The traditional site of Lazarus' tomb in Bethany.

When Jesus arrived at Bethany, he had conversations with Martha (vv. 20–27) and Mary (vv. 28–32) that revolved around his fifth "I am" saying—"I am the resurrection and the life" (v. 25).

1. Martha and Jesus (vv. 20–27)

True to her type A personality,[4] Martha first engaged Jesus in conversation (v. 20). Martha expressed her sadness that Jesus had not come earlier before Lazarus died (v. 21). But her faith was confident that even now Jesus could remedy the situation (v. 22), though in light of verses 23–24, she apparently did not have in mind a present resurrection. When Jesus assured Martha that Lazarus would be resurrected from the dead (v. 23), Martha confessed what ancient Jews believed—that the dead would be raised at the end of time (v. 24; cf. 5:21, 25–29; Dan. 12:1–2; Acts 23:8; Josephus, *Ant.* 18.1.3/14; *J.W.* 2.8.14/163; *b. Sanh.* 90b; *m. Sanh.* 10.1; *m. Ber.* 9.5; et al.). Jesus altered Martha's response—the resurrection of the last day was *now* taking place through faith in Christ (John 11:25a), which would shortly be illustrated by Lazarus's resurrection. Here we have the combination of final/futuristic eschatology (the resurrection of the last day, v. 24) and realized eschatology (resurrection in the present through Christ, v. 25a). Though believers in Jesus may die physically, they have spiritual life beginning now (realized eschatology) and the promise of the resurrection of the body later (final eschatology; v. 25b). Stated another way, believers alive now physically will never die spiritually (v. 26a).

Jesus asked Martha if she believed him (v. 26b), and her response reminds one of Peter's confession: "Yes ... you are the Christ, the Son of God, who was to come into the world" (v. 27; cf. esp. Matt. 16:16). The reader has already been introduced by John to these three messianic titles, which anticipate the key verses of the fourth gospel—20:30–31.

2. Mary and Jesus (vv. 28–32)

After Martha's confession of faith in Jesus, she reentered her home and told Mary of Jesus' arrival (vv. 28–31). Mary's meeting with Jesus indicates she had a strong faith in him, as did her sister, Martha (v. 32). Yet Mary's faith, like Martha's, was also incomplete, for she did not perceive that Jesus possessed present resurrection power.

C. Jesus' Seventh Sign (vv. 33–44)

Verses 33–44 describe Jesus' raising of Lazarus from the dead, the seventh sign miracle recorded by John. The verses begin with Jesus' own display of emotions. The scene is

---

4. Luke 10:38–42 contrasts Martha the energetic one with Mary the meditative one.

touching. Mary and the mourners were weeping over the loss of Lazarus. Strong emotions welled up in Jesus. He was deeply moved and troubled with feelings of anger he felt toward Satan and death (vv. 33–37). Upon arriving at Lazarus's tomb, Jesus shed tears for Lazarus (v. 38). The tomb was a cave with a stone laid across the entrance. Though the shaft of the cave could have been vertical or horizontal, from the way Lazarus came out, as well as archaeological evidence and Mishnaic regulations, it appears that the cave was horizontal.[5] The tomb was outside the village so as not to render the villagers ritually impure. Jesus' own burial would later occur in a similar tomb (John 19:41).

Another verbal interchange occurred between Jesus and Martha at the tomb. Jesus' command to take away the stone prompted Martha to express her concern about the stench of Lazarus's decaying body. Jesus gently chided Martha by reminding her of what he had told her earlier—that if she believed, she would see the glory of God (vv. 39–40).

> When the stone was removed, Jesus offered a prayer to God, thanking him in advance that he was going to raise Lazarus from the dead.

When the stone was removed, Jesus offered a prayer to God, thanking him in advance that he was going to raise Lazarus from the dead. This public prayer was not showmanship on Jesus' part, but rather for the purpose of the crowd coming to belief in Jesus, the one sent from God (vv. 41–42).

Then Jesus cried for Lazarus to come out of the tomb, which he did, wrapped with strips of linen and with a cloth around his face. The grave clothes were removed, and Lazarus was now alive and free (vv. 43–44). Donald Carson provides important background for this scene:

> The corpse was customarily laid on a sheet of linen, wide enough to envelop the body completely and more than twice the length of the corpse. The body was so placed on the sheet that the feet were at one end, and then the sheet was drawn over the head and back down to the feet. The feet were bound at the ankles, and the arms were tied to the body with linen strips.... Jesus' body was apparently prepared for burial in the same way (cf. 19:40; 20:5, 7).[6]

> Clearly ... the raising of Lazarus was a foreshadowing of Jesus' upcoming death and resurrection.

From this description we can clearly see that the raising of Lazarus was a foreshadowing of Jesus' upcoming death and resurrection. This was the "sign" value of the miracle.[7]

II. THE PLAN TO KILL JESUS (11:45–56)

As usual, the reaction to Jesus was mixed; some believed in him (v. 45) while others divulged to the Pharisees what Jesus had just done (v. 46). Not surprisingly, the Jerusalem

---

5. See M. Avi-Yonah, *The World of the Bible: The New Testament* (Yonkers, N.Y.: Educational Heritage, 1964), 147; and R. M. Mackowski, *Jerusalem, City of Jesus* (Grand Rapids: Eerdmans, 1980), 157–59.

6. D. A. Carson, *The Gospel according to John*, Pillar New Testament Commentary (Grand Rapids: Eerdmans, 1991), 418–19.

7. The raising of Lazarus ranks with the other raisings of the dead in the Bible: the raising of the Shunammite's son by Elisha (2 Kings 4:8–37) and the raisings of Jairus's daughter (Matt. 9:18–19; cf. Mark 5:22–42; Luke 8:41–56) and the widow's son at Nain (Luke 7:11–15) by Jesus.

authorities (Pharisees and chief priests, which were Sadducees) wanted to do away with Jesus (vv. 47–53). Perhaps the best way to summarize the last-mentioned group would be to point out the ironies of the situation.

First, the Jerusalem authorities called a "gathering" (*synēgagon*) of the Sanhedrin, the ruling body of ancient Israel, to determine how to proceed regarding Jesus (v. 47). Yet Jesus' death and resurrection were destined to gather (*synagagō*) the true people of God into one people (believing Jews and believing Gentiles, v. 52).

Second, the Jerusalem authorities were doing nothing to stop Jesus, who was performing sign miracles on behalf of God (v. 47). The contrast between the futile attempts of the authorities and Jesus' mighty accomplishments is striking.

Third, the Sanhedrin feared that the Romans would punish Israel if they followed a "false Messiah" like Jesus, but, in fact, in the purposes of God, the Jerusalem temple was destroyed by the Romans precisely because the nation did not believe in Jesus (v. 48).

Fourth, Caiaphas, the high priest that year (AD 30 or 33; recall my discussion of John 2 [see chap. 4, n. 2]), unwittingly prophesied that Jesus' death would be vicarious (vv. 49–52).

Fifth, Jesus' raising of Lazarus to life was the catalyst for the authorities seeking his death (v. 53).

In light of the imminent danger the Pharisees and chief priests posed to Jesus, he could no longer move about publicly (vv. 54, 57). This piqued the curiosity of the Jews on the eve of Passover:[8] would Jesus come to Jerusalem at that time or not (vv. 55–56)?

---

8. This is the third Passover mentioned in the fourth gospel; the first Passover is referred to in John 2:13, the second in 6:4. Estimates of the number of tourists and inhabitants in Jerusalem during Passover vary from 100,000 to 2.5 million (the latter is Josephus's calculation and is undoubtedly exaggerated; *J.W.* 6.9.3/422–25).

REVIEW QUESTIONS

1. Discuss John's usage of irony in chapter 11.

2. According to John 11:4–6, why did Jesus allow Lazarus to die?

3. How are final/futuristic and realized eschatology operative in John 11:24–26?

4. What was the "sign" value of the resurrection of Lazarus?

KEY TERMS

Bethany and Bethphage

Caiaphas

final eschatology

"I am the resurrection and the life"

irony

Lazarus

Martha

Mary

realized eschatology

seventh sign miracle

CHAPTER 14

The Anointing of Jesus,

His Triumphant Entry into Jerusalem,

and His Discourse on the Last Hour

JOHN 12

Objectives

After reading this chapter, you should be able to:

- Relate what the theological message is of Mary's anointing of Jesus' feet.

- Identify the five messianic titles applied to Jesus by the crowd on Palm Sunday.

- Identify the eight aspects of realized eschatology at work in Jesus' discourse on the Last Hour.

INTRODUCTION

John 12 concludes the Book of Signs[1] and the public ministry of Jesus. In doing so, it prepares the reader for Jesus' soon-to-follow death and resurrection. Three episodes comprise the chapter: verses 1–11: the anointing of Jesus; verses 12–19: Jesus' entry into Jerusalem; verses 20–50: Jesus' discourse on his coming hour, which is a summary statement of Jesus' public ministry.

I. THE ANOINTING OF JESUS (12:1–11)

"Six days before the Passover" no doubt refers to Saturday evening, if indeed Jesus was crucified on Friday (v. 1). The mention of Lazarus, Martha, and Mary (vv. 2–3) ties John

Perfume jars and other artifacts found in the excavations at Masada.

12 with the previous chapter. Who made the meal and where it was held are ambiguous. During the meal, Mary, using her hair, anointed Jesus' feet with a pound of nard, a costly perfume made in northern India (v. 3).

Two actions of Mary especially call for comment. First, the amount of expensive perfume she used to anoint Jesus was extravagant. A normal flask held one ounce of perfume, but this alabaster container held almost a pound.[2] We learn later that the cost of the perfume was three hundred denarii, about one year's salary (v. 5). Some have suggested from this that such an expensive gesture on Mary's part symbolized a royal anointing, which would make sense in light of Jesus' triumphant entry, the next narrative (12:12–19).

Second, Jesus' feet, not his head, were anointed by Mary (v. 3). The anointing of the latter was done to a king, while the former was usually performed on the deceased as a part of the burial procedure. But these two points—that Jesus was anointed as royalty (hence the expensive perfume and the triumphant entry) and that the anointing of his feet was symbolic of his coming death—are not contradictions. Rather, they represent Johannine irony: Jesus' royal enthronement was to occur on the cross!

Judas's complaint that Mary instead should have sold the perfume and given it to the poor (vv. 5–8) was but a feigned attempt by him to show concern for others. In reality, Judas the treasurer was a thief, pilfering the money box's funds for himself (v. 6). Worse yet, Judas was the one who would betray Jesus (v. 4) in the face of Mary's faithfulness to her Lord, another instance of Johannine irony.

The party for Jesus attracted numerous Jews who also wanted to see Lazarus. The miracle of the raising of Lazarus brought many in the crowd to faith in Jesus. That, in turn,

---

1. The Book of Signs is John 1–12 and contains the seven sign miracles of Jesus in contrast to the Book of Glory (John 13–21), which exalts Jesus' death and his moment of glory.
2. Craig S. Keener, *The Gospel of John: A Commentary*, vol. 2 (Peabody, Mass.: Hendrickson, 2003), 294.

prompted the Jerusalem authorities to plan to kill Lazarus—that is, to do away with the evidence that Jesus was the Messiah who raised the dead (vv. 9–11).

II. JESUS' ENTRY INTO JERUSALEM (12:12–19)

Jesus' triumphant entry into Jerusalem, or "Palm Sunday," is recorded in all four gospels (John 12:12–19; cf. Matt. 21:1–11; Mark 11:1–11; Luke 19:28–44). John's perspective on Jesus' triumphant entry will emerge as we summarize the episode.

A road on the Mount of Olives. Jerusalem is visible in the distance.

Jesus entered into Jerusalem "the next day," that is, Sunday (cf. v. 12 with v. 1), which, along with the mention of palm branches (v. 13), is the origin of the title "Palm Sunday." Furthermore, Jesus' raising of Lazarus was the catalyst for the gathering of the crowds that day (vv. 17–18).

Five messianic/nationalistic responses to Jesus by the crowd can be identified in John's episode. First, the crowd greeted Jesus by waving palm branches (v. 13), a national Jewish symbol (see Josephus, *Ant.* 3.10.4/245; 13.13.5/372). Second, the description of the crowd "going to meet him" (*eis hypantēsin*, cf. v. 13) was the normal Greek expression used to describe the joyful escort of Hellenistic sovereigns into a city.

Third, the shout of "Hosanna!" by the crowd meant "save now" (v. 13; see 2 Sam. 14:4; 2 Kings 6:26; and esp. Pss. 113–18 [the Hallel]), and definitely conveyed Jewish aspirations for deliverance from the Romans.

Fourth, so also did the phrase "Blessed is he who comes in the name of the Lord" (v. 13), a quotation of Psalm 118:26.[3] Later rabbinic interpretation viewed this psalm messianically (*Midr. Ps.* 118:22 on Ps. 118:24); indeed, the fourth gospel associates Jesus the Coming One with the Messiah (John 4:25; 7:27, 31, 41, 42; 11:27; cf. 6:14).[4]

Fifth, the next acclamation of the crowd—"Blessed is the King of Israel!" (v. 13)—obviously was nationalistic. The crowd on Palm Sunday, like the crowd in John 6:15, wanted to make Jesus their king and the restorer of Israel's former glory.

> Judas's complaint that Mary instead should have sold the perfume and given it to the poor (vv. 5–8) was but a feigned attempt by him to show concern for others.

---

3. The Old Testament citations in John 12:13, 15 are the verses in John that do not have an introduction formula.

4. See Andreas J. Köstenberger, *John*, Baker Exegetical Commentary on the New Testament (Grand Rapids: Baker, 2004), 370.

Woman riding on a donkey.

In John's narrative, it is only after these acclamations that Jesus found a donkey and rode upon it into Jerusalem (v. 14). What follows, then, was Jesus' *rejection* of the crowd's nationalistic craze to make him king in order to exalt Israel. More specifically, Jesus offered himself as the suffering Messiah who came to spiritually deliver *both* Jews and Gentiles. Four pieces of data indicate that this is what Jesus was doing. First, he rode on a donkey, not the warhorse of a conquering king. That such a gesture signified humility and even death will be made clear in verses 20–36. Second, in verse 15, right before John quotes Zechariah 9:9 ("See, your king is coming, seated on a donkey's colt") comes a quotation from Zephaniah 3:16 ("Do not be afraid, O daughter of Zion"). The last-mentioned passage envisions the salvation of both Jews and Gentiles.[5] Third, ironically in John 12:19 the Pharisees confirm Jesus' mission to the Gentiles: "Look how the whole world has gone after him." Fourth, verses 20–36 explicitly connect Jesus' triumphant entry with his outreach to the Gentiles. And it was this aspect of Jesus' Palm Sunday appearance that the disciples also failed to understand.

> What follows, then, was Jesus' *rejection* of the crowd's nationalistic craze to make him king in order to exalt Israel.

III. JESUS' DISCOURSE ON THE LAST HOUR (12:20–50)

John 12:20–50 records Jesus' discourse on the last hour. More specifically, some eight end-time events would be set in motion by Jesus' death and resurrection—his last hour. I now summarize those eight aspects of realized eschatology.

A. The Conversion of the Gentiles (vv. 20–23a, 32)

The Old Testament prophets prophesied that in the end times Gentiles will stream into Jerusalem to worship God (Isa. 42:4; 49:6; Zech. 8; Tobit 13:11). It is interesting in that regard to observe that the attempt of Gentiles to see Jesus prompts him to announce that his hour—his death and resurrection—has arrived (v. 23). In other words, the nations of the world were beginning to stream into Jerusalem to worship God through Christ. The "Greeks" referred to here may have come from the Decapolis area or even beyond Israel. They approached Philip, who enlisted the help of Andrew, perhaps because those two men had Greek names.

---

5. Brown's discussion of this point is insightful, Raymond E. Brown, *The Gospel according to John I–XII*, Anchor Bible 29A (Garden City, N.Y.: Doubleday, 1966), 462–63.

B. Resurrection (vv. 23b–26)

We have already observed from John 5:19–30 that the end-time resurrection began in Jesus' life and ministry. John 12:23b–26 specifies that Jesus' resurrection/glorification (v. 23b) will come because of his obedient suffering on the cross (v. 24). And those who want a share in his resurrection must also suffer with him (vv. 21–26; cf. Matt. 16:24–28// Mark 8:34–38//Luke 9:23–27).

C. The Messianic Woes (vv. 28–30)

Much of Second Temple Judaism (519 BC to AD 70) expected that Israel would undergo unprecedented affliction immediately before the Messiah came (Dan. 12:1; *4 Ezra* 7:37; Jub. 23:11, *2 Bar.* 55:6; *1 Enoch* 80:4–5; 1QM; et al.). Jesus' reference in John 12:27 to his soul being troubled should be linked with John 15:18–16:4, a section devoted to describing the messianic woes that Jesus and his disciples undergo.

D. Holy War (v. 31)

Much of Second Temple Judaism expected that God's Messiah would appear at the end of the age to fight and defeat Satan (Ezek. 38–39; Dan. 7:8, 25; 11:36, 40–41; 1 John 4:3; Rev. 11:7, 13; 13:2, 5, 7; 1QM). That concept is the backdrop for verse 31: Jesus' death/ resurrection will be the scene of the end-time holy war and the defeat of Satan, the prince and ruler of this world.

E. The Appearance of the Messiah/Son of Man (vv. 33–34)

That Jews in Jesus' day longed for the Davidic Messiah to appear at the end of the age and exalt Israel is clear from verse 33. "Son of Man" was also a messianic figure in some Jewish texts (Dan. 7:13–14; *1 Enoch* 46:1; 47:3; *4 Ezra* 7:28–29; 13:32; 4Q246). It seems that the crowd was surprised to hear Jesus speak of the suffering and death of the Messiah/ Son of Man (v. 34), probably because Judaism before New Testament times had not yet connected the Messiah with Isaiah's Suffering Servant (see Isa. 42:1–7; 49:1–6; 50:4–9; 52:13–53:12).

F. Dualism (vv. 35–36)

Jewish apocalypticism was famous for its temporal and ethical dualistic (either/or) categories. The former was expressed in terms of the opposition of the two ages: this age versus the age to come.[6] The latter was expressed in terms of the contrast between the righteous and the wicked. Both of these aspects occur in the Dead Sea Scrolls, especially the Community Rule (1QS) 3:1–4:26. There the language of the sons of light versus the sons of darkness is strikingly similar to John 12:35–36 (cf. 1 John 1:5–7; 2:8–11; Rev. 21:23–25; 22:5). The sons of light in John's gospel are those who believe in Jesus, while those who do not follow him remain in darkness. Verse 36 conveys an ominous note: Jesus hid from the crowds to symbolize the reality that the light was passing from view; the opportunity to accept Christ was fading away.

---

6. For a discussion of this concept, see C. Marvin Pate, *The End of the Age Has Come: The Theology of Paul* (Grand Rapids: Zondervan, 1995).

G. Apostasy (vv. 37–43)

Jewish apocalyptic literature also expected that in the end time many of the people of God would abandon the faith rather than face the persecution of the messianic woes (*Jub.* 23:14–23; *4 Ezra* 5:173; *1 Enoch* 90:3–10; cf. Matt. 24:10–13; Mark 13:20–23; Luke 21:34–36; 1 Tim. 4:1–5; 2 Tim. 3:1–5; Rev. 13:15–18; et al.). John 12:37–43 seems to apply that sign of the time to Jesus' audience. Such apostasy on their part was based on their rejection of Jesus the Suffering Servant.

H. Judgment Day (vv. 44–50)

As is frequently noted by commentators, end-time judgment in the fourth gospel has become a present reality. One's response to Jesus now seals one's destiny: to believe in him is to receive eternal life now; to reject him is to receive condemnation now (vv. 46–50).

As a whole, John 12:44–50 echoes John 1:11–12: Jesus' own rejected him, but those who do accept him become his children. Thus 12:44–50 is a fitting conclusion to Jesus' public ministry and the Book of Signs (see also v. 37).

REVIEW QUESTIONS

1. What was the theological message conveyed by Mary's anointing of Jesus' feet?

2. What were the five messianic/nationalistic responses to Jesus' triumphant entry?

3. What is the message of John 12 relative to Jesus' triumphant entry?

4. What are the eight aspects of realized eschatology at work in Jesus' discourse on the last hour (John 12:20–50)?

TERMS

anointing of Jesus	dualism	Palm Sunday
Antiochus Epiphanes	holy war	resurrection
apostasy	judgment day	Son of Man
book of signs	messianic woes	triumphant entry
conversion of the Gentiles	palm branches	

CHAPTER 15

The Last Supper

JOHN 13

Objectives

After reading this chapter, you should be able to:

- Discuss the relationship between the Passover meal and the Last Supper as recorded in John 13.

- Discuss why Jesus' Upper Room Discourse was a "farewell speech."

- Explain why Jesus washed the disciples' feet.

INTRODUCTION

John 13 begins the episode of the Last Supper, the meal Jesus ate with his disciples before his death. The description of the Last Supper extends from John 13 to 17, beginning with two short reports (the foot washing, 13:1–20; and the prediction of Judas's betrayal, 13:21–30). After those comes the last discourse, which goes all the way from 13:31 to 17:26. Before discussing each of the preceding chapters, we need first to touch upon four introductory matters regarding the Last Supper: its chronology, composition, genre, and eschatology.

> The description of the Last Supper extends from John 13 to 17.

First, there continues to be a lively debate among scholars about the relationship between John's chronology and that of the Synoptics concerning the nature of the Last Supper. Was it a Passover meal or not? According to the Synoptics, Jesus ate a Passover meal with the disciples on the night before he died (Thursday; Mark 14:12//Mark 26:17//Luke 22:7) and was crucified on Friday.

John, however, seems to give a different picture: the Last Supper occurred *before* Passover (John 13:1; cf. 18:28; 19:14, 36, 42). Thus Jesus would have eaten the Last Supper on Wednesday evening and then been crucified on Thursday, the day of Passover (though see 19:31).

The following chart pinpoints the differences between the preceding two chronologies:

Meal	Synoptics	John
Nature	Passover	Not Passover meal
Time	Thursday night	Wednesday night
Day	15th of Nisan/Passover	14th of Nisan

Many scholars argue that the Synoptics' chronology of the Last Supper reflects the actual situation and John adapted that to his message. That is, John equated Jesus with the Passover Lamb (19:14; cf. vv. 29, 36). Therefore the Last Supper for the fourth gospel could not have been a Passover meal, because the Passover Lamb (Jesus) had not yet been slain. All this is to say that John adapted the Synoptics' chronology in order to equate Jesus with the Passover lamb.[1]

Second, the composition of John 13–17 is disputed. Following Raymond Brown, many argue that John 13:31–14:31 and 16:4b–33 are duplicates. Note the major similarities between the two:

A model of the sacrificial altar in the Court of the Priests of the Jerusalem temple.

---

1. Such "poetic license" on the part of the fourth evangelist should not be construed as undermining the inspired, inerrant nature of John's text, for as the *Chicago Statement of Inerrancy* observes, the gospel writers were free to arrange their chronologies to make a topical/theological point.

13:31 – 14:31[2]	16:4b – 33
Jesus is going away (14:28).	Jesus is going away (16:5 – 7).
"Do not let your hearts be troubled" (14:1).	"You are filled with grief" (16:6).
First Paraclete passage (14:15 – 17).	First Paraclete passage (16:7 – 11).
"The Prince of the World is coming" (14:30).	"The Prince of this World now stands condemned" (16:11).
Second Paraclete passage (14:26).	Second Paraclete passage (16:13 – 15).
"Before long, the world will not see me anymore, but you will see me" (14:19).	"In a little while you will see me no more" (16:16).
Prayer in Jesus' name (14:13, 14).	Prayer in Jesus' name (16:23 – 24).
Loving Jesus is loving the Father (14:21, 23).	Loving Jesus is loving the Father (16:27).
Peace upon the disciples (14:27).	Peace upon the disciples (16:33).

Others, however, disagree, arguing against any theory of duplication between the two.[3] Because John elsewhere seems to provide duplicate accounts (13:19 – 25/26 – 30; 6:35 – 50/51 – 59), I would not be surprised if he (or a later student of John's) did something similar here.

Third, there is a consensus among interpreters of John that the Last Supper Discourse (13:31 – 17:26) fits nicely the genre of farewell speech. Patterned after Moses' farewell discourse in Deuteronomy (31 – 33) and other similar Old Testament farewells (Gen. 49; Josh. 23 – 24; 1 Sam. 12; 1 Kings 2:1 – 2; 1 Chron. 28 – 29), Second Temple Judaism produced an entire genre of such literature (e.g., 1 Macc. 2:49 – 70; *Assumption of Moses*; *Jub.* 22:10 – 30; *Testaments of the Twelve Patriarchs*; Josephus, *Ant.* 12.6.3/279 – 84).[4] These works include the following features, which others have applied to John 13 – 17:

---

2. I have adopted Raymond E. Brown's chart, which argues that the two are duplicates. See his *The Gospel according to John XIII–XXI,* Anchor Bible 29B (Garden City, N.Y.: Doubleday, 1970), 589-93.

3. That seems to be the trend these days. See Andreas J. Köstenberger's bibliography supporting the literary unity of the Farewell Discourse in his *John,* Baker Exegetical Commentary on the New Testament (Grand Rapids: Baker, 2004), 398n9.

4. See Brown, *Gospel according to John XIII–XXI,* 597 – 601; Köstenberger, *John,* 396; Francis J. Moloney, *The Gospel of John,* Sacra Pagina, ed. Daniel J. Harrington (Collegeville, Minn.: Liturgical Press, 1998), 377 – 78 (see his bibliography, pp. 389 – 91). For Greco-Roman farewell passages, see Bruce J. Malina and R. L. Rohrbaugh, *Social-Science Commentary on the Gospel of John* (Minneapolis: Fortress, 1998), 221 – 22.

1. A great man predicts his death and departure (John 13:33, 36; 14:5–6, 12, 28).
2. He also predicts future challenges for his followers (John 15:18–16:4a).
3. The great leader makes arrangement for his succession or continuation (John 14:16; cf. 14:26; 15:26–27; 16:7–11).
4. He gives exhortations to his followers for moral behavior (John 13:34; 14:15, 21; 15:10, 14).
5. The leader affirms the renewal of God's covenant (John 14:23).
6. He offers a closing prayer (John 17).
7. He adds a final commission (John 17:18–23).[5]

Fourth, commentators commonly observe that realized eschatology dominates the last discourse, especially the coming of the Holy Spirit. That is to say, the return of Christ recedes in importance compared to the presence of the Spirit. While this is true, it should not be overstated, because the return of Christ does receive mention in John 14:1–6. Moreover, the predicted persecution of the disciples (John 15:18–16:4a) also bespeaks the fact that the age to come is not yet fully realized.

---

5. See the discussions by Brown, *Gospel according to John XIII–XXI*, 597–601, and Köstenberger, *John*, 396–97. The latter points out differences between John 13–17 and the farewell speeches (Jesus' farewell is temporary; it contains no extended predictions of the future [but see 15:18–16:4a]). Köstenberger, rather, roots John 13–17 solely in Deuteronomy 31–33, Moses' farewell speech.

The upper room. A historical tradition locates the Last Supper in the Cenacle on Mount Zion. This present structure was reconstructed by Franciscans in 1335.

Old Testament Sacrifices			
Sacrifice	**OT References**	**Elements**	**Purpose**
Burnt Offering	Lev 1; 6:8-13; 8:18-21; 16:24	Bull, ram or male bird (dove or young pigeon for the poor); wholly consumed; no defect	Voluntary act of worship; atonement for unintentional sin in general; expression of devotion, commitment and complete surrender to God
Grain Offering	Lev 2; 6:14-23	Grain, fine flour, olive oil, incense, baked bread (cakes or wafers), salt; no yeast or honey; accompanied burnt offering and fellowship offering (along with drink offering)	Voluntary act of worship; recognition of God's goodness and provisions; devotion to God
Fellowship Offering	Lev 3; 7:11-34	Any animal without defect from herd or flock; variety of breads	Voluntary act of worship; thanksgiving and fellowship (it included a communal meal)
Sin Offering	Lev 4:1—5:13; 6:24-30; 8:14-17; 16:3-22	1. Young bull: for high priest and congregation 2. Male goat: for leader 3. Female goat or lamb: for common person 4. Dove or pigeon: for the poor 5. Tenth of an ephah of fine flour: for the very poor	Mandatory atonement for specific unintentional sin; confession of sin; forgiveness of sin; cleansing from defilement
Guilt Offering	Lev 5:14—6:7; 7:1-6	Ram	Mandatory atonement for unintentional sin requiring restitution; cleansing from defilement; make restitution; pay 20% fine

I. THE FOOT WASHING (13:1–20)

The apparent setting of John's episode of the Last Supper was probably Passover Eve (Wednesday; see 13:1; and recall my comments above). The hour of Jesus' death and resurrection was now upon him, a time that would reveal his steadfast love for his disciples (v. 1). The ensuing act of foot washing, then, would be a picture of Jesus' sacrificial love for his own. Judas Iscariot, inspired by Satan, had already apparently conspired with the Jewish leaders to hand Jesus over to them (*paradidōmi*, v. 2). The stage was now set for Jesus' last discourse.

As a dramatic, prophetic picture of his upcoming sacrifice, Jesus disrobed himself (*tithenai* is the same word Jesus used of laying down his life for his sheep in 10:11, 15, 17, 18), took a towel and basin of water, and washed his disciples' feet (vv. 3–5). Washing the feet of one's guests was an act of hospitality performed by the servant of the host (see Gen. 18:4;

19:2; 24:32; 43:24; Judg. 19:21; 1 Sam. 25:41; *Mek. Exod.* 21.2).[6] Peter misunderstood Jesus' action, believing that it was beneath Jesus' dignity. But he needed to understand that the intent of Jesus' washing of the disciples' feet was to symbolize his sacrificial death for them and his cleansing of their sin (vv. 7, 12). Jesus then challenged his disciples to serve others, just as he had served them (vv. 13–17). Jesus' cleansing, however, did not extend to Judas (vv. 10, 18–20), for the latter was about to betray Jesus.

II. THE PREDICTION OF JUDAS'S BETRAYAL (13:21–30)

After Jesus washed the disciples' feet, he became deeply troubled (*tarassō*; cf. 11:33; 12:27).[7] With prescience Jesus predicted that one of his disciples was about to betray him (v. 21).

The disciples were shocked at Jesus' announcement (v. 22). Peter signaled to the "Beloved Disciple" (probably John),[8] sitting next to Jesus to ask Jesus to clarify his statement, which the Beloved Disciple did (vv. 23–25). Jesus told John that the one to whom he gave the morsel (bitter herbs dipped in a bowl of fruit and wrapped in unleavened bread) was the betrayer (v. 26). At that, Jesus gave the sop to Judas and told him to leave quickly to do his evil deed. The episode concludes on an ominous note: Judas left and it was night (v. 30)—both literally and figuratively. Satan had entered Judas to propel him to betray Jesus to the authorities (v. 27).[9]

This is the only mention of Satan in the fourth gospel. The next time we hear of Judas, he will lead the temple guard to Jesus at Gethsemane (18:2–5).

III. INTRODUCTION TO THE LAST DISCOURSE (13:31–38)

Verses 31–38 introduce Jesus' last discourse, or at least the first part of it (chap. 14).[10] The outline of 13:31–38 is this: Jesus' glorification (vv. 31–32) and return to the Father (v. 33); the new commandment to be followed in the absence of Jesus (vv. 34–35); Peter's misunderstanding (vv. 36–38).

A. Jesus' Glorification (vv. 31–32)

Judas's departure set in motion the "hour" of Jesus' passion. It also cleansed the disciples of the presence of evil. Verses 31–32 then describe Jesus' glorification, which involved his suffering, death, and resurrection. In other words, Jesus' glorification was broader than just

---

6. The references come from Köstenberger, *John*, 404. Two different words are used for washing with water in v. 10: *luoō* ("bathe"), and *niptō* ("wash").

7. We are reminded here of Jesus' agony in the Garden of Gethsemane, which is recorded in the Synoptics but not in John.

8. This description occurs again in 19:26–27; 20:2–9; 21:20–27; 21:24–25 and is probably to be equated with "the other disciple" in 18:15–16 and 20:2–9. Most likely the two labels refer to John in a discreet way.

9. The word used here of Satan entering Judas is *eiserchomai*, which in the Synoptics refers to demonic possession (see, e.g., Mark 5:2; Luke 8:30; 11:26).

10. Brown and others argue that there are duplicate last discourses: 13:31–14:31 and chaps. 15–16, *Gospel according to John XIII–XXI*, 608–9. John 13:31–38, then, would be the introduction to the first discourse.

With prescience Jesus predicted that one of his disciples was about to betray him.

The episode concludes on an ominous note: Judas left and it was night (v. 30)—both literally and figuratively.

his resurrection; it included his humiliation. Moreover, Jesus' obedient submission to the whole process of glorification brought glory to God. And soon, God would glorify Jesus at his return to the Father in heaven (v. 32).[11]

B. Jesus' Return to the Father (v. 33)

Teknia ("my little children") occurs only here in John but several times in 1 John (2:1, 12, 28; 3:7, 18; 4:4; 5:21). Like the patriarch of the family who called the Passover guests his "children," so Jesus hosted the Last Supper with his disciples/children. He informed them that his departure was imminent and they would not be able to follow him.

Judas' departure set in motion the "hour" of Jesus' passion.

C. The New Commandment (vv. 34–35)

In the meantime, the presence of Jesus would be mediated to his disciples when they loved one another as he loved them. This would be the mark that distinguished the disciples as followers of Jesus. Jesus called this commandment to love the "new commandment," because it was to become the basic requirement of the new covenant.

D. Peter's Misunderstanding (vv. 36–38)

Peter did not understand what Jesus meant when Jesus said he was leaving the disciples. Peter boasted that he would lay down his life for Jesus to prevent him from leaving (vv. 36–37). Jesus pointed out to the contrary that Peter would deny Jesus three times before the rooster crowed.[12] Jesus' words would prove to be true (18:17–18, 25–27).

---

11. There has been much discussion as to why John uses two tenses in vv. 31–32—the past and the future. The situation seems to be, however, that the aorist is complexive while the future alludes to Jesus' soon to be received glory in the presence of the Father, as I mentioned above.

12. The Romans used the label "cock crow" for the watch between midnight and 3:00 a.m. (cf. Mark 13:35); so D. A. Carson, *The Gospel according to John,* Pillar New Testament Commentary (Grand Rapids: Eerdmans, 1991), 487.

REVIEW QUESTIONS

1. Does John equate the Last Supper with the Passover meal?

2. Are John 13:31 – 14:31 and 16:4b – 33 duplicate accounts of the Last Supper Discourse?

3. What are some of the features of John's farewell speech/Last Supper Discourse?

4. What did Jesus' washing of the disciples' feet symbolize?

KEY TERMS

foot washing

new commandment

Last Supper Discourse

Passover

CHAPTER 16

Predictions about Jesus' Departure

and the Spirit's Arrival

JOHN 14

Objectives

After reading this chapter, you should be able to:

- Identify the two themes that dominate John 14.
- Differentiate the "comings" of the Paraclete, Jesus, and the Father.

INTRODUCTION

Two themes dominate John 14: Jesus' predictions about his soon departure to the Father and the Holy Spirit's arrival from the Father. We will move through the chapter by following three divisions: verses 1–14: Jesus' departure; verses 15–24: the Spirit's arrival; verses 25–31: concluding comments on the two themes.

Two themes dominate John 14: Jesus' predictions about his soon departure to the Father and the Holy Spirit's arrival from the Father.

I. JESUS' PREDICTIONS OF HIS SOON DEPARTURE (14:1–14)

John 13:31–38 introduced the prediction that Jesus was soon to be removed from his disciples. John 14:1–14 develops that theme. It begins with Jesus' comforting words to his followers not to let their hearts be troubled (v. 1a). The "heart" was considered to be the seat of one's decisions and emotions. The word "trouble" was used earlier of Jesus' deep feelings for Lazarus (11:33) as well as his sense of betrayal by Judas (13:21). It is now used of the disciples, who are facing an unknown future without Jesus (cf. 14:27; 16:16, 22).

Jesus' response to the disciples' fear was to encourage them to believe in God, much as ancient Israel was challenged to believe in God before entering the Promised Land (Deut. 20:1, 3; Josh. 1:9).

There is a debate among the commentators as to whether the first verb — *pisteuete* (v. 1b) — is an imperative or an indicative. It seems that the first occurrence of *pisteuete* is indicative, and the second, imperative: "You believe in God ... believe[!] in me."

Jesus provided the basis for the disciples' comfort in verses 1–4: he was going to his Father's house of many dwellings to prepare a place for his followers and then return to take them there.[1] The word *monē* occurs in the New Testament only here in verse 2 and in verse 23. The latter is the spiritual indwelling of the Father and the Son in the believer, but verse 2 seems to refer to a physical dwelling, a place (*topos*, v. 3). Several metaphors may form the background of the heavenly dwellings of verse 2: the patriarchal extended family; Ezekiel's new temple of the end times; Jewish apocalypticism's equation of heaven with the believer's future resting place; and Greco-Roman villas.[2]

Deror avi/Wikimedia Commons

Remains of a Herodian-era home discovered in Jerusalem. Similar to the Roman villa.

---

1. Verse 2 is probably a second-class conditional statement: "If it were not so [but it is], I would have told you."
2. Andreas J. Köstenberger provides the references and backgrounds in *John*, Baker Exegetical Commentary on the New Testament (Grand Rapids: Baker, 2004), 426–27.

Ezekiel's Temple

- **A.** Wall (40:5,16-20)
- **B.** East gate (40:6-14,16)
- **C.** Portico (40:8)
- **D.** Outer court (40:17)
- **E.** Pavement (40:17)
- **F.** East inner court (40:19)
- **G.** North gate (40:20-22)
- **H.** North inner court (40:23)
- **I.** South gate (40:24-26)
- **J.** South inner court (40:27)
- **K.** Gateway (40:28-31)
- **L.** Gateway (40:32-34)
- **M.** Gateway (40:35-38)

- **N.** Priests' rooms (40:44-45)
- **O.** Court (40:47)
- **P.** Temple portico (40:48-49)
- **Q.** Outer sanctuary (41:1-2)
- **R.** Most Holy Place (41:3-4)
- **S.** Temple walls (41:5-7,9,11)
- **T.** Base (41:8)
- **U.** Open area (41:10)
- **V.** West building (41:12)
- **W.** Priests' rooms (42:1-10)
- **X.** Altar (43:13-17)
- **AA.** Rooms for preparing sacrifices (40:39-43)
- **BB.** Ovens (46:19-20)
- **CC.** Kitchens (46:21-24)

Ezekiel uses a long or "royal" cubit, c. 21 inches or 52 cm ("cubit and a handbreadth," Eze 40:5) as opposed to the standard Hebrew cubit of c. 18 inches or 45 cm.

Scripture describes a floor plan, but provides few height dimensions. This artwork shows an upward projection of the temple over the floor plan. This temple existed only in a vision of Ezekiel (Eze 40:2), and was never actually built as were the temples of Solomon, Zerubbabel and Herod.

Floor plan of sanctuary

Side rooms

CUBITS 0 50 100 150 200 250 300

H. NORTH

NORTH

Height of this wall has been exaggerated slightly to avoid optical illusion

J. SOUTH

F. EAST

Kitchens were in all four corners

Ezekiel's end-time temple (chaps. 40 – 48).

The Gospel of Thomas

The *Gospel of Thomas* is a second-century AD Gnostic reinterpretation of Jesus. The Gnostics were a group of professing Christians who were considered heretical by the mainstream church. Akin to the Greek philosopher Plato, they taught that the human body is evil and only the soul is good. According to them, in the beginning there was one cosmic spirit being and no matter. But an evil creator god turned from the one true God and created the world.

Gnostics believed that they were not of this world, but descendants of the one true God. They thought of themselves as sparks of divine light entrapped by the evil creator god in the material world of his creation. Their goal — their salvation — was to escape this world and reascend to the heavenly realm of their origin.

In Christian Gnosticism, the redeemer figure was identified with Christ. He came, as in other Gnostic systems, to remind Gnostics of their true nature, to awaken them from forgetfulness, and to tell them of their heavenly home. This Christ shared with them secret knowledge — *gnosis* — which was the means by which they could escape the world of evil and return to God.

The *Gospel of Thomas* reflects the outlook of the Gnostic movement in significant aspects. Jesus, for example, speaks as the redeemer come from God. He reminds his followers of humanity's forgetfulness and tells how humanity is in need of enlightenment (*Thomas* 28). He deprecates the world (*Thomas* 21:6; 27:1; 56:1 – 2; 80:1 – 2; 110; 111:3). He reminds people of their origin (*Thomas* 49) and tells them of their needed return to the heavenly home (*Thomas* 50). He also speaks of his own return to the place from which he has come (*Thomas* 38).

Jesus' promise to return to take the disciples with him (v. 3) most likely refers to the parousia (the second coming of Christ; cf. 21:22 – 23), though many take it to mean the coming of Jesus in the Holy Spirit at Pentecost (cf. vv. 16 – 17; et al.).

There followed, then, an interchange between Jesus and Thomas: Jesus assured the disciples that they knew the way he was going (v. 4), but Thomas was confused (v. 5). Jesus then named himself as the exclusive way to the Father (v. 6). There has been much discussion of the relationship of the three nouns in verse 6: "way," "truth," and "life." Most commentators today rightly see "way" as the head noun, from which the other two proceed. Most likely, therefore, Jesus asserted the following: "I am the true way to life."

> Most commentators today rightly see "way" as the head noun, from which the other two proceed. Most likely, therefore, Jesus asserted the following: "I am the true way to life."

Many interpreters think that the two ways tradition of Deuteronomy 30:15 – 20 forms the backdrop to John 14:6: obeying Jesus is the stipulation for entering and staying in the new covenant.[3] This is opposed to the "false" way to enter the covenant proposed by the Jerusalem leadership.

---

3. See the study by A. Lacomara, "Deuteronomy and the Farewell Discourse (Jn 13:31 – 16:33)," *CBQ* 36 (1974): 65 – 84.

A similar contrast is prominent in the Dead Sea Scrolls. The Essenes are the true way to the new covenant (1QS 9:17–18), while those who apostatized have turned from that way (CD 1:3). The regulations of the Essene community were "the regulations of the way" (1QS 9:21). They prepared the "way" for the Messiah and the new covenant (1QS 8:12–16). Those opposed to the Essenes are the "way" of iniquity (1QS 4:15–16). As followers of Jesus, the early Christians called themselves the "way" (Acts 9:2; 19:9, 23; 22:4; 24:14, 22).

"Knowing" the way of Christ, and thereby God, is rooted in the knowledge of God the new covenant brings (cf. John 14:5–7 with Jer. 24:7; 31:34).[4] John's twist to this is that Christ, not the law of Moses, is the means of entrance into the new covenant.

The second-class conditional sentence in verse 7 implies that Thomas and the disciples do not really know Christ and God yet: "If you really knew me [—and you don't—], you would know my Father as well." But verse 26 offers the encouragement that Thomas and the disciples will indeed come to know Jesus and the Father as a result of Christ's passion.

Philip continued to display his spiritual obtuseness by requesting Jesus to show the Father to the disciples (v. 8).[5] Jesus' curt reply reminded Philip and the disciples that to see Jesus is to see God, for the former is on par with the latter (v. 9). The two — the Son and the Father — experience mutual indwelling. Thus Jesus' words are those of his Father, and his miracles prove that to

> The two ways tradition of Deuteronomy 30:15–20 forms the backdrop to John 14:6: obeying Jesus is the stipulation for entering and staying in the new covenant. This is opposed to the "false" way to enter the covenant proposed by the Jerusalem leadership.

---

4. So Raymond E. Brown, *The Gospel according to John XIII–XXI*, Anchor Bible 29B (Garden City, N.Y.: Doubleday, 1970), 631.

5. As did Moses in Exodus 33:18; cf. 24:10 and Merkabah (throne) proponents in general in Second Temple Judaism.

Deuteronomy 30:15–20

See, I set before you today life and prosperity, death and destruction. For I command you today to love the LORD your God, to walk in his ways, and to keep his commands, decrees and laws; then you will live and increase, and the LORD your God will bless you in the land you are entering to possess.

But if your heart turns away and you are not obedient, and if you are drawn away to bow down to other gods and worship them, I declare to you this day that you will certainly be destroyed. You will not live long in the land you are crossing the Jordan to enter and possess.

This day I call heaven and earth as witnesses against you that I have set before you life and death, blessings and curses. Now choose life, so that you and your children may live and that you may love the LORD your God, listen to his voice, and hold fast to him. For the LORD is your life, and he will give you many years in the land he swore to give to your fathers, Abraham, Isaac and Jacob.

be so (vv. 10–11). Once again, Jesus drew here on the concept of *ṣālîaḥ*, the Jewish principle of representation (see *m. Ber.* 5.5).

Verses 12–14 record two amazing promises Jesus made to his disciples. The first was that they would do greater works, or miracles, than Jesus did (v. 12). Though it is debated, it does seem that the basis of this promise is the future coming of the Spirit (see vv. 16–17, 25–26). While Jesus was on earth, he was the primary miracle worker, but when he departed and sent his Spirit to indwell his followers, Jesus' miracles were multiplied through them, as Acts records (3:6; 5:1–11; 9:34, 40).

The second promise Jesus made to the disciples regarded answers to their prayers. Raymond Brown identifies four types of such statements in Jesus' last discourse and in 1 John:

(a) xiv 13: "Whatever you ask in my name I will do [*poiein*]."
 xiv 14: "If you ask anything of me in my name, I will do [*poiein*] it."
(b) xv 16: "Whatever you ask the Father in my name He will give you."
 xvi 23: "If you ask anything of the Father, He will give it to you in my name."
(c) xvi 24: "Ask and you shall receive."
 xv 7: "Ask for whatever you want and it will be done [*ginesthai*] for you."
(d) A free form (found also in I John):
 xvi 26: "On that day you will ask in my name; and I do not say that I shall have to petition the Father for you."

I John iii 21–22: "If conscience [heart] knows nothing damaging, we can have confidence before God and receive from Him whatever we may ask, because we are keeping His commandments and doing what is pleasing in His sight."

I John v 14–15: "Now we have confidence in God that He hears us whenever we ask for anything according to His will. And since we know that He hears us whenever we ask, we know that what we have asked Him for is ours."[6]

> What becomes clear from these four variants and 1 John is that prayer is not a carte blanche affair.

What becomes clear from these four variants and 1 John is that prayer is not a carte blanche affair. Rather, answered prayer results from praying in the "name" of Christ (14:13, 14; 15:16; 16:26), which means to keep God's commandments (1 John 3:21–22) and do his will (1 John 5:14–15). These are all variations of the same theme, namely, answered prayer results when Jesus' followers seek his will in their lives.

II. THE SPIRIT'S ARRIVAL (14:15–24)

Introduction

This section introduces Jesus' prophecies about the coming of the Paraclete (*paraklētos*), the Holy Spirit. There are five such texts in the Last Discourse: 14:16–17, 26; 15:26; 16:7–11, 12–15. We will touch upon each of these texts as we summarize the Upper Room Discourse.

It is clear that the theme of John 14:15–24 is love for, and obedience to, Christ, the consequence of which is the promise of divine indwelling. This refrain occurs three times in verses 15–24, resulting in a threefold division:

---

6. Brown, *Gospel according to John XIII–XXI*, 634.

- Love/obey: The Paraclete will come (vv. 15–17).
- Love/obey: Jesus will come (vv. 18–21).
- Love/obey: The Father will come (vv. 22–24).

What is not so clear, however, is the timing of the comings of the Paraclete, Jesus, and the Father. Most likely, the referent of their comings to followers of Christ is the same. But what is that referent? The postresurrection appearances of Jesus, Pentecost, or the parousia? The scope of Jesus' promise of divine indwelling seems to rule out the first option, for the divine indwelling will happen to all of Jesus' disciples (John 17:20–26), not just the first-century apostles. The third option is logical, but the Paraclete passage introduced above makes it more likely that it was Pentecost when Jesus' promise of divine indwelling was fulfilled.[7] Thus the coming indwellings of the Spirit, Jesus, and the Father occurred at Pentecost. Indirectly, then, John 14:15–24 attests to the residence of the Trinity in the hearts of believers. I will presume this interpretation as I now summarize verses 15–24.

A. Love/Obey and the Coming of the Paraclete (vv. 15–17)

Verses 15–17 record Jesus' first promise to the disciples of the divine indwelling of the Paraclete. This is conditional upon their love for Jesus by obeying his command(s).[8] The commandments of Jesus are to believe in him (14:1–14) and to love the brethren (13:34; 15:12–17; cf. 1 John 2:8–10; 3:11–24; 4:7–21). These constitute the stipulations of the new covenant (cf. Deut. 6:5–6).

B. Love/Obey and the Coming of the Son (vv. 18–21)

Once, again, Jesus challenged his disciples to love and obey him (v. 21). The result would be that he would come to live within them by his Spirit (vv. 18–20). Presumably, this promise came true at Pentecost.

C. Love/Obey and the Coming of the Father (vv. 22–24)

In response to the question of Judas (not Iscariot) as to why Jesus was revealing himself to the disciples and not the world (v. 22), Jesus challenged his audience for a third time to love and obey him (vv. 23–24). This would result in God the Father taking up his residence within the followers of Jesus.

III. CONCLUSION (14:25–31)

Those who argue that John 13:31–14:31 and chapters 15–16 are duplicate accounts of Jesus' last discourse see 14:25–31 as the conclusion to the original speech. Indeed, verse 31 would seem to indicate Jesus completed his comments at that point. Alternatively, those who disagree with the duplicate theory see verses 25–31 as a transition to Jesus' further remarks.

---

7. Brown argues that the three comings originally referred to the parousia, but two factors caused the Johannine community to reidentify the comings with the Spirit's arrival at Pentecost: (1) the delay of the parousia and (2) the death of John. Brown, *Gospel according to John XIII–XXI*, 1142–43.

8. Verse 15 is most likely a subjunctive conditional clause that states a commonly accepted principle—"Those who love me keep my commandments."

"All this" (v. 25; cf. v. 29) refers to the two predictions of Jesus that dominate John 14: his imminent departure (vv. 1–14) and the coming of the Paraclete (vv. 15–24). When the Spirit comes, he will remind the disciples of those truths and, indeed, all that Jesus had taught them (vv. 25, 29).

The "peace" that Jesus promised to the disciples is the result of the believer's communion with God and Christ through the indwelling of the Holy Spirit. Yet such a peace would be no exemption for them from trouble and persecution at the hands of the ruler of this world (v. 30). But Jesus' death and resurrection would overcome the evil one, and thereby so would the disciples (vv. 30–31). This should bring joy to them (v. 28).[9]

---

9. The words "for the Father is greater than I" (v. 28) strike the balance presumed in the gospel of John (cf. 1:1–5; 20:18–31) and in the New Testament as a whole: Jesus is equal to God in essence but subordinate to the Father in his mission (see esp. 1 Cor 15:28). That is to say, Jesus is God's (essence) Son (subordinate). Such a balance may have been accented by John to answer Jewish accusations that Christianity was polytheistic, not monotheistic.

REVIEW QUESTIONS

1. What are the two themes that dominate John 14?

2. What does the phrase — "I am the way and the truth and the life" — mean?

3. What is the *Gospel of Thomas*? Should it have been included in the New Testament canon?

4. What do the four types of prayer promises in John have in common?

5. When did the coming of the Paraclete, Jesus, and the Father take place, according to John 14:15–24?

KEY TERMS

answers to prayer	Paraclete	two ways tradition of Deuteronomy 30:15–20
Gospel of Thomas	"The way and the truth and the life"	
Jesus' departure		

CHAPTER 17

The Vine, the Branches, and the World

JOHN 15:1–16:4A

Objectives

After reading this chapter, you should be able to:

- Discuss the Old Testament background of Jesus' allegory of the vine and the branches.

- Identify the unfruitful and fruitful branches.

- Explain how covenant themes shed light on John 15.

- Explain how the messianic woes inform John 15:18–16:4a.

- Address the two major themes of John 15:1–16:4a.

INTRODUCTION

John 15:1 – 16:4a seems to form a self-contained unit, focusing on two main themes: the vine and the branches (15:1 – 17), and the hatred of the world for Jesus and his disciples (5:18 – 16:4a).

I. THE VINE AND THE BRANCHES (15:1 – 17)

John 15:1 – 17 contains the majestic description of Jesus as the vine and his followers as the branches. The commentators agree that John 15:1 – 17 divides into two parts: the allegory of the vine and the branches (vv. 1 – 6), and the explanation of that allegory (vv. 7 – 17).

> John 15:1 – 16:4a seems to form a self-contained unit, focusing on two main themes: the vine and the branches (15:1 – 17), and the hatred of the world for Jesus and his disciples (5:18 – 16:4a).

A. The Allegory of the Vine and the Branches (vv. 1 – 6)

John 15:1 – 6 is an allegory, an extended metaphor. Unlike parables, which tend to make one basic point, an allegory makes several points. Here in verses 1 – 6 Jesus' horticultural allegory emphasizes three symbols: the vine, the gardener, and the branches.

1. The Vine (v. 1a)

"I am the true vine" is the last of the seven "I am" sayings in John. The background of Jesus' usage of the vine imagery is Old Testament Israel, which is called the vineyard of God in several famous passages: Psalm 80:8 – 18; Isaiah 5:1 – 7; Jeremiah 2:21; Ezekiel 15:1 – 5; 17:1 – 2; 19:10 – 14; Hosea 10:1 – 2; cf. *Leviticus Rabbah* 36 (133a); Matthew 20:1 – 16; Mark 12:1 – 12; Luke 13:6 – 9.

The striking characteristic of the above Old Testament and New Testament passages is that Israel as the vineyard of God was placed under divine judgment due to its spiritual fruitlessness. This is no doubt the key to understanding Jesus' self-reference "I am the *true* vine." Jesus represents true Israel precisely because he is the obedient vineyard of God and

Left: A vineyard near the tell, or mound, of Lachish. *Right:* A watchtower in the hills of Samaria.

his community is the new covenant people. In John's day that applied as well to his churches who had replaced rabbinic Judaism as God's vineyard.

> "I am the true vine" is the last of the seven "I am" sayings in John.

2. The Gardener (vv. 1–2b)

God is compared to the vinedresser or the gardener. As such he performs two roles: (1) he cuts off the branches that are fruitless (v. 2a), and (2) he prunes those branches that are fruitful (v. 2b). The next point explores what this means.

3. The Branches (vv. 2–8)

The branches in this allegory are divided into two camps: unfruitful branches and fruitful branches.

Some branches are unfruitful because they do not abide/remain in Christ (vv. 2a, 6). Most likely Jesus has in mind Judas, who once was in union with Jesus the vine but removed himself by betraying his Lord (13:18–30). In John's day the imagery was probably thought to apply to those who departed from the Johannine community (1 John 2:18–19; 4:1–6; 5:16–17). Whether the branches of John 15:2, 6 should be considered genuine Christians or no more than professing believers is a matter of debate. These spiritually barren branches are cut off from the vine (v. 2) and burned (v. 6). While the imagery of fiery destruction is figurative, the gravity of the fate of such individuals should not be downplayed. They have committed apostasy.

Things are altogether different, however, for the fruitful branches (vv. 2b, 3–5). Jesus made three remarks about these branches that remain in him. First, God prunes them (vv. 2b, 5b). Such a painful action springs from God's love for his own, knowing that trials and discipline mature the Christian (see John 15:18–16:4a; cf. Heb. 12:4–11). Second, the fruitful branches are pruned by God to bear more fruit (John 15:2b, 5b). Such fruit, as verses 10–17 make clear, involves loving other believers. Furthermore, as Aelred Lacomara has shown, such fruitfulness is to be understood against the background of the covenant blessing of fruitfulness in the land of Canaan[1] but is now applied to spiritual fruitfulness in Christ. Third, the fruitful branches have been cleansed by Jesus' word spoken to them (v. 3). More specifically, Jesus' sacrificial death, symbolized in his washing the disciples' feet (13:1–17), provided the ultimate word of cleansing for his own.

> The branches in this allegory are divided into two camps: unfruitful branches and fruitful branches.

The key, of course, to spiritual productivity is to remain in Jesus the Vine. "Remain/abide" (menō) occurs eleven times in John 15:4–10 alone. The term, as Edward Malatesta has demonstrated, is heavily indebted to Old Testament covenant theology (see Ex. 25:8; 29:45; Lev. 26:11–12; Ezek. 37:27–28; 43:9), where God's presence and Law come to

---

1. Aelred Lacomara, "Deuteronomy and the Farewell Discourse (Jn 13:31–16:33)," *CBQ* 36 (1974): 79. As Andreas J. Köstenberger observes, *karpos* (fruit) occurs 8 times in John 15:1–16 and only twice in the rest of the gospel of John (4:36; 12:24). Andreas J. Köstenberger, *John*, Baker Exegetical Commentary on the New Testament (Grand Rapids: Baker, 2004), 452.

> The key to spiritual productivity is to remain in Jesus the Vine.

reside in the hearts of his people, empowering them to obey him.[2] For John, however, one enters the new covenant by believing in Jesus the Christ, not by keeping the law of Moses.[3]

B. The Explanation of the Vine and Branches Allegory (vv. 7–17)

The covenant theme continues to exert itself in verses 7–17. Three components of the Deuteronomic theology can be identified therein. Beginning in verse 6, we find the influence of the Deuteronomic/covenantal curses, while in verses 7–17 one can see the covenantal blessings and stipulation at work. These components are reworked by John along the lines of the new covenant in Christ. I now touch upon these three components.

1. Covenant Curses (v. 6)

I touched on verse 6 above, but here I note that the contrasting conditional statements in verses 6–7 distinctly remind one of the antithetical pronouncements of the covenantal curses from Mount Ebal and the covenantal blessings from Mount Gerizim (Deut. 27:9–28:68):

verse 6 — "If anyone does not remain in me (Christ), he is ... burned"
verse 7 — "If you remain in me (Christ) ... whatever you wish ... will be given to you."[4]

---

2. Edward Malatesta, *Interiority and Covenant* (Rome: Biblical Institute Press, 1978), chap. 8.

3. The new covenant background of John 15 has suggested to some a sacramental/Eucharistic nuance, despite the lack of any reference to "wine" in these verses. See Raymond E. Brown, *The Gospel according to John XIII–XXI*, Anchor Bible 29B (Garden City, N.Y.: Doubleday, 1970), 672.

4. Verses 1–6 have the third person, while vv. 7–17 address the second person. Some think this suggests that the two paragraphs were once separate but later brought together by a Johannine editor. See Brown, *Gospel according to John XIII–XXI*, 666–67.

Women picking grapes.

Overhead vines near Hebron.

2. New Covenant Stipulation (vv. 7–17)

As we saw in verse 4, abiding/remaining in Christ is the stipulation of the new covenant. This stipulation is expressed in various ways in verses 7–17: "Remain in me and [let] my words remain in you" (v. 7); "Remain in my love" (vv. 9b, 10b); "Obey my commands" (v. 10a). The essence of the stipulation of remaining in the new covenant is to believe in Christ, according to verses 1–6. That is expanded in verses 7–17 to include love for one's fellow Christians (vv. 12–13, 17).

3. New Covenant Blessings (vv. 7–17)

Remaining in Christ by believing in him and loving his followers produces some four new covenant blessings, which I simply list here: answers to prayer (cf. John 15:7b, 16b with Neh. 1:5–11; 9:1–37; et al.); spiritual fruitfulness (see John 15:8, 16a); being loved and chosen by God (cf. John 15:9a, 14–16a with Deut. 4:37; 7:8; et al.); joy (cf. John 15:11 with Isa. 25:9; 35:10; et al.).

II. HATRED FOR JESUS AND HIS DISCIPLES (15:18–16:4A)

The most distinguishing feature of John 15:18–16:4a is its eschatological makeup, in particular its parallels with Jesus' Olivet Discourse in the Synoptics (Matt. 24:9–10; Mark 13:9–13; Luke 21:12–17). Comparing John and the Synoptics indicates that Jesus' disciples were in their lifetimes already undergoing the messianic woes/Great Tribulation.

The term *messianic woes* refers to the time of great sorrow and tribulation to come upon God's people immediately prior to the coming of the Messiah; that is, the signs of the times. The concept is adumbrated in the Old Testament in association with the day of Yahweh (e.g., Isa. 24:17–23; Dan. 12:1–2; Joel 2:1–11a, 28–32; Amos 5:16–20; Zeph. 1:14–2:3) and developed in Jewish apocalypticism (e.g., *2 Bar.* 55:6; *1 Enoch* 80:4–5; *4 Ezra* 7:37ff.; *Jub.* 23:11; 24:3). The term itself, however, does not occur until the writing of the Talmud (e.g., *b. Shab.* 118a; *b. Pes.* 118a). There is striking agreement in the literature under consideration that there will be intense persecution of God's people, which will sorely tempt them to depart from the faith.[5]

John 15:18–16:4a particularly illustrates the last-mentioned sign—persecution of Jesus' followers and their temptation to commit apostasy. I now briefly remark on the four divisions that comprise John 15:18–16:4a, which form a chiasm:

  A The world's persecution of the disciples (15:18–21)

    B The guilt of the world (15:22–25)

    B' The Spirit's exposure of the guilt of the world (15:26–27)

  A' The world's persecution of the disciples (16:1–4a)[6]

---

5. For further details, see C. Marvin Pate and Douglas W. Kinnard, *Deliverance Now and Not Yet: The New Testament and the Great Tribulation* (2003; repr., Baltimore: Peter Lang, 2005).

6. The outline is Brown's, *Gospel according to John XIII–XXI*, 695–702. Here I list the reasons for extending John 15:1 to 16:4a: (1) The theme of persecution begun in 15:18 ends in 16:4a. (2) The fact that 15:18–16:4a goes together is confirmed by the parallels between these verses and Matthew 10:17–25. (3) That the section stops at 16:4a is confirmed by the inclusion between 16:1 and 16:4a ("I have told you these things"). (4) John 16:4b–33 is a section that duplicates 13:32–18:31; so 16:4b–33 should be separated from 16:1–4a in terms of delineation (for these reasons, see Brown, *Gospel according to John XIII–XXI*, 693).

A. The World's Persecution of the Disciples (15:18–21)

Four conditional statements unfold in John 15:18–21. The first and third statements express real conditions, while the second and fourth express unreal conditions. I provide their meaning accordingly:

> Since the world hated me [Jesus], it will hate you [disciples] (v. 18).

> If you were of the world (and you are not), then the world would love you (and it does not) (v. 19).

> Since they (the world) persecuted me, they will persecute you (v. 20a).

> If the world kept my word (and it did not), then it will keep your word (and it will not) (v. 20b).

These statements indicate that, because of the reciprocal union between Jesus and his disciples, the way the world treated Jesus is the way the world (implied the Jews) treats his followers (cf. John 1:10–11; cf. Acts 9:4).

B. The Guilt of the World (15:22–25)

Verses 22–25 also unfold in conditional statements, which are unreal statements. These conditional sentences divide the paragraph into two parallel statements:

Jesus' Words (vv. 22–23)	Jesus' Works (v. 24)
1. If I did not speak my word to them [the world—and I did] then they would not be guilty of sin [but they are].	1. If I did not perform my works among them [and I did], then they would not be guilty of sin [but they are].
2. They hate Jesus and therefore the Father.	2. They hate Jesus and therefore the Father.

C. The Spirit's Exposure of the Guilt of the World (15:26–27)

The Spirit's witness and the disciples' witness are placed side by side in verses 26–27. When the Spirit comes to the disciples, he will be a witness to Jesus (v. 26) through the disciples (v. 27).[7] The context suggests that this witness will be one of convicting the world of its sin of rejecting Jesus.

---

7. The words "who comes (*exerchesthai*) from the Father" (v. 26) became the subject of debate between the Eastern and Western church fathers in the fourth and fifth centuries AD. The former thought the words indicated that the Spirit proceeded eternally only from the Father, while the latter emphasized the Spirit's procession from both the Father and the Son. This was called the "filioque debate." But actually, the present tense of the verb "coming" along with the parallel statement "I shall send" (v. 26) merely applies to the Spirit's mission to humans, not his preexistent relation with the other members of the Trinity.

D. The World's Persecution of the Disciples (16:1–4a)

That 16:1–4a is a paragraph is clear from the words "All this I have told you," which form an inclusion (v. 1a and v. 4a). The "this" refers to 15:18–27—the coming persecution of the disciples. Having been forewarned, they should not be caught off guard and thus forsake Christ (vv. 1–4a). The nature of the persecution inflicted upon Jesus' followers will include being expelled from the synagogue and killed (v. 2a). The Jews who do this will think they are serving God, but the reason the disciples' enemies do these things is because they do not truly know God (v. 3).

CONCLUSION

We have seen that John 15:1–16:4a addresses two themes: the need for followers of Jesus to abide in Christ by believing in him and loving one another (15:1–17) and the prediction of future persecution of the disciples by the world (15:18–16:4a).

REVIEW QUESTIONS

1. What is the Old Testament background of Jesus' allegory of the vine and the branches (John 15:1–6)?

2. Who are the unfruitful branches (John 15:2, 6)?

3. Who are the fruitful branches (John 15:2–6)?

4. How does the covenant themes of curses, stipulations, and blessings relate to John 15:7–17?

5. What are four covenantal blessings mentioned in John 15:7–17?

6. How does John 15:18–16:4a relate to the messianic woes as predicted by Jesus in the Synoptics' eschatological discourse?

7. What are some of the "signs of the times"?

8. Summarize the four divisions of John 15:18–16:4a.

9. What are the two major themes addressed in John 15:1–16:4a?

fruitful branches

Israel, the vineyard of God

messianic woes

Synoptic eschatological discourse

unfruitful branches

CHAPTER 18

Summary of the Last Discourse

JOHN 16:4B–33

Objectives

After reading this chapter, you should be able to:

- Explain how the convicting work of the Spirit is a type of "retrial" of Jesus.

- Explain the six end-time events recast in terms of realized eschatology in John 16:14b–33.

INTRODUCTION

Though it is debated, John 16:4b–33 may well be a duplicate of John 13:31–14:31, the first part of Jesus' last discourse.[1] Like John 13:31–14:31, 16:4b–33 addresses two key themes: Jesus' departure and the Spirit's arrival (albeit in reverse order). The unit divides into two sections: verses 4b–15 and verses16–33. The former deals with the Spirit's arrival, while the latter focuses on Jesus' departure.

> Like John 13:31–14:31, John 16:4b–33 addresses two key themes: Jesus' departure and the Spirit's arrival.

I. THE SPIRIT'S ARRIVAL (16:4B–15)

Verses 4b–15 form their own section. Verse 4a forms an inclusion with verse 1, centering on the theme of Jesus' words. Verse 4b, then, begins a new section. That section concludes at verse 15, where the last of the Paraclete passages occurs. Verse 16 begins a new theme—Jesus' departure. John 16:4b–15 can be outlined as follows:

A. The introduction of the twofold theme (vv. 4b–7).

　　1. Jesus' departure (vv. 4b–6).

　　2. The Spirit's arrival (v. 7).

B. The convicting work of the Spirit (vv. 8–11).

　　1. Summary statement of that conviction (v. 8).

　　2. Detailed statement of that conviction (vv. 9–11).

C. The assurance of the Spirit (vv. 12–15).

A. The Introduction of the Twofold Theme (vv. 4b–7)

Verse 4b reports that Jesus told the disciples that he did not mention to them early on that they too would face persecution on behalf of his name (15:18–16:4a). He did not need to tell them at that time, for he was the focus of the opposition of the Jews. However, upon his departure, the persecution of his disciples would pick up where it left off with Jesus, and understandably this thought saddened the disciples (vv. 5–6).[2] But there was good news in all of this: Jesus had to go back to the Father (via death/resurrection/ascension) so that the Spirit could come to the disciples (v. 7). Though the rationale for this is not made explicit here, it seems to be implied that while the historical Jesus was on earth, he could only be at

---

1. Recall my discussion of John 13. See Raymond E. Brown's argumentation for this position in his *The Gospel according to John XIII–XXI*, Anchor Bible 29B (Garden City, N.Y.: Doubleday, 1970), 709. See also the chart on p. 145 identifying the parallels between John 13:31–14:31 and 16:4b–33. It should be observed that this duplicate view is being challenged today, most notably by the work of L. Scott Kellum, *The Unity of the Farewell Discourse: The Literary Integrity of John 13.31–16.33*. JSOTSup 256 (London and New York: T. & T. Clark, 2004). He argues that the style and structure of the Farewell Discourse both point to unity of authorship therein. He concludes that John 14:31d ("Come now; let us leave") is not interrupted by the following chapters, which would result in forming a literary seam only to be resumed at John 18:1, but is integrally related to what follows. Kellum's important work demands more attention than can be given in this introductory text, but it seems to this author that John 21 is added by an editor after John's death (at least that is still the majority view among interpreters), which provides precedent for allowing for a later addition to the Farewell Discourse as well.

2. Verse 5b ("No one asked Jesus where he was going") is in tension with 13:36 (Peter asked Jesus where he was going) and 14:5 (Thomas said to Jesus that he did not know where he was going).

one place at one time. But when he came back in the form of the Holy Spirit, he could be in all of his followers at once.

B. The Convicting Work of the Spirit (vv. 8 – 11)

The Spirit's arrival, the topic of verses 8 – 15, will serve two functions: he will convict the world (vv. 8 – 11) but assure the disciples (vv. 12 – 15). Verse 8 lists the three items of conviction the Spirit will bring against the world: sin, righteousness, and judgment. The "world" here refers especially to those Jewish leaders (though not exclusively) who tried and convicted Jesus. Verses 9 – 11, then, in a kind of retrial of Jesus, detail the convictions brought against Jesus' enemies by the Spirit.

> The Spirit's arrival, the topic of verses 8 -- 15, will serve two functions: he will convict the world (vv. 8 – 11) but assure the disciples (vv. 12 -- 15).

The key in verses 9 – 11 to understanding how it is that the Spirit is the one who convicts the world is to realize that the Spirit is the resurrected presence of *Jesus* now sent to the disciples. The Spirit will convict the world of sin because the world did not believe in Jesus (v. 9). In particular, the Jewish leadership did not believe Jesus was the Son of God (John 19:7, 14 – 15, 19 – 22; cf. 3:19; 12:37). But the very fact that God raised him from the dead and sent his Spirit to indwell the disciples is proof that Jesus was who he claimed to be.

Verse 10 makes a similar point. "Righteousness" (*dikaiosunē*) here involves vindication. The trial of Jesus condemned him as a criminal—a blasphemer (19:7) and an insurrectionist (19:12 – 16). Yet once again Jesus' resurrection and ascension to his Father proved he was who he claimed to be and vindicated him before God. The presence of Jesus in his disciples was proof of that too. Verse 11 continues the theme of the retrial of Jesus: though Jesus was condemned and handed over to judgment by crucifixion, that very judgment was his victory over Satan, the prince of the world, and over Satan's cohorts—the Jewish and Roman authorities (18:36 – 37; 19:11; cf. 12:31; 14:31). And the presence of Jesus in his disciples through the Spirit was proof of Jesus' victory over the world.

C. The Assurance of the Spirit (vv. 12 – 15)

Things will be much different for Jesus' disciples after Jesus' resurrection (v. 15); he will send his Spirit to the disciples, who will guide them into all truth (v. 13; cf. 14:26). In John 14:6 Jesus identified himself with the true way to life, and that is a blessing that will belong to the disciples, because they will possess the Spirit (cf. 16:13 with 20:22). But the Spirit will not teach the disciples anything new; rather, he will remind the disciples of Jesus' message and interpret that for them (vv. 13b – 15).[3]

> The presence of Jesus in his disciples through the Spirit was proof of Jesus' victory over the world.

One detects in all of this a chain of revelation from the Father to the Son to the Spirit to the disciples. The word "declare" (*avangellō*; NIV "speak") is used three times in verses

---

3. It is unlikely that the Spirit will bring new revelation; rather, he will only illumine Jesus' teaching (see John 14:26; 16:13 – 14).

13–15 (vv. 13, 14, 15); a key term in the Johannine tradition (see our comments on 1 John 1:1–5). It is the passing on of the official pronouncement of the truth of Jesus.

I conclude this section by calling attention to the eschatological influence on verses 4b–33, in particular realized eschatology. Six events that Judaism associated with the last days and the arrival of the kingdom of God are presented in this passage as already operative as a result of the death and resurrection of Jesus: final judgment (vv. 8–15), glory (v. 14), the messianic woes (vv. 20–23), knowledge of God (vv. 23–30), apostasy brought on by persecution (vv. 31–32), and end-time holy war (vv. 32–33).[4] I will briefly comment on the first two of these now, as they occur in 16:4b–15, reserving discussion of the other four themes for verses 16–33.

According to verses 8–15, final judgment has broken into the present, depending on one's response to Christ. Those who reject Jesus are already judged and convicted (vv. 8–11). Those who believe in Jesus are accepted by God and indwelled by the Spirit of Jesus (vv. 12–15).

Furthermore, Judaism anticipated that the Messiah would come with power and glory to establish the kingdom of God (see Mark 13:26//Matt. 24:30//Luke 21:27; 2 Thess. 1:7–10; Titus 2:13; Rev. 1:6–7). According to John 16:14, that reality has already dawned through the work of the Spirit.

> Six events that Judaism associated with the last days and the arrival of the kingdom of God are presented in this passage [John 16:4b–33] as already operative as a result of the death and resurrection of Jesus.

II. JESUS' DEPARTURE (16:16–33)

Verses 16–33 divide into two parts: (1) the disciples' confusion about Jesus' departure (vv. 16–19) and (2) Jesus' explanation of his departure (vv. 20–33).

A. The Disciples' Confusion about Jesus' Departure (vv. 16–19)

The contrast between seeing Jesus no more and seeing Jesus in a little while dominates verses 16–19, occurring in verses 16, 17, and 19. The meaning of seeing Jesus no more is obvious: he will soon leave the disciples by dying and being resurrected to return to his heavenly Father. But the words "after a little while you will see me" are debated. Do they refer to the parousia, the postresurrection appearances of Jesus, or the coming of the Spirit?

The following remarks of Jesus help to answer that question, for verses 20–33 talk about events connected with the end of the age: the messianic woes (vv. 20–22), the knowledge of God (vv. 23–30), apostasy (vv. 31–32), and holy war (v. 33). Indeed the phrase meaning "a little while" (NIV "very soon" or "in a very short time") frequently occurs in passages anticipating the eschatological action of God (e.g., Isa. 10:25; 29:17; Jer. 51:33; Hos. 1:4).[5] While these portents heralding the kingdom of God and the age to come could suggest that Jesus' second coming is in mind here, most likely John's realized eschatology is once again at work.

---

4. Recall my earlier comments on the comparisons between John 15:18–16:4a and the Synoptics' Olivet Discourse.

5. So George R. Beasley-Murray, *John,* Word Biblical Commentary 36 (Nashville: Thomas Nelson, 1999), 285.

Events associated with the end of history are for him a present reality because of the presence of the resurrected Jesus by his Spirit. In other words, the words "after a little while you will see me" probably include all three options: Jesus' postresurrection appearances, which gave way after fifty days to the Spirit's arrival at Pentecost, which anticipates the parousia.

The words "after a little while you will see me" are debated. Do they refer to the parousia, the postresurrection appearances of Jesus, or the coming of the Spirit?

B. Jesus' Explanation of His Departure (vv. 20–33)

Jesus' explanation of his departure occurs in verses 20–33. He speaks therein of end-time events that will occur *in* history. In other words, Jesus' death, resurrection, and sending of his Spirit inaugurated the age to come. Four such eschatological happenings are mentioned.

1. Messianic Woes (vv. 20–22)

Jesus' metaphor of the sorrow of birth pains that give way to the joy of birth is an allusion to the apocalyptic idea of the birth pangs of the Messiah (Isa. 26:16–21; 66:7–14; Dan. 12:1; Zeph. 1:14–15; Matt. 24:8; Mark 13:8; Rev. 12:2–5; 1QH 3:8ff.). That is, the suffering of God's people will be replaced with the joy of the arrival of the Messiah.[6] Indeed, John's use of the word *thlipsis* ("tribulation") for the disciples' suffering no doubt is to be equated with the Great Tribulation that will immediately precede the return of Christ (cf. vv. 21, 33 with Mark 13:19, 24).

2. Knowledge of God (vv. 23–30)

One of the great Old Testament promises regarding the end times is that the people of God will come to a genuine knowledge of God (see Isa. 11:9; Jer. 31:33–34; Hab. 2:14). John 16:23–30 seems to promise the same end-time knowledge of God.

3. Apostasy (vv. 31–32)

But things would get worse for the disciples (and Jesus) before they got better. Jesus predicted that his disciples would forsake him at his darkest hour—the cross. They would be "scattered" (*skorpisthēte*) like sheep are dispersed when their shepherd is struck down (Zech. 13:7; Matt. 26:31; Mark 14:27). As Dale C. Allison has demonstrated, the Zechariah reference is understood in the Gospels as signifying end-time apostasy; that is, out of fear for their own lives the disciples will forsake Jesus and the faith (cf. Zech. 13:7; Matt. 26:31; Mark 13:5; 14:27 with Matt. 24:10–12; 2 Thess. 2:3; 1 Tim. 4:1).[7] But, as John 16:33 indicates, Jesus will prevail and reclaim his disciples.

4. Holy War (v. 33)

I have already noted that the fourth evangelist perceived the cross and resurrection to be Jesus' moment of triumph over the prince of this world (12:31; cf. 3:14; 8:28). John 16:33

---

6. Beasley-Murray (ibid., 286) finds it interesting that Isaiah 26:16–21 contains three pertinent words or concepts found in John 16:20–22: "little while," "labor pangs," "resurrection."

7. Dale C. Allison, *The End of the Age Has Come. An Early Interpretation of the Passion and Resurrection* (Philadelphia: Fortress, 1985), 36.

reiterates that point. The word "overcome" (*nikaō*) occurs elsewhere in Johannine literature with reference to Jesus' triumph over Satan in the end-time holy war that was waged at the cross (1 John 2:13, 14; 4:4; 5:4, 5; Revelation — 12 times; especially Rev. 2–3; cf. 1 Cor. 15:57). What in Jewish literature was to be the climactic battle between God and the forces of evil (Ezek. 37–38; 1QM), for John had already happened at Jesus' cross and resurrection.

CONCLUSION

John 16:4b–33 treats two interrelated themes: the Spirit's arrival (16:4b–15) and Jesus' departure (16:16–33). The former brought about the latter. Indeed, the very presence of the Holy Spirit, the Spirit of Jesus, with the disciples was proof that the unbelieving world was wrong in judging Jesus, just as much as his presence vindicated the disciples. The arrival of the Spirit is clearly eschatological in meaning for the fourth gospel, as is the departure of Jesus. Thus both the new covenant and the age to come were present realities for Jesus' followers then, and they are now.

1. What two themes again dominate John 16:14b – 33?

2. How is the Spirit's convicting work a type of retrial of Jesus, according to John 16:8 – 11?

3. What six end-time events are recast according to John's realized eschatology in John 16:14b – 33?

4. How does final judgment relate to John 16:8 – 15?

5. How does the end-time promise of glory relate to Jesus and the kingdom of God?

6. To what end-time event do "birth pains" allude in John 16:20 – 22?

7. How was knowledge of God connected with the end times according to John 16:23 – 30?

8. Who fell into end-time apostasy according to John 16:31 – 32?

9. When was the end-time holy war fought according to John 16:33?

KEY TERMS

apostasy	end-time holy war	messianic woes
arrival of the Spirit	final judgment	*War Scroll*
departure of Jesus	knowledge of God	

CHAPTER 19

Jesus' Farewell Prayer

JOHN 17

Objectives

After reading this chapter, you should be able to:

- Identify the threefold outline of John 17.
- Explain the three phrases: "before the world," "in the world," "not of the world."
- Discuss the spiritual union of God the Father, Christ, and the Christian.

INTRODUCTION

John 17 concludes Jesus' farewell speech. The prayer divides into three parts: Jesus prayed to be glorified (vv. 1–5); Jesus prayed that his present disciples would be sanctified (vv. 6–19); Jesus prayed that his future disciples would be unified (vv. 20–26). We now briefly interact with these three divisions.

I. JESUS PRAYED TO BE GLORIFIED (17:1–5)

Two themes occur in John 17:1–5: glory (vv. 1, 4–5) and eternal life (vv. 2–3). And they are related: Jesus' death would both glorify God and become the basis of eternal life for his followers.

A. Jesus' Glory (vv. 1, 4–5)

Jesus prayed for his Father to glorify him (vv. 1, 4–5). "Glory," as I mentioned earlier, is eschatological: the future resurrection body will exude brilliant light (see Dan. 12:1–3). So when the Father raised him from the dead, Jesus would be glorified, clothed in a splendorous resurrection body. Verses 1, 4–5a speak as if Jesus' death and resurrection had already happened. The completion of Jesus' work on earth would reinstate the glory he enjoyed before his incarnation (v. 5b), and by the same token, Jesus' obedient death would glorify the Father (vv. 1b, 4).

B. Eternal Life (vv. 2–3)

Jesus' obedient death was not only his and the Father's moment of glory; it was also the basis for the eternal life to be given to the disciples. Such life comes from knowing God and Christ.

> Jesus' obedient death was not only his and the Father's moment of glory; it was also the basis for the eternal life to be given to the disciples. Such life comes from knowing God and Christ.

While an older generation of scholars rooted John's reference to knowledge (v. 3) in Gnosticism, most today rather relate it to the prophetic promise that God's children will know him with the advent of the new covenant in the age to come (Jer. 31:33–34; cf. 24:7). That covenantal background also explains two other descriptions in John 17:2–3: "eternal life" and "the only true God." The first is rooted in the life of the covenant promised to those who obey God (Deut. 30:16), except that it is eternal and spiritual, not temporary and material. The other description, "the only true God" alludes to the Shema ("hear"; Deut. 6:4), Israel's statement of monotheism and the basis of their covenant with God. Jesus Christ provides both blessings for his followers. They come to know God through Christ's revelation, which results in eternal life.

II. JESUS PRAYED THAT HIS PRESENT DISCIPLES WOULD BE SANCTIFIED (17:6–19)

The theme of holiness may form an inclusion around John 17:6–19. In verse 6 Jesus referred to the revelation of God's name to the disciples. A significant aspect of God's name is his holy character (cf. "Holy Father" in v. 11 and "Righteous Father" in v. 25). In the Old Testament, God is characteristically called "the Holy One" of Israel, while in Jewish prayers he is addressed as holy (2 Macc. 14:36; 3 Macc. 2:2; cf. *Didache* 102 in Christian literature). Verses 17–19 explicitly mention the theme of holiness/sanctification (*hagios*). If God and Jesus are sanctified, so should the disciples be set apart. To Israel God said, "I am holy, so you be holy" (cf. Lev. 11:44; 19:2; 20:26).

Synonymous with the disciples' sanctification is God's protection of them while they are in the world: "Holy Father, protect them by the power of your name" (v. 11; cf. vv. 12, 15).

So the theme of John 17:6–19 is the disciples' sanctification/protection. This will happen for three reasons: the disciples are chosen by God; they keep God's word; and they are persecuted by the world. These reasons respectively correlate with the following phrases: "before the world," "in the world," and "not of the world."

A. "Before the World": The Disciples Were Chosen by God (vv. 6, 9–10, 24; cf. v. 12)

The first reason the disciples will be sanctified—that is, remain holy by being faithful to Christ and God—is that they were chosen by God before the world began. In other words, they were predestined. If God chose Israel to be his holy people in the Old Testament, so the disciples are God's predestined people in Christ (John 17:6, 9–10, 24; cf. 15:16; Rom. 9:6–32; Eph. 1:4–5).[1] By way of contrast, Judas was predestined to be an apostate, a son of perdition (v. 12; cf. 6:64, 70; 13:2, 27, 30).[2]

B. "In the World": The Disciples Keep Jesus' Word (vv. 6–8, 17; cf. vv. 11–12)

The disciples will be sanctified because they keep Christ's word (vv. 6–8, 17) and therefore will be protected by God's name (vv. 11–12).

The former consists of Jesus' message to the world—he is God's Son whose death atones for all sin (cf. John 3:16 with 17:19;[3] 1 John 2:1–2). The disciples—minus Judas—continued to believe that Jesus is the Christ, the Son of God and therefore received life through his name (cf. John 20:31). In other words, the disciples abided in Christ (15:1–17). Similarly, by abiding in Jesus, God's Son, the "I Am," the disciples were protected by the power of God's name (vv. 11–12).

> The first reason the disciples will be sanctified—that is, remain holy by being faithful to Christ and God—is that they were chosen by God before the world began.

---

1. For a thorough discussion of the preexistent divine choice of the disciples, see R. G. Hamerton-Kelly, *Pre-Existence, Wisdom, and the Son of Man. A Study on the Idea of Pre-Existence in the New Testament*, SNTSMS 21 (Cambridge: Cambridge University Press, 1973), 215–24, who roots his discussion in the idea that the messianic community is preexistent.

2. See Brown's discussion of the possible Old Testament verse behind v. 12, whether Psalm 41:10 (9); Isaiah 57:4; or some other possibility, in Raymond E. Brown, *The Gospel according to John XIII–XXI*, Anchor Bible 29B (Garden City, N.Y.: Doubleday, 1970), 760.

3. As Burge observes, the phrase "for them" (*hyper*) in v. 19 implies sacrificial death throughout John (see 6:51; 10:11, 15; 11:50–52; 13:37; 15:13; 18:14; cf. Mark 14:24; Luke 22:19; Rom. 8:32; 1 Cor. 11:24). See Gary M. Burge, *John*, NIV Application Commentary (Grand Rapids: Zondervan, 2000), 467.

C. "Not of the World": The Disciples Are Persecuted by the World (vv. 14–16)

Just as the world (nonbelieving Jews) persecuted Jesus because he was not of this world, so will be the lot of the disciples, according to verses 14–16. This shows that they live holy lives. Nevertheless, the disciples are to remain in the world in order to be a witness to Christ (Matt. 5:10–15).[4]

III. JESUS PRAYED THAT HIS FUTURE DISCIPLES WOULD BE UNIFIED (17:20–26)

In verses 20–26 Jesus prayed for his future disciples; those who would believe[5] because of the witness of the eleven apostles (cf. John 10:16; 11:52). His intercession for them is that they will be unified. The unity of Jesus' future believers will proceed from their spiritual union with the Father and the Son (vv. 21–23).

With that as background, we may now note from verses 20–26 three points about the unity of Jesus' future disciples: the expression of that unity (vv. 23b, 24b, 26), the results of that unity (vv. 21–24), and the rejection of that unity (vv. 25–26).

A. The Expression of Unity (vv. 23b, 24b, 26)

The expression of unity among Jesus' followers would be love (vv. 23b, 24b, 26). God's love for Jesus would be extended to his disciples, which, in turn, they would manifest to one another (cf. John 13:35; 1 John 3:11).

> The disciples' love for and unity with one another would be a testimony to the watching world that Christ had come.

B. The Results of Unity (vv. 21–24)

The results of unity among future Christians would be twofold. First, such unity would cause the world to know that God had sent his Son into the world. Verses 21 and 23 parallel each other on this point:

v. 21: oneness of disciples = world will believe — God sent Jesus

v. 23: oneness of disciples = world will know — God sent Jesus

The disciples' love for and unity with one another would be a testimony to the watching world that Christ had come.[6]

The second result of the unity of Jesus' followers is that they would one day share his preexistent glory (vv. 22, 24; cf. 1:14), presumably at the parousia (cf. John 14:1–6). This stands to reason, for if Jesus' disciples were united to him now, then they would also be united to him in his resurrection glory.

---

4. How can John 3:16 — "for God so loved the world" — be reconciled with John 17:9 — "I do not pray for the world"? One answer is that between John 3:16 and 17:9 the world had rejected Jesus and therefore placed itself outside Christ's concern. Another possibility is that in the Upper Room Discourse Jesus was primarily concerned about the disciples and not, for the moment, about the world. A third alternative answer to this question is that even though Jesus' prayer in John 17 was not for the world, still he continued to love it. I believe the second and third options are closer to the truth than the first answer.

5. The present participle — "believing" (NIV, "will believe") — in v. 20 is prophetic; it refers to the future.

6. Though the Spirit is not explicitly mentioned, he is implied to be the means of the disciples' mystical union with the Father and Son.

C. The Rejection of Unity (vv. 25 – 26)

Jesus concluded his farewell prayer: while the disciples believe in Jesus' heavenly origin, the world does not (vv. 25 – 26). At first glance, this seems to contradict verses 21 and 23, but not really. Tragically, the world, though seeing Jesus' love and unity manifested in the disciples, chose not to believe in him (cf. 1:10 – 11).

CONCLUSION

We thus conclude Jesus' farewell prayer. As we have seen, this prayer is concerned with the glory of Jesus (vv. 1 – 5), the sanctity of the eleven disciples (vv. 6 – 19), and the unity of Jesus' future followers (vv. 20 – 26).

REVIEW QUESTIONS

1. In what ways does John 17 conclude Jesus' farewell speech that began in John 13?

2. What is the threefold outline of John 17?

3. What are the two themes of John 17:1 – 5?

4. What are the two key themes in John 17:6 – 19? How do these relate to the following phrases about the disciples of Jesus: "before the world," "in the world," and "not of the world"?

5. What three points about unity are made in John 17:20 – 26?

6. Please describe the spiritual union of God, Christ, and believers as John understood it.

KEY TERMS

farewell speech   sanctification/protection   spiritual union

CHAPTER 20

The Passion of Christ

JOHN 18:1–27

Objectives

After reading this chapter, you should be able to:

- Explain the intimate connection between John's passion narrative and the overall message of the fourth gospel.

- Identify Jesus' actions in the Garden of Gethsemane that indicate he was in control of his destiny.

- Discuss Peter's three denials of Jesus.

INTRODUCTION

John 18–19 records the passion narrative, which is divided into three parts: Jesus' arrest and interrogation by the high priest (18:1–27), Jesus' trial by Pilate (18:28–19:16a), and Jesus' crucifixion, death, and burial (19:16b–42). Before discussing these points over the next few chapters, however, we must make an introductory comment regarding the theology of John's passion narrative as a whole.

> John 18–19 records the passion narrative, which is divided into three parts: Jesus' arrest and interrogation by the high priest (18:1–27), Jesus' trial by Pilate (18:28–19:16a), and Jesus' crucifixion, death, and burial (19:16b–42).

While John agrees in general with the Synoptic Gospels' presentations of Jesus' passion, he omits some important details and adds others. And therein we arrive at the particular theological bent of John's passion narrative.

John's major omissions from the Synoptic picture are: (1) Judas's betrayal with a kiss, (2) Jesus' prayer in the Garden of Gethsemane, (3) the disciples' sleepiness, (4) the healing of the servant's ear, (5) Simon of Cyrene, (6) the mocking crowds, (7) Jesus' cry from the cross.

John's major additions to the Synoptic passion narrative include: (1) Roman soldiers falling to the ground in the arrest scene when Jesus identifies himself, (2) Jesus' conversation with Annas, (3) Jesus' conversation with Pilate, (4) John's emphasis on the inscription on the cross, (5) a full description of Jesus' garments, (6) Mary mother of Jesus given to the Beloved Disciple at the cross, (7) Jesus' body threatened with the breaking of his legs, (8) Jesus pierced with a soldier's lance, (9) Nicodemus's joining Joseph at Jesus' burial.

These omissions and additions convey three key Johannine theological items. First, in John's passion narrative Jesus is in complete control over his destiny, death included (see the seven omissions above, along with additions 1, 4, and 6). Second, Jesus' death is that foretold by the paschal lamb in the Old Testament (see additions 5, 7, 8, and 9). The discussion to follow on John 18–19 will fill out the details of these two theological items—Jesus was in control of his destiny, and he was the prophesied paschal lamb.

> In John's passion narrative Jesus is in complete control over his destiny.

The third theological message conveyed by John's passion narrative concerns "the Jews'" involvement in the interrogation of Jesus. Simply put, the Jewish authorities receive especially bad press in John's record of Jesus' trial (among other details, see additions 2 and 3 above).

While all four of the Gospels attest that the Sanhedrin broke Jewish jurisprudence in its handling of the interrogation of Jesus (see discussion below), John's statements against "the Jews" crescendo in his passion narrative, pointing a finger of blame at them some twenty-two times in chapters 18–19. This accent on the culpability of "the Jews" is in stark contrast to the positive treatment Pilate receives in those same chapters.

We turn now to a survey of John 18:1–27, which divides into two parts: the arrest of Jesus (vv. 1–12) and the interrogation of Jesus by the high priest (vv. 13–27).

Left: The Kidron Valley. *Right:* An olive grove in the Garden of Gethsemane.

I. THE ARREST OF JESUS (18:1–12)

John's record of the arrest of Jesus unfolds in three points: the setting (vv. 1–3), the authority of Jesus before the authorities (vv. 4–9), and Peter's response (vv. 10–12).

A. The Setting (vv. 1–3)

After Jesus finished the Upper Room Discourse, he and his disciples left Jerusalem to go to the Mount of Olives, passing via the Kidron Valley. The Kidron Valley is a wadi (a dry river bed that fills up during Israel's rainy season) that runs between the eastern side of Jerusalem and the western slopes of the Mount of Olives. Jesus probably did not want to stay in Jerusalem during the crowded conditions of Passover.

Because Passover observers were required to stay within Jerusalem's city district, however, Jesus could not lodge at Bethany (on the eastern side of the Mount of Olives), his customary stay-over place, because it was outside Jerusalem's city limits. The western slopes of the Mount of Olives were considered to be within the city's limits yet afforded secluded spots. That, plus the fact that Jesus had spent time before in the Garden of Gethsemane (see Matt. 26:36; Mark 14:32), made the Mount of Olives the logical place for his stay for the night. There in the Garden of Gethsemane (meaning "oil press"), Jesus and the disciples could sequester themselves and pray. But Judas, the betrayer (cf. 12:4; 13:2, 11, 21), knew the place and led both Roman soldiers and Jewish police there to apprehend Jesus. The detachment of Roman soldiers (*speira*) numbered between two hundred and six hundred soldiers and was led by a Roman tribune (*chiliarchos*, v. 12), along with the temple police of the Sanhedrin.

John is the only gospel writer who mentions the presence of the Roman soldiers. Truly the world (Roman and Jew) rejected Jesus

> The Jewish authorities receive especially bad press in John's record of Jesus' trial.

An olive press with a millstone in the center.

Left: Model of Roman soldier. A soldier's equipment included a crested helmet, breastplate, belt with short sword, shield, and lance. *Center:* Copy of Roman standards. The emblems of the Roman legions and their use in religious ceremonies were offensive to Jewish sensibilities about idolatry. *Right:* Tombstone of a centurion. Marcus Favonius Facilis was stationed in Britain in the mid-first century. Centurions, indicated by the stick and sword, were the backbone of the Roman army.

(1:10). The lanterns and torches attest to the time of the arrest—it was night. But they also convey a symbolic message—darkness was trying to overtake the light (John 1:5).

B. The Authority of Jesus before the Authorities (vv. 4–9)

Verses 4–9 reveal that the apprehension of Jesus was no ordinary arrest. Jesus took three actions that showed he was in control of the situation. First, knowing the divine time had arrived for his death, Jesus went out to meet the authorities—not the reverse (v. 4). He asked them who they were seeking, and they responded, "Jesus the Nazarean"[1] (NIV, "Jesus of Nazareth," v. 5). Second, Jesus responded, saying, "I am he" (the name of God—Yahweh, v. 5) which supernaturally knocked the authorities off their feet (vv. 6–7)! Third, Jesus protected his disciples from being arrested (vv. 8–9; cf. 17:12).[2]

> Jesus took three actions that showed he was in control of the situation.

C. Peter's Response (vv. 10–12)

In keeping with his impetuous character (see 13:6–11; 13:37–38), Peter tried to deliver Jesus from the authorities. His aim fared no better than his intentions, merely cutting off the earlobe of Malchus, the high priest's servant (vv. 10–11).

---

1. "Nazarean" may allude to the Hebrew word *nēser* in Isaiah 11:1, with reference to the coming messianic branch.
2. The implication is that Judas was not one of the chosen.

Jesus, however, prevented any more retaliation on the part of his disciples, commanding them to sheath their swords (Luke 22:38 says there were two of them). Resisting arrest was not what Jesus was called to do. Rather, it was time now for him to drink the cup of divine suffering (cf. Mark 14:36; John 12:27–28; Pss. 16:5; 60:3; Isa. 29:9–10; 51:17; Jer. 25:15–19a; et al.). Because of Peter's actions, the Roman and Jewish authorities bound Jesus and whisked him away to Annas (John 18:12–13).

> Upon his arrest, Jesus was immediately taken to Annas, the father-in-law of the high priest Caiaphas.

II. THE INTERROGATION OF JESUS BY THE HIGH PRIEST (18:13–27)

We may conveniently divide John 18:13–27 into two uneven parts: the setting (vv. 13–14) and the contrasting responses of Peter and Jesus (vv. 15–27).

A. The Setting (vv. 13–14)

Upon his arrest, Jesus was immediately taken to Annas, the father-in-law of the high priest Caiaphas. The former of these was appointed as high priest of Israel by the Roman prefect Quirinius in AD 6 and deposed by Valerius Gratus in 15 (so Josephus, *Ant.* 18.2.1/26; 18.2.2/34). But even after his removal from office, Annas remained powerful because his five sons became high priests (Josephus, *Ant.* 20.9.1/198). His family was known for its greed, wealth, and power. Besides John, only Luke mentions Annas (Luke 3:2; Acts 4:6). One gets the impression from John and Josephus that, though Annas was no longer the official high priest, he continued to rule that office behind the scenes.[3] To John alone we owe the details that Jesus appeared before Annas before being whisked away to Caiaphas and that the latter was son-in-law to Annas. The reader already met Caiaphas the official high priest in John 11:50, who unknowingly prophesied Jesus' upcoming vicarious death.

Artistic interpretation of the Jewish high priest.

B. The Contrasting Responses of Peter and Jesus (vv. 15–27)

Peter's three denials of Jesus (vv. 15–18; 25–27) frame Annas's interrogation of Jesus (vv. 19–24).

1. Peter's First Denial (vv. 15–18)

There is no contradiction between John 16:32, Jesus' prediction that his disciples would forsake him, and 18:15, Peter following Jesus to Annas's palace, because before the night was over, Peter had indeed forsaken Jesus by denying him three times.

---

3. Apparently, former high priests retained their titles as a courtesy; see Raymond E. Brown, *The Gospel according to John XIII–XXI*, Anchor Bible 29B (Garden City, N.Y.: Doubleday, 1970), 820. Also, Jews may have continued to recognize deposed high priests because the Old Testament declared they were appointed for life (Num. 35:25).

Possibly, the House of Caiaphas. *Top left:* The Church of St. Peter Gallicantu. *Top right:* A wealthy Herodian era home discovered in excavations of the Jewish quarter in Jerusalem. *Bottom right:* This area north of the Dormition Church on Mount Zion is a possible location for Caiaphas's home. This is a portico of an Armenian shrine under restoration.

The other disciple who accompanied Peter most likely was John. The two are often paired together in the fourth gospel (13:23–26; 20:2–10; 21:7, 20–23).

At John's request, a servant girl of Annas opened the gate for Peter to leave the courtyard and enter the palace proper.[4] At that time, the girl asked if Peter was a follower of Jesus, which Peter promptly denied. Apparently the girl knew that John was a disciple of Jesus and assumed the same for Peter. Peter's denial presumably permitted him to remain with Annas's attendants as they warmed themselves by the night fire (vv. 16–18).

2. Jesus' Interrogation (vv. 19–24)

In the meantime, inside the palace Annas interrogated Jesus, trying to elicit a confession of guilt from him (v. 19). Jesus, however, dodged Annas's question about the nature of his teaching by challenging the high priest himself to ask those many Jews who had heard Jesus teach often and publicly in the synagogues and in the temple precincts (vv. 20–21). In other words, Jesus was calling Annas's bluff: if this was an official trial, then let the high priest gather witnesses against Jesus or (implied) let him go. Jesus' response met with physical abuse at the hands of one of the temple police. Jesus, however, challenged the perpetra-

---

4. Annas is thought by some scholars to have lived in his own palace located on the southern part of the west hill of Jerusalem. Others think Annas lived in a different wing of the same palace shared by Caiaphas; see Brown, *Gospel according to John XIII–XXI*, 823.

The Ossuary of Caiaphas

In November 1990, while constructing a children's recreational water park in Jerusalem's Peace Park, workmen using bulldozers unearthed an ancient burial cave. When Israeli archaeologists arrived, they found a dozen ossuaries or bone burial boxes. The most elaborate ossuary had an exquisitely decorated façade featuring two large circles, each composed of five rosettes surrounding a center rosette. The sides and top were framed with stylized branches. On the back and on one side were slightly varied inscriptions that read, "Yehosef bar Qafa" ("Joseph son of Caiaphas"). Excavators discovered the bones of six different people inside the ossuary, which were determined to be the bones of two infants, a child between two and five years, a boy between thirteen and eighteen years, an adult woman, and a man about sixty years old. The remains of the man very well could be those of the high priest Caiaphas, who directed the Sanhedrin's trial of Jesus. The tomb therefore was determined to be the burial cave of Caiaphas's family or clan, typical of tombs that were reserved for temple aristocracy, landed gentry, and wealthy merchants. This is a remarkable find, because, as Jewish scholar David Flusser remarks, "Caiaphas is the most prominent Jewish personality of the Second Temple period whose ossuary and remains have been discovered."[1]

The Jews, for about a hundred years ending in AD 70, had developed a practice chiefly in Jerusalem of regathering from a burial chamber the bones of a decayed corpse and placing them with the bones of family members in a depository called an ossuary, a small, rectangular coffinlike box made of a single block of limestone (approximately two feet long, one foot wide, and a little more than one foot high). The ossuary lids varied, some flat, others triangular (gabled) or curved (vaulted). The ossuaries were often decorated with geometric designs, and many were inscribed with graffiti-like inscriptions to commemorate and preserve the deceased.

This discovery gives remarkable insight into burial practices of the Jewish aristocracy and offers an electrifying archaeological link to real-life persons involved in the events of Jesus' final days before going to the cross.

Ossuary of Caiaphas. © Dr. James C. Martin (bibleworldseminars@gmail.com). Collection of The Israel Museum, Jerusalem, and Courtesy of The Israel Antiquities Authority, Exhibited at The Israel Museum, Jerusalem.

---

1. David Flusser, *Jesus* (Jerusalem: The Magnes Press, 1997), 195. *Zondervan Illustrated Bible Backgrounds Commentary*: *Matthew, Mark, Luke* (Grand Rapids: Zondervan, 2002), 160.

tor to supply any evidence of falsehood on his part (vv. 22–23). Apparently neither Annas nor the temple police had any hard evidence against Jesus, so they sent him to Caiaphas, the official high priest; perhaps he would have better luck at convicting Jesus (v. 24).

3. Peter's Second and Third Denials (vv. 25–27)

In stark contrast to Jesus' courage under fire before Annas, Peter now cowered in fear as he denied two more times that he was a follower of Jesus. His second denial was in response to the insinuation by those also warming themselves by the fire that he was Jesus' follower. Peter's third denial came as a relative of Malchus recognized Peter as the one who cut off the ear of the high priest's servant! Upon Peter's final denial, the cock crowed.[5]

---

5. The cock crow occurs in Jerusalem between midnight and 3:00 a.m.

REVIEW QUESTIONS

1. Encapsulate the theology of John's passion narrative.

2. What actions of Jesus in the Garden of Gethsemane indicate he was in control of the situation, according to John 18:4–9?

3. Summarize Peter's three denials of Jesus as recorded in John 18:15–18, 25–27.

4. Who was Caiaphas, and what was his relationship to Annas?

KEY TERMS

Annas	Garden of Gethsemane	Peter's denials
Caiaphas	ossuary of Caiaphas	theology of John's passion
	passion narrative	

CHAPTER 21

Jesus before Pilate

JOHN 18:28–19:16A

Objectives

After reading this chapter, you should be able to:

- Summarize the seven episodes that unfold the relationship between Jesus and Pilate.

- Discuss the ironies of Jesus' trial before Pilate and the Jewish authorities.

- Summarize the three stages of Jesus' trial.

INTRODUCTION

The trial of Jesus before Pontius Pilate is recorded in John's gospel in 18:28 – 19:16a, which is my reason for treating chapters 18 and 19 together. As recent interpreters have pointed out, the Roman trial of Jesus unfolds in seven episodes that form a chiasm. Moreover, the episodes alternate between Pilate's movement inside and outside of the palace (praetorium):

Stanza A, 18:28 – 32 (outside Pilate's chamber)
It was early
Passover
Jewish leaders cannot put a man to death (lawfully)
The type of Jesus' death
A Jewish plea for Jesus' death

> **Stanza B, 18:33 – 38a (inside)**
> Pilate does not speak on his own accord
> Jesus' origins: not of this world
> Jesus is passive: he is not of this world

> > **Stanza C, 18:38b – 40 (outside)**
> > Pilate finds no crime in him
> > Pilate brings Jesus out: he *may* be set free

Stanza D, 19:1 – 3 (inside)
1 Jesus flogged
    2 Jesus crowned
        3 Jesus arrayed in a royal robe
    2' Jesus hailed as "king"
1' Jesus struck

> > **Stanza C', 19:4 – 8 (outside)**
> > Pilate finds no crime in Jesus
> > Pilate brings Jesus out: will he be set free?

> **Stanza B', 19:9 ~ 12a (inside)**
> Pilate's power is not his own
> "Where are you from?"
> Jesus is passive: Pilate's authority is from above

Stanza A', 19:12b – 16a (outside)
It was late (the sixth hour)
Passover
The Jewish crowds call for death
Crucifixion
The Jewish leaders obtain Jesus' death[1]

---

1. Except for some minor changes in verse divisions, I follow Gary M. Burge, whose outline is typical of that found in other commentaries on John; see his *John*, NIV Application Commentary (Grand Rapids: Zondervan, 2000), 488.

The impression that this increasingly frantic movement of Pilate back and forth, inside and outside, gives is that he, not Jesus, is on trial. Pilate is on trial for his response to Jesus Christ, the truth. Will he embrace it or not? We now survey these verses by proceeding through the above seven episodes.

The impression that this increasingly frantic movement of Pilate back and forth, inside and outside, gives is that he, not Jesus, is on trial.

I. EPISODE 1: OUTSIDE PILATE'S CHAMBER: JEWS DEMAND JESUS' DEATH (18:28–32)

John does not mention Jesus' nighttime and dawn sessions before Caiaphas and the Sanhedrin (the grand jury, so to speak) recorded in the Synoptics (Matt. 26:57, 59–68//Mark 14:53, 55–65; cf. Luke 22:54, 63–65).[2] But "the Jews" in John 18:28 may allude to the members of the Sanhedrin. The Jewish authorities (implied) and temple police took Jesus to the praetorium. The praetorium denoted the place of residence of the chief Roman official in subjugated territories. In Palestine the Roman governor's permanent residence was at Caesarea by the Mediterranean Sea (see Acts 23:33–35). But

during volatile times such as Passover, the Roman governor resided in Jerusalem. Many equate this residence with the fortress Antonia, a Hasmonean castle converted as a palace for Herod the Great (ca. 35 BC) and named after Mark Antony. It stood on the east hill just north of the temple precincts. The fortress's elevation over the temple mound afforded the Roman soldiers stationed there a clear view of the surroundings of the temple. In 1870 a pavement of massive stone slabs was discovered at the location of the now demolished Antonia fortress (The *Lithostrotos* or "Stone Pavement"). Supporters of this view argue that such a discovery fits well with John 19:13.

Jesus was taken to the praetorium at *prōi* (daybreak), the last division of the Roman reckoning of the night (coming after the "cock crow," which was between midnight and 3:00 a.m.; 18:28).

The Jews did not enter the praetorium for fear of becoming ritually unclean (v. 28). Such ritual impurity could have stemmed from the general Jewish belief that Gentiles were unclean before God (Acts 10:28). There is sadistic irony in verse 28: the Jewish authorities wanted to be

Caesarea, now seafront ruins, was constructed by Herod the Great. The city became the Roman center of administration in Palestine.

---

2. Luke records no night meeting of the Sanhedrin.

Model of the fortress of Antonia. The four towers mark the location of this palace on the northwest corner of the Temple Mount.

ritually pure so that they could celebrate Passover, while they were unjustly condemning Jesus.[3] The contrast between ritual purity and moral integrity couldn't be stronger.

The Lithostrotos — a Roman era pavement stone found near the location of the fortress where Jesus carried his cross. It now is in the monastery of the Sisters of Zion.

Jesus was brought before Pilate. Only Luke refers to him as Pontius Pilate (Luke 3:1; Acts 4:27; cf. Josephus [*Ant.* 18.2.2/35]). Pilate went outside the palace, apparently to the courtyard, to meet Jesus and the Jewish authorities. Because the authorities had just met as a grand jury, Pilate sought their verdict. The Jews' response was one of sarcasm. Verse 30 is a second-class conditional sentence, making a contrary-to-fact statement. Thus they said, "If Jesus were not guilty (and he is), we would not be handing him over to you (as we are)!" Sensing their insolence, Pilate curtly told them that they, then, should pass judgment on Jesus (v. 31). The Jews' retort — that they had no authority to execute a criminal — is corroborated by ancient testimony (so Josephus and Talmud).

---

3. See Raymond E. Brown, *The Gospel according to John XIII–XXI*, Anchor Bible 29B (Garden City, N.Y.: Doubleday, 1970), 846. For the second possibility, see Burge, *John*, 498n37. Incidentally, v. 28 mentions that the Jewish authorities were preparing to eat Passover, perhaps a further indication that the fourth evangelist does not equate Jesus' meal with the disciples in the upper room with the Passover seder. For John, Jesus' death is the true Passover to be celebrated. If those authorities included priests, then according to Numbers 9:6–12, the Passover would have to be delayed for seven days until the impurity was removed. This was so because the priests took part in slaying the Passover lambs.

Our author recognizes the hand of God in all of this: the fact that Jews could not execute criminals meant that Jesus would be dealt with the Roman way—by crucifixion: lifting him up on a cross by which he would draw all people unto himself, just as Jesus predicted (cf. v. 32 with 12:32, 33).[4]

II. EPISODE 2: INSIDE PILATE'S CHAMBER: PILATE QUESTIONS JESUS ABOUT KINGSHIP (18:33–38A)

With John's second episode, Pilate the judge began to be judged; he was being placed on trial before Jesus the Truth. One senses from Pilate's uneasy movement (outside, now inside, then back and forth) that he was losing control of the situation.

All four Gospels record Pilate's question to Jesus, "Are you the king of the Jews?" (v. 33). The title "The King of the Jews" goes back perhaps to the Hasmonean priest kings, the last independent rulers of Judea before Rome's takeover of that province. So it is clear that Pilate's interest in Jesus was born out of political concern: have the Jews made Jesus their king in an attempt to rebel against Rome? We know from the fourth gospel that the Jewish authorities tried to allay any such fear on the part of the Roman officials (see 11:47–53). But we also know that the Jewish authorities were mainly motivated to prove Jesus to be a blasphemer (19:7; cf. 10:36; 16:2; cf. Mark 14:64//Matt. 26:65). Either way, in their eyes—insurrectionist or blasphemer—Jesus should be executed!

John's record of Jesus' reply to Pilate (vv. 34–38) is more developed than the Synoptics'. They have Jesus respond to Pilate's question ("Are you the king of the Jews?") by simply saying to Pilate, "Yes, it is as you say" (Matt. 27:11//Mark 15:2//Luke 23:3). In John, Jesus placed Pilate on the defensive by asking him whose idea that title was—his or the Jews? (v. 34) Pilate winced at the thought that he could be associated with Jews (v. 35).[5] Jesus proceeded to answer the question. No, he was not a rival political king to Caesar. If he were, his servants (angels?) would conquer all would-be opponents (v. 36a). But, yes, Jesus did have a kingdom, the kingdom of God, one that is spiritual in nature and not of this world (vv. 36b–37). This kingdom is a kingdom of truth (v. 37). Pilate's rather sarcastic response, "What is truth?" indicated his skepticism for matters religious and philosophical and began to tip his hand regarding his decision about Jesus.[6]

---

4. Brown's comments about Jews' view of crucifixion is helpful: "Incidents where crucifixion was practiced were looked on with horror, for instance, when Alexander Jannaeus crucified the Pharisees (Josephus, *War* I.iv.6;#97; 4QpNahum 1:7). In Jewish eyes the execution of Jesus on a cross would bring him into disrepute. It was considered the same as hanging (Acts v 30; x 39), and Deut xxi 23 enunciates the principle: 'A hanged man is accursed by God' (see Gal iii 13). As for how the Sanhedrin itself would have executed Jesus, we are not totally certain of what the Sadducees would have regarded as acceptable forms of capital punishment. Of the four forms mentioned in the later Pharisaic law (Mishnah, *Sanhedrin* 7:1), namely, stoning, burning, beheading, and strangling, the first three were recognized in the OT and should have been acceptable to the Sadducees (see note on viii 5). In the Gospels the most common Jewish charge against Jesus is blasphemy, for which execution by stoning is the penalty specified in the OT (Lev xxiv 16), in the NT (John x 33; Acts vii 57–58), and in the Mishnah (*Sanhedrin* 7:4, 9:3)."
5. Pilate's patron back in Rome was Aelius Sejanus, who was avowedly anti-Semitic; this perspective may have rubbed off on Pilate.
6. The reader will find Andreas J. Köstenberger's article on this topic helpful. See his "'What Is Truth?' Pilate's Question in Its Johannine and Larger Biblical Context," in *Whatever Happened to Truth?* ed. Andreas J. Köstenberger (Wheaton: Crossway, 2005), 19–51.

Although a somewhat positive picture of Pilate evolves in the Gospels (especially in John), in sources outside of the New Testament the portrait of that Roman governor does not fare well. Pilate was of equestrian rank, that is, lower nobility, as contrasted with Roman senatorial rank. He ruled Judea from AD 26 to 36. Before Emperor Claudius (AD 41–54), the title given to governors of lesser provinces like Judea was "prefect." This is confirmed by the discovery in 1961 at Caesarea of Pilate's Inscription, which uses that term for him. After Claudius, the title was changed to "procurator."[1]

Pilate, the governor (AD 26–36), and the Pontius Pilate Inscription.

Philo accused Pilate of robbery, murder, and inhumanity (*Ad Gaium* 38/302). Even the first-century Roman historian Tacitus acknowledged that "Christ had been executed in Tiberius's reign by the procurator of Judea, Pontius Pilate" (*Ann.* 15.50.44). Moreover, Josephus rehearsed Pilate's failed relationships with the Jews (*Ant.* 18.3.55–62; 4.85–89).

1. So according to A. H. M. Jones, "Procurators and Prefects in the Early Principate," in his *Studies in Roman Government and Law* (Oxford: Oxford University Press, 1960), 115–25.

III. EPISODE 3: OUTSIDE: PILATE FINDS JESUS INNOCENT (18:38B–40)

Pilate went back outside to face the Jewish authorities. For the first of three times, the Roman prefect declared Jesus' innocence (cf. 38b with 19:4, 6).

> Pilate went back outside to face the Jewish authorities. For the first of three times, the Roman prefect declared Jesus' innocence.

Pilate hoped to solve the problem at hand by offering to release Jesus as a courtesy of the Roman Passover amnesty provision by which one Jewish prisoner was released during the festival. While we have no extrabiblical record of such a practice, two of the Synoptics also mention the custom (Matt. 27:15; Mark 15:8). The Jewish authorities shocked Pilate by rejecting Jesus and calling for the release of Barabbas, a revolutionary (v. 40).[7]

Episode 3 is filled with irony. (1) Pilate mockingly called Jesus "the king of the Jews," when in fact he was. (2) The Jewish authorities, who earlier had decided to kill Jesus because they feared he would stir up rebellion among the Jews, thus bringing down upon them the wrath of Rome (11:48–51), now demanded the release of Barabbas the revolutionary. (3) Barabbas — "son of the Father" — was a mockery of the true "son" of the Father — Jesus (18:40; cf. Mark 14:36).

IV. EPISODE 4: INSIDE: PILATE HAS JESUS FLOGGED (19:1–3)

Roman law allowed three types of flogging, which increased in order of severity: *fustigatio*, *flagellatio*, *and verberatio*. Jesus seems to have been exposed to the last-mentioned form,

7. "Bandit" (*lēstis*) is used by Josephus to describe the revolutionary bandits who kept ancient Israel in constant insurrection (*J.W.* 2.13.2–3/253–54); cf. Josephus's similar description of the Zealots (*J.W.* 2.21.1/585).

which involved the ripping to shreds of the person's flesh by pieces of bone and metal attached to two or three leather thongs and administered by professional soldiers. As the next episode makes clear, sadistic as it was, Pilate's treatment of Jesus was born out of concern for his innocence. The governor hoped his reducing of Jesus to shredded flesh and bones might arouse pity for him among the Jews. But Pilate's plan failed.

V. EPISODE 5: OUTSIDE: PILATE FINDS JESUS INNOCENT AGAIN AND AGAIN (19:4−8)

Pilate escorted Jesus outside to face the Jewish authorities, declaring Jesus' innocence for a second time. Pilate then paraded Jesus, freshly flogged, before the audience. Pilate's address to the audience, *"Ecce homo!"* ("Behold the man!") was designed to show how humiliated Jesus now was—not a regal dignity but a broken and defeated man.[8] Nevertheless, the beating evoked no pity from the crowd. Jesus' scourging only egged the Jewish leaders on to demand his crucifixion. Pilate's third declaration that Jesus was innocent fell on deaf ears (v. 6). The Jewish authorities insisted that Jesus be executed for blasphemy, as the Old Testament prescribed (cf. Lev. 24:16 with Matt. 26:63−64; Mark 14:61−64; John 19:7). Now Pilate was really unnerved. To let Jesus go would mean he would be breaking Jewish law.

VI. EPISODE 6: INSIDE: PILATE FURTHER INTERROGATES JESUS (19:9−12A)

In episode 6 Pilate demonstrated his ineptness at understanding spiritual matters. Three such spiritual deficiencies can be detected in John 19:9−11. First, after Pilate returned to his chamber, he asked Jesus where he was from (vv. 9−10). Pilate's question had to do with Jesus' geographical origin. In Luke 23:6−7 Pilate learned at this point that Jesus was from Galilee, and so he sent him to Herod Antipas, the Jewish tetrarch of Galilee. But in the fourth gospel, Pilate's question failed to take into account Jesus' earlier answer—that his kingdom was not of this world (18:36−37).

Second, Jesus' silence prompted Pilate to warn the bleeding man that, as governor, he had the authority to free or crucify Jesus (vv. 9b−10). Jesus, however, informed Pilate that his authority was merely derivative—it came from God (v. 11a). Pilate was only carrying out the divine will in executing Jesus. Jesus' next comment—"the one who handed me over to you is guilty of the greater sin" (v. 11b)—does not let Pilate off the hook morally. Pilate was still responsible for his part in the unjust trial of Jesus. But the Jewish authorities (Caiaphas, Annas, Judas, et al.) would receive the greater condemnation for rejecting their own Messiah.

Third, hearing all of this, Pilate kept trying to free Jesus (v. 12a). The imperfect, *ezētei* ("kept seeking"), suggests Pilate was frantically trying to find a way to release Jesus. But, again, Pilate misperceived the situation spiritually: no matter what he did, he could not free Jesus, because Jesus' divine destiny was to be enthroned on the cross.

---

8. In Jerusalem the *Ecce Homo* Convent (the Convent of the Sisters of Zion) is located in the remains of the Antonia Fortress, the traditional location of these events. The *Ecce Homo* Arch attached to it (which crosses the *Via Dolorosa*) belongs to the later period of Hadrian.

VII. EPISODE 7: OUTSIDE: PILATE DELIVERS JESUS TO CRUCIFIXION (19:12B–16)

Pilate's repeated attempts to deliver Jesus came to a crashing halt with the Jews' threat, "If you let this man go, you are no friend of Caesar. Anyone who claims to be a king opposes Caesar" (v. 12b). "Friend of Caesar" was an official title (Lat., *amicus Caesaris*) bestowed on select persons, such as senators, who showed their loyalty to the emperor.[9] Conversely, Roman emperors were noted for eliminating those who fell out of their favor (so according to the Roman historian Seutonius [*Lives of the Caesars*, 3.58]).[10] This threat, along with Pilate's storied failed relationships with Palestinian Jews (not to mention, Emperor Tiberius's earlier warning to Pilate about his mishandling of Rome's affairs with Jews), caused the Roman prefect to bow to the crowd's pressure (v. 13). Pilate returned to the porch outside with Jesus, where he occupied the governor's judgment seat (*bema*; cf. Acts 25:6; 17; Rom. 14:10; 2 Cor. 5:10) and prepared to render an official decision.[11]

> Pilate's repeated attempts to deliver Jesus came to a crashing halt with the Jews' threat, "If you let this man go, you are no friend of Caesar..." (v. 12b).

John added a footnote at this point as he mentioned that the *bema* was located at the place called "the stone pavement" (Gk., *Lithostrotos*) and added the Hebrew (Aramaic) note that it was called the "*Gabbatha*" (which probably meant "platform" or "high place"; v. 13).[12]

Two details in verse 14 likely reflect John's theological bent, namely, Jesus is the Passover Lamb. Thus the meal Jesus celebrated the night before was not the Passover seder (it was the preparation of the Passover, v. 14), and the hour of Jesus' crucifixion was not at 9:00 a.m. (so Mark 15:25//) but noon — the hour of the slaying of the Passover Lamb (Mark 15:33; Matt. 27:45; Luke 23:44).[13]

---

9. Conclusively proven by E. Bammel, "φίλος του Καίσαρος (John 19:12)," *Theologische Literaturzeitung* 77 (1952): 205–20.

10. The late first-century Roman historian Suetonius tells of one C. Cornelius Gallus who lost favor with Emperor Augustus and consequently was banished from the imperial provinces. He committed suicide (*Lives of the Caesars* 12:66). A similar fate befell the aforementioned Sejanus, once considered a friend of Caesar Tiberius. He, along with many of his friends, were executed. This took place in AD 31 and may have overlapped with Pilate's trial of Jesus. If so, Caiaphas's remark about not being a friend of Caesar would have struck a note of terror in Pilate's heart (see Burge, *John*, 506nn53, 54).

11. Some have translated the verb in v. 13 — *ekathisin* — as transitive; that is, Pilate caused Jesus to sit down. If so, then Pilate's gesture would have been a further act of scorn heaped on Jesus — he was seated on Pilate's bema in mockery. However, the verb can also be translated as intransitive, requiring no complement: Pilate sat down on the bema. This usage is attested in Josephus, interestingly enough, who uses the same syntax of Pilate sitting on his tribunal (*J.W.* 2.9.3/172). Moreover, Pilate's frantic attempt to free Jesus does not square with such a nonchalant response on his part.

12. This "stone pavement" is today claimed to be uncovered in the Convent of the Sisters of Zion on Jerusalem's *Via Dolorosa* and is a valued traditional site to pilgrims. This pavement at the convent is within the ruins of the Antonia Fortress. Josephus describes an outdoor judgment seat for the governor Florus in *J.W.* 2.14.8/30.

13. For a different view, see Burge, *John*, 507–8, following D. A. Carson, *The Gospel according to John: An Introduction and Commentary*, Pillar New Testament Commentary (Grand Rapids: Eerdmans, 1991), 603–4, who argues that John intended to say that Jesus celebrated a Passover meal.

Verses 14b–16 end episode 7 on a pathetic note of irony: the Jewish authorities rejected Jesus, the true King of the Jews—and the world—while they embraced the Roman caesar as their king.[14]

Pilate, then, handed Jesus over to be crucified.

CONCLUSION

I conclude my discussion of John 18:28–19:16a by calling attention to two points: the historical reconstruction of the trial of Jesus and its legal implications.

A. A Historical Reconstruction of the Trial of Jesus

There has been much debate among gospel scholars about how the trial(s) of Jesus actually unfolded.[15] John's gospel is unique in two

> The Jewish authorities rejected Jesus, the true King of the Jews—and the world—while they embraced the Roman caesar as their king.

respects regarding Jesus' appearance before the Jewish authorities. First, unlike the Synoptics, John records Annas's interrogation of Jesus (18:13–15, 19–24). Second, John does not record Jesus' interrogation before the Sanhedrin and Caiaphas, the official high priest (Matt. 26:57, 59–68; Mark 14:53, 55–65; Luke 22:54, 63–65). But John's mention in passing that Jesus appeared before Caiaphas (18:24, 28) no doubt presumes such a meeting.

Pulling together the four Gospels, then, the following three stage historical reconstruction seems to explain Jesus' trial before the Jewish authorities and Pilate:

1. Arrest and Interrogation by Annas

The arrest and interrogation of Jesus by Annas may well have been instigated by Pilate, who may have grown suspicious of Jesus' activity. The Jewish leaders helped that suspicion along by casting Jesus as an insurrectionist.

2. Grand Jury by Caiaphas and the Sanhedrin

Jesus' appearance before the official high priest and the Sanhedrin was probably more of a grand jury investigation rather than an actual trial.[16] Here the purpose was to inquire if there was enough evidence against Jesus to warrant placing him on trial before Pilate. The Sanhedrin indicted Jesus on two counts: he was a blasphemer and he was a political revolutionary. The latter accusation was what most concerned Pilate.

3. Trial before Pilate

Jesus was officially placed on trial before Pilate, being accused of insurrection. Though Pilate determined this allegation to be false, he nevertheless handed Jesus over to execution by crucifixion.

---

14. It was an Old Testament axiom that God alone is King over Israel (see 1 Sam. 8:7).

15. Brown's discussion and historical reconstruction of the trial of Jesus is superb, *Gospel according to John XIII–XXI*, 829–30. For his more detailed treatment of the death of Jesus, see Raymond E. Brown, *The Death of the Messiah—from Gethsemane to Grave: A Commentary on the Passion Narratives in the Four Gospels*, 2 vols. (New York: Doubleday, 1994).

16. Traditionally, Jesus' appearances before the authorities have been divided into two separate trials: one before the Jews (Annas, Caiaphas, the Sanhedrin, Herod Antipas) and another before the Roman authorities (Pilate).

Therefore we can say that the ancient Jewish authorities were involved in arresting, interrogating, and indicting Jesus. They comprised the grand jury. Then the Romans carried out the "legal" formalities. Yet the modern reader must be careful not to generalize from this information that Jews beyond Jesus' day are culpable for the injustice perpetrated against him. Not to recognize this would be anti-Semitic.

B. The Legal Implications of Jesus' Trial

Based on later Jewish law, several aspects of the legal proceedings surrounding Jesus' trial would have been considered unjust.[17] At Jesus' interrogation before Annas, (1) Annas tried to coerce a confession from him. Such self-incrimination was wrong then in Jewish culture and now in Western jurisprudence. (2) Furthermore, the temple police physically abused Jesus in trying to extract a confession from him. (3) At the grand jury before the Sanhedrin, the witnesses called to testify against Jesus were inconsistent to the point of canceling each other out. (4) And at the trial before Pilate, Jesus was crucified even though the Roman prefect found him to be innocent. The last-mentioned item was obviously a breech of Roman jurisprudence.

The ultimate irony of Pilate's decision to protect his own "skin" was that in AD 36 Caesar removed Pilate from office in Palestine anyway, banishing him for poor conduct relative to the Jews. Rather than go with his conscience and let Jesus go free, Pilate's condemnation of an innocent man eventually came back to haunt him.

---

17. Keener offers a sound discussion of the relation of later Mishnaic law to the Jewish jurisprudence followed at Jesus' interrogation. Craig S. Keener, *The Gospel of John: A Commentary*, vol. 1 (Peabody, Mass.: Hendrickson, 2003), 1086–87. The pertinent Mishnaic passages are *m. Sanhedrin* 4:1; 5:1–4; 7:5; 11:2.

QUESTIONS

1. Can you summarize the seven episodes that unfold between Jesus and Pilate in John 18:28–19:6a?

2. What is the overall impression one gets from these episodes?

3. Where was Jesus' trial before Pilate?

4. What was the irony about the Jewish leadership's concern not to be ritually tainted, according to John 18:28?

5. Describe the irony of John 18:38b–40.

6. Discuss Barabbas's relationship with the Jewish revolutionaries of the first century.

7. What did Pilate hope flogging Jesus would accomplish (John 19:1–3)?

8. What were the likely three stages of Jesus' trial?

Antonia fortress

arrest/interrogation

Barabbas

blasphemer

capital punishment

grand jury

insurrectionist

Lithostrotos/Stone Pavement

Pilate

Praetorium

prefect/procurator

trial of Jesus

CHAPTER 22

The Crucifixion of Christ

JOHN 19:16B–42

Objectives

After reading this chapter, you should be able to:

- Explain the significance of the title on Jesus' cross.
- Identify what Old Testament prophecies were fulfilled by Jesus' crucifixion.
- Describe the difference between Joseph of Arimathea and Nicodemus as compared with Pilate.

INTRODUCTION

John 19:16b–42 records the crucifixion of Christ. As Raymond Brown demonstrates, the narrative unfolds in seven episodes: Jesus' crucifixion (vv. 16b–18); Jesus' inscription (vv. 19–22); Jesus' clothes (vv. 23–24); Jesus' mother and the Beloved Disciple (vv. 25–27); Jesus' death (vv. 28–30); Jesus' blood and water (vv. 31–37); Jesus' burial (vv. 38–42).[1]

After summarizing each of these episodes, I will offer two concluding remarks on verses 16b–42.

> Jesus carried the crossbeam, or *patibulum*, without help from others.

I. EPISODE 1: JESUS' CRUCIFIXION (19:16B–18)

The Roman soldiers escorted Jesus to the place of his execution. Jesus carried the crossbeam, or *patibulum*, without help from others, though the Synoptics record that Simon of Cyrene was enlisted by the soldiers to help Jesus with his load (Matt. 27:32; Mark 15:21; Luke 23:26).

There may be a theological reason for John's omission of that detail (see below in my concluding remarks). Jesus was taken outside the city limits of Jerusalem to be crucified

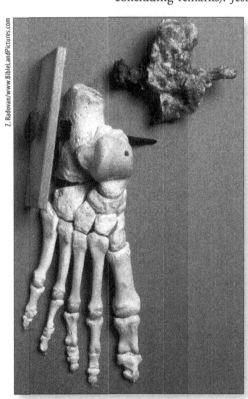

The heel bone of a man crucified with an iron nail that pierced the bone and fastened him to the wood. The bone was found in an ossuary (burial box) in a Jerusalem tomb.

at a place called the "skull" (Aram., Golgotha; Lat., Calvary). The name of the site probably stemmed from its topological formation, namely, that it was a hill that resembled a skull, perhaps an abandoned quarry where manmade caverns were used for burial and that was visible to all passersby. The two others crucified with Jesus are only mentioned in passing by the fourth evangelist. Matthew 27:38 and Mark 15:27 (cf. 15:7) refer to these two individuals as *lēstai* (revolutionary bandits). Luke 23:39–43 tells of one of these men's conversion to Christ.

II. EPISODE 2: JESUS' INSCRIPTION (19:19–22)

Criminals executed by Rome were required to carry a placard called a *titulus* around their necks on the way to being crucified, listing their names and crimes. Even though the Jewish authorities protested Jesus being called "the King of the Jews," Pilate mustered up the courage to let stand what he had handwritten. Posting the titulus in the three spoken languages of Israel—Hebrew, Latin, and Greek—afforded all observers, Jews and Gentiles alike, the opportunity to read the sign. This was the beginning of the fulfillment of John 12:32: "I, when I am lifted up from the earth, will draw all men to myself." Pilate was unwittingly God's instrument for accomplishing that prophecy. Moreover, John intends the reader to understand by this that Jesus' death on the cross was his enthronement as the true King of the Jews—and Gentiles.

---

1. Raymond E. Brown, *The Gospel according to John XIII–XXI*, Anchor Bible 29B (Garden City, N.Y.: Doubleday, 1970), 911. See his extended treatment, pp. 911–31.

III. EPISODE 3: JESUS' CLOTHES (19:23–24)

Confiscation of goods was a common penalty accompanying execution or other sentences of judgment. Jesus probably only owned the clothes on his body, which the (four?) soldiers removed and divided among themselves. They then gambled over who would get Jesus' loincloth, his undergarment. The Romans crucified their victims naked, though sometimes due to Jewish sensitivities, they left the undergarment on the criminal.[2] Apparently that was not the case for Jesus.

> Criminals executed by Rome were required to carry a placard called a *titulus* around their necks on the way to being crucified, listing their names and crimes.

Two points emerge from verses 23–24. First, the casting of lots for Jesus' loincloth fulfilled Psalm 22:18. Fulfillment of Old Testament Scripture played an important theological role in Jesus' crucifixion, as we will see later. Second, the fact that Jesus' loincloth was seamless indicates that he was the true High Priest (see Ex. 28:4; Lev. 16:4; cf. Josephus, *Ant.* 3.8.4/161). As such, Jesus was both priest and sacrifice. He was thus both Israel's rightful King (John 19:19–22) and faithful High Priest (vv. 23–24).

IV. EPISODE 4: JESUS' MOTHER AND THE BELOVED DISCIPLE (19:25–27)

Probably verse 25 enumerates four women who witnessed Jesus' crucifixion firsthand. Mary, Jesus' mother, receives the main attention, but it is interesting that her sister is also mentioned. Brown makes a good case for equating her with Salome, the mother of James and John, the sons of Zebedee (Matt. 27:56). This would make Jesus and John, the Beloved Disciple, cousins.[3] And that in turn makes sense of why Jesus commissioned John to care for Jesus' mother after his death (John 19:26–27), though there is more to the story than that, as you will see in my concluding remarks. We don't know anything about Mary of Clopas, but Mary of Magdala (a village north of Tiberius on the west side of the Sea of Galilee) was a cured demoniac who followed Jesus (Mark 16:9; Luke 8:2). The Beloved Disciple, as I argued earlier, was John.

> Confiscation of goods was a common penalty accompanying execution or other sentences of judgment.

V. EPISODE 5: JESUS' DEATH (19:28–30)

The Old Testament enters into the picture again in verses 28–30, once explicitly invoked and twice alluded to. First, Jesus said, "I am thirsty," with reference to Psalm 22:15 (John 19:28). Second, the soldiers used a hyssop plant with a wet sponge attached to it to give Jesus watered-down wine to drink (vv. 29–30a).[4] Surely this action recalled the ancient Israelites spreading the blood of the Passover lamb on the lintels and doorposts of their homes by means of the hyssop

---

2. Craig S. Keener makes this point in his *The Gospel of John: A Commentary*, vol. 1 (Peabody, Mass.: Hendrickson, 2003), 1138.

3. Brown, *Gospel according to John XIII–XXI*, 906; and more extensively, idem, *The Death of the Messiah — from Gethsemane to Grave: A Commentary on the Passion Narratives in the Four Gospels* (New York: Doubleday, 1994), 2:1013–26.

4. This offer of drink seems to be different from the offer of a narcotic/anesthetic recorded in Mark 15:23.

plant (Ex. 12:22). These two Old Testament passages—Psalm 22:15 and Exodus 12:22—portray Jesus as the Suffering Servant, the paschal lamb whose death delivers the people of God.

Third, Jesus, in complete control of his destiny, chose to give up his spirit in death (v. 30). This may be an allusion to the coming of the Paraclete upon Jesus' death. As such, it harks back to the Old Testament promise of the new covenant and the sending of the Spirit to indwell believers (Ezek. 36:25–28).

VI. EPISODE 6: JESUS' BLOOD AND WATER (19:31–37)

The Jewish authorities, with hypocritical piety, requested that Pilate have the three victims' legs broken to hasten death, so that the soon-approaching Sabbath would not be spiritually polluted (v. 31). Going back to Deuteronomy 21:22–23, Jewish custom forbade that hanged criminals remain overnight on a tree. The Jews' piety was contradicted by their execution of a just man.

Because death by crucifixion could extend over a period of days, Roman soldiers, using a heavy mallet, broke the criminals' legs to hasten asphyxiation and cause profuse bleeding. The bones of a first-century crucified Jew discovered in Israel in 1968 attest to this practice. The Romans applied this procedure to the two thieves but found Jesus to already be dead. Therefore they did not break his bones. This was in compliance with Exodus 12:46, which proscribed the breaking of any bones of the Passover lamb (vv. 32–36).

John 19:37 furthers the description, equating Jesus' death with the piercing of the messianic Shepherd as prophesied in Zechariah 12:10. The atoning nature of Jesus' death is made clear in all of this: he was the Passover Lamb/messianic Shepherd who embraced the covenant curses.

John 19:34–35 is not so clear, however, in its meaning. To what do the "blood and water" that flowed from Jesus' side refer? Several possibilities emerge, none of which are mutually exclusive. First, the "blood and water" could be the fulfillment of John 7:38–39, where Jesus promised that from his body would flow the water of the Spirit. In other words, Jesus' death (blood) was the means for dispensing the Holy Spirit to his followers (water). This is the language of the new covenant.[5]

Second, the "blood and water," as in 1 John 5:6, may be a polemic against the Docetic secessionists from John's community. Those people taught that the divine Spirit came upon the man Jesus at his baptism but left him before his death on the cross. John, then, would be refuting such a notion in John 19:34–35: Jesus was God both in his baptism (water) and at his death (blood). This view would be strengthened if John knew the Gnostic claim that Simon of Cyrene secretly took Jesus' place on the cross, leaving the latter to escape death

---

5. Verse 34 may be informed by a particular Passover practice—to make sure the paschal lamb was not already dead, the temple authorities watched for the strong flow of blood that would spurt forth when the lamb's throat was cut. J. Massyngberde Ford has convincingly applied this practice to v. 34's statement that "immediately" blood and water flowed forth from Christ's body, mingled with blood from his side (John xix. 34). "'Mingled Blood' from the Side of Christ," *NTS* 15, no. 3 (1968–69): 337–38.

Top: A courtyard by the entrance of the Church of the Holy Sepulchre. Ancient tradition associates the location of this church with both the crucifixion and burial of Jesus. *Below right:* Chamber inside the Church of the Holy Sepulchre.

(see Irenaeus, *Haer.* 3.22.2; 4.33.2). This would explain why John does not mention Simon; John wants to avoid any such connotation.

Third, "blood and water" could also be an allusion to the sacraments of the Eucharist (blood) and baptism (water). In light of John 6, such a theory is not out of the question.[6]

John, the Beloved Disciple, was an eyewitness of the flowing blood and water from Jesus' side, attesting to his death (v. 35).

VII. EPISODE 7: JESUS' BURIAL (19:38–42)

Upon Jesus' death, Joseph of Arimathea and Nicodemus went public with their faith in Jesus by requesting of Pilate that they be allowed to bury Jesus. Receiving permission to do so, they anointed Jesus' body with perfumes befitting a kingly burial (vv. 38–39). Then they wrapped Jesus' body with cloth and placed it in Joseph's new tomb (vv. 40–42). Many today believe the Shroud of Turin is the very grave cloth that covered Jesus before his res-

---

6. For discussion of the possible medical interpretations of the blood and water flowing from Jesus' side, see Gary M. Burge's treatment in *John*, NIV Application Commentary (Grand Rapids: Zondervan, 2000), 531–32. The theories have ranged from Jesus dying of a broken heart to the spear penetrating Jesus' heart and producing blood with water coming from the pericardial sac, to the trauma of the flogging causing the buildup of fluid between the body lining and the lung.

urrection, though this is difficult to confirm. Note the irony of the situation: Joseph and Nicodemus, in effect, declared their allegiance to Jesus before Pilate, who had cowered in his decision about Jesus for fear of the Jews.

> Upon Jesus' death, Joseph of Arimathea and Nicodemus went public with their faith in Jesus by requesting of Pilate that they be allowed to bury Jesus.

CONCLUSION

I conclude my discussion of John 19:16b–42 by making two extended comments on its polemical perspective and theological message.

First, John 19:16b–42 seems to be taking aim at two opponents of the Johannine community: Docetism and Judaism.

John's Docetic opponents argued that God was not truly incarnate in the man Jesus. First John obviously counters such a position, claiming that the man Jesus was the Christ all the way from baptism to the cross and beyond (recall 1 John 5:6). We saw above that John 19:34–35 shares in that same anti-Docetic sentiment. Possibly, we are also to understand John's omission of the detail about Simon the Cyrene in the same light. This anti-Docetic background, I suggest, also informs John 19:26–27. Without detracting in any way from the literal reading of that text—John, the Beloved Disciple, was charged with the care of Jesus' mother—we may also discern symbolism at work therein. As has long been argued, the Beloved Disciple and Mary represent more than individuals; they represent entities. John stands for the Christian in general, while Mary embodies the church.[7] And in the two, we have the symbol of the beloved community.[8] More specifi-

> John 19:16b–42 seems to be taking aim at two opponents of the Johannine community: Docetism and Judaism.

cally, John 19:26–27 seems to imply that true Christianity—the Christian and the church—will be continued through John's community, not by the Docetic, Gnostic community of the late first century and second centuries AD.[9]

John 19:16b–42 also takes on ancient Judaism, especially its rejection of the suffering Messiah. The death of Jesus the Messiah on a cross scandalized Judaism of the first and second centuries. John 19:16b–42 answers that objection: Jesus was ordained of God to be the Suffering Servant whose sacrificial death, like the Passover lamb, atoned for sin. Recall the Old Testament underpinning of this section in John:

---

7. See Brown's discussion in *Gospel according to John XIII–XXI*, 922–27. If it be objected that this is too allegorical a reading of this passage, one could respond that since the miracles in John are signs—literal events that point to a deeper reality—why cannot some of the narrative in the fourth gospel be understood in a similar light?

8. The term recalls Raymond Brown's book on the Johannine church, *The Community of the Beloved Disciple: The Life, Loves and Hates of an Individual Church in New Testament Times* (New York: Paulist, 1978).

9. It is no doubt the case that Jesus did not commit the care of his mother to his natural brothers because they were not believers in him; and obviously they were not at the cross.

Old Testament	John 19:16b – 42
Psalm 22:18	v. 24
Psalm 22:15	v. 28
Exodus 12:22	vv. 29 – 30
Isaiah 53:12	v. 30
Deuteronomy 21:22 – 23	v. 31
Ezekiel 36:26 – 27/Zechariah 12:10	vv. 34 – 35
Exodus 12:46	v. 36

This theme of Jesus as the Lamb of God who takes away the sin of the world forms an inclusio with John 1:29 and thus governs the whole perspective of the fourth gospel.

Second, the theological message of John 19:16b – 42 is that Jesus was in control of his destiny. We saw this earlier in the garden at Jesus' arrest when his "I am he" leveled the Roman soldiers. Jesus' control over his destiny surfaced again in his trial before Pilate, where the roles of accuser and judge were reversed. We see that theme also in John 19:16b – 18, where Jesus carried his cross alone, without the help of Simon of Cyrene, and again in verses 29 – 30 where Jesus himself gave up his Spirit to death. This, along with the Old Testament underpinning of his crucifixion, indicates that Jesus' death was not an accident but, rather, was divinely planned.

> The theological message of John 19:16b – 42 is that Jesus was in control of his destiny.

REVIEW QUESTIONS

1. How was Pilate's title for Jesus' death a fulfillment of prophecy (John 19:19 – 21)?

2. Explain the Old Testament underpinnings of Jesus' crucifixion.

3. What is the meaning of John 19:34 – 35, which refers to the flow of "blood and water" from Jesus' side?

4. How did Joseph and Nicodemus differ from Pilate in their relationship to Jesus (John 19:38 – 41)?

5. What two groups do John 19:16b – 42 take aim at?

KEY TERMS

blood and water	Joseph of Arimathea	Pilate
docetism	Judaism	Simon of Cyrene
Golgotha/Calvary	Nicodemus	*titulus*

CHAPTER 23

The Resurrection of Jesus Christ

JOHN 20

Objectives

After reading this chapter, you should be able to:

- Discuss the three actions Jesus performed after his resurrection.

- Identify titles applied to Jesus after his resurrection.

INTRODUCTION

John supplements the Synoptic Gospels' records of the resurrection by adding to it Jesus' extended conversation with Mary Magdalene (20:1–18) and his twofold appearance to the disciples, the last of which involved the famous verbal exchange with doubting Thomas (20:19–29). The chapter concludes with a statement of the purpose for the writing of the gospel of John. I now unpack these three points.

I. JESUS' POSTRESURRECTION APPEARANCES TO MARY MAGDALENE (20:1–18)

Verses 1–18 can be divided into three scenes: Mary at the empty tomb (vv. 1–2); Peter and John at the empty tomb (vv. 3–9); Jesus' postresurrection appearance to Mary Magdalene (vv. 10–18).

A. Mary at the Empty Tomb (vv. 1–2)

As Sunday morning[1] was nearly dawning, Mary Magdalene[2] approached the tomb where Jesus had been placed and found the stone rolled away from its entrance. She did not

---

1. This constitutes the third day, on which Christ was raised (see 1 Cor. 15:4). For Jews, any part of a day was counted as a whole day. Thus Friday evening = one day; Saturday = one day; Sunday morning = one day.
2. Magdala is located north of Tiberias on the west coast of the Sea of Galilee.

An alternative (although unlikely) site of Jesus' tomb. The tomb is associated with the site that General Charles Gordon suggested as the location of Golgotha in 1883.

Answers to Objections to the Resurrection of Christ

Objections	Answers
1. STOLEN BODY THEORY: Someone stole the body of Jesus, giving the false impression that Christ arose.	
But who stole the body?	A. Not the disciples, because they were hiding for their lives. B. Not the Jews; otherwise they could have put an end to Christianity by producing the body of Jesus. C. Not the Roman soldiers; they were to guard the tomb on pain of their deaths.
2. SWOON THEORY: Jesus fell unconscious on the cross but awoke in the dampness of the tomb. He then slipped away to die a normal death.	
But:	A. The human soldiers who executed Jesus were experts at inflicting death. B. And how did Jesus move the heavy stone after he was flogged and crucified?
3. WRONG TOMB THEORY: Jesus was placed in one tomb at his death, but the disciples went to the wrong tomb, which was empty. They therefore erroneously concluded that Jesus had risen from the dead.	
But:	A. Did the Romans go to the wrong tomb too? B. Did the Jewish leadership also go to the wrong tomb? C. Did Joseph of Arimathea, who owned the tomb in which Jesus was buried, go to the wrong tomb?
4. HALLUCINATION THEORY: The disciples so grieved over Jesus' death that they hallucinated that they saw Jesus.	
But:	A. The postresurrection appearances of Jesus were varied, not falling into one pattern. B. The disciples did not expect Jesus to arise. His resurrection surprised them as much as anyone. C. More than five hundred people saw the resurrected Jesus. D. Hallucinations don't occur only to stop suddenly.

ARTISTIC RECONSTRUCTION OF JESUS' TOMB.

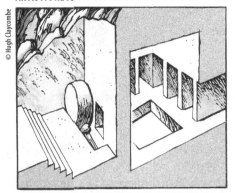

© Hugh Claycombe

ORIGINAL TOMB CUT INTO SOLID BEDROCK

TOTAL DESTRUCTION BY THE ROMAN EMPEROR HADRIAN (After A.D. 135)

After suppressing the second Jewish Revolt Hadrian demolished the rock hillside down to about the level of the bench and built a temple to Venus over the area. Jerome stated that the sacred resurrection spot was occupied by a statue of Jupiter.

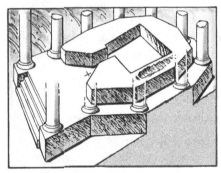

CONSTANTINE'S MONUMENTS
(After A.D. 326 when Christianity was official)

Following the Roman custom of building an "above ground" tomb for an important person, Constantine carved out all around the bench, lowered the floor and built a "small building" or "edicule". Around and above it he later erected a rotunda and dome. As reported by the traveler Egeria, by 395 pilgrims had chipped away pieces of the burial bench for souvenirs and it "began to resemble a trough". Marble slabs later covered it, as they do to this day.

Hadrian's Destruction and Constantine's Monuments

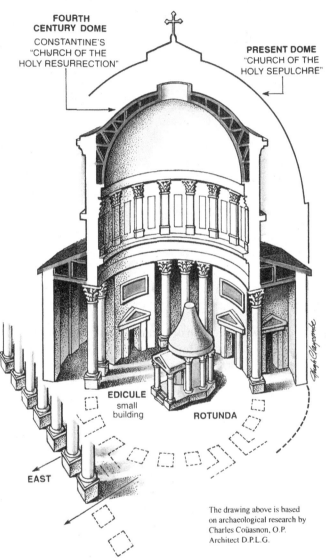

FOURTH CENTURY DOME
CONSTANTINE'S "CHURCH OF THE HOLY RESURRECTION"

PRESENT DOME "CHURCH OF THE HOLY SEPULCHRE"

EDICULE small building

ROTUNDA

EAST

The drawing above is based on archaeological research by Charles Coüasnon, O.P. Architect D.P.L.G.

Constantine's architects did not erect the dome exactly over the burial bench where Jesus' body had lain, but rather 48" to the South and 20" to the East. The focus point of the rotunda (the exact center) and centered under the dome was the outer edge of the entrance, precisely where the risen Christ first stepped out of the tomb into the world of the living. Thus the entire building complex commemorated the resurrection. Eastern churches still celebrate Easter at midnight, when closed doors are opened and pastors step out into the congregation proclaiming "Christ has Risen.

enter into the tomb but rather ran to inform Peter and the Beloved Disciple (John) of the situation.

B. Peter and John at the Empty Tomb (vv. 3–9)

Peter and John darted to the tomb, with John outrunning the presumably older Peter. John saw the grave clothes in the tomb but did not enter in at first. Peter arrived and entered the tomb; he also saw Jesus' grave clothes. They consisted of a shroud, or large cloth, that was wrapped around the body and a napkinlike cloth that covered Jesus' face. The two linen pieces were separated from one another (vv. 3–7). Then John entered the tomb and, after seeing the burial clothes of Jesus, believed (implied) in his resurrection. Still, neither disciple made the connection between Old Testament prophecy and Jesus' resurrection (cf. v. 9 with Luke 24:26–27, 44–47). Apparently Jesus' grave clothes collapsed flat on the stone slab after his resurrection. When John saw this, he knew that Jesus' body had not been stolen or removed, because the clothes would not have been left behind, and rather

Were Jesus and Mary Magdalene Married?

Dan Brown's *The Da Vinci Code* was a runaway best-seller. It sold millions of books, sat atop the *New York Times* best-seller list for over two years, and generated a movie directed by Ron Howard, thus creating no small stir within and outside the church. Its formula for success is the mixture of a conspiracy theory, a potent long-held secret, and a good dose of vilifying historic Christianity, especially the Roman Catholic Church. There is no doubt about it: *The Da Vinci Code* is a brilliant, thrilling page turner. But is it true? No, it is not! There are three main errors on which *The Da Vinci Code* is based:

Error 1: The true gospels are the *Gospel of Mary* (Magdalene) and the *Gospel of Philip*, not the canonical Gospels. The *Gospel of Mary* (Magdalene) and *Gospel of Philip* claim that Jesus and Mary Magdalene were marital companions. But these two writings date no earlier than the second century AD and were produced by Gnostic authors who reinterpreted the canonical gospels.

Error 2: Jesus is a mere human in the earliest historical sources who was only later divinized at the Council of Nicea in AD 325. This was due to the oppressive tactics of Emperor Constantine, who suppressed the earlier (Gnostic) gospels and replaced them with the four canonical Gospels. But nothing could be further from the truth. Already the New Testament declared Jesus is God (e.g., John 1:1–4; 20:31; Phil. 2:9–11; 2 Peter 1:2; Rev. 4–5). The Nicea Council only confirmed the witnesses of the New Testament and the early church fathers.

Error 3: Jesus was married to Mary Magdalene. But the Gospels' references to Mary Magdalene show no indication whatsoever that she and Jesus were married or even lovers. Here are the references:

- Jesus cast seven demons out of Mary (Luke 8:2).
- Mary witnessed Jesus's crucifixion (Matt. 27:55–56; Mark 15:40–41; John 19:25).
- Mary was present at the burial of Jesus (Matt. 27:57–61; Mark 15:47; cf. Mark 16:1).
- Mary was the first to see Jesus in his resurrection body (John 20:10–17).
- Mary, along with the other women, announced Jesus' resurrection to the apostles (Luke 24:10; John 20:18).

neatly at that. He had to have been raised from the dead. John, then, was the first to believe in Jesus' resurrection.

C. Jesus' Appearance to Mary Magdalene (vv. 10–18)

Mary Magdalene must have returned to the tomb during the disciples' discovery. When they left, Mary remained outside the tomb, crying. She ventured into the grave and saw two angels in white, one seated at the place where Jesus' head lay and the other at the foot. The angels asked Mary why she was crying, and she responded that someone had taken away the body of Jesus (vv. 10–13). The question came to Mary again, this time from the risen Jesus, whom Mary did not recognize. Mary thought Jesus was the gardener and asked if he knew where the body of Jesus had been taken (vv. 14–15). Jesus called her by her name, and recognizing him, she addressed Jesus as *Rabboni* (Aramaic for Teacher).

What did Jesus mean when he told Mary to stop clinging to him because he had not yet returned to the Father?

Verse 17 has puzzled many a reader.[3] What did Jesus mean when he told Mary to stop clinging to him because he had not yet returned to the Father?

Most likely Jesus was announcing to Mary that she should not expect him to remain on earth in his new glorified body but rather that he would abide with them in the person

---

3. Gary Burge lists the following: Jesus prohibits a literal touching; Jesus really said, "Do not fear" rather than "Do not hold on to me." Gary M. Burge, *John*, NIV Application Commentary (Grand Rapids: Zondervan, 2000), 556.

of the Paraclete, the Holy Spirit (cf. v. 22). But this would not happen until Jesus ascended to his heavenly Father (recall John 14:3, 18, 26; 16:7). Jesus' return to God his Father would make God the Father of his followers (v. 17). Mary returned to the disciples' meeting place, telling them that she had seen the Lord (v. 18). If John was the first to believe in Jesus' resurrection, then Mary Magdalene was the first to see the risen Jesus and testify of him.

II. JESUS' TWOFOLD APPEARANCE TO THE DISCIPLES (20:19–29)

This episode falls quite naturally into two scenes: Jesus' resurrection appearance to the ten disciples, without Thomas (vv. 19–23); Jesus' resurrection appearance to the eleven disciples, including Thomas (vv. 24–29).

A. Jesus' Appearance to the Ten Disciples (vv. 19–23)

That same night Jesus appeared to ten of the disciples behind closed doors. By now, Judas had committed suicide and Thomas was not present with the group. Jesus' postresurrection appearance to the ten disciples was both discontinuous and continuous with his earthly body. It was discontinuous because, as a *glorified* form, he could pass through solid substances like doors and walls (v. 19b). But Jesus' postresurrection mode was continuous with his earthly existence in that he still possessed a body—the disciples could touch his hands and side once pierced by nails and a spear (v. 20).

John records three actions of Jesus toward his disciples. First, he granted them peace (vv. 19, 21), which overjoyed them (v. 20). "Peace" and "joy" were two qualities Jesus promised the disciples in his farewell speech (14:27; 15:11; 16:19–24; 17:13).

Second, Jesus commissioned his disciples. As he was sent into the world by the Father, so now would they be sent into the world (cf. v. 21b with 17:18). This is the key to understanding Jesus' third action relative to the disciples.

Third, Jesus gave the disciples the Holy Spirit and thereby empowered them to proclaim his message to the world (vv. 22–23). The first half of this statement has been called the "Johannine Pentecost." Whether Jesus' bestowal of the Spirit in this scene was only symbolic or anticipatory of Acts 2,[4] either way it does seem to be the case that this was a genuine anointing of the Holy Spirit. The disciples actually received the Spirit, in fulfillment of Jesus' promise to send the Paraclete upon his return to the Father. The second half of the statement (v. 23) probably connects to Jesus' commissioning of the disciples in verse 21.

The greatest doubter had uttered the greatest confession of faith.

B. Jesus' Appearance to the Eleven Disciples (vv. 24–29)

At that meeting on the night of Jesus' resurrection, Thomas was not present with the disciples. A little later he expressed his doubts to the ten about the reality of Jesus' resurrection. One week later, the next Sunday night, Thomas was gathered with the other disciples in the same house. Once again Jesus appeared, his form both glorified (v. 26) and corporal (v. 27). Jesus bid Thomas do what Thomas demanded had to happen before he would believe in Jesus' resurrection—touch Jesus' hands and side. Thomas did that and believed, confessing

---

4. See Burge's classification of the theories of the interpretation of the Johannine Pentecost (symbol, partial anointing, genuine anointing). Ibid., 559–61.

Jesus to be Lord and God; in other words, Yahweh! With that, the greatest doubter had uttered the greatest confession of faith.

III. THE PURPOSE OF THE GOSPEL OF JOHN (20:30–31)

If John 21 is an appendix added to the fourth gospel after the death of the Beloved Disciple (see my remarks on that chapter), then originally John 20:30–31 concluded the gospel of John. In it the purpose of the fourth gospel is stated: out of the many miracles or signs that Jesus performed, the ones that John chose to record were intended to bring his audience to faith in Christ and thus receive (eternal) life. In concluding this chapter, I make several comments about verses 30–31.

First, John only recorded some seven signs of Jesus when, in fact, he performed many others (v. 30). Those miracles probably occurred both in Jesus' earthly ministry and in connection with his postresurrection appearances. They may have been remembered by John by being collected in a signs source.

Second, there is a textual variant regarding the word "believe" (v. 31). For example, Codex Alexandrinus (fifth century AD) has an aorist subjunctive—*pisteusēte*, while p^{66} (John Bodmer papyrus, second century AD) and Codices Sinaiticus and Vaticanus (fourth century AD) have a present subjunctive—*pisteuēte*.

If the former reading is correct, then John would be encouraging non-Christian readers to believe in Jesus. But if the latter is the original, then John would be challenging Christians to continue in their faith in Jesus. It should be noted that the identical phrase in John 19:35 is also aorist. Even though Greek grammarians no longer think we can press the aorist tense, most commentators—rightly, I believe—think the Johannine phrase is evangelistic in its thrust.[5]

Third, "Christ, the Son of God," joins the repertoire of titles applied to Jesus throughout the fourth gospel, along with Rabbi, Prophet, Son of Man, the Coming One, the King of Israel, Lord, and God. That being the case, John 20:30–31 forms an inclusio with John's prologue (1:1–18).

Fourth, believing that Jesus is the Christ, the Son of God, brings (eternal) life (v. 31). This life is covenantal and eschatological. It is the life of the new covenant and the life of the kingdom of God/age to come, of which the fourth gospel has had much to say.

---

5. For further discussion, see D. A. Carson, "The Purpose of the Fourth Gospel: Jn 20:31 Reconsidered," *JBL* 106 (1987): 639–51.

REVIEW QUESTIONS

1. How does John 20 distinguish itself in reporting Jesus' resurrection?

2. Why did John the Beloved Disciple come to believe in Jesus' bodily resurrection?

3. What does John 20:17 most likely mean when it says that Mary should not "cling" to Jesus?

4. What three actions did the resurrected Jesus perform, according to John 20:19–23?

5. Is John 20:30–31 speaking to Christians, or is it more evangelistic in tone?

6. What are some of the titles for Jesus in the fourth gospel (see, e.g., 20:30–31)?

KEY TERMS

Beloved Disciple

Johannine Pentecost

Mary Magdalene

Peter

purpose of the Gospel of John (20:30–31)

Thomas

CHAPTER 24

The Epilogue

JOHN 21

Objectives

After reading this chapter, you should be able to:

- Discuss the literary problem of John 21.
- Discuss Jesus' threefold question to Peter.
- Identify the historical setting of John 21.

INTRODUCTION

John 21 functions as the epilogue[1] to the fourth gospel, drawing out the conclusion of John 20:30–31 (yet another sign is reported in John 21—another postresurrection appearance of Jesus—that is designed to elicit faith in Christ) and balancing the prologue (1:1–18). But John 21 poses a literary difficulty: how do we account for the fact, on the one hand, that the style of John 21 matches that of the rest of the gospel while, on the other hand, John 21 was probably written *after* the death of the Beloved Disciple?

The solution to this problem that has commended itself to many interpreters is that an editor from the Johannine school assembled in John 21 other stories recorded by the Beloved Disciple not found in John 1:19–20:31.

Assuming the accuracy of the preceding solution to the literary problem of John 21, I now cover two major points: I offer a summary of John 21, and I hypothesize the original setting that occasioned the writing of John 21.

I. A SUMMARY OF JOHN 21

John 21 records three topics of interest: Jesus' postresurrection appearance to the disciples at the Sea of Tiberias (vv. 1–14), the rehabilitation of Peter (vv. 15–23), and the second conclusion to the fourth gospel (vv. 24–25).

A. Jesus' Postresurrection Appearance to the Disciples at the Sea of Tiberias (vv. 1–14)

It is clear that verses 1–14 address a self-contained topic. The passage begins and ends with a reference to Jesus' revealing of himself to the disciples (vv. 1, 14), a third such appearance in John 20–21. This postresurrection appearance occurred at the Sea of Tiberias (Galilee, v. 1). The disciples witnessing this sighting of Jesus were Peter, Thomas, Nathanael, John and James (the sons of Zebedee), and two other unnamed disciples (v. 2). We are not told why Peter and the other-mentioned disciples would leave Jerusalem after encountering the risen Christ and return to their former vocation of fishing. Perhaps it was Peter's impetuousness that got the best of them.

---

1. John 21 is not an *appendix*, if by that term we mean an addition to a work that is not related to the completeness of the work. Nor is it a *supplement*, because, while supplemental material is acquired later, some of the information in John 21 may actually predate the events of John 20 (see below). Most scholars today prefer the term *epilogue* for John 21, for it concludes some of the lines of thought left unfinished in the fourth gospel as a whole. See Raymond E. Brown, *The Gospel according to John XIII–XXI*, Anchor Bible 29B (Garden City, N.Y.: Doubleday, 1970), 1078–79. Note also that a number of scholars do not think that John 21 is a later addition to the fourth gospel. Andreas J. Köstenberger, e.g., argues that John wrote his own appendix: "'I Suppose' (*oimai*): The Conclusion of John's Gospel in Its Literary and Historical Context," in *The New Testament in Its First-Century Setting: Essays on Context and Background in Honour of B. W. Winter*, ed. P. J. Williams et al. (Grand Rapids: Eerdmans, 2004), 72–88. This is an important article that compares the words "I suppose" in v. 25 with the same verb used by ancient first-century writers like Diodorus of Sicily, Josephus, and Plutarch. Köstenberger concludes that the verb is used by those writers and the apostle John to convey the notion of authorial modesty in commending a claim or a comment by the writer to his or her audience. In other words, "I suppose" indicates that John is the author, not a later editor. This may be, but the reference to John in the third person and the mention of the first person plural in vv. 24–25 still seem to best be accounted for by some sort of later redacting of John 21.

Left: The musht fish, also known as Saint Peter's fish. *Right:* Various fish from the Sea of Galilee.

The disciples fished at night, a desirable time to catch fish, but this night to no avail. Just after daybreak, Jesus appeared on the shore of the Sea of Galilee and directed the disciples to recast their net. They did not yet recognize Jesus (vv. 3–6). Nevertheless, the disciples obeyed and immediately landed a large catch of fish. This prompted the Beloved Disciple to recognize Jesus. Hyperactive Peter jumped into the water, presumably to reach shore before the boat did, which was still a hundred yards out (vv. 7–8).

On shore, Jesus cooked breakfast for the disciples. The amazing catch of 153 fish had not broken the net. By now all the disciples recognized Jesus (vv. 9–14).

Although the other disciples are mentioned, Peter and John are singled out for attention in John 21. John's recognition of Jesus in verse 7 is reminiscent of John 20:8; in both cases John was the first to correctly perceive spiritual reality: Jesus' resurrection in 20:8, and now the appearance of the risen Jesus.

John 21:9 recalls Peter's denial of Jesus at the charcoal fire outside Annas's palace (John 18:18).

Jesus' present appearance to Peter was for the purpose of rehabilitating that disciple to become a fisher of men, the topic of verses 15–23. Other New Testament references seem to allude to Jesus' postresurrection appearance to Peter for the purpose of reclaiming him (Matt. 16:16b–19; Luke 5:1–11; 1 Cor. 15:5).

> John 21:9 recalls Peter's denial of Jesus at the charcoal fire outside Annas's palace (John 18:18).

B. The Rehabilitation of Peter (vv. 15–23)

Verses 15–23 cover two related themes: the recommissioning of Peter (vv. 15–19) and Peter's concern about John's fate (vv. 20–23).

1. The Recommissioning of Peter (vv. 15–19)

After feeding the disciples breakfast, Jesus addressed Peter, calling him by his formal name—Simon Peter. Probably Jesus thereby communicated that his friendship with Peter was distant because of the latter's threefold denial of his Lord (v. 15). The point of Jesus' threefold question and response to Peter was both to emphasize Peter's failure in denying

Left: Remains of basalt homes. The modern structure in the background is built over the top of the site identified as the home of Peter. *Right:* Remains of the home of Peter in Capernaum. The property was converted into a church during the second – fourth centuries AD.

Christ three times (hence the reason Jesus asked Peter three times, "Do you love me"?) and to offer Peter forgiveness and recommissioning as an apostle. Jesus predicted that this time Peter would prove his faithfulness to Christ, even by being crucified upside down (vv. 18, 19).[2] Like Jesus the Good Shepherd (John 10), Peter would lay down his life for the flock of God (cf. 1 Peter 5:1–4).

2. Peter's Concern about the Fate of John (vv. 20–23)

Verses 20–23 reveal that, though Peter was now rehabilitated for the cause of Christ, he still had some maturing to do. As he was "following" Christ (he was now on the right path again), he asked Jesus what would become of the Beloved Disciple (vv. 20–21).[3] Since Peter had just been told his fate (crucifixion), he inquired about the fate of John. Jesus' response was that it was his decision as to whether John would survive until the parousia (vv. 22–23). In the meantime, Peter should not worry about John's walk with the Lord but rather should concentrate on his own spiritual journey with Jesus.

It is clear from verse 23 that John's death had confused some of the Johannine community, for some of them had mistakenly thought that Jesus promised that John would live to see the return of Christ, when in fact John did not.

C. The Second Conclusion to the Gospel of John (vv. 24–25)

If indeed John 21 is a later edition to the fourth gospel, verses 24–25 constitute a second conclusion to it (the first conclusion was John 20:30–31). The disciple who added John 21:24–25 may well be the same person referred to in 19:35: a follower of the Beloved Disciple and, therefore, one who accurately passed along the message of his mentor. The

---

2. The stretched-out hands correspond to crucifixion, while the binding of the belt alludes to tying the victim before leading him to crucifixion.

3. Raymond E. Brown observes that v. 20 is a mosaic of statements from John 13: "During supper" (v. 2); "Jesus was betrayed" (v. 21); "the disciple whom Jesus loved" (v. 25). See his *Gospel according to John XIII–XXI*, 1109.

context of "these things" he wrote is probably John 21. The many other things Jesus did included another postresurrection appearance.

II. A HYPOTHESIS FOR THE ORIGINAL SETTING OF JOHN 21

Without detracting from the historicity of the events recorded in John 21, I am inclined to agree with Brown that John 21 reflects tension between Johannine and Petrine Christianity in the late first century AD. John 21, then, is an appeal to those communities to be unified.[4] We now develop this hypothesis in four statements.

1. Peter died a martyr's death in the late AD 60s (vv. 18–19). This, along with the fact that Peter was the chief disciple (Matt. 16:16–19), caused many early Christians to venerate him as their apostle.

2. John died in the late AD 90s of natural causes. Even though he was persecuted for his faith, John survived Domitian's inquisition of Christianity (vv. 21–23). The Johannine churches venerated John.

3. Upon John's death, tension broke out between Petrine and Johannine Christianity over which of the two apostles was the greatest. Those who adhered to Petrine Christianity pointed to the facts that the risen Jesus appeared to Peter (vv. 1–14) and that Peter died a martyr's death (vv. 18–19). Those who championed Johannine Christianity could claim that John was closer to Jesus, something that made Peter jealous (vv. 20–21).

4. The editor of John 21 tried to bring harmony between the above two factions by arguing two things. First, John was equal to Peter as an apostle. Thus John's death, though not a martyr's death, was still a reliable witness to Christ (vv. 21–23). Furthermore, John was associated with Peter and thus was on par with him in importance (vv. 1–23). Moreover, Jesus mildly rebuked Peter but not John (v. 22).

   Second, the editor of John 21 encouraged unity between Petrine and Johannine Christianity by reminding the latter that Peter was rehabilitated to discipleship and therefore held a high spiritual status among the churches. Furthermore, the 153 fish caught may well have symbolized the unity of the world at that time (153 species of fish populated the world, according to ancient writers[5]). Also, the mention of the net not breaking may also have represented the unity of the church.

---

4. Ibid., 1120–21, and the commentators he mentions there.
5. Gary M. Burge provides a list of the symbolic interpretations of the 153 fish, including the one I mention above in *John*, NIV Application Commentary (Grand Rapids: Zondervan, 2000), 584–85. Others object to a symbolic interpretation of the number of fish, arguing that this count would be typical of fishermen dividing up the catch among themselves (J. Carl Laney, *John*, Moody Gospel Commentary [Chicago: Moody Press, 1992], 377).

1. What is a possible solution to the literary problem of John 21?

2. Why did Jesus pose the threefold question to Peter (John 21:15 – 19)?

3. Did Jesus promise that John the Beloved Disciple would live to see the Second Coming of Christ (John 21:20 – 23)?

4. How is John 21:24 – 25 a second conclusion to the gospel of John?

5. What is a plausible historical setting of John 21?

KEY TERMS

153 fish

epilogue

Johannine Christianity

Johannine school

Petrine Christianity

Sea of Tiberias

PART 2

The Epistles of John

CHAPTER 25

Introduction to the Epistles of John

Objectives

After reading this chapter, you should be able to:

- Identify the similarities between New Testament letters and ancient Greco-Roman letters.

- Discuss whether Paul's letters and the New Testament letters in general are public or private correspondences.

- Discuss the process whereby 1, 2, and 3 John were considered canonical.

- Explain the six steps in the production of the Johannine literature.

INTRODUCTION

As I did for the gospel of John, so now I will offer some introductory remarks relative to the epistles of John. I will cover the following points: ancient letter writing and the New Testament epistles, including 1, 2, 3 John; the canonicity of the epistles of John; the authorship of the epistles of John; the historical setting of 1, 2, 3 John as compared to that of the gospel of John; the literary sequence of 1, 2, 3 John; the genre of the epistles of John; the structure of 1 John; and the Greek manuscript evidence for 1, 2, 3 John; and a summary of the theology of the epistles of John.

I. ANCIENT LETTER WRITING AND NEW TESTAMENT EPISTLES

This section answers two important questions about ancient letter writing and the New Testament epistles: (1) Was there a common form for the letters? (2) How should we classify ancient letters, and how do the New Testament epistles relate to that classification?

A. Was There a Common Form for the Letters?

Biblical scholar William G. Doty answers the question of whether there was a common form for ancient letter writing in the affirmative. A typical letter from one Serapion to his brothers shows this to be the case:

> Serapion to his brothers Ptolemaeus and Apollonius greeting. If you are well, it would be excellent. I myself am well. I have made a contract with the daughter of Hesperus and intend to marry her in the month of Mesore. Please send me half a chous of oil. I have written to you to let you know. Goodbye. Year 28, Epeiph 21. Come for the wedding-day, Apollonius.[1]

Thus the typical letter in antiquity contained three components: (1) introduction (prescript or salutation), including sender, addressee, greetings, and often additional greetings or a wish for good health; (2) text or body; and (3) conclusion, including greetings; wishes, especially for persons other than the addressee; final greetings or prayer sentence; and sometimes dating.[2]

The best New Testament example of the preceding components can be found in Paul's writings. Although the rest of the New Testament letters do not follow the preceding pattern as closely as Paul does, they still contain elements of the ancient letter, except 1 John.

B. How Should We Classify Ancient Letters, and How Do the New Testament Epistles Relate to That Classification?

Ancient letters, or epistles, proceeded along a continuum from private correspondences to public essays. Moreover, they were personal, financial, philosophical, and official in nature,

---

1. Quoted in William G. Doty, *Letters in Primitive Christianity* (Philadelphia: Fortress Press, 1973), 13. BCE (before the Common Era) and CE (Common Era) are designations, often used by the Jews, that extend from 519 BC to AD 70. This period is often labeled Second Temple Judaism because Solomon's temple (destroyed by the Babylonians in 586/587 BC) was rebuilt by the Jews in 519 BC. That temple was later refurbished by Herod the Great but destroyed by the Romans in AD 70.

2. See Doty, *Letters*, 14. For examples in antiquity and further discussion, see E. Randolph Richards, *Paul and First-Century Letter Writing: Secretaries, Composition and Collection* (Downers Grove, Ill.: InterVarsity, 2004), 122–27.

to name only a few types. There is a well-known debate among scholars as to where the New Testament letters, especially Paul's, fit in the above classification: private or public? In the early twentieth century, Adolf Deissmann, a leading philologist in his day, made a sharp distinction between ancient epistles and letters. After studying numerous Greek papyri discovered in Egypt, where the dry climate preserved them well, Deissmann made a now-famous statement:

> An epistle is an artistic literary form ... just like the dialogue, the oration, or the drama. It has nothing in common with the letter except its form.... [while] a letter is something non-literary, a means of communication between persons who are separated from each other ... it is intended only for the person or persons to whom it is addressed, and not at all for the public or any kind of publicity.[3]

According to Deissmann, the contrasts between epistle and letter had far-reaching ramifications, as the following chart highlights:

Epistle	Letter
Public	Private
General setting	Occasional in situation
Upper class	Lower class
Classical Greco-Roman writers	Egyptian papyri

The upshot of Deissmann's claim was that Christianity as reflected in the New Testament letters, especially Paul's, was indicative of the poor masses whose education was barely above the illiterate level.

Today, however, most scholars think Deissmann posed too sharp a divide between ancient letters and epistles. Rather, especially beginning with the Roman statesmen Cicero (106–43 BC), the private letter was elevated to the literary level. And it is that hybrid form that informs the New Testament letters. Hence, they were meant to be read in the public setting of the Christian congregations and they follow the literary features of introduction, body, and conclusion. Thus we are justified in interchanging the terms "epistle/literary" and "letter" for that New Testament genre. For our purposes, 2 and 3 John nicely fit the above epistle/letter genre, while 1 John does not. See my discussion to follow.

> Today most scholars think Deissmann posed too sharp a divide between ancient letters and epistles.

---

3. Adolf Deissmann, *Light from the Ancient East: The New Testament Illustration by Recently Discovered Texts of the Greco-Roman World*, trans. Lionel R. M. Strachan (1927; repr., Peabody, Mass.: Hendrickson, 1995), 228–29.

II. CANONICITY OF THE EPISTLES OF JOHN

The canonicity of the epistles of John is intimately related to the authorship of said writings and, shortly, I will address the latter subject.

Even though 1, 2, and 3 John were drawn upon by the church fathers by AD 250, it took time for all three epistles to be accepted as inspired Scripture. That process seems to have occurred in three steps. First, 1 John was widely accepted as canonical by AD 325, because early in the second century, followers of the apostle John, such as Polycarp and Papias, attributed that work to the apostle John. But, second, Papias also suggested that the author of 2 and 3 John, "the Presbyter" (NIV "elder"), was a different John from the apostle John. This distinction apparently cast suspicion enough over those two letters such that Eusebius classified them as "disputed" books in his day (AD 325). Third, however, between the time of Eusebius and Athanasius's festal letter to the churches (AD 367), which lists all twenty-seven books that now comprised the New Testament, 2 and 3 John had been accepted as Scripture. This seems to have stemmed from the argument that the apostle John and the presbyter were one and the same; the apostle simply humbly called himself the "presbyter," or the elder, even as Peter did (1 Peter 5:1).[4]

In my next section, I will demonstrate that there is good reason to posit one author—the apostle John—for the gospel and the three epistles.

> Even though 1, 2, and 3 John were drawn upon rather early in the life of the church, it took time for all three epistles to be accepted as inspired Scripture.

III. THE AUTHORSHIP OF THE EPISTLES OF JOHN

The epistles of John are commonly grouped with other writings often attributed to the apostle John—the gospel of John and Revelation. Together they comprise the Johannine corpus, or body of writings. Scholars, however, have been and continue to be divided over the authorship question of these materials, with three scenarios competing for acceptance. Here I will simply state those opinions and then offer a defense of my view.

The three conflicting perspectives regarding the authorship of the Johannine corpus are as follows: (1) The same author, the apostle John, wrote all three works—the gospel, the epistles, and Revelation.[5] Thus, in terms of authorship, the gospel of John = the epistles of John = Revelation. (2) Scholars at the other end of the spectrum contend that three different authors composed the Johannine corpus. While the beloved apostle John might have provided the original core of testimony to Jesus, a differ-

> The epistles of John are commonly grouped with other writings often attributed to the apostle John—the gospel of John and Revelation.

---

4. For further discussion on the process of recognizing the canonicity of 1, 2, and 3 John, see the helpful comments by Raymond E. Brown, *The Epistles of John*, Anchor Bible 30 (Garden City, N.Y.: Doubleday, 1982), 12–13; and Georg Strecker, *The Johannine Letters*, trans. Linda M. Maloney, Hermeneia (Minneapolis: Fortress, 1996), xxxii–xxxv.

5. See Donald Guthrie, *New Testament Introduction* (Downers Grove, Ill.: InterVarsity, 1978), 864–69; and D. A. Carson, Douglas J. Moo, and Leon Morris, *An Introduction to the New Testament* (Grand Rapids: Zondervan, 1992), 446–50.

ent person, "the evangelist," actually wrote the gospel of John, while the presbyter, or the elder (also called John), wrote the epistles of John, leaving a third individual to write Revelation. Therefore, in terms of authorship, the gospel of John ≠ the epistles of John ≠ Revelation.[6] (3) In between the preceding two views, other interpreters equate the author of the gospel of John with the writer of the epistles of John but posit a second, different author for Revelation. Thus the author of the gospel of John = the author of the epistles of John ≠ the author of Revelation.[7]

The only commonality among the preceding opinions is that 1 and 2–3 John were written by the same author, whoever he may have been. This is a near consensus view today.[8]

There are good reasons to posit one author for the gospel of John and 1 John.

There are also good reasons to posit one author for the gospel of John and 1 John. First, the internal evidence is strong for linking the two writings. The prologues of the gospel of John and 1 John are similar, as the following verbal links reveal:

Gospel of John 1:1 – 18	1 John 1:1 – 4
1. In the *beginning* (vv. 1, 2) . . . *word* became flesh	That which was from the *beginning* . . . *word* of life (v. 1)
2. He *was with God* (v. 2)	was *with the Father* (v. 2)
3. In him was *life* (v. 4)	the word of *life* . . . The *life* appeared (vv. 1, 2)
4. *We have seen* his glory (v. 14)	*we have seen* the life (v. 2)
5. John the Baptist *testifies* to the light (v. 7)	we *testify* to the life (v. 2)

The distinct impression one gets from these comparisons is that these prologues are rooted in an eyewitness account of the historical Jesus.

Next, the purposes of the fourth gospel and 1 John are identical: to elicit faith in Christ resulting in eternal life (cf. John 20:31 with 1 John 5:13). Moreover, numerous other similarities exist between the gospel of John and 1 John, as Colin Kruse documents:

> Compare, e.g., the following: the word of life from the beginning — 1 John 1:1 – 2/John 1:1 – 4; the light — 1 John 1:5 – 7/John 1:6 – 9; the Paraclete — 1 John 2:1/John 14:16, 26; 15:26; 16:7; the new commandment — 1 John 2:7/John 13:34; the love of fellow believers

6. See Brown, *Epistles of John*, 21 – 30, though Brown deals primarily with the gospel and the epistles.

7. See I. Howard Marshall, *The Epistles of John*, NICNT (Grand Rapids: Eerdmans, 1978), 42 – 48.

8. The major exception is Georg Strecker, who argues for differing authors of 1 and 2–3 John, in "Die Anfänge der johanneischen Schule" ("The Origins of the Johannine School"), *New Testament Studies* 32 (1986): 31 – 47; cf. his *Johannine Letters*, xxxv – xlii.

and the world's hatred—1 John 3:13/John 15:9–25; passing from death to life—1 John 3:14/John 5:24; Jesus lays down his life for us—1 John 3:16/John 10:11, 15, 17, 18; 15:12–14; God's command to believe in Jesus Christ—1 John 3:23/John 6:29; no one has ever seen God—1 John 4:12/John 1:18; the "Saviour of the world"—1 John 4:14/John 4:42; being born of God—1 John 5:1/John 1:12–13; water and blood—1 John 5:6/John 19:34; eternal life—1 John 5:13/John 3:16; the love commandment—2 John 5–6/John 13:34.[9]

This is not to say, however, that there are no variants between the gospel of John and the epistles of John. As I will discuss later, there are indeed key contrasts between the two.

Regarding the external evidence, early Christian tradition unanimously ascribed 1 John to the apostle John. Thus Papias (*Exposition of Oracles of the Lord* [AD 130–40], as recorded by Eusebius [*Eccl. Hist.* 3.39]); Irenaeus (d. AD 202; *Haer.* 3.16.5, 8); Dionysius of Alexandria (d. ca. AD 265; cited in Eusebius, *Eccl. Hist.* 7.25.6ff.); Tertullian (d. ca. AD 220; *Prax.* 15; *Scorp.* 12); and Jerome (d. ca. 419; *Lives of Illustrious Men*, 13) all equate the author of 1 John (and 2 and 3 John as well, for Revelation it is a different matter) with the apostle John, the author of the gospel.[10] So, even though numerous scholars today disassociate the gospel of John from the epistles of John, the internal and external evidence overwhelmingly attributes them to one author—the apostle of John.

---

9. Colin Kruse, *The Letters of John*, Pillar New Testament Commentary (Grand Rapids: Eerdmans, 2000), 5n3; cf. Brown's extensive list of 119 links between the gospel and the epistles (*Epistles of John*, 757–59), though Brown concludes the two are written by *different* authors!

10. Some key church fathers distinguished the author of Revelation from the apostle John, namely Papias (as quoted in Eusebius, *Eccl. Hist.* 3.39), Dionysius (as quoted in Eusebius, *Eccl. Hist.* 7.25.6), and Eusebius himself (also in *Eccl. Hist.* 3.39). I will defer discussion of this issue to my later treatment of the authorship of Revelation.

Remains of the fourth-century AD Church of St. John, near Ephesus.

IV. THE HISTORICAL SETTING OF 1, 2, AND 3 JOHN

The last section broached the subject of the situation in life that produced the epistles of John. Here I offer a fuller discussion of that issue. The careful reader of the gospel of John and 1, 2, and 3 John will notice that there are considerable differences between the gospel and epistles.

A. Historical Differences

Most interpreters agree that the historical settings are different for John's gospel and his epistles. Thus historically, the gospel was written for the purpose of refuting Palestinian Jews' accusation that Jesus was less than God, while 1, 2, and 3 John were written in Ephesus for the purpose of refuting the claims of those who had recently seceded from the Johannine community.

> The careful reader of the gospel of John and 1, 2, and 3 John will notice that there are considerable differences between the gospel and epistles.

B. Differences in Christology

Next, the Christology in the gospel of John is as exalted as any other New Testament work, if not more so. Unlike the Synoptic Gospels and comparable only to Paul (Phil. 2:5–11; Col. 1:15–20), John begins with a prologue (John 1:1–18) that equates Jesus with God from eternity past, which is reaffirmed in John 8:58 and 17:5. Moreover, as commentators have long noted, throughout the gospel of John, Jesus' deity is emphasized seemingly over his humanity. This is especially clear in John's passion narrative, where the Jewish and Roman guards do not capture Jesus, rather, he voluntarily surrenders to them (18:1–11); and on the cross when Jesus gives up his spirit to death, rather than death overtaking him (19:30). On the other hand, 1, 2, and 3 John make a point to emphasize both Jesus' deity and humanity (1 John 1:1–4; 2:22–23; 4:1–3; 5:6; 2 John 7).[11]

C. Differences in Eschatology

Furthermore, the differing eschatologies of the gospel and the epistles are well known. The gospel of John espouses realized eschatology more so than futurist eschatology, as we saw earlier. The epistles of John, however, take a somewhat different tack on eschatology. Urban C. von Wahlde observes:

> When eschatology is spoken of in the first epistle, we find a different emphasis than in the gospel. 1 John takes pains to indicate that the correct answer to the problem of eschatology revolves around another "both/and": the Christian has eternal life "both" in the present "and" in the future.
>
> In 1 John there are clear indications of realized eschatology: we already walk in the light (1:7; 2:9–10); the true light is already shining (2:8); we are children of God now (3:1); the evil one has been conquered (2:13–14); we have eternal life in us now (implicit in 3:15; 5:11–13, 16). Yet in spite of this present possession of eschatological gifts, there is clearly a future element

---

11. Although Jesus' humanity is certainly presented in John as well. Jesus is tired and thirsty at Jacob's well (John 4); he weeps at Lazarus's death (John 11); and most significantly Jesus is the Word made flesh (John 1:14).

in the author's thought. This future element deals with what we will be at the second coming of Jesus [cf. 2:28 – 3:3; 4:17 – 18].[12]

Von Wahlde goes on to point to 1 John 2:28 – 3:3, which envisions a second coming of Christ, the thought of which should motivate Christians to walk in holiness. First John 4:17 – 18 continues the epistles' futurist eschatology by highlighting the hope of the parousia.[13] We should add to these passages 1 John 2:18, which declares that in the future the Antichrist will come, but in the author's day the foreshadowing of that event coincides with the false teachers' departure from the Johannine community. These are called in 1 John 4:3 the "spirit of the antichrist."

> Many interpreters today believe that the resolution to the preceding differences lies in the hypothesis that the epistles of John correct a *misinterpretation* of the gospel of John at an earlier stage, one that was promoted by the secessionists' departure from the Johannine churches in and around Ephesus.

D. A Proposed Resolution to the Above Differences

Many interpreters today believe that the resolution to the preceding differences lies in the hypothesis that the epistles of John correct a *misinterpretation* of the gospel of John at an earlier stage, one that was promoted by the secessionists' departure from the Johannine churches in and around Ephesus.

I turn now to that discussion, because it will provide the basis for my ensuing explanation of the entire letters of John.

Our task here is to identify the teachings of the opponents of the apostle John as reflected in the latter's three epistles. Although we do not have primary documents composed by these individuals, we can essentially reconstruct their beliefs by tracking John's polemical statements about them. Three classifications of such remarks surface: the opponents were once a part of John's community of faith; these teachers denied that Christ had come in the flesh; they regarded themselves as spiritually perfect, having therefore no need for ethics. I now unpack these three categories.

1. The Opponents Left John's Community

First, it is clear that these dissenters once belonged to the church(es) in Ephesus but later departed from it (see 1 John 2:19 – 26; cf. 3:23; 4:1 – 3; 5:13).

2. The Opponents' Christology

Second, John expressly disagrees with his opponents' Christology because they deny the son (1 John 2:23), deny that Jesus Christ has come in the flesh (1 John 4:2; 2 John 7), and deny that *Jesus* (his humanity) is the Christ (his deity, 1 John 2:22).

John counters their claims: Jesus is the Christ (1 John 5:1); Jesus Christ has come in the flesh (1 John 4:2); Jesus is the Son (1 John 2:23; 3:23; 5:11) or the Son of God (1 John

---

12. Urban C. von Wahlde, *The Johannine Commandments: 1 John and the Struggle for the Johannine Tradition* (New York and Mahwah, N.J.: Paulist, 1990), 180 – 81.

13. Ibid., 181.

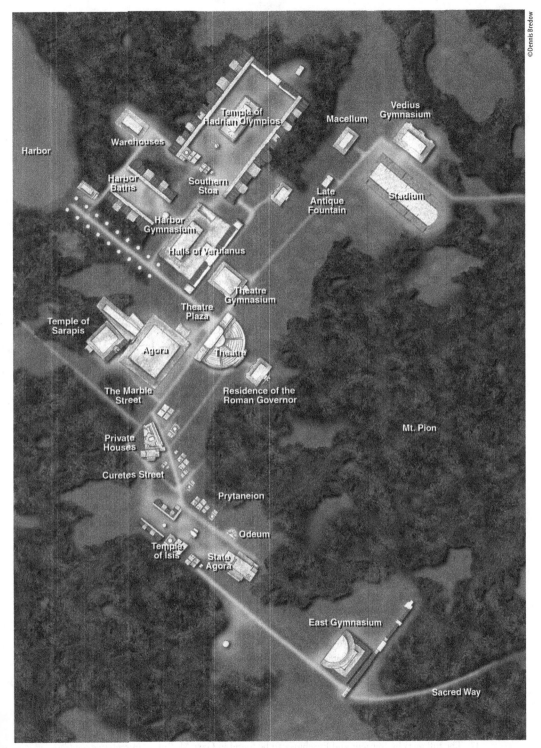

©Dennis Bredow

Harbor

Warehouses

Temple of
Hadrian Olympios

Macellum

Vedius
Gymnasium

Harbor
Baths

Southern
Stoa

Late
Antique
Fountain

Stadium

Harbor
Gymnasium

Halls of Verulanus

Theatre
Gymnasium

Theatre
Plaza

Temple of
Sarapis

Agora

Theatre

The Marble
Street

Residence of the
Roman Governor

Mt. Pion

Private
Houses

Curetes Street

Prytaneion

Odeum

Temple
of Isis

State
Agora

East Gymnasium

Sacred Way

Drawing of ancient Ephesus.

1:3, 7; 3:8, 23; 4:9, 10, 15, et al.); Jesus Christ came "by water and blood" (1 John 5:6).[14] The opponents' view of Christ apparently carried with it disastrous results, namely, the denial of the incarnation and the atonement of Jesus.

3. The Opponents' Ethics

Third, the secessionists had no regard for ethics and therefore claimed to be sinless (1 John 1:8, 10; see John's counterclaim in v. 9). They boasted that they had fellowship with God, but they walked in the darkness (1 John 1:6) and were disobedient (1 John 2:4; see John's response in 1 John 1:7). They said they loved God and walked in the light, yet they hated their brothers and sisters (1 John 2:9; 4:20; note John's opposite claim in 1 John 3:11–18).[15] It is possible to root the preceding lack of moral disposition in realized eschatology. That is, based on their reading of the gospel of John, the adversaries believed themselves to be fully in the kingdom of God and therefore perfect spiritually. Or perhaps the opponents succumbed to a Platonic/Gnostic-like dualism of spirit and flesh, believing that because they were in the Spirit the body no longer mattered. On either reading, the adversaries considered themselves to be above needed ethical constraints.

V. HISTORICAL SETTINGS OF THE GOSPEL AND THE EPISTLES

Most modern interpreters of the gospel of John and the epistles of John posit that two historical settings inform these respective writings. The gospel of John itself reflects two settings: the life of Jesus (AD 30s) and the life of the later churches of Asia Minor (AD 90s). The first setting was recorded for the purpose of presenting Jesus as the Christ, the Son of God (John 20:31), especially in the face of Palestinian Jews' rejection of the message of the historical Jesus. The second setting, now identified as Ephesus, alludes to the synagogue debate in Asia Minor, where non-Christian Jews in the early 90s were expelling Christian Jews from the synagogues, thus exposing them to the Roman demand to worship Caesar.[16] Since Julius Caesar, Jews had been exempt from emperor worship, and as long as Jewish Christians were perceived as Jews who worshiped in the synagogues, so were they. But when the synagogue leaders kicked out Christian Jews, the latter ceased being Jewish to the mind of Rome and hence were obligated to submit to the cult of Caesar.

These two settings point to the apostle John composing his gospel in ca. AD 90, after moving from Israel to Ephesus. Early tradition makes clear that John came to reside in Ephesus. Polycarp (early second-century bishop of Smyrna), who was a student of John, says that John came to Ephesus from Israel and enjoyed a widespread ministry in the area, planting various churches in Ephesus. Irenaeus and Eusebius confirm that report.[17] Indeed,

---

14. Gary M. Burge nicely tabulates this information in *The Letters of John*, NIV Application Commentary (Grand Rapids: Zondervan, 1996), 28.

15. This paragraph draws on Burge's comments. Ibid., 31.

16. J. L. Martyn's groundbreaking study develops this theme. See his *History and Theology in the Fourth Gospel*, rev. ed. (Nashville: Abingdon, 1979). The key text in this regard is John 9:22, where the parents of the sightless man whom Jesus healed feared that they would be expelled from the synagogue. I discussed this theme earlier with regard to John, and we will later see it at work in Revelation.

17. The full texts by Irenaeus and Eusebius can be found in Gary M. Burge, *Interpreting the Gospel of John* (Grand Rapids: Baker, 1992), 46–50.

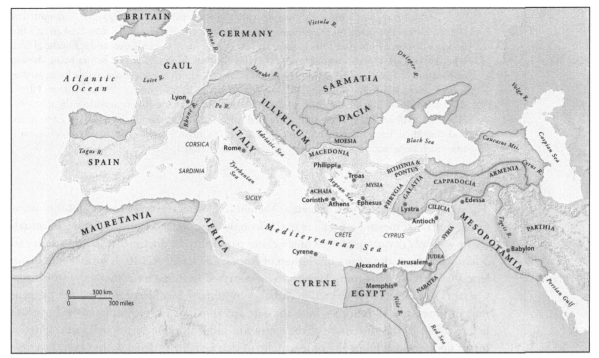

The Roman Empire.

John was buried in Ephesus.[18] In addition to dealing with Jewish opponents outside of the Johannine churches, John now, in the epistles, had to handle an in-house struggle, one that resulted in the dissenters exiting the Johannine community.

Can we put a name on these dissenters? Three second-century heretics have often been associated with the opponents of John as culled from his epistles: Cerinthus, the Docetists, and the Gnostics. We now provide portraits of each of these heresies based on the writings of those church fathers who opposed them, comparing them with 1, 2, and 3 John.

A. Cerinthus

Irenaeus (AD 120–202), bishop of Lyons, in his magnum opus *Against Heresies*, provides firsthand information concerning the heretic Cerinthus. Irenaeus records Polycarp's famous story about John the disciple of the Lord meeting Cerinthus in the bath house in Ephesus, and provides a description of Cerinthus's teaching.[19] The upshot of this quote is to claim that Cerinthus denied the real humanity of Jesus Christ.

> There are also those who heard from him [Polycarp] that John, the disciple of the Lord, going to bathe at Ephesus, and perceiving Cerinthus within, rushed out of the bath-house without bathing, exclaiming, "Let us fly, lest even the bath-house fall down, because Cerinthus, the enemy of the truth, is within" (*Against Heresies* 3.3.4).

---

18. See Burge's documentation in *Letters of John*, 21–22.
19. The following primary texts are collected by Kruse, *The Letters of John*, 20–26. I follow his translations.

Cerinthus, again, a man who was educated in the wisdom of the Egyptians, taught that the world was not made by the primary God, but by a certain Power far separated from him, and at a distance from that Principality who is supreme over the universe, and ignorant of him who is above all. He represented Jesus as having not been born of a virgin, but as being the son of Joseph and Mary according to the ordinary course of human generation, while he nevertheless was more righteous, prudent, and wise than other men. Moreover, after his baptism, Christ descended upon him in the form of a dove from the Supreme Ruler, and that then he proclaimed the unknown Father, and performed miracles. But at last Christ departed from Jesus, and that then Jesus suffered and rose again, while Christ remained impassible [unaffected], inasmuch as he was a spiritual being (*Against Heresies* 1.26.1).

B. The Docetists

The writings of Ignatius, and references therein to his Docetic opponents ("docetic" is the Greek word that means "appear," as in Christ only appeared to be human, while, in actuality, he was only divine), provide a much closer parallel to the doctrines rejected in 1, 2, and 3 John than Cerinthus. Ignatius, bishop of Antioch, Syria (d. AD 107), wrote a number of letters while on his way from Antioch to be martyred in Rome for denying the worship of Caesar. These letters were written to churches in western Asia Minor shortly after the penning of the epistles of John. So, both the date and proximity in geography make Ignatius's letters salient to this discussion of the epistles of John. In those correspondences, Ignatius insists upon the real humanity of Jesus Christ, that he truly suffered death upon the cross, and that he rose bodily from the dead. He warns his readers against those who deny the preceding christological truths and who fail to love those in need.[20] Of the various pertinent passages by Ignatius related to this topic, one especially merits quoting:

> Be deaf therefore when anyone speaks to you apart from Jesus Christ, who was of the family of David, and of Mary, who was truly born, both ate and drank, was truly persecuted under Pontius Pilate, was truly crucified and died in the sight of those in heaven and on earth and under the earth; who also was truly raised from the dead, his Father raised him up, as in the same manner his Father shall raise up in Christ Jesus us who believe in him, without whom we have no true life (Ign. *Trall.* 9:1–2). For love they have no care, none for the widow, none for the orphan, none for the distressed, none for the afflicted, none for the prisoner, or for him released from prison, none for the hungry or thirsty (Ign. *Smyrn.* 6:1–7:1). It is monstrous to talk of Jesus Christ and to practise Judaism. For Christianity did not base its faith on Judaism, but Judaism on Christianity, and every tongue believing on God was brought together in it (Ign. *Magn.* 10:1–3).

That the Docetists denied Jesus Christ's humanity is clear in all of this.

C. The Gnostics

A third possible identification of John's opponents is the second-century Gnostics, who were led by Basilides and Valentinus. Irenaeus also provides a description of these men, which he seems to differentiate from Cerinthus. In Cerinthus one finds only the beginning stages of the Gnosticism that later characterized the teachings of Basilides and Valentinus. The last two taught that the universe is comprised of the Pleroma, which contains 365

---

20. See ibid., 21–22.

heavens and was created by mini-gods. The God of the Old Testament was chief among those mini-gods who created the lowest level—earth. That same God created Christ, who came upon the man Jesus for the purpose of revealing to humans their divine origins and thereby deliver them from this world. But it was Jesus who died on the cross, not Christ. More particularly, it was Simon the Cyrene who died in Christ's place, and Irenaeus writes:

> Wherefore he did not himself suffer death, but Simon, a certain man of Cyrene, being compelled, bore the cross in his stead; so that this latter being transfigured by him, that he might be thought to be Jesus, was crucified, through ignorance and error, while Jesus himself received the form of Simon, and, standing by, laughed at him. (*Against Heresies* 1.24.3–4; cf. 3.16.1)

The above Gnostic teaching that Christ was not human resonates with the message of John's opponents as extracted from the epistles. Moreover, we know that second-century Gnostics claimed the gospel of John as their own, especially its exalted Christology.[21] But the Gnostic teaching about the Pleroma as containing 365 heavens and as created by mini-gods has no parallel in the opponents of 1, 2, and 3 John. It is more likely that the latter provides only the seeds of later Gnostic thought such as propounded by Basilides and Valentinus.[22] In any event, Gnosticism did not arise until after the writing of John's epistles.

Of the three heresies described above—Cerinthus, the Docetists, and the Gnostics—Cerinthus and the Docetists refuted in Ignatius's letters seem to have more in common with the portrait of John's opponents, especially in the way they denied salvation through Jesus' flesh and blood.

I now pull these last two sections together on the historical settings of the gospel of John and the epistles of John by offering six commonly accepted steps in the generation of the Johannine literature that was intimately related to the struggles of John's community.[23]

1. Somewhere in the late 80's, the apostle John compiled what would turn out to be an early draft of the gospel of John, essentially 1:19–20:31.[24] This document apparently worked at two levels: one that presented the historical Jesus as the Christ, the Son of God—and that in the face of Palestinian Jewish opposition to Jesus from about AD 27–30 (or alternatively AD 29–33; recall my earlier discussion of the issue of the dates of Christ's life); the other with reference to the expulsion of Jewish Christians from synagogues in western Asia Minor, dating in the late 80s.

2. In the late 80s to early 90s, some in the Johannine churches in and around Ephesus began to seriously misinterpret the above early form of the gospel of John circulating at that time in Asia Minor. These professing Johannine Christians emphasized

---

21. See, e.g., works such as *Gospel of Thomas*, *Gospel of Truth*, and *Apocryphon of John*, which reinterpret John along Gnostic lines.

22. The last twenty years or so have witnessed the emergence of a near consensus view among New Testament scholars, namely, that any full-blown Gnostic system did not appear until the second century AD. Therefore we can speak only of the beginning stages of Gnosticism in the first century AD, often labeled "incipient Gnosticism."

23. For helpful summaries of these steps, though with their various respective nuances, see Brown, *Epistles of John*, 47–115; Burge, *Letters of John*, 27–33; Kruse, *Letters of John*, 15–27. We will not yet factor Revelation in this scenario.

24. Though it should be noted that no manuscript exists without John's prologue in it.

Left: Traditional site of the burial place of St. John near Ephesus. *Right:* An icon of St. John's burial in the Monastery of St. John on Patmos.

Jesus' deity to the exclusion of his humanity. Moreover, they argued that the kingdom of God had fully arrived with the first coming of Christ and the possession of the Holy Spirit; hence, they were now spiritually perfect, without sin. They were the elite. It was apparently at this time that these misinterpreters of the gospel of John seceded from the Johannine churches. It may even be that they were the wealthier constituency of the churches in Ephesus and their departure created a harsh financial situation for the Christians who did not leave with the false teachers.[25]

3. In the early 90s, subsequent to the departure of the secessionists, the apostle John countered the claims of the false teachers. He did so, first, by editing his earlier draft of John, perhaps adding to it the prologue (1:1–18), especially verse 14's emphasis on the humanity of Jesus: "the Word became flesh." John may also have added John 19:34–35 to the original text; the reference to blood and water flowing from Jesus' side at the thrust of the soldier's spear. This is another indication that Jesus was fully human, even at his death. So this edition of the gospel ran from 1:1–20:31. Second, John composed the epistles of John for the purpose of countering the Docetic eschatological and ethical claims of the secessionists I previously identified.

4. Around the mid-90s John, the disciple of Jesus, died.

5. John's faithful followers then provided two finishing touches to the gospel of John. First, they probably added the references therein that refer to John as the Beloved Disciple (John 13:23; 19:26; 20:2; 21:7, 20), the guarantor of the Jesus tradition. Second, they added John 21 as an epilogue to the gospel. This final form of the gospel matches what we have today—John 1:1–21:25.[26]

---

25. Hans-Josef Klauck makes the interesting point that the secessionists had financial resources, whereas those who remained in the Ephesian churches did not. "Internal Opponents: The Treatment of the Secessionists in the First Epistle of John," *Concilium* 200 (1988): 55–65, especially 56–57.

26. It is possible, but less certain, that John 5:26–30, with its emphasis on futuristic eschatology, was also added to the gospel in this editing. This will have balanced out the realized eschatology of John 5:19–25. For

6. John's community and literature became part of the received tradition of early Christianity, the Scriptures. But the Johannine secessionists fragmented into splinter groups in the second century, associating themselves, or perhaps even forming, the heresies I earlier described: Cerinthus, Docetists, and Gnostics.

VI. THE SEQUENCE OF 1, 2, AND 3 JOHN

In light of the preceding discussion, we may now ask, What was the sequence of the writing of 1, 2, and 3 John? Many commentators posit that a theological consideration accounts for the sequence of the three letters. Kruse believes that 1 John was written first as a general letter landing a broadside against the opponents I discussed above, while 2 and 3 John were then designed to convey personal notes warning individual churches of the false teachers.[27]

---

more discussion see Raymond E. Brown, *The Gospel according to John I–XII*, Anchor Bible 29A (Garden City, N.Y.: Doubleday, 1966), 219–21. Recall my previous comments on that passage.

27. Kruse, *Letters of John*, 8.

The Epistolary Format of 2–3 John		
Epistolary Components		
	2 John	3 John
Sender	the presbyter (v. 1)	the presbyter (v. 1)
Addressee	the chosen lady and her children (v. 1)	the beloved Gaius (v. 1)
Greeting	"Grace, mercy and peace from God the Father and from Jesus Christ" (v. 3).	
Thanksgiving		"I pray that you may enjoy good health and that all may go well with you, even as your soul is getting along well" (v. 2).
Body	vv. 4–12	vv. 3–14
Closing	"The children of your chosen sister send their greetings" (v. 13).	"Peace to you. The friends here send their greetings. Greet the friends there by name" (v. 15).

For a fuller discussion of the matter, see Brown, *Epistles of John*, 788–95.

VII. THE GENRE OF THE EPISTLES OF JOHN

Second and Third John essentially follow the epistolary format, as the accompanying chart indicates.

But 1 John is another matter all together, since it has no epistolary components. This prompted B. F. Westcott, over a century ago, to say of 1 John that it has "no address, no subscription, no name is contained in it of person or place; there is no direct trace of the author, no indication of any special destination."[28] One wonders, then, how 1 John was ever classified as a General Epistle. If not a letter, what then is the genre of 1 John? Four possibilities surface: universal religious tractate, circular epistle, homily, or reworking of the gospel of John. The last possibility seems most likely. Thus, 1 John is a type of commentary on the gospel of John, particularly an exposé of the secessionists' misinterpretation of the gospel of John.

First John is thus a corrective piece for John's community to read and follow. Accordingly, the following parallels surface between the gospel of John and 1 John:

Gospel of John	1 John[29]
A. Prologue: 1:1–18 The word that was from the beginning entered the world in Christ.	A. Prologue: 1:1–4 Christ who was from the beginning was manifested to the disciples.
B. The Book of Signs: 1:19–12:50 The light shined in the darkness of Judaism but was rejected.	B. Part 1: 1:5–3:10 God is Light, and like Jesus, we must walk in the light.
C. The Book of Glory: 13:1–20:29 Jesus cares for and loves his own (believers in him).	C. Part 2: 3:11–5:12 God is love, and those who know him must love one another.
D. Conclusion: 20:30–31 The purpose is to bring people to faith in Jesus the Christ, the Son of God.	D. Conclusion: 5:13–21 The purpose is to bring people to faith in Jesus the Christ, the Son of God.

According to this approach, 1 John corrects the misinterpretation of the gospel of John by Gnostic-like teaching of the secessionists. The result of their teaching creates a theological domino effect: if one denies the incarnation, then one necessarily denies the atonement,

---

28. B. F. Westcott, *The Epistles of St. John*, new ed. (1883; repr., Grand Rapids: Eerdmans, 1966), xxix.
29. See Brown, *Epistles of John*, 90–129. The chart is my adaptation of the charts in Brown, *Epistles of John*, 124; and Burge, *Letters of John*, 44.

after which one will inevitably deny the need for ethics in the Christian life. These statements will become clear in my comments to follow on the epistles of John.

VIII. THE STRUCTURE OF 1 JOHN

The preceding debate over the genre of 1 John leads us now to a discussion of the structure of 1 John. As we have already seen, 2 and 3 John are easily outlined according to epistolary format, but not so 1 John. What, then, is the structure of 1 John? Three major theories of the outline of 1 John have vied for acceptance among interpreters: a three-part outline, a two-part outline, or no structure at all. I now interact with those theories.

A. A Tripartite Schema

The threefold division made famous by Robert Law has commended itself to many interpreters of 1 John. According to Law, 1 John presents three tests for true believers as opposed to those who had departed from the Johannine community: righteousness, love, and belief. Moreover, these three tests are repeated three times in 1 John, forming a sort of spiral effect.

> *Three major theories of the outline of 1 John have vied for acceptance among interpreters: a three-part outline, a two-part outline, or no structure at all.*

Prologue (1:1–4)

1. *First Cycle (1:5–2:28).* The Christian life as fellowship with God (walking in the Light), tested by righteousness (1:8–2:6), love (2:7–17), and belief (2:18–28).
2. *Second Cycle (2:29–4:6).* Divine sonship tested by righteousness (2:29–3:10a), love (3:10b–24a), and belief (3:24b–4:6).
3. *Third Cycle (4:7–5:21).* Closer correlation of righteousness, love, and belief.[30]

Unfortunately, the secessionists do not pass the tests: they do not engage in *righteous* behavior. By their not *loving* the brethren, they show that they do not have genuine *belief* in Jesus. Only John's community truly passes the three tests.

> *The threefold division made famous by Robert Law has commended itself to many interpreters of 1 John.*

But as many commentators have readily acknowledged, Law's theory, though ingenious, does not actually work. While the three tests are clearly delineated in the second unit, 1 John 2:29–4:6, they are not in the other two units. Regarding the first unit, 1:5–2:28, love (2:3–6) occurs in the section on righteousness (1:8–2:6), and conversely, love does not occur in 1 John 2:12–14, the heart of the love section; and righteousness does not occur in the third unit at all (4:7–5:21). For these reasons, many interpreters have abandoned the tripartite approach.[31]

---

30. Robert Law, *The Tests of Life: A Study of the First Epistle of St. John* (Edinburgh: T. & T. Clark, 1909), 1–24.
31. See Brown's critique, *Epistles of John*, 121–22.

B. A Bipartite Approach

Brown's argument that 1 John is patterned after the gospel of John is the basis for his thesis that 1 John should be divided into two parts, each respectively marked off by two declarations: God is light (1:5), and God is love (3:11; cf. 4:16b).

I supply the resulting outline, adding my descriptions along the way:

Prologue (1:1–4)

I.   First part (1:5–3:10).

    A. This is the message: God is light (1:5).

    B. Three claims and counterclaims (1:6–2:2).

        1. Claim to have fellowship (1:6a), *but* walk in darkness, not in light (1:6b–7).

        2. Claim to be sinless (1:8a), *but* truth is not in them (1:8b–9).

        3. Claim to be without sin (1:10a), *but* his word is not in them (1:10b–2:2).

    C. Three claims in need of testing by one's walk (2:3–11).

        1. We know him if we obey him (3/6 inclusio) (2:3–5).

        2. We abide in him by walking in him (2:6–8).

        3. We are in the light if we love the brothers (2:9–11).

    D. True believers walk in the light (2:12–17).

    E. Secessionists are not in the light (2:18–27).

    F. Two destinies: children of light versus followers of darkness (2:28–3:10).

II.   Second part (3:11–5:12).

    A. This is the message: God is love (3:11; cf. 4:16b).

    B. True believers love one another (3:12–24).

    C. The Spirit of truth versus the spirit of error (4:1–6).

    D. Love is the key (4:7–5:4a).

    E. Faith is the victory (5:4b–12).

III. Conclusion: Author's purpose (5:13–21).[32]

As mentioned earlier, this approach has much to commend it.

C. No Structure

Because of the difficulty of detecting a clear-cut outline for 1 John, some scholars discount any structure for it, claiming 1 John is held together only by a free association of ideas.[33] I, however, agree with Brown and others that there is an overarching logic to 1 John — the bipartite approach centering around two truths: God is light and God is love.

---

32. The bipartite approach was earlier defended by A. Feuillet, "The Structure of First John: Comparison with the 4th Gospel," *Biblical Theology Bulletin* 3 (1973): 194–216; and developed by Brown, *Epistles of John*, 123–29. One should note that there are anomalies even in Brown's approach. Thus love (1 John 2:9–10) is in the unit on light (1:5–3:10), but the theme of light does not occur in the second unit on love (3:11–5:12). These details, however, do not seem to overturn his bipartite thesis.

33. See, e.g., Marshall, *Epistles of John*, 26.

IX. THE GREEK MANUSCRIPT EVIDENCE FOR 1, 2, AND 3 JOHN

Now we briefly turn to the question of the Greek manuscript evidence for the epistles of John. William L. Richards has provided the most thorough investigation of the textual tradition of the Johannine letters. He concludes that there are three principal text groups that contain 1, 2, and 3 John: Alexandrian, Byzantine, and a mixed group.[34] We will have occasion to interact with these text types later as we make our way through the epistles, especially concerning 1 John 5:7–8, the famous "Johannine comma" (clause).

X. THE THEOLOGY OF THE EPISTLES OF JOHN

Every key aspect of John's theology in his epistles is presented in terms of its opposition to his Docetic/Gnostic opponents: Theology proper, Christology, Pneumatology, Soteriology, and Eschatology.

A. Theology

I reduce the teachings of the epistles of John about God to five beliefs. First, God is the true and holy God (1 John 5:20–21). This is vintage Old Testament monotheism. The flipside of this truth is that the Docetists are idolatrous; in other words, in distorting the word of God (see below) the secessionists have left the worship of the one true God.

Second, God is light; he is holy (1 John 1:5–2:14). As such, he is good (3 John 11–12). These thoughts remind the reader of Genesis 1, which proclaims the light and goodness of God's creation. But herein lay the error of the Docetists: in Platonic fashion they viewed the material world as evil—hence their rejection of Christ's humanity. In the epistles of John, then, the apostle thoroughly debunks the Docetic rejection of the goodness of God's creation as manifested in Jesus Christ.

Third, God is love, which was ultimately demonstrated through his giving up of his Son for the sins of humanity (1 John 3:7–19). The secessionists, to the contrary, have not experienced God's love because they rejected God's love in Christ.

Fourth, as such, the fact that Jesus Christ came in the flesh to atone for the sins of the world is the word and testimony of God (1 John 1:1–4; 5:9–12; 2 John 7). But because John's opponents rejected Christ they remain in their sins.

Fifth, those who embrace Jesus Christ are God's children (1 John 2:1, 28; 3:1–10; 5:4). These have forgiveness of sins (1 John 3:20–21; 5:16) and eternal life. But the Docetists are not truly born of God and consequently have neither forgiveness nor life.

B. Christology

The Christology of the epistles of John is straightforward: Jesus Christ is both God and human, whose death was an atoning sacrifice for the sins of the world. That message places two requirements on John's readers. First, they are to believe it (1 John 1:5–3:10; 2 John

> I agree with Brown and others that there is an overarching logic to 1 John—the bipartite approach centering around two truths: God is light and God is love.

---

34. William L. Richards, *The Classification of the Greek Manuscripts of the Johannine Epistles*, SBLDS 35 (Missoula, Mont.: Scholars, 1977).

1–5, 7–11), and second, they are to love their fellow believers in Jesus (1 John 3:11–5:12; 2 John 5–6; 3 John 3). The Docetists do neither. Regarding the first, they bought into the lie that Jesus Christ was only God and not human. Regarding the second, in leaving the Johannine community, they betrayed the brothers.

But those who believe in Jesus Christ and love his followers have fellowship with God (1 John 1:3), forgiveness (1 John 1:8–2:2), and the indwelling of the Spirit (1 John 2:27; 4:1–6); they are the children of God (1 John 3:11–16); they overcome Satan and the world (1 John 5:1–12); and they have spiritual union with the Father and the Son (1 John 4:7–21).

C. Pneumatology

The epistles of John do not provide a description of the essence of the Holy Spirit in the sense that he is the third member of the Trinity (though they no doubt assume that to be the case). Rather, in the epistles of John, the function of the Holy Spirit is highlighted, namely, he is the Spirit of truth who opposes the Spirit of error (1 John 4:1–6; 5:6–7). As the Spirit of truth, he bears witness to the fact that Jesus Christ is God and human. And the Spirit's indwelling and teaching of Christians remind them of that truth (1 John 2:20–27). Therefore, as such, the Spirit opposes the spirit of error that denies the humanity of Christ (1 John 4:1–6), which is the lie Satan propagates through the Docetists.

D. Soteriology

Like the Christology of the fourth gospel, the basis of salvation according to John's epistles is twofold: first, one must believe that Jesus is the Christ whose substitutionary death on the cross atones for sin (1 John 1:5–3:10; et al.), and second, one must have love for the true followers of Jesus Christ (1 John 3:11–5:12; et al.). These two are closely related: the former leads to the latter. To these belong all of the blessings mentioned above that Christ gives to his disciples: fellowship, forgiveness, the Spirit, the family of God, victory and union with the Trinity. The secessionists, however, in departing from the Johannine community, showed themselves to still be in the world and therefore unsaved (1 John 2:15–27; et al.).

E. Eschatology

The eschatological concept that governs the epistles of John is the overlapping of the two ages. This idea is showcased in 1 John 2:15–18a (cf. v. 8): the age to come already dawned with the first coming of Christ, which is overcoming this present evil age/world. That victory will be completed at the second coming of Christ.

According to the epistles of John, then, some five end-time events were set in motion at Christ's first coming that will continue and even intensify until his parousia. John's contribution to this subject is to align the Johannine community with the age to come while relegating the secessionists to this age/world which is passing away. I simply state these five events, leaving for later our discussion of them. (1) The messianic woes/Great Tribulation have been unleashed on the Johannine community in the form of the secessionists' heretical teaching (1 John 2:18, 22; 4:3). (2) This is the vanguard movement of the Antichrist (1 John 2:18–19). (3) Those who have departed from John's Christology have succumbed to end-time apostasy (1 John 2:18–19). (4) The heretics' opposition to the Johannine community constitutes the end-time holy war between the sons of darkness and the sons of light (1 John 1:5–7; 2:8–11; 3:1–10; 4:1–6). (5) But those who are faithful to John's message are the people of the new covenant (1 John 1:5–2:2; 4:20–21).

CONCLUSION

With the preceding introductory matters in mind, along with my earlier treatment of the gospel of John, we now proceed to an analysis of the epistles of John.

REVIEW QUESTIONS

1. What three features do the epistles of the New Testament share with ancient letters?

2. Were the letters of Paul private or public?

3. How does the "letter" of 1 John differ from the other letters of the New Testament?

4. What three steps seemed to be involved in the canonization of the epistles of John?

5. What are the three conflicting perspectives regarding the authorship of the Johannine literature?

6. What are the differences between the gospel of John and his epistles?

7. What theory might account for the above differences?

8. Evaluate the three possible identities of John's opponents.

9. What six steps seem to explain the generation of the Johannine literature?

10. How might the theological explanation account for the sequence of the writing of 1, 2, and 3 John?

11. What is the bipartite proposal for the outline of 1 John?

12. What are the problems with Robert Law's "tripartite schema" of 1 John?

KEY TERMS

authorship of 1, 2, and 3 John

bipartite schema

canonicity of 1, 2, and 3 John

Cerinthus

Christology

Docetists

Elder/Presbyter

epistle/letter

epistolary form of 2 and 3 John

eschatology

form of ancient letters

Gnostics

historical setting of 1, 2, and 3 John

prologues of John and 1 John

secessionists

sequence of 1, 2, and 3 John

tripartite schema

CHAPTER 26

Prologue

1 JOHN 1:1–4

Objectives

After reading this chapter, you should be able to:

- Understand the usage of the relative pronoun in 1 John 1:1, 3.
- Identify who the "we" are in 1 John 1:1–4.
- Explain key titles for Jesus in John's prologue (1 John 1:1–4).
- Relate the background of John's term "fellowship" (1 John 1:3–4).

INTRODUCTION

Prologue means "first" or "before word." For our purposes, we may say that John's prologue serves as an introduction to the letter as a whole, stressing as it does the humanity of Jesus Christ.

It does so in the face of the teaching of the Docetic opposition to the Johannine churches. The Greek text of the prologue consists of one long sentence, extending from verse 1 to verse 4, in which occur five relative clauses along with a puzzling alternation of tenses that pervades the entire prologue—from imperfect (continuous action in the past) to perfect (action completed in the past, the result of which continues into the present) to aorist (undefined action, often in the past) to present, and then roughly the reverse order of those tenses.

> John's prologue serves as an introduction to the letter as a whole, stressing as it does the humanity of Jesus Christ.

To grasp the meaning of the prologue of 1 John, we need to resolve a number of key issues: Why the use of the neuter relative pronoun? Related to this, what does John mean by the phrase "from the beginning"? What does the apostle mean by "we"? Why does the author use the sensory verbs "heard," "seen," "touched," and "appeared"? What do the words "Word of life" mean? And how do these relate to "eternal life"? How are we to understand the two titles attributed to Jesus in the prologue—"Son" and "Christ"? What do "fellowship" and "joy" have to do with the prologue? I now attempt to answer these questions.

I. THE RELATIVE PRONOUN (*HO*) IS USED FIVE TIMES IN THE PROLOGUE (VV. 1, 3)

The relative pronoun *ho* introduces the following clauses: "that which was from the beginning," "that which we have heard," "that which we have seen," "that which we have looked at" (v. 1), "that which we have seen and heard" (v. 3). Verse 3 makes it clear that the "that which" refers to Jesus Christ, but how so? Do the relative clauses refer to Christ's preincarnational existence like the prologue introducing John's gospel does, especially with its identification of Jesus as the preexistent "word" (*logos*, John 1:1) that gives "life" (*zōē*, John 1:4)? No doubt, 1 John 1:1–4 presupposes that background. But the relative pronouns in verses 1 and 3 are neuter in gender and therefore do not modify the masculine noun, *logos* ("word" v. 1), nor the feminine noun, *zōē* ("life," v. 1). Consequently, most commentators today recognize that *ho* is referring to the earthly career of Jesus—his life, death, and resurrection.

II. THIS CONCLUSION CLEARS UP THE CONFUSION SURROUNDING JOHN'S FIRST PHRASE (V. 1).

It would be understandable to equate "beginning" (*ap' arxēs*, v. 1) here with Jesus' preexistent state with God in eternity past, modeled after John 1:1 (cf. Genesis 1:1)—"In the beginning was the Word, and the Word was with God, and the Word was God." And, once again, John no doubt presumes that truth here. But it is more likely that 1 John 1:1 specifically has in mind the beginning of Jesus' ministry, namely, his baptism by John the Baptist, which commenced Jesus' earthly ministry.

This is so for two reasons. First, the same phrase—"from the beginning"—occurs eight other times in 1 and 2 John and never implies that Jesus' preexistence is in view (1 John 2:7, 13, 14, 24; 3:8,11; 2 John 5, 6). Second, the relative clause initiating verse 1 ("that which was from the beginning") is parallel to the other four relative clauses in the prologue introduced by *ho*, and they all refer to observing Jesus' life. (John could not have used such personal sensory terms—"heard," "seen," "looked," and "touched"—of Jesus' preexistence, because he wasn't there!)

III. WHO ARE THE "WE" (VV. 1–3)?[1]

> That ... which *we* have heard, which *we* have seen with our eyes, which *we* have looked at and our hands have touched—this *we* proclaim.... *we* have seen it and testify to it, and *we* proclaim to you.... *We* proclaim to you what *we* have seen and heard ... (1 John 1:1–3).

Most modern commentators agree that "we" here is a genuine first-person plural, rather than being merely an editorial way for the author to refer to himself. But what is the specific nuance of "we" if it is truly to be interpreted as a first-person plural? For many, the answer is that John is referring to himself and the other apostles who were eyewitnesses of the historical Jesus, beginning from his baptism and all the way to his death and resurrection.

Indeed, John 19:35 and 20:29–31 seem to say as much, since they declare that the author of the gospel of John personally witnessed the events described therein. The same should be said of the "we" statements in 1 John 1:1–4.

Positing that the author of 1 John 1:1–4 is the apostle John nicely explains the various tenses used in the prologue. The imperfect verbs (continuous action in the past) used of Jesus, the Son of the Father, and the Christ (vv. 1, 2), implying Jesus' preexistence with God in eternity past, also focus on the earthly career of Jesus from his baptism to his death and resurrection. The perfect verbs (continuous action in the past whose results continue in the present)—we "heard," "saw," "looked at"—indicate that John and the other apostles were personally associated with Jesus during his life and continue to report that association in the present. The aorist verbs (undefined action in the past; which is described as a whole)—"looked," "touched," "revealed"—refer to the whole life of Christ witnessed by John and others. The present verbs (continuous action in the present)—"testify," "proclaim," "write"—refer to the ongoing testimony of John to his churches concerning the reality of the events to which he attests. All of this confirms the eyewitness interpretation of 1 John 1:1–4.

> First John 1:1 specifically has in mind the beginning of Jesus' ministry, namely, his baptism by John the Baptist, which commenced Jesus' earthly ministry.

> John is referring to himself and the other apostles who were eyewitnesses of the historical Jesus, beginning from his baptism and all the way to his death and resurrection.

---

1. In the Greek New Testament, the person is reflected in the verb or separately by means of the personal pronoun.

IV. WE ARE NOW IN A POSITION TO ANSWER THE QUESTION OF WHY THE AUTHOR USES THE SENSORY VERBS IN THE PROLOGUE.

"Heard," "seen," "looked," and "touched" are tactile terms describing the physical nature of Christ. Jesus could be heard, seen,[2] and touched because he was flesh and blood. Such verbs, then, of eyewitness accounts counter the Docetic claim that Christ was God but not truly human.

> Such verbs, then, of eyewitness accounts counter the Docetic claim that Christ was God but not truly human.

V. THE CONTENT OF THE MESSAGE OF THE APOSTOLIC WITNESSES IS THE "WORD OF LIFE" (V. 1).

Although "Word" is reminiscent of John 1:1, where it is said that Jesus is the "Word," here the "Word" is the message proclaimed (see 1 John 1:10; 2:5, 7, 14; 3:18; 3 John 10). It is a message, or word, about life. But that life is further characterized in verse 2 as "eternal life," and according to 1 John 5:20, Jesus Christ is that eternal life. Verse 2 undergirds the fact that Jesus Christ is eternal life in that it announces that Christ was in God the Father's presence (implied) from eternity past. That is the truth that God revealed about Jesus to John and his eyewitness associates (v. 2). "Father" is a key Johannine term expressing Jesus' relation to God. Twenty-three times in the gospel of John Jesus speaks of God as "my father," and another sixty-five times of God as "the Father."[3] This divine relationship is presupposed in the epistles of John.

---

2. "Looked" (*theaomai*) and "see" (*horaō*) are synonymous.
3. So Raymond E. Brown, *The Epistles of John*, Anchor Bible 30 (Garden City, N.Y.: Doubleday, 1982), 169.

The Shrine of the Book, Jerusalem, where some of the Dead Sea Scrolls are housed.

Berthold Werner/Wikimedia Commons

VI. THE SPECIAL BOND BETWEEN JESUS AND GOD IS HIGHLIGHTED BY THE TERMS "SON" AND "CHRIST" (V. 3).

"Son" (*huios*) is used of Jesus' relationship to God twenty-seven times in the gospel of John and another twenty-four times in 1 and 2 John. So, obviously, Jesus' divine Sonship is of great importance to the apostle John. Interestingly enough, only Jesus is called God's Son in the gospel of John and his epistles; Christians are instead labeled the children of God[4] (see, e.g., 1 John 2:1; 3:1, 2, 10; 5:2).

> Only Jesus is called God's Son in the gospel of John and his epistles.

Next, Jesus is called "Christ" (*Christos*). *Christos* is the Greek word for "anointed," while "Messiah" is the Hebrew term for the same. We examined this term earlier, but here we note that the Old Testament equated the Davidic King, God's Anointed (Messiah), with God's Son (see 2 Sam. 7:14 and Ps. 2:7). This may be the impetus for John's assigning of the two titles—Son and Christ/Messiah—to Jesus here in verse 3.

VII. JOHN PROCLAIMS THE MESSAGE SO THAT HIS READERS WILL HAVE *KOINŌNIA* AND JOY WITH HIM, GOD, AND CHRIST (VV. 3–4).

Koinōnia can be translated "fellowship" or "community." While koinōnia described ancient Roman societies and schools, the idea of community was especially dear to the Dead Sea Scrolls (1QS = the Community Rule), where the Qumran community considered itself to be the new covenant eschatological community. Thus, like "joy," "fellowship" is understood by John to be the present experience of the eschatological age to come, or kingdom of God, that comes by abiding in Christ (John 15:11; 16:20–24; 17:13). Fellowship and joy, then, are rooted in the true understanding and relationship with Jesus Christ, the Son of God the Father. More specifically, the Johannine churches will experience the complete joy of the age to come if they remain in John's community of faith—that is, if they don't follow after the Docetic secessionists.

The "House of David" Inscription: a ninth-century BC Aramaic inscription found in Dan mentioning the battle of Ben-Hadad, king of Aram, against "the house of David."

CONCLUSION

In conclusion, 1 John 1:1–4 is the apostle's testimony that Jesus Christ come in the flesh is the true means to experiencing fellowship with God, that is, the new covenant.

---

4. Ibid., 171.

1. What does the relative pronoun (*ho*) refer back to in time in 1 John 1:1, 3?

2. What does the phrase in 1 John1:1, "that which was from the beginning," refer back to?

3. Who are the "we" mentioned several times in 1 John 1:1 – 4?

4. What do the words "Word of life" (1 John 1:1) mean?

5. What is the Old Testament background for the titles of Jesus — "Son" and "Christ" — in 1 John 1:3?

6. How do the words koinōnia and "joy" relate to each other in 1 John 1:3 – 4?

KEY TERMS

aorist tense	imperfect tense	prologue of 1 John
Christ/Messiah	joy	relative pronouns
"From the beginning"	*koinōnia*	Son
"heard," "seen," "touched," "appearance"	perfect tense	"we"
	personal eyewitness	Word of life

CHAPTER 27

Three Claims and Three Counterclaims

1 JOHN 1:5–2:2

Objectives

After reading this chapter, you should be able to:

- Summarize the three sets of conditional sentences that comprise 1 John 1:5–2:2.

- Explore the Docetic arguments behind 1 John 1:5–2:2, which John refutes.

INTRODUCTION

That 1 John 1:5–2:2 forms a self-contained section is clear from the structure of these verses, which consists of six conditional sentences divided into three sets:

That 1 John 1:5–2:2 forms a self-contained section is clear from the structure of these verses, which consists of six conditional sentences divided into three sets.

1. 1:6–7: two conditional sentences (each beginning with the subjunctive *ean*), the first of which is the opponents' claim, while the second conditional sentence provides John's counterclaim.
2. 1:8–9: two conditional sentences (each beginning with *ean*), the first of which is the opponents' claim, while the second conditional sentence provides John's counterclaim.
3. 1:10–2:2: two conditional sentences (each beginning with *ean*), the first of which is the opponents' claim, while the second conditional sentence provides John's counterclaim. Verse 2a in this set is John's pastoral aside comment.

ANALYSIS

First John 1:5 introduces the section "This is the message we have heard from him and declare to you: God is light; in him there is no darkness at all." The word *angelia* is used only twice in the New Testament—here and in 1 John 3:11. It introduces the two major units of 1 John (1:5–3:10 and 3:11–5:12). Most commentators take angelia to mean "message." This message was given by Jesus ("from him")[1] to John and the other apostolic eyewitnesses and now to the churches in and near Ephesus. The content of that message is straightforward, namely, that God is light and in him there is no darkness.

I. 1:6–7

Now comes the first of three claims made by the Docetists. Each one begins with the words "if we claim" (*ean eipōmen*), with John then supplying the opponents' boast.

Now comes the first of three claims made by the Docetists. Each one begins with the words "if we claim" (*ean eipōmen*), with John then supplying the opponents' boast. Thus, "if we claim that we have fellowship with God" (the opponents' boast) but "walk in darkness" (the true nature of the opponents' situation), then "[they] lie and do not live by the truth" (John's assessment of the opponents).[2] We now discuss each of these three statements.

John's opponents claim to have "fellowship" with God. I earlier suggested that the word taps into the idea of the covenant community. Wolfgang Nauck, in particular, roots all of 1 John 1:6–2:2 in the covenant context. He argues that John's affirmations in these

---

1. "From him" (v. 5a) must refer back to Christ, the last third person antecedent mentioned (v. 3b).

2. The grammatical construction of v. 6 consists of the subjunctive particle (*ean*) plus a subjunctive verb (*eipōmen*) in the protasis part of the conditional sentence with a present tense verb in the apodosis (*pseudometha, poioumen*), thus expressing an axiomatic statement. As such, v. 6, as well as vv. 8 and 10, are a type of third-class conditional sentence.

verses ("walk in the light," v. 7; "confess our sins," v. 9; et al.) are based on the moral demands of the Pentateuch, which are intimately related to God's covenant with Israel.[3] So the point to be made from this background is that the opponents of John claimed to be in fellowship with God, thus constituting them as the new covenant community.

According to John, however, the reality is that the secessionists form nothing of the kind. Actually, they left the new covenant community! Consequently, they walk in spiritual darkness, lie, and do not practice the truth. The term "walk" (*peripateō*) already had a long history in the Old Testament with reference to one's way of life (Ps. 119; Prov. 8:20; Isa. 2:5. cf. Mark 7:5; Acts 21:21; Eph. 5:8; et al.). The phrase "to walk" is common in the Johannine writings (John 8:12; 11:9, 10; 12:35; 1 John 1:6, 7; 2:11; Rev. 21:24).

In the Johannine literature "lying," the opposite of "doing the truth," is not a matter of ignorance but of willful distortion of the truth (John 8:44; 1 John 2:21, 22; 2:4; 4:20).

"Truth" (*alētheia*) is significant for the Johannine epistles, occurring some twenty times therein (cf. its some 25 occurrences in the gospel of John). Truth is God's revelation, which, if received, makes a person's character godly.[4] So John is declaring that those who have been faithful to God are the true covenant community, not those who abandoned it.

The second conditional sentence in verses 6–7 occurs in verse 7, where John describes the situation of true believers: they walk in the light (just as God is light), have fellowship with him, and the shed blood of Jesus, God's Son, cleanses them from all sin. Because the audience has remained true to the message of the incarnational Christ, they are walking in God's purity, and they do participate in God's true covenant community. As a result, their sins are forgiven because of Christ's sacrificial death on the cross (cf. 1 John 2:2; Lev. 17:11; cf. also Ps. 19:13; Prov. 20:9; Jer. 33:8 with John 6:53–56; 19:34; Rev. 1:5; 5:9; 7:14; 12:11; see also Acts 20:28; Rom. 5:9; Eph. 1:7; 2:13; Col. 1:20; Heb. 9:14; 1 Peter 1:18–19). Most likely 1 John 1:7 refers, not to the forgiveness of sins initiating conversion to Christ, but rather to the Christian life in general.

We may detect in verse 7, then, the following nuance of meaning: the secessionists denied the truth that Jesus Christ's death was real—that is, they said that Jesus the man died on the cross, not the divine Christ.

But for John such teaching was a lie, and it removed the Docetists from the truth of the covenant community, leaving them to walk in spiritual darkness.

II. 1:8–9

First John 1:8–9 consists of two more conditional sentences that follow the same pattern as verses 6–7. Verse 8a records the opponents' claim, while verse 8b is John's assessment of

---

3. Wolfgang Nauck, *Die Tradition und der Charakter des ersten Johannesbriefes,* WUNT 3 (Tübingen: Mohr, 1957).

4. Raymond E. Brown, *The Epistles of John,* Anchor Bible 30 (Garden City, N.Y.: Doubleday, 1982), 199.

their true status, and in verse 9 John supplies his counterclaim to the secessionists. These three components will occupy our attention below.

We may detect in verse 7, then, the following nuance of meaning: the secessionists denied the truth that Jesus Christ's death was real — that is, they said that Jesus the man died on the cross, not the divine Christ.

Verse 8 registers the claim of the opponents, "We are without sin." The expression "to have sin" (NIV, "guilty of sin") occurs four times in John (9:41; 15:22, 24; 19:11). First John 1:8 seems to refer to a state of guilt and sin. In other words, John's opponents in 1 John 1:8 claim no longer to be in a state of sin and guilt, because they have the truth about Jesus Christ.[5] Their Docetic understanding no doubt contributed to such confidence, for if Christ was not truly human, then, by extension, what is committed by the body is of no importance. So sin committed by the Docetists through the instruments of their bodies did not matter since they became enlightened about the real nature of Christ. John's response to this outlandish notion is that the Docetists were self-deceived and the truth did not abide in them (v. 8b).

It is significant that John elsewhere uses the language of deception for the Docetists, who are of the spirit of the Antichrist (1 John 2:26; 2 John 7; cf. 1 John 2:18, 19, 22; 3:8–10; 4:1–6), because they deny that Christ has come in the flesh.

The second conditional sentence in 1 John 1:8–9 occurs in verse 9, which follows the same pattern we identified above. "If we confess our sins" is a conditional clause, as the commentaries observe, that probably is communal in nature; that is, it involved mutual confession of sin in the church body (cf. 1 John 1:9 and 5:16 with Matt. 3:6; Mark 1:5; Acts 19:18; James 5:16; see also 1QS 1:23–26; *Didache* 4:14). John's word "to confess" (*homologein*) Christ is also public in reference (John 1:20; 9:22; 12:42; cf. also 1 John 2:23; 4:2, 15; 2 John 7).

Verse 8 registers the claim of the opponents, "We are without sin." John's response to this outlandish notion is that the Docetists were self-deceived and the truth did not abide in them (v. 8b).

The attributes of being "faithful and just" bespeak God's faithfulness to his covenant, as Deuteronomy 7:9 makes clear, "Know therefore that the LORD your God is God; he is the faithful God, keeping his covenant of love [Gk. *dikaios*; Heb. *chesed*] to … those who love him and keep his commands." Deuteronomy 32:4 makes the same connection in the context of God's covenant with Israel: God is faithful and just (cf. Jer. 42:5).

Likewise, the words in 1 John 1:9, "Forgive us our sins and purify us from all unrighteousness" (two synonymous statements), are rooted in the Old Testament sacrificial system (Lev. 4:20; 19:22; Num. 14:19), which is intimately related to the covenant with God. One remains in the covenant, then, by confessing one's sin and being forgiven (*aphienai* — see the above three Old Testament references) of sin.

---

5. Ibid., 205–6.

The upshot of John's counterclaim in 1 John 1:9 is that those who remain in the Johannine churches are the ones who are members of the new covenant, whose forgiveness of sins are based on Christ's sacrificial death on the cross, not some phantom who was whisked away before suffering in his body for sin.

III. 1:10 – 2:2

The third set of conditional sentences meets us in 1:10 – 2:2. Verse 10a reflects the opponents' claim; verse 10b provides John's assessment of their true status; after a pastoral aside in 1 John 2:1a, comes John's counterclaim in 2:1b – 2. I now unpack these three points.

The secessionists had apparently claimed that they committed no sin. While 1:8a records a similar boast, verse 10 seems to refer to specific sins, not just the abiding state of sin or guilt. Therefore the opponents believed themselves to be free of sins (implied — since coming to the knowledge that Christ was not fully human).

But John believed nothing of the kind and therefore labeled the secessionists "liars" and devoid of the "word," or message, of Christ. The logic behind John's accusation seems to be something like this: to deny the reality of sin is to deny the need for the incarnation and thus the sacrifice of Christ, which, in turn, makes God a liar!

First John 2:1a is a pastoral aside comment. John's use of the word *teknia* ("children") is interesting. As Raymond Brown has pointed out, three different terms for children occur in the epistles of John. *Teknon*, "child," is used in 1 John of Christians in general as the children of God (cf. 1 John 3:1, 2, 10; 5:2; 2 John 1, 4, 13; 3 John 4). However, *teknion* — "child" — (the diminutive form of *teknon*) refers to John's addressees, namely, his spiritual children, the ones who have been faithful to his message by remaining in the Johannine churches (cf. 1 John 2:1, 12, 28; 3:7, 18; 4:4; 5:21). So also, *paidion* — "child" — is a term of direct address for John's churches (cf. 1 John 2:14, 18).[6]

First John 2:1b – 2 is the last of the six conditional sentences in this section, and it conveys John's counterclaim to 1:10a — but if we do sin, we have in Christ a *paraclete* ("advocate") and an atoning sacrifice. The two images just mentioned dominate verses 1 – 2. While the gospel of John equates the Paraclete with the Holy Spirit (John 14:16, 26; 15:26: 16:7 – 15), 1 John 2:1 identifies Jesus by that title. This switch could be due to the secessionists' overemphasis on the Holy Spirit to the downplaying of Christ (see my later discussion of 1 John 2:20 – 27). Also, no doubt the fact that the Holy Spirit is called "another paraclete," according to John 14:16 – 17, implies that Jesus himself is a paraclete, thus intimately associating Jesus and the Spirit.

Jesus Christ is the "righteous" paraclete, or "advocate" (John 14:16 TNIV). It may well be that this description plays off the biblical idea that Satan accuses the people of God before God's throne (Job 1:6 – 2:7; Zech. 3:1 – 3; cf. Rev. 12:10). But, according to

---

6. Ibid., 213 – 14. *Teknia* in 1 John 2:12a is used interchangeably with *padia* in 1 John 2:13.

The Tabernacle
A portable temple for the wilderness journey

The new religious observances taught by Moses in the desert centered on rituals connected with the tabernacle, and amplified Israel's sense of separateness, purity, and oneness under the Lordship of Yahweh.

A few desert shrines have been found in Sinai, notably at Serabit el-Khadem and at Timnah in the Negev, and show marked Egyptian influence.

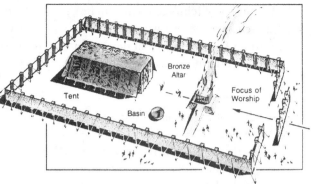

Specific cultural antecedents to portable shrines carried on poles and covered with thin sheets of gold can be found in ancient Egypt as early as the Old Kingdom (2800–2250 B.C.), but were especially prominent in the 18th and 19th dynasties (1570–1180). The best examples come from the fabulous tomb of Tutankhamun, c. 1350.

Comparisons of construction in the text of Ex. 25–40 with the frames, shrines, poles, sheathing, draped fabric covers, gilt rosettes, and winged protective figures from the shrine of Tutankhamun are instructive. The period, the Late Bronze Age, is equivalent in all dating systems to the era of Moses and the Exodus.

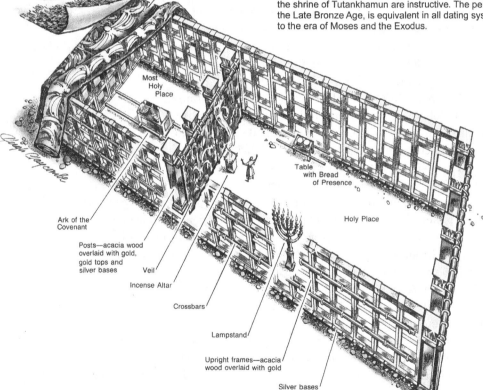

The tabernacle.

© Hugh Claycombe 1997

Sacrifice at the tabernacle.

John, Jesus Christ has defeated Satan and replaced him with his own righteous defense of God's people (cf. 1 John 3:8).

The other dominant image in 1 John 2:1–2 is that of Jesus' atonement (*hilasmos*) for sin. That "propitiation" is the correct translation of *hilasmos* seems assured in light of Leviticus 25:9, where *hilasmos* is the Greek word used in the Septuagint for the Hebrew *yom* (day) *kippur* (covering/atonement). This verse describes the fall Jewish festival of the Day of Atonement. On that day, the high priest offered a bull

Animals appointed for sacrifice.

and a goat as a sacrifice for the sins of Israel. He then poured the blood of those sacrificed animals onto the mercy seat (the *hilasmos* or *kippur*) on the ark of the covenant (see Lev. 16:16). This background is certainly applied to Jesus by the writer of the Hebrews in chapters 9–10, and the same is true of 1 John 2:2. Indeed, the reference to Jesus' shed blood in 1 John 1:7 seems to confirm that understanding.

Items from the Holy Place. *Left:* A model of the golden table of showbread with two stacks of bread and two golden bowls of incense. *Right:* The golden lampstand (menorah).

Left: A representation of the high priest sprinkling blood on the mercy seat (or atonement cover) in the Most Holy Place on the Day of Atonement. *Right:* Contents of the ark of the covenant in the Holy of Holies: a model of the ark, Aaron's rod, the two stone tablets, and the golden pot of manna.

CONCLUSION

First John 1:5–2:2 pits the Johannine community against the Docetic secessionists who turned away from the apostle John's teaching that Jesus Christ has come in the flesh. The former constitute the new covenant church, while the latter left it.

REVIEW QUESTIONS

1. Summarize the three sets of conditional sentences that comprise 1 John 1:5 – 2:2 relative to John's opponents and the apostle's response to them.

2. Why did the Docetists not have fellowship with the Son, according to 1 John 1:6 – 7?

3. Why did John's opponents think they had no sin, according to 1 John 1:8 – 9 and 1:10 – 2:2?

4. What does John mean by Jesus' "atonement" for sin (1 John 2:2)? What is the Old Testament background of 1 John 2:2?

KEY TERMS

angelia	conditional sentences	*hilasmos*
atonement	Docetic	"If we claim"
"child"	fellowship	Paraclete

CHAPTER 28

Three More Claims and Counterclaims

1 JOHN 2:3–11

Objectives

After reading this chapter, you should be able to:

- Explain the three claims of the Docetists that John refutes in 1 John 2:3–11.

- Explain John's view of what it means that God indwells his people.

INTRODUCTION

First John 2:3–11 contains three more claims of John's opponents and then three counterclaims of the apostle. Each of the claims of the secessionists begins with the participle "saying" (*legōn*) — verses 4, 6, and 9[1] — followed by John's rebuttals. The passage, then, can be outlined as follows:

I. General theme: We can be sure we know God by keeping his commandments (v. 3).[2]

II. The first wrong claim picks up on the theme of knowing God (vv. 4–5).

   A. The opponents claim to know God but do not follow his commandments (v. 4a).

   B. John's assessment: they are liars and the truth is not in them (v. 4b).

   C. John's rebuttal: whoever keeps God's word is perfected in his love; this is what it means to be in God (v. 5).

III. The second wrong claim picks up on the last statement of being in God (vv. 6–8).

   A. The opponents claim they abide in God (v. 6a).

   B. John's assessment: then they must walk as Christ walked (v. 6b).

   C. John's rebuttal: the commandment of Christ is to love, which is both old and new. Obeying this commandment is proof that one is in the light (vv. 7–8).

IV. The third wrong claim picks up on the previous theme of light (vv. 9–11).

   A. The opponents claim to be in the light (v. 9a).

   B. John's assessment: because they hate their brothers, the opponents are in the dark (v. 9b).

   C. John's rebuttal: those who love the brothers are in the light (the Johannine community); those who hate the brothers are in the dark (the secessionists) (vv. 10–11).

First John 2:3–11 contains three more claims of John's opponents and then three counterclaims of the apostle.

ANALYSIS

I now analyze the paragraph.

"By this" (*en toutō*, v. 3, which the NIV does not translate) refers to what follows; namely, the way we know that we truly know God is that we obey his commands. "Knowledge" (*gnōsis* and its derivatives) is a key term in the gospel of John (it occurs 56 times) and the epistles (25 times in 1 John, 1 time in 2 John). Most scholars base the Johannine idea of knowledge in God's revelation to Israel in the Old

---

1. The NIV obscures this by offering two different translations of *legōn*: "the man who says" (v. 4) and "whoever claims" (vv. 6, 9).

2. I am indebted to Raymond E. Brown, *The Epistles of John*, Anchor Bible 30 (Garden City, N.Y.: Doubleday, 1982), 277, for the following outline, though I have adapted it to my own argumentation.

Testament. Through God's self-disclosure in his mighty acts and by his Spirit, Israel could know God in an experiential way. Such knowledge was to be the crowning quality of the new covenant and would result in obedience to God from the heart (Jer. 31:33–34; Ezek. 36:26–27).

John's statement in verse 3 is an opening salvo in the paragraph against his opponents, whose three claims follow. First, they claim to know God but do not obey his "commandments" (*entolas*, v. 4a).[3] But this only proves that the secessionists are liars and that the truth is not in them (v. 4b), for knowing God and obeying him cannot be divorced. Verse 5 contains the apostle's counterclaim: whoever obeys God's word, God's love is perfected in him. "Word" (*logos*) is synonymous with "commandment," as can be seen in verse 7 where the two are equated. For the first time, God's love is mentioned in the epistles of John. *Agapē* is not a love originating in the human heart but, rather, is a spontaneous, unmerited, love flowing from God to the Christian and from the Christian to a fellow believer.

What do the words, "God's love is truly made perfect [NIV 'complete'] in him [the Johannine Christian]" mean? The Greek word for "perfect" is *teleioō*, which means "I complete." Thus, for example, in John's gospel Jesus speaks repeatedly using *teleioō* of completing the work(s) assigned to him by his Father (4:34; 5:36; 17:4). Besides 1 John 2:5, *teleioō* occurs three times in John's letters: in 4:12 (God's love for us is completed in us when we love one another), 4:17 (God's love for us completes its work in us when we have confidence on the day of judgment), and 4:18 (perfect love casts out fear; conversely, the presence of fear indicates God's love is not yet completed in the believer). This idea of completion suggests that 2:5 means that God's love is perfected/completed in those who obey God's command to love one another.[4]

First John 2:5 closes with the clause "This is how we know we are in him," which forms an inclusio with verse 3. The last-mentioned words, "in him," introduce the reader to John's theme of immanence — the indwelling of God — which is best discussed in connection with verse 6.

The second claim of the opponents and John's counterclaim occur in verses 6–8. The secessionists boast that they are "in" (*menein*) God, but John begs to disagree: if they were truly in God, then they would walk as Christ walked, namely, by loving the brethren, which they do not. The positive counterpart of verse 6 is that the one walking as Jesus walked is in God.

Although an earlier generation of scholars argued that John's concept of immanence is indebted to the mystery religions, whereby worshipers believed themselves to be united with the deity, most interpreters today recognize that the Old Testament is the closer source

---

3. "Command/commands" occurs 18 times in John's epistles (10 times in the singular, 8 times in the plural). They are interchangeable, giving a comprehensive sense to the one command to love one another. Ibid., 251.

4. Colin G. Kruse, *The Letters of John*, Pillar New Testament Commentary (Grand Rapids: Eerdmans, 2000), 80.

for John's thinking, particularly God's indwelling the tabernacle (Ex. 33:7–11) and the temple (2 Chron. 7:1–3; Ezek. 48:35; Zech. 2:10–11; cf. Sir. 24:3, 8; *Jub.* 1:17, 26). But the prophets of the new covenant longed for the day when God would indwell the hearts of his people, not just the temple (Jer. 24; 31; Ezek. 36). This principle of internalizing obedience, not just following laws on tablets of stone, continues with John, beginning with Jesus (John 1:14) and extending to his followers (i.e., "to be in" or "abide in" God/Christ).

Verse 7 fills in the details as to how Jesus walked: he loved others. That is why John can say, on the one hand, that love is not a new command, because loving one another goes back to Jesus (John 13:34–35). But, on the other hand, the command to love one another is new in the sense that Jesus' death and resurrection inaugurated the age to come or the kingdom of God. And the command to love is new in that it is a key sign of the presence of the new covenant (see again John 13:34).

Verse 8 furthers the eschatological aspect of the new command to love by announcing that God's light, or righteousness, has already dawned and is dispelling darkness, or sinfulness (cf. 2:15–17). The full light of God will be revealed at the return of Christ, according to 1 John 2:28.

The third claim and counterclaim occur in 1 John 2:9–11. Picking up on the contrast between light and darkness, the apostle says that even though his opponents boast that they are in God's light, they are nevertheless still in darkness, as is evident in the fact that they hate their brothers. How the Docetists hated their brethren is specified in 1 John 2:19: they seceded from the Johannine community; and in 3:11–17: they deprived the community of financial assistance. John's response comes in 2:10–11: those who love the brethren are in the light and will not be scandalized ("stumble"); in other words, they will not falter in the Christian faith by departing from the truth that John holds dear (v. 10). Conversely, those who hate the brethren are spiritually blind and in the dark ethically.

We may now summarize 1 John 2:3–11 using a syllogism:

Premise A: To know God is to keep his commandment.

Premise B: God's commandment is to love the brethren.

Therefore: To know God is to love the brethren.

This is what those faithful to John's teaching are doing and what the secessionists are precisely not doing. No doubt the apostle wanted his audience to get the connection here between Christology and ethics: to deny that Christ has come in the flesh (Christology) leads to hating the brethren, Christ's community of flesh and blood (ethics).

REVIEW QUESTIONS

1. What are the three claims of the Docetists that John refutes in 1 John 2:3 – 11?

2. What is the most probable background of John's term "knowledge"?

3. What is Christian love?

4. What does John mean by the word "perfect"?

5. Summarize John's understanding of God's indwelling.

6. How did the Docetists hate their brothers?

KEY TERMS

abide in God	knowing God	"perfect"
commandments	knowledge	"saying"
"in the light"	love	to be in/to abide in

CHAPTER 29

Assurances and Admonitions

1 JOHN 2:12–17

Objectives

After reading this chapter, you should be able to:

- Discuss how many groups John is addressing in 1 John 2:12–14.

- Explain the three titles in 1 John 2:12–14: "children," "fathers," "young men."

- Identify John's usage of the term *world* and what the world's future is (1 John 2:15–17).

INTRODUCTION

First John 2:12–17 divides into two easily identifiable parts: verses 12–14—assurances to John's followers that they are on the right side; and verses 15–17—admonitions to those believers to remain on the right side.

First John 2:12–14 consists of six clauses that divide into two sets. Gary M. Burge nicely shows the symmetry of the two sets:[1]

I write to you:		
children (*teknia*)	because	sins are forgiven
fathers (*pateres*)	because	you have known him from the beginning
young men (*neaniskoi*)	because	overcome the evil one
I have written to you:		
children (*paidia*)	because	you have known the Father
fathers (*pateres*)	because	you have known him from the beginning
young men (*neaniskoi*)	because	you are strong, word of God/overcome evil one

Before summarizing verses 12–14, we must attempt to solve two interpretive issues in this paragraph. (1) How many groups are addressed here—one, three, or two? (2) Are the three titles—"children," "fathers," "young men"—to be taken literally (chronologically) or figuratively (spiritually)?

First, how many groups are referred to in verses 12–14: one, three, or two? One possibility is that one group is in mind here, with three different names applied to it: all Christians are "children" because they are born again to become children of God; all Christians are "fathers" because they believe in Christ who was from the beginning; and all Christians are "young men" because they are conquerors of the devil.[2] Other interpreters assign three different groups to the three names: "children" are the new converts; "fathers" are long-standing Christians; "young men" are those in between the prior two stages of spiri-

---

1. Gary M. Burge, *The Letters of John*, NIV Application Commentary (Grand Rapids: Zondervan, 1996), 111–12. He correctly observes, however, that two different terms are used for "children" (*teknia* and *paidia*), and the clauses in the second set are rearranged. The change of tense from "I write" to "I have written" is stylistic. In both cases the apostle is referring to 1 John, not another correspondence. Moreover, I take it that *hoti* should be translated as "that" (rather than "because"); this better accounts for the admonitory tone of the clauses in vv. 12–14.

2. See the discussion in I. Howard Marshall, *The Epistles of John*, NICNT (Grand Rapids: Eerdmans, 1978), 138.

tual growth.[3] Still others say the three groups correspond to three church offices according to their hierarchal structure: deacons (children), presbyters (young men), and bishops (fathers) — this despite the fact that such a threefold structure does not occur in the New Testament.

One simple fact, however, shows that two groups as a part of the whole are in mind in verses 12–14 — namely, as I noted earlier, John uses the interchangeable terms *teknia* (v. 12a) and *paidia* (v. 13c) for his readers because they are his spiritual children. So "children" is the name for the group as a whole, which is subdivided into two parts — "fathers" and "young men."[4] This detail dismisses at once the one group and three group views. Who these two groups are will be seen below.[5]

Second, should the three titles — "children," "fathers," and "young men" — be interpreted literally/chronologically or figuratively/spiritually? If, indeed, "children" is John's affectionate term for his followers, then the latter view seems to best explain the titles. The fathers are mature Christians, and the young men are progressing in their faith but have not yet reached the spiritual level of the fathers; though, admittedly, more mature believers generally tend to be older than less mature Christians.

> The fathers are mature Christians, and the young men are progressing in their faith but have not yet reached the spiritual level of the fathers.

ANALYSIS

Having resolved the preceding interpretive issues, I am now free to briefly explain verses 12–14. I will follow Burge's handy outline above.

Two descriptions are applied to the "children," John's disciples. First, their sins are forgiven (*aphienai*, v. 12). The perfect tense is employed here, meaning the readers' sins were forgiven in the past (when they believed in Christ) and such forgiveness continues in the present. And that forgiveness is because of his (Christ's) name (cf. v. 8 where the third person personal pronoun also stands for Christ). The "name" here and in 3:23; 5:13; and 3 John 7 refers to Jesus Christ. Second, forgiveness of sins comes because John's children have "known" (*egnōkate*, v. 13c) God, the Father. Again, the usage of the perfect tense means that John's recipients have known God and continue to know him. That is, they know God and the forgiveness he offers because they believe in Christ.

Now the first part of the group is addressed — the fathers. Two identical statements are made about these individuals: they have known him from the beginning and continue to know him (vv. 13b, 14b). The "him" is Jesus Christ. So the spiritually mature individuals in John's churches have a long-standing faith in Christ.

> The spiritually mature individuals in John's churches have a long-standing faith in Christ.

The content of that faith was revealed by Jesus Christ to his apostles, including John, and the latter passed that message along to the present audience.

---

3. See Raymond E. Brown's bibliography, including Clement of Alexandria, Origen, F. F. Bruce, and John Stott in *The Epistles of John*, Anchor Bible 30 (Garden City, N.Y.: Doubleday, 1982), 297–98.

4. Ibid., 298–300. Brown's defense of this position is most convincing.

5. See ibid.; Colin G. Kruse, *The Letters of John*, Pillar New Testament Commentary (Grand Rapids: Eerdmans, 2000), 87–88; Burge, *Letters of John*, 111–14.

The second group is labeled "young men," of whom two very similar statements are made: they have overcome the evil one, and because they are strong in the word of God, they again have overcome the evil one (vv. 13c, 14c). *Nikaō*—"I overcame"—is used by John frequently: seven times in 1 John and seventeen times in Revelation. The word consistently projects triumph over the Christian's spiritual enemy, especially the devil and his Antichrist (see, e.g., 1 John 2:13, 14; 3:8; 5:18, 19). For John, the skirmish between believers and secessionists is a part of the apocalyptic, end-time holy war. The "young men" are those in John's congregations who have resisted the evil one's allure to leave the Johannine flock. They are spiritually strong because they are rooted in the word of God, especially the apostolic tradition John passed on to them.

> The "young men" are those in John's congregations who have resisted the evil one's allure to leave the Johannine flock.

The second part of the passage under consideration is verses 15–17: admonitions to John's audience to remain on the right side of the spiritual battle. These verses pit the people of God against the world. Accordingly, three points can conveniently guide our discussion: the definition of the world (v. 15); the characteristics of the world (v. 16); the defeat of the world (v. 17).

In verse 15 John commands his audience not to love the world, for whoever loves the world does not love God. The "world" (*kosmos*) is not nature or humankind, for God created the former (see John 1:3–5) and loves the latter (John 3:16). Rather, the world is the satanic system that controls humankind and is therefore opposed to God.

In the gospel of John, such an understanding of "world" applies to those who rejected Jesus, especially Jesus' own people, the Jews (see John 1:10–11; cf. 9:39; 12:31; 14:30). In 1 John the world has attracted the secessionists to join its side of the eschatological holy war (cf. 1 John 2:15 with verses 18–19; 3:11–15; 4:1–6). If we contrast the "world" (v. 15) with the age to come (v. 17), we see that the two are opposites: this world/age and the age to come. Christians live in the overlapping of the two ages. They are citizens of the kingdom of God, yet as citizens of this world, they still live in this present age. This is the eschatological background of the "world," and this is why Christians should not align themselves with it.[6]

Verse 16 attributes three fundamental vices to this world. "The lust of the flesh" (KJV; NIV, "cravings of sinful man") is not denigrating the human body (which is a gift of God). Rather, the description pinpoints the flesh—here used to mean humanity set against God—as the source

Z. Radovan/www.BibleLandPictures.com

"The world and its desires. . . ." Roman gold coins with image of the emperor.

---

6. I have devoted a book to the subject: Marvin C. Pate, *The End of the Age Has Come: The Theology of Paul* (Grand Rapids: Zondervan, 1995).

of unwarranted desires. This sin nature is further described as "the lust of [the] eyes" (KJV), because the eyes are the medium for exciting the flesh to generate unhealthy lusts, whether financial, sensual, intellectual, or emotional in nature. The "pride of life" (KJV; NIV, "boasting of what he has and does") communicates the idea that one's accomplishments can be a source of ill-advised pride.

The third overall point about the "world" in verses 15–17 comes in verse 17—the defeat of the world. According to John, the one who does the will of God, or serves the kingdom of God/age to come, is the victor. The secessionists, however, have aligned themselves with this present evil age/world, which since the appearance of the historical Jesus, has begun to pass away. All of this is thoroughly eschatological in tone, and such a tone continues in verses 18–27.

REVIEW QUESTIONS

1. What is the twofold division of 1 John 2:12–17?

2. How many groups are referred to in 1 John 2:12–14? Why?

3. Should the three titles in 1 John 2:12–14 be understood chronologically or figuratively?

4. What is the key characteristic of the "fathers" of verses 12–14?

5. What is the key characteristic of the "young men" of verses 12–14?

6. What does John mean by "world" in 1 John 2:17?

KEY TERMS

children   world

fathers   young men

overcome

CHAPTER 30

The Antichrist Is Here!

1 JOHN 2:18–28

Objectives

After reading this chapter, you should be able to:

- Make five observations about the Antichrist.

- Define what John means by the "anointing" (1 John 2:20–23).

- Discuss the five end-time events developed in 1 John 2:18–28.

INTRODUCTION

First John 2:18–28 comprises a self-contained section. My proposed outline of 1 John 2:18–28 proceeds along its topical intent: verse 18a introduces the theme of the section, which is the announcement of the presence of the eschatological signs of the times, and then verses 18b–28 delineate those end-time occurrences, which John believes have begun to happen in his day: rise of the Antichrist (v. 18b), apostasy (v. 19), presence of the Holy Spirit (vv. 20–23), eternal life (vv. 24–27), and parousia (second coming) of Christ (v. 28).

I now analyze the passage along this line of thought.

I. THE LAST DAYS ARE HERE! (V. 18A)

John's opening words in this section herald the arrival of the last days: "Dear children, this is the last hour." "Children" (*paidia*) is an address, like *teknia*, for John's followers, as I noted earlier. "Last" — *eschatē* — is the word from which "eschatology" — "a word about the end" — is derived. Although "hour" (*hōra*) is without an article, it is nevertheless still definite, because John is treating "last" as an ordinal number that substitutes for the definite article. In other words, it is *the* last hour (cf. John 1:39; 4:6; 19:14, where the ordinal number makes "hour" definite). Thus the last hour/last days alludes to the belief of the early church that the first coming of Christ began the end-time, which will continue in history until its completion at the second coming.

What follows, then, in verses 18b–28 is the actualization of some five events in connection with the first coming of Christ, which early Jews expected to happen at the end of time in connection with the arrival of the kingdom of God.

II. SIGNS OF THE TIMES (VV. 18B–28)

A. The Antichrist (v. 18b; cf. v. 22)

"*Anti*christ" means "against or in place of" Christ, with reference to that end-time personage ancient Jews and Christians expected to appear for the purpose of opposing once and for all God and his people (Dan. 8:11, 13, 25; 9:27; 12:11; 1 Macc. 1:54; 2 Macc. 9:12; *As. Moses* 8:1–2; 10:1–2; Matt. 24:24; Mark 13:22; 2 Thess. 2:2–10; 1 John 2:18, 20; Rev. 13:1–6; et al.)

A number of observations emerge from the preceding passages regarding the Antichrist: First, there are various names for this end-time malevolent figure: "Antichrist," "false christ," "false prophet," "man of lawlessness," and "the beast." Second, the expectation of a coming Antichrist was pervasive in early Christian thinking. Third, there is an intermingling of one Antichrist with many antichrists. This idea is at work in 1 John 2:18b, which equates the work of the secessionists with the machinations of the Antichrist. They are offering a Christology at odds with the Christ of the early church. Fourth, there is also an intermingling of the ideas of a human and a

---

John's opening words in this section herald the arrival of the last days: "Dear children, this is the last hour."

Verse 18a introduces the theme of the section, which is the announcement of the presence of the eschatological signs of the times, and then verses 18b–28 delineate those end-time occurrences.

supernatural Antichrist(s). This is clear in Revelation 13:1–7. Fifth, all of the above passages indicate that the Antichrist of the last days is partially here now.

B. Apostasy (v. 19)

John vehemently equates his opponents with the Antichrist, which is a firm indication that the apostle believes the last days are here (v. 18). Verse 19, then, declares that the secessionists departed from the Johannine community and that such an exit proved his opponents left the true faith. This statement immediately calls to mind the notion of apostasy, a Jewish apocalyptic idea that the end of time would witness a large-scale turning away from the faith by the people of God (see *Jub.* 23:14–23; *1 Enoch* 71:3–10; *4 Ezra* 5:1–3; et al.).

Jesus, in his Olivet Discourse, also refers to that expectation (Matt. 24:10–13; Mark 13:20–23; [cf. Luke 21:34–36]), as does Paul (1 Cor. 11:19; 2 Thess. 2:3; 1 Tim. 4:1–5; 2 Tim. 3:1–5), the gospel of John regarding Judas (John 6:70; 13:2, 27; 14:30; 17:12), and Revelation (13:15–18 et al.). First John 2:18, 22; 4:3; 2 John 7 fit that concept as well. So, according to those verses in 1 John, the apostate secessionists embody the message of the Antichrist in that they deny the humanity of Christ.

C. The Holy Spirit (vv. 20–23)

"But you" (v. 20) serves to contrast John's audience with the secessionists. *Chrisma* ("anointing") occurs only in these verses in the New Testament (vv. 20, 27 [2 times]). Most recent commentaries identify the "anointing" with the Holy Spirit.[1] "From the Holy One" could be God but more likely is Christ.

The NIV rightly translates verse 20 as "all of you know (*pantes oidate*) the truth," rather than "you know all things (*panta oidate*)" (as some translations read). The immediate context of verse 20 indicates that the author wants to give his adherents confidence in the face of the secessionists' claims to knowledge. Thus John encourages his faithful followers by informing them that they—all of them—possess the Holy Spirit and therefore are privy to the true knowledge of who Christ is (cf. v. 20 with v. 22).

Verses 21–23 proceed from that assurance: John's readers possess the Holy Spirit and therefore know the truth and abide in Christ and God, but the secessionist antichrists have bought into the lie that the man *Jesus* is not the Christ (cf. 1 John 4:2; 2 John 7). In doing so they deny not only the Son but also God the Father.

I conclude my discussion of 1 John 2:20–23 by calling attention to the early church's eschatological perspective toward the Holy Spirit. More than one

Roman emperors who were candidates for the title "Antichrist" in the first century: *Top:* Caligula (AD 37–41; 2 Thess. 2:4). *Middle:* Nero (AD 54–68; Rev. 13). *Bottom:* Domitian (AD 81–96; Rev. 13:17).

---

1. Rather than the "word of God"; see Colin G. Kruse's comments in his *The Letters of John*, Pillar New Testament Commentary (Grand Rapids: Eerdmans, 2000), 109–10.

Aerial view of Masada. Herod built a palace and fortress at this easily defensible site near the Dead Sea. Zealots occupied the site in the first revolt against Rome (AD 66–73) and held out at least three years after the temple in Jerusalem fell (AD 73).

modern theologian has rightly characterized the Holy Spirit in the New Testament as the sign par excellence that the end-times had arrived.

Joel 2:28–32 is the classic Old Testament text heralding the pouring out of God's Spirit and the arrival of the last days. Acts 2:16–21 is the classic New Testament text that declares that in Christ the Spirit of the end-times has been poured out on God's people. John's gospel also highlights that theme by way of anticipation (see John 14:15–21, 25–31; 15:26–16:16). This is the background of the anointing/Holy Spirit passages in 1 John (vv. 20, 27): the followers of John possess the Holy Spirit, the sign that they are members of the kingdom of God and participate in the age to come; not so the secessionist antichrists.

D. Eternal Life (vv. 24–27)

Verses 24–27 further contrast John's readers with his opponents. The opponents deny the Son and the Father and thus do not abide in them (vv. 22–23), while John's followers confess the Son and the Father and therefore abide in them (v. 24). The Johannine Christians remain faithful to their confession of Christ, which probably occurred at their

Silver coin from the time of Simon Bar Kokba, who was a messianic-type leader of the failed Jewish revolt against Rome (AD 134–35).

baptism. This message that Jesus the man is Christ the Lord began with Jesus himself (v. 24). As a result of their abiding or remaining in Christ and the Father (v. 24), John's followers have received the promise of eternal life.

And it is the anointing of the Holy Spirit that teaches them the truth about the Son. Conversely, the lack of such an anointing is the cause of the lies and deception of the secessionists (vv. 26–27).

E. Parousia (v. 28)

Verse 28 is a transitional verse. On the one hand, it continues the theme of abiding in verses 24–27 as well as the topic of the signs of the times of the last days in 2:18–27. But on the other hand, verse 28 begins with the words, "And now, dear children," which seem to initiate a new section. Verse 28 also introduces the theme of ethics—right living prepares one for the return of Christ.

"Little ["Dear," NIV] children" (*teknia*) identifies the readers as John's followers. The challenge for them to abide in the truth about Christ as the author interpreted it is now connected with the return of Christ. Two terms are used for the return of Christ: "appears" (*phaneraō*) and "coming" (parousia). First John speaks several times of the appearing of Jesus Christ, either with reference to his incarnation (1:2 [2 times]; 3:5, 8) or with reference to Jesus' future return (here in 2:28 and again in 3:2).[2] The subjunctive *ean* does not convey uncertainty about the fact of Christ's return but rather regarding its timing. The passive voice of "appear" implies that Christ will be made visible at his return by God.

The other term for Christ's return in verse 28 is *parousia*, one of three technical terms for the return of Christ in the New Testament (*epiphaneia* and *apocalypsis* being the other two).

Abiding in Christ brings two synonymous results: "confidence" and "not being ashamed" at the second coming of Christ. The first of these forms a play on words with *parousia* and *parrēsia* ("confidence"). "Confidence" occurs nine times in John and four times in 1 John. According to the latter, we have: confidence before God on judgment day at the parousia (2:28; 4:17), confidence before God in prayer (5:14), or both (3:21–22). Its counterpart is "not being ashamed" (*aischynesthai*), a word also used of the return of Christ. Those who are ashamed of Christ now will find that he will be ashamed of them in the future (Matt. 10:32–33; Mark 8:38).

To summarize verse 28: those who abide in the truth about Christ as taught by John will be confident and not ashamed at Christ's return.

> As a result of their abiding or remaining in Christ and the Father (v. 24), John's followers have received the promise of eternal life.

> The other term for Christ's return in verse 28 is *parousia*, one of three technical terms for the return of Christ in the New Testament (*epiphaneia* and *apocalypsis* being the other two).

---

2. Kruse makes this point in ibid., 112.

1. What five observations can be made about the Antichrist from 1 John 2:18, 22 and related New Testament texts?

2. What was the nature of the secessionists' apostasy?

3. What is the "anointing" referred to in 1 John 2:20 – 23?

KEY TERMS

Antichrist	eternal life
apostasy	last days
chrisma	parousia

CHAPTER 31

Children of God versus Children of the Devil

1 JOHN 2:29–3:10

Objectives

After reading this chapter, you should be able to:

- Explain the structure of 1 John 2:29–3:10.
- Discuss the contrasts between the children of God and the children of the Devil as recorded in 1 John 2:29–3:10.

INTRODUCTION

First John 2:28–3:10 is a self-contained unit, remarkable for the fact that *pas* ("everyone"), or the definite article plus a participle ("the person who"), occurs nine times therein (which we here render literally from the Greek):[1]

2:29b: Everyone who acts justly	has been begotten by God
3:3a: Everyone who has this hope based on him	makes himself pure
3:4a: Everyone who acts sinfully	is really doing iniquity
3:6a: Everyone who abides in him	does not commit sin
3:6b: Everyone who does commit sin	has never seen him
3:7b: The person who acts justly	is truly just
3:8a: The person who acts sinfully	belongs to the devil
3:9a: Everyone who has been begotten by God	does not act sinfully
3:10a: Everyone who does not act justly	does not belong to God

This feature creates a series of running contrasts throughout the section, as I will detail later in my discussion. Furthermore, 1 John 2:28–3:10[2] divides into two paragraphs: 2:28–29/3:4–6 and 3:7–10 (we will see later that 3:1–3 is parenthetical to the first subsection). The first subsection (2:28–29/3:4–6) begins with the address "Dear children,"[3] as does the second subsection (3:7–10).

I now turn to a brief discussion of the logic of 2:28–29 followed by an explanation of the aside comments in 3:1–3. Then I will discuss the preceding two paragraphs (2:28–29/3:4–6 and 3:7–10) in terms of the contrasts presented therein between the children of God and the children of the Devil.

I. THE LOGIC OF 2:28–29

The logic of 2:28–29 is this: those who are begotten of God (the Johannine community) abide in Christ and therefore practice righteousness; that righteousness instills within them confidence at the soon-appearing parousia of Christ. I earlier discussed the terms "abide," "just/righteous," "parousia." Here I will briefly examine the idea "begotten of God" (NIV, "born of him"). The background of the concept of divine begetting seems to be rooted in the Old Testament, which speaks of Israel as God's covenant people who are his children (Ex. 4:22–23; 2 Sam. 7:14; Jer. 31:9; Hos. 11:1; cf. the Dead Sea Scrolls [1QH 4:32–33; 11:9; 1QS 1:9; 2:16; 3:13, 24, 25; 4:22; 1QS 2:8–9]; cf. also Rev. 21:7); this implies their divine begetting. And, as God is holy, so must they be holy, Lev. 19:2; cf. 1 Peter 1:16). This may well be what informs John's phrase "begotten of God."

---

1. See Brown, *The Epistles of John,* 418.
2. The reader will recall that v. 28 is a hinge verse between v. 27 and v. 29.
3. *Teknia*, used here and in 1 John 3:7, is to be distinguished from *teknion* and *paidion* in that it is an address to Christians in general, not just the Johannine community.

II. AN ASIDE COMMENT ON THE WONDER OF BEING GOD'S CHILDREN (3:1–3)

As commentators note, 3:1–3 is a parenthetical paragraph expanding on the idea that Christians are begotten of God.[4] The paragraph can be divided into two points, both of which exclaim awe at being the children of God.

1. *According to verse 1, Christians are the children of God, and two points flow from that.* First, they are so because of the heavenly Father's love for them. We are "called" the children of God because we really are by spiritual nature the children of God. Second, however, because John's readers are the children of God, the world rejects them just as it rejected God and Christ (see John 1:10; 3:6; 4:9; 8:19; 16:3; 17:25).

2. *According to verses 2–3, Christians are the children of God, and two more points are added for clarification.* First, even though Christians are presently the children of God, their understanding of what all that means is incomplete; only the parousia will fully reveal the full extent of that wonder.

Second, in the meantime the "hope" of Christ's parousia motivates Christians to walk in purity as Christ is "pure." The noun "hope" (*elpis*) is used only here in Johannine literature and is rooted in eschatological expectation; it is the hope of the return of Christ (see 1 Thess. 1:3, 10; 2:19–20; 4:13–18; et al.). The word "pure" (*agnizō, agnos*) is rare in the New Testament, and even more so in Johannine literature (John 11:55 is its only occurrence). Its background is the Old Testament sacrificial system, wherein the slain animal purified Israel and made them acceptable in God's presence (see especially Ex. 19:10–11; Num. 8:21). Like 1 John 2:1–2 (cf. John 17:19), 3:3 draws on Jesus' sacrificial death/atonement as the means by which his followers are purified, both now and at his return (cf. James 4:8; 1 Peter 1:22–23).

> John 3:1–3 is a parenthetical paragraph expanding on the idea that Christians are begotten of God.

III. THE PURITY OF CHRIST VERSUS THE INIQUITY OF THE ANTICHRIST (3:4–6)

As I mentioned earlier, a series of contrasts resulting from the construction *pas*, or the definite article plus a participle, runs throughout 2:29–3:10, not including the aside comments in 3:1–3.

First John 2:29–3:6 is the first paragraph of the section; it highlights three contrasts between the children of God and John's opponents. I now discuss those antitheses.

> The "hope" of Christ's parousia motivates Christians to walk in purity as Christ is "pure."

1. 2:29: Everyone (*pas*) who acts justly (*poiōn tēn dikaiosyēn*) has been begotten of God.
   3:4: Everyone (*pas*) who acts sinfully (*lo poiōn tēn hamartian*) participates in the iniquity of the Antichrist.

---

4. See, e.g., Colin G. Kruse's remarks in this regard in his *The Letters of John*, Pillar New Testament Commentary (Grand Rapids: Eerdmans, 2000), 114; and Raymond E. Brown's observations in his *The Epistles of John*, Anchor Bible 30 (Garden City, N.Y.: Doubleday, 1982), 422.

First John 2:29 is clear — God is righteous/just, and those born of him will practice righteousness. The words "doing righteousness" occur here and again in 3:7 and 9. The present participle — "doing" — seems to convey the notion of habitual action, namely, consistently doing righteousness. If we track John's usage of "begotten of God," we see that there is an ontological relationship involved: like God, like his children; and this family resemblance is righteousness (cf. 2:29 with 3:9; 4:7; 5:1, 5, 18). Conversely, 3:4 captures the family resemblance between sinners and the Antichrist: sin/lawlessness. The words, "everyone who does sin" is the negative counterpart to "doing righteousness" (2:29); they occur again in verse 8. The present participle — "doing sin" — probably also conveys habitual action. Such sin breaks (God's) law — *anomia*. More particularly, "doing sin," says John, is "*the* lawlessness." As commentators recognize, John has more in mind than general libertine, or immoral, behavior on the part of the secessionists; he is thinking of the end-time lawlessness brought on by the Antichrist (see Matt. 7:22 – 23; 13:41; 24:11 – 12; 2 Thess. 2:3 – 8; *Didache* 16:3 – 4). Thus John is announcing that the sin the secessionists are committing is the manifestation of the lawlessness of the Antichrist (cf. 1 John 2:18). So the opponents are Antichrist in their wrong belief about Jesus (1 John 2:8, 22) and in their sinful actions (1 John 3:4).[5]

2. 3:5a: Christ takes away sin
    3:5b: No sin is in Christ.

"That one" (*ekeinos*, v. 5; NIV, "he") is Christ (cf. v. 3), whose appearance during his life and death took away sin. "To take away" (*airein*) connotes the sacrificial death of Christ, as it does in John 1:29 — "the Lamb of God, who takes away (*airein*) the sin of the world" (cf. 1 John 1:7; 2:2).

Verse 5b spells out the contrast of verse 5: the fact is that Christ took away sin rather than sin was found in him and, in so doing, proclaims the sinlessness of Jesus (see John 8:46; 14:30; 1 John 2:1 – 2; cf. 2 Cor. 5:21; Heb. 4:15; 1 Peter 2:22).

3. 6a: Everyone (*pas*) who abides (*ho menōn*) in him will not sin.
    6b: Everyone (*pas*) who sins (*ho hamartanōn*) has not seen/not known Christ.

Verse 6 registers another contrast: those who abide in Christ/God do not sin (John's followers), but those who continue to sin (John's opponents) have neither seen nor known God/Christ. One might have expected the author to express the following contrast: whoever abides in God/Christ does not sin, but whoever does not abide in God/Christ does sin. But John is even harsher: whoever sins has never seen or known God! John has seen Jesus (John 19:35) and made him known to his community, but his opponents' departure proves that they never really had a spiritual relationship with God through Christ. Verse 6 raises an issue that we will take up later in our discussion of verse 9: does John contradict himself in 3:6, 9 — the Christian does not sin — since in 1:8, 10 he proclaimed just the opposite — the Christian does sin?

---

5. Kruse's comments are helpful on this point. *Letters of John*, 117 – 18.

IV. THE CHILDREN OF GOD VERSUS THE CHILDREN OF THE DEVIL (3:7–10)

Two more contrasts surface in this section in 3:7–10:

1. 7: Everyone (*pas*) who does righteousness (*ho poiōn tēn dikaiosynēn*) is righteous, just as he is righteous.
   8: He (*ho*) who does sin (*poiōn tēn hamartian*) is of the Devil, who sinned from the beginning.

2. 9: No one (*pas*) who is born of God (*ho gegennēmenos*) sins, because God's Son is in him.
   10: Everyone (*pas*) who does not do righteousness (*ho mē poiōn dikaiosynēn*) is not a child of God.

Because we have already touched upon some of the key words in this contrast ("do righteousness," "he is righteous," "do sin," "born of God"), we will only briefly give attention to four ideas that are new here in 1 John: "the devil has sinned from the beginning"; "the Son of God appeared to destroy the works of the devil"; "God's Son abides in him"; and "no one who is born of God will [continue to] sin."

1. The "devil" (occurring 3 times in 3:8; see also 3:10; cf. John 6:70; 8:44; 13:2; Rev. 12:7–17) is Satan, the lawless one, who opposes God and his people. He did so "from the beginning" (1 John 3:8) is probably an allusion to Satan's instigation of the fall of Adam and Eve and to Cain's murder of Abel (see Gen. 3–4; cf. also 1 John 3:12), and Satan continues to sin against God through the antichrist secessionists.

2. The statement in verse 8 that Christ, the Son of God, appeared the first time to destroy the works of the Devil most likely means that Jesus engaged Satan in an apocalyptic showdown at his death and resurrection and there defeated the Devil (see John 12:30–33; 16:11; Rev. 19; cf. the Dead Sea Scrolls [1QM]).

3. Although the identification of God's "seed" (*sperma*) is debated, it most probably is to be equated with the Holy Spirit, especially since the new birth is effected by God through the Spirit (John 3:5–8) and the Spirit is the one who remains in believers (1 John 2:20, 27).[6]

4. First John 3:6, 9 declares that the Christian does not sin. But does this contradict what John said earlier in 1:8, 10 — that Christians do, in fact, sin? This issue is hotly debated

> The statement in verse 8 that Christ, the Son of God, appeared the first time to destroy the works of the Devil most likely means that Jesus engaged Satan in an apocalyptic showdown at his death and resurrection and there defeated the Devil.

---

6. J. du Preez lists six different interpretations of *sperma autou*: children of God; the proclaimed word of God; Christ; the Holy Spirit; new life from God; and the new nature, before opting himself for the "new life of being pure and doing right through practicing brotherly love in communion with God (Christ) and according to the example of Christ" as the best interpretation. "'*Sperma autou*' in 1 John 3:9," *Neot* 9 (1975): 105–10.

The Hallowing of Hell, depicted in the Petites Heures de Jean de Berry, 14th c. illuminated manuscript.

among commentators.[7] It seems to me that two considerations demonstrate that our author is not contradicting himself. First, 1 John 3:6–9 seems to say that those who are born of God do not *habitually* sin, even though they may occasionally lapse into sin; thus 1:8–10.[8] Second, the eschatological tension that is attested to throughout the New Testament — "the already–not yet" — is at work in these verses in 1 John as well. Thus, because Christians are *already* in the kingdom of God, they have victory over sin. But because they are *not yet* in heaven, they still will struggle with sin in this life until the parousia.[9] Perhaps if John were to state the matter the way Paul does, he might say that Christians are perfect in their *position* in Christ, but their *practice* of overcoming sin lags behind (see Rom. 6 especially).

7. See Brown's excellent discussion of the options: (1) two different authors are involved; (2) the one author is addressing two different adversaries; (3) the author is thinking of specific kinds of sins when he says that Christians cannot sin; (4) only super-spiritual/elite Christians are in the author's mind; (5) Christians don't habitually sin; (6) the author speaks from two levels: one from a pastoral perspective (1:8; 2:1–2), the other as an ideal goal (3:6, 9; 5:18); (7) the author speaks in two contexts: one is kerygmatic (1:8; 1:10–2:2), the other apocalyptic (3:6, 9; 5:18). See also Kruse's discussion in Letters of John, 126–32.

8. But this explanation is not without difficulty, because the present tense is used in *both* 3:6–9 and 1:8.

9. This understanding of the problem is well argued by P. P. A. Kotze, "The Meaning of 1 John 3:9 with Reference to 1 John 1:8 and 10," *Neot* 13 (1979): 63–83, esp. 81; cf. Rudolf Schnackenburg, *The Johannine Epistles* (Spring Valley, N.Y.: Herder & Herder, 1992), 257–58.

REVIEW QUESTIONS

1. Please explain the structure of 1 John 2:29 – 3:10, including its twofold division and manifold use of "everyone."

2. What is the logic of 1 John 2:28 – 29?

3. What is so wonderful about being the children of God, according to 1 John 3:1 – 3?

4. What does it mean to say that the parousia is imminent?

5. What are the three contrasts between the children of God and the children of the Devil that are highlighted in 1 John 2:29 – 3:6?

6. What two contrasts are discussed in 1 John 3:7 – 10?

7. Does 1 John 3:6, 9 (the Christian does not sin) contradict 1 John 1:8, 10 (the Christian does sin)?

KEY TERMS

"abides"/"not abides"

already – not yet

begotten of God

Devil

doing righteousness/doing sin

imminence of the parousia

CHAPTER 32

Loving One Another

1 JOHN 3:11–24

Objectives

After reading this chapter, you should be able to:

- Explain how 1 John 3:11 begins the second division of 1 John.

- Identify the overarching theme of 1 John 3:11–24.

- Discuss how the Old Testament story of Cain (Genesis 4) sheds light on 1 John 3:11–24.

- Discuss the results of loving one's brother, according to 1 John 3:18–22.

INTRODUCTION

A number of commentators rightly see a natural break occurring in 1 John 3:11.[1] Gary Burge supplies three reasons they say there is a break. First, 3:11 divides the letter into two near equal halves (1:5–3:10 and 3:11–5:12). Second, if the gospel of John was the model for the structure of 1 John, its emphasis on the light and truth of God in the first half of John is followed by an emphasis on love in the community, themes that occur in the above two sections of 1 John. Third, 1 John 3:11 begins the second part of 1 John with the words "This is the message (*angelia*) you heard from the beginning," a near copy of 1:5, "This is the message (*angelia*) we have heard from him."[2] All of this suggests, then, that 1 John 3:11 begins the second part of the letter.

> First John 3:11 begins the second part of the letter.

That 1 John 3:23 concludes a self-contained section that begins in verse 11 is clear from the inclusion the two verses form. Thus both begin with the phrase "This is the message [v. 11]/command [v. 23]," which is followed by a *hina* (purpose) clause and a command to love. Verse 24 is a hinge verse connecting verse 23 to 4:1.

In light of the preceding, I suggest the following outline for 3:11–24:

I. Introduction.

A. This is the message of love (v. 11).

B. Cain as a foil to love (v. 12).

II. Brotherly love contrasted to brotherly hate (vv. 13–17).

A. General command to love (vv. 13–15).

1. Loving others is a sign of eternal life (v. 14a).

2. Not loving others is a sign of death (vv. 13, 14b–15).

B. Specific command to love (vv. 16–17).

1. Loving others by dying for others, like Christ (v. 16).

2. Not loving others by neglecting to help them financially (v. 17).

III. Results of loving in deed (vv. 18–22).

A. Abiding in the truth (vv. 18a–19a).

B. Assurance before God (vv. 19b–21).

C. Answers to prayers (v. 22).

IV. Conclusion.

A. This is the message of love (v. 23).

B. The presence of the Spirit (v. 24).

---

1. Gary M. Burge, *The Letters of John*, NIV Application Commentary (Grand Rapids: Zondervan, 1996), 159–60; Colin G. Kruse, *The Letters of John*, Pillar New Testament Commentary (Grand Rapids: Eerdmans, 2000), 132; Raymond E. Brown, *The Epistles of John*, Anchor Bible 30 (Garden City, N.Y.: Doubleday, 1982), 442.

2. Burge, *Letters of John*, 159.

I. INTRODUCTION (3:11–12)

Verse 11 introduces 1 John 3:11–24 and, in doing so, begins the second half of the letter. Like 1:5, it begins with the words "This is the message." The two verses provide the two key themes of 1 John: "This is the message: God is light" (1:5) and "This is the message: God is love" and "we should love one another" (3:11). The message heard from the beginning (3:11) is no doubt the message of Christ passed on to the apostles and now to John's community. The message is that followers of Jesus should love one another (see John 13:34; 15:12, 17), which in 1 John is translated as loving one's brothers (this command occurs 5 times in 1 John), the Johannine churches in particular.

Verse 12 is a foil to verse 11: John's audience should love others (v. 11), not be like Cain who hated his brother Abel (v. 12; cf. Gen. 4).

The Cain story, then, casts its shadow over verses 12–17 and is the only direct appeal to the Old Testament in 1 John. The point John makes from all of this is that Cain represents the secessionists who have turned on their brothers, the Johannine community. Verses 13–17 proceed to highlight the contrasts between the two: John's followers and the secessionists.

> Verse 12 is a foil to verse 11: John's audience should love others (v. 11), not be like Cain who hated his brother Abel (v. 12; cf. Gen. 4).

II. BROTHERLY LOVE CONTRASTED TO BROTHERLY HATE (3:13–17)

Verse 13[3] records the only usage of "brothers" as an address to fellow Christians in the epistles of John, even though it occurs frequently in the rest of the New Testament. It no doubt stems from the mention of "Cain" in verse 12, whose brother he killed. So the reader is thereby alerted to the most famous biblical illustration of sibling rivalry.

And it may be that the story's historical outcome as recorded in Genesis 4 — Cain/life and Abel/death — is ironically reversed in 1 John 3:12–15: Cain/secessionists/spiritual death and John's community/Abel/spiritual life.

> Those who have remained true to John and his community are true believers and have passed from death to eternal life.

A. General Command to Love (vv. 13–15)

1. Loving Others Is a Sign of Eternal Life (v. 14a)

Those who have remained true to John and his community are true believers and have passed from death to eternal life (cf. John 5:24).

2. Not Loving Others Is a Sign of Death (vv. 13, 14b–15)

Just as Abel was hated by his brother Cain because Abel's deeds were righteous and Cain's were evil, so the secessionists now hate John's followers.

---

3. According to the Greek uncial Sinaiticus, v. 13 began with a *kai* ("and" or "then"). It probably was omitted in other Greek manuscripts because *kai* resembles *dikaia* ("righteous"), the last word in v. 12. Apparently the scribe inadvertently confused the two, which is called *homoeoteleuton* by text critics. If the *kai* is original, it would introduce the idea "Brothers, do not be surprised, *then*, when the world hates you.

Just as Abel was hated by his brother Cain because Abel's deeds were righteous and Cain's were evil, so the secessionists now hate John's followers.

But this only proves that John's opponents never had life; they continue to be dead spiritually before God.

B. Specific Command to Love (vv. 16–17)

Verses 16–17 specify how it is that believers are to love one another and how, conversely, the secessionists are not loving one another.

1. Loving Others by Dying for Others, Like Christ (v. 16)

"By this" (en touto; NIV, "This is how") introduces what is to follow: By this we know what love is, namely, laying down one's life for others like Christ did. "That one" (NASB) is Christ who "put off" (ethēken, from tithēmi; NIV, "laid down") like a garment his life (cf. especially John 13:4 where tithēmi is used of Christ taking off his outer garment to wash the disciples' feet). Christ's death for others is reinforced by the "atonement" preposition, hyper— "for us" (twice here in v. 16 and once in 2:2; cf. John 10:15; Mark 14:24; Rom. 5:8). Such sacrifice for others is incumbent on believers to do the same, "and we ought to put off (theina, from tithēmi; NIV, "lay down") our lives for (hyper) our brothers" (cf. John 15:12–13). As verse 17 makes clear, the sacrifice John has in mind is the selfless giving of one's possessions to others.

2. Not Loving Others by Neglecting to Help Them Financially (v. 17)

Here the opponents of John become a foil to Christ and true believers in that they "see"[4] their brothers (the Johannine community) in financial need but fail to help alleviate that need.

This only proves that the love of God[5] does not abide[6] in them. As recent commentaries observe, it may well be that the secessionists took their considerable material resources with them when the Johannine church(es) suffered division, leaving John's true followers with no financial base.

Here the opponents of John become a foil to Christ and true believers in that they "see" their brothers (the Johannine community) in financial need but fail to help alleviate that need.

III. RESULTS OF LOVING IN DEED (3:18–22)

Three consequences follow for those who love in deed:

A. Abiding in the Truth (vv. 18a–19a)

Verse 18 begins with the second address in 3:11–24, thus suggesting that "Little children [NIV, 'Dear friends']" begins the second half of the section. John challenges his followers not to love merely in word or tongue but rather in deed and truth.

---

4. The word "see" here is theōrein, one of five different verbs for seeing in Johannine literature. They are all basically synonymous (see Brown, Epistles of John, 449–50).

5. There is a debate among commentators as to whether the "love of God" (v. 17) is an objective genitive = love for God, or a subjective genitive = love from God; but it is most likely the latter.

6. Menien is probably a future subjunctive rather than a present indicative. The former, more so than the latter, admits to doubt as to whether the love of God abides in a person who does not love others.

B. Assurance before God (vv. 19b–21)[7]

I propose that verses 19b–21 express a major-minor argument: "If God does not condemn our hearts even when we do [cf. v. 20, major argument], how much more so will God not condemn us when our hearts do not [cf. v. 21, minor argument]."

The upshot of verses 19–21, then, is that the Johannine community has assurance before God that he accepts them; not so the secessionists.

C. Answers to Prayer (v. 22)

The third result of loving others in deed, not with mere words, is answers to prayers. This is the first time the epistles of John mention prayer; it will happen again in 5:14–15. Receiving answers to prayer from God in Jesus' name is a common theme in the gospel of John (14:14–16; 15:7, 16; 16:23–26; cf. Matt. 7:7). But this should not be misunderstood to mean that prayer before God is a carte blanche. Rather, "in Jesus' name" is the equivalent of "in keeping with Jesus' character." In other words, answers to prayer are conditioned on obedience. This is clear from the second half of 1 John 3:22, "because we obey his commands," which is the same as "do what is pleasing before him."

IV. CONCLUSION (3:23–24)

Verses 23–24 conclude this section by nicely summarizing the two themes of 1 John: the commands to believe that Jesus is the Christ, the Son of God, and to love the brothers. John's followers do these because they possess the Holy Spirit.

> The upshot of verses 19–21, then, is that the Johannine community has assurance before God that he accepts them; not so the secessionists.

---

7. A hermeneutical thicket awaits the interpreter of 1 John 3:19–21, the details of which cannot occupy us here. Rather, I will simply list the exegetical issues and state my opinion on each. For further discussion, see Brown, *Epistles of John*, 454–60; and Kruse, *Letters of John*, 139–42. (1) What does "By this" (*en toutō*, v. 19a; NIV, "This is how") refer to? Though normally referring to what follows in the epistles of John, these words here probably refer to the preceding v. 18: loving in deed shows that one is abiding in the truth. (2) *Emprosthen* (v. 19b) may be forensic: judgment *before* God, especially given the context of 1 John 2:28–3:3. If (3) *kardia* has the unusual meaning of "conscience" in v. 19b (as is probably the case), then (4) *peithein* (v. 19b) probably means "convince" rather than "rest" (see NIV). (5) *Hoti ean* (v. 20a) most likely is to be taken as concessive — "that if" or "even if," rather than as causal — "because if." (6) *Kataginōskē* (v. 20a) is to be taken negatively — "know against" or "condemn." It conveys a legal sense, so the NIV. (7) *Hoti* (v. 20b) is resumptive, meaning "that," probably not causal, meaning "because." (8) *Panta* (v. 20c) = God knows all things and is merciful rather than God knows all things and is judgmental. (9) *Mē kataginōskē* (v. 21a), like v. 20, means "the heart/conscience does not condemn us." See my discussion above of the major to minor argument these verses form.

1. What is the overarching theme of 1 John 3:11 – 12?

2. Please explain the running contrast in 1 John 3:13 – 17 between loving and hating one's brothers.

3. How might finances have played a role in the preceding contrast?

4. Please explain the three results of loving one's brother, according to 1 John 3:18 – 22.

KEY TERMS

abiding in the truth	assurance before God	*hyper*
angelia	brotherly hate	major/minor argument
answers to prayer	brotherly love	*tithēmi*
	Cain and Abel	

CHAPTER 33

Testing the End-Time Spirits

1 JOHN 4:1–6

Objectives

After reading this chapter, you should be able to:

- Discuss the eschatological themes presented in 1 John 4:1–6.

- Distinguish the Spirit of truth from the Spirit of error, according to 1 John 4:1–3.

- Summarize the expressions used in 1 John that affirm the humanity of Christ.

- Explain the differing responses to John's message as mentioned in 1 John 4:4–6.

- Explain how the doctrines of the incarnation, Christ's atonement, and ethics are related in 1 John.

INTRODUCTION

First John 4:1–6 is easily identified as a section: the theme of the Spirit introduced in 3:24 is developed in 4:1–6. Furthermore, we saw that 3:23 summarized the two commands emphasized in 1 John: believe in Jesus Christ and love the brothers. John 4:1–6 addresses the first command: believe in Jesus Christ; while 4:7–5:4a highlights the second command: love the brothers.

First John 4:1–6 reminds one of 1 John 2:18–27 in its emphasis on eschatology. Consider the following themes: the Holy Spirit, the sign of the presence of the eschaton (4:1–3); the Antichrist (4:3); end-time false prophets (4:1); the end-time holy war (4:4); and end-time judgment now in history, depending on one's response to Christ (4:5–6). The overarching theme of 4:1–6 is testing the end-time spirits.

First John 4:1–6 divides into two parts, each beginning with an address to the recipients:

4:1–3: "Beloved" (NIV, "Dear friends"): Test 1: What do the spirits say about Jesus?

4:4–6: "Little [NIV, 'Dear'] children": Test 2: What does the world think about the spirits?

Verse 1a introduces the theme of verses 1–6: test the end-time spirits to see if they are of God. *Dokimazete*—"test"—occurs only here in the Johannine literature but is common in the rest of the New Testament (22 times). The idea of testing the spirits to weed out false prophets is rooted in the Old Testament (Deut. 13:2–6; 18:15–22). The same challenge is echoed in the Dead Sea Scrolls (1QS 3:13–14; 5:20–21, 24). Indeed, the closest parallel to 1 John 4:1–6 on testing the two spirits is to be found in 1QS 3:17–21.

I. BELOVED: TEST 1: WHAT DO THE SPIRITS SAY ABOUT JESUS? (4:1–3)

It is clear in verse 1 that more than one spirit is intended to be tested (*panti pneumatic*, "every spirit"; *ta pneumata*, "the spirits"). Actually, there are two: the Spirit of truth and the spirit of deceit (v. 6).

A. The Spirit of God (Truth) (vv. 1a, 2)

"Spirit of God" occurs only here in the Johannine literature, but no doubt the author means by this the Holy Spirit. This supernatural Spirit says or confesses that Jesus Christ has come in the flesh and thereby proves that he (that Spirit) proceeds from God.

B. The Spirit of False Prophets/Antichrist (Deceit) (vv. 1b, 3)

It would be helpful at this point for the modern reader of 1 John to contextualize the author's challenge to test the spirits to see which was genuine. In the early years of Christianity, before the New Testament was completed (AD 100) and before the first creeds of the church were formulated (AD 325), there were no official, universal theological benchmarks for evaluating Christian preaching and teaching. To complicate matters, the early Christians were pneumatics; that is, they believed themselves to be filled with the Spirit of God, which provided divine backing for their messages. This is why Paul said in 1 Thessalonians 5:19–21 that Christians should, on the one hand, not despise prophecies of the Spirit, while, on the other hand, they should discern whether the spokesperson truly was inspired by the Holy Spirit. John is calling for much the same in 4:1–6: his community needed to discern whether a speaker was inspired by the Holy Spirit. For John, however, there was indeed at least one theological benchmark: if the person confessed that Christ was the man Jesus, the Son of God, then the spirit inspiring him or her was God's Spirit. If not, the spirit was an evil spirit, one inspiring false prophets and the spirit of Antichrist.

Just as the pouring out of the Holy Spirit upon the people of God was expected to happen in the end-time (Joel 2:28, 32; see Acts 2:17–21), so too was the spirit of Satan expected to inspire false prophets in the end-time (cf. 1 John 4:1 with Matt. 24:11; Rev. 13:11–18; 16:13), not to mention the Antichrist himself (cf. 1 John 4:3; 2 John 7 with 1 John 2:18–27; Rev. 13:1–10).

Verse 3 spells out the reason for John's condemnation of the secessionists—these false prophets and antichrists "do not confess Jesus" (NIV, "do not acknowledge"); that is, they deny Christ's humanity.

II. TEST 2: WHAT DOES THE WORLD THINK ABOUT THE SPIRITS? (4:4–6)

The address to the letter's recipients in verse 4—"little [NIV, 'dear'] children"—suggests a development in the thought of 4:1–6, namely, a second test of the two spirits is offered: What does the world think about them?

A. The Spirit of Deceit (v. 5)

Simply put, the world—that human system alienated from God and energized by Satan— accepts the spirit of deceit, who guides the secessionists. There is a hint in verse 5 that the secessionists were successful in propagating their Docetic message, drawing a larger following than those who remained in the Johannine community.

B. The Spirit of Truth (vv. 4, 6)

The followers of John, however, possess the Holy Spirit, the Spirit of truth—so little wonder that the world does not hear their message (cf. John 15:19; 17:14, 16). Not to worry, however, because the true believers belong to God (v. 6); not only that, but John's followers have defeated the world (v. 4). There are probably two historical aspects to the Johannine idea that Christians have defeated the world and the secessionists. First, they defeated their spiritual enemy by remaining in the Johannine community during the church split (cf. 1 John 2:18–27). Second, because these believers abide in God and Christ, they share in Christ's victory over the Devil, the prince of this world, which happened at the cross and resurrection (John 12:31; 14:30; 16:11). Thus John can say in verse 4, "The one who is in you is greater than the one who is in the world."

CONCLUSION

I conclude 1 John 4:1–6 by summarizing the spiritual domino effect that occurs with the Docetic message, toppling three cardinal Christian doctrines: incarnation, atonement, and ethics. John well knew this and responded by writing 1, 2, and 3 John:

Doctrine	Deniers of Christ's humanity	John affirms Christ is human
Incarnation	**Denied:** 1. Jesus (man) = Christ (1 John 2:22). 2. Christ came in flesh (1 John 4:2; 2 John 7). 3. Therefore both his humanity and his deity show that Jesus Christ is the Son of God (1 John 2:23).	**Affirmed:** 1. Jesus = Christ (1 John 5:1). 2. Christ has come in flesh (1 John 1:1 – 4; 4:2). 3. Jesus Christ is Son of God (1 John 1:7; 2:23; 3:23; 4:9, 10, 15; 5:5). 1. Summary: the eternal Son of God, second member of the Trinity in eternity past, became human = Jesus (via Mary) and deity = Christ (via God). Thus Jesus Christ = the God-Man at birth, baptism, ministry, death, resurrection.
Atonement	**Implicitly denied atonement:** 1. Sufficiency of atonement = Jesus died, not Christ; therefore death of mere man not deity. 2. Need for the cross = human dilemma is ignorance (so Gnostics), not sin (1 John 1:8, 10).	**Affirmed Atonement:** 1. Sufficiency of atonement: Christ died (1 John 2:1 – 2; 4:10). 2. Need for the cross: 1 John 1:8, 10 = if no sin, that makes God to be a liar, when what we need to do is confess sin, (v. 9).
Ethics/Sanctification	**Denied that Christian life should impact the body:** 1. sinless (1 John 1:8 – 10) 2. elite (1 John 2:20, 27 = special anointing).	**Affirmed that Christian life should impact the body:** 1. confess sin; otherwise walk in darkness (1 John 1:8 – 10) 2. love brethren; otherwise liar (1 John 2:9; 3:11 – 18; 4:20).

1. What is the message of 1 John 4:1 – 6?

2. What eschatological themes are present in 1 John 4:1 – 6?

3. What distinguishes the Spirit of Truth from the spirit of error, according to 1 John 4:1 – 3?

4. Why does the world accept the message of the Docetists (1 John 4:4 – 6)?

5. How does denying the humanity of Christ topple the doctrines of incarnation, atonement, and ethics?

KEY TERMS

1QS 3, 5	end-time holy war	Holy Spirit
Antichrist	end-time judgment	incarnation
atonement	ethics	testing the Spirits
	false prophets	

CHAPTER 34

Love in Motion

1 JOHN 4:7–5:4A

Objectives

After reading this chapter, you should be able to:

- Identify the four aspects of love that emerge in 1 John 4:7–5:4a.

- Explain John's concept of perfection.

INTRODUCTION

The reader will recall that 1 John 3:23 delineates two commands for believers to follow: believe in Jesus Christ and love others. First John 4:1–6 unpacks the first command, while 4:7–5:4a develops the second command. Love is clearly the theme of 4:7–5:4a; it is a pervasive topic throughout the section. Though scholars debate how 1 John 4:7–5:4a should be outlined, we can agree that four aspects of love emerge in this passage: the origin of love—God (4:7–10); the revelation of love—the Christian (4:11–16b); the opposite of love—fear (4:16c–19); the test of love—authenticity (4:20–5:4a). We now summarize each of these aspects of love.

I. THE ORIGIN OF LOVE—GOD (4:7–10)

Agapētoi, "beloved," has been used in 1 John before (2:7; 3:2, 21) and will be used one more time in this letter (4:11) and four times in 3 John (vv. 1, 2, 5, 11). It is John's term of endearment for his followers. His message is clear here: those loved of God need to love others; this is proof that they know God (v. 7b). Conversely, those who do not love their brothers have not begun to know God (i.e., the secessionists).[1]

The Greek for "by this" (*en toutō*) occurs five times in this section (4:9, 10, 13, 17; 5:2). Here the phrase refers to what follows: God's love was revealed in the fact that he sent his only Son into the world (v. 9). Two key words call for comment here: "sent" (*apestalen*, from which we derive the English word *apostle*) is found seventeen times in John and three times in 1 John (4:9, 10, 14). Here, "sent" implies that Jesus Christ was sent from heaven to earth at his incarnation.[2]

The second key word in our statement is "only" (cf. John 1:14, 18; 3:16, 18). The NIV rightly translates *monogenēs* "one and only," not "begotten." If John had intended the latter word, he would have used the Greek word *gennaō*—"I give," "beget," or "I give birth."

I conclude this section by calling attention to the phrases in 1 John 4:7–10 that indicate that God is the origin of love: "love comes from God" (v. 7b); "love has been born of God" (v. 7c); "God is love" (v. 8b); "This is how God showed his love among us: He sent his one and only Son" (v. 9); "not that we loved God, but that he loved us" (v. 10). These statements make clear that God took the initiative to show his love to us in Christ before we cared for him at all.

II. THE REVELATION OF LOVE—THE CHRISTIAN (4:11–16B)

The second aspect of love developed in 1 John 4:7–5:4a is the revelation of love (4:11–16b), more particularly God's love as manifested through Christians. It is clear that verse 11 is patterned after John 3:16, "God so loved the world," except that God's love for us in Christ is now being extended to others. In other words, we are to imitate God's love for us by showing his love to others (cf. 1 John 3:16; John 13:14).

---

1. *Egnō*, "has known," is probably an inceptive aorist: the secessionists have not even begun to know God!
2. See Eduard Schweizer, "Zum Religionsgeschichtlichen Hintergrund der 'Sendungsformel' Gal. 4.4f., Röm 8.3f., Joh 3.16f., 1 Joh 4.9" ("On the School of Religion's Background of the Send Formula"), *ZNW* 57 (1966): 199–200, 207.

The claim in verse 12 that no one has seen God draws on John 1:18; 5:37; 6:46; 1 John 4:20).[3] While the verb for "see" (*heōraken*) occurs in the preceding references, *theasthai* is used here in verse 12. It may be that John is engaging in a word play: *Theos* ("God") and *theasthai* ("see").[4] Two results follow when Christians love others. First, God lives in them (see 1 John 3:24; 4:13, 15, 16). Second, God's love is perfected or completed in believers when they love others (see 1 John 2:5; 4:17, 18). In other words, the circuit of God's love is completed when we love one another. All this is to say that God's love was set in motion through Christ and now through believers to others. Christians have become the locale of God's revelation of love. Their love for others makes visible the invisible God.

Verse 13 continues the theme of the mutual indwelling of God and the believer (cf. 1 John 3:24; 4:15, 16), rooting it in the presence of the Spirit within Christians. It is the Spirit of God who indwells believers, which creates a vital spiritual union with God.

Verse 14 adds a note of solemnity to the discussion: John and his community have seen and testify that the Father has sent his Son to be the Savior of the world. This assertion is of the same piece of cloth as other testimony statements in the Johannine literature.

"Savior of the world" has a storied background. In the Old Testament, Yahweh is the salvation of Israel and of the individual Israelite (Deut. 32:15; Ps. 24:5; Isa. 12:2), passages that the Septuagint renders "Savior." In the New Testament, "Savior" is used of Christ (see, e.g., John 4:42; Phil. 3:20; the Pastorals [10 times]; Luke-Acts [4 times]; 1 and 2 Peter [5 times]). In classical paganism, "Savior" was applied especially to Zeus, to the gods of the mystery religions, and in the first century AD, to the Roman emperor. Although there is no polemic against this pagan background in John and the epistles, there is in Revelation, as we will see.[5]

Colin Kruse provides an insightful discussion of how the "Savior of the world" changes meaning between John 4:42 and 1 John 4:14. On the lips of the Samaritans, "Savior of the world" in the former means Christ is Savior of Jew and Samaritan alike and indeed of the whole world. But in 1 John 4:14, "Savior of the world" is a polemical statement against the secessionists, in particular their denial of their sin and therefore any need for Jesus' atoning death as Savior.[6]

Verse 15 repeats the idea of the mutual indwelling of God and believer, a condition based on confessing (*homologeō*) "that Jesus is the Son of God." Kruse offers another insight into 1 John when he suggests verse 15, like other verses in the letter, is a shorthand reference to the full orthodox formula that needs to be adhered to by the Johannine community. That formula reads as follows: Jesus is the Christ, the Son of God, who came in the flesh as the Savior of the world and gave himself as an atoning sacrifice for the sins of the whole world.[7]

---

3. See the discussion by Wendy E. Sproston, "Witness to What Was *ap' archēs*: 1 John's Contribution to Our Knowledge of Tradition in the Fourth Gospel," *JSNT* 48 (1992): 43–65. Of course, the gospel of John teaches that Jesus has made the invisible God visible (see John 1:18).

4. So according to P. W. van der Horst, "A Wordplay in 1 John 4.12?" *ZNW* 63 (1972): 280–82.

5. Raymond E. Brown provides a good discussion of this background in his *The Epistles of John*, Anchor Bible 30 (Garden City, N.Y.: Doubleday, 1982), 523.

6. Colin G. Kruse, *The Letters of John*, Pillar New Testament Commentary (Grand Rapids: Eerdmans, 2000), 164.

7. 14. Ibid., 165.

Verse 16a–b concludes the paragraph—to know is to believe or rely on God's love for us. Thus God's love flows outward to others through Christ and should continue to flow to others through Christians. God's love should be revealed through believers to others.

III. THE OPPOSITION TO LOVE—FEAR (4:16C–19)

Verse 16c consists of yet another statement about the mutual indwelling of God and the believer that results from love. And it is by loving others that believers perfect or complete the flow of the love of God (v. 17a). Such love from God and to others creates within the Christian confidence (*parrēsian*) at the approaching day of judgment (cf. 1 John 2:28; 3:21).

Verse 17c—"because in this world we are like him"—should be taken to mean that Christians in this life are like Christ (because they have accepted him). Verse 18 amplifies the Christian's confidence at the approaching day of judgment: experiencing and expressing God's love drives out fear of divine disapproval. God's love and fear of judgment are mutually exclusive realities.

Verse 19 ties into the previous statement in verse 18—"the one who fears is not made perfect in love"—by emphatically contrasting those who are afraid with "we" who love because we are loved by God. *Agapōmen* should be translated as an indicative—"we love"—not as a subjunctive—"let us love"—because the tone of verse 19 is one of reassurance and comfort. John's readers are being encouraged because, in fact, they love God and their brothers. Thus God's love in motion has come full circle in this section: God loved Christ, who loved us, who love others, which in turn is to love God.

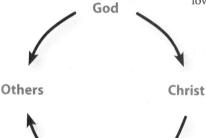

IV. THE TEST OF LOVE—AUTHENTICITY (4:20–5:4A)

The final two paragraphs of 1 John 4:7–5:4a reiterate the theme that resounds through this unit: love is the true test of Christian authenticity. I offer now a summary statement of 4:20–5:4a.

Verse 20a is antisecessionist in orientation: despite the secessionists saying they love God, their hatred for their brothers (the Johannine community from which they departed) belies their profession (cf. 1:6, 8, 10; 2:4, 6, 9). Then comes in verse 20b a minor-to-major argument: if the secessionists do not love their brothers whom they see (minor argument), how can they possibly love God whom they have not seen? (major argument)[8] According to the author, loving God and loving one's brother are inseparable commands. Love is both vertical and horizontal (v. 21).[9]

First John 5:1 provides a shorthand of the orthodox formula noted above: the one who believes that Jesus is the Christ (that Christ is human) is the one who has been born of God, that is, is authentically Christian. The moment of belief in Christ is the moment of being born of God (see John 1:12–13). Then follows a general maxim applied to the Christian

---

8. To this point 1 John speaks of loving others or one another. Here it speaks of love for one's brother.
9. What in the gospel of John is *Jesus'* command to love one another (13:34; 14:15, 21; 15:10, 12) becomes in 1 John *God's* command to love one another (2:3–4; 3:22–24; 5:2–3; 2 John 4).

life: if one loves one's father (the one who begot), then one will love the children begotten of the father. The meaning is clear. Genuine Christians love their heavenly Father as well as the family of God, something the secessionists were not doing.

Verse 2 throws a curve at the reader. Heretofore, John has said that the test of loving God is to love others. Now he switches by saying the test of loving others is loving God. But there is no real contradiction between these two statements, for divine love, according to John, is reciprocal in nature. The illustration here shows how this is so.

Verse 3 begins to conclude 1 John 4:7–5:4a by restating the principle that to love God is to obey his commands. "Obeying" his commands is synonymous with "carrying out" his commands (v. 2; see also 1 John 3:22).

Verses 3b and 4a are related: God's commands are not burdensome (v. 3b), because everyone born of God overcomes (*nika*) the world. In other words, for the one born of God spiritually, obeying his commands comes rather naturally—loving God and others (4:7–5:4a) and believing in Christ (4:1–6; 5:4b–12); therefore, they are not a burden (cf. Matt. 11:30). Furthermore, knowing that the authentic Christian has overcome the world (including the secessionists) lightens any of the load of obeying God.

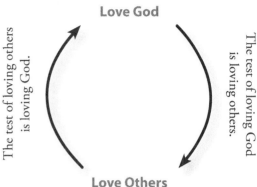

Love God

The test of loving others is loving God.

The test of loving God is loving others.

Love Others

REVIEW QUESTIONS

1. What is the overall theme of 1 John 4:7–5:4a?

2. What are the four aspects of love that emerge in 1 John 4:7–5:4a?

3. Through whom does God reveal his love to others, according to 1 John 4:11–16b?

4. How does 1 John 4:14 use the phrase "Savior of the world" against the Docetists?

5. What full orthodox formula lies behind John's shorthand reference to Christ's humanity?

6. What is the true test of authenticity (1 John 4:20–5:4a)?

confess

confidence

monogenēs

overcomes

Savior of the world

CHAPTER 35

Faith Is the Victory

1 JOHN 5:4B–12

Objectives

After reading this chapter, you should be able to:

- Explain how the theme of faith is developed in 1 John 5:4b–12.

- Discuss the threefold testimony about Christ in 1 John 5:4b–8.

- Explain the key phrase "water and blood" (1 John 5:6a).

INTRODUCTION

First John 5:4b–12 clearly forms its own section, with faith as the theme.[1] The noun *pistis* ("faith") occurs once therein, while various forms of the verb *pisteuō* ("I believe") occur four times in the short space of nine verses. The object of faith or belief in 1 John 5:4b–12 is the divine testimony that Jesus is the Son of God (another shorthand reference to the orthodox christological formula I identified earlier, pp. 304–5). For 1 John 5:4b–12 faith is both commitment to Christ and the right belief about who Christ is.

One may easily detect two parts to 5:4–12: the threefold testimony about Christ (vv. 4b–8) and God's testimony about Christ (vv. 9–12).[2] I now briefly discuss these two points.

I. THE THREEFOLD TESTIMONY ABOUT CHRIST (5:4B–8)

Verse 4b registers a change of tense in the usage of the verb "overcome" (*nikaō*):

> Verse 4a: present indicative of overcome (*nika*)
>
> Verse 4b: aorist participle of overcome (*nikēsasa*)
>
> Verse 5: present participle of overcome (*nikōn*)

So why the change from present tense in verses 4a and 5 to aorist in verse 4b? Assuming that the tenses are not simply stylistic, the past victory was the expulsion of the secessionists from the Johannine community, while the present victory referred to is the latter's continued stance against the allurement of John's opposition.[3]

The noun "faith" is found only here in the epistles of John. John far and away prefers the verb "believe." This is so because, for the beloved disciple, faith is dynamic (a verb) not static (a noun). In the epistles, faith is belief in the orthodox confession of who Christ is. The correct understanding of Christ is stated in verse 6a—Jesus Christ came not only by water but also by blood. To what does "by water and blood" refer? The majority view of 1 John 5:6 is that "water and blood" sum up the totality of Jesus' incarnational ministry on earth. Jesus' baptism (water, see John 1:34) and crucifixion (blood, John 19:34) frame his ministry. On this reading, then, "water and baptism" refute the Docetic denial that Christ was only divine (beginning probably at his baptism). Even more specifically, perhaps John has in mind Cerinthian-like teaching that claimed that Christ the deity came upon the man Jesus at his baptism by John, but that Christ left Jesus before his crucifixion. If so, then to the contrary, John is asserting that Christ and Jesus were one and the same throughout his life and death. This interpretation does not seem to have any flaw in it (contra Brown).[4]

It is the Holy Spirit who testifies to the reality of who Christ is (v. 6b). "Testify" and "testimony" occur ten times in this section, obviously highlighting the importance of that

---

1. That 5:13 begins the conclusion to 1 John and is separate from 5:4b–12 is signaled by the change to the first person in v. 13, "I write these things to you."

2. See Raymond E. Brown, *The Epistles of John*, Anchor Bible 30 (Garden City, N.Y.: Doubleday, 1982), 592–93.

3. I have been following Brown, ibid., 570–71.

4. Ibid. Brown rejects a full-blown docetic interpretation in general and Cerinthian teaching in particular, because he restricts his reconstruction of secessionist teaching to what can be culled from the gospel of John. But this approach seems to me to be too restrictive.

theme for John. Already in the gospel of John, as Alfred Plummer notes, there were seven agents of divine testimony to Jesus the Son of God: Scripture, John the Baptist, the disciples, Jesus' own works, Jesus' words, the Father, and the Paraclete/Spirit.[5] In 1 John 5:6b, it is the Holy Spirit who has given to the Beloved Disciple and his school the true interpretation of Jesus to be passed on to the Johannine community.

The Spirit, the water, and the blood combine into a threefold testimony to the orthodox view of Christ (vv. 7–8). The commentators agree that the background for this statement is Deuteronomy 19:15, which calls for two or three witnesses to confirm the validity of a testimony. But after that the consensus of interpretation of verses 7–8 breaks down, with two basic approaches surfacing in the debate.

1. *The Spirit, the water, and the blood are sacraments through which God outwardly confirms that Jesus Christ is the Son of God.* The Spirit is a prebaptismal anointing; the water is baptism; the blood is the Eucharist. But the problem with this perspective is that there is no New Testament instance of a prebaptismal sacramental anointing of the Spirit. Indeed, the chrism ("anointing") is the Spirit, not a prebaptismal ritual (1 John 2:20, 27).

2. *The Spirit is not a sacrament, but the witness through the Johannine tradition that the true view of Jesus is that he was both God and human in life (made public at his baptism—water) and in death (blood).* This approach seems to me to be the more correct interpretation of verses 7–8.[6]

---

5. A. Plummer, *The Epistles of John*, Cambridge Greek Testament (Cambridge: Cambridge University Press, 1886), 115.

6. There is a longer version of 5:7–8 that reads: "For there are three that testify in heaven, the Father, the Word and the Holy Spirit, the water and the blood, and these three are one." This longer version, known as the "Johannine Comma" ("comma" meaning "sentence"), is preserved in only a few later Byzantine Greek manuscripts (dating from the tenth to the eighteenth centuries). It is thought that the Johannine Comma found its way into the Greek manuscripts via the Latin manuscripts of the ninth century. The Johannine Comma is

II. GOD'S TESTIMONY ABOUT CHRIST (5:9–12)

The second paragraph of 1 John 5:4b–12 begins with a first-class conditional sentence and should be translated, "Since we accept the testimony of men, then the testimony of God is greater" (cf. v. 9).[7] Two questions are raised by this remark: What is the testimony of man? And what is the testimony of God?

The testimony of man cannot be the previous three witnesses invoked concerning Jesus (vv. 7–8), because they are obviously divine in nature. It is possible that the testimony of man could be a grand maxim, but Raymond Brown is probably closer to the truth when he equates it with the witness of John the Baptist. Although John the Baptist was from God, his witness was inferior to God through Christ.

The "testimony of God" most likely is an additional witness to the threefold witness to Jesus by the Spirit, the water, and the blood. This is precisely what one finds in John 5:31–40. There the Father's testimony is added to other divine witnesses to Jesus: Jesus' own words, John the Baptist, Jesus' miraculous works.[8] The content of God's testimony to Jesus is stated in verses 10–12: he who believes in Jesus has eternal life. Proper belief in Jesus the Christ, the Son of God, divides humanity into two groups: those who have eternal life and those who do not because they do not believe in him. This is the conclusion to 1 John 5:4b–12.

---

found in no early Greek manuscripts and is not found in the Old Latin versions before the seventh century, nor in the Vulgate before the eighth century. It is correctly omitted from all modern translations of the New Testament. For a full discussion of the textual traditions, see Brown, *Epistles of John*, 775–87; Georg Strecker, *The Johannine Letters*, trans. Linda M. Maloney, Hermeneia (Minneapolis: Fortress, 1996), 188–91; Colin G. Kruse, *The Letters of John*, Pillar New Testament Commentary (Grand Rapids: Eerdmans, 2000), 180.

7. The NIV omits this nuance of v. 9 in its translation.

8. See Brown, *Epistles of John*, 586–87.

REVIEW QUESTIONS

1. What is the theme of 1 John 5:4b–12?

2. How is that theme developed in two parts?

3. What is the threefold testimony about Christ in 1 John 5:4b–8?

4. Why the change from past to present tense in 1 John 5:4–5?

5. What does the phrase "water and blood" (1 John 5:6a) mean?

6. What is meant by the "hypostatic union"?

7. To what does "the testimony of men" probably refer (1 John 5:9)?

8. To what does "the testimony of God" refer (1 John 5:10–12)?

KEY TERMS

hypostatic union

pisteuō

testify/testimony

water and blood

CHAPTER 36

Conclusion

1 JOHN 5:13–21

Objectives

After reading this chapter, you should be able to:

- Identify the two main divisions of 1 John 5:13–21.

- Discuss the three blessings that result from true belief in Christ, according to 1 John 5:13–17.

- Explain what the "sin that leads to death" (1 John 5:16) is and is not.

- Discuss the certainties mentioned in 1 John 5:18–21.

- Explain 1 John 5:21 and the words "keep yourselves from idols."

INTRODUCTION

First John 5:13–21 serves as the conclusion to the letter and, as such, reminds one of John 20:31 (see especially 1 John 5:13). Furthermore, 1 John 5:13 forms an inclusio with the prologue of 1 John (1:1–4) just as John 20:31 forms an inclusio with the prologue of John (1:1–18).[1] First John 5:13–21 divides into two parts: verses 13–17 and verses 18–21. The first part treats the theme of the blessings of belief. The second part, easily identified by the threefold usage of "we know" (vv. 18, 19, 20), deals with the theme of the certainties of belief.

I now discuss 1 John 5:13–21 in more detail.

I. THE BLESSINGS OF BELIEF (IN THE SON OF GOD) (5:13–17)

"I write these things" (v. 13) is modeled after John 20:31, both of which serve to conclude their respective writings by summarizing their main messages. Those messages of 1 John and the gospel of John are the same: belief in Jesus Christ as the Son of God results in eternal life.

"I write these things" (v. 13) forms an inclusio with the prologue of 1 John, especially 1:4: "We write this." "Know" occurs six times in 1 John 5:13–21 (vv. 13, 15 [2 times], 18, 19, 20), signaling the theme of this section: knowledge, confidence, and certainty result from the proper belief in Jesus (v. 13). Verses 13–17 record three blessings that flow from such faith.

> Those messages of 1 John and the gospel of John are the same: belief in Jesus Christ as the Son of God results in eternal life.

A. Eternal Life (v. 13)

"Eternal life" in 1 John conveys two notions. First, it is eschatological; that is, it is the life of the age to come or the kingdom of God that comes to an individual because he or she believes in the name of the Son of God. Second, it is covenantal; eternal life is the life that proceeds from being in the new covenant of Christ. The Johannine Christians believe in the true understanding of who Christ is and therefore are in the new covenant, but the secessionists are not, because they believe misinformation about Jesus.

B. Answers to Prayer (vv. 14–15)

The second blessing of true faith in Christ is divine answers to prayer. Some form of "asking"—prayer—is found six times in verses 14–16 (*aiteō*, vv. 14, 15 [one verb, one noun], 16; *eōraō* [vv. 15, 16]),[2] indicating the theme of these verses.

John supplies a condition for receiving answers to one's prayer—one must pray according to the will of God (v. 14). In terms of prayer, the logic of verses 14–15 is this: if we pray according to God's will, he hears us; and if he hears us, God will answer our prayers.

C. Forgiveness of Sins (vv. 16–17)

Verses 16–17 identify two types of sins: sins that do not lead to death and the sin that leads to death.

---

1. The prologue of John may also have been added to the fourth gospel at a later stage; perhaps at the time of the addition of the epilogue, John 21.

2. *Aiteō* and *eōraō* are probably synonymous.

The former category is understood by John to be the sinning Johannine Christian. If his fellow brother prayers for him, God (understood) will forgive the erring brother and restore spiritual life to him.

On the other hand, if the person (he is not called a brother) commits the sin unto death, prayer for him will not help. Concerning the specific identification of the "sin that leads to death" in 1 John 5:16–17, most modern commentators say, rightly, I believe, the sins that can be forgiven are those by the Johannine community, while the sin unto death, which cannot be forgiven, is the secession of John's opponents.

The context of 1 John 5:16 and the letter itself assures us that this is what John had in mind.[3] By way of comparison, the Dead Sea Scrolls provide us with an analogue of John's sin unto death in the way they castigate the secessionists from their community (1QS 10:20–21). In both cases, 1 John and 1QS, the sin that cannot be forgiven is that of leaving the fellowship of the new covenant community.

Verse 17 concludes John's comments on sin and forgiveness, which serve a twofold purpose. First, when the author asserts "all wrongdoing is sin," he is communicating the truth that Christians should not be lax on sin. So this is a challenge to the Johannine community. But then John assures his readers that not all sin is deadly. That is, their sins are forgivable; not so the secessionists.

> Most modern commentators say, rightly, I believe, the sins that can be forgiven are those by the Johannine community, while the sin unto death, which cannot be forgiven, is the secession of John's opponents.

II. CERTAINTIES OF BELIEF (5:18–21)

On a slightly different note, John now transitions from discussing the blessings of belief to the *certainties* of belief. The latter topic emerges with the author's usage of "we know" three times in verses 18–21 (18, 19, 20). Three assurances are delineated therein.

A. Deliverance from Evil (v. 18)

The one who has been spiritually begotten (born) of God (cf. 2:29; 4:7; 5:1, 4) does not commit sin (cf. 3:6, 9). How this compares with John's other statements acknowledging that Christians sin (1:9; 2:1–2; 5:16–17) has already been discussed. No doubt, the usage of the present tense here—sins (*hamartanei*)—signifies habitual sin.

The next phrase in verse 18 is "the one who was born of God [the Christian] keeps him safe, and the evil one cannot harm him." This certainty of divine protection of God's children reminds one of Job 2:5—and Satan's desire to "touch" Job.

---

3. Thus, e.g., Colin G. Kruse, *The Letters of John*, Pillar New Testament Commentary (Grand Rapids: Eerdmans, 2000), 193–94; Raymond E. Brown, *The Epistles of John*, Anchor Bible 30 (Garden City, N.Y.: Doubleday, 1982), 617–19; Gary M. Burge, *The Letters of John*, NIV Application Commentary (Grand Rapids: Zondervan, 1996), 215–18; John Painter, *1, 2, and 3 John*, Sacra Pagina, ed. Daniel J. Harrington (Wilmington, Del.: Michael Glazier, 2008), 317–20. Refer to these works for the ten possibilities of what the sin unto death is for John.

B. Separation from the World (v. 19)

Verse 19 continues 1 John's dualism by dividing humanity into two sides: those who belong to God (the true Christians) and everybody else (especially the secessionists) who belongs to the world of the evil one. Informing this dualism is the apocalyptic division of the two ages:

This Evil Age	The Age to Come (The Kingdom of God)
Sinners	Believers

C. Union with Christ and God (vv. 20–21)

Besides the certainties of the protection of God and separation from the world, Johannine Christians have the assurance they are in spiritual union with Christ and God (vv. 20–21). This is so because Christ the Son of God has come and given knowledge of God, the one who is true (v. 20a). It is interesting that John does not use the noun *gnosis* (knowledge), but rather *dianoia* (insight). This may be because he did not want to cater to the Gnostics' word for "knowledge." "True One" is a title for God in the Johannine literature based on Isaiah 65:16 (John 17:3), but so also is it predicated of Jesus (John 14:6; Rev. 3:7, 14; 19:11). So the reason we are in the one who is true—God—is because we are in Jesus who is true. We have met with this concept of the mutual divine indwelling in the believer before. The result of such a union for the believer is eternal life (v. 20).

Most modern interpreters identify "idols" with the idolatry of the secessionists who left the worship of the true God to follow after a false Christology.

Verse 21 concludes the section and 1 John as a whole: "Dear children, keep yourselves from idols." Most modern interpreters identify "idols" with the idolatry of the secessionists who left the worship of the true God to follow after a false Christology (cf. the application of idolatry to secessionist apostasy in 1QH 4:9–11, 15; CD 20:8–10; 1QS 2:11–12, 16–17).[4]

---

4. See Brown, *Epistles of John*, 627–29.

REVIEW QUESTIONS

1. What evidence indicates that 1 John 5:13–21 forms the conclusion to that epistle?

2. What are the two main divisions of 1 John 5:13–21?

3. What are the three blessings that result from true belief in Christ according to 1 John 5:13–17?

4. What does the "sin that leads to death" (1 John 5:16) most likely mean?

5. What are the certainties of belief discussed in 1 John 5:18–21?

6. Who is the one "who was born of God" (1 John 5:18)?

7. What most likely does "keep yourselves from idols" in 1 John 5:21 mean?

KEY TERMS

answers to prayers	forgiveness of sins	sin unto death
deliverance from evil	separation from the world	union with Christ and God
eternal life	sin not unto death	

CHAPTER 37

Walk in Truth and Love

2 JOHN

Objectives

After reading this chapter, you should be able to:

- Identify the epistolary components of 2 John.

- Explain the meaning of "presbyter."

- Discuss who the "lady" is to whom 2 John is addressed.

- Explain how the words "In truth I love you" encapsulate the message of 2 John.

INTRODUCTION

Second John, unlike 1 John, follows the epistolary format I noted in my introduction:

I. Sender (v. 1a)

II. Recipient (vv. 1b–2)

III. Greetings (v. 3)

IV. Body (vv. 4–12)

V. Concluding formula (v. 13)

I now discuss 2 John following the preceding epistolary outline. In doing so, I will cover key background issues, such as the identification of the author and recipients, and the theme of the letter.

Second John, unlike 1 John, follows the epistolary format.

I. SENDER (V. 1A)

Second John begins with, "The presbyter" (NIV, "The elder"). Most interpreters argue that "presbyter" means an elderly man, which is in keeping with the thesis that John, an aged apostle, wrote the letter. This view also appeals to 3 John 4, where the same writer calls his recipients "my [spiritual] children." This suggests an elderly man of dignity and importance, which fits the advisory tone of our author in 2 John. This view also finds confirmation in the fact that the apostle Peter called himself a "presbyter" (NIV, "elder") as well (1 Pet. 5:1).

II. RECIPIENT (VV. 1B–2)

The recipient of 2 John is the "elect lady" (NIV, "chosen lady) and "her children." Two basic views compete for the identification of the "elect lady" (*eklektē kyria*): she is a literal woman and has physical children, or the title is a figurative expression for one of the presbyter's churches.

Two basic views compete for the identification of the "elect lady."

Some identifying the elect lady as an individual think her name was "the lady Electa" (referring to a certain Babylonian woman called "Electa"), while others believe the title is for an esteemed unnamed woman — "the dear lady."[1]

Most commentators identify the recipient as a local Johannine church. I can do no better than to quote Colin Kruse's four arguments for this view:

> (i) While the addressees are referred to as "the chosen lady and her children" in verses 1 and 2,... in the rest of the letter (vv. 6, 8, 10, 12) John addresses all his readers in the second person plural ("you"), suggesting that "the chosen lady and her children" is another way of addressing all members of a local church. (ii) In the OT and the Apocrypha Israel is referred to as a wife, bride, mother, and daughter, indicating that there would have been some precedent for a Christian community to be addressed in similar terms. (iii) In 1 Pet 5:13 the church in Rome is described as "she who is in Babylon," indicating that NT Christians could speak of a Christian community as a woman. (iv) The letter closes with the words "the children of your chosen sister send their greetings" (v. 13), which appears to be a way of

---

1. Raymond E. Brown, *The Epistles of John*, Anchor Bible 30 (Garden City, N.Y.: Doubleday, 1982), 652–54.

conveying the greetings of the elder's Christian community to his readers. If this is the case, then the letter opens and closes with references to Christian communities: the one to which this letter is sent ("the chosen lady and her children") and the one to which the elder belongs ("the children of your chosen sister").[2]

The literal Greek, "In truth I love you," combines in one clause the two commandments that dominate 1 John: walk in truth and walk in love.[3]

The combination occurs again in verses 2 and 3, the latter of which forms an inclusio with verse 1b. As 1 John made clear and now 2 John will reiterate, "truth" is believing the correct theological interpretation about Jesus, while "love" is loving fellow Johannine Christians because they believe the truth. The "truth" will be developed in this letter in verses 4, 7–11, while "love" is discussed in verses 5–6. In verses 1b–2, John expresses his love for the local church addressees and all such congregations because they have embraced the truth about Jesus Christ.

> "In truth I love you" combines in one clause the two commandments that dominated 1 John: walk in truth and walk in love.

III. GREETINGS (V. 3)

Most New Testament letters begin with a greeting, in particular that God's grace (*charis*) and peace (*eirēnē*) would rest upon their readers; so also 2 John 3.

IV. BODY (VV. 4–12)

The body of 2 John essentially is devoted to the two Johannine commandments: walk in the truth of who Jesus is (vv. 4, 7–11) and walk in love of the brethren (vv. 5–6).

A. Walk in Truth (vv. 4, 7–11)

The joy that John speaks of (v. 4) reminds one of 1 John 1:3–4—fellowship with the truth brings joy. The phrase "some of your children" need not imply that some of the elect lady's (church) were walking in truth and others were not. They would not be called children of the elect lady (v. 1b) if they were not all adhering to the commandment of truth. What that truth is, is mentioned in verses 7–11. Verse 7 is another shorthand reference to the orthodox view of Christ occurring throughout the epistles of John: "Jesus Christ as coming in the flesh" (cf. 1 John 2:22; 4:2–3, 15; 5:1, 5, 6).

The total formula encompasses the following: Jesus was the Christ, the Son of God come in the flesh, whose death atoned for our sins.

"Coming" is a present participle, *erchomenon*, leading some interpreters to see in this a reference to the parousia: Jesus

> Verse 7 is another shorthand reference to the orthodox view of Christ occurring throughout the epistles of John: "Jesus Christ coming in the flesh" (cf. 1 John 2:22; 4:2–3, 15; 5:1, 5, 6).

---

2. Colin G. Kruse, *The Letters of John*, Pillar New Testament Commentary (Grand Rapids: Eerdmans, 2000), 204–5.

3. The NIV is correct in treating "in truth" as a theological statement, not merely as an adverb.

Christ will come *again* in the flesh.[4] But most commentators take "coming" to refer to Jesus' incarnation, especially since 2 John 7 matches 1 John 4:2, the latter of which clearly speaks of the incarnation, not the parousia.[5] The perfect participle in 1 John 4:2 (*elēluthota*, "has come") pinpoints the time of Jesus Christ becoming flesh, namely, at the incarnation. The present participle in 2 John 7 ("coming") attributes a timeless character to Christ's humanity — it began at the incarnation and continues even to this day. Those who do not confess that Jesus Christ is come in the flesh — the secessionists — are deceivers and antichrist (cf. 1 John 2:18, 19; 4:1).

Verses 8–9 seem to suggest that even Johannine Christians can lose sight of the truth and thereby remove themselves from the new covenant. If they do not persist in the true view of Christ, according to verse 8, they will lose what they have worked for, which, based on John 6:27, 29, is their faith.

Verses 10–11 prohibit welcoming those who embrace the teaching of John's opposition.

The first-class conditional sentence (v. 10) indicates that John is not uttering an idle threat — the secessionists, in fact, are trying to secure a hearing before Johannine believers. "Do not take him into your house (*oikian*)" means a couple of things. First, the Johannine believers John is addressing should not welcome the false teachers into their homes; that is, they are not to provide private hospitality to the secessionists. The provision of hospitality for itinerant Christians was very important in the early years of the church. There were inns, but these were of ill repute, and most travelers preferred to find lodging with friends, relatives, and acquaintances, or those to whom they bore letters of introduction and recommendation (see Matt. 10:9–13; 2 Cor. 3:1; Heb. 13:1–2; 3 John 8).[6] By the second century, spiritual charlatans were taking advantage of Christian hospitality, using such as the occasion to mooch off their hosts or even to spread false teaching at their expense (see *Didache* 11:1–2 and Ignatius's letters [*Eph.* 7:1; 8:1; 9:1; *Smyrn.* 4:1; 5:1; 7:2]).

Second, however, "house" probably means more than private house; it also could refer to the house church, the meeting places of Christians for public worship during the first centuries of Christianity (see Rom. 16:5; 1 Cor. 16:19; Col. 4:15; 1 Tim 3:15; Philem. 2). If so, then the presbyter is advising the members of the house church not to receive heretical teachers into the assembly of the church so they would not be given the opportunity to propagate their beliefs.

B. Walk in Love (vv. 5–6)

The second Johannine commandment flows from the first: believing the truth about Jesus (vv. 4, 7–11) involves loving those of kindred spirit (vv. 5–6).

---

4. So Georg Strecker, *The Johannine Letters*, trans. Linda M. Maloney, Hermeneia (Minneapolis: Fortress, 1996), 234–36.

5. So, e.g., Kruse, *Letters of John*, 210; John Painter, *1, 2, and 3 John*, Sacra Pagina, ed. Daniel J. Harrington (Wilmington, Del.: Michael Glazier, 2008), 349–50; Gary M. Burge, *The Letters of John*, NIV Application Commentary (Grand Rapids: Zondervan, 1996), 234.

6. See the groundbreaking study by Abraham J. Malherbe, "Hospitality and Inhospitality in the Church," in his book *Social Aspects of the Early Church*, 2nd ed. (Philadelphia: Fortress, 1983), 92–112; cited from 94–96.

The commandment to love is not new but originated with Jesus (cf. v. 5 with John 13:34; 15:12, 17; 1 John 3:23; 4:21).

Verse 12 concludes the body of the letter by calling attention to the quality of joy that obedience to the two commandments (truth and love) produces; in doing so, it returns us to the beginning of 2 John (v. 4). This the presbyter will discuss more fully when he visits the church of "the elect lady."

V. CONCLUDING FORMULA (V. 13)

Second John closes with a greeting from "the children of your chosen [*eklektēs*] sister" (cf. 3 John 14). Verse 13 follows the Greek grammatical rule: a neuter subject—"the children"—(*tekna*) requires a singular verb "greets" (*aspazetai*). This gives a collective sense to "children"; namely, it is the local church to which John refers; in particular, the congregation over which John presides. The implication of all of this is that the children of God are those who believe the truth about Jesus and love one another.

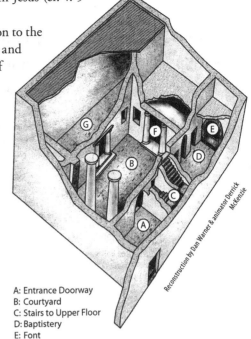

Reconstruction by Dan Warner & animator Derrick McKenzie

A: Entrance Doorway
B: Courtyard
C: Stairs to Upper Floor
D: Baptistery
E: Font
F: "Sunday School"
G: "Church"

Cross-sectional drawing of the earliest Christian church building discovered, a converted house in the eastern Syrian city of Dura.

REVIEW QUESTIONS

1. What are the epistolary components of 2 John?

2. What does "presbyter" mean?

3. Is the recipient of 2 John a lady or a church?

4. How do the words "In truth I love you" encapsulate the message of 2 John (and 1 John)?

5. Does John warn the church that the false teachers should not be allowed in members' homes, or in their house churches, or both?

KEY TERMS

children	hospitality	presbyter
elect lady	house church	truth
	love	

CHAPTER 38

House Churches in Conflict

3 JOHN

Objectives

After reading this chapter, you should be able to:

- Explain the relationship between 2 and 3 John.
- Discuss the relationship between John and Diotrephes.
- Explain how Gaius and Demetrius factor into the above relationship.
- Reconstruct the historical situation that lies behind 3 John.

INTRODUCTION

It would be helpful to raise and attempt to answer the key questions generated by 3 John before analyzing the letter in more detail. Three key relationships have to be grasped in order to understand 3 John.

I. THE RELATIONSHIP OF 3 JOHN TO 2 JOHN

Three key relationships have to be grasped in order to understand 3 John.

First, what is the relationship of 3 John to 2 John? Several links between these two epistles indicate that they were written by the same individual. Both claim to be authored by the "presbyter." Both use the same key words: "truth," "love," "welcome." And both letters conclude with the identical closing sentences. Therefore, there is no doubt that the same author wrote 2 and 3 John. And as I argued in the introduction, the author of 1, 2, and 3 John is one and the same—the apostle John. But it is possible that there is an even closer relationship between 3 John and 2 John, namely, 3 John 9 ("I wrote to the church …") might actually be referring to 2 John. And, if it is, then an important issue is thereby cleared up, namely, the relationship between the presbyter John and Diotrephes.

II. THE RELATIONSHIP BETWEEN JOHN AND DIOTREPHES

Second, what was the relationship between John and Diotrephes, the latter of which is the villain in the story behind 3 John? Three answers have been offered by scholars to explain the hostility between the two: ecclesiastical, doctrinal, and social.

A. An Ecclesiastical Dispute

Some interpreters posit that the hostility between John and Diotrephes was rooted in the contrasting style of church governance observed by these two individuals.

Thus Diotrephes is the first monarchial bishop that we know from the first century who abused his authority by excommunicating John's missionaries from his churches. This interpretation is based on 3 John 9–10, where it is said that Diotrephes loved to be the first and denied hospitality to the brothers of John.[1]

But the problem with the ecclesiastical interpretation, as most commentators recognize today, is that there is no evidence in the New Testament era for the existence of bishops. Rather, we do not meet such an individual until in the second-century writings of Ignatius of Antioch. In fact, it is clear from 1 John 2:27 that the apostle John did not consider the church to have need of an authoritative teacher because it possessed the Spirit.

B. A Doctrinal Dispute

Others have argued that the conflict between the elder and Diotrephes was theological in nature. Diotrephes was a secessionist heretic, while the elder stood for the orthodox

---

1. Adolf von Harnack, "Über den dritten Johannesbrief" ("On the Third Johannine Letter"), *TV* 15 (1897): 16ff.; cited by Jens-W. Taeger, "Der Konservative Rebell: Zum Widerstand des Diotrephes gegen den Presbyter" ("The Conservative Rebel: The Opposition of Diotrephes against the Presbyter") *ZNW* 78 (1987): 267–87; citation from 268.

faith.[2] In my judgment, three considerations combine to indicate that Diotrephes did indeed align himself with John's Docetic opponents. First, if the connection between 3 John 9 and 2 John stands (that the previous letter the elder wrote was 2 John), then 3 John deals with the same theological aberration that is spelled out in 2 John, namely, Docetic Christology. And it is that which Diotrephes welcomed, prompting him to turn John's representatives away.

Second, 3 John focuses on the same two words emphasized in 2 John — "truth" and "love." These two words in 3 John convey the same meaning they did in 2 John: the "truth" is believing in correct Christology, while "love" means to welcome those who spread that message of orthodoxy.[3]

Third, as John Painter has demonstrated, 3 John 10 recalls 2 John 10 – 11. The latter passage refers to the secessionists who propagated their false Docetic Christology, labeling their efforts "evil works" (*ergois … ponērois*; NIV, "wicked work"), the same description of Diotrephes' efforts found in 3 John 10 (*ta erga … ponērois*). This seems to confirm the theological nature of the above dispute[4] — John opposes Diotrephes because of the latter's acceptance of the secessionists' teaching.

C. A Social Dispute

These days most interpreters of 3 John follow Abraham J. Malherbe's construct, which roots the dispute between the elder and Diotrephes in a failed social relationship. In his groundbreaking study, Malherbe argued that Diotrephes was the host of one of the churches among the Johannine congregations. But when John's emissaries arrived at that house church, Diotrephes refused to offer them hospitality — that despite the fact the missionaries brought a letter of recommendation from John. The refusal of Diotrephes to receive the emissaries amounted to a refusal of John himself. Therefore the dispute was not doctrinal in nature, but purely social. John was rejected and embarrassed by one of his own churches![5]

In my opinion, Malherbe's theory makes sense, except that I see no reason to exclude from it the theological viewpoint. That is to say, it was precisely because Diotrephes sided with the secessionists that his house church refused hospitality to John's representatives and, thereby, John himself. Indeed, it seems reasonable to conclude that the very grouping together of John's three epistles suggests that author saw a theological connection among them. So, on this reading, the combination of the doctrinal and social components nicely explains the nature of the relationship between John and Diotrephes.

---

2. Walter Bauer, *Orthodoxy and Heresy in Earliest Christianity* (Philadelphia: Fortress, 1971), 93. I must disagree, however, with Bauer's larger theory, which was that orthodoxy did not clearly develop until the second century AD.

3. See my analysis of 3 John to follow.

4. John Painter, *1, 2, and 3 John*, Sacra Pagina, ed. Daniel J. Harrington (Wilmington, Del.: Michael Glazier, 2008), 364 – 65.

5. Abraham J. Malherbe, "Hospitality and Inhospitality in the Church," in his *Social Aspects of the Early Church*, 2nd ed. (Philadelphia: Fortress, 1983), 92 – 112.

III. THE RELATIONSHIP OF GAIUS, DIOTREPHES, AND DEMETRIUS

Third, what was the relationship of Gaius, Diotrephes, and Demetrius? Most scholars say that Gaius and Diotrephes were hosts to separate house churches in the same general area. I concur with this conclusion.[6]

Assuming the above conclusions, the following scenario best explains the historical situation informing 3 John:

1. John sent his representatives to those churches under his spiritual authority at a distance from Ephesus, his base of operation, for the purpose of warning them of the advances of the secessionists (recall 2 John is written to one such house church).

2. The house church over which Diotrephes presided rejected John's missionaries most probably because Diotrephes had already sided with the Docetic teachers (3 John 9–10).

3. Those emissaries then traveled to Gaius's house church, where they were welcomed and received support (3 John 5–8). This was so because Gaius was "faithful to the truth" (3 John 3–4).

4. John praised Gaius for his hospitality shown to the orthodox missionaries (3 John 3–8) and encouraged him to do the same regarding Demetrius, whom John would be sending shortly to that area (vv. 11–12).

We will now explore this scenario in more detail as we make our way through 3 John.

IV. ANALYSIS

Third John adheres to the ancient epistolary style more than any other New Testament letter, especially with its inclusion of the health wish:

A. Sender (v. 1a)

B. Addressee (v. 1b)

C. Health wish (v. 2)

D. Body (vv. 3–12)

E. Conclusion (vv. 13–14a)

F. Concluding formula (v. 14b)

I now summarize the contents of 3 John by following its epistolary format.

A. Sender (v. 1a)

The author, like that of 2 John, identifies himself as the presbyter, or elder, whom I take to be the apostle John.

---

6. See Raymond E. Brown, *The Epistles of John*, Anchor Bible 30 (Garden City, N.Y.: Doubleday, 1982), 729–30.

B. Addressee (v. 1b)

"Gaius" was a common name in the Roman Empire. Beside 3 John's addressee, several other men named Gaius can be found in the New Testament in connection with Paul's ministry (Gaius of Corinth whom Paul baptized, 1 Cor. 1:14; Rom. 16:23; a Macedonian Gaius who was a traveling companion of Paul, Acts 19:29; and a Gaius who accompanied Paul to Jerusalem at the conclusion of the apostle's third missionary journey, Acts 20:4).

Gaius is called the "beloved" (*agapētos*; NIV, "dear friend"). "Beloved" occurs often in the epistles of John (6 times in 1 John and 4 times in 3 John, here and vv. 2, 5, 11). Putting these references together reveals a chain reaction: Christ is the beloved of God, whose incarnation and atonement make Christians the beloved of God, who should then love others. As 3 John unfolds, Gaius is the beloved of God who demonstrates God's love to John's missionaries by showing them hospitality.

The presbyter "loves" Gaius "in the truth," even as Gaius himself loves the truth (vv. 3, 4, 6; cf. v. 8). It seems clear that the terms "truth" and "love" recall the two Johannine commandments: walk in the truth of correct Christology and love those who embrace the orthodox view of Jesus Christ.

C. Health Wish (v. 2)

A health wish, such as that from John to Gaius, is a typical feature in ancient letters and need not imply a "health and wealth" gospel.

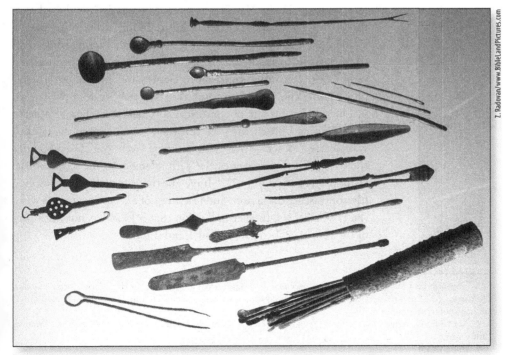

Tools of a Roman doctor.

D. Body (vv. 3–12)

The body of the epistle of 3 John is devoted to discussing three individuals: Gaius (vv. 3–8), Diotrephes (vv. 9–10), and Demetrius (vv. 11–12).

1. Commendation of Gaius (vv. 3–8)

The presbyter praises Gaius, the recipient of the letter, for two reasons. First, he is commended because of his theological affirmation of the truth (vv. 3–4). That is, Gaius walks in the truth. As mentioned before, walking in the truth is one of the two key commandments in the gospel and the epistles of John. It means to embrace the proper view of Jesus: that he was the Christ, whose life and death served as atonement for humanity. Gaius's action brings joy to John (cf. vv. 3–4 with 1 John 1:4; 2 John 4); even as do all of John's spiritual children when they walk in such truth.[7]

Second, Gaius is commended by John for his practical expression of the truth: he loves those of kindred spirit (vv. 5–8). In other words, Gaius's reception of John's missionaries demonstrated that he obeyed God, the second key Johannine commandment—to walk in love. Those whom Gaius's house church showed hospitality to were called "brothers" (v. 5) who were sent out for the sake of the "Name." *Proempō* ("send them on their way," v. 6), functions as a technical term for missionary support in the early church (Acts 15:3; 20:38; 21:5; Rom. 15:24; 1 Cor. 16:6, 11; 2 Cor. 1:16; Titus 3:13; cf. Polycarp, *Philip.* 1:1).[8] "In a manner worthy of God" no doubt means that Gaius should provide for these brothers/missionaries of John in a way that befits those who serve God (cf. 1 Thess. 2:12, the only other place the expression, "worthy of God," occurs in the New Testament). The words "for the sake of the Name" (*hyper tou onamatos*, v. 7) are found in five other places in the New Testament, often in the context of suffering for Christ (Acts 5:41; 9:16; 15:26; cf. 21:13; Rom. 1:5).[9] So, John's emissaries went to the Johannine churches in Gaius's area for the purpose of proclaiming the true Christ, and they suffered for it at the hands of Diotrephes. By way of contrast, Gaius accepted these brothers, thus aligning himself with the truth (cf. "coworkers of the truth," v. 8). Verse 7 observes that these brothers "went out" (*exerchomai*), the term used three times earlier with reference to the secessionists (1 John 2:19; 4:1; 2 John 7).[10] It may be that the presbyter is implicitly contrasting the actions and teachings of his representatives with the false teachers, further indication that 3 John has not lost sight of the theological controversy of 1 and 2 John.

> It may be that the presbyter is implicitly contrasting the actions and teachings of his representatives with the false teachers, further indication that 3 John has not lost sight of the theological controversy of 1 and 2 John.

---

7. The term here for "children" is *teknia* (*teknon*), whereas normally John uses the diminutive form, *teknion*. The usage in 3 John 4 may reflect the fact that the apostle is writing to a church under his spiritual jurisdiction but not known to him personally.

8. See Colin G. Kruse, *The Letters of John*, Pillar New Testament Commentary (Grand Rapids: Eerdmans, 2000), 223.

9. Ibid., 224.

10. See Brown, *Epistles of John*, 712.

2. Condemnation of Diotrephes (vv. 9–10)

That which John wrote to the church (house church) may have been 2 John, though that is debated. But if the allusion is to 2 John, as I believe it is, then John's condemnation of Diotrephes was doctrinally based: Diotrephes was aiding and abetting the secessionists. Consequently, John condemns several actions of Diotrephes in verses 9–10: (1) He loves to be first in the church, probably meaning Diotrephes took control of the house church (was he its host?), leading it to reject John's representatives and thus the apostle himself. (2) Diotrephes went further than that and slandered John. (3) Diotrephes refused to show hospitality to the orthodox brothers. (4) He restrained those in his church who wanted to help John's emissaries by expelling them from the congregation. All of this earned Diotrephes the label of "evil" worker (v. 11). As such, Diotrephes had not really "seen God," the same indictment John earlier leveled against the secessionists (1 John 3:6; cf. 4:12, 20).

> Diotrephes had not really "seen God," the same indictment John earlier leveled against the secessionists (1 John 3:6; cf. 4:12, 20).

3. Commendation of Demetrius (vv. 11–12)

The only other Demetrius in the New Testament is Demetrius the silversmith of Ephesus (Acts 19:24, 38). It is an attractive hypothesis that 3 John refers to the same individual who has now become a Christian. Yet there is no evidence the two individuals are the same. The Demetrius of verses 11–12 is another representative of the presbyter who has been sent to Gaius and other Johannine churches nearby. Demetrius may well be the carrier of 3 John and will read and interpret its contents to John's congregations. Thus verse 11 encourages Gaius not to act like Diotrephes (who rejected John's earlier missionaries) but, rather, to welcome Demetrius even as he did the previous emissaries of the presbyter. Demetrius should be received because he is well spoken of by all, the truth itself, and by John himself.

The first testimony speaks of the praise of Demetrius by the other Johannine churches. The second testimony of commendation comes from the truth: Demetrius continues the message of orthodox Christianity regarding Jesus Christ. The third testimony—John's—is 3 John itself, which is a letter of recommendation to Gaius from John on Demetrius's behalf. Similar letters of recommendation are mentioned in the New Testament (Acts 18:27; Rom. 16:1–2; 1 Cor. 16:3; 2 Cor. 3:1; Phil. 2:25–30; Col. 4:7–9), paving the way for hospitality—prayer, lodging, and financial support for Christian missionaries.

> Demetrius should be received because he is well spoken of by all, the truth itself, and by John himself.

E. Conclusion (vv. 13–14a)

John concludes this letter as he did in 2 John (v. 12), by sharing his desire to visit with the recipient in person.

F. Concluding Formula (v. 14b)

Verse 14b is a concluding formula that conveys a benediction from John and his churches to Gaius and his house church. "Peace" reminds one of Jesus' benediction to his disciples after his resurrection (cf. John 20:19, 26 with 14:27). "Friends" (*philoi*) derives from John 15:13–15, where Jesus characterizes his disciples as his "friends." There he says that no one has greater love for his friends than to lay down his life for them—something Jesus did, and something the beloved community of John must do as well. This is what it means to be a part of the new covenant in Christ.

REVIEW QUESTIONS

1. What is the relationship of 3 John to 2 John?

2. What was the relationship between John and Diotrephes: ecclesiastical, doctrinal, or social?

3. What was the relationship of Gaius, Diotrephes, and Demetrius?

4. Can you explain the historical situation informing 3 John?

5. Why does the presbyter commend Gaius (vv. 3–8)?

6. Why is Diotrephes condemned (vv. 9–10)?

7. Why is Demetrius commended (vv. 11–12)?

KEY TERMS

Demetrius	Gaius	monarchial leadership
Diotrephes	health-wealth gospel	the "Name"
doctrinal dispute	hospitality	social dispute
	house church	

PART 3

Revelation

CHAPTER 39

Introduction to Revelation

Objectives

After reading this chapter, you should be able to:

- Discuss the three genres that comprise Revelation.

- Defend the Johannine authorship of Revelation.

- Evaluate the Neronian and Domitian possible dates for the writings of Revelation.

- Identify some of the background materials informing Revelation.

- Explain the four major schools of interpretation of Revelation and subcategories of each.

- Summarize the theology of Revelation.

INTRODUCTION

We come now to the third writing that comprises the Johannine corpus: Revelation. The Apocalypse (the Greek name for Revelation) forms the climax of John's inspired thought and, indeed, of biblical prophecy.

Of all the books in the Bible, Revelation requires some introductory remarks before one can properly interpret it. Such an introduction should include the genre of Revelation; its authorship; the date and historical setting of its writing; traditional materials in Revelation; the Greek text of the Apocalypse; the major schools of interpretation of the book; Revelation's relationship to the gospel of John and the epistles of John; and the theology of Revelation.

I. GENRE

Before one can properly interpret any piece of literature, the Bible included, one must determine its genre or literary type.[1] This principle is acutely important for Revelation, and its neglect has resulted in a morass of conflicting viewpoints. The difficulty is heightened by the fact that Revelation consists of a mixture of three genres: apocalyptic, prophetic, and epistolary.

---

1. For an excellent "genre" approach to the Bible, see Gordon D. Fee and Douglas Stuart, *How to Read the Bible for All Its Worth: A Guide to Understanding the Bible*, 2d ed. (Grand Rapids: Zondervan, 1993); cf. J. Scott Duvall and J. Daniel Hays, *Grasping God's Word: A Hands-On Approach to Reading, Interpreting, and Applying the Bible* (Grand Rapids: Zondervan, 2005).

An icon in the monastery at Patmos of St. John receiving his revelation.

Wikimedia Commons

Modern Patmos. Orthodox monastery of St. John with its massive fifteenth-century walls and seventeenth-century battlements.

Alan F. Johnson succinctly describes the first of these genres:

> Revelation is ... commonly viewed as belonging to the body of nonbiblical Jewish writings known as apocalyptic literature. The name for this type of literature (some nineteen books) is derived from the word "revelation" (*apocalypsis*) in Revelation 1:1.... The extrabiblical apocalyptic books were written in the period from 200 B.C. to A.D. 200. Usually scholars stress the similarities of the Apocalypse of John to these noncanonical books—similarities such as the use of symbolism and vision, the mention of angelic mediators of the revelation, the bizarre images, the expectation of divine judgment, the emphasis on the kingdom of God, the new heavens and earth, and the dualism of this age and the age to come.[2]

While significant parallels do indeed exist between Revelation and early Jewish and Christian apocalyptic materials, there are critical differences between them as well, none the least of which is that Revelation is a prophetic book (1:3; 22:7, 10, 18–19), while the others make no such claim.[3] Revelation

> Revelation consists of a mixture of three genres: apocalyptic, prophetic, and epistolary.

2. Alan F. Johnson, "Revelation," in *The Expositor's Bible Commentary*, ed. Frank E. Gabelein (Grand Rapids: Zondervan, 1981), 12:400. See Johnson's helpful bibliography on apocalypticism, 400–401n3. Johnson also cites John J. Collins, who has supplied the most influential definition of the apocalypse genre: " 'Apocalypse' is a genre of revelatory literature with a narrative framework, in which a revelation is mediated by an otherworldly being to a human recipient, disclosing a transcendent reality which is both temporal, insofar as it envisages eschatological salvation, and spatial, insofar as it involves another, supernatural world" (Collins, "Pseudonymity, Historical Reviews and the Genre of the Revelation of John," *CBQ* 39 1977.). Others have updated this definition to include the social function of ancient apocalypses, namely, to reinforce the convictions of a persecuted minority by transforming their vision of reality. Such a symbolic world is created by the stock imagery of apocalyptic, in which the reader is invited to participate in the kingdom of God, which is actualized in the present by faith. See Richard Bauckham, *The Climax of Prophecy: Studies in the Book of Revelation* (Edinburgh: T. & T. Clark, 1993), 5–12, 17–22.

3. Studies describing John as a prophet include David Hill, *New Testament Prophecy* (Richmond: John Knox, 1979), 87–89; "Prophecy and Prophets in the Revelation of St. John," *NTS* 18 (1971–72): 401–18; Wayne Grudem, *The Gift of Prophecy in 1 Corinthians* (Washington, D.C.: University Press of America, 1982), 106–9; David E. Aune, *Revelation 1–5*, WBC 52A (Dallas: Word, 1997), lxxv–lxxvi.

is not pseudonymous (1:1; 22:8); neither is it pessimistic about God's intervention in history. Furthermore, while many apocalyptic writers recast past events as though they were futuristic prophecies (*vaticinia ex eventu*), thus lending credibility to their predictive prowess, John (the author of Revelation) does not follow this procedure. On the contrary, he places himself in the contemporary world of the first century AD and speaks of the coming eschatological consummation in the same manner as did the Old Testament prophets—a consummation that, for John, has already begun to break into history in the death and resurrection of Jesus Christ (1:4–8; 4–5).

In addition to being apocalyptic and prophetic in nature, Revelation is encased by an epistolary framework (1:4–8 and 22:10–21). This convention alone sets it apart from apocalyptic materials. The prescript (1:4–8) contains the typical epistolary components—sender, addressees, greetings, and the added feature of a doxology. The postscript (22:10–21), in good ancient letter form, summarizes the body of the writing, as well as legitimates John as its divinely inspired composer. The combined effect of the prescript and the postscript, not to mention the letters to the seven churches of the Roman province of Asia (chaps. 2–3), is to root Revelation in the real history of its day. How different from other ancient noncanonical apocalypses. Consider, for example, the opening statement in *1 Enoch*, that what the author saw was "not for this generation but the distant one that is coming" (*1 Enoch* 1:2).[4]

II. AUTHORSHIP

In ascertaining the identity of the author of Revelation, two lines of evidence need to be assessed: external and internal.[5] The external evidence consists of the testimony of the church fathers, which is nearly unanimously in favor of the opinion that the apostle John was the author of the Apocalypse. These include Papias, Justin Martyr, the Muratorian Fragment, Irenaeus, Clement of Alexandria, Tertullian, Hippolytus, Origen, and Methodius. The notable exceptions to this testimony are Dionysius, bishop of Alexandria (AD 247–64), and Eusebius, the church historian, who himself was persuaded by Dionysius's arguments against Johannine authorship of the book (though Eusebius expressed his doubts less vigorously than did Dionysius).

In turning to the internal evidence for determining the authorship of Revelation, Dionysius's four categories continue to convince many against Johannine authorship,[6] which I summarize here: (1) the writer's self-identification, (2) the construction of Revelation as compared with the genuine writings of John the apostle, (3) the character of these writings, and (4) the writing style of these materials.

1. The first internal argument offered by Dionysius is that whereas Revelation identifies its author as "John" (1:1, 4, 9; 22:8), neither the gospel of John nor the letters of John do the same. The assumption here is that if the apostle John had written Revelation, he would

---

4. The epistolary influence on Revelation probably comes from Paul and the liturgical setting of Revelation.

5. I am indebted to Robert L. Thomas's work, *Revelation 1–7: An Exegetical Commentary*, ed. Kenneth Barker (Chicago: Moody, 1992), 2–19, for the following discussion. The question of the authorship of Revelation is closely related to its canonicity, at least in terms of the discussion of the church fathers. Those who accepted the Johannine authorship of Revelation accepted its canonicity. But those who questioned or even denied Johannine authorship questioned or rejected its canonicity (notably Dionysius and, to a lesser degree, Eusebius).

6. This influence can especially be seen in the monumental work by R. H. Charles, *The Revelation of St. John*, ICC, 2 vols. (Edinburgh: T. & T. Clark, 1920).

not have felt any compulsion to identify himself as its author. This reasoning, however, is an argument from silence and therefore is not convincing. Moreover, the apocalyptic nature of the book may have necessitated the author identifying himself, even as other works fitting that genre do. Actually, the fact that the author mentions his name—John—without any appeal to credentials, suggests he was well known to the Asia Minor churches. This lends support to the claim that John the apostle authored the Apocalypse.

2. With regard to the construction of Revelation and that of John's gospel and letters, Dionysius argued that the former does not begin with the identification of Jesus as the "Word" nor with the author's eyewitness vantage point, whereas the latter do (cf. John 1:1–18 with 1 John 1:1–4). But this observation overlooks Revelation 1:2 and its connection of the word of God with Christ. It also misses the significance attached to the concept of "witness" in Revelation and in the other Johannine literature (cf. Rev. 1:2; 22:16 with John 1:19–34; 5:32; 8:18; 15:26; 1 John 1:1–4; 5:6–11).

3. Dionysius also maintained that the vocabulary of Revelation differs significantly from the genuine Johannine writings. Yet Dionysius's assertion does not hold up under careful scrutiny. Twelve of the nineteen Johannine terms that are supposedly not found in Revelation do in fact occur (e.g., "life," "blood," "judgment," "devil"). Moreover, three of the terms not occurring in Revelation are also absent from the gospel of John ("forgiveness," "Antichrist," "adoption"), and one of them ("conviction") is not present in 1 John. Furthermore, while "truth" is not in the Apocalypse, its synonym, "genuine," is. Also, while "joy" is absent in the Apocalypse, it only occurs once each in the three letters of John. We are left then with one term, "darkness," that occurs frequently in the other Johannine writings and not in Revelation—hardly enough evidence upon which to base a major distinction.

4. Finally, Dionysius claimed that Revelation is written in poor Greek, in contrast to the good Greek style of the other Johannine materials. However, this overlooks three factors: (a) An author's writing style is not always consistent. (b) John, like his contemporaries, may well have used an amanuensis (a professional secretary) through whom he composed his gospel and the letters (cf. Rom. 16:22; 1 Peter 5:12). Exiled on the island of Patmos, however (cf. 1:9), he presumably did not have access to such an individual. (c) Revelation (apocalyptic) is a different genre than John (gospel) or the epistles of John (letter). This might also account for differing styles.

On balance, then, the external and internal evidence seem to point to the apostle John as the author of the Apocalypse.

III. DATE AND HISTORICAL SETTING

The date and historical setting of Revelation are integral to how one interprets that work. Later in this introduction I will overview the four major schools of interpretation of Revelation, but here I observe that two major periods qualify as candidates for its historical setting: the period of the reign of Emperor Nero (AD 54–68), especially AD 64–68; and the time of Domitian's reign (AD 81–96), especially the last few years. I now summarize the arguments for those respective views.

Some five arguments are often put forth to defend a pre–AD 70 writing of Revelation.

A. Neronian Date

Some five arguments are often put forth to defend a pre–AD 70 writing of Revelation.[7]

1. Revelation 11:1–2 speaks of the Jerusalem temple as still standing. Since the temple was not destroyed by the Romans until AD 70, it is surmised that Revelation was written before that catastrophe occurred.

2. Revelation 17:10 speaks of seven kings: "five have fallen, one is, the other has not yet come." The one who is, the sixth king, is the one in power at the writing of Revelation. The kings are often identified with the Roman emperors of the first century, beginning with Augustus.

Augustus (31 BC—AD 14)

Tiberius (AD 14–37)

Caligula (AD 37–41)

Claudius (AD 41–54)

Nero (AD 54–68)

Galba (AD 68–69)

Otho (AD 69)

Vitellius (AD 69)

Vespasian (AD 69–79)

Titus (AD 79–81)

Domitian (AD 81–96)

The advocates of a Neronian date for Revelation argue for one of two options regarding Revelation 17:10. One option is to equate the first king with Augustus, the first official Roman emperor, and the sixth as Galba, who reigned briefly after Nero's death. The other possibility is to begin with Julius Caesar, who first claimed the rights of Roman emperor (47–44 BC); then the sixth king would be Nero, with Galba being the seventh. Either way, these two approaches relate Revelation 17:10 to Nero.

3. The number 666 (Rev. 13:18) is no doubt John's usage of the Jewish numerological technique of gematria. Gematria was a mathematic cryptogram that assigned numerical values to letters of the alphabet. More than one scholar has seen a possible referent of this number in *Neron Kaiser*. The Hebrew numerical valuation for *Nrwn Qsr* is as follows: N = 50, R = 200, W = 6, N = 50, Q = 100, S = 60, and R = 200, which add up to 666.

4. "Babylon" is thought to represent Jerusalem in Revelation (see Rev. 11:8; 18:10, 16, 18, 19, 21; cf. 14:8; 17:5). This is so because Jerusalem/ancient Judaism crucified Christ, persecuted early Christians, and was exempt from Caesar worship (see below). These actions earned the city the name "Babylon," the nemesis of the people of God in the Old Testament.

---

7. For the following discussion, I am indebted to these scholars: Aune, *Revelation 1–5*, lvi–lxx; Craig S. Keener, *Revelation*, NIV Application Commentary (Grand Rapids: Zondervan, 2000), 35–39; Grant R. Osborne, *Revelation*, Baker Exegetical Commentary on the New Testament (Grand Rapids: Baker, 2002), 6–9; G. F. Beale, *The Book of Revelation: A Commentary on the Greek Text*, NIGTC (Grand Rapids: Eerdmans, 1999), 4–27.

5. Related to the previous point, Revelation 1:7, according to those advocating a pre–AD 70 date for Revelation, is a prophecy of Jesus' coming judgment on Jerusalem, which was fulfilled in AD 70 at the hands of the Romans (cf. Zech. 12:12).

While these arguments are impressive at first glance, there are problems with them.

1. Regarding Revelation 11:2, most commentators rightly recognize that symbolic Jerusalem is being described therein, not the literal city. Thus a post–AD 70 setting better fits the description of the destruction of the city but the preservation of the true people of God as portrayed in that verse.

> While these arguments are impressive at first glance, there are problems with them.

2. There are other viable ways of numbering the emperors in Revelation 17:10, if indeed they represent Roman caesars.[8] According to R. H. Charles, one way is to begin with Augustus, the first recognized Roman emperor. Thus Nero would be the fifth king. Because the reigns of Galba, Otho, and Vitellius were brief and disputed, they should be omitted in the count. That would make Vespasian the sixth ruler and his son, Titus, the seventh. The eighth king would be Vespasian's other son Domitian.[9]

3. It does seem that "666" is alluding to Nero, but it is Nero *Redivivus* (revived) that John has in mind (see Rev. 13:3). After Nero committed suicide on June 9, AD 68 (right after the Roman Senate condemned his rule), the legend developed that Nero returned from the dead and was about to lead the Parthians from the east to attack Rome. It seems that this myth did not gather force until the end of the first century AD.

4. The problem with equating "Babylon" with Jerusalem in Revelation is that there is not one example elsewhere of "Babylon" being used as a symbolic name for Israel.[10] On the other hand, "Babylon" was often used of the city of Rome in post–AD 70 Jewish literature (cf. Rev. 14:8; 16:19; 17:4; 18:2, 10, 21 with *4 Ezra* 3:1–2, 28–31; *2 Bar.* 10:1–3; 11:1; 67:7; *Sib. Oracles* 5.143, 159). Babylon was an appropriate symbol for Rome, because just as Babylon captured Jerusalem and destroyed the temple in 587 BC (2 Kings 25), so Rome captured and destroyed Jerusalem and its temple in AD 70.[11]

5. As we will see later in my treatment of Revelation, Revelation 1:7 and the other references to Jesus' parousia better refer to his second coming in the future than to his past coming in judgment on Jerusalem in AD 70.

B. Domitian Date

Most scholars today argue for a Domitian date of the writing of Revelation.

> Most scholars today argue for a Domitian date of the writing of Revelation.

The following considerations are often enlisted:

1. The pertinent church fathers thought so, including Irenaeus, Eusebius, Victorinus, Jerome, Clement of Alexandria, Justin Martyr, et al.[12]

---

8. Some equate Revelation 17:10 with world kingdoms, not individual emperors; see Osborne, *Revelation*, 620.

9. Charles, *Revelation of St. John*, 2:69–70.

10. See Beale, *Book of Revelation*, 25.

11. So A. Yarbro Collins, "Dating the Apocalypse of John," *Biblical Research* 26 (1981): 33–45.

12. See Aune's references, *Revelation 1–5*, lx.

2. As mentioned above, Revelation 11:2 best fits a post–AD 70 date; Revelation 17:10 is quite capable of supporting a Domitian setting; "666" is better taken as an allusion to Domitian (or, better, as a type of Nero); "Babylon" fits post–AD 70 Rome; Revelation 1:7 refers to Jesus' second coming, not the fall of Jerusalem in AD 70.

3. The problem posed to early Christians by Roman emperor worship is extensive in Revelation (Rev. 2–3; 13:4, 14–17; 14:9; 15:2; 16:2; 19:20; 20:4), and such a practice gained momentum under Domitian, especially in Asia Minor, home of the seven churches of Revelation.[13]

4. Related to the previous point, persecution of those who did not worship Caesar became intense and more widespread under Domitian.[14] This was in contrast to Nero's persecution of Christians, which was restricted to Rome.

5. The historical background of the seven churches in Asia Minor support a post-Neronian date for Revelation. Thus Grant Osborne delineates events reflected in the letters that point to a later date than the 60s:

> (1) The unaided recovery of Laodicea (3:17) best fits the earthquake and subsequent reconstruction of the city in A.D. 80; (2) their great wealth reflects better the 90s than the 60s; (3) "do not harm the oil and the wine" (6:6) most likely refers to an edict of Domitian in A.D. 92 restricting the growing of vines in Asia; (4) the "synagogues of Satan" (2:9; 3:9) can best be situated in conflicts that took place under Domitian; (5) the church of Smyrna (2:8–11) may not have existed in the 60s; (6) the idea of the beast's "mortal wound that is healed" (13:3, 12, 14) may well reflect the Nero redivivus legend that developed in the 80s and 90s.[15]

In my estimation, then, the date (at least the final editing) of the writing of Revelation was circa AD 90–95, at a time when Christians in Asia Minor were being pressed to worship Domitian.[16]

IV. TRADITIONAL MATERIALS IN REVELATION

While Revelation draws on various traditional materials (e.g., Greco-Roman court ceremonial, chaps. 4–5; Jewish apocalyptic, chaps. 4–5; et al.; the Olivet Discourse, chap. 6; the dragon drama, chap. 12; the Nero myth, chap. 13; Roman coinage, chaps. 17–18), by far the dominant source of its information is the Old Testament. While Revelation does not contain a single specific quotation of the Old Testament, nevertheless out of 404 verses in it, 278 contain allusions to the Old Testament, especially from the Pentateuch and some of the prophets, particularly Daniel.

---

13. Key works analyzing the imperial cult as the immediate background to Revelation include Wm. M. Ramsay, *The Letters to the Seven Churches* (London: Hodder & Stoughton, 1904); C. J. Hemer, *The Letters to the Seven Churches of Asia in Their Local Setting*, JSNTSup 11 (Sheffield: JSOT, 1986); S. R. Price, *Rituals and Power: The Roman Imperial Cult in Asia Minor* (Cambridge: Cambridge University, 1984).

14. See Aune for discussion of the development of the debate over whether Revelation in fact reflects the imperial cult (*Revelation 1–5*, lxiv–lxix). Cf. also Beale's judicious assessment of the evidence, *Book of Revelation*, 28–33. He concludes that the Caesar cult did indeed make its presence known in Asia Minor under Domitian.

15. Osborne, *Revelation*, 9. Many assume number 6 above reflects a reapplication of the title Beast for Nero to Domitian.

16. Aune thinks Revelation was first written before AD 70 and then revised in the AD 90s (*Revelation 1–5*, lviii).

Colosseum in Rome (outside and inside view; floor missing). Site of the persecution of early Christians.

V. THE TEXT OF REVELATION

From a text-critical point of view, there are fewer extant Greek manuscripts for reconstructing the original reading of the Apocalypse than any other part of the New Testament. Nevertheless, there is a sufficient amount to accomplish the task with assurance (approximately 230 Greek manuscripts). The major witnesses to Revelation are the uncials — Codex Sinaiticus (fourth century), Codex Alexandrinus (fifth century), Codex Ephraemic (fifth century); the papyri, the most important of which is p^{47} (third century); the minuscules (eighth to tenth centuries); the church father quotations (second to fifth centuries); and a Greek commentary on Revelation by Andreas (sixth century).[17]

VI. THE MAJOR SCHOOLS OF INTERPRETATION

Traditionally, four major interpretations have been put forth in attempting to unravel the mysteries of the Apocalypse: preterist, historicist, futurist, and idealist. Except for the historicist view, the other three perspectives enjoy many followers today. But because the historicist view restricted itself to the battle between the Protestant Reformation and the papacy in the sixteenth century, that school of interpretation long ago fell out of favor with readers of Revelation.

After discussing the three remaining interpretations, I will offer my own eclectic approach.

A. The Preterist Interpretation

The preterist ("past") viewpoint wants to take seriously the historical interpretation of Revelation by relating it to its original author and audience. That is, John addressed his book to real churches that faced dire problems in the first century AD. Two quandaries in particular provided the impetus for the recording of the book. Kenneth L. Gentry Jr. writes of these:

---

17. For further discussion of the manuscript evidence, consult Robert Thomas, *Revelation 1–7: An Exegetical Commentary* (Chicago: Moody, 1992), 1–7, 42–43; and Aune, *Revelation 1–5*, cxxxiv–cxlviii.

Revelation has two fundamental purposes relative to its original hearers. In the first place, it was designed to steel the first century Church against the gathering storm of persecution, which was reaching an unnerving crescendo of theretofore unknown proportions and intensity. A new and major feature of that persecution was the entrance of imperial Rome onto the scene. The first historical persecution of the Church by imperial Rome was by Nero Caesar from A.D. 64 to A.D. 68. In the second place, it was to brace the Church for a major and fundamental re-orientation in the course of redemptive history, a re-orientation necessitating the destruction of Jerusalem (the center not only of Old Covenant Israel, but of Apostolic Christianity [cf. Ac. 1:8; 2:1ff.; 15:2] and the Temple [cf. Mt. 24:1–34 with Rev. 11]).[18]

Thus the sustained attempt to root the fulfillment of the divine prophecies of Revelation in the first century AD constitutes the preterist's distinctive approach.

The origin of preterism can be traced to the theological system known as postmillennialism, which teaches that Christ will return after the millennium, a period of bliss on earth brought about by the conversion of the nations because of the preaching of the gospel. Preterists locate the timing of the fulfillment of the prophecies of Revelation in the first century AD, specifically just before the fall of Jerusalem in AD 70 (though some also see its fulfillment in both the falls of Jerusalem [first century] and Rome [fifth century]). Despite the opinion of many that Revelation was written in the 90s during the reign of Domitian (81–96), much of evangelical preterism holds the date of the book to be Neronian (54–68). But recall my arguments above against that view.

The preterist view might outline Revelation as follows:

I. John's vision of the risen Jesus (chap. 1).

II. The situation of early Jewish Christianity (chaps. 2–3).

III. The heavenly scene of Christ's reign (chaps. 4–5).

IV. Parallel judgments on Jerusalem (chaps. 6–18).

V. The coming of Christ to complete the judgment of Jerusalem (chap. 19).

VI. Christ's rule on earth (chaps. 20–22).

B. The Idealist Interpretation

The idealist approach to Revelation has sometimes been called the "spiritualist" view in that it interprets the book spiritually, or symbolically. Revelation is seen from this perspective as representing the ongoing conflict of good and evil, with no immediate historical connection to any social or political events. Accordingly, Raymond Calkins captures the chief message of Revelation in terms of five propositions:

1. It is an irresistible summons to heroic living.

2. It contains matchless appeals to endurance.

---

18. Kenneth Gentry Jr., *Before Jerusalem Fell: Dating the Book of Revelation* (Tyler, Tex.: Institute for Christian Economics, 1989), 15–16. We should remember, however, that preterism is comprised of two camps — one that locates the fulfillment of Revelation largely in the first century relative to the fall of Jerusalem, and another that sees the fulfillment of Revelation in *both* the first century (the fall of Jerusalem) and fifth century (the fall of Rome). This section on the schools of interpretation comes from C. Marvin Pate, ed., *Four Views on the Book of Revelation* (Grand Rapids: Zondervan, 1998), 19–34.

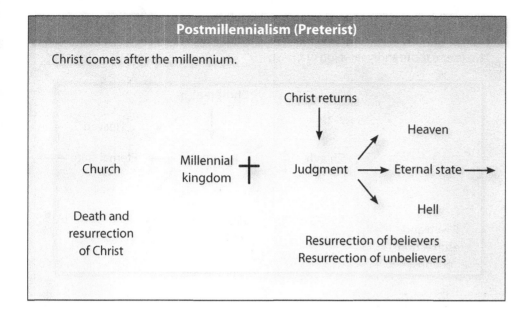

Postmillennialism (Preterist)

Christ comes after the millennium.

Church

Millennial kingdom

Death and resurrection of Christ

Christ returns

Judgment → Eternal state →

Heaven

Hell

Resurrection of believers
Resurrection of unbelievers

3. It tells us that evil is marked for overthrow *in the end*.
4. It gives us a new and wonderful picture of Christ.
5. It reveals to us the fact that history is in the mind of God and in the hand of Christ as the author and reviewer of the moral destinies of men.[19]

While all of the schools of interpretation surveyed here resonate with these affirmations, the idealist view distinguishes itself by refusing to assign the preceding statements to any historical correspondence and thereby denies that the prophecies in Revelation are predictive except in the most general sense of the promise of the ultimate triumph of good at the return of Christ.[20]

The origin of the idealist school of thought can be traced back to the allegorical or symbolic hermeneutic espoused by the Alexandrian church fathers, especially Clement and Origen. Akin to the Alexandrian interpretation of Revelation was the amillennial view propounded by Dionysius, Augustine, and Jerome. Thus the Alexandrian school, armed with the amillennial method, became the dominant approach to Revelation until the Reformation.

As mentioned above, idealists do not restrict the contents of Revelation to a particular historical period, but rather see it as an apocalyptic dramatization of the continuous battle between God and evil. Because the symbols are multivalent in meaning and without specific historical referent, the application of the book's message is limitless. Interpreters can

> The idealist approach to Revelation has sometimes been called the "spiritualist" view in that it interprets the book spiritually, or symbolically.

---

19. Raymond Calkins, *The Social Message of the Book of Revelation* (New York: Woman's Press, 1920), 3–9.
20. Merrill C. Tenney provides a helpful summary of the idealist interpretation of Revelation, as well as the other viewpoints in *Interpreting Revelation* (Grand Rapids: Eerdmans, 1957), 143–44.

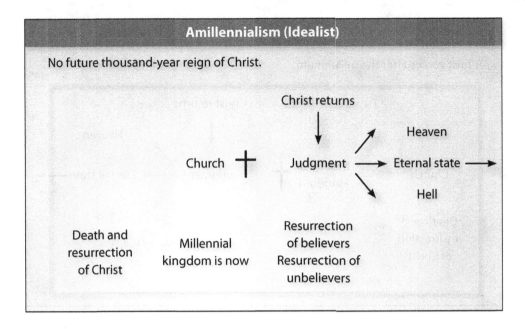

Amillennialism (Idealist)

No future thousand-year reign of Christ.

Christ returns

Church ✝ Judgment → Heaven / Eternal state → / Hell

Death and resurrection of Christ

Millennial kingdom is now

Resurrection of believers
Resurrection of unbelievers

therefore find significance for their respective situations. There does not seem to be a hard-and-fast rule for the idealist in delineating the structure of Revelation.

C. The Futurist View

The darling of the masses regarding the interpretation of Revelation is the futurist view. *The Scofield Bible*, Hal Lindsey's *The Late Great Planet Earth*, and Jerry Jenkins and Tim LaHaye's Left Behind series have ensured that. While the futurist view tends to interpret Revelation 4–22 as still unfulfilled (awaiting the events surrounding the second coming of Christ), it is not completely unified, dividing into two camps of interpretation: dispensationalism and historic premillennialism. I now introduce each of these:

1. Dispensationalism

The name *dispensationalism* is derived from the biblical word *dispensation*, a term referring to the administration of God's earthly household (KJV, 1 Cor. 9:17; Eph. 1:10; 3:2; Col. 1:25). Dispensationalists divide salvation history into historical eras or epochs in order to distinguish the different administrations of God's involvement in the world. C. I. Scofield, after whom the enormously popular *Scofield Bible* was named, defined a dispensation as "a period of time during which man is tested in respect of obedience to some specific revelation of the will of God."[21] During each dispensation, humankind fails to live in obedience to the divine test, consequently bringing that period under God's judgment and thus creating the need for a new dispensation. Read this way, the Bible can be divided into the following eight dispensations (though the number of names vary in this school of

---

21. The *Scofield Reference Bible* (New York: Oxford, 1909), note to Genesis 1:28 heading. For an updated definition that emphasizes faith as the means for receiving the revelations in the various dispensations, see Charles C. Ryrie, *Dispensationalism Today* (Chicago: Moody, 1965), 74.

thought): innocence, conscience, civil government, promise, Mosaic law, church and age of grace, tribulation, millennium.[22]

The hallmark of dispensationalism has been its commitment to a literal interpretation of prophetic Scripture. This has resulted in three well-known tenets cherished by adherents of the movement. First, a distinction between the prophecies made about Israel in the Old Testament and the church in the New Testament must be maintained. In other words, the church has not replaced Israel in the plan of God. The promises he made to the nation about its future restoration will occur. The church is, therefore, a parenthesis in the outworking of that plan. The dispensational distinction between Israel and the church was solidified in the minds of many as a result of two major events in this century: the Holocaust (which has rightly elicited from many deep compassion for the Jewish people) and the rebirth of the State of Israel in 1948.

> The hallmark of dispensationalism has been its commitment to a literal interpretation of prophetic Scripture.

Second, dispensationalists are premillennialists; that is, they believe Christ will come again and establish a temporary, one-thousand-year reign on earth from Jerusalem.

Third, dispensationalists believe in the pretribulation rapture; that is, Christ's return will occur in two stages: the first one for his church, which will be spared the Great Tribulation; the second one in power and glory to conquer his enemies.

The dispensationalist's understandings of the time frame of Revelation and its structure go hand in hand. Because this school of thought interprets the prophecies of the book literally, their fulfillment, therefore, is perceived as still future (especially chaps. 4–22). Moreover, the magnitude of the prophecies (e.g., one-third of the earth destroyed; the sun darkened) suggests that they have not yet occurred in history. The key verse in this discussion is 1:19, particularly its three tenses, which are thought to provide an outline for Revelation: "what you have seen" (the past, John's vision of Jesus in chap. 1), "what is now" (the present, the letters to the seven churches in chaps. 2–3), and "what will take place later" (chaps. 4–22). In addition, the dispensationalist believes that the lack of mention of the church from chapter 4 on indicates that it has been raptured to heaven by Christ before the advent of the Great Tribulation (chaps. 6–18).

2. Historic Premillennialism

The historic premillennial interpretation agrees with its sibling viewpoint — dispensationalism — that Christ will return to establish a thousand-year reign on earth at his parousia. But sibling rivalry ensues between the two approaches on the issue of the relationship of the church and the Great Tribulation (Rev. 6–18). According to historic[23] premillennialism, the church will undergo the messianic woes, the Great Tribulation. This

---

22. C. I. Scofield, *Rightly Dividing the Word of Truth* (New York: Loizeaux, 1896). Many modern dispensationalists, however, have grown uncomfortable with these periodizations, preferring rather to talk about the Bible in terms of its two divisions — the old and new covenants.

23. The name "historic" premillennialism comes from the conviction that this was the earliest view of the church fathers; see C. Marvin Pate and Douglas Welker Kennard, *Deliverance Now and Not Yet* (New York: Peter Lang, 2003), 3. For a helpful, detailed investigation of the four schools of interpretation relative to Revelation, see Steve Gregg, ed., *Revelation: Four Views*, A Parallel Commentary (Nashville: Thomas Nelson, 1997).

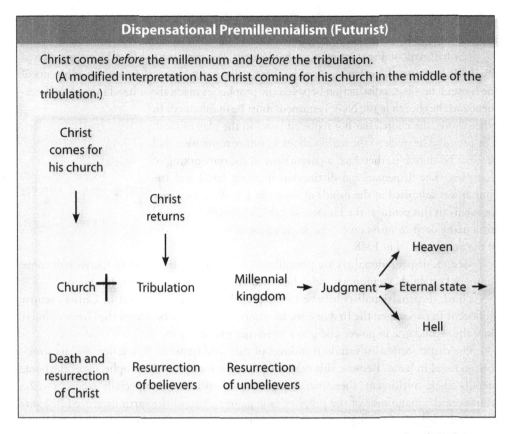

Dispensational Premillennialism (Futurist)

Christ comes *before* the millennium and *before* the tribulation.
(A modified interpretation has Christ coming for his church in the middle of the tribulation.)

Christ comes for his church ↓

Christ returns ↓

Church ✝   Tribulation   Millennial kingdom → Judgment → Eternal state →

↗ Heaven

↘ Hell

Death and resurrection of Christ   Resurrection of believers   Resurrection of unbelievers

is so because the church has replaced Old Testament Israel as the people of God (Rom. 2:26–28; 11; Gal. 6:16; Eph. 2:11–22; 1 Peter 2:9–10; Rev. 1:5–6; 7:1–8; et al.). Like, amillennialism, the historic premillennial view is based on the already–not yet eschatological hermeneutic: the kingdom of God dawned with the first coming of Christ, but it will not be completed until the second coming of Christ. And in the between period the church encounters the messianic woes, which will intensify and culminate in the return of Christ.

My own view of Revelation, like that of many, is an eclectic approach. That is, I find an element of truth in all of the above viewpoints (with the exception of the historicist interpretation). Thus the preterists are correct to root much of Revelation in the first century, especially the early church's battle with Caesar worship. Yet, with the futurist, I believe that the parousia did not happen at the fall of Jerusalem. Rather, it awaits the future return of Christ. And the idealist perspective helps one to vigilantly apply the message of Revelation until that day, especially the challenge therein to worship Christ alone. I will substantiate my approach to Revelation as we move through the book.

VII. THE RELATIONSHIP OF REVELATION TO THE GOSPEL AND THE EPISTLES

Although there are linguistic differences between Revelation and the gospel of John and the epistles of John, it seems to me that John the apostle wrote Revelation, for at least two reasons.

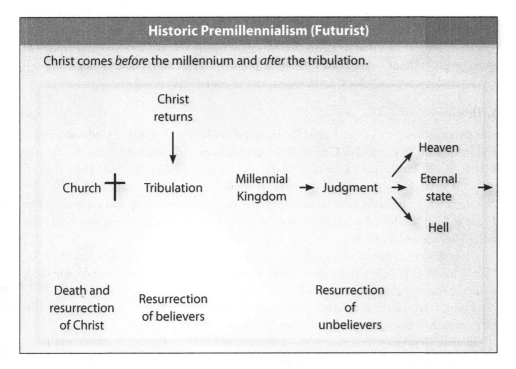

Historic Premillennialism (Futurist)

Christ comes *before* the millennium and *after* the tribulation.

Christ returns

Church ✝ Tribulation → Millennial Kingdom → Judgment → Eternal state → Heaven / Hell

Death and resurrection of Christ — Resurrection of believers — Resurrection of unbelievers

First, the eschatology of Revelation matches the epistles of John — they both are characterized by inaugurated eschatology; see my comments to follow. Second, the history presumed in Revelation matches that of the gospel of John. The expulsion of Jewish Christians from the synagogue alluded to in the fourth gospel continues in Revelation (especially chaps. 2–3). The added feature of the Apocalypse is that now those expelled Christians face persecution from the Roman emperor cult. Indeed, by the time John the apostle wrote Revelation (ca. AD 95), his churches in Asia Minor faced three opponents: (1) Jewish leadership in Asia Minor persisted in expelling Jewish Christians from the synagogues. How they did so will occupy us later as we explore Revelation 2–3. (2) With the increased emphasis on Caesar worship in Asia Minor, John's congregations now faced the other side of the coin of excommunication from the synagogues: they were forced to worship the emperor because they were no longer regarded as Jews (Judaism was exempt from the imperial cult; see my comments on Rev. 2–3). (3) The Docetic interpreters of the gospel of John thought they had a ready-to-hand solution to this dilemma: Christians should go ahead and play along with Caesar worship because, after all, there was only one God (1 Cor. 8:1–3). In other words, the Docetists seem to have encouraged believers to pay lip service to Caesar. Since one's body and actions did not appear to matter to these incipient Gnostics, no harm would be done in saying, "Caesar is Lord." When we look at Revelation 2–3, a part of John's counterclaim to this third group of opponents was that they were, in reality, aligning themselves with the Beast/Caesar. For those who overcome, however, by being true to Christ and refusing to worship the Beast, belong the blessings of the new covenant.

> By the time John the apostle wrote Revelation (ca. AD 95), his churches in Asia Minor faced three opponents.

VIII. THE THEOLOGY OF REVELATION

I conclude my introduction to Revelation by summarizing the major theological aspects of John's prophetic book—the book's theology (proper), Christology, pneumatology, angelology, soteriology, anthropology, ecclesiology, and of course, eschatology.

A. Theology

Four characteristics of God surface as Revelation unfolds. The first is that God is sovereign; he is in control. In particular, God is the Lord of history and eternity: he was, is, and will be (1:4, 8; 4:8; 11:17; 16:5). Likewise, God is the "Beginning and the End" (1:8; 21:6; cf. 1:17; 22:13). God, not Caesar, is "Almighty" (*pantokrator*; see 1:8; 4:8; 11:17; 15:3; 16:7, 14; 19:6, 15; 21:22). Similarly, God is enthroned over heaven and earth, spatial categories. The throne of God is referred to some forty-six times in Revelation, signifying that God rules both in heaven and on earth.

Second, God is holy and therefore should be worshiped (see especially Rev. 4–5; cf. 7:11; 11:16; 15:4; 19:4; 20:4). Hymns in Revelation are the centerpiece of worshiping God, occurring some sixteen times therein.

Third, God is a trinity: Father, Son, and Holy Spirit (1:4–6; 4:1–5:14; et al.), yet this does not detract from John's commitment to monotheism.

Fourth, Revelation is a theodicy—a defense of God's righteous character and judgment. Osborne identifies four points relative to God's ways in Revelation: (1) God's judgment reveals his righteous character, especially against evil in the world (6:16–17; 11:18–19; 15:1, 7; 16:1, 19; 19:15). (2) Even though God judges the depraved earth dwellers, the followers of the Beast, God still offers them the opportunity to repent (2:21–23; 9:20–21; 16:9, 11; et al.). (3) God's judgment executes his righteousness by turning sin upon itself (2:23; 11:18; 14:13; 18:6; 20:12–13). This is the principle of *lex talionis*, the law of retribution. (4) God's justice is demonstrated in his vindication of the righteous (6:11, 15–17; 7:17; 8:2–5; 21:4; 22:5).[24]

B. Christology

Four major truths characterize Christ in the Apocalypse. First and foremost, Christ is the sacrificial Lamb. *Arnion* ("lamb") is used of Christ in Revelation twenty-nine times. It is through his atoning death that Christ the Lion-Lamb overcame evil at his cross and resurrection (5:6, 9, 12; 7:14; 12:11; 13:8; cf. John 1:29). In other words, Jesus is the Davidic Messiah who conquered by becoming the Suffering Servant, paschal lamb (1:6; 5:6–10; et al.). Second, Jesus is equal to God, as the same doxologies to God and Christ make clear (Rev. 4–5). Third, Jesus is the Divine Warrior who will come and put Caesar and all future world empires in their rightful place (Rev. 19). Fourth, Jesus will reward his followers, especially the martyred saints, by having them rule with him in his kingdom (1:6; 2:26–27; 3:21; 5:10; 20:4, 6). Simply put, Jesus, not Caesar, is Lord.

> Four major truths characterize Christ in the Apocalypse.

---

24. Osborne, *Revelation*, 38–39.

C. Pneumatology

At first glance, the Holy Spirit seems to be tangential to the book of Revelation. Yet, in reality, the Spirit is an essential component of the book. Three things can be said about the pneumatology of Revelation. (1) The Spirit is all-knowing (1:4; 3:1; 4:5; 5:6). (2) The Spirit is a member of the divine Trinity (see again 1:4–6; 4:1–5:14). (3) The Spirit inspires end-time prophecy—both John's visions (1:10; 2:7, 11, 17, 29; 3:6, 13, 22; 22:6–7, 9–10, 16, 18–19) and the witness of his community (22:9).

D. Angelology

In Revelation there are two kinds of angels: righteous angels and evil angels. Righteous angels in the Apocalypse do God's bidding, including representing the seven churches of Asia Minor (Rev. 2–3), serving as interpreters of John's visions (5:2; 10:1–11; 17:1, 7, 15; 21:6, 9, 15; 22:1, 6, 9–10; et al.), executing judgment on the earth (Rev. 8–9; 11:15–19; 14:6–12; 15–18), and, of course, worshiping God (Rev. 4–5).

Satan seems to be portrayed as the leader of the fallen angels; those angels who rebelled against God in the past (Rev. 12:7–9). As Osborne well notes:

> Everything Satan does in Revelation is a parody of God. Thus: the mark of the beast (13:16–17) on the right hand or forehead is a mere copy of God sealing the saints in the forehead (7:3). The false trinity (the dragon, beast, and false prophet, 16:13) is an obvious copy of the triune Godhead. The mortal wound that is healed (13:3, 12) imitates the death and resurrection of the Lord. The dragon giving the beast his power, throne, and "great" authority (13:2) copies the relationship between God and Christ. The demand for the nations to worship the beast and dragon (13:8, 14–15) follows the constant commands in Scripture to worship God.[25]

But the doom of Satan and his demonic followers (fallen angels, Rev. 9) is sealed. Christ defeated them at the cross and will mop them up at the parousia (Rev. 19).

E. Soteriology

The soteriology (salvation) of Revelation is based on persevering in one's faith in Christ, despite being persecuted by the antichrist world system. This is especially clear in the admonitions the risen Jesus includes in his messages to the seven churches in Asia Minor (Rev. 2–3); see the discussion below.

F. Anthropology

John's view of human nature is dualistic: either a person is walking with Christ or a person is aligned with the Beast. Such dualism is very close to the teachings of the Dead Sea Scrolls (1QS 3–4, etc.). According to the Apocalypse, there is no in-between status for humanity (see, e.g., 21:27). The decision is up to each individual.

---

25. Ibid., 34.

At first glance, the Holy Spirit seems to be tangential to the book of Revelation. Yet, in reality, the Spirit is an essential component of the book.

In Revelation there are two kinds of angels: righteous angels and evil angels.

John's view of human nature is dualistic: either a person is walking with Christ or a person is aligned with the Beast.

G. Ecclesiology

John's concept of the church as depicted in Revelation is striking, especially involving three metaphors. First, the church is the true Israel. The promises that once pertained to Israel now belong to the church: priests (1:6), twelve tribes (Rev. 7; 14; 21:12), new Jerusalem (Rev. 21–22), kingdom of God (20:1–6), new covenant (15:5, et al.). Second, the church will be the messianic army at the parousia (Rev. 7; 14; 19:19–21; 20:9–10), though it seems that Christ will do all the fighting against evil. Third, the church is the bride of Christ, the new Jerusalem (19:9; 21:2; et al.)

> John's concept of the church as depicted in Revelation is striking, especially involving three metaphors.

H. Eschatology

The book of Revelation is patently eschatological in its focus. The key perspective of eschatology in Revelation is showcased in 1:19, where the already–not yet framework is highlighted.

I illustrate this eschatological tension in chart form, by calling attention to five major aspects in Revelation:

Already	Not Yet
1. The age to come has dawned (Rev. 1:1, 3, 19).	1. The age to come will not be complete until the parousia or millennial kingdom and eternal state (Rev. 1:19; 19–22).
2. Christians are rulers with Christ in heaven now (Rev. 1:6; 5:10; et al.).	2. But Christians do not yet rule on the earth; that awaits the millennium (Rev. 20:1–6).
3. The Great Tribulation has already begun (Rev. 1:9; 2–3).	3. The Great Tribulation is not yet complete (Rev. 6–18).
4. The fall of Jerusalem has already occurred (Rev. 6–16).	4. The fall of Babylon/Rome has not yet occurred but soon will (Rev. 17–18).
5. Satan has already been defeated at the cross (Rev 12:1–12).	5. Satan will not be banished forever until after the millennium (Rev. 20:9–15).

This concludes my introduction to the Apocalypse. I turn now to a summary of its contents.

REVIEW QUESTIONS

1. What three works comprise the Johannine literature?

2. What three genres make up the book of Revelation?

3. How would you refute Dionysius's categories of "evidence" against the Johannine authorship of Revelation?

4. What are the five arguments for a Neronian date for Revelation?

5. How do advocates of a Domitian date for Revelation respond to the five arguments in question 4?

6. What are some of the background materials informing Revelation?

7. Please describe each of the four major schools of interpretation of Revelation.

8. What are the two types of futurist interpretations of Revelation?

9. What are the three tenets of dispensationalism?

10. What distinguishes historic premillennialism from dispensationalism?

11. Summarize the historical-theological picture producing the Johannine literature.

12. Summarize the overall theology of Revelation.

KEY TERMS

666/Nero *Redivivus*

already – not yet

amillennialism

Apocalypse

Babylon

biblical postmillennialism

Caesar worship

classical dispensationalism

Dionysius

dispensationalism

Domitian date of Revelation

expulsion from the synagogue

external evidence of authorship

futurist

genre of Revelation

historic premillennialism

historicist

idealist

internal evidence of authorship

liberal postmillennialism

messianic woes/ Great Tribulation

Neronian date of Revelation

postmillennialism

premillennialism

preterist

pretribulation rapture

Roman emperors

CHAPTER 40

The Apocalypse of Jesus Christ

REVELATION 1

Objectives

After reading this chapter, you should be able to:

- Explain the "chain" of revelation as recorded in Revelation 1:1–3.
- Discuss the timing of the fulfillment of the events of Revelation.
- Explain the outline of Revelation as reflected in 1:19.

INTRODUCTION

The opening chapter of Revelation consists of an introduction (vv. 1–8) and a vision of the risen Jesus (vv. 9–20).

> The opening chapter of Revelation consists of an introduction (vv. 1–8) and a vision of the risen Jesus (vv. 9–20).

The introduction calls attention to the mixed genre of the book: it is an apocalypse (vv. 1–3) and a letter (vv. 4–8) written by a prophet (v. 3). As an apocalyptic piece, John's work unfolds God's plan for the end times, especially as it is related to the second coming of Jesus Christ. As a letter, the Apocalypse begins with the typical epistolary format of the day: author—John (v. 4); recipients—the seven churches of Asia (v. 4); salutation—greetings and blessings from the Father, the Holy Spirit, and the Son. The vision of the risen Jesus (vv. 9–20) combines descriptions of the heavenly Son of Man and God, the Ancient of Days found in Daniel 7.

I now unpack these opening statements.

I. INTRODUCTION (1:1–8)

Revelation begins with an introduction, which consists of a prologue (vv. 1–3) and a prescript (vv. 1–8).

A. Prologue (vv. 1–3)

Verses 1–3 and 22:6–21 frame the book of Revelation with an inclusio highlighting the key themes of John's vision: the soon appearing of Christ, the claim of authenticity for the book, and the blessing for those who obey the book's message.

I offer comments on five aspects of this critical opening statement about Revelation, its content (v. 1a), chain of revelation (vv. 1b–2), timing (vv. 1b, 3), manner (v. 1b), and blessing (v. 3).

1. The Content of Revelation (v. 1a)

The words "The revelation of Jesus Christ" (Rev. 1:1a), serve as both the title of the book and its content. Jesus Christ is the content of the book, the book's focus. Revelation features his sacrificial death, victorious resurrection, and triumphant second coming (cf. 1:5–20; chaps. 5; 19; et al.). But Jesus Christ is also the one who revealed the prophecies of the future about his kingdom to John.

2. The Chain of Revelation (vv. 1b–2)

Verses 1b–2 mention several links in the chain of Revelation: from God to Jesus, from Jesus to an interpreting angel, from the angel to John, from John to his community (the servants).

3. The Timing of Revelation (vv. 1b, 3)

In the words "soon" (*en tachei*, [v. 1b]) and "the time is near" (*ho kairos eggus* [v. 3]) we meet with an interpretive difficulty that has generated conflicting views.

First, preterists argue that the prophecies were *immediately* fulfilled in Christ's judgment upon Jerusalem in AD 70. Second, dispensationalists argue that "soon" and "the time is near" mean *imminent*, not immediate. In other words, there might be an interval between John's day and the fulfillment of his prophecies, but when those prophecies begin to be fulfilled—whenever that may be—they will unfold rapidly. Third, historical premillennialists and amillennialists appeal to the already–not yet eschatological tension in order to interpret the two preceding phrases. This view can be stated as follows: (a) "soon" and "the time is near" meant *immediate*, but in reality, the return of Christ was delayed (for more than two thousand years!). (b) This delay, however, was not terribly unsettling to the early church, for it viewed the first coming of Christ as the most climactic event in history. And the eschatological significance of it prevented the church from worrying about when the parousia would occur. I concur with this last view.

In the words "soon" (*en tachei*, [v. 1b]) and "the time is near" (*ho kairos eggus* [v. 3]), we meet with an interpretive difficulty that has generated conflicting views.

4. The Manner of Revelation (v. 1b)

The heavenly visions granted to John were "signified" (v. 1b; NIV, "made ... known"), the verbal form of the noun *sign*, so important to the gospel of John. Just as the miracles recorded in the fourth gospel were literal occurrences but pointed to a deeper, symbolic meaning, so the visions of Revelation point to figurative meanings in need of decoding the reality behind them.

5. The Blessing of Revelation (v. 3)

A blessing is pronounced on the reader of Revelation (the one who reads the contents of the scroll to the congregation) and on the one who obeys its message to persevere in the faith despite persecution (cf. 1:3 with 14:13; 16:15; 19:9; 20:6; 22:7, 14).

B. Prescript (vv. 4–8)

The prescripts of ancient letters, the New Testament included, contained three elements: sender, recipient, and salutation or greeting. Revelation 1:4–8 contains those components, adapting them to its theological message.

1. Sender (v. 4a)

"John" (cf. v. 1 with vv. 4, 9; 22:8) received his prophetic vision from the Lord (vv. 1–3) and now passes it on to his congregations in Asia Minor.

2. Recipients (v. 4b)

The recipients of Revelation were the seven churches of Asia Minor. The order listed in verse 11 and in chapters 2–3 no doubt reflects the fact that that was the geographical order in which a courier would deliver this letter from John. The number "seven" refers to actual churches of that Roman province, but probably also typifies the universal church then and

Roman province of Asia.

now (though one need not subscribe to the historicist's theory that the seven churches correspond to seven periods of church history).

3. Salutation (vv. 4c–8)

The salutation, or greeting, to the seven churches is both conventional and unconventional compared to other New Testament salutations, especially Paul's. Revelation 1:4c–8 is conventional in that it offers "grace" and "peace" to the recipients from two members of the Trinity—God and Christ (cf. Rom. 1:7b; 1 Cor. 1:3; 2 Cor. 1:2; Gal. 1:3; Eph. 1:2; Phil. 1:2; 2 Thess 1:2).

But John's salutation is unconventional in that it adds "the seven spirits" as a member of the greeting, while theologizing significantly on the Trinity as a whole. We may treat this aspect of the greeting and more by using four words: *Trinity* (vv. 4c–6a), *doxology* (v. 6b), *liturgy* (vv. 6c, 8), and *summary* (vv. 7–8).

a. Trinity (vv. 4c–6a)

John records greetings from each member of the Trinity.

1. God is described as, "him who is, and who was, and who is to come" (v. 4d; cf. 1:8; 4:8; 11:17; 16:5). The title conveys the truth that God controls the past, present, and future.

2. The seven spirits (v. 4e; cf. 4:5; 5:6) most likely are the Holy Spirit, based on the qualities ascribed to the Spirit in Isaiah 11:2. The "Spirit" is mentioned before Christ, perhaps because in Revelation the Spirit is above all the Spirit of prophecy (Rev. 1:10–11; 22:6). Thus it is the Spirit of God (v. 4) who reveals the destiny of Christ (vv. 5–7).

3. "Jesus Christ" is the third member of the Trinity mentioned in the greeting (vv. 5–6a). Two descriptions of Christ are provided: who he is (v. 5a) and what he has done (vv. 5b–6a). Three things characterize who Christ is. (a) He is "the faithful witness," an allusion to Christ's obedient death before God (cf. 3:14; cf. John 5:31–47; 8:13–18; 10:25). This is the same path his followers must tread (Rev. 1:9; 6:9; 12:11, 17; 17:6; 19:10; 20:4). (b) Christ is the "firstborn (*prōtotokos*) from the dead" (cf. Ps. 89:27 LXX with Rom. 8:29; Col. 1:18; Heb. 1:6). (c) He is ruler of the earth (cf. again Ps. 89:27), which in Revelation means that Christ is triumphant over Caesar and any other kings of the earth (Rev. 6:5–17; 17:14; 19:16, 18–19).

Two things characterize what Christ has done for his people (vv. 5b–6a): he has saved his people from their sins by means of his loving, sacrificial death (cf. v. 5b with 5:6, 9, 12;

> John records greetings from each member of the Trinity.

7:14; 12:11; 13:8), and he has made them a kingdom (cf. v. 6a with Ex. 19:6; Rev. 2:26; 3:21; 5:10; 20:4, 6) of priests before God (cf. v. 6a with Ex. 19:5–6; Rom. 12:1; Heb. 10:19–20; 1 Peter 2:5).

b. Doxology (v. 6b)

Verse 6b includes a doxology to God, ascribing to him glory (*doxa*) and power (*kratos*). This is a reminder that God is in control, not Caesar.

c. Liturgy (vv. 6, 8)

As the commentators observe, "Amen"—a congregation's agreement with a prophetic word or praise to God (cf. v. 7)—suggests a liturgical context for Revelation 1:4–8. The "Amen," plus the doxology and the reference to the "reader" (v. 3), seems to confirm such a worship setting.

d. Summary (vv. 7–8)

Verses 7–8 contain a prophetic oracle about the parousia of Christ and a majestic manifold description of God. Together these summarize the message of Revelation. The prophetic oracle in verse 7 is taken by preterists as referring to Jesus' coming in judgment on Jerusalem in AD 70. Most, however, think this refers to the second coming of Christ at the end of time.

Verse 8 concludes the salutation by listing four majestic titles of God. "I am" is a reference to the name "Yahweh" used of God first in Exodus 3:14. "Alpha and Omega"—the first and last letters of the Greek alphabet—indicate that God controls the beginning and the end. Moreover, God "was, is, and is to come"—that is, he is eternal. Finally, God is the "Almighty." If Caesar was called *autokrator* ("emperor"; see Josephus, *Ant.* 14.199), then God is called, even better, *pantokratōr* ("the all-powerful emperor"). This was a message Christians in Asia Minor (and today) sorely needed to hear.

II. JOHN'S PROPHETIC COMMISSION (1:9–20)

Revelation 1:9–20 records the risen Jesus' commissioning of John to deliver the prophetic vision of Revelation. Verses 9–10a provide the setting of the vision, while verses 10b–20 give the vision itself of the risen Jesus. The prophetic oracle to the seven churches is outlined in Revelation 2–3 and then developed in the rest of the book.

A. The Setting of the Vision (vv. 9–10a)

The setting for the prophetic vision/oracle revealed to John was the island of Patmos, for there John was imprisoned for preaching the gospel ("the word of God"/"the testimony of Jesus"). Patmos (now Patino), one of the Sporades Islands, is thirty miles in circumference

Verse 6b includes a doxology to God, ascribing to Him glory (*doxa*) and power (*kratos*). This is a reminder that God is in control, not Caesar.

Verses 7–8 contain a prophetic oracle about the parousia of Christ and a majestic manifold description of God. Together these summarize the message of Revelation.

Orthodox monastery of St. John on the island of Patmos.

and is located fifty miles from ancient Ephesus. Emperor Domitian was famous for banishing dissidents to Patmos and other nearby islands.

John identifies himself as a brother and companion in the suffering (*thlipsis*), kingdom (*basileia*), and endurance (*hypomonē*) in Jesus. One article governs the three nouns, intimately associating the three words. Thus we are to understand John to be saying that the kingdom (of God)—glory—comes through enduring the Great Tribulation/messianic woes—suffering.[1] *Thlipsis* is a famous word in Revelation for the Great Tribulation or the messianic woes.

The key response of Christians that John calls for is to endure these messianic woes by being faithful to Jesus. This will result in their ultimate possession of the kingdom of God.

John received his vision on the Lord's Day (i.e., Sunday; cf. *Didache* 14.1; Pliny, *Epistles* 10.96; Acts 20:7; 1 Cor. 16:2), the day early Christians chose to weekly commemorate Jesus' resurrection (John 20:19, 26). John was in the "Spirit," probably with reference to his spiritual ascent to heaven (cf. Ezek. 2:2; 3:12–14; 11:5, 24, with Rev. 1:10; 4:2; 17:3; 21:10).

> The key response of Christians that John calls for is to endure these messianic woes by being faithful to Jesus. This will result in their ultimate possession of the kingdom of God.

---

1. For the same pattern—suffering the messianic woes now so as to inherit the glory of the kingdom of God later—see C. Marvin Pate, *The Glory of Adam and the Afflictions of the Righteous: Pauline Suffering in Context* (New York: Edwin Mellen, 1993), which traces that motif in ancient Jewish and early Christian apocalyptic literature.

B. The Vision of the Risen Jesus (vv. 10b–20)

The trumpetlike sound (of Jesus) that John heard was as loud as it was clear. The voice commanded John to write down the ensuing vision (2:1, 8, 12, 18; 3:1, 7, 14; 14:13; 19:9; 21:5). The vision that John is about to record should be sent to seven churches in Asia Minor: Ephesus, Smyrna, Pergamum, Thyatira, Sardis, Philadelphia, and Laodicea. These were chosen because they followed the order of mail delivery, and each in turn served as a hub for cities near it. In that fashion, the contents of Revelation could reach the seven churches under John's jurisdiction and beyond.

The vision in verses 12–20 follows the typical pattern of visions in the Old Testament and in Jewish apocalyptic literature: (1) the initial vision (vv. 12–16) followed by (2) the seer's response (vv. 17–19) and then (3) an interpretation of the vision (v. 20).

1. The Vision (vv. 12–16)

The voice John "saw" was among the seven golden lampstands (v. 13). The menorah was the most common symbol of Israel and Judaism (Ex. 25:31–35; 37:18–21; 2 Chron. 4:7, 20). Its application to the seven churches of Asia Minor (cf. v. 20) suggests that the church is the new, true Israel. Jesus' presence among the lampstands indicates that he is Lord of the churches.

> The message of this combination is clear — Jesus is God.

The appearance of the risen Jesus to John combines the personages of the heavenly Son of Man (Dan. 7:13–14; 10:5–6)[2] and the Ancient of Days (Dan. 7:9–10, 13). Note the combination:

Heavenly Son of Man	Ancient of Days
Like Son of Man (Dan. 7:13–14)	Head/hair = wool/snow (Dan. 7:9)
Eyes like fire (Dan. 10:6)	Face of the sun (Dan. 7:9–10)
Legs like bronze (Dan. 10:6)	
Voice like sound of multitudes (Dan. 10:6)	

The message of this combination is clear — Jesus is God.[3]

He is also the great High Priest, as his robe and golden sash indicate (cf. Ex. 28:4; 39:29; Lev. 8:7).

Jesus had seven stars in his right hand (v. 16a), which, according to verse 20, are to be identified with the "angels" of the seven churches. The fact that they are in Jesus' right

---

2. The identity of the heavenly Son of Man in Daniel 7 — now an individual messianic figure, now a corporate symbol for Israel — is much discussed in the commentaries. *First Enoch* 37–71 (ca. 150 BC) individualizes that personage, equating him with the Messiah; this is the background of Revelation 1:12–16. There is also debate as to whether Daniel 10:5–6 refers back to the Son of Man of Daniel 7 or to an angel separate from the heavenly Son of Man, or perhaps both.

3. For John, Jesus is God, but Jewish monotheism is still preserved; see David E. Aune, *Revelation 1–5.* WBC 52A (Dallas: Word, 1997), 92.

hand (Ps. 110:1; Matt. 26:64) conveys the idea that he is in control of them. The two-edged sword proceeding from Jesus' mouth is symbolic of his word of judgment (Isa. 11:4; 49:2) spoken against the enemies of God, especially Caesar (cf. Rev. 2:12, 16; 6:8; 19:15, 21).

2. John's Reaction (vv. 17–19)

Falling down with fear before visions of the Deity or his angelic messengers was common in ancient Judaism (cf. Rev. 1:17; 19:10; 22:8 with Josh. 5:14; Ezek. 1:28; Dan. 8:17–18; 10:7–9; Matt. 17:6; John 18:6; *1 Enoch* 14:4). Jesus reassured John by placing his right hand on John and telling him not to be afraid. Two honorific titles of Jesus are then given. He is the "I am" (Ex. 3:14; Rev. 1:8), "the first and last" (Isa. 41:4; 44:6; 48:12). These two titles, used earlier of God, indicate that Jesus is the same and is therefore sovereign over history and death.

The risen Jesus then commanded John to write what he saw—what is and what will be (v. 19). The threefold clause, "what you have seen, what is now and what will take place later" is correctly understood as significant for grasping the chronological outline of the Apocalypse.

> The threefold clause "what you have seen, what is now and what will take place later" is correctly understood as significant for grasping the chronological outline of the Apocalypse.

Futurists usually take them as referring to the past (the vision of the risen Christ, chap. 1), the present (the seven churches, chaps. 2–3), and the future (the Great Tribulation, the parousia, the temporary messianic kingdom, and the eternal state, chaps. 4–22). Preterists understand the clauses as being on the verge of fulfillment, accomplished at the fall of Jerusalem in AD 70. Many amillennialists and historic premillennialists, however, understand the verse in the following manner: "what you have seen" refers to the whole of the vision given to John—that is, the book of Revelation (cf. 1:11),[4] which consists of two time frames: "the things that are," the already (the kingdom of God in heaven), and "the things that will be," the not yet (the kingdom of God descended to earth). My reading of Revelation will develop this last viewpoint.

3. The Interpretation (v. 20)

The heavenly Christ then provided the interpretation of the vision of the mystery of the seven stars and the seven golden lampstands (vv. 12–16): the former are the angels of the lampstands; the latter are the churches. Even though it is much debated, it seems that we should understand these to be literal angels assigned to their respective churches, based on the idea that "patron angels" protected Israel and the righteous (Pss. 34:7; 91:11; Dan. 10:13–21; Matt. 18:10; Acts 12:15; Heb. 1:4).

But what are the angels (cf. Rev. 1:20 with 2:1, 8, 12, 18; 3:1, 7, 14)?

The point the risen Christ made to John in verse 20, then, is that he (Jesus) is Lord of the churches and their angelic guardians.

---

4. "Write" (*graphon*) is an epistolary aorist; this is so because, by the time the seven churches receive John's vision/oracle, the sending of it will already have occurred. My earlier perspective on Revelation, progressive dispensationalist (in C. Marvin Pate, ed., *Four Views on the Book of Revelation* (Grand Rapids: Zondervan, 1998), has changed to the historic premillennial interpretation (see C. Marvin Pate and Douglas Welker Kennard, *Deliverance Now and Not Yet* [New York: Peter Lang, 2003], 479–502).

REVIEW QUESTIONS

1. What is the content of the book of Revelation (Rev. 1:1)?

2. What is the timing of the events of Revelation; that is, when will they happen (Rev 1:1, 3)?

3. How is the Trinity described in Revelation 1:4 – 6?

4. What are some titles for God in Revelation 1:7 – 8?

5. How do Daniel 7 and 10 shed light on the vision of Jesus recorded in Revelation 1:12 – 16?

6. How do the various schools of interpretation view Revelation 1:19?

KEY TERMS

Ancient of Days

angel

heavenly Son of Man

hour/"the time is near"

kratos ("power")

parousia

Revelation of Jesus Christ

seven churches of Asia Minor

Trinity

"What you have seen, what is now and what will take place later"

CHAPTER 41

The Seven Churches of Asia Minor

REVELATION 2

Objectives

After reading this chapter, you should be able to:

- Explain the mixed genre informing Revelation 2–3.
- Discuss how the covenant components shed light on Revelation 2–3.
- Describe the Caesar worship the seven churches of Asia Minor faced.
- Explain the strengths and weaknesses of the church at Ephesus.
- Explain why the church at Smyrna is only praised and not criticized.
- Explain what John meant by "the synagogue of Satan."
- Explain the strengths and weaknesses of the church at Pergamum.
- Discuss how the guilds and Caesar worship related to each other.
- Discuss the strengths and weaknesses of the church at Thyatira.

INTRODUCTION

Revelation 2–3—the "letters" to the seven churches of Asia Minor—is a part of the vision/oracle revealed to John; thus 1:9–3:22 forms a self-contained literary unit. Three introductory matters regarding these letters need to be addressed before discussing each one separately: their genre, background, and interpretation.

> Three introductory matters regarding these letters need to be addressed before discussing each one separately: their genre, background, and interpretation.

A. The Genre of the Seven Letters

In discussing the genre of the seven letters, we must both examine their internal structure and their external fit with similar types of Old Testament literature.

1. The Internal Structure

On the one hand, the messages of the risen Jesus in Revelation 2–3 are typically understood to be ancient letters, but on the other hand, they only bear a superficial resemblance to such. They have no formal introduction (sender, recipient, greeting), body, or conclusion shaping the messages of Revelation 2–3.[1]

Each of these "letters" contains some seven features, though with slight alterations:

1. Command to write to an angel of a church.
2. Christ's self-description derived from the description in chapter 1 and introduced by the formula "These are the words."
3. Commendations of the church's good works.
4. Accusation because of some sin.
5. Exhortation to repent with a warning of judgment or an encouragement.
6. Exhortation to discern the truth of the preceding message ("He who has an ear ...")
7. Promise to the conquerors.

2. External Match with Old Testament Literature

Do the above seven features compare with any other type of literature in the ancient world? I believe they do. With others, I think that the format of these letters is a mixed genre of Old Testament literature consciously styled so by John[2]: prophetic oracle, which is included in the larger structure of the covenantal format. I now discuss each of these genres as they pertain to Revelation 2–3: prophetic oracle and covenantal format.

a. Prophetic Oracle

F. Hahn, U. B. Müller, and D. E. Aune have convincingly argued that the messages to the seven churches match the Old Testament prophetic salvation—judgment oracle (cf. Rev. 2–3 with Isa. 13–23; Jer. 46–51; Ezek. 25–32; Amos 1–2; et al.).[3]

---

1. David E. Aune rightly rules out genres like the heavenly letter and the prophetic letter in his *Revelation 1–5*, WBC 52A (Dallas: Word, 1997), 124–26.
2. Ibid., 124–29; G. F. Beale, *The Book of Revelation: A Commentary on the Greek Text*, NIGTC (Grand Rapids: Eerdmans, 1999), 224–38.
3. F. Hahn, "Die Sendschreiben der Johannesapokalypse: Ein Beitrag zur Bestimmung prophetischen Re-

Essentially two components comprise that genre: (1) Old Testament prophetic messenger formula: "Thus says the Lord" (cf. "These are the words of ... [Jesus]" in Rev 2:1, 8, 12, 18; 3:1, 7, 14); and (2) salvation-judgment oracle (2:2–6; 2:9–10 [salvation only]; 2:13–16; 2:19–25; 3:1–4; 3:8–11 [salvation only]; 3:15–20 [judgment only]).

b. Covenantal Format

Intimately related to the genre of salvation-judgment oracle, W. H. Shea and, in revised form, G. F. Beale have insightfully rooted Revelation 2–3 in the covenantal format of the Old Testament, especially Deuteronomy. It should not be surprising that there is a blend of prophetic oracle and covenantal format in Revelation 2–3, because in the Old Testament the prophets' oracles reinforced the covenant stipulations and blessings/curses.

W. H. Shea has proposed that each letter contains five essential segments, which thematically reflect the fivefold ancient Near Eastern covenant form imposed on Israel by Yahweh in Exodus 21–23 and throughout Deuteronomy: (1) preamble (the words of Christ ["these are the words"] and descriptive titles from chapter 1; (2) prologue ("I know your deeds ...," which concludes the two sections labeled above as commendation and accusation); (3) stipulations (expressions built around variants of "therefore ... repent," along with other hortatory words); (4) witness to the covenant ("Hear what the Spirit says to the churches"); (5)concluding blessings and curses ("to him who overcomes, I will give ...").[4]

Beale offers a revision of Shea's proposals that basically factors in the initial command to write and separates the blessings and curses.[5]

Following Shea's proposal and Beale's adjustments, I now offer my own reconstruction of the prophetic salvation-judgment oracle and covenantal format of Revelation 2–3, which I unpack in this chapter and the next.

B. The Background of the Seven Letters of Revelation 2–3

I noted earlier that the book of Revelation as a whole reflects the early church's struggle with the Roman imperial cult, beginning with Nero and intensifying during the reign of Caesar Domitian. That background specifically informs Revelation 2–3, as Colin J. Hemer has carefully shown[6]. See my discussion to follow.

> The messages to the seven churches match the Old Testament prophetic salvation—judgment oracle.

> It should not be surprising that there is a blend of prophetic oracle and covenantal format in Revelation 2–3.

deformen" ("The Letters of the Johannine Apocalypse: An Investigation of the Voice of Prophetic Speech Formation"), in *Tradition und Glaube: Das frühe Christentum in seiner Umwelt* (*Tradition and Faith: Early Christianity in Its Environment*), Festschrift K. G. Kuhn, ed. G. Jeremias, H.-W. Kuhn, and H. Stegemann (Göttingen: Vandenhoeck & Ruprecht, 1971), 372–94; U. B. Müller, "Literarische und formgeschichtliche Bestimmung der Apokalypse des Johannes als einem Zeugnis frühchristlichen Apokalyptik" ("Literary and Formhistorical Setting of the Apocalypse of John as a Witness to Early Christian Apocalyptic") in *Apokalypticism in the Mediterranean World and the Near East* (Tübingen: Mohr-Siebeck, 1983), 599–619; Aune, *Revelation 1–5*, 126.

4. W. H. Shea, "The Covenantal Form of the Letters to the Seven Churches," *AUSS* 21 (1983): 71–84.

5. Beale, *Book of Revelation*, 227; see the application of the covenant structure to Revelation as a whole by K. A. Strand, "A Further Note on the Covenantal Form in the Book of Revelation," *AUSS* 21 (1983), 251–64.

6. C. J. Hemer, *The Letters to the Seven Churches of Asia in Their Local Setting*, JSNTSup 11 (Sheffield: JSOT, 1986). Recall my earlier discussion of the twelfth benediction as it might have related to the gospel of John (pp. 31–33).

Genre	Ephesus	Smyrna	Pergamum	Thyatira	Sardis	Philadelphia	Laodicea
Introduction: Messenger Formula: A. "These are the words of Christ" = "Thus says the Lord" B. "To the angel of the church in ... write"	2:1	2:8	2:12	2:18	3:1	3:7	3:14
Preamble: Description of Christ	2:1	2:8	2:12	2:18	3:1	3:7	3:14
Prologue: Christ's relationship with the church	Commendation (salvation) — 2:2, 3, 6	Commendation (salvation) only — 2:9	Commendation (salvation) — 2:13	Commendation (salvation) — 2:19	Commendation (salvation) — 3:4	Commendation (salvation) only — 3:8–9	Condemnation (judgment) only — 3:15–17
	Condemnation (judgment) — 2:4		Condemnation (judgment) — 2:14–15	Condemnation (judgment) — 2:20–24	Condemnation (judgment) — 3:1		
Stipulation	2:5	2:10	2:16	2:25	3:2–3	3:10–11	3:18–20
Curses	2:5		2:16	2:22–25	3:2–3		3:16, 18–19
Blessings	2:7	2:11	2:17	2:26–28	3:5	3:10, 12	3:21
Witness	2:7	2:11	2:17	2:28	3:6	3:13	3:22

The covenantal structure of the seven letters suggests John regarded unbelieving Jews and followers of Caesar as under the covenant curses.

I will delve a little more into this background as I touch on each of the seven letters below.

C. The Interpretation of the Seven Letters

The interpretation of the seven letters to the churches of Asia Minor has been essentially divided into two camps. Historicists (and a few futurists) have called attention to certain parallels between the individual letters and subsequent periods of church history from John's day until the end. They conclude that the seven letters present a panorama of the age of the church.

But two related considerations confirm the majority view of the seven letters — that the letters do not correspond to specific periods in the history of the church. First, the imperial cult background of all of the seven churches in Revelation 2–3 roots them in the first century AD. Second, as Beale has noted, the majority of the churches (five out of seven) are spiritually unhealthy. This was due to the influence of the imperial cult in the first century. There is no hint here of any correspondence with later church history.[7]

I turn now to a brief discussion of each of the seven letters, following the above chart, which combines the genres of prophetic oracle and covenantal format, all the while detecting an anti-Caesar polemic.

I. THE "LETTER" TO EPHESUS (2:1–7)

A. Historical Background

Ephesus enjoyed pride of place in western Asia Minor in the first century AD. This was so for at least three reasons. Politically, Ephesus was the unofficial capital of the Roman province of Asia. Culturally, it enjoyed abundant commerce because of its harbor location where the Cayster River met the Aegean Sea and because of its intersection with three trade routes. Religiously, Ephesus enjoyed diverse traditions: the cult of Diana (Artemis), whose temple was acclaimed one of the seven wonders of the ancient world (cf. Acts 19:23–41); the imperial cult (boasting six temples to Caesar: Julius, Augustus [two], Domitian [one plus a colossal statute of him], and Hadrian [two]); magic (Acts 19:19–20); Judaism (Acts 18:26; 19:8); and Christianity (Acts 19:1–40; 20:17, 28).

Fig. 41.1. Graeco-Roman deities.

B. Covenantal Format/Prophetic Oracle

1. Introductory-Messenger Formula (v. 1)

a. "To the angel of the church in ... write ..."
b. "These are the words of him ..."

---

7. Beale, *Book of Revelation*, 226–27.

Chapter 41: The Seven Churches of Asia Minor

369

Graeco-Roman Deities

Greek Name	Roman Name	Position	Scripture Reference
Aphrodite	Venus	Goddess of love	
Apollo	Sol (also identified with Helios)	Shepherd-god; sun-god; associated with poetry, music, prophecy, and hunting	
Ares	Mars	War-god; also linked with agriculture; Areopagus (Mars hill, AV) named after him	Acts 17:22
Artemis	Diana	Goddess of fertility	Acts 19:21–40
Asklepios (Asclepius)		Goddess of medicine	
Athena	Minerva	Goddess of wisdom, fertility, and war; guardian of Athens	
Cronus	Saturn	Father of Zeus; agriculture	
Dike		Justice	Acts 28:4
Demeter	Ceres	Corn-goddess; guardian of marriage	
Dionys(i)us	Bacchus (Liber)	Phrygian god; associated with nature, wine, and revelry	
Hades	Pluto (Dis)	God of the underworld	
Hephaistos (Hephaestus)	Vulcan	God of fire; patron of craftsmen	
Hera	Juno	Goddess of women	
Hermes	Mercury	God of heralds	Acts 14:12
Hestia	Vesta	Goddess of fire; cf. vestal virgins	
Pan	Faunus	Goat-god of shepherds	
Poseidon	Neptune	Water-god; also linked with earthquakes	
Prometheus		God of fire; created man from clay	
Tyche	Fortuna	God of destiny	
Zeus	Jupiter	Sky-god; controller of weather; ruler of all gods and men	Acts 14:12, 13
	Cybele	Mother-earth	
	Emperor	Julius Caesar and Augustus Caesar were deified posthumously; Caligula, Nero, and Domitian demanded worship in their lifetime.	

Top left: Ruins of the temple of Apollo at Didyma. *Above:* The scant remains of the temple of Artemis at Ephesus. The Byzantine-era church of St. John is in the background. *Bottom left:* Remains of the temple of Domitian in Ephesus.

2. Preamble (v. 1)

The one holding the seven stars and walking among the lampstands.

3. Prologue (vv. 2, 3, 6)

a. Commendation/Salvation (vv. 2, 3, 6)

In the past, the Ephesian Christians rejected the false apostles—those itinerant preachers claiming to be messengers from God, yet whose works were evil.[8] In the present, the Ephesians reject the Nicolaitans, a term meaning "overcome (*nikaō*) the people (laity)." Although their identity is much debated, the Nicolaitans, like the Balaamites (Rev. 2:14–15) and Jezebel (Rev. 2:20–23), probably advocated syncretism, resulting in accommodating the pagans by participating in practices like emperor worship.

Like Balaam of old who "overcame Israel"[9] with idolatry, so the Nicolaitans did the same in John's day.

---

8. "Apostles" seems to be a generic sense of the word—"one who is sent"—rather than the technical term Luke-Acts uses for the twelve disciples.

9. In the third century BC the Romans began to award palm branches to the winners at the games, a custom taken over from the Greeks. Palm branches are depicted on many coin types from Asia, and a particular favorite was a standing Nike with a wreath and palm. This may also be a part of the background of John's usage of *nikaō* in the book of Revelation.

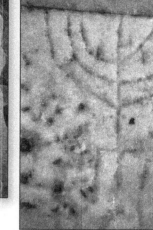

Left: A relief of Nike holding a palm branch in Ephesus. *Right:* Lampstand graffito. This depiction of a menorah was inscribed on the pavement near the Library of Celsus in Ephesus.

b. Condemnation/Judgment (v. 4)

Nevertheless, the Ephesian Christians so concentrated on maintaining theological orthodoxy that they lost their original love for Christ and each other.

4. Stipulation (v. 5)

They need to repent and return to the fervor of their first love.

5. Curses (v. 5)

If the Ephesian church did not repent, Christ would remove their lampstand — that is, obliterate the church.

6. Blessings (v. 7)

If they overcome by repenting, they will receive eternal life (eat of the tree of life and enter paradise).[10]

7. Witness (v. 7)

The Spirit testifies to the truth of Jesus' oracle to the churches.

II. THE "LETTER" TO SMYRNA (2:8 – 11)

A. Historical Background

Smyrna (modern Ismir) was a center of emperor worship located thirty-five 35 miles north of Ephesus.

---

10. See Hemer's discussion, *Letters to the Seven Churches*, 44 – 47, which roots this promise/parody in the cult of Artemis, which was originally a tree shrine.

In AD 26 Smyrna beat out ten other cities for the privilege of building a temple to Emperor Tiberias. Under Domitian emperor worship was compulsory on the threat of death. Once a year Smyrna's citizens were required to burn incense on the altar to Caesar. For refusing to call Caesar "Lord," Polycarp, one-time disciple of John and bishop of Smyrna, was martyred for his faith in Christ (AD 155).

> Smyrna (modern Ismir) was a center of emperor worship located thirty-five miles north of Ephesus.

Smyrna had a large Jewish population that virulently opposed Christians, which seems to have manifested itself in local Jews serving as informants (*delatores*) to Roman officials, divulging to them the names of Jewish Christians who were recently expelled from the synagogues because they were not true Jews. No longer exempt from Caesar worship, Jewish Christians were rounded up by the local authorities, imprisoned, and some were put to death (see Rev. 2:13).

Because the church at Smyrna refused to participate in the imperial cult, they no doubt endured economic sanctions as well (Rev. 2:9). For John's part, the apostle called the Jewish opposition what it was — "a synagogue of Satan" (v. 9).

B. Covenantal Format/Prophetic Oracle

1. Introductory Messenger Formula (v. 8)

a. "To the angel of the church in ... write ..."
b. "These are the words of him ..."

The agora at Smyrna with Mount Pagus in the background.

2. Preamble (v. 8)

The First and the Last/resurrected Christ (which would have comforted the church at Smyrna as they potentially faced death for their faith).

3. Prologue (v. 9)

a. Commendation/Salvation (v. 9)
They are faithful to Christ despite persecution.
b. Condemnation/Judgment: None

4. Stipulation (v. 10)

Persevere in resisting Caesar worship.

5. Curses: None

6. Blessings (v. 11)

Although they may die for their faith, believers at Smyrna have eternal life and will not experience eternal judgment ("the second death").

7. Witness (v. 11)

The Spirit testifies to the truth of Jesus' oracle to the churches.

III. THE "LETTER" TO PERGAMUM (2:12–17)

A. Historical Background

Pergamum (modern Bergama) is located seventy miles north of Smyrna. It was well-known culturally for its famous library, rivaling the one at Alexandria, Egypt. Its very name — Pergamum — comes from the term *parchment*, the skin of animals used for writing material.

Politically, Pergamum was the residence of the Roman proconsul,[11] before whose bench (*bēma*) people from outlying areas would come to be tried. Religiously, Pergamum was the center of the imperial cult of Asia Minor.

> Pergamum was the center of the imperial cult of Asia Minor.

Pergamum was the first city in that province to be permitted to build a temple to Caesar (Augustus, 29 BC), and to *Dea Roma* (Rome personified as a deity, 20–18 BC). Its citizens proudly called their city the "temple warden" (*neōkrōsis*) — that is, guardian of the imperial cult. The famous altar to Zeus *Soter* (Savior) and the temple to Asclepius, the god of healing, symbolized by a snake on a pole, could also be found in Pergamum, along with a cult to Dionysius (god of wine).

Pergamum is called "Satan's throne" (Rev. 2:13; cf. "where Satan lives," v. 14), because it was a major center of the imperial cult.

And the rub against the church at Pergamum was that, even though they resisted the imperial cult, by participating in the guilds' temple banquets (which served meats offered

---

11. There were two kinds of Roman provinces in the first century AD. One was a "senatorial province" run by the Senate in a nonvolatile area, which appointed a proconsul to rule on behalf of the Senate. The other type was the "imperial province," governed by Caesar and the military due to the hostile setting of the area. It was governed by a procurator who reported to Caesar. Asia Minor was a senatorial province, while Judea/Syria was an imperial province.

The theater on the side of the acropolis of Pergamum.

to idols—see 1 Cor. 8–10), they undermined their loyalty to Christ (Rev. 2:14–15). This was so because the temple banquets were held in honor of both pagan deities *and* Caesar. The Balaamites (Heb., meaning "overcome the people"[12]), or Nicolaitans, encouraged the Christians in Pergamum to eat the meats offered to idols, knowing that there was no true God but Christ (1 Cor. 8:1–3). For John, however, such action compromised their witness for Christ.

But those who overcome by being faithful to Christ will be provided hidden manna, a white stone, and a new name (v. 17). The "hidden manna" probably referred to the Jewish belief that Jeremiah hid the manna in the ark so it would not be destroyed by the Babylonians. But when the Messiah comes, he will produce that manna for the righteous (cf. Ex. 16:33–34 with *2 Bar.* 29:8; *Sib. Oracles* 7:149). John challenges his readers to eat this manna rather than meat offered to idols.

The white stone could allude to the guild banquets held in pagan temples that required a magical amulet (often white) to be worn for entrance. On the one side of the amulet/coin was the image of the patron deity of the temple, while on the other side—hidden from view—was a secret name[13] (of the worshiper?). On this reading of Revelation 2:17, the white amulet (used for entrance and magical protection) with the image of the patron deity provided entrance into the guild to eat the meat that had been offered to idols. But

---

12. According to Numbers 22–24, Balaam was a Gentile prophet consulted by Balak, king of Moab, to curse Israel who, instead, pronounced a blessing on the Israelites. According to Numbers 25:1–3, Balaam then helped to bring about Israel's fall by having their men cohabitate with the pagan women of Moab. The idolatrous and immoral feast that followed brought about God's judgment on Israel in the wilderness (cf. 1 Cor. 10:7–8).

13. So Aune, *Revelation 1–5*, 190–91.

Left: A tunnel to the sacred pools in the Asklepion at Pergamum. *Right:* A view of the acropolis of Pergamum from the walkway at the Asklepion.

according to John, faithful Christians—those who do not frequent the pagan temples—will eat hidden manna because their "amulet" is Christ, which has become their new name (cf. Isa. 62:2 with Rev. 3:12; 19:12).

B. Covenantal Format/Prophetic Oracle

1. Introductory Messenger Formula (v. 12)

a. "To the angel of the church in ... write ..."
b. "These are the words of him ..."

2. Preamble (v. 12)

These words written to the church in Pergamum are those of the one who has the two-edged sword.

3. Prologue (vv. 13–15)

a. Commendation/Salvation (v. 13)
Christ commended the church in Pergamum for being faithful in the midst of the imperial cult.
b. Condemnation/Judgment (vv. 14–15)
He told the believers in Pergamum that they compromised their witness by frequenting the guild banquets in the pagan temples.

4. Stipulation (v. 16)

The church at Pergamum was to repent of the syncretistic, compromising teaching of the Balaamites/Nicolaitans.

5. Curses (v. 16)

If they did not repent, the risen Jesus would come and use his sword against them.

6. Blessings (v. 17)

To those who overcome by not compromising, the risen Jesus would provide new manna, a white stone, and a new name.

7. Witness (v. 17)

The Spirit testified to the truth of Jesus' oracle to the churches.

IV. THE "LETTER" TO THYATIRA (2:18–29)

A. Historical Background

Thyatira (modern Akhisar) is forty miles southeast of Pergamum. The most noticeable feature about ancient Thyatira was its trade guild associations, especially the shoemakers, makers and sellers of dyed cloth (cf. Acts 16:14), and the bronze smiths. These guilds governed the economic, social, and religious life of the citizens of Thyatira and controlled the local work force, because one would have a hard time getting a job in these industries without belonging to the respective guilds (compare modern American unions). Furthermore, the trade guilds each had their own patron god or goddess and often held events in those gods' temples. There meat was served (meat was a luxury in the ancient world) that had been dedicated to the patron deity of the temple and guild. This posed a serious problem for Christians, as we saw from Revelations 2:14–17. Above all the gods at Thyatira, Apollo (Son of Zeus, who embodied the Roman emperor) enjoyed pride of place.

> The most noticeable feature about ancient Thyatira was its trade guild associations, especially the shoemakers, makers and sellers of dyed cloth (cf. Acts 16:14), and the bronze smiths.

This background explains Revelation 2:18–29. The risen Jesus, the true Son of God (not Apollo or the caesar, v. 18), with eyes of fire and feet of bronze (purer than any brass provided by the bronze guild at Thyatira), is the one who addressed the church at Thyatira.

He commended them for their love, which produced good works (v. 19). But this strength was overshadowed by the fact that the church there tolerated the teaching of Jezebel (vv. 20–25). Jezebel (no doubt an unnamed female prophet analogous to the sibyl, the Greek-Roman prophetess) apparently was the leader of the Nicolaitan/Balaamite cult. Like Jezebel of the Old Testament (1 Kings 16:31–34; 21:25–26; 2 Kings 9:22), she led the people of God at Thyatira into idolatry and immorality by teaching that Christians could belong to the trade guilds and join in the temple feasts (see again 1 Cor. 8–10). "Satan's so-called deep secrets" were probably related to her proto-Gnostic teaching[14] based on a misunderstanding of 1 Corinthians 8:1–3: that since there is only one true God, Christians are permitted to eat meat offered to idols without it affecting them. John, however, warned that it was because of such teaching that Christ was about to judge Jezebel and her followers. The "bed of suffering" (v. 22; Gk., *klinē*) may be an allusion to the type of dining couch used in the guild feasts. That could well become the occasion for Christ inflicting sickness and even death upon Jezebel and her devotees (vv. 22–25).

---

14. This same teaching probably informed the Docetists who left the Johannine community (see 1 John 1:8–10; 2:18–3:10).

To those who reject Jezebel's teaching, however, are promised corulership with Christ over the nations (vv. 26–27 with Ps. 2:8–9).

B. Covenantal Format/Prophetic Oracle

1. Introductory Messenger Formula (v. 18)

a. "To the angel of the church in ... write ..."
b. "These are the words of ... the Son of God ..."

2. Preamble (v. 18)

Christ, not Caesar, is the Son of God whose eyes of fire and feet of bronze (contra the bronze guild at Thyatira), will judge the church if it does not reject the Jezebel cult.

3. Prologue (vv. 19–24)

a. Commendation/Salvation (v. 19)
The church is commended for its love resulting in good works.
b. Condemnation/Judgment (vv. 20–24)
Yet Jesus was against the church's toleration of Jezebel's teaching.

4. Stipulation (v. 25)

They were to hold on to the truth by rejecting Jezebel.

5. Curses (vv. 22–25)

The risen Christ would come to judge Jezebel and her followers, the church at Thyatira included, if it did not repent.

6. Blessings (vv. 26–28)

The followers of Jesus would rule the nations with him.

7. Witness (v. 28)

The Spirit testifies to the truth of Jesus' oracle to the churches.

CONCLUSION

The covenantal format/prophetic oracle pattern of Revelation 2 communicates the truth that those who overcome by being faithful to Jesus are the ones who share in the blessings of the new covenant. However, those who are not faithful to Christ are under the curses of the covenant; pagans, Jews, and apostate Christians alike.

1. What is the mixed genre that informs the letters of Revelation 2 – 3?

2. How do the covenant components factor into the genre of the letters of Revelation 2 – 3?

3. Review how Caesar worship is the key historical background to Revelation 2 – 3.

4. Why was Ephesus praised and criticized (Rev. 2:1 – 7)?

5. Who were the Nicolaitans (Rev. 2:6)?

6. Why was Smyrna only praised (Rev. 2:8 – 11)?

7. What was the synagogue of Satan in Smyrna (Rev. 2:9)?

8. What distinguished Pergamum, labeled in Revelation 2:13 "Satan's throne"?

9. How did the guild banquets in Pergamum incorporate the worship of Caesar?

10. Who were the Balaamites (Rev. 2:14)?

11. What was the city of Thyatira noted for?

12. Why is the name Jezebel used in connection with the church at Thyatira (Rev. 2:20)?

KEY TERMS

Balaamites	guilds	prophetic oracle
caesar worship	Jezebel	Satan's throne
covenantal format	Nicolaitans	Smyrna
Ephesus	overcomers	Thyatira
	Pergamum	

CHAPTER 42

The Churches of Asia Minor

REVELATION 3

Objectives

After reading this chapter, you should be able to:

- Discuss the strengths and weaknesses of the church at Sardis.
- Explain why the church at Philadelphia is only praised.
- Explain why the church at Laodicea is only criticized.

I. THE "LETTER" TO SARDIS (3:1–6)

A. Historical Background

Sardis (modern *Sart*), located forty miles southeast of Thyatira and forty-five miles east of Smyrna, had a storied past by the time of John's letter to the church there. Founded in ca. 1200 BC, Sardis became the capital of the wealthy and powerful Lydian kingdom. Sardis's geographical setting ensured its safety for hundreds of years, situated as it was on a hill surrounded on three sides by a fifteen-hundred-foot precipice and a steep approach on the south side. Sardis's location on a major trade route enriched its economy, one already famous for gold in the Springs of Pactolus that ran through the city. Accordingly, Sardis was the first to mint gold and silver coins. Sardis was a religiously diverse city as its (unfinished) temples to Artemis and Augustus and massive synagogue attest.

> But Sardis's glory had long since passed by the late first-century AD. Twice its impregnable city was captured because its guards did not bother to watch the steep cliffs.

But Sardis's glory had long since passed by the late first-century AD. Twice its impregnable city was captured because its guards did not bother to watch the steep cliffs (546 BC to Cyrus; 214 BC to Antiochus III). In AD 17 an earthquake devastated the city. Though rebuilt by Emperor Augustus, Sardis lost its prestige to Pergamum and Smyrna, both of which became major centers of the imperial cult. This background illuminates Revelation 3:1–6.

B. Covenantal Format/Prophetic Oracle

1. Introductory Messenger Formula (v. 1)

a. "To the angel of the church in … write …"
b. "These are the words of him …"

The temple of Artemis near the Acropolis of Sardis.

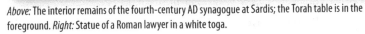

Above: The interior remains of the fourth-century AD synagogue at Sardis; the Torah table is in the foreground. *Right:* Statue of a Roman lawyer in a white toga.

2. Preamble (v. 1)

The one speaking is the one who holds the seven spirits of God (Holy Spirit) and seven stars (angels of the churches).

3. Prologue (vv. 1, 4)

a. Commendation/Salvation (v. 4)
The minority remnant who were faithful to Christ were commended.
b. Condemnation/Judgment (v. 1)
The majority who compromised by syncretistic worship were reprimanded.

4. Stipulation (vv. 2–3)

Jesus tells the church to wake up and repent.

5. Curses (vv. 2–3)

If they don't wake up and repent, Christ will come like a thief.

6. Blessings (v. 5)

The faithful will be victorious (dressed in white) and not be blotted out of the Book of Life.

7. Witness (v. 6)

The Spirit testifies to the truth of Jesus' oracle to the churches.

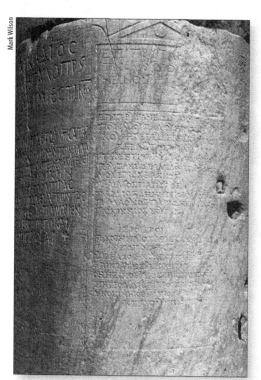

This pillar in the Ephesian city council building is inscribed with the names of the priests of Artemis.

There is powerful irony in Revelation 3:5: the synagogue expelled Jewish Christians, thus placing them under the "curses" of the covenant; but, in fact, those expelled are assured the blessings of the new covenant—Christ's approval, while the synagogue unwittingly placed itself under the curse of God!

II. THE "LETTER" TO PHILADELPHIA (3:7–13)

A. Historical Background

Philadelphia (modern Alashehir) is thirty miles southeast of Sardis on the main trade route from Smyrna to the east. Philadelphia ("lover of his brother") was supposedly named after Attalus Philadelphus's (ruler of the city) devotion to his older brother Eumenes II (189 BC). The earthquake that leveled Sardis in AD 17 also devastated Philadelphia, making it susceptible thereafter to seismic activity. Because of the damage, Emperor Tiberius exempted Philadelphia from paying tribute to Rome for five years. Out of gratitude, the city renamed itself Neo-Caesarea. In the AD 80s the city again adopted a name humoring Rome, Flavia (after the Flavian dynasty). In the third century AD (AD 211–17), Philadelphia earned the name *neōkoros* (temple guardian). The first mention of Christianity in Philadelphia occurs in Revelation 1:4; 3:7–13. Ignatius wrote a letter to the church there in AD 110. We learn of a Jewish presence in Philadelphia from Revelation 3:7–13.

The risen Jesus identified himself as "holy and true" (cf. v. 7 with Rev. 6:10). The reference to Jesus as the one holding the key of David who opens and closes the door (Isa. 22:22) was perhaps an allusion to the Davidic, or messianic, kingdom. This description would have been a comfort to the Philadelphian Christians who had been expelled from the "synagogue of Satan." But the tables will be turned one day: Jews will bow down before the church, the true people of God (vv. 8–9).

B. Covenantal Format/Prophetic Oracle

1. Introductory Messenger Formula (v. 7)

a. "To the angel of the church in ... write ..."
b. "These are the words of him ..."

2. Preamble (v. 7)

The holy and true one holds the key of David. What he opens no one can shut; what he shuts no one can open.

3. Prologue (vv. 8–9)

a. Commendation/Salvation (v. 10)

The ruins of the ancient stadium at Philadelphia.

The church at Philadelphia is commended for being faithful to Christ in the midst of imperial worship and Jewish opposition.

4. Stipulation (v. 11)

The church is encouraged to hold on to what they have so that no one will take their crown.

5. Curses: none

6. Blessings (vv. 10, 12)

Since they have kept Jesus' command to endure patiently, he will preserve them through the Great Tribulation. He will also make them a pillar in the temple of God and give them his new name.

7. Witness (v. 13)

The Spirit testifies to the truth of Jesus' oracle to the churches.

III. THE "LETTER" TO LAODICEA (3:14–22)

A. Historical Background

The Seleucid King Antiochus II (261–246 BC) founded Laodicea, which he named after his divorced wife Laodice. Laodicea was located at the junction of two trade routes, which contributed to its rise to wealth. Under Roman rule, Laodicea became a banking center and was associated with the production of black wool for the making of garments. Laodicea had a famous school of medicine connected with the temple of Menkarou ("God of the Valley"), the god of healing. Laodicea became famous for Phrygian powder, an eye salve.

Calcified water pipes at Laodicea.

But the city faced two drawbacks. First, it was prone to earthquakes, and in AD 60 one practically destroyed the city. Yet because of its financial wealth, Laodicea rejected aid from Rome. Second, Laodicea had no water supply; this was in contrast to nearby Hierapolis and its medicinal hot springs and Colossae with its cool, refreshing water. By the time Laodicea piped water in from its nearest spring of five miles away, it was tepid and emetic.

Laodicea was religiously syncretistic, comprised of a combination of local and Roman gods,[1] including Zeus, men, Apollo, and an imperial temple.

This background informs Revelation 3:14–22.

B. Covenantal Format/Prophetic Oracle

1. Introductory Messenger Formula (v. 14)

a. "To the angel of the church in ... write ..."
b. "These are the words of the Amen ..."

2. Preamble (v. 14)

The Amen/faithful witness/ruler of creation.

3. Prologue (vv. 15–17)

a. Commendation/Salvation: None
b. Condemnation/Judgment

Jesus rebukes the church for being lukewarm and says they are "wretched, pitiful, poor, blind and naked."

4. Stipulation (vv. 18–20)

They are to repent and come to Christ.

5. Curses (vv. 16–19)

If they do not repent, Jesus will spew them out of his mouth.

6. Blessings (v. 21)

The one who overcomes will rule with Christ.

7. Witness (v. 22)

The Spirit testifies to the truth of Jesus' oracle to the churches.

---

1. Laodicea was one of three cities in the Lycus Valley, along with Hierapolis and Colossae. Probably Paul's associate—Epaphras—was the founder of the churches there (see Col. 1:7; 4:12–13). Paul wrote a letter to the church at Laodicea (Col. 4:16), which is lost to us. For a thorough investigation of the religious syncretism that influenced the Lychus Valley churches, see Clinton E. Arnold, *The Colossian Syncretism: The Interface between Christianity and Folk Belief at Colossae*, WUNT 2/77 (Tübingen: J. C. B. Mohr/Paul Siebeck, 1995).

Ruins of the ancient city of Laodicea.

CONCLUSION TO REVELATION 2–3

Again and again we have seen how the covenantal format impacted the letters to the seven churches of Asia Minor. Those faithful to Christ are promised the blessings of the new covenant. Those outside that covenant — pagans, non-Christian Jews, even apostate Christians — are threatened with divine curses. These have caved in under the pressure to worship Caesar.

1. What was an embarrassing part of Sardis's history?

2. What is the irony of the synagogue's casting out of Jewish Christians (Rev. 3:5)?

3. What was the synagogue of Satan referred to with regard to the church at Philadelphia (Rev. 3:9)?

4. What major problem at Laodicea offset that city's accomplishments?

5. What was the greatest need of the church of Laodicea?

KEY TERMS

Laodicea	"synagogue of Satan"
Philadelphia	tepid water
Sardis	"thief"

CHAPTER 43

The Throne of God and Christ

REVELATION 4–5

Objectives

After reading this chapter, you should be able to:

- Define *merkabah* mysticism.

- Explain how Revelation 4–5 relates to ancient Roman imperial ceremonial.

- Identify the concentric circles that make up John's vision of heaven.

- Explain what the seven-sealed scroll is.

- Explain why the doxologies to God and Christ are essentially the same.

- Explain what qualities applied to Caesar are reapplied to God and Christ.

- Identify the four living creatures.

- Identify the twenty-four elders.

INTRODUCTION

In good Jewish apocalyptic fashion, John is raptured to heaven to receive a vision of the throne room of God (cf. Rev. 4:1 with Ezek. 1; *1 Enoch* 14; *4 Ezra* 14; *3 Enoch*).

Revelation 4–5 is John's description of the divine heavenly court, using the imagery of concentric circles: (1) the throne of God and Christ is the center of the circle (4:3; 5:6); (2) the four living creatures (cf. Ezek. 1:5–25) comprise the next circle (Rev. 4:6–9);

> In good Jewish apocalyptic fashion, John is raptured to heaven to receive a vision of the throne room of God.

(3) the twenty-four elders and their thrones form the next one (4:4, 10–11); (4) an innumerable heavenly host makes up the last circle around the throne (5:11–13). The nearly identical doxologies to God (4:7–11) and to Christ (5:11–14) indicate that the two are equal in divine status (see the discussion to follow).

I now summarize Revelation 4–5 by intertwining their descriptions of the throne of God and Christ, and the heavenly attendants to the divine throne.[1] I begin by investigating the nature of John's ascent to heaven.

I. JOHN'S MYSTIC ASCENT TO HEAVEN (4:1–2)

Revelation 4:1–2 introduces John's vision of the throne of God by recording his mystic ascent to heaven. By the end of the first century AD, *merkabah* (Heb. for chariot/throne [of God]) mysticism had become entrenched in certain sectors of Judaism (see 2 Cor. 12:1–7; Col. 2; Rev. 4–5; *1 Enoch* 14; *3 Enoch*; .*Ḥag.* 11b–16a; *Hekalot Rab.* [the last mentioned three works date to around the second to third centuries AD]). From the preceding literature, we see that the components of *merkabah* include (1) rigorous preparation for the heavenly ascent via prayer and fasting; (2) mystic ascent through the seven "houses" or palaces of heaven; (3) negotiations with the angels assigned to each of the palaces by the use of magical formulae, seals, etc.; (4) danger accompanying the ascent; (5) vision of the glorious divine throne/chariot (*merkabah*).

John's mystic experiences throughout Revelation do comply with key features of *merkabah*: rigorous preparation—worship in the Spirit on Sunday (Rev. 1:10), mystic ascent to heaven (Rev. 4:1–2), angelic interpretation (Rev. 7:13; et al.), vision of the divine throne (Rev. 4; 5; et al.). There are differences, however. The danger motif does not fit John's mystic experience, and no mention of a plurality of heavens is listed in Revelation.[2]

---

1. Revelation 4:1 probably does not allude to the rapture of the church to heaven before the onslaught of the Great Tribulation on earth.

2. I. Gruenwald denies that John's mystic experience was of the *merkabah* variety and identifies a number of features in Revelation 4–5 that distinguish John's experience from *merkabah* mysticism: (1) The author knows only one heaven, not the plurality of as many as seven heavens found in Jewish apocalypses and *merkabah* literature. (2) The twenty-four elders, while they have some parallels in Jewish literature, are not part of the *merkabah* tradition and betray the eclecticism of the author. (3) The throne of God has two peculiar features: (a) that the four living creatures are "in the midst of the throne and round about the throne" may reflect the Jewish tradition that the four living creatures bear the firmament over their heads and that the throne is located on the firmament (so they *cannot* see God); and (b) that the four living creatures are listed in different order from that found in Ezekiel 1. (4) Gruenwald then turns to the *Apocalypse of Paul* (a composition dependent in part on Revelation) and points out that the throne of God appears to be located in the heavenly temple; though apart from Isaiah 6 the temple is never mentioned in *merkabah* visions. This suggests that the author of the

But, as David Aune has demonstrated, there is yet another background for Revelation 4–5, namely, the Roman imperial ceremonial court. The following points of contact with that milieu emerge in the symbolism of chapters 4–5: (1) Greco-Roman kings were considered to be divine, their courtrooms often artistically expressed in terms of being cosmic, portrayed in concentric circles. (2) Their attendants were often associated with astrology (seven planetary spheres [cf. Rev. 4:5], twenty-four [the doubling of the twelve signs of the Zodiac] devotees [cf. 4:4, 10; 5:6–10]). (3) These attendants sang hymns of worship to the divine king (cf. 4:8–11; 5:9–14). (4) The king dispensed justice over his empire, symbolized by a scroll (cf. 5:1–8). These considerations, along with the competing claims for their respective deities throughout Revelation between John and the imperial cult of the first century (god, son of god, lord's day, savior of the world), suggest that the two cultures clash in the imagery employed in Revelation 4–5.[3]

II. THE THRONE OF GOD AND CHRIST (4:3, 6; 5:6)

A. The Throne of God (4:3, 6)

The inner circle of John's heavenly vision was the throne of God (Rev. 4:3, 6), the ultimate goal of Jewish-Christian mysticism. Four things are said about God on his throne, three of which refer to translucent stones. (1) Jasper, perhaps an opal or diamond, often red tinted at times with other colors, bespeaks God's glory (cf. Rev. 21:11, 18, 19–20). (2) Carnelian (*sardiō*, cf. Sardis?) is a fiery red stone that was popular in the ancient world. (3) An emerald-like rainbow (cf. Rev. 10:1) encircled the divine throne like a green halo. The imagery comes from Ezekiel 1:27–28 (cf. DSS [4Q 405 20–22 i 10–11]) and reminds one of Genesis 9:13, where God hangs up his warrior's bow as a promise that he will never again destroy the world by flood. Two of these stones are found in Revelation's description of the New Jerusalem: jasper (4:3; 21:11, 18, 19) and carnelian (4:3; 21:20); a third also occurs—crystal (cf. 4:6 with 22:1). (4) Spreading out before the heavenly throne was something like a sea of glass (crystal; 4:6). This alludes to the firmament that separated the waters in Genesis 1:7 (cf. Ezek. 1:22) and perhaps also the bronze sea in Solomon's temple (1 Kings 7:23–26; 2 Chron. 4:2). God is portrayed as sovereign and separated by holiness from his creation.

> There is yet another background for Revelation 4–5, namely, the Roman imperial ceremonial court.

Apocalypse of Paul, like the author of Revelation, has produced a blend of literary motifs, not recorded a personal mystic ascent to heaven. I. Gruenwald, *Apocalyptic and Merkavah Mysticism*, Arbeiten zur Geschichte des antiken Judentums und des Urchristentums (Works on the History of Ancient Judaism and Early Christianity) 14 (Leiden: Brill, 1980), 62–72. These criticisms, however, are not weighty. Regarding point 1, I suggest later that John assumed the seven heavens tradition. Concerning point 2, the imagery of the twenty-four elders, as we will see, draws on the belief that angels lead the heavenly host in worship, a concept compatible with *merkabah* mysticism. Clearly, the throne of God is the centerpiece of Revelation 4–5, regardless of the exact position of the four living creatures (point 3). In any event, the blending of literary motifs (point 4) need not rule out *merkabah* mysticism, especially since *merkabah* and apocalypticism comingled before AD 70. Moreover, John's reliance upon literary motifs no longer suggests to many scholars that John's vision was not real.

3. David E. Aune, "The Influence of Roman Imperial Court Ceremonial on the Apocalypse of John," *Papers of the Chicago Society of Biblical Research* 28 (1983): 1–26.

B. The Throne of Christ (5:1–14)

Revelation 5 clearly shows that John's vision of Christ placed him on par with God. Three items make this point: Christ is seated on the throne with God; Christ alone, like God, is worthy to open the sealed book; the doxologies to God and Christ are similar. I now summarize these three items.

Carnelian stones.

1. God and Christ on the Heavenly Throne (4:2–11; 5:1–14)

Like God, Christ is seated on the heavenly throne (cf. 4:2–11 with 5:1–14). This is made explicit in Revelation 5:13, "To him who sits on the throne [God] and to the Lamb." The ancient world was familiar with the image of a *bisellium*, a double throne (see *Orphic Hymns* 62:2, of Dike and Zeus; Lucian, *Peregrinus* 29, of Hephaestus and Herakles; the Roman imperial cameo, *Gemma Augustea*, of Augustus and Dea Roma). The double throne places the dual deities on par with each other. Revelation 12:5 and 22:1, 3 depict this as well.[4]

Gemma Augustea: Caesar Augustus seated on a bisellium on the righthand side of the goddess Roma.

2. The Seven-Sealed Scroll (5:1–14)

The identity of the seven-sealed scroll of Revelation 5 has prompted much debate. Most agree that it is an *opistograph*;[5] an ancient document written on the front and back, signifying fullness and completeness (cf. Ezek. 2:9–10). And all agree that the function of the opening of the scroll by the exalted Jesus is to equate him with God: Christ alone is worthy to open the contents of the heavenly book. Revelation 5 therefore serves as the investiture of the Lamb — the public acknowledgment of who he is, namely, God.[6] But, beyond that, the identity of the scroll is disputed. The possibilities include the book of the destiny of the world with emphasis on its eschatological finale, the Lamb's Book of Life, Yahweh's bill of divorce of Israel, a Roman legal document, a last will and testament, a covenant promise.[7]

---

4. David E. Aune, *Revelation 1–5*, WBC 52A (Dallas: Word, 1997), 267.

5. Most papyrus and parchment scrolls were written on one side, the side with the grain running horizontally (*recto*). For a description of how papyrus and parchment were used for ancient writing materials, see Grant R. Osborne, *Revelation*, Baker Exegetical Commentary on the New Testament (Grand Rapids: Baker, 2002), 247.

6. Of the three possible genres informing Revelation 5 — enthronement, commission, or investitures — Aune convincingly argues for the last (*Revelation 1–5*, 332–38).

7. See the discussions by Aune, ibid., 338–46; G. F. Beale, *The Book of Revelation: A Commentary on the Greek Text*, NIGTC (Grand Rapids: Eerdmans, 1999), 339–48; Osborne, *Revelation*, 247–50.

While all of the preceding theories are good possibilities and not necessarily mutually exclusive, I find the last suggestion especially attractive and, in what follows, I bring out that nuance of meaning.

Revelation 5 is the investiture of the Lamb with the authority and honor of God. Only Christ is worthy to open the book, because only he is God. Two messianic titles are applied to Christ in verse 5: the Lion of Judah (Gen. 49:9–10; *4 Ezra* 12:31–34; *T. Jud.* 24:5) and the root of David (Isa. 11:1; *4 Ezra* 12:32; 4QFlor 1.11–12; cf. Mark 12:35–37; John 7:42).

> When John sees the Lion, he turns out to be, paradoxically, a slain Lamb.

And yet when John sees the Lion, he turns out to be, paradoxically, a slain Lamb (5:6, 12)![8] Three possible backgrounds inform John's imagery here: (1) Jesus is the horned, apocalyptic lamb who defeats the enemies of God at the end of history (*1 Enoch* 90). (2) Jesus is the Passover lamb (Ex. 11–12). (3) Jesus is the Suffering Servant who is like a lamb led to the slaughter (Isa. 53:7; John 1:29, 36; Acts 8:32; 1 Cor. 5:7; 1 Peter 1:19). Yet these three backgrounds are not contradictory: Jesus is the conquering, apocalyptic lamb precisely through his death on the cross as a paschal lamb/suffering servant. Thus Jesus overcame (*nikaō*, Rev. 5:5) paradoxically by dying (Rev. 5:6). As a result of Jesus' triumphant death, he has made the people of God a kingdom and priests (cf. Rev. 5:10; 1:6; 20:6). This is reminiscent of God's salvation of Israel, his covenant people (Ex. 19:6).

The content of the scroll unfolds in Revelation 6–18, and it is none other than the blessings of the covenant promised to those who worship Christ and the curses of the covenant pronounced upon those who worship the Beast (Caesar).[9] More particularly, like the blessings uttered over the obedient in Deuteronomy from Mount Gerizim and the curses pronounced on the disobedient from Mount Ebal (chaps. 28–30), so God's blessings rest on those whose deaths for Christ usher them to heaven, while God's curses fall on the disobedient earth-dwellers.[10]

> The content of the scroll is none other than the blessings of the covenant promised to those who worship Christ and the curses of the covenant pronounced upon those who worship the Beast (Caesar).

The scroll (*biblion*, "book") opened by Christ was written on the front and the back, which the commentators recognize to be an allusion to Ezekiel 2:9–10. There the prophet Ezekiel is shown a divine book written on the front and the back, which contained the Deuteronomic curses of the old covenant now realized in Israel's exile (ca. 586 BC). But this would give way to the blessings of the new covenant (Ezek. 36). This seems to match the scroll of Revelation 5 with its blessings and curses; moreover, it is interesting that Deuteronomy, which contains the covenantal blessings

---

8. The Gospel of John uses *amnos* for "lamb" to signify the sacrificial aspect of Jesus' death, while Revelation uses *arnion* for "lamb" to signify the conquering aspect of Jesus' death. See C. Marvin Pate and Douglas Welker Kennard, *Deliverance Now and Not Yet* (New York: Peter Lang, 2003), 282–86, 514.

9. As I have shown elsewhere, apocalyptic authors contemporary to John's day believed the messianic woes were the culmination of the covenantal curses, *Deliverance*, 146–48.

10. Duvall's comments highlight this theme for Revelation 21–22. See J. Scott Duvall, J. Daniel Hays, E. Randolph Richards, W. Dennis Tucker, and Preben Vang, *The Story of Israel: A Biblical Theology*, ed. C. Marvin Pate (Downers Grove, Ill.: InterVarsity, 2004), 276.

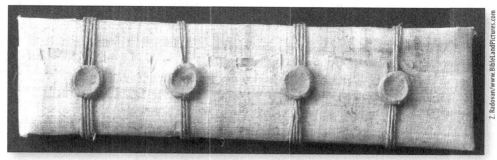

A model of a papyrus document sealed with four bulae (clay seals).

and curses (especially chaps. 28–30), later became known as the "Book of the Covenant" (Sir. 24:3).

All of this is to say that the handing over and the opening of the scroll by Christ expresses John's view that Jesus is God.

3. The Doxologies

The heavenly hymns sung to God and Christ in Revelation 4 and 5, respectively, serve two functions. First, they equate Jesus with God. Second, they set God and Christ in opposition to Caesar. Both of these aspects exalt the risen Jesus and God.[11]

1. The hymns to Jesus in Revelation 5 essentially match the hymns to God in Revelation 4, as the following chart highlights:[12]

God (Revelation 4)	Christ (Revelation 5)
v. 8: "Holy, holy, holy" (see Isa. 6:3)	vv. 1–6: alone worthy—(implied) holy
v. 8: "was, and is, and is to come" = eternal	v. 13: "for ever and ever" = eternal
v. 9: "glory, honor and thanks"	v. 12: "power and wealth and wisdom and strength and honor and glory and praise"
v. 11: "glory and honor and power"	v. 13: "honor and glory and power"
v. 11: worthy	vv. 9, 12: "worthy"
v. 11: Creator	vv. 9–10: Redeemer
vv. 2–3: sits on the throne	v. 13: sits on the throne

---

11. The Spirit is not left out of this picture of worship; the reference in Revelation 5:6–7 to "seven horns and seven eyes" seems to allude to the third member of the Trinity.

12. There are some sixteen heavenly hymns to God and Christ in Revelation; see Aune's analysis, *Revelation 1–5*, 314–17.

The conclusion John wishes his readers to draw from these virtually equivalent hymns to God and Jesus is that God and Jesus are equal in divine status (cf. Rev. 1:13–16).

2. The hymns to God and Christ in Revelation 4–5 also contain titles included in hymns sung to Caesar during the first century AD, titles that John reapplies to God and Christ. In doing so, the seer is exalting God/Christ over the Roman emperor. Following is a list of titles in Revelation 4–5 commonly used of Caesar now reapplied by John to God/Christ:[13]

Almighty (cf. Rev. 4:8 with Josephus, *Ant.* 14.199)

Worthy (cf. Rev. 4:11; 5:9–12 with Statius, *Silvae* 1.03)

Lord and God (cf. Rev. 4:11 with Suetonius, *Dom.* 13.2; Martial, 1.4.2; 7.55; 8:32–6)

Glory (cf. Rev. 4:11; 5:12, 13 with Martial 2.91.1)

Holy One (cf. Rev. 6:10 with Martial 5.1.190; 5.2.177)

Power (cf. Rev. 4:11; 5:12–13 with Martial 9.79.7; Dio Cassius, 4.1)

John's reappropriation of these titles for Caesar demonstrate his conviction that Christ/God—not Caesar—is Lord.

III. HEAVENLY ATTENDANTS

Arranged in concentric circles around the throne of God and Christ are three groups of heavenly attendants who worship God and the Lamb day and night: the four living creatures, the twenty-four elders, and the vast throng.

A. The Four Living Creatures (Rev. 4:6–9; 5:6, 8–10)

Nearest the divine throne are the four living creatures—lion, ox, man, eagle, which are a composite image of Isaiah's fiery seraphim (Isa. 6:2–3) and Ezekiel's cherubim supporting God's throne (Ezek. 1:5–21; 10:1–20; 11:22).[14] As Craig Keener observes, these four creatures represented the most powerful and regal of animals to communicate the majesty of God's creation.[15]

B. Twenty-four Elders (Rev. 4:4, 10–11; 5:6, 8–10)

The next circle around the divine throne consists of the twenty-four elders. The identity of this group is much debated, but it is probably the case that, just as the four living creatures are a composite portrait of the visions of Isaiah and Ezekiel, so also the twenty-four elders combine a number of images: angels, priests, people of God, and attendants to Caesar's throne. Note the following chart of characteristics:

> Arranged in concentric circles around the throne of God and Christ are three groups of heavenly attendants who worship God and the Lamb day and night: the four living creatures, the twenty-four elders, and the vast throng.

---

13. I am indebted to Aune, *Revelation 1–5*, 316–17, for the following analysis.

14. The difference is that *each* of Ezekiel's creatures has the four faces, whereas in Revelation 4–5 each of the creatures is represented by one face.

15. Craig S. Keener, *Revelation*, NIV Application Commentary (Grand Rapids: Zondervan, 2000), 174. The idea that a heavenly, royal court surrounds the throne of God goes back to the Old Testament (see 1 Kings 22:19; Dan. 7:9; et al.).

Angels	Priests	People of God	Caesar's Court Attendants
Lead in heavenly worship (Rev. 4:4, 10–11; 5:8–11)	24 courses of service (1 Chron. 23:6; 24:7–18)	12 tribes of Israel/12 apostles = Israel + church = people of God	24 devotees
Separate from the saints (Rev. 5:8)	White robes (Rev. 4:4; cf. Ex. 28:4; Lev. 16:4)	Elders (Ex. 24:9–10; Isa. 24:23)	Incense to Caesar
Yahweh's royal court (cf. 1 Kings 22:19; Job 1:6; 2:1)	Bowls of incense/ prayer (Rev. 5:8; cf. Ex. 25:29; Ps. 141:2)	Rule with Christ (cf. Rev. 4:8; 5:10; 20:6)	Cast crowns/ wreaths before emperor
			Lord and God
			Almighty, worthy, glory, power, etc.[16]

At the very least, the twenty-four elders represent the worship ascribed to God and the Lamb by the angelic realm and thus are the counterpart to the animal realm of the four living creatures. More particularly, the twenty-four elders are probably the angelic representation of the people of God (a kingdom of priests) who worship God and Christ, not Caesar.[17]

C. The Vast Throng (Rev. 5:11–13)

The last of the concentric circles around the divine throne is the vast throng that worships God and Christ (cf. Dan. 7:10 with Rev. 5:11–13). This innumerable group of worshipers encompasses all of creation.

CONCLUSION

Revelation 4–5 records the most awe-inspiring, breathtaking vision of the throne of God in all of the Bible and, probably, in all of literature. The thrice-holy God, the Lion-Lamb, honorific language second to none, the majesty and mercy of God and Christ, thunder and lightning, heaven and earth, friend and foe are all a part of John's kaleidoscopic, mystic ascent to the throne. Revelation 4–5 is a heavenly cinematic wonder, outdoing the likes of the Star Wars, Lord of the Rings, and Chronicles of Narnia films combined. Such a vision, at the very least, should command our attention and our eternal worship!

---

16. Recall the hymnic titles sung to Caesar referred to above.
17. Recall that in Revelation 1:20 the stars are the angelic counterparts of the seven churches. Something similar seems to be behind the concept of the twenty-four elders. The angels represent the church in heavenly worship.

1. Discuss *merkabah* mysticism relative to John's mystic ascent to heaven (Rev. 4:1 – 2).

2. How does Revelation 4 – 5 relate to ancient Roman imperial ceremonial?

3. What are the concentric circles that make up John's vision of heaven?

4. What beautiful stones are used by John to describe God' throne (Rev. 4:3, 6)?

5. What is a *bisellium*, and how do God and Christ relate to it?

6. Explain the seven-sealed scroll (Rev. 5:1 – 14).

7. Why is Jesus described as the Lion-Lamb (Rev. 5:6, 12)?

8. What are the three possible backgrounds behind the Lion-Lamb imagery?

9. What are some of the traits Jesus and God share according to the doxologies in Revelation 4 – 5?

10. What qualities applied to Caesar in the first century are reapplied to God and Christ?

11. Who are the four living creatures in Revelation 4 – 5?

12. Who are the twenty-four elders in Revelation 4 – 5?

KEY TERMS

bisellium

doxologies to God and
Christ

four living creatures

Lion-Lamb

merkabah

opistograph

Roman imperial
ceremonial

seven-sealed scroll

titles for Caesar

twenty-four elders

CHAPTER 44

The Seal Judgments

REVELATION 6

Objectives

After reading this chapter, you should be able to:

- Compare and contrast the seal, trumpet, and bowl judgments.
- Explain whether the three sets of judgments above are sequential or simultaneous in nature.
- Compare the seal judgments with the Synoptics' Olivet Discourse.
- Explain the "already" fall of Jerusalem in AD 70 and the "not yet" imminent fall of Rome background to Revelation 6.
- Identify the meaning behind the six seal judgments.
- Relate the curses of the covenant to the seal judgments.

INTRODUCTION

Revelation 6 presents the terrifying four horsemen of the Apocalypse as divine agents of judgment. They form a part of the seven seal judgments, which, in turn, are intimately related to the trumpet judgments (Rev. 8–9) and the bowl judgments (Rev. 15–18). Together these three sets of seven judgments are commonly known as the messianic woes or Great Tribulation.

The chart[1] on the next page helps us to see the order and extent of the three sets of judgments.

This chapter will deal with two topics. First, we will discuss the structure of the seal, trumpet, and bowl judgments. Second, we will survey the seal judgments of Revelation 6.

The Four Horsemen of the Apocalypse by Albrecht Dürer.

I. THE STRUCTURE OF THE SEAL, TRUMPET, AND BOWL JUDGMENTS

Here we enter briefly into the debate over whether the seal, trumpet, and bowl judgments are sequential or parallel in structure. That there is partial recapitulation or some overlapping in the judgments is probable. But that the three judgments are parallel and therefore identical is improbable because of a number of considerations: (1) The sixth seal unfolds into the period of wrath poured out on the worshipers of the Beast but does not actually advance to the event of the parousia (6:12–17). (2) The seventh seal introduces the trumpet judgments, which run their course, and the seventh trumpet seems to bring one into the kingdom of Christ (11:15–18). (3) The seventh bowl then brings one to the culmination point in the return of Christ (chaps. 16–17). (4) Interludes come between the sixth and seventh seals and between the sixth and seventh trumpets but not between the sixth and seventh bowls, which would be expected if the trumpets were strictly parallel to the bowls.

---

1. The chart is based on G. F. Beale, *The Book of Revelation: A Commentary on the Greek Text*, NIGTC (Grand Rapids: Eerdmans, 1999), 128.

Four Catastrophes

Seals	Trumpets	Bowls
6:1–2: white horse; rider held a bow; was given a crown; bent on conquest	8:7: hail, fire, blood	16:2: sores
6:3–4: red horse; rider given a sword and power to take peace from the earth	8:8–9: fiery mountain in sea, {dec63} sea became blood	16:3: sea turned to blood
6:5–6: black horse; rider held scales	8:10–11: star named Wormwood fell on 1/3 of rivers and springs and turned water bitter; many died	16:4–7: rivers turned to blood
6:7–8: pale horse; its rider was Death and had power over ¼ of the earth to kill by sword, famine, plague, and wild animals	8:12: 1/3 sun, 1/3 moon, and 1/3 stars struck and turned dark	16:8–9: sun given power to scorch people with fire

Woes Intensify as the End Approaches

6:9–11: martyrs under altar asked, "How long," and were told, "A little longer"	8:13–9:12: "Woe! Woe! Woe ..." Demon locusts came from abyss	16:10: kingdom of Beast plunged into darkness
6:12–17: earthquake; sun turned black; moon turned red; stars fell; all feared the wrath of the Lamb	9:13–21: 200 million demon cavalry released from Euphrates	16:12–16: kings of east crossed Euphrates to prepare for Armageddon

Interlude

7:1–9: 144,000 sealed; great multitude seen in heaven	10:1–11: John eats scroll 11:1–3: 2 witnesses prophesy	(pattern broken)

The End

8:1: silence	11:15: end announced and celebrated but not described	16:17–21: theophany "God remembered Babylon the Great"; earthquake
		17–18: the seventh bowl is a continuation and elaboration of the fall of Babylon

II. THE SEAL JUDGMENTS (REV. 6–7)

We now proceed to survey the seven seal judgments recorded in Revelation 6–7. We begin by noting the oft-mentioned parallel structure between the seal judgments of Revelation 6–7 and the signs of the times as delineated in Jesus' Olivet Discourse:[2]

Matthew 24:6–7, 9a, 29	Mark 13:7–9a, 24–25	Luke 21:9–12a, 25–26	Revelation 6:2–17; 7:3
1. Wars	1. Wars	1. Wars	Seal 1. Wars
2. International strife	2. International strife	2. International strife	Seal 2. International strife
3. Famines	3. Earthquakes	3. Earthquakes	Seal 3. Famine
4. Earthquakes	4. Famines	4. Famines	Seal 4. Pestilence (Death and Hades)
5. Persecutions	5. Persecutions	5. Pestilence	Seal 5. Persecutions
6. Eclipses of the sun and moon; falling of the stars; shaking of the powers of heaven	6. Eclipses of the sun and moon; falling of the stars; shaking of the powers of heaven	6. Persecutions; earthquakes and signs in the sun, moon and stars	Seal 6. Earthquakes, eclipse of the sun, ensanguining of the moon

My thesis for the seal judgments is that they represent John's *reapplication* of the Olivet Discourse to a future fall of the Roman Empire. In other words, the fall of Jerusalem to Rome in AD 70 (the already aspect) is the backdrop for John's forecast of the imminent fall of Rome (the not-yet aspect).

That there is partial recapitulation or some overlapping in the judgments is probable. But that the three judgments are parallel and therefore identical is improbable.

John's oracles of judgments are directed against Rome because of its treatment of Jews and Jewish Christians beginning with the Jewish Revolt (AD 66–73), and continuing in John's own day.

That the signs of the times delineated in the Olivet Discourse in some way predicted the fall of Jerusalem to the Romans in AD 70 is recognized by many scholars. Yet the scope of the judgments portrayed in Revelation 6–7 go beyond what happened in the Jewish Revolt, for they envision God's wrath poured out worldwide and even cosmically. So

---

2. So R. H. Charles, *A Critical and Exegetical Commentary on the Revelation of St. John*, ICC (Edinburgh: T. & T. Clark, 1920), 1:158; cf. Louis A. Vos, *The Synoptic Traditions in the Apocalypse* (Kampen: Kok, 1965), 181–92.

my task here is to show that the seal judgments draw on the Olivet Discourse/fall of Jerusalem but with a view to forecasting the future fall of the Roman Empire.

A. The First Seal: The White Horse of the Antichrist (6:2)

The interpretation of the conquering cavalier on the white horse, with bow and crown, falls into two camps: positive and negative. Positively, the first seal has been identified with either Christ (cf. Rev. 19:11–16) or the triumph of the gospel before the return of Christ forecast in the Olivet Discourse (cf. Matt. 24:14; Mark 13:10; Luke 21:12). Alternatively, the cavalier on the white horse has sometimes been equated with the Antichrist or the false messiahs Jesus predicted would come before and after the fall of Jerusalem (Matt. 24:4–5, 11, 23; Mark 13:5–6, 21–23; Luke 21:8) or Nero and the Parthian army (cf. Rev. 13:3; 17:11). This is the negative interpretation.

The negative interpretation of the white horse of the Apocalypse seems to me to be the most accurate. And one need not choose among its options. Josephus records some ten Jewish messianic claimants that eventually brought about the Jewish Revolt, thus demonstrating that they were false christs (*J.W.* 1.10.6/209; *Ant.* 10.1.3/19).[3] Moreover, in a classic turning of the tables, John would be alluding to gloating over Rome's future defeat at the hands of its former emperor, Nero, especially if Revelation 6 also draws on the Roman fear of a Parthian invasion. The Parthians were expert horsemen and archers, and they posed a constant threat to the Roman Empire in the first century. They were always poised to cross the Euphrates River, and in AD 62 their military leader, Vologesus, did attack some Roman legions. The Parthians rode white horses, and their founder, Seleucus, was named Nikator, "the victor."

Furthermore, if, as a number of scholars feel, the beast of 13:3 (cf. 17:11), who received a mortal wound in the head but was revived draws on the Nero Redivivus (revived) story, the Parthian background of 6:2 is strengthened. Although Nero's first five years as emperor were relatively good, it was downhill after that. He perpetrated one monstrosity after another, including the murders of foes, friends, and family; sodomy; tyranny; and persecution of Christians (beginning in AD 64). Indeed, the title "beast" was a fitting one for him (13:1). So unpopular was Nero toward the end of his reign (AD 67–68) that there were open revolts against his authority in Gaul and Spain.

> The interpretation of the conquering cavalier on the white horse, with bow and crown, falls into two camps: positive and negative.

> The Parthians were expert horsemen and archers, and they posed a constant threat to the Roman Empire in the first century.

---

3. Flavius Josephus was a Jewish historian who lived from AD 37 to 101. He served as a general in the Jewish forces during the Jewish war against Rome in AD 66–70. During the war the Romans defeated Josephus's forces at Jotapata. Josephus surrendered to the Roman general Flavius Vespasian, whom he befriended by interpreting a prophetic oracle to mean that Vespasian would one day be emperor of Rome. He then worked with Vespasian in attempting to persuade the Jews to surrender their helpless cause. After the war, Josephus moved to Rome and changed his name from the very Jewish Joseph Ben Matthias to the Roman Flavius Josephus, taking on his benefactor's name. Vespasian did indeed become emperor of Rome in AD 69 and sponsored Josephus's works: *The Jewish Wars*, *The Antiquities of the Jews*, and others. Josephus completed his *Jewish Wars* in AD 75, just five years after the fall of Jerusalem. In this work Josephus wrote as an eyewitness historian who happened to be in action on both sides of the conflict. His reputation, however, was obviously questioned by his compatriot Jews, and to this day his historical reliability continues to be debated among scholars.

Left: Parthian cavalry archers. *Right:* The "Great Horse" raised by the Parthians for battle.

Eventually the Praetorian guard and the Senate proclaimed him to be a public enemy and approved Galba as his successor.

Nero fled and reportedly committed suicide by thrusting a sword through his throat on June 9, AD 68. However, the rumor spread that he had not died but escaped to Parthia and would return with the Parthian army to regain his throne — hence the story of Nero Redivivus. This fearful expectation of the return of Nero, a type of the Antichrist, leading the Parthian cavalry riding on white horses with bows and arrows, going forth to conquer, makes good sense of the first horseman of the Apocalypse (cf. *Sib. Oracles* 4:119 – 27).

This reading of Revelation 6:2 takes into account both the fall of Jerusalem in AD 70 to the Romans (thanks to the false messiahs) and a future fall of Rome to Nero Redivivus (see Rev. 13) and the Parthians.

B. The Second Seal Judgment: The Red Horse of War (6:3 – 4)

Ceramic plaque of a mounted archer.

In the Olivet Discourse, Jesus acknowledged the certainty of war but added that that was not necessarily the sign that the end had totally arrived (Matt. 24:6 – 7//Mark 13:7 – 8//Luke 21:9 – 10; Rev. 6:3 – 4). It, like the other signs of the times, was only the beginning of "birth pains" or the signs of the times. Many interpreters believe that Jesus' reference to the increase of wars here and in Revelation 6:3 – 4 (the second horseman) alludes to the first century.

The peace that Caesar Augustus (31 BC – AD 14) established (*pax Romana*) throughout the Roman Empire was short-lived. Wars broke out in Britain, Germany, Armenia, and Parthia under Emperor Claudius (AD 41 – 54). The period following Nero's death (AD 69) saw three emperors, Otho, Galba, and Vitellius, quickly rise and fall amid civil upheavals and political chaos. So devastating was the period following Nero's death that it threatened to reduce the Roman Empire to rubble (Josephus, *War* 4.9.2; cf. Tacitus, *Histories* 1.2 – 3; Suetonius, *Lives*, "Vespasian" 1).

Especially relevant to the end-time sign of wars and rumors of wars was the Jewish revolt against Rome, which culminated in the fall of Jerusalem (AD 66–73).

The Jewish war against Rome witnessed the deaths of multiple thousands of Jews in Judea and the enslavement of thousands more. Josephus estimates that as many as 1.1 million Jews were killed at that time (though he undoubtedly exaggerated the figure). Titus, the Roman general, razed the city to the ground and took fifty thousand more Jewish captives back to Rome to form a part of his triumphant processional (*War*, preface to 1 and 4; cf. 7.1.1).

A coin depicting Emperor Nero (AD 54–68).

For John, the Jewish Revolt was but one of a number of civil wars that threatened to undo the Roman Empire, and no Roman emperor could stop it — not Vespasian, Titus, or Domitian. Added to this foreboding concern was the ever-ready Parthian cavalry stationed across the Euphrates River and poised to strike at the heart of the Roman Empire (see Rev. 8:13–9:21).

C. The Third Seal Judgment: The Black Horse of Famine (6:5–6)

The inevitable consequence of war is famine, nowhere so starkly portrayed as in Revelation 6:5–6 (cf. vv. 7–8), with its description of the third horseman. It would have been easy for the seer of the Apocalypse to envision war and famine.

During Claudius's reign, famine occurred in Rome in AD 42, and food shortage was reported in Judea in 45–46, in Greece in 49, and in Rome again in 51, and quite often in Asia Minor, including the time of Domitian, 92. The reference to the pair of scales and the inflated prices for food in 6:5–6 cannot help but recall the severe famine that occurred in Jerusalem during its siege by the Roman army (Matt. 24:7//Mark 13:8//Luke 21:11). During that time the inhabitants of Jerusalem had to weigh out their food and drink because of the scarcity of those necessities. So severe was it that even a mother would eat her child (*War* 6.3.4; see also *War* 5.10.5; cf. 6.5.1; Luke 21:23).

A reconstruction of a Roman scale utilizing the original parts.

The fall of Jerusalem and the resulting famine may also explain the ironic statement in Revelation 6:6, "and do not damage the oil and the wine." The command to spare the oil and the wine is possibly an allusion to General Titus's order that even during the ransacking of Jerusalem, olive trees (for oil) and grapevines (for wine) were to be spared.[4] If so, the fall of Jerusalem serves as the perfect backdrop for the third seal judgment (6:5–6), as it does for the Olivet

---

4. The order could also allude to Domitian's regulations on the grapevines in Asia Minor in AD 92. Recall my introduction.

Discourse prophecy about the eventuality of famines. Indeed, Jesus' statement that such horrors were but the beginning of the end (Mark 13:7), the initiation of the messianic woes (13:8), points in that direction (cf. Rev. 6:7–8 with the fourth seal judgment).

D. The Fourth Seal Judgment: The Pale Horse of Death (6:7–8)

The fourth seal judgment is death personified (cf. Rev. 1:18; 20:13, 14). As mentioned above, multiple thousands of Jews were killed in the first revolt against Rome. But according to Revelation 6:7–8, the four horsemen of the Apocalypse would one day retaliate against the Roman Empire, killing one-fourth of its people. And that would only be the beginning (see Rev. 8–16).

E. The Fifth Seal Judgment: Christian Martyrdom (6:9–11)

There are three interlocking destinies delineated in the Olivet Discourse and the fifth seal judgment of Revelation: the persecution of Jesus' disciples, Jesus' crucifixion, and the destruction of Jerusalem. The apparent connection to be made from this is that Israel's crucifixion of Jesus and subsequent persecution of his disciples brought about divine destruction on Jerusalem.

> There are three interlocking destinies delineated in the Olivet Discourse and the fifth seal judgment of Revelation: the persecution of Jesus' disciples, Jesus' crucifixion, and the destruction of Jerusalem.

The Olivet Discourse ominously predicts that Jesus' disciples will be persecuted (Matt. 24:9–10//Mark 13:9–19//Luke 21:12–19). Luke's second volume, Acts, records the fulfillment of Jesus' prediction, describing the persecutions of Peter and John (Acts 4:1–12; cf. 12:3–19), Stephen (6:8–7:60), James (12:1–2), Paul (16:22–30; 21:27–23:35), and many other Jewish Christians (8:1–4). In being delivered up to the Jewish and Roman authorities, the disciples were repeating the destiny of Jesus (notably, his crucifixion).

Later church tradition understood that the fall of Jerusalem in AD 70 came about as a result of divine judgment because of the Jewish persecution of Jesus' followers. For example, the fourth-century church historian Eusebius refers to the belief of many that God judged Jerusalem because it killed the half brother of Jesus, James the Just (*Eccl. Hist.* 2.23). Even Josephus attributed Jerusalem's fall to divine judgment. Writing of the burning and destruction of the temple in late August or early September AD 70, he writes that the fire was not ultimately ignited by the Romans: "The flames ... owed their origin and cause to God's own people" (*War* 6.4.5).

The same threefold intertwined destinies surface in Revelation 6:9–11, the fifth seal judgment. That the martyrs described therein are Christians is plain. Corresponding descriptions of these saints occur in 7:9–17 and 14:1–5. Their exemplar in suffering for righteousness is Jesus, the Lamb who was slain (5:6–14). But who were the perpetrators of such injustice and violence on the people of God? Revelation 6:10 provides a clue: It was "the inhabitants of the earth" (cf. 3:10; 11:10). Alan J. Beagley understands these "earth-dwellers" to have been Jerusalemites who killed Jesus.[5]

---

5. Alan J. Beagley, *The "Sitz im Leben" of the Apocalypse with Particular Reference to the Role of the Church's*

But Rome also had a hand in persecuting early Christianity, beginning with Nero, as the preceding references in Revelation suggest. And it is probably the case that Revelation 6:9 (cf. 12:11) alludes to the Neronian slaughter of Christians in Rome in AD 64 as a scapegoat for the emperor's burning of that city. Indeed, the reference in Revelation 6:10 to God as *despotēs* is an affront to the emperor's claim to be *despotēs* ("lord/master") (see Philo, *Flacc.* 4.23; Dio Chrysostom, *Orations 45: In Defense of His Relations with His Native City,* 1).

The same threefold intertwined destinies surface in Revelation 6:9 – 11, the fifth seal judgment.

But one day the tables will be turned: Christ will avenge the blood of his followers (v. 10).[6] This will happen when the divinely predetermined number of Christians will be martyred (cf. Rom. 11:25; *2 Bar.* 23.5; *1 Enoch* 47:4; *4 Ezra* 4:36; *Mart. Pol.* 14; Eusebius, *Hist. Eccl.* 5.1.13).

F. The Sixth Seal Judgment and Cosmic Upheaval (6:12 – 17)

The Old Testament associated cosmic disturbances with the coming of divine judgment, especially the day of the Lord (Isa. 34:4; Ezek. 32:7; Joel 3:3 – 4; Hab. 3:6, 11). That Jesus should use such apocalyptic imagery to describe the fall of Jerusalem (see Matt. 24:29// Mark 13:24//Luke 21:11, 25 – 26) was not unusual. Josephus did the same (*War* 6.5.1.3). The sixth seal judgment of the Apocalypse (6:12 – 17) also utilizes apocalyptic language to rehearse cosmic disturbances in the first century.

The opening of the sixth seal (6:12 – 17) introduces several spectacular physical phenomena that strike terror into people of every social rank so that they seek to hide from God and the Lamb. Beagley believes that refers to various earthquakes in the first century, three being referred to by Tacitus (*Annals* 12.43, 58; 14.27) — in AD 51, 53, and 60 — and others during the seventh decade (mentioned by Seneca, *Naturales Quaestiones* 6.1; 7.28). The darkening of the sun perhaps refers to solar eclipses that occurred between AD 49 and 52 or to phenomena associated with the eruption of Vesuvius in 79. Beagley also suggests that the islands being moved from their places (Rev. 6:14) is connected with "the sudden formation of new islands" (e.g., Thera and Terasia; cf. Seneca, *Nat.* 6.2, 6). He also calls attention to the connection between Revelation 6:16 and Luke 23:30, both of which allude to the destruction of Jerusalem in AD 70.[7]

The sixth seal judgment of the Apocalypse (6:12 – 17) also utilizes apocalyptic language to rehearse cosmic disturbances in the first century.

Indeed, the cosmic upheaval promised in Revelation 6:12 – 17 is reminiscent of Roman prodigies, pagan prophetic warnings of the coming divine judgment upon Rome because

---

Enemies (New York and Berlin: Walter de Gruyter, 1987), 36.

6. The martyrs' prayer for vindication is rooted in the imprecatory Psalms (7, 35, 55, 58, 59, 69, 79, 83, 109, 137, 139); cf. *1 Enoch* 47:4; *4 Ezra* 4:35 – 37; *Sib. Oracles* 3:313.

7. Beagley, *"Sitz im Leben" of the Apocalypse,* 44 – 45. The seal and trumpet judgments in Revelation follow the same pattern: the first four deal with earthly judgments, while the next two deal with heavenly events, with the last judgment becoming the next seven judgments; thus 4 + 2 + 1. The bowl judgments do not, however, follow this pattern.

of her impiety (so, e.g., Tacitus, *Hist.* 1.3.3; 1.86; *Annals* 12.64; 14.12; 15.47). Revelation 6:12–17, then, is John's way of applying apocalyptic judgment to Jerusalem and Rome. Did Rome destroy Jerusalem? Then God will one day destroy Rome!

CONCLUSION

I conclude this chapter by noting that the seal judgments of Revelation 6 are set against the backdrop of the curses of the covenant.[8] The four horsemen of the Apocalypse draw their imagery from Zechariah 1:8–11; 6:1–8. In those passages God sends out his four angel-driven chariots as his patrol over the earth, which inflict punishment on Israel's enemies. This was so even though those nations were raised up by God to exact the covenantal curses on disobedient Israel.[9] Furthermore, it is commonly known that the day of the Lord's wrath (Rev. 6:12–17) is rooted in the Old Testament prophets' threat of divine punishment on wayward Israel — that is, the curses of the covenant (see Joel 2:11, 31; Zeph. 1:14; Mal. 4:5; et al.). According to John, such judgment is to be executed upon disobedient Israel and the unbelieving (Roman) world by the Messiah.

---

8. This supports my earlier contention that the messianic woes are viewed in Jewish and Christian apocalypticism as the culmination of the Deuteronomic curses.

9. So Beale, *Book of Revelation*, 372.

REVIEW QUESTIONS

1. Summarize the chart on the seal, trumpet, and bowl judgments.

2. Are the seal, trumpet, and bowl judgments simultaneous or sequential? How do you know?

3. Please summarize the chart on the parallels between the seal judgments of Revelation 6 and the Synoptics' account of Jesus' Olivet Discourse.

4. What is our thesis for the seal judgments of Revelation 6?

5. How are we to interpret the rider on the white horse of Revelation 6:2?

6. What particular war might especially inform Revelation 6:3–4 and the red horse of war?

7. What famine may Revelation 6:5–6 have in mind?

8. What three interlocking destinies are behind Revelation 6:9–11?

9. Did cosmic upheaval occur at the fall of Jerusalem in AD 70, according to Revelation 6:12–17?

10. How do the curses of the covenant compare to the seal judgments?

KEY TERMS

black horse

bowl judgments

Christian martyrdom

cosmic upheaval

curses of the covenant

four horsemen of the Apocalypse

Jewish Revolt

messianic woes/ Great Tribulation

Nero Redivivus

Olivet Discourse

pale horse

Parthians

red horse

seal judgments

trumpet judgments

white horse

CHAPTER 45

The 144,000

REVELATION 7

Objectives

After reading this chapter, you should be able to:

- Summarize the reasons why some interpreters equate the 144,000 (Rev. 7:1–8) with the innumerable multitude (Rev. 7:9–17).

- Summarize why other interpreters distinguish the 144,000 and the innumerable multitude.

- Discuss what historical incident might be behind Revelation 7:1–8.

- Discuss what historical situation might inform Revelation 7:9–17.

INTRODUCTION

Revelation 7 is an interlude in the drama of the seal judgments. It creates suspense as the reader awaits the unfolding of the seventh seal. The identity of the 144,000 who receive the seal of God in their foreheads is debated by religious traditions ranging from evangelicalism to Jehovah's Witnesses. History, as we will see, may well provide the answer to that quandary.

We will survey Revelation 7 by covering three points: the interpretive issue of whether the 144,000 in verses 1–8 is to be equated with the innumerable multitude of verses 9–17, the historical setting of Revelation 7, and a summary of verses 1–17.

I. THE INTERPRETIVE ISSUE OF REVELATION 7

The question of who experiences the Great Tribulation as detailed in Revelation 6–18 largely depends on the identification of the 144,000 sealed servants of God as described in Revelation 7:1–8 (cf. 14:1–5; 17:14), and how that relates to Revelation 7:9–17.

> The question of who experiences the Great Tribulation as detailed in Revelation 6–18 largely depends on the identification of the 144,000 sealed servants of God as described in Revelation 7:1–8.

We may state the issue like this: If the 144,000 (7:1–8) are to be equated with the innumerable multitude of believers (7:9–17), then the posttribulationists would be correct; but if the two are not the same, the pretribulationists would be right. The assumption of the latter view is that the church will be raptured before the advent of the tribulation and that during the tribulation 144,000 Jews (7:1–8) become Christians who then evangelize the world (7:9–17). But if the former view is accurate, then the church (144,000 = innumerable multitude) undergoes the tribulation (v. 14). Before we finish our discussion of Revelation 7, we will see that both views have merit.

A. The 144,000 = Innumerable Multitude

Three key reasons are often put forth in defense of the view that the 144,000 are the innumerable multitude. (1) There was no record of the twelve tribes of Israel during John's day, and therefore his order of tribes symbolically replaces Israel with the church. (2) In the rest of the New Testament, the church is portrayed as the replacement of Israel (Rom. 2:29; 9:6–8; Gal. 3:29; 6:16; Phil. 3:3; James 1:1; 1 Peter 1:1; 2:4, 9). (3) The sealing of the 144,000 is a symbol of Christian baptism, something all New Testament Christians submitted to. Therefore the sealing of the 144,000 is to be understood as the church's identification with Christ through baptism, not the setting apart of a Jewish Christian remnant in the Great Tribulation.

But there are significant problems with the preceding arguments. (1) Against the first argument, Josephus (AD 90) reckoned with the existence of the twelve tribes of Israel in his day (*Ant.* 11.133). Moreover, there was a widespread Jewish eschatological hope of the regathering of the twelve tribes of Israel that was based on the assumption of their actual existence in the world (Isa. 49:6; 63:17; Ezek. 47:13, 21–23; 48:30–31; Zech. 9:1; Sir. 36:10;

4 Ezra 13:12–13, 39–49; *Pss. Sol.* 17:26–28, 43–44; 1QM 2:2–3; 3:13–23; 1QSa 1:15, 29; *Shemoneh Esreh* [Eighteen Benedictions]; Josephus, *Ant.* 11.133; et al.).

(2) The above references to the supposed replacement of Israel by the church need to be seen alongside another line of witness in the New Testament, namely, that God will one day restore ethnic Israel to their Messiah (see Matt. 10:23 and especially Rom. 11). Furthermore, there is no clear-cut example of the church being called "Israel" in the New Testament or in the church fathers before AD 160.[1]

> Three key reasons are often put forth in defense of the view that the 144,000 are the innumerable multitude.

(3) Sealing[2] in the ancient world could mean various things: a barbarian custom, a mark of disgrace, a sign of ownership/protection, a sacral rite in some cults, circumcision, or a term for Christian baptism.[3] In my estimation, sealing as a mark of ownership/protection is the best meaning of Revelation 7:4, because it is based on Ezekiel 9:4. That passage describes the Hebrew letter taw being placed on the foreheads of the Jewish remnant so that they would not be destroyed with the rest of Israel. This background precisely fits the sealing of the Jewish Christian remnant during the Great Tribulation period, as we will see below.

B. The 144,000 ≠ the Innumerable Multitude

For several reasons, I am convinced that Revelation 7:1–8 is not to be equated with Revelation 7:9–17. (1) The numbers are obviously different: 144,000 and an uncountable number. (2) The twelve tribes of Israel are best taken as ethnic Jews (the remnant), while the innumerable host is best seen as the fulfillment of God's promise to Abraham that his seed would consist of all nations, not just Jews (Gen. 17:4–6; Rom. 4:16–18; 9:6–13; Gal. 3:16). (3) The 144,000 are on earth, but the uncountable host is in heaven. (4) The 144,000 face the imminent danger of the Great Tribulation, while the innumerable host of Gentile Christian martyrs are now safely home in heaven.

> For several reasons, I am convinced that Revelation 7:1–8 is not to be equated with Revelation 7:9–17.

(5) The idea that a Jewish remnant could be protected in the land of Israel while enduring the Great Tribulation is amply attested in ancient Judaism (Dan. 12:12; Mark 13:13; 1 Thess. 4:15–17; *2 Bar.* 29:1–2; 40:2; 71:1; *4 Ezra* 9:7–8; 12:34; 13:26, 48–49; 1QH 3).[4] Such protection undoubtedly recalls God's preservation of the Hebrews during the Egyptian plagues (cf. Rev. 7:1–8; 14:1–5; 17:14 with Rev. 8:1–9:21; 15:1–18:21; Ex. 7:8–12:36). Some would label this aspect of John's eschatology midtribulationist (the church will undergo only the first half

---

1. See Peter Richardson, *Israel in the Apostolic Church*. SNTSMS (Cambridge: Cambridge University Press, 1969), 74–84, 206.

2. The seal, *sphragis*, was the impression of a seal in clay or wax. Seals could be worn suspended from a chain or cord around the neck or the seal could form the ring on the monarch's finger.

3. See David E. Aune's discussion in his *Revelation 6–16*, WBC 52B (Nashville: Thomas Nelson, 1998), 456–59. The seal on the foreheads of the 144,000 is the righteous counterpart to the mark of the Beast (Rev. 13:16–18). The seal also reminds one of Jewish phylacteries on the male's forearm and forehead; see my later discussion of Revelation 13.

4. W. D. Davies makes this point. *The Gospel and the Land* (Berkeley/Los Angeles: University of California, 1974), 49–52; see also Aune, *Revelation 6–16*, 443–45.

of the tribulation). It seems more accurate to say, however, that the divine seal upon the 144,000 reflects John's belief that the kingdom of God (which is advanced by the activity of that group) has dawned. But this already perspective is tempered by the grim reality that these saints will, though protected, still have to endure the entirety of the Great Tribulation. In actuality, it is they who most likely form part of the righteous warriors in the end-time holy war (cf. Rev. 14:1–5 with Rev. 19).[5]

(6) Further support for not equating the 144,000 (Jewish Christians) with the innumerable host (Gentile Christians) comes from those Old Testament passages that speak pro-

5. 119. Some might want to label this interpretation as "midtribulational" (so Gleason L. Archer, ed., *Three Views on the Rapture* [Grand Rapids: Zondervan, 1996], 139–44), but there are two problems with that assumption: (1) the 144,000 are on earth, not raptured to heaven; and (2) according to Revelation 6:19, the first three and a half years are also included in the wrath of God, something midtribulationists and pretribulationists want to avoid saying the church will endure.

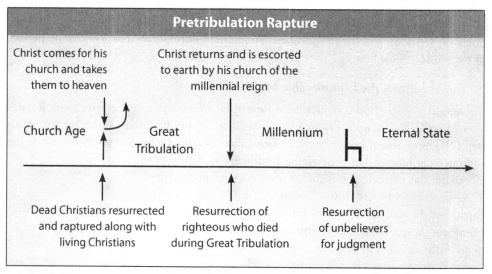

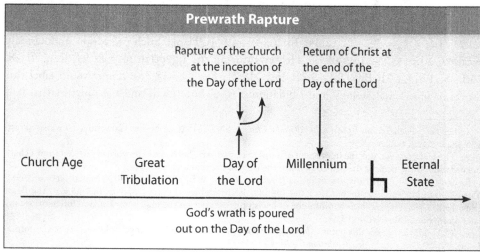

phetically of Gentiles joining Israel in worshiping God at the temple in Jerusalem during the end times (e.g., Isa. 2:2; 49:6; 56:6–8; Zech. 14:16). This notion seems also to inform Revelation 7.[6]

(7) If the 144,000 is the same group as Revelation 14:1–5 (which it undoubtedly is), then the combined passages should be seen as presenting the Jewish Christian remnant as God's soldiers who engage in the eschatological holy war that results in the restoration of Israel (cf. the following passages on Israel's restoration: Deut. 30:3–5; Isa. 11:11–16; 27:12–13; 49:5–6; 54:7–16; Pss. 106:47; 147:2; Jer. 31:7–14; Ezek. 37:15–23; Hos. 11:10–11; Tobit 13:13; Sir. 36:11; Bar. 5:5–9; 2 Macc. 2:7; *2 Bar.* 78:5–7; *1 Enoch* 57; 90:33; *4 Ezra* 13:12–13, 39–47; *Pss. Sol.* 11:2–7; 17:26; *T. Jos.* 19:4; *Shemoneh Ezreh*

---

6. This view would be enhanced if an eschatological reading of the Feast of Booths behind Zechariah 14 is operative in Revelation 7, especially since the Jewish remnant win the nations to God in the end times; see Aune, *Revelation 6–16*, 448–50.

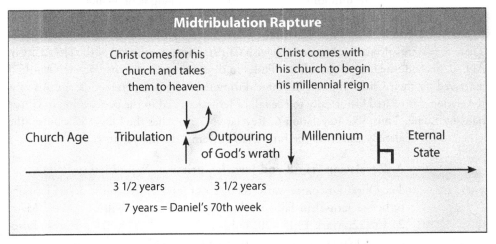

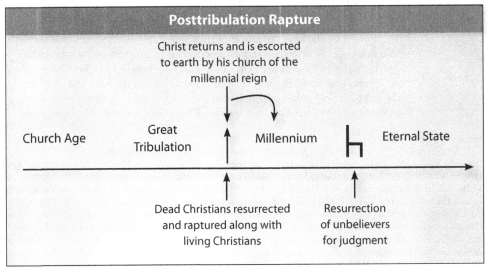

10; Matt. 24:31 = Mark 13:27; 1 Thess. 4:16 – 17; 2 Thess. 2:1 with Dan. 7:21 – 22; Ezek. 40 – 48; Zech. 14; *Pss. Sol.* 17:26 – 28, 43 – 44; 1QM; Matt. 19:28//Luke 22:30; Rev. 19).[7]

I conclude this first point on the interpretive issue of Revelation 7 by stating my opinion in the matter: the 144,000 are not the innumerable host (so the pretribulationist view), but, nevertheless, *both* groups undergo the Great Tribulation (so the posttribulationist view). How history might shed light on this anomaly is addressed in my next major point on Revelation 7.

> The 144,000 is a figurative number for the Jewish Christians who fled from Jerusalem to Pella before AD 68.

II. THE HISTORICAL BACKGROUND OF REVELATION 7

If we were correct to relate the seal judgments of Revelation 6 to, among other things, the Olivet Discourse and the events preceding and including the fall of Jerusalem in AD 70, then Revelation 7 — the beginning of the unfolding of the seventh trumpet judgment — should also be seen in light of that same historical setting. I now make two observations: First, 144,000 is a figurative number for the Jewish Christians who fled from Jerusalem to Pella before AD 68. There they were safe and reconstituted Jewish Christianity after the fall of the Holy City in AD 70. Second, the innumerable host alludes to those many Christians (largely Gentiles?) martyred for their Christian faith in Rome during the Neronian persecution. In this way, Revelation 7 is related historically to the fall of Jerusalem and to the persecution of Christians by Rome. Thus, like Revelation 6, Revelation 7 reapplies the Olivet Discourse (the already aspect) to the future fall of Rome (the not-yet aspect).

> The innumerable host alludes to those many Christians (largely Gentiles?) martyred for their Christian faith in Rome during the Neronian persecution.

A. Revelation 7:1 – 8 and Jewish Christians Who Fled to Pella

The Olivet Discourse warns followers of Jesus to flee to the desert for safety before Jerusalem falls; in this way the elect few will be spared (Matt. 24:16 – 22; Mark 13:15 – 20; Luke 21:18 – 24). The church historian Eusebius (AD 263 – 339) connected this warning with a prophetic oracle exhorting Jewish Christians to leave Jerusalem (ca. AD 68):

> But before the war, the people of the Church of Jerusalem were bidden in an oracle given by revelation to men worthy of it to depart from the city and to dwell in a city of Perea called Pella. To it those who believed in Christ migrated from Jerusalem. Once the holy men had completely left the Jews and all Judea, the justice of God at last overtook them, since they had committed such transgressions against Christ and his apostles. Divine justice completely blotted out

---

7. Reid identifies three militaristic aspects of the description of the 144,000 in Rev. 7:1 – 8. "(1) In Revelation 7:1 – 8 we learn that the number is derived by multiplying twelve tribes by 12,000 from each tribe. The Hebrew *'elep,* 'thousand,' may have served as a technical term for a military unit in Israel (Nu 1; 26; Jdg 5:8; 1Sa 17:18; 1Ch 13:1) and may have been so intended in Revelation. (2) The census list of the 144,000 recalls in some aspects the listing in Nu 1:20 – 46 of able-bodied male Israelites prepared for war (Rev 14:4 also implies males). (3) The seer's list is headed by Judah, from which the lion of 5:5 comes, an image associated with the son of David's prowess in war" (Tremper Longman III and Daniel G. Reid, *God Is a Warrior* [Grand Rapids: Zondervan, 1995], 185). To these Aune adds a fourth possible military characteristic: the chastity of the 144,000 as depicted in Rev. 14:4 may reflect the purity regulations required of participants in a holy war (Lev. 15:16; Deut. 23:9 – 10; 1 Sam. 11:11; 1QM 7:3 – 7), *Revelation 6 – 16,* 812.

Masada as seen from the air. In this mountaintop fortress, Jewish rebels held out against the Romans until AD 73. Notice the assault ramp on the right built by the Romans.

that impious generation from among men (*Ecc. His. III. V. 3*). [Cf. Epiphanius, *De Mensuris et Ponderibus* 15, and his *Ad. Haer.* 29.7; 30.2.]

Kenneth Gentry adds a detail to the preceding picture — the suicide of Nero in AD 68 prompted the Roman generals Vespasian and his son, Titus, to cease operations against Jerusalem, withdrawing for a year because of the subsequent turmoil in Rome. When Vespasian was declared emperor in AD 69, he directed Titus to proceed with the siege of Jerusalem (see Josephus, *J.W.* 4.9.2; 4.10.2; 4.10.5).[8]

It may well be, then, that the command to the angels to seal the 144,000 before divine judgment fell (Rev. 7:1–3) alludes to the flight to Pella by the Jewish Christians in about AD 68 (cf. also Rev. 12:15–17).

B. Revelation 7:9–17 and the Innumerable Host and the Neronian Persecution

Revelation 7:9–17 may well allude to the Neronian persecution of Roman Christians from November AD 64 to Nero's suicide in June AD 68 (forty-two months; cf. Rev. 13:5–7; 1 Peter 4:12–19).

---

8. Kenneth L. Gentry Jr., in *Four Views on the Book of Revelation*, ed. C. Marvin Pate (Grand Rapids: Zondervan, 1998), 57. He draws on Josephus for that background. In AD 68 generals Vespasian and Titus "had fortified all the places round about Jerusalem ... encompassing the city round about on all sides" (*J.W.* 4.9.1). But when Vespasian and Titus were "informed that Nero was dead" (4.9.2), they "did not go on with their expedition against the Jews" (4.9.2; cf. 4.10.2) until after Vespasian became emperor in 69. Then "Vespasian turned his thoughts to what remained unsubdued in Judea" (4.10.5). Gentry's general preterist treatment of the seals and the fall of Jerusalem in AD 70 is as fascinating as it is illuminating (pp. 37–92).

The Roman historian Tacitus provides a gruesome account of Nero's persecution of Christians in Rome, noting that he "inflicted unheard-of punishments on those who … were vulgarly called Christians" (*Ann.* 15.44). The persecution claimed "an immense number" (*Ann.* 15:44; cf. Livy, 2.39.9; 4.33.2; 5.7.2; 9.23.16; 34.29.51; *1 Clem.* 6:1).

This interpretation of Revelation 7:9–17 is strengthened by comparing these verses to the Roman triumph processional, a ceremony that exalted the conquering Roman general and his victorious return to Rome. The wearing of a white toga, waving of palm branches (Livy 10.47.3), and receiving of the accolades of the crowds remind one of the Christian martyrs who give honor to Christ (Rev. 7:9–17). This, then, can be seen as a parody of the Roman triumph ceremony: Roman Christians overcome Nero precisely through their faithful witness to Christ unto death (cf. Rev. 19:11–21).

And one day that victory will be made manifest to the world at the fall of Rome.

> Revelation 7:9–17 may well allude to the Neronian persecution of Roman Christians from November AD 64 to Nero's suicide in June AD 68 (forty-two months; cf. Rev. 13:5–7; 1 Peter 4:12–19).

III. SUMMARY OF REVELATION 7:1–17

I now offer a summary of Revelation 7:1–17: The four angels hold back the winds of divine judgment (upon Jerusalem?) until the 144,000 are sealed (Jewish Christians who fled to Pella? [vv. 1–3]).

The order of the twelve tribes of Israel (vv. 4–8) begins with Judah, probably because the Messiah was connected with that tribe (Rev. 5:5). Dan is omitted because of its association with idolatry (Judg. 18:30; 1 Kings 12:29) and possibly because of the (later?) legend that the Antichrist would come from Dan (Irenaeus, *Haer.* 5.30.2). The removal of Dan allowed the inclusion of the tribe of Levi. Joseph was the father of Manasseh and Ephraim (the latter is not mentioned in John's list). The reordering of the twelve tribes thus delineated in verses 4–8 need not, therefore, mean that John is subtly replacing Israel with the church.

While the 144,000 live protected during the Great Tribulation, the innumerable multitude (Christian martyrs in Rome?) do not. Rather, they die for their faith. Washing their robes white in the blood of the Lamb paradoxically indicates that they followed Christ's sacrificial path (Rev. 5:6) and thus now enjoy his glory in the heavenly temple of God. Accordingly, they give all honor to the Lamb, as do the four creatures, twenty-four elders, and hosts of angels (vv. 9–17; cf. 21:4).

1. Summarize the reasons why some interpreters equate the 144,000 (Rev. 7:1 – 8) with the innumerable multitude (Rev. 7:9 – 17).

2. Why do other interpreters disassociate the two?

3. What difference does it make?

4. What historical incident might be related to Revelation 7:1 – 8?

5. What persecution might be behind Revelation 7:9 – 17?

KEY TERMS

144,000	Neronian persecution	pretribulation rapture
innumerable multitude	Pella	seal
midtribulation rapture	posttribulation rapture	white toga

CHAPTER 46

The Trumpet Judgments

REVELATION 8–9

Objectives

After reading this chapter, you should be able to:

- Explain the relationship between the seventh seal judgment and the seven trumpet judgments.

- Discuss how the Old Testament events of the Egyptian plagues, the fall of Jerusalem to the Babylonians, and the Persian defeat of Babylon inform Revelation 8–9.

- Discuss how more recent events in John's day, such as the eruption of Mount Vesuvius and the impending Parthian invasion explain Revelation 8–9.

- Discuss the meaning of the locust plague, Parthian army, and demonic host in terms of the meaning of the fifth and sixth trumpet judgments.

INTRODUCTION

The seventh seal judgment, like one firecracker exploding into several more, becomes the seven trumpet judgments (8:1–9:21). After the seventh seal is opened heaven is silent for a half an hour. The silence creates suspense before the trumpet judgments are implemented. It may also quiet the heavenly hosts so that the martyrs' prayers for vindication can be heard (8:3). The trumpets are blown by the seven archangels who attend God's throne (Rev. 8:2). From extrabiblical literature we learn that their names are Uriel, Raphael, Raguel, Michael, Saraga'el, Gabriel, and Remiel (*1 Enoch* 20:2–8; cf. *Jub.* 2:1–2; Tobit 12:15; *3 Enoch* 17; *T. Lev.* 8:2; 4Q 404).

> The seventh seal judgment, like one firecracker exploding into several more, becomes the seven trumpet judgments (8:1–9:21).

In the Old Testament, the trumpet (whether the shofar, yobel, or hasusra) was used for several purposes, including as a general means of warning (Num. 10:1–8), as a warning of imminent attack (Jer. 20:16), as an announcement of victory in battle (Ps. 47:5), or as a part of a theophany scene (Ex. 19:13, 16, 19). The militaristic usage of trumpets in Second Temple Judaism became associated with eschatological holy war (1QM 2:16–3:11; *4 Ezra* 6:23; *Sib. Oracles* 4.174–75; *Apoc. Moses* 22:3; 18th Benediction; cf. Isa. 27:13; Zech. 9:14–15).[1]

The seven trumpets of Revelation 8–9 no doubt are blown by the seven archangels to herald the eschatological holy war that inflicts the messianic woes on the earth's inhabitants. Like the seal judgments, they take the form of 4 + 2 + 1 (four earthly judgments + two cosmic judgments + one last judgment) that becomes the seven bowl judgments (8:1–11:15), with an interlude (10:1–11:13) comparable to Revelation 7.

My thesis for the trumpet judgments is that they, too, like the seal judgments (though more intensely), predict the imminent fall of the Roman Empire at the hands of Christ. These predictions are given against the backdrop of ancient Israelite history (the Egyptian plagues and the prophet Joel's prediction of a coming locust invasion) and recent Roman events (the eruption of Mount Vesuvius and an impending Parthian invasion of Rome).

We will incorporate these historical influences into our survey of the seven trumpets, but it would be helpful at the start to discuss the influence of the Egyptian plagues on Revelation 8–9; 15–16.

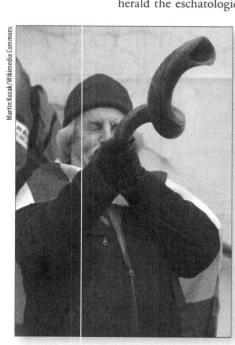

Martin Kozak/Wikimedia Commons

A shofar, a ceremonial Jewish trumpet made of ram's horn.

I. THE TRUMPET AND BOWL JUDGMENTS AND THE EGYPTIAN PLAGUES

Commentators commonly recognize that the trumpet judgments (Rev. 8:1–11:15) and the bowl judgments (15:1–16:21) parallel

---

1. So David E. Aune, *Revelation 6–16*, WBC 52B (Nashville: Thomas Nelson, 1998), 510–11.

some of the ten plagues on ancient Egypt (Ex. 7:8 – 13:16), as the following synoptic table[2] illustrates.

Seven Trumpets (Rev. 8 – 9)	Ten Plagues (Ex. 7 – 11)	Seven Bowls (Rev. 16)
1. Earth hit with hail, fire, and blood (8:7)	7. Hail (9:13 – 34) 6. Boils (9:8 – 11)	1. People with Beast's mark afflicted with sores (16:2)
2. 1/3 of sea turned to blood and 1/3 of sea creatures die (8:8 – 9)	1. Blood (7:14 – 21)	2. Sea turned to blood and all sea creatures die (16:3)
3. 1/3 of fresh waters embittered by Wormwood (8:11)	1. Blood (7:14 – 21)	3. Rivers and springs turned to blood (16:4)
4. 1/3 of sun, moon, and stars darkened (8:12)	9. Darkness (10:21 – 23)	4. Sun scorches people with fire (16:8 – 9)
5. Locusts released on earth after Abyss is opened (9:1 – 11)	8. Locusts (10:3 – 19) 9. Darkness (10:21 – 23)	5. Darkness on earth and sores break out (16:10 – 11)
6. 200 million troops at Euphrates River released by 4 angels (9:13 – 16)	2. Frogs (8:2 – 14)	6. Kings from east gathered to Euphrates River by 3 unclean spirits resembling frogs (16:12 – 13)
7. Heavenly temple opens, accompanied by lightning, earthquake, and hail (11:15, 19)	7. Hail (9:18 – 34)	7. Lightning, severe earthquake, and plague of large hail (16:18 – 21)
	Egyptians wail loudly because of loss of firstborn (12:30)	People curse God because of the plagues (16:9, 21)
Survivors of plagues refuse to repent (9:20 – 21)	Pharaoh hardens heart (7:22; 8:15, 19, 32; 9:7, 12, 34 – 35; 10:20, 27; 11:10)	Survivors of plagues refuse to repent (16:9, 11)

The major difference between the trumpet and bowl judgments is that the former affects one-third of the earth while the latter's effect on the earth is total.

---

2. This chart comes from Mark Wilson, *Charts on Revelation* (Grand Rapids: Kregel, 2007), 80.

The colossal statue of Ramses II, part of the rock-cut façade of the great temple at Abu Simbel, measuring about 69 feet (21 m.) high. Ramses II (ca. 1250 BC) may have been the pharaoh against whom the plagues of Moses were directed.

II. THE SEVEN TRUMPET JUDGMENTS (REV. 8–9)

The seven trumpet judgments mix together at least two images: Israelite history (the Egyptian plagues, but also the prophet Joel's prediction of the coming locust invasion of Israel) and recent events in Rome's history (the eruption of Mount Vesuvius and an imminent Parthian invasion). The seer of Revelation uses these past happenings as the backdrop to foretell the coming fall of the Roman Empire. I now survey Revelation 8–9 in that light.

A. The First Trumpet Judgment: Hail, Fire, Blood (8:6–7)

The raining down on earth from heaven of hail and fire recalls the seventh plague God inflicted on ancient Egypt (Ex. 9:13–34). The additional image of blood probably stems from Joel 2:30–31, where blood stains the heavens in the last days.

But, as Osborne observes, we should no doubt also view the imagery of raining blood that resulted from volcanic eruptions in the Aegean islands in the first century, which were said to have turned the sky red, as background to the first trumpet. These eruptions formed part of the Roman prodigy lists warning of impending doom (Cicero, *Div.* 1.43.98; Pliny, *Nat.* 2.57.147; *Sib. Oracles* 5.377–80).[3] This volcanic background is all the more likely in light of Revelation 8:8–12, which alludes to the eruption of Mount Vesuvius in AD 70 (see below).

The references to the destruction of one-third of the earth, trees, and grass (Rev. 8:7; cf. vv. 8, 9, 10, 12) allude to Ezekiel 5:2, where Ezekiel's hair and beard were divided into thirds, each representing a type of destruction to come upon ancient Jerusalem (ca. 587 BC).[4]

We may pull these comments together by suggesting that John reapplies the plagues on Egypt and the destruction of Jerusalem by Babylonia (587 BC) to Rome. Soon that city will fall under the covenantal curses of God as Jerusalem did and will be brought to its knees as Egypt was by the plagues. Indeed, the ongoing seismic activity in the Aegean and the recent devastation of Vesuvius (AD 79) are but portents of the coming end-time leveling of the Roman Empire.

> We should no doubt also view the imagery of raining blood that resulted from volcanic eruptions in the Aegean islands in the first century, which were said to have turned the sky red, as background to the first trumpet.

---

3. Grant R. Osborne, *Revelation*, Baker Exegetical Commentary on the New Testament (Grand Rapids: Baker, 2002), 350–51 (cf. Pseudo-Philo's *Bib. Ant.* 11:4; Cicero, *Div.* 1.43.98; Pliny, *Nat.* 2.57.147; *Sib. Oracles* 5.377–80).

4. Aune points this out. *Revelation 6–16*, 519.

B. The Second Trumpet Judgment: Burning Mountain and Blood (8:8–9)

Next, a burning mountain fell into the seas, turning a third of them into blood and destroying a third of the fish and ships. This second trumpet judgment recalls the first Egyptian plague, which turned the Nile River and its tributaries into blood (Ex. 7:14–21). But here it is not Moses' staff placed into the waters that turns them to blood, but a falling burning mountain. There are several viable interpretations of the identity of this burning mountain, none of them mutually exclusive. (1) Jeremiah 51:25 proclaims that God will turn Babylon into a burned-out mountain in return for its attack on Jerusalem (587 BC). (2) First Enoch 18:13, in good Jewish apocalyptic fashion, predicts that God will throw out of heaven fallen angels who are like shooting stars. It is interesting that *Sibylline Oracle* 5.158–59 applies the imagery of the burning star to Rome (there called Babylon), which will be destroyed by God. (3) The burning mountain that sheds blood may be Mount Vesuvius, which in AD 79 buried Pompeii and Herculaneum.[5] Debris from the eruption of Vesuvius radically affected the Bay of Naples from Capri to Cumae, making it impossible to land boats. The eruption of Vesuvius is described in *Sibylline Oracle* 4.130–34 (AD 80) in the context of divine judgment: "But when a firebrand, turned away from a cleft in the earth in the land of Italy, reaches to broad heaven, it will burn many cities and destroy men. Much smoking ashes will fill the great sky, and showers will fall from heaven like red earth."[6]

> The burning mountain that sheds blood may be Mount Vesuvius, which in AD 79 buried Pompeii.

---

5. Osborne, *Revelation*, 352–53.
6. Aune points this out. *Revelation 6–16*, 520. The translation comes from James H. Charlesworth, *Apocalyptic Literature and Testaments,* TOTP, Vol. 1 (New Haven: Yale University Press, 1983), 387.

Mount Vesuvius.

Dio claims that "it wrought much injury of various kinds, as chance befell, to men and farms and cattle, and in particular it destroyed all fish and birds" (66.23.2; LCL trans.). Pliny the Younger, an eyewitness of the eruption of Vesuvius, observed that the sea level went down and many sea creatures were left stranded on the dry sand (*Ep.* 6.20.9). It has been estimated that from twelve thousand to fifteen thousand people lost their lives.

The message of this imagery is clear: as God defeated Israel's enemies in the past — Egypt and Babylon — so he will defeat true Israel's (the church's) enemy — Rome. And Vesuvius is only the beginning of the judgment to come.

C. The Third Trumpet Judgment: Wormwood (8:10 – 11)

The next judgment, which also resembles the first Egyptian plague, encompasses the inland waters, such as rivers and springs, for a meteorite falls into them polluting one-third of the drinking water and killing many people. The name of the "star" is *Apsinthos* (Wormwood), a bitter-tasting shrub, symbolizing Old Testament Israel's future defeat (Deut. 29:18; Jer. 9:15;[7] 23:15; Lam. 3:15, 19). It is also customary to see in Revelation 8:10 – 11 a reversal of the miracle of Marah (Ex. 15:23), when Moses threw a piece of wood into the bitter water, turning it sweet. Moreover, an allusion to Mount Vesuvius here is probable, for many interpreters believe Revelation 8:10 is a duplicate of 8:8.[8] All of this is the backdrop for John's prediction here of the future fall of Rome.

D. The Fourth Trumpet: Cosmic Darkness (8:12)

The fourth angel sounded the trumpet, and one-third of the sun, moon, and stars were darkened. The motif of darkness here alludes to the ninth Egyptian plague (Ex. 10:21 – 23). That plague was picked up later in Jewish apocalypticism to describe the coming day of the Lord (Ezek. 32:7; Joel 2:10; Amos 5:18 – 20; 8:9; Mark 13:24 – 25//Matt. 24:29; Rev. 6:12 – 13; *1 Enoch* 17:6; 1QM 11:10; 13:11 – 12). Also, the eruption of Vesuvius was reported to have darkened the sun for days because of the airborne volcanic ash (Pliny the Younger, *Ep.* 6.16.17; 16.20.15). The message here is that darkness will one day fall upon Rome as an expression of divine wrath; indeed, it has already begun with Vesuvius.

After the sounding of the fourth trumpet, a flying eagle announced the next three trumpet judgments, identifying them as the three "woes" (8:13). The "woe" oracle in the Old Testament announced the coming covenantal curses upon unfaithful Jerusalem (Ezek. 16:23; cf. Isa. 5:8 – 9; Amos 6:1 – 2; Hab. 2:9 – 10). According to Revelation 8:13 (cf. 18:10, 16, 19), such judgment will soon be dispensed upon the new Babylon — Rome — and the followers of the Beast.

E. Fifth, Sixth, and Seventh Trumpets (9:1 – 19)

The fifth, sixth, and seventh trumpet judgments comprise the three woes (Rev. 8:13), though the seventh trumpet is delayed, essentially becoming the seven bowl judgments. On the one hand, it is clear that John distinguishes between the fifth and sixth trumpets, especially since the former does not take human life while the latter does. Also, Revela-

---

7. Wormwood is bitter but not poisonous. The poisonous reference comes from Jeremiah 9:15.
8. So Aune, *Revelation 6 – 16*, 519.

Glazed reliefs (now in the Istanbul Museum) of roaring lions, which lined the processional way at Babylon during the time of Nebuchadnezzar II (605 – 562 BC).

tion 9 and its two images of a locust plague and an invading army come from the book of Joel (ca. 600 BC?), which seems to distinguish the two, much like Revelation 9:1 – 12 (locust plague) and 9:13 – 21 (invading army); see Joel 1:4 – 6; 2:4 for the former and Joel 2:11, 20, 25; 3:9 – 12 for the latter. But, on the other hand, the images of locust, invading army, and demonic host are mixed together throughout Revelation 9, indicating that these two trumpet judgments are similar in nature, if not the same. Indeed, Aune makes a good case that Revelation 9:13 – 19 is a duplication of Revelation 9:1 – 12.[9] Accordingly, I will summarize Revelation 9 by discussing the three metaphors that dominate that chapter: locust plague, invading army (Parthians), and demonic host. Having done that, we will see that the overarching message of the fifth and sixth trumpet judgments is that, from the divine perspective, just as the Medo-Persians destroyed ancient Babylon (539 BC) for destroying Jerusalem (587 BC), so the contemporary Parthians (New Medo-Persians) will destroy Rome (New Babylon, cf. Rev. 16 – 18) for destroying Jerusalem (AD 70).

III. LOCUST PLAGUE, PARTHIAN ARMY, AND DEMONIC HORDE

A. Locust Plague

Although the fifth trumpet judgment recalls the eighth Egyptian plague (Ex. 10:3 – 19), it is more intimately rooted in Joel's prophecy of a coming locust plague upon disobedient Israel as a part of the covenant curses (see, again, Joel 1:4 – 6; 2:4; ca.

The famous Cylinder of Cyrus, the Lord's "anointed" (Isa. 45:1), which tells how he captured Babylon and liberated the prisoners from Babylonia. It was made of baked clay from Babylon (ca. 536 BC).

---

9. Ibid., 497.

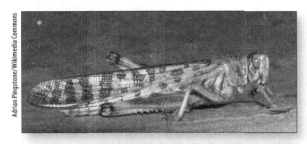

Top: Desert locust. *Bottom:* Locusts feeding.

600 BC?). The massive number of locusts mentioned in Revelation 9 darken the sky (v. 2), though paradoxically the locusts are forbidden (by God) from eating precisely what they are known for eating—grass, plants, and trees (v. 4). They can only harm those not protected by the seal of God (v. 4; cf. Rev. 7:1–8). The five-month period of pain they strike probably corresponds to the locust's life span (spring-summer? v. 5). Their "lion's teeth" symbolize locusts' destructive power (see Joel 1:6), and the chariot sound captures their noisy, thunderous advance (see Joel 2:5; Rev. 9:9). The "breastplate of iron" reminds one of the locust's scaled body (Rev. 9:9).

B. Parthian Army

Another key image of Revelation 9, as the commentators recognize, is the ancient Roman fear of the Parthians.

Concerning John's mention of the Euphrates River (Rev. 9:14), Craig Keener writes:

> The mention of "the great river Euphrates" leaves no doubt that Parthians are in view, for the Euphrates repeatedly appeared as the traditional boundary between Roman and Parthian territories throughout Mediterranean literature. Pompey had established this boundary in the first century BC, and it remained in John's day. When Parthians crossed the Euphrates, it was to fight Romans. A later writer observes that these two most powerful empires in the world were separated only by a river.[10]

The human faces of the locusts (9:7) indicate that John is combining the images of a locust plague and a human army invasion, and the long hair was characteristic of Parthian warriors. The war horses described by John, with breastplates and helmets for rider and horse (9:7, 9), match ancient descriptions of the Parthian cavalry[11] as does their ability to shoot arrows while turning backward when riding their horses (9:10, 19).

The mention of the four angels stationed at the Euphrates who incite a Parthian invasion reminds one that the Parthian invasion of Rome will be divinely inspired (cf. *1 Enoch* 56:5–6 [ca. 150 BC]). The Nero Redivivus legend of the emperor leading a Parthian invasion of Rome fits the fear described here in Revelation. Indeed, Nero identified himself as Apollo (Apollyon, Rev. 6:2; 9:11),[12] the ancient Greek god, one of whose emblems was the locust (Aeschylus, *Agamemnon* 1080–86).

> Another key image of Revelation 9, as the commentators recognize, is the ancient Roman fear of the Parthians.

10. Craig S. Keener, *Revelation*, NIV Application Commentary (Grand Rapids: Zondervan, 2000), 270.

11. See Aune, *Revelation 6–16*, 533.

12. See Kenneth L. Gentry Jr. in *Four Views on the Book of Revelation*, ed. C. Marvin Pate (Grand Rapids: Zondervan, 1998), 68.

C. Demonic Horde

But the fifth and sixth trumpets exceed the imagery of locust plague and Parthian invasion. They encompass the demonic realm. (1) The locusts/Parthians emerge out of the pit, the place reserved for Satan in the future (Rev. 20:3, 7) and the present home of fallen angels (2 Peter 2:4; Jude 6). (2) Their leader, Abaddon (Heb., meaning "death"), or Apollyon (Gk., meaning "destruction") = Nero is satanically inspired. (3) Their scorpion or serpentlike sting reminds one of the description of Satan in Revelation 12. (4) Their number—200 million—finds no earthly correspondence; rather, it is a demonic horde. (5) "Fiery red, dark blue, and yellow as sulfur" seems to describe their hellish, supernatural aura. (6) The combined portrait of lion, serpent-scorpion, and belching fire would bring to mind the horrifying monster called the chimera or Medusa with her snake-like hair.[13]

Roman chariot and horses.

CONCLUSION

I will now pull together my comments on Revelation 8–9 by restating my thesis: just as God raised up the Medo-Persians to destroy ancient Babylon for destroying Jerusalem (587 BC), so John predicts God will raise up a new Medo-Persian army—the Parthians—to destroy Rome—new Babylon—because of its treatment of Jerusalem in AD 70. In other words, like the seal judgments, the trumpet judgments present the imminent destruction of Rome (the not yet) against the backdrop of the fall of Jerusalem (the already). The following chart summarizes the trumpet judgments according to that perspective:

Revelation 8–9	History (Already)	Prophecy (Not Yet)
8:1–13: 1st–4th Trumpet Judgments	Egypt's enslavement of Jews; cf. Roman destruction of Jerusalem (AD 70)	Future destruction of Rome using imagery of the eruption of Mount Vesuvius against backdrop of Egyptian plagues
9:1–19: 5th–7th Trumpet Judgments	Babylon defeated Jerusalem (587 BC)/Medo-Persian defeat of Babylon (539 BC)/Rome—now Babylon—defeated Jerusalem (AD 70)	Future end-time invasion of Rome by new Medo-Persian army (demonic, Parthian attack, with locustlike effort)

---

13. See Keener's comments, *Revelation*, 271–72.

1. What does the seventh seal judgment turn into (Rev. 8:1 – 9:21)?

2. For what main purpose was the trumpet used in the Old Testament?

3. What is the numerical pattern of the seal and trumpet judgments?

4. What thesis does the author present for Revelation 8 – 9?

5. Summarize the chart comparing the trumpet/bowl judgments and the Egyptian plagues.

6. How do the themes of the Egyptian plagues and the eruption of Mount Vesuvius inform the first four trumpet judgments (Rev. 8:1 – 13)?

7. How do Joel's prophecy of a locust invasion and the threat to Rome of a Parthian invasion enlighten the last three trumpets judgments (Rev. 9:1 – 19)?

8. How does the demonic horde factor into the discussion of the last three trumpet judgments?

9. Please summarize the already/history and not yet/prophecy dynamic behind Revelation 8 – 9.

KEY TERMS

4 + 2 + 1 pattern	locust plague	Persian defeat of Babylonia
Abaddon/Apollyon	Medo-Persians	seven angels/archangels
Babylonian invasion of Jerusalem	Mount Vesuvius	trumpet
Egyptian plagues	Nero Redivivus	wormwood
	Parthian invasion	

CHAPTER 47

The Little Scroll

REVELATION 10

Objectives

After reading this chapter, you should be able to:

- Discuss how the Colossus of Rhodes served as the background to Revelation 10.
- Discuss the five points made about prophecy.

INTRODUCTION

Revelation 10 continues the theatrics of the Apocalypse by revealing the little scroll but concealing the nature of the seven thunders therein. Though it is debated by commentators, the contents of the little scroll seem to be unfolded in chapters 11 – 16, the bowl judgments.

I now look at two of the background components of Revelation 10, then summarize this brief chapter.

I. BACKGROUND OF REVELATION 10

Two backgrounds inform Revelation 10 — one of minor importance and the other of major significance.

A. The Colossus of Rhodes

Commentators rightly see in the description of the mighty angel whose face is like the sun and whose feet stride sea and land the Colossus of Rhodes, one of the seven ancient wonders of the world. This marvel was a 105-foot-high bronze statue of Helios (the sun patron deity of the city) built in 280 BC and destroyed by an earthquake in 224 BC. A popular myth stated that its feet were on two huge piers guarding the harbor, and ships would pass between its legs. However, it was actually on a promontory overlooking the harbor, and the ruins of the magnificent statue were still visible on the ground in John's day.[1]

B. The Book of the Covenant

The identity of the little scroll whose contents are revealed to John is debated, particularly whether it is to be equated with the great scroll of Revelation 5. Those who equate the two point out that the same word is used of both — *biblion*, except that Revelation 10:2 calls it *biblaridion*, a diminutive of *biblion*. Accordingly, the chain of revelation of events would be as follows: chapter 5: Christ opens the unopened scroll, the book of the covenant, which will unfold as the seal and trumpet judgments; chapter 10: John is recommissioned as a prophet, who reports that a high-ranking angel of God opens more of the contents of the same scroll — namely, the bowl judgments (Rev. 11 – 16). Those who disagree with this interpretation, however, argue that the diminutive word in Revelation 10 should be taken seriously; it is a "little" scroll contrasted to the "great" scroll of Revelation 5.

The Colossus of Rhodes by Ferdinand Knab/Private Collection/Archives Charmet/The Bridgeman Art Library International

Der Koloß zu Rhodos.

This drawing of *Colossus of Rhodes*, which illustrated The Grolier Society's 1911 *Book of Knowledge*, is probably fanciful, as it is unlikely that the statue stood astride the harbor mouth.

---

1. Descriptions of the Colossus of Rhodes come from Pliny, *Nat.* 34.18.41; Strabo, *Geographia* 14.2.5; and Sextus Empiricus, *Math.* 7.107.

Actually, both views are viable here. Thus the diminutive form should stand—it is a small scroll to be included in the contents of the great scroll. Therefore, the great scroll of Revelation 5 should be understood to reveal the entire plan of God's covenant—Revelation 6–16—while the little scroll reveals one significant part of that plan—the bowl judgments.

II. SURVEY OF REVELATION 10

Revelation 10–11:13 forms an interlude between the trumpet and bowl judgments just as Revelation 7 formed an interlude between the seal and trumpet judgments. Indeed, as we will see, just as God sealed his own for protection in Revelation 7, so he will do the same in Revelation 10–11. The dominant theme connecting Revelation 10 and 11 is prophecy. Thus Revelation 10 describes the prophecy contained in the little scroll while Revelation 11 dramatizes the prophetic ministry of God's servants. Indeed, prophetic activity occurs throughout Revelation 10–11: 10:7, 11; 11:3, 6, 10; cf. 1:3; 11:18; 22:9, 18–19).[2] The effect of this is to indicate that John is being (re)commissioned as a prophet, whose prophecy will unfold in Revelation 10–16. I now summarize Revelation 10 and the motif of prophecy therein under five points:

> The great scroll of Revelation 5 should be understood to reveal the entire plan of God's covenant—Revelation 6–16—while the little scroll reveals one significant part of that plan—the bowl judgments.

A. The Angel of the Prophecy (v. 1)

The mighty angel descending from heaven is unnamed. "He" may be the anonymous angel of Revelation 5:2, or he may be Michael (Dan. 12:1) or Gabriel (Dan. 10:5–14) since Daniel 12 is a part of the Old Testament substructure of Revelation 10. I can at least say that the angel most likely is not Christ.[3] The "rainbow" over the angel's head is reminiscent of God's throne (Rev. 4:3; cf. Ezek. 1:28). "Robed in a cloud" and "legs ... like fiery pillars" recall God's guidance of the Israelites in the wilderness (Ex. 13:21, cloud by day and fire by night). Besides, this Old Testament background is the backdrop of the Colossus of Rhodes, which accounts in part for the gigantic size of the angel who stands astride the sea and land (vv. 1–2).

B. The Scope of the Prophecy (v. 2)

I have already suggested that the little scroll is a part of the book of the covenant, unfolding the covenantal blessings on the faithful followers of Christ and Deuteronomic curses upon those who are not. The posture of the mighty angel—standing astride sea and land—symbolizes the universality

> Besides this Old Testament background is the backdrop of the Colossus of Rhodes, which accounts in part for the gigantic size of the angel who stands astride the sea and land (vv. 1–2).

---

2. C. H. Giblin points this out in "Revelation 11.1–13: Its Form, Function and Contextual Integration," *NTS* 30 (1984): 433–59; citation is from 434.

3. Contra Beale, who argues that the angel is Christ. G. F. Beale, *The Book of Revelation: A Commentary on the Greek Text*, NIGTC (Grand Rapids: Eerdmans, and Carlisle: Paternoster, 1999), 522–24.

and sovereignty of God's rule. This counters the Beast's claim to control the same territory (Rev. 13:1–10 [over the sea]; Rev. 13:11–18 [over the earth]).

C. The Sealing of the Prophecy (vv. 3–4)

The angel with the little scroll loudly proclaimed the seven thunders yet to be poured on the earth (v. 3), but John was commanded to seal that prophecy; to not reveal it (for this reveal-conceal component, see Dan. 8:26; 12:4, 9; 2 Cor. 12:4; *4 Ezra* 14:5–6). Apparently the seven thunders would be poured out on the earth unannounced, perhaps in conjunction with the upcoming bowl judgments.

D. The Content of the Prophecy (vv. 5–7)

The angel swore an oath before heaven that God would soon impose his will on the earth (vv. 5–6a). This oath is rooted in Deuteronomy 32:40–41 where God swears he will enforce the curses of the covenant on those disobedient to him, especially Israel (cf. Dan. 12:7). Verses 6b–7 make it clear that the content of the prophecy of the little scroll has to do with the seventh trumpet judgment (see 11:15–19—seven bowl judgments, chaps. 15–16).

> Verses 6b–7 make it clear that the content of the prophecy of the little scroll has to do with the seventh trumpet judgment (see 11:15–19—seven bowl judgments, chaps. 15–16).

The angel, therefore, swears that the blowing of the seventh trumpet will begin the last judgments on the earth (the seven bowl judgments, chaps. 10–16), which will immediately bring the kingdom of God from heaven to earth. Those judgments will be the beginning of the end. In other words, the last judgments announced here will be the means by which God finally and awesomely purges and prepares the earth for the descent of his kingdom. That this is what John means is clear from his choice of words to describe the content of the scroll—"the mystery (*mystērion*) of God" which is "announced" (*euēggelisen*) to his "servants, the prophets" (cf. Rev. 14:6; Matt. 11:2–6; Mark 1:14–15; Luke 7:18–23).[1] Unfortunately, their message will be rejected.

E. The Reception of the Prophecy (vv. 8–11)

Like Ezekiel the prophet, John ate the little scroll of the prophetic word of God, symbolizing his reception of its message (cf. Ezek. 2:9; 3:3). Its content at first tasted sweet to the seer (symbolizing the fact that the message was God's word). But then the content of the scroll became bitter, symbolizing the fact that the word of prophecy that John was about to utter was distasteful; it is the wrath of the covenant curses to be poured out on the unfaithful inhabitants of the earth (vv. 8–11). Just as Ezekiel prophesied against Jerusalem and then the nations that defeated Jerusalem, so John will prophesy against Rome who destroyed Jerusalem. Revelation 11–18 makes this clear.

---

1. See David E. Aune's excellent discussion in his *Revelation 6–16*, WBC 52B (Nashville: Thomas Nelson, 1998), 568–69. Daniel 2–7 and the pesher commentaries in the Dead Sea Scrolls accentuate the idea that the divine mystery is the kingdom of God now revealed to his servants.

CONCLUSION

I have suggested that the background of Revelation 10 is twofold. The mighty angel John describes is portrayed against the backdrop of the Colossus of Rhodes, and the little scroll is a part of the book of the covenant, the unfolding of the covenantal curses on the followers of the Beast in the last days. As we will see, Revelation 11–16 gives new meaning to the statement "Things will get worse before they get better"!

REVIEW QUESTIONS

1. What is most likely the content of the little scroll of Revelation 10?

2. How did the Colossus of Rhodes influence John's portrait of the angel of Revelation 10?

3. Summarize the five points made about prophecy in Revelation 10.

KEY TERMS

biblion

Colossus of Rhodes

little scroll

mystery of God

seven thunders

CHAPTER 48

The Temple, the Two Witnesses, and the Blowing of the Seventh Trumpet

REVELATION 11

Objectives

After reading this chapter, you should be able to:

- Discuss whether the temple referred to in Revelation 11 is literal, figurative, or both.

- Contrast the Jewish Christians' flight to Pella with the Jewish Zealots' stand in Jerusalem.

- Discuss the identity of the two witnesses mentioned in Revelation 11.

- Identify the referent of "the great city."

INTRODUCTION

Our chapter title above, "The Temple, the Two Witnesses, and the Blowing of the Seventh Trumpet," succinctly captures the contents of Revelation 11: the fall of the temple (of Jerusalem, vv. 1–2), the ministry of the two witnesses (vv. 3–14), and the blowing of the seventh trumpet judgment (vv. 15–19).

> Our chapter title above … succinctly captures the contents of Revelation 11: the fall of the temple (of Jerusalem, vv. 1–2), the ministry of the two witnesses (vv. 3–14), and the blowing of the seventh trumpet judgment (vv. 15–19).

Interpretations of Revelation 11 widely differ. Many futurists take these events as referring exclusively to the end times: the Antichrist will attack the rebuilt eschatological temple in Jerusalem—this despite the powerful, miraculous preaching of Elijah and Moses, now descended from heaven.[1] Preterists take a completely different tack in interpreting Revelation 11: the events described therein either accompanied the fall of Jerusalem in AD 70[2] or are expected by John to transpire in the imminent fall of Rome.[3] My view is a combination of these two subcategories of the preterist view: the fall of Jerusalem in AD 70 is the backdrop for John's assumption that Rome will soon be destroyed. This is very much what we saw at work in the seal and trumpet judgments and, as we will see, in

---

1. Popularized in print and films by the Left Behind series of Jerry Jenkins and Tim LaHaye. The books were published by Tyndale House Publishers.

2. So Kenneth L. Gentry Jr. in *Four Views on the Book of Revelation*, ed. C. Marvin Pate (Grand Rapids: Zondervan, 1998), 65–66.

3. This is my view, which will be developed below.

A model of Herod's temple in Jerusalem.

the bowl judgments. Idealists take Revelation 11, as usual, to be a picture of the general struggle between the church and Satan throughout the ages.[4] Historicists tried to pin down the happenings of Revelation 11: the two witnesses represent those opposed to the papacy before the Protestant Reformation.[5]

My treatment of Revelation 11 will unfold in two broad points: interpretive issues in Revelation 11 and a survey of the material therein.

I. INTERPRETIVE ISSUES IN REVELATION 11

There are at least three key hermeneutical issues in Revelation 11: Do verses 1–2 refer to the literal temple in Jerusalem, the figurative temple — the church — or perhaps both? Who are the two witnesses described in verses 3–12? And what is the "great city" that persecutes the two witnesses (v. 8) — Jerusalem, Rome, or both? We now examine these three issues.

An imperial bronze coin commemorating the Roman victory over the Jews in AD 70. It is inscribed with the words "Captive Judea" (*IVDEA CAPTA*).

A. The Temple (vv. 1–2)

1. Literal Temple in Jerusalem

The temple that John is commanded to measure is identified by many commentators as the literal temple in Jerusalem that fell in AD 70,[6] with the forty-two months corresponding to the time between the Jewish Revolt and the siege of Jerusalem — AD 66–70. Since Julius Wellhausen, many have interpreted 11:1–2 as a fragment of a Zealot prophecy from the weeks before the fall of Jerusalem to the Romans, expressing the belief that the Romans would overrun the city and the temple court but would be unable to penetrate the inner parts of the temple, which were held by the Zealots themselves and therefore thought by them to be divinely protected.[7] Toward the end of the war, the Zealots retreated into the sanctuary itself, the Holy Place and the Holy of Holies, as a place of last resort (Josephus, *J.W.* 6.122). The major problem with this view is that the prophecy of protection for those sealed did not come true, for the Zealots were killed along with the rest of the inhabitants of Jerusalem (Josephus, *J.W.* 6.285–87).

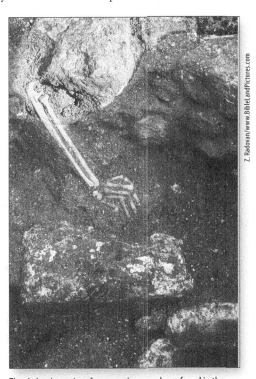

The skeletal remains of a woman's severed arm found in the charred ruins of a first-century Jewish home in Jerusalem after the city's destruction by Rome.

---

4. So Sam Hamstra, in *Four Views on the Book of Revelation*, ed. Pate, 110.

5. See Steve Gregg, ed., *Revelation: Four Views*, A Parallel Commentary (Nashville: Thomas Nelson, 1997), 217ff.

6. See the bibliography for this view in David E. Aune, *Revelation 6–16*, WBC 52B (Nashville: Thomas Nelson, 1998), 596.

7. Recorded in ibid., 594–95. There are two other subviews under the rubric of literal temple here — the heavenly temple (see the bibliography in ibid., 596) and a rebuilt eschatological temple (so, according to many dispensationalists and the Left Behind series).

2. Figurative Temple

Therefore many interpret the temple of Revelation 11:1–2 figuratively as the church, the new temple of God contrasted to the old temple of Judaism (1 Cor. 3:16–17; 2 Cor. 6:16; Eph. 2:19–22; 1 Peter 2:5).[8] On this reading of Revelation 11:1–2, the Jerusalem temple fell and therefore ceased to function as the dwelling place of God (it actually ceased being such with Jesus' death and resurrection). That honor now belongs to the church.

My view is that the literal identification of verses 1–2 with the Jerusalem temple of AD 70, plus the figurative equation of the temple with the church is correct, but with a powerful irony/parody introduced by John: it was not the Zealots in the holy places who represented the remnant of Israel, for they were destroyed; rather, it was the Jewish Christians who fled Jerusalem to Pella in AD 68 who were the true remnant. These were sealed (cf. Rev. 7:1–8) and protected (11:1–2) by God (cf. Rev. 12). These, along with Gentile Christians, constituted the true temple of God. Such preservation, however, was not extended to the two witnesses (the rest of the church), which leads us to discuss the identification of those personages (vv. 3–14).

Map of the Decapolis showing the location of Pella.

B. The Two Witnesses (vv. 3–14)

The task of identifying the two witnesses of Revelation 11:3–14 must take into account the Old Testament background drawn upon therein. Zechariah 3–4 and 6:9–15 speak of two eschatological figures in terms of two olive trees and two menorahs, which were probably Joshua the high priest and Zerubbabel the Davidic prince. Revelation 11:4 presumes this background.

Furthermore, the miraculous preaching and works of the two witnesses in Revelation 11 recall Elijah (cf. vv. 5–6a and the shutting up of the heavens from raining and con-

---

8. See, e.g., Alan J. Beagley, *The "Sitz im Leben" of the Apocalypse with Particular Reference to the Role of the Church's Enemies* (New York and Berlin: Walter de Gruyter, 1987), 61; R. H. Mounce, *The Book of Revelation*, rev. ed. NICNT (Grand Rapids: Eerdmans, 1998), 220.

Ancient ruins of Pella.

suming enemies with fire from heaven with 1 Kings 17–18 and 2 Kings 1, respectively) and Moses (cf. v. 6b and turning water into blood and other plagues with Ex. 7:14–19; 7:14–11:10).

Some futurists believe Moses and Elijah will return during the tribulation period to preach against the Antichrist once the eschatological temple has been rebuilt. Others—some preterists—think the two witnesses were Peter and Paul who met with martyrdom in Rome under Nero (AD 64–68). Many interpreters, however, view the two witnesses as a symbolic portrayal of the prophetic witness of the church in the first century AD. Thus the two olive trees/menorah picture the witness of the church in its priestly (Joshua) and kingly (Zerubbabel) functions. Indeed, Revelation 1:6; 5:10; 20:6 describe the church as "a kingdom and priests." And the church also fulfilled the roles of the law (Moses) and the prophets (Elijah) in its testimony to Christ. I think it possible that John intended to call to mind Peter and Paul as representatives of the church there in Rome.

I agree with this figurative interpretation of the identity of the two witnesses as the church of the first century (represented by Peter and Paul)[9] and would hasten to add one other point: the 1,260 days of the church's witness coincides with the time of Nero's persecution of the church in Rome (AD 64–68).[10] If this is so, then what we have in Revelation 11 is the same pattern we discovered in Revelation 7: a handful of believers—the Jewish Christian remnant (Rev. 7:1–8; 11:1–2)—was spared death at the fall of Jerusalem, while

9. Another set of candidates for the two witnesses is Enoch and Elijah, both of whom did not die, according to the Old Testament (for Enoch, see Gen. 5:24; cf. *1 Enoch*; for Elijah, see 2 Kings 2:11–12). Yet nothing in Revelation 11 seems to point toward Enoch as one of the two witnesses.

10. The slight difference between forty-two months (Rev. 11:2) and 1,260 days (Rev. 11:3) might hint at the Neronian persecution in Rome rather than the siege of Jerusalem. Or it could be that John, as his custom is, assigns various meanings to symbols and numbers.

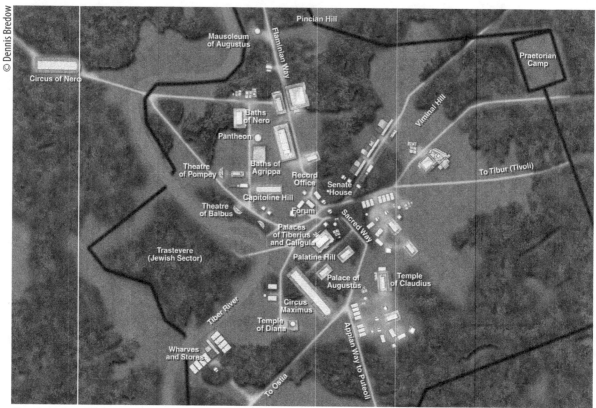

Rome in the time of Paul.

many in the church suffered martyrdom at the hands of the Neronian persecution in Rome (Rev. 7:9–17; 11:3–14). This theory also fits in with my argument below that both Jerusalem and Rome are alluded to in Revelation 11.

C. The Great City: Jerusalem or Rome, or Both?

To what does the "great city" (v. 8) refer?

1. Jerusalem

The reference to the city where "their Lord was crucified" (v. 8), along with its title "holy city" (v. 2) and other factors, suggest that John is thinking here of Jerusalem (not to mention the Zealot prophecy mentioned above).

2. Rome

Yet other clues in Revelation 11 point to Rome as the great city (v. 8). Everywhere else in Revelation, the "great city" alludes to Rome (16:19; 17:18; 18:10, 16, 18, 19, 21 = Babylon the Great, a euphemism for Rome; cf. 1 Peter 5:13). The "beast" that makes war on the two witnesses (v. 7) elsewhere in Revelation is Rome, and Nero in particular (13:1; 17:8; et al.). Rome, too, shed the blood of the prophets and saints (cf. Rev. 11:8 with 18:24).

3. Both Jerusalem and Rome

I believe the great city was Jerusalem in AD 70 and yet Rome in John's day. Multivalence in symbol is typical of John (see my discussion of Revelation 12). We saw this to be the case for Jerusalem and Rome in Revelation 6–9.

II. A SURVEY OF REVELATION 11

Revelation 11 contains three self-contained sections: verses 1–2, 3–14, and 15–19. I now summarize their content.

A. The Fall of the Temple (vv. 1–2)

The command to measure the inner courts of the temple[11] (Holy Place, Holy of Holies) is inspired by Ezekiel 40–42, where the eschatological temple in Jerusalem is revealed by God (cf. 11Q Temple 3–48). While measuring can mean different things in the Old Testament, here it signifies the protection of the Jewish Christian remnant, the true worshipers of God, because they are the true temple (v. 1).

Contrasted to the safety of the remnant is the destruction of the temple of Jerusalem by the Romans in AD 70.

The "forty-two months" (cf. Rev. 13:5) comes from Daniel 7:25; 12:7. There it is a term for the length of the eschatological tribulation that will come upon Israel right before the Messiah arrives (Dan. 12:1–4). Daniel understands that to be the three and one-half years the temple of Jerusalem was desecrated by Antiochus Epiphanes (167–164 BC).[12] For John, the three and one-half years applied to the Jewish Revolt until the siege of Jerusalem (AD 66–70).

B. The Two Witnesses (vv. 3–14)

Earlier I argued that while the two end-time witnesses could be Moses and Elijah returned to earth, most likely John had in mind the church, a kingdom of priests whose testimony to Jesus fulfills the Law and the Prophets. Perhaps he also thought of Paul and Peter as representing the church.

The 1,260 days could be a repeat of the forty-two months (v. 2), but they could also allude to the period of Neronian persecution of the church in Rome (AD 64–66), which claimed the lives of Paul and Peter (vv. 3–4). The church's witness in Rome was apparently powerful, miraculous, and invincible until the beast (Caesar Nero) was permitted to overcome them (v. 7). One is reminded here of the miraculous ministries of Peter (Acts 2:12)

---

11. *Naos* in Revelation refers to the inner courts of the temple (Holy Place, Holy of Holies; see Rev. 11:19) as opposed to *hieron*, which refers to the temple and its outer court (cf. Josephus, *J.W.* 2.400; 5.198–99; Matt. 21:12; Mark 11:15–16; Luke 19:45, 47; John 10:23). The outer court—the Court of the Gentiles—was demarcated from the other temple courts by warnings posted on a low stone barrier that enclosed the temple. They read, "No foreigner is to enter within the balustrade and enclosure around the temple area. Whoever is caught will have himself to blame for his death which will follow" (Josephus, *Ant.* 15.410–17; *J.W.* 5.193–94; 6.124–26; Eph. 2:14; *Corpus Inscriptionum Judaicarum* 2:1400).

12. For fuller discussion, see C. Marvin Pate and Calvin B. Haines Jr., *Doomsday Delusions: What's Wrong with Predictions about the End of the World* (Downers Grove, Ill.: InterVarsity, 1994), chap. 3.

and Paul (Acts 13:8–12). Yet through their faithfulness in dying for Christ's sake, they overcame the beast (see Rev. 12:11). The shameful treatment of Christians by Nero is well known. They were not buried but were used as torchlights in Nero's gardens, or mauled and eaten by the lions in the amphitheater, or killed by some other torturous method (cf. v. 8).

> Revelation 10:1–11:13 serves as an interlude between the trumpet and bowl judgments, just as Revelation 7 served as an interlude between the seal and trumpet judgments.

Moreover, ancient reports say that the bodies of the two apostles mentioned above were not buried (John Malalas, *Chron.* 10.37). The dead bodies of the two witnesses were exposed for three and one-half days (v. 9), an allusion to the length of Jesus' death. The deaths of the Christians at Rome occasioned great celebration among Roman citizens (vv. 9b–10). But the resurrection of the martyred Christians was soon to be a reality (vv. 11–12). And like the earthquake that accompanied Jesus' resurrection (Matt. 28:2), so John envisioned the imminent destruction of Rome by an earthquake (Rev. 16:18–20). John also believed that the destruction of Rome would be the catalyst for the conversion of Israel to Christ at his return (v. 13). In all of this, Jerusalem and Rome are the key cities in which the drama of Revelation unfolds.

C. The Seventh Trumpet and the Ark of the Covenant (vv. 14–19)

Revelation 10:1–11:13 serves as an interlude between the trumpet and bowl judgments, just as Revelation 7 served as an interlude between the seal and trumpet judgments.

Moreover, the fifth and sixth trumpet judgments (the first and second woes — Rev. 9), will now give way to the seventh trumpet, or third woe (v. 14).

Revelation 11:15–19 is an antiphonal hymn sung to God by his heavenly attendants. The first part of the hymn (v. 15), sung by unnamed voices, announces that the kingdom of God and Christ, though reigning over the world invisibly, will now make that rule known by overtaking the earth (vv. 16–19). This will be accomplished by the unfolding of the seventh trumpet (= seven bowl judgments; Rev. 15–16). This episode shows that heaven is the true ark of the covenant.

A model of the ark of the covenant with two cherubim.

GerthMedien

CONCLUSION

For John, Revelation blends the past fall of Jerusalem with the imminent fall of Rome. Did the Romans destroy Jerusalem? Then God will destroy the Romans; not only for destroying the holy city in AD 70 but also for attempting to destroy the church, the true temple, during the Neronian persecution and during Domitian's reign of terror. It is for these reasons that divine wrath will fall on Rome.

REVIEW QUESTIONS

1. What data suggest that the temple referred to in Revelation 11:1 – 2 was the Jerusalem temple?

2. What evidence might indicate that the temple was figurative?

3. Can the preceding two views be reconciled?

4. How did the Jewish Christians' flight to Pella contrast with the Zealots' stand in Jerusalem?

5. Who are the two witnesses mentioned in Revelation 11:3 – 14?

6. Was the "great city" Jerusalem, Rome, or both?

KEY TERMS

ark of the covenant	Jewish Revolt	temple of Jerusalem
church, the new temple	Neronian persecution	two witnesses
great city	Pella	Zealot prophecy

CHAPTER 49

The Woman, the Dragon, and the Child

REVELATION 12

Objectives

After reading this chapter, you should be able to:

- Describe the mythical imagery behind the woman, the Dragon, and the child.

- Explain how the messianic woes inform the above dramatic characters.

- Explain the three reference points for the heavenly war recorded in Revelation 12.

- Identify the historical event behind the flight of the woman in Revelation 12:13–16.

- Identify the covenant components in Revelation 12.

INTRODUCTION

Revelation 12–14 seems to be the third of three interludes in Revelation (cf. 7:1–17; 10:1–11:19). Like Revelation 10:1–11:19, Revelation 12–14 anticipates the seven bowl judgments (chaps. 15–16). There is no consensus as to how chapters 12–14 should be outlined, but one popular approach is to regard those chapters as introducing a new set of seven: seven dramatic personages that play key roles in the unfolding events of the rest of the Apocalypse. Those personages are the woman with child (12:2), the Dragon (12:3), the male child (12:5), Michael the archangel (12:7), the Jewish remnant (12:6, 13; chap 14), the beast from the sea (13:1–10), and the beast from the earth (13:11–18).

> The drama of Revelation 12 unfolds in three acts: war on the mother and child (vv. 1–6), war in heaven (vv. 7–12), and war on earth with the woman and her seed (vv. 13–17).

The common denominator of these seven personages is that they either are, or participate in, the supernatural world. The first two are called "signs,"[1] with reference to their appearance in heaven. The child is the Messiah. Michael is an angel. The Jewish remnant (if that indeed is who they were) are delivered by God. And the beasts of the sea and earth, along with the Dragon, form the evil supernatural trinity.

The drama of Revelation 12 unfolds in three acts: war on the mother and child (vv. 1–6), war in heaven (vv. 7–12), and war on earth with the woman and her seed (vv. 13–17).

I. WAR ON THE MOTHER AND CHILD (12:1–6)

A. Background of the Woman, Dragon, and Child

Commentators commonly recognize that the three characters dramatized in verses 1–6—woman, Dragon, and child—formed a mythological story well known in John's day. Craig Keener identifies the Egyptian and Greco-Roman origins of the story of the Dragon who attacks the woman and her child and the latter's subsequent escape and eventual victory over their enemy:

> In Egyptian mythology, Isis (Hathor), portrayed with the sun on her head, birthed Horus, and the red dragon Typhon sought to slay her, but she escaped to an island and her son Horus overthrew the dragon. In the Greek version of the story, the great dragon Python warned that he would be killed by Leto's son, pursued the pregnant Leto, who was hidden by Poseidon on an island, which he then temporarily submerged. After Python had left, Leto birthed the god Apollo, who in four days was strong enough to slay the dragon....
>
> Compare this to Roman propaganda in Asia Minor that the goddess Roma was the new mother goddess and the Roman emperor her child, the world's savior.[2]

However, John's Jewish heritage helps him reinterpret the pagan story for his audience. The apostle combines three Old Testament images of the Dragon in Revelation 12: Levia-

---

1. These signs seem to be different from the ones in the gospel of John. The former symbols do not appear for the purpose of inducing faith like the latter do.

2. Craig S. Keener, *Revelation*, NIV Application Commentary (Grand Rapids: Zondervan, 2000), 316, 317.

Cylinder seal from Tell Asmar (in ancient Mesopotamia) dated ca. 2500 BC showing two gods spearing a four-legged, seven-headed hydra, four of whose heads hang dead and three still live and show projected forked tongues; six tongues of flame arise from the monster's back; two worshipers and a star in the field are also seen. See Revelation 12:3 – 4; 13:1, 3, 14; 17:3, 8 – 11.

than, the many-headed sea monster tamed by God at creation (Ps. 74:14),[3] the serpent who deceived Eve and Adam (cf. Rev. 12:17 with Gen. 3:15), and the devil/Satan (1 Chron. 21:1; Job. 1:6, 9, 12; 2:3, 4, 6, 7; Zech. 3:1, 2).

In addition, John adds to the mix the Old Testament narrative of the fall of Satan in Isaiah 14:12 – 15[4] (see Rev. 12:4), which is recast as an end-time holy war (Rev. 12:7 – 12). Furthermore, the imagery of the woman in the pangs of childbirth comes from Isaiah 26:17 – 19, which is interpreted in later Judaism as the birth pangs of the Messiah, that is, the messianic woes.

Yet this pagan and Jewish background is historicized by John to allude to the flight of Jewish Christians to Pella in AD 68, as we will see below. These are the true Israel who undergo the messianic woes but nevertheless enjoy God's protection.

> The imagery of the woman in the pangs of childbirth comes from Isaiah 26:17 – 19, which is interpreted in later Judaism as the birth pangs of the Messiah, that is, the messianic woes.

B. Summary of vv. 1 – 6

The woman clothed in the sun with the moon under her feet and a crown of twelve stars is rooted in Joseph's dream (Gen. 37:1 – 9) and signifies the woman's exalted status. The twelve stars symbolize the twelve tribes of Israel. Indeed, righteous Israel, true Israel, is portrayed as a mother in the Old Testament (Isa. 54:1; 66:7 – 10; Mic. 4:9 – 10; 5:3; cf. Isa.

---

3. Which comes most likely from the Canaanite Baal Epic 67.1 – 3.
4. Old Testament scholars debate whether Isaiah 14:12 – 15 refers only to the fall of the king of Tyre or also to the fall of Satan presumed in Genesis 3.

7:14; 9:6; 26:18–19; cf. *4 Ezra* 10:44–46). The woman here is the remnant, whose suffering births the Messiah (vv. 1–2).[5]

The Dragon that awaits the birth of the Messiah for the purpose of devouring him (vv. 3–4) is an allusion to Herod the Great's attempt to kill baby Jesus so that he would not grow up to become a rival king (Matt. 2:1–18). Empowering Herod was Satan and the fallen angels (cf. Gen. 3; Isa. 14:12–15; cf. 2 Peter 2:4–5; Jude 6). The reference to the Dragon's seven heads/crowns and ten horns both draws on the ancient Near Eastern conceptions of Leviathan and contemporary Rome, with its seven hills and ten caesars in the first century (see my discussion of Revelation 13 and 17; cf. also Dan. 7:7–8, 20, 24).[6] So standing behind Herod was Rome, and both were inspired by Satan.

Verse 5 speaks of Christ's birth and then fast forwards to his resurrection/ascension to the throne of God, from whence he began his messianic reign (Ps. 2:9; cf. Rev. 2:27; 19:15).

In the meantime, the woman fled to the desert to be protected by God for 1,260 days (v. 6). This episode is expanded upon in verses 13–17. Verse 6 seems to allude to those Jewish Christians who fled to Pella around AD 68 before the destruction of Jerusalem in AD 70.

II. WAR IN HEAVEN (12:7–12)

The war in heaven between Michael and the Dragon has three points of reference: protological, eschatological, and historical. After examining this background, I will then summarize verses 7–12.

A. Points of Reference for the War in Heaven

As I noted above, there is a *protological*, or primeval, point of reference to the casting of Satan out of heaven described in verses 7–9, and it is the fall of Satan and his angelic followers at or before the time of creation (recall Isa. 14:12–15; Gen. 3; et al.). But second, this spiritual holy war also seems to envision a final, *eschatological* battle in which Satan will be cast out of heaven for good.

Apparently, for now, Satan still has access to heaven as the accuser of the brethren (cf. v. 10 with Job 1:6, 7, 9, 12; Zech. 3:1; see also Eph. 6:10–17). But one day that will change.

Yet there is also a *historical* perspective to Revelation 12:7–9—Jesus' death and resurrection. We saw in the gospel of John that Jesus' death on the cross began the defeat of Satan, the prince of this world (John 12:31–33; cf. Luke 10:18–19), and Revelation 12:7–8 concurs.

B. Survey of Verses 7–12

John envisions Michael the archangel as prevailing over the Dragon/Serpent/Devil/Satan/accuser of the brethren (all one and the same) and casting him to earth (vv. 7–8). Probably

---

5. There are three broad schools of interpretation of the identity of the woman in Revelation 12. (1) Catholics tend to identify her with Mary the mother of Jesus (cf. v. 4). (2) Dispensationalists identify her as Israel, not the church, who undergoes the Great Tribulation. (3) Most other interpreters equate the woman with the church, true Israel, who undergoes the Great Tribulation.

6. The references in Daniel allude to the three and one-half years that the Jerusalem temple was desecrated due to the abominable act of Antiochus Epiphanes in 167 BC (167–164 BC).

John believed Satan's defeat began at the cross of Christ but that its final fulfillment still lay in the imminent future (no doubt in connection with the imminent fall of Rome).

As Revelation 13–18 will make clear, in John's day the Dragon was the Roman imperial cult that was deceiving the world to follow Caesar (v. 9).

III. WAR ON EARTH WITH THE WOMAN AND HER SEED (12:13–17)

Two fates of Christians are described in Revelation 12:13–17: the protection of the woman (vv. 13–16) and the martyrdom of her seed (v. 17).

A. The Protection of the Woman (vv. 13–16)

With verse 13 the narrative of verses 1–6 is resumed, in particular the flight of the woman into the desert (cf. vv. 1b, 6 with vv. 13–16). It seems to me that the woman is true Israel (recall my earlier comments on vv. 1–2) and especially the remnant—the faithful Jews who are Christians. These are the ones who fled to the desert city of Pella before the fall of Jerusalem in AD 70.

The "desert" in the Bible signifies not just testing and trial (Matt. 3/Luke 3) but also divine comfort and protection (Ex. 16:32; Deut. 1:31; 8:2; Ps. 78:52; cf. John 6:31; Acts 7:36).

The reference to Satan spewing out water from his mouth to destroy the woman but the earth swallowing it up is an obvious allusion to ancient Israel's exodus through the Red/Reed Sea on dry ground (vv. 15–16). Moreover, the image of the woman being given two wings for her flight draws on the Exodus tradition. Thus Exodus 19:4 says of that event, "I

> Two fates of Christians are described in Revelation 12:13–17: the protection of the woman (vv. 13–16) and the martyrdom of her seed (v. 17).

Todd Bolen/www.BiblePlaces.com

Judean wilderness.

carried you on eagle's wings and brought you to myself" (cf. Deut. 32:10–11; Isa. 40:31; 1 Enoch 96:2; *T. Moses* 10:8).

The time period of the woman's safe stay in the desert was "a time, times and half a time"—that is, three and one-half years (cf. 11:2, 3; 12:6). The plural "times" is two years; the "time" is one year; and the "half" is a half year (cf. again Dan. 7:25; 12:7).

There seem to be two historical events behind Revelation 12:6 and 12:13–16. First, Jewish Christians fled east of Jerusalem about AD 66–68 to the desert city of Pella, which necessitated their crossing the Jordan River. Apparently they did so safely. But later in AD 68, when many Jews fled Jerusalem before the attacking Roman army, the Jordan River flooded, blocking the Jews' escape. According to Josephus, the Romans slaughtered them there en masse (*J.W.* 4.7.5/433–36). The former group was spared from the wrath of the Dragon (Romans) while the latter group was not.

B. The Martyrdom of the Woman's Seed (v. 17)

Frustrated in his plan to destroy the woman (the Jewish Christians), the Dragon turned his attention to the woman's offspring (v. 17).

Although commentators debate the identity of the seed of the woman, it is most likely to be associated with Gentile Christians—probably Gentile Christians martyred during the Neronian persecution (for Nero as the Beast/Dragon, see my comments on Rev. 13).

If so, we have here two different referents of the three and one-half years: divine protection during the siege of Jerusalem of the sealed Jewish Christians (Rev. 11:2; 12:6, 14) and divine permission for the martyrdom of many Gentile Christians in Rome under Nero (11:3; cf. 12:17). Nevertheless, the seed of the woman overcame the serpent (an allusion to the *protoevangelium* of Gen. 3:15) by remaining faithful to the commandments of God and the testimony of Jesus (v. 17).[7]

CONCLUSION

Thus Revelation 12 reminds one of Revelation 7 and 11: the Christian Jewish remnant is spared during the tribulation while the Gentile Christian masses are not.

---

7. Genesis 3:15 is often thought to predict the coming of the Messiah from the seed of the woman—Eve/Mary—who will crush the head of Satan. Therefore Genesis 3:15 is called the *protoevangelium*—first, or original, gospel.

REVIEW QUESTIONS

1. What are the seven personages that unfold in Revelation 12 – 14?

2. What ancient myths provide the backdrop for the woman, Dragon, and child episode in Revelation 12:1 – 6?

3. How does the life of Christ factor in that discussion?

4. How do the messianic woes factor in that discussion?

5. Who is the woman of Revelation 12:1 – 6?

6. What are three points of reference informing the war in heaven described in Revelation 12:7 – 12?

7. What historical event might lie behind the protection of the woman as depicted in Revelation 12:13 – 16?

8. What historical event seems to be behind the martyrdom of the seed of the woman as described in Revelation 12:17?

KEY TERMS

birth pangs of the Messiah

desert

Dragon

Herod the Great

Michael the archangel

Nero

Pella

protoevangelium

protological

woman with child

CHAPTER 50

The Two Beasts

REVELATION 13

Objectives

After reading this chapter, you should be able to:

- Explain who the beast from the sea is (Rev. 13:1–10).
- Discuss the Nero Redivivus legend.
- Explain who the beast from the earth is (Rev. 13:11–18).
- Discuss the meaning of the "mark of the Beast."
- Explain the meaning of "666."

INTRODUCTION

"The mark of the Beast," "666," "the Antichrist"! What Christian has not shuddered at the sound of those words, yet all the while secretly harboring excitement and suspense about pinpointing their meaning?

"The mark of the Beast," "666," "the Antichrist"! What Christian has not shuddered at the sound of those words, yet all the while secretly harboring excitement and suspense about pinpointing their meaning?

All three of these well-known apocalyptic images come together in Revelation 13 and its portrayal of the "two beasts." Although many within the futurist school have let their imaginations run wild in trying to identify the two beasts, the preterist school far and away has the better chance of nailing down the meaning of these three characters, especially those who rightly see the first-century Roman Empire in general and the imperial cult in particular as the background to Revelation 13. We will follow that procedure as we survey the two main points of the chapter: the beast from the sea (vv. 1–10) and the beast on the land (vv. 11–18).

I. THE BEAST FROM THE SEA (13:1–10)

Revelation 12:17 connects the Dragon—Satan—with the two beasts to be presented in Revelation 13: the beasts are inspired by the Devil. My working hypothesis for Revelation 13 is that the two beasts were the Roman procounsuls of the Asian province who enforced the worship of Caesar therein (Nero, then later Domitian, vv. 1–10) through the imperial cult priests who implemented the wishes of the procounsul at the local level (vv. 11–18).

I now discuss the beast from the sea (vv. 1–10) by covering the following points: his identity (13:1–2), worship (vv. 5b–6, 8), and persecution of the saints (vv. 7, 9–10).

A. The Identity of the Beast (vv. 1–3a)

The beast from the sea is empowered by the Dragon (12:17; 13:2, 4) to coerce worship for himself and the Dragon. We saw in Revelation 12 that the Dragon was a multivalent symbol, standing for Herod the Great in Jesus' day and, in John's day, Caesar. That Revelation 13:1–10 envisions Nero Caesar to be the Dragon who persecutes the people of God is clear enough; thus the two beasts represent Nero and the imperial cult. The ten horns could be the first ten caesars of Rome,[1] or in light of Revelation 13:12–14, they could be the ten

---

1. The book of Daniel forms a significant part of the Old Testament substructure of Revelation 13. Craig S. Keener (*Revelation*, NIV Application Commentary [Grand Rapids: Zondervan, 2000], 336) calls attention to the following parallels, to which I add a couple of others.

Revelation	Daniel
13:1	7:2–3, 7
13:2	7:3–6
13:4	7:6, 12
13:5a	7:8, 25
13:5b	7:25 (cf. 12:7, 11–12)
13:6	7:25 (cf. 8:10–11; 11:36)
13:7a	7:21
13:7b	cf. 7:14
13:11	8:3–25
13:14	3:1–7

provinces that comprised Rome in the first century AD. Or they could be ten client kings under Rome's auspices (see my later discussion of Revelation 17:12–14). Whichever of the above three alternatives is correct, any of them point to the Roman Empire as the key to identifying the ten horns of the beast from the sea.

The seven heads (hills, too, according to Rev. 17:9–10) are kings, most likely the seven Roman emperors who appeared and had passed from the scene by John's day.

My suspicion is that Revelation 13 was written by John between AD 68 and AD 70 but later updated during the reign of Domitian. This would account for both the Neronian persecution of Christians in Rome from 64 to 68 and Domitian's persecution of Christians in Asia Minor in the 90s that Revelation 13 presupposes. If we factor in here the enumeration of the seven kings from Revelation 17:9–11 (which, I suspect, was written by John *after* AD 70; see my later discussion), we might arrive at the following configuration of caesars:

Revelation 13:1–18/17:9–11	Roman Emperors	New Testament[2] Correlation
	Julius Caesar (44 BC)	
	Augustus (27 BC–AD 14)	Birth of Christ
	Tiberius (AD 14–37)	Life of Christ
	Caligula (37–41)	2 Thess. 2:4: attempted to set a statue of himself in the Jerusalem temple in AD 41
	Claudius (41–54)	Emperor during expansion of early church
"Is"	Nero (54–68)	Persecuted Christians in Rome, including Peter and Paul; the beast of Rev. 13 (AD 64–68)
Will reign briefly	Galba, Otho, Vitellius (68–69): three Caesars during Rome's brief civil war after Nero's death	Not alluded to
Has not yet come	Vespasian (69–79): the beginning of the Flavian dynasty (including his two sons Titus and Domitian)	Started the siege of Jerusalem in AD 68; proclaimed emperor in AD 69
	Titus (79–81)	Finished the siege and destruction of Jerusalem; proclaimed emperor in AD 79
	Domitian (81–96)	John exiled under his regime
	Nerva (96–98)	Released Domitian's exiles, including John

2. As we will see in our discussion of Revelation 17:9–14, John seems to update his identification of the Antichrist—from Nero (Rev. 13) to Domitian (Rev. 17:9–14), though for John, Domitian is Nero Redivivus.

The beast from the sea in Revelation 13:2 combines in one figure the four images of the four empires in Daniel 2, 7, 8, and 11: leopard, bear, mouth like a lion, and hideous beast.[3] But behind them all is the inspiration of the Dragon, Satan (Rev. 13:2b). Furthermore, the beast blasphemously claims to be deity (Rom. 13:1b), which reminds one of Nero's demand to be worshiped.

Megalomaniac that he was, Nero had coins minted on which he was called "Almighty God" and "Savior." Nero's portrait also appears on coins as the god Apollo playing a lyre. While earlier emperors were proclaimed deities upon their deaths, Nero abandoned all reserve and demanded divine honors while still alive (as did also Caligula before him, AD 37–41).

> The beast blasphemously claims to be deity (Rom. 13:1b), which reminds one of Nero's demand to be worshiped.

A statue of Emperor Nero from the Corinth Museum.

The reference in Revelation 13:3 to the Beast receiving a fatal wound but recovering from that wound no doubt alludes to the Nero Redivivus legend, now applied to Domitian.[4]

---

3. The identification of the four empires that Daniel sees in his visions is debated. One view interprets the data like this:

	Kingdom	Leader	Date
1.	Babylonian	Nebuchadnezzar	ca. 570 BC
2.	Medo-Persian	Cyrus	ca. 539 BC
3.	Greek	Alexander the Great	ca. 330 BC
4.	Revived Roman Empire	Antichrist	In the end time

But a more widely accepted view interprets the date like this:

	Kingdom	Leader	Date
1.	Babylonian	Nebuchadnezzar	ca. 570 BC
2.	Media	Astyages	ca. 550 BC
3.	Persian	Cyrus	ca. 539 BC
4.	Greek	Alexander the Great	ca. 330 BC

4. The Nero Redivivus myth is mentioned by, among others, Suetonius (*Nero*, 57), *Sib. Oracles* 4.119–22, 137–39; 5.137–54, 214–27; 8.68–72; 12.78–94; Dio Chrysostom (*Orations* 21.10); Tacitus (*Hist.* 2.8); Dio Cassius 63.9.3; 66.19.3; all of whom lived in the first century AD. Aune points out that there were perhaps three false Neros in the later first century: (1) an unnamed imposter who resembled Nero appeared in AD 69. He gathered an army in the desert with the purpose of attacking the Romans, but he was captured and executed. His body was taken via Asia to Rome. (2) The false Nero of AD 80 was Terentius Maximus, an Asiatic who looked and spoke like Nero, and who gathered followers from Asia to the Euphrates. (3) A third pretender appeared in AD 88. We do not know the name of this individual nor his fate or that of Terentius Maximus, because that part of the account of Tacitus (*Hist.* 2.8.1) is lost. It is interesting that the Roman satirist Juvenal calls Domitian "Nero" (*Satires* 4.38). Although Nero was public enemy number one in the West, he was very popular in the East among the Parthians. David E. Aune, *Revelation 6–16*, WBC 52B (Nashville: Thomas Nelson, 1998), 737–40.

B. The Worship of the Beast (vv. 3b–6)

If Nero was the Beast before AD 70, in John's day that "honor" fell to Domitian who, like Nero, demanded to be worshiped.

As commentators observe, the imperial cult of Domitian was pervasive in Asia Minor in the AD 90s. The beast from the sea may well have been, then, the procounsul representing the Roman emperor who arrived each year in the Roman province of Asia and was bound to set foot first in Ephesus. Since he necessarily arrived by boat, it could be said that he came "from the sea."[5] Indeed, at the time of the writing of Revelation, a 22- to 23-foot stave, or image, of Caesar had arrived in Ephesus.

The worship of the Beast is mentioned in verse 4 and elsewhere in Revelation (vv. 8, 12, 14; 14:9, 11; 16:2; 20:4). It is interesting that Roman senators were compelled to worship an empty chair representing the emperor Gaius (Caligula) in Rome (Dio Cassius 49.24.4; cf. Philo, *Leg.* 116). Also, everyone (except Jews) was expected to pray to Caesar and sacrifice to him as a god.[6] Indeed, Gaius, Nero, and Domitian required all to prostrate themselves in worship before them as a part of the imperial court ceremonial (Seneca, *Ben.* 2.12.1–2; Suetonius, *Vit.* 2; Dio Cassius 59.19.5; 59.24.4; 49.27.4–6; Philo, *Leg.* 116–17).

Jay King

Image of Emperor Augustus on Roman coin.

And the acclamation "Who is like the beast?" alludes to Old Testament hymns to Yahweh (Ex. 15:11; Pss. 18:31; 35:10; 89:6; 113:5; et al.) now blasphemously applied to Caesar. Verse 5 draws on Daniel 7:8, 20 where the little horn (Antiochus Epiphanes) blasphemed God and desolated the Jerusalem temple for three and one-half years, according to Daniel 7:25; 8:14; 9:27. Revelation 13:5 may well allude to Nero's persecution of Christians from AD 64 to 68. Revelation 13:6 says that the Beast blasphemed both God and his people ("dwelling place").[7]

C. The Persecution of the Saints (vv. 7–10)

Those who worship the Beast are not part of the slain Lamb's Book of Life (cf. 17:8; 1 Peter 1:19–20). But the true believer refuses to bow

---

5. As mentioned earlier, Leviathan appears in the Old Testament as the sea creature/monster created on the fifth day of creation, as was Behemoth, the land creature/monster.

6. S. R. F. Price's masterful documentation of the pervasive presence of the imperial cult in Asia Minor is a must-read for the background of Revelation: *Rituals and Power: The Roman Imperial Cult in Asia Minor* (Cambridge: Cambridge University Press, 1984).

7. The commentators rightly translate *skçnç* (v. 6) figuratively—the people of God, i.e., the saints—not literally—the Jewish temple.

If Nero was the Beast before AD 70, in John's day that "honor" fell to Domitian who, like Nero, demanded to be worshiped.

Indeed, Gaius, Nero, and Domitian required all to prostrate themselves in worship before them as a part of the imperial court ceremonial.

before Caesar and is persecuted by the Beast for not doing so. These verses recall Nero's persecution of Christians in Rome as well as Domitian's and, later, Trajan's persecution of Christians who did not bow before the imperial statue (see vv. 14–17; Pliny, *Ep.* 10.96.5; see my discussion below).

II. THE BEAST ON THE LAND (13:11–18)

The second beast that John saw emerged from the earth. I'll comment on three aspects of it: its description (v. 11), its role (vv. 12–17), and its number (v. 18).

A. The Description of the Second Beast (v. 11)

If "Antichrist" is a fitting description of the first beast, then "False Prophet" is an appropriate name for the second beast. This is so because the second beast performs religious functions that generate worship of the first beast. Most likely, the second beast from the land is the imperial priesthood of Asia Minor, which promoted the worship of Caesar at the local level. Priests of the imperial cult wore crowns that displayed the busts of the deified emperors and the gods whose cult they served.[8] The two horns are undefined but probably allude to Daniel 8:3 (two kings, the Medes and Persians, but one empire), perhaps suggesting that the second beast and the first beast form a powerful union. Or perhaps the two horns indicate the secondary importance of the second beast compared to the first beast with ten horns (Rev. 13:1a).[9] The second beast speaks on behalf of the first beast.

B. The Role of the Second Beast (vv. 12–17)

The role of the False Prophet was to facilitate the worship of the beast from the sea, who is Nero Redivivus—Domitian (vv. 12, 14). The beast did this in two ways: by manipulation through miracles (vv. 13–15) and by overt force (vv. 16–17).

1. Manipulation by Miracles (vv. 13–15a)

The imperial priesthood performed miracles ("signs") designed to deceive the people into worshiping Caesar (cf. 13:13, 14; 16:14; 19:20; cf. 2 Thess. 2:9–13; Mark 13:21–23//Matt. 24:23–25 based on Deut. 13:1–3). Two miracles are mentioned. First, the beast caused fire to fall from heaven (vv. 3–14), a parody of Elijah's miracle of fire (1 Kings 18:38; 2 Kings 1:10). Keener documents ancient priests like the Roman imperial priests who used machines to stage thunder or fire (cf. *Sib. Oracles* 3.63–74).[10] Second, he set up an image or statue to Caesar and caused it to speak (vv. 14–15). The creating of a cult image to generate worship to the emperor recalls Daniel 3:4–5, where Nebuchadnezzar set up a golden image presumably to himself to be

---

8. Aune discusses the sculptures displaying the garb of the imperial priests in *Revelation 6–16*, 756.
9. *Arnion* (13:11) here is a ram, not a lamb, for the latter does not have horns.
10. Craig S. Keener, *Revelation*, NIV Application Commentary (Grand Rapids: Zondervan, 2000), 351.

These verses recall Nero's persecution of Christians in Rome as well as Domitian's and, later, Trajan's persecution of Christians who did not bow before the imperial statue.

The role of the False Prophet was to facilitate the worship of the beast from the sea, who is Nero Redivivus—Domitian (vv. 12, 14).

worshiped. L. Thompson points out the proliferation of shrines and statues that were part of the imperial cult in Asia Minor. They were in buildings, porticoes, fountains, city gates, streets, and temples. Incense, wine, and bulls were sacrificed at shrines on behalf of Caesar.[11]

An entire branch of magic, called *theurgy*, was devoted to animating images representing Greco-Roman deities, including Caesar. David Aune supplies ancient reports of cult statues turning, sweating, weeping, or speaking, all designed to communicate oracles from the images.[12]

> An entire branch of magic, called *theurgy*, was devoted to animating images representing Greco-Roman deities, including Caesar.

2. Overt Force (vv. 15b – 17)

The second beast also enforced the worship of Caesar by show of force. Those Christians who did not bow before the emperor were executed (v. 15b; cf. 2:13 and Antipas's death).

Furthermore, the imperial priesthood forced all people to receive a mark on their right hand or forehead, without which they could not do business (vv. 16 – 17). The two motifs of the brand and the worship of the Beast are connected here in verses 15 – 17 and also in 14:11; 15:2; 19:20; and 20:4. The mark or brand (*charagma*) of the Beast could have been one of five things: (1) It could have been a parody of Jewish *tephillim* or phylacteries, leather boxes containing Scriptures emphasizing monotheism and worn on the hand and forehead. John considered Jews idolatrous for sacrificing on behalf of Caesar.[13] (2) The charagma could have been a brand for slaves. (3) It could have been Roman coins that bore the portraits and names of Roman emperors. Inability to buy and sell would result from refusing to use Roman coins. (4) The charagma could have been the imperial seal.[14] (5) A fifth possibility is that in the third century AD only those who worshiped Caesar received a charagma—a certificate—for use in the marketplace.[15] Perhaps this regulation was already in place during Domitian's reign. All of the above options, except for number 2, associate the mark of the Beast in some way with the imperial cult. Furthermore, the guilds in Asia Minor required their members to participate in eating meals dedicated to their patron gods,

A Jewish boy celebrating his bar mitzvah at the Western Wall, Jerusalem. Notice the tephillim (phylacteries) on the wrist and forehead of both man and boy.

© Dr. James C. Martin (bibleworldseminars@gmail.com).

---

11. L. Thompson, *The Book of Revelation: Apocalypse and Empire* (New York: Oxford University Press, 1990), 162–63.

12. Aune, *Revelation 6–16*, 763.

13. Josephus says that Jews were granted the right not to worship the Roman emperors as deity, but they did offer sacrifices in honor of them as "worthy men," which probably also included prayers for but not to the emperors (*Ag. Ap.* 2.6); cf. Philo (*Legat.*, 349–67; esp. 357).

14. Aune, *Revelation 6–16*, 767.

15. J. Nelson Kraybill, in his thoroughly documented work, *Imperial Cult and Commerce in John's Apocalypse*, JSNTSup 132 (Sheffield: Sheffield Academic, 1996), 137–39, points this out.

The Hebrew numerical valuation for NRWN QSR is as follows:

N = 50, R = 200, W = 6, N = 50, Q = 100, S = 60, and R = 200, which add up to 666.

including Caesar. Not to do so was to invoke excommunication from the guild and thereby loss of one's livelihood (cf. Rev. 2:18–29).

C. The Number of the Beast (v. 18)

The number of the Beast, who is supported by the procounsul and the imperial priesthood, is 666. In this number, one can detect the apocalyptic seer's usage of *gematria*, a mathematic cryptogram that assigns numerical values to letters of the alphabet. More than one scholar has seen a possible referent of this number in *Neron Kaiser*. The Hebrew numerical valuation for NRWN QSR is as follows: N = 50, R = 200, W = 6, N = 50, Q = 100, S = 60, and R = 200, which add up to 666.

This interpretation of 666 has been confirmed by the discovery of a document from the Judean desert dating to the mid-second century AD that spells Nero's name the same way.[16] So, for John, Domitian is Nero returned (13:3, 12, 14), the new and "improved" Antichrist.

CONCLUSION

The mark of the Beast, 666, and the Antichrist were first-century symbols applied to the Roman imperial cult, including at the very least the worship of Nero and Domitian. But according to the apostle John, Rome's power was vastly inferior to that of the Lion-Lamb (Rev. 5), and the empire's glory was about to crumble before the watching world (so Rev. 15–18)!

---

16. Quoted in Aune, *Revelation 6–16*, 770.

REVIEW QUESTIONS

1. What two basic topics does Revelation 13 discuss?

2. Who was the beast from the sea (Rev. 13:1–10)?

3. How could John call both Nero and Domitian the "Antichrist"?

4. What Roman emperors correlate with the New Testament?

5. Which first-century Roman emperors demanded to be worshiped?

6. Who was the beast on the land (Rev. 13:11–18)?

7. Discuss how the second beast evoked worship through the manipulation of miracles (13:13–15a) and overt force (vv. 15b–17).

8. What do you think the mark of the Beast was (Rev. 13:16–17)?

9. What did "666" stand for (Rev 13:18)?

KEY TERMS

666	*charagma*	Nero
Antichrist	Domitian	Neron Kaiser
Antiochus Epiphanes	False Prophet	seven heads/hills
beast from the earth	*gematria*	*tephillim*
beast from the sea	mark of the Beast	theurgy

CHAPTER 51

The Return of the 144,000

REVELATION 14

Objectives

After reading this chapter, you should be able to:

- Compare and contrast the setting of the 144,000 in Revelation 14 with that of Revelation 7:1–8.

- Discuss who the 144,000 in Revelation 14 are.

- Explain the two judgment motifs in Revelation 14.

INTRODUCTION

For the second time now we are introduced to the 144,000 (cf. Rev. 7:1–8). There is a key similarity and a key difference between Revelation 14 and Revelation 7.

On the one hand, both refer to the same group of people—the 144,000—who, in my estimation, were the Jewish Christian remnant that fled Jerusalem before it fell in AD 70 to the Romans. But on the other hand, the 144,000 of Revelation 14 find themselves in a different role than that in Revelation 7: here they constitute the Messiah's eschatological army ready to trounce the Roman forces (see 14:8). In other words, Revelation 7 records the flight of the 144,000 before the fall of Jerusalem, while Revelation 14 anticipates the imminent fall of Rome at their hands. Thus the fall of Jerusalem before AD 70 becomes the backdrop for the imminent fall of Rome post–AD 70. As we have seen so far, this twofold dynamic undergirds the book of Revelation. A simple chart highlights the differing roles of the same group of 144,000 (Jewish Christian remnant):

> For the second time now we are introduced to the 144,000 (cf. Rev. 7:1–8). There is a key similarity and a key difference between Revelation 14 and Revelation 7.

144,000 in Revelation 7	144,000 in Revelation 14
Fled Jerusalem	Lead the attack on Rome
To the desert, to prepare for the final battle	Poised for the final battle
Defensive	Offensive

Revelation 14 divides into four easily defined sections: the return of the 144,000 (vv. 1–5); the three angelic messages of judgment on the earth (vv. 6–12); a beatitude for the faithful (v. 13); and the twofold image of the final judgment (grain, vv. 14–16; winepress, vv. 17–20). I now summarize these four sections.

I. THE RETURN OF THE 144,000 (14:1–5)

Though commentators debate their identity, the 144,000 are in my mind the Jewish Christian remnant who fled Jerusalem before AD 70 but are now envisioned by John as the vanguard of the final battle against Rome. Some six reasons combine to suggest that the 144,000 are Christ's end-time holy warriors who will exact vengeance on Rome because the latter defeated Jerusalem.

1. The "Lamb" (v. 1) is the apocalyptic lamb/Messiah expected to judge Israel's enemies at the end of history (cf. Rev. 5:6 with *1 Enoch* 90:9, 38). Jesus, the slain paschal Lamb, will become the Lion/apocalyptic Lamb at his second coming.
2. The Lamb is standing on Mount Zion (v. 1). In Jewish apocalyptic literature the Messiah comes to Mount Zion—Jerusalem—in the end times to deliver Israel

and establish his kingdom in Jerusalem (Isa. 24:23; 31:4; Joel 2:32; Mic. 4:7; Zech. 14:4–5; *2 Bar.* 41:1–4; *4 Ezra* 13:29–50; *Jub.* 1:28; cf. Rev. 17:14; *Sib. Oracles* 5.414–33; 19:14; 1QM).

3. The mention in verse 4 of the 144,000 not defiling themselves with women indicates they are all males, who alone were permitted to fight in ancient Israel. Their commitment to celibacy alludes to the temporary refraining from sex with their wives that characterized ancient Israelite soldiers (Deut. 23:10; 1 Sam. 21:5). This was to be the pattern for the end-time holy war (1QM 7:3–6; et al.).

4. The 12,000 from each tribe alludes to ancient Israel's practice of drafting for war an equal number of soldiers from each of the twelve tribes (cf. Rev. 14:1–5; Rev. 7:4–8 with Num. 1:3, 18, 20; 26:2, 4; 31:1–6; 1 Chron. 27:23; 2 Chron. 25:5), here cast as the end-time military roster (cf. 1QM).

5. "Without guile" (v. 5; NIV, "blameless") is an expression used of the remnant in Zephaniah 3:13 (NIV, "do no wrong") and of the remnant as apocalyptic warrior-priests ("holy," "without guile") in the Dead Sea Scrolls, 1QM 7:4.

6. The 144,000 follow the Lamb (v. 4). This, in Revelation 19:14, refers to the Christian army fighting with the Messiah against his enemies.

These reasons from Revelation 14:1–5 combine to suggest that John presents therein the 144,000 as holy warriors who fight with Christ against Rome at the end of time.[1] The vision is proleptic; the war against Rome has not yet happened, but it will very soon.

If the 144,000 are to be contrasted with the martyred believers in the Great Tribulation (Rev. 14:12–13), as I suspect they should, then we find continued in Revelation 14 the pattern we detected earlier in Revelation 6–7 and 11–13: the Jewish Christian remnant who fled Jerusalem will survive the Great Tribulation (i.e., the persecution by Rome), while the majority of Christians will not. But in a classic turning of the table, the 144,000 who survive the tribulation will lead the army of Christians (who do not survive the tribulation) to exact vengeance upon the Dragon and his two beasts at the return of Christ. Revelation 14:6–20 envisions that coming judgment upon Rome.

> The vision is proleptic; the war against Rome has not yet happened, but it will very soon.

II. ANGELIC ANNOUNCEMENTS OF JUDGMENT (14:6–12)

At this point in John's visions of the past and the future, three angels announce for all the world to hear that God is about to judge the world, which he will do by turning up the heat in the next seven (bowl) judgments.

1. The first angel flies in midheaven (where all can see and hear), announcing to the earth that God the Creator is about to judge the world (vv. 6–7). Although the term *euangelion* refers to the gospel of the good news of Christ's death and resurrection elsewhere in the New Testament (see, e.g., 1 Cor. 15:3–4), here in Revelation it is not good news. Rather, it is the proclamation of coming destruction. The warning itself, however, is an opportunity for the earth to repent of following the Beast.

---

1. Later in this chapter we will show that Babylon in v. 8 is a code name for Rome.

2. A second angel then appeared with a more specific announcement of judgment, namely, Babylon is about to fall under divine wrath (v. 8; cf. 18:3). Three comments are in order here. First, the past tenses — "Fallen! Fallen is Babylon" — are prophetic perfects; the action has not yet occurred, but it is as certain as if it already happened. Second, Babylon is a code name for Rome (see Rev. 16:19; 17:6; 18:2, 10, 21; cf. 1 Peter 5:13; *Sib. Oracles* 5.143, 159; cf. the "kittim" [the Romans] in the DSS [1Qp Hab; 1QM]; Josephus, *Ant.* 10.276–77). Babylon and Rome are comparable because both were world empires and both destroyed Jerusalem and its temple. Third, Rome will fall because it has corrupted the nations with its immorality and idolatry (see Rev. 18 for more detail).

3. A third angel followed with an even more specific pronouncement of judgment, detailing the reason for God's upcoming wrath (vv. 9–12): those who follow the Beast by receiving his mark will be the recipients of divine wrath (cf. 13:16, 17; 14:11; 16:2; 19:20; 20:4). The "cup of wrath" is an Old Testament concept often connoting the covenantal curses upon either Israel or their enemies (Isa. 51:17, 22; Jer. 49:12; 51:7; Lam. 4:21; Ezek. 23:31–33; Obad. 16; Hab. 2:15–16; Zech. 12:2).

III. THE BEATITUDE FOR THE FAITHFUL (14:13)

That the ark of the covenant in the heavenly temple is still in view is clear from verse 15 (cf. v. 17; 11:19).

At this point in John's visions of the past and the future, three angels announce for all the world to hear that God is about to judge the world, which he will do by turning up the heat in the next seven (bowl) judgments.

This may well be the background to verse 13, which blesses those who die because they are faithful to the Lord; consequently, they go to their heavenly rest.[2] The blessing of rest is the Deuteronomic promise par excellence for those who obey the commandments of the Lord (Deut. 12:9; 29:9; Josh. 21:44; 2 Sam 7:11; 1 Kings 8:54–56; 4QFlor. 1:1–9; Matt 11:25–30; Heb. 3:1–4:13), which, in this case, means to be faithful to Jesus (v. 12; cf. 12:17).

IV. THE GRAIN/WINEPRESS JUDGMENT (14:14–20)

Revelation 14:14–20 forecasts the coming judgment upon Rome using two metaphors: the grain harvest (vv. 14–16) and the winepress (vv. 17–20).[3] I now touch upon these metaphors.

A. Grain Harvest Judgment (vv. 14–16)

Now there appeared before John's eyes one "like a son of man," seated upon a white cloud, with a crown of gold on his head and a sharp sickle in his hand (v. 14; cf. 1:7, 13; Dan. 7:13). That this personage is not Christ is clear from two points. First, he is referred to in verse 15 as another angel, whereas Christ is not called an angel elsewhere in Revelation. Second, the angel who exits the heavenly temple (v. 15)

---

2. This is one of seven beatitudes pronounced on the righteous in Revelation (1:3; 14:13; 16:15; 19:9; 20:6; 22:7, 14). All of them seem to be colored by the nuance of the covenantal/Deuteronomistic blessings.

3. David E. Aune demonstrates that Revelation 14:16–18 and vv. 17–20 are duplicates in *Revelation 6–16*, WBC 52B (Nashville: Thomas Nelson, 1998), 798–800. The only difference in the two accounts is that the first is that of grain judgment while the other is the winepress judgment.

orders him to begin the grain harvest; but nowhere else is Christ ordered about in Revelation. Like the winepress harvest to follow (vv. 17–20), so the grain harvest alludes to Joel 3:13 (Matt. 21:41). The role of angels as reapers is mentioned in Matthew 13:39 (cf. Matt. 24:30–31//Mark 13:26–27). The sickle as a metaphor for God's judgment alludes to, among other passages, Zechariah 5:1–5. For the harvest (grain, grape, or olive) as a symbol for divine judgment, see Isaiah 17:5; 18:4–5; 24:13; Jeremiah 51:33; Hosea 6:11; Joel 3:13 (Matt. 21:41); Mic. 4:12–13; Matt. 13:24–30, 36–43; Mark 4:29; *2 Bar* 70:20; *4 Ezra* 4:28–32.[4] The action of the angel swinging the sickle harvesting the earth is proleptic of the coming destruction of Rome at the second coming of Christ (v. 16).

> Revelation 14:14–20 forecasts the coming judgment upon Rome using two metaphors: the grain harvest and the winepress.

B. The Winepress Judgment (vv. 17–20)

Yet another angel exited the heavenly temple with a sharp sickle and called out to other angels to proceed ahead with gathering the grape clusters from the vineyard for the purpose of putting them into the great winepress of the wrath of God (vv. 17–19). Like the grain harvest, the gathering of grapes to be crushed in the winepress is a symbol in Scripture for divine judgment (see the above references). The connection of crushed grapes to blood is obvious, for they both have a similar color.

The height and distance of the flood of blood is extraordinary—up to the horses' bridles and across a space of 1,600 stadia, or about 184 miles (v. 20). As some commentaries have pointed out, such a distance was approximately the size of Israel from the Syrian border in the north to the Egyptian border in the south. Moreover, as Kenneth Gentry has rightly noted, the blood flow mentioned in verse 20 may well allude to the Romans turning ancient Israel into a killing field during the Jewish Revolt of AD 66–73 (see Josephus, *J.W.* 6.8.5).[5] In my estimation, verse 20 is a divine turning of the tables against Rome: Did it shed the blood of Israel? Then God will shed the blood of Rome very shortly.

The surface of a winepress in a village near Hebron.

---

4. The references are from ibid., 844. Furthermore, Aune shows convincingly that Revelation 14:16–20 as a whole is a pastiche of themes occurring elsewhere in Revelation (795–96).

5. See Kenneth L. Gentry Jr. in *Four Views on the Book of Revelation*, ed. C. Marvin Pate (Grand Rapids: Zondervan, 1998), 72–73.

REVIEW QUESTIONS

1. How do the 144,000 as depicted in Revelation 14 compare and contrast with Revelation 7:1 – 8?

2. What evidence indicates that the 144,000 are end-time holy warriors who will accompany Christ at his return for the purpose of destroying "Babylon" (Rev. 14:1 – 5)?

3. Is the "good news" announced by the angel actually good news (Rev. 14:6 – 7)?

4. What is the cup of wrath (Rev. 14:9 – 12)?

5. What is the Old Testament background for the beatitude pronounced upon the faithful (Rev. 14:13)?

6. What are the two metaphors used of the coming judgment when Christ returns (Rev. 14:14 – 20)?

7. What do the 1,600 stadia roughly correspond to (Rev. 14:20)?

KEY TERMS

1,600 stadia	end-time holy warriors	Lamb
144,000	gospel	Mount Zion
Babylon	grain harvest	rest/blessing
covenant	Jewish Christians/Pella	

CHAPTER 52

The Seven Bowl Judgments

REVELATION 15–16

Objectives

After reading this chapter, you should be able to:

- Correlate the trumpet and bowl judgments with the Egyptian plagues.

- Discuss how Revelation 15–16 portrays the imminent fall of Rome with the past fall of Jerusalem in 587 BC and AD 70.

- Explain the three new items the bowl judgments include compared to the trumpet judgments.

- Discuss the relationship between the fall of Rome and Megiddo.

INTRODUCTION

Revelation 15–16 records the unleashing of the seven bowl judgments—the last measure of the wrath of God—upon the beast and his followers on earth.

Revelation 15 announces the impending bowl judgments while Revelation 16 delineates the destruction they produce on the whole of physical existence—earth and the heavens. Before surveying these two chapters, I will first put forth my working hypothesis regarding the bowl judgments.

> Revelation 15–16 records the unleashing of the seven bowl judgments—the last measure of the wrath of God—upon the Beast and his followers on earth.

I. MY WORKING HYPOTHESIS

My thesis for interpreting Revelation 15–16 is that the bowl judgments, like the trumpet judgments (Rev. 8–9), portray the imminent fall of Rome against the backdrop of the fall of Jerusalem in 587 BC and again in AD 70.

Did ancient Egypt enslave Israel? Then, consequently, God defeated Egypt through the plagues of Moses and the exodus. So will God upend the Romans with a new, unprecedented barrage of Egyptian-like plagues for defeating Jerusalem in AD 70 and carrying away into slavery fifty thousand Jews (bowls

Left: Cyrus II of Persia, The Great. *Right:* Cyrus and the Hebrew exiles.

1–5; Rev. 16:1–11). Moreover, did Babylonia destroy Jerusalem and its temple in 587 BC? Then, consequently, God defeated Babylonia through Cyrus and the Medo-Persians. So will God defeat Rome through a new Medo-Persian Empire—the Parthian Empire from east of the Euphrates (bowls 6–7; Rev. 16:12–21).

The new material related to the bowl judgments—the battle of Armageddon (Rev. 16:16)—furthers the above connection: Did Rome invade Israel and destroy the holy city and the temple (AD 66–73)? Then God will soon regather the Roman Empire in Israel at Armageddon for the purpose of destroying that arrogant nation (cf. Rev. 16:12–21; 19:11–14; 20:9 with the Gog and Magog oracle in Ezek. 38–39 [especially 38:8; 39:2, 4, 17]; cf. also Joel 3:2; Zech. 14:2; *2 Bar.* 70:7–10; *1 Enoch* 56:5–8; *4 Ezra* 13:34–35; *Sib. Oracles* 3.663–68; 1QM 1:10–11; 15:2–3; see my discussion of Rev. 16:16 to follow).

God will do this, in part, through the Parthians ("the kings of the whole world," Rev. 16:14); the new Medo-Persians. Another way to say it is that the seal judgments announce *that* Rome will fall shortly; the trumpet judgments proclaim *how* that will happen—through Egyptian-like plagues and a Parthian invasion; while the bowl judgments tell *where* the defeat of Rome will occur—at Armageddon in Israel.[1]

All of this bespeaks the divine turning of the tables on Rome: did she defeat Jerusalem? Then God will defeat her.

II. SURVEY OF REVELATION 15–16

A. The Announcement of the Impending Bowl Judgments (chap. 15)

The unleashing of the bowl judgments is called a "sign in heaven," the third such reference in Revelation (cf. 15:1 with 12:1, 3). Seven angels are charged with carrying out these last judgments, which empty out the wrath of God on the totality of the earth (v. 1). For "the wrath (*thumus*) of God," see Revelation 14:10, 19; 15:1, 7; 16:1; cf. 9:15.

Before the throne of God proceeds a sea of glass mingled with fire as well as those who overcame (*nikaō*) the Beast (implied) by faithfully dying for Christ (v. 2). The fire represents the judgment that is about to fall on the earth. It may also communicate the conviction that the martyrs had come through the fire of the Great Tribulation and were thereby purged (see Matt. 3:11–12; Luke 3:16–17). The martyrs sang the song of Moses, the victory hymn sung after the exodus crossing (Ex.

> God will soon regather the Roman Empire in Israel at Armageddon for the purpose of destroying that arrogant nation.

> Another way to say it is that the seal judgments announce *that* Rome will fall shortly; the trumpet judgments proclaim *how* that will happen—through Egyptian-like plagues and a Parthian invasion; while the bowl judgments tell *where* the defeat of Rome will occur—at Armageddon in Israel.

---

1. David E. Aune insightfully shows that Revelation 16:12–16 and 19:19–21 form a continuous narrative about the end-time battle of Armageddon. That narrative was broken up to insert Revelation 16:17–19:18—the fall of Babylon/Rome (*Revelation 6–16*, WBC 52B [Nashville: Thomas Nelson, 1998], 866–67). We will explore later the implications of this literary structure.

A model of the tabernacle showing the entrance.

15:1 – 18; cf. Deut. 31:30 – 32:43; Ps. 90). The song by the martyrs is one of praise to God for his great and wonderful deeds, righteous and true ways, and holiness. Because of who God is, he will soon avenge the deaths of his children by judging the Beast and his followers (vv. 3 – 4). This is all accomplished through Christ; hence also the name of the hymn to God, the song "of the Lamb" (v. 3). Still, however, there is time for the nations to repent and worship God in the end-times (cf. v. 4 with Ps. 86:9 – 10 [LXX 85:9 – 10]; Isa. 2:2 – 4; 14:1 – 2; 45:14; 60:1 – 3; 66:18; Jer. 16:19; Zech. 8:20 – 23; Rev. 21:24).

Then the seven angels assigned to pour out the last seven plagues exited the temple (vv. 5 – 6).[2] The smoke-filled heavenly temple implies that the fire of divine wrath is about to be served up on the Beast and his followers (cf. vv. 7 – 8 with the smoke-filled Solomonic temple at its dedication; for smoke as a symbol for the presence of God, see 1 Kings 8:10 – 12; 2 Chron. 5:1 – 7:10). The seven libation bowls (v. 7) are the heavenly counterparts to the Jerusalem cultic utensils used for offering sacrifice and prayer to God. Jeremiah 7:20; 10:25; and 14:16 talk about God pouring out his wrath from libation bowls.

B. The Pouring Out of the Bowl of Judgments (chap. 16)

Chapter 16 records the actual dispensing of the bowl judgments (v. 1). The first bowl judgment poured out falls on the followers of the Beast (cf. v. 2 with the fifth trumpet judgment; sixth Egyptian plague). The second bowl judgment turned the saltwater into blood (cf. v. 3 with the second trumpet judgment; first Egyptian plague). The third bowl judgment turned all fresh water into blood (cf. v. 4 with the third trumpet judgment; first Egyptian plague).

Accompanying the third bowl judgment are two doxologies to God pronounced by the third angel (vv. 5 – 7).

These are known by scholars as a "judgment doxology" — praise to God for his righteous acts of judgment against evil (see

> Accompanying the third bowl judgment are two doxologies to God pronounced by the third angel.

---

2. The combination of temple/tent (*naos, skçnç*) is unusual, but in Psalms 26:8; 46:4 [MT 5]; 74:7 the term *tabernacle/tent* is used for the tent (cf. Heb. 8:2; 9:11; 4QMMT 32 – 35). The combination probably stems from the assumption that the earthly tabernacle was but the earthly copy of the heavenly tabernacle (Ex. 25:9, 40; 26:30; 27:8). It is interesting that in Rome the temple of Janus was opened as a declaration of war (Vergil, *Aenid* 1.294; Livy 1.19.2 – 4; et al.). Augustus closed the doors of the temple of Janus three times, the first time in January 29 BC, at the end of the civil war inaugurating *pax Romana* (the peace of Rome); a second time in 25 BC; and a third unspecified time (see Aune, *Revelation 6 – 16*, 878). The opening of the heavenly temple in Revelation 15:5 may, therefore, suggest that God is declaring all-out war on the Roman caesar and his devotees.

the earliest occurrence of this in the Achan episode, Josh. 7:19–21). God's holy wrath is poured out on the earth because its inhabitants shed the blood of his people/prophets. God is called here "the one who is and was" (cf. Rev. 11:17; cf. 1:4, 8; 4:8) and the "Almighty" (*pantokratôr*; see 15:3; et al.) in contrast, no doubt, to the grandiose claims of Nero and Domitian.

The fourth bowl judgment consists of intense, scorching heat from the sun, which burned the Beast and his followers (cf. perhaps seventh Egyptian plague). But instead of repenting, they become entrenched in their sin like Pharaoh of old (cf. vv. 8–9 with Ex. 7:13, 22; 8:15, 19, 32; 9:7, 12, 34–35; 10:1, 20; 11:9–10; 14:4; see also Rev. 9:20–21; 16:11). Blaspheming God constitutes breaking the third commandment (Ex. 20:7//Deut. 5:11).

The fifth bowl judgment is spelled out in Revelation 16:10–11: darkness is poured out on the throne of the Beast (Rome) and his kingdom (cf. the fourth trumpet judgment and the ninth Egyptian plague), which results in more intense pain. The connection between darkness and pain is left unexplained, but it is probably the cumulative effect of the previous bowl judgments.

The sixth bowl judgment is similar to the fifth and sixth trumpet judgments in that it probably envisions the invasion of the Roman Empire by the Parthians, "the kings of the east" (Nero Redivivus who leads the Parthian tribes, from across the Euphrates). But the sixth bowl judgment supplements the fifth and sixth trumpet judgments with three new pieces of information.

First, the Euphrates River is said to dry up (v. 12), something unheard of in the ancient Near East. The drying up of the Euphrates alludes to the exodus crossing of the Red/Reed Sea (Ex. 14) and thereby symbolizes a new exodus for the people of God. John apparently thinks God will use the Parthians to bring about that deliverance by defeating the Roman Empire.

Second, the symbolism of three frogs/demonic spirits sent by the evil trinity (the Dragon, the Beast [from the sea], and the False Prophet [the beast from the land]; see Rev. 13) also alludes to Israel's experience in Egypt, in particular the second plague consisting of the proliferation of frogs (Ex. 8:1–7). That plague is adapted here to say that the evil trinity is demonically inspired to stir up world war, probably the Beast and his client kings of the west versus the Parthians and the client kings of the east (vv. 13–14).[3] Yet behind it all is the plan of God, who will bring about Rome's ultimate defeat (at the hands of the Parthians?). That this battle is the end-time battle that immediately precedes the return of Christ is evident from verse 15, which admonishes believers to be spiritually alert and ready for the parousia (cf. 19:17, 19; 20:8).

Third, the place of that end-time battle will be "Armageddon" (v. 16), a name that most likely means "mountain of Megiddo." The town of Megiddo overlooks the bountiful Valley of Jezreel, which borders between Samaria and Lower Galilee. The international

> The sixth bowl judgment supplements the fifth and sixth trumpet judgments with three new pieces of information.

---

3. There is debate among interpreters of Revelation 16:12–16 and 19:19–21 as to whether the kings of the east (Parthians) and the kings of the west (Romans) meet at Armageddon to fight or to form a coalition against Jerusalem and Christ. The fifth and sixth trumpet/bowl judgments seem to presume the former, while Revelation 19:19–21 might presume the latter. I have opted for the conflict between the Parthians and Romans.

trade route — the Way of the Sea/Via Maris — (Isa. 9:1; Matt. 4:15) ran through Jezreel. Thus that valley, the breadbasket of Lower Galilee, and its strategic travel route became an important site to control militarily. Consequently, major battles were fought there, not only to control Israel, but also to dominate the gateway between north and south and east and west.

Third, the place of that end-time battle will be "Armageddon" (v. 16), a name that most likely means "mountain of Megiddo."

Thus its strategic setting and storied history made it inevitable that Megiddo was expected to be the location of the eschatological battle between Israel and the nations as the latter gathered to destroy Jerusalem. But God was expected to intervene on behalf of Israel, destroying their end-time enemies (Rev. 19:19; 20:9; cf. Ezek. 38–39; Joel 3:2; Zech. 14:2; *1 Enoch* 56:7; *4 Ezra* 13:34–35; *Sib. Oracles* 3.663–68).

From all of this, it seems that we are to understand John to say that God will lure the Roman army to Armageddon for the purpose of fighting the Parthians and, along the way, of finally destroying Jerusalem. But the Romans, in fact, will be the ones who are defeated by God at the hands of the Parthians.[4]

The seventh bowl judgment is the grand finale of all three sets of judgments in Revelation (seals, trumpets, bowls; see Rev. 16:17–18:24). Revelation 16:17–21 anticipates that event.

The seventh angel poured out his libation bowl into the air, resulting in cosmic upheaval, for this was the last and greatest of the divine judgments (vv. 17–21). Lightning,

---

4. That Rome was not done with attacking Israel in AD 73 is clear from the fact that Emperor Hadrian destroyed Jerusalem "for good" in AD 135 in order to put down the Second Jewish Revolt (AD 134–35).

An aerial view of the tell at Megiddo.

Todd Bolen/www.BiblePlaces.com

thunder, an unprecedented earthquake, islands and mountains disappearing, and massive hailstones (cf. seventh Egyptian plague, Ex. 9:22–26) all combined to topple the great city, Rome (cf. Rev. 17:18; 18:10, 16, 18, 19, 21), the New Babylon (see 14:8; 18:2; Isa. 30:30; *Sib. Oracles* 3.689–92). The division of the city into three parts alludes to Ezekiel's prophecy that Babylonia would destroy Jerusalem in three parts (Ezek. 5:2, 12). Now Rome, the New Babylon, will fall in three parts—divine turnabout is fair play! As far as John was concerned, God's patience with a disobedient world that worshiped the beast had run out. The time for repentance was over. All that remained was facing the terrifying wrath of God.

CONCLUSION

Nothing in Revelation 15–16 would indicate that the author of the Apocalypse has changed his perspective that God will shortly judge Rome because it once destroyed the Holy City and continues to persecute the followers of the Lamb. The seal, trumpet, and bowl judgments are unified in this assumption. Moreover, the bowl judgments continue the theme of the other two prior judgments—namely, the curses of the covenant are falling on the disobedient world of John's day while the covenantal blessings abide on the faithful followers of the Lion-Lamb.

REVIEW QUESTIONS

1. How do the bowl, trumpet, and Egyptian judgments line up with each other?

2. What is our working hypothesis for Revelation 15–16?

3. What three pieces of new information do the bowl judgments add to the fifth and sixth trumpet judgments?

4. Please discuss the historical and eschatological aspects of Megiddo.

KEY TERMS

Armageddon	Jezreel Valley	three frogs
bowl judgments	judgment doxologies	trumpet judgments
Cyrus	Medo-Persians	wrath of God
Egyptian plagues	Parthians	

CHAPTER 53

The Harlot and the Beast

REVELATION 17

Objectives

After reading this chapter, you should be able to:

- Discuss why Rome is the Babylon of Revelation 17.
- Explain the relationship between the harlot and the Beast.
- Identify the seven heads of Revelation 17:9 – 11.

INTRODUCTION

Revelation 17 records the beginning of the end of Rome, which by 19:10 has finally received its just deserts. Revelation 17:1–19:10 imaginatively paints a picture of Rome as a harlot riding a beast—this in contrast to the church, the pure bride of Christ (Rev. 21:9–22:9). Revelation 17 has bewildered many a reader, but it will be best negotiated by firmly keeping in mind the first-century background of the Roman imperial cult. The chapter is easily outlined: introduction to the vision of the harlot (vv. 1–3a), description of the harlot and the Beast (vv. 3b–6), and angel's interpretation of the vision (vv. 7–18).

> Revelation 17 records the beginning of the end of Rome, which by 19:10 has finally received its just deserts.

I. INTRODUCTION TO THE VISION OF THE HARLOT (17:1–3A)

One of the angels dispensing the seven bowl judgments revealed to John the harlot (*pornç*; cf. 5, 15, 16) who sits on many waters (nations, v. 1; cf. Ps. 144:7; Isa. 8:6–7; 17:12–14). The image of the prostitute is applied in the Old Testament to godless cities (Isa. 23:16–17 [Tyre]; Nah. 3:4 [Nineveh], including Jerusalem [Isa. 1:21]; cf. Jer. 3:6–10; Ezek. 16:15–22; 23:1–49; Hos. 4:12–13; 5:3). The adulterous lifestyle of the whore and her suitors is an Old Testament metaphor for Israel as being spiritually unfaithful to her covenant with Yahweh, her husband (Lev. 17:7; 20:5–6; Num. 14:33; 15:39; Deut. 31:16; Jer. 2:20; 3:2, 9; Hos. 1:2; 2:4 [Matt. 6]; 4:15; 9:1; et al.), now applied to Rome. The idea here is that Rome's political and economic liaisons with the nations seduced them to worship the Beast (v. 2). That Rome is in mind here is clear from the allusion to its seven hills (Capitol, Aventine, Caelin, Esquiline, Quirinal, Viminal, and Palestine, 17:9). Also, Rome was located on the river Tiber (cf. 17:1, 15). Moreover, Rome was called "Babylon" in the first century (1 Peter 5:13; *Sib. Oracles* 5.155–70).

> The idea here is that Rome's political and economic liaisons with the nations seduced them to worship the Beast (v. 2).

The revelation of the prostitute came to John as the Spirit whisked him away into the desert (v. 3a). Though "desert" is a positive place in Revelation 12:6, 14, here it is negative, signifying wicked Babylon, the desert by the sea (Isa. 21:1–10). The desert was thought to be the home of the demons, so Babylon (Isa. 13:21; Tobit 8:3).

II. DESCRIPTION OF THE HARLOT AND THE BEAST (17:3B–6)

According to verse 3b, there in the desert John saw the harlot, Rome, sitting on the Beast, inspiring Caesar to promote the imperial cult (blasphemous names). The seven heads, as verses 9–11 will reveal, are probably Augustus (27 BC–AD 14), Tiberius (AD 14–37), Gaius/Caligula (AD 37–41), Claudius (AD 14–54), Nero (AD 54–68), Vespasian (AD 69–79), Titus (AD 79–81), and the eighth—Domitian (AD 81–96), Nero Redivivus. The ten horns, as verses 12–14 suggest, are probably ten unnamed client kings of Rome.

The scarlet color of the woman's clothing is in keeping with the wealthy attire of ancient courtesans. The purple attire (cf. v. 4 with Rev. 18:16)[1] in antiquity symbolized status and royalty (Judg. 8:26; Esth. 8:15; Dan. 5:7; et al.), as did expensive jewelry.[2] Rome's "cup of abomination" alludes to LXX Jeremiah 28:7 and the metaphor there for Babylon. It is clear from this that Rome is New Babylon.

The mysterious name on the harlot's forehead may have been *Amor* (*Roma*, the goddess of Rome, spelled backward).

Rome's "love" polluted the souls of all who trafficked with her (v. 5). The woman was drunk with the blood[3] of the martyred followers of Jesus, an allusion to the Neronian persecution of Christians between AD 64–68 and, more current in John's day, to Domitian's tyrannical treatment of believers (v. 6).[4]

An image of the goddess Roma on a Roman coin.

III. THE ANGEL'S INTERPRETATION OF THE VISION (17:7–18)

John was perplexed by the vision of the harlot and the Beast, so the angel interpreted it for him (v. 7). Most likely Nero is the Beast who was, but had died (AD 68) by the time of the final writing of Revelation. Yet Nero was expected to appear again (Nero Redivivus), leading the Parthian armies against Rome (v. 8; see vv. 16–17). Thus the Beast (Nero) will turn on the harlot (Rome). Non-Christians will be enamored by Nero's return (probably in the person of Domitian) and will worship him. The utter contrast with the faithful followers of Christ is striking (v. 6). But Nero revived will meet with destruction at the hands of God (v. 8), at which time Christians will be vindicated.[5]

> The mysterious name on the harlot's forehead may have been *Amor* (*Roma*, the goddess of Rome, spelled backward).

The meaning of verses 9–11 is hotly debated,[6] but many interpreters prefer the following scenario: the "seven heads/hills" (vv. 9–11) are the seven caesars of the first century leading up till the time of John (assuming his first draft of Revelation was written at the time of the reign of Vespasian):

Fifth king = Nero (AD 54–68)[7]

Sixth king = "is" = Vespasian (AD 69–79)

Seventh king who will reign briefly = Titus (AD 79–81)

Eighth king is Beast who was—Domitian (AD 81–96), Nero Redivivus.[8]

---

1. See David E. Aune, *Revelation 17–22*, WBC 52C (Nashville: Thomas Nelson, 1998), 935, for the references.

2. Ibid.

3. "Drunk with blood" is a metaphor based on Ezekiel 39:18–19 (cf. Judith 6:4).

4. We may have two settings in Revelation 17: Nero/Vespasian (vv. 1–6/15–18), which is updated during the reign of Domitian (vv. 7–14).

5. Verses 8b and 14 represent two antithetical predestined fates: the wicked (v. 8b) and the righteous (v. 14).

6. Aune lists as many as nine configurations in *Revelation 17–22*, 947.

7. "Fallen" (*epesan*) alludes to the violent deaths of many of the Roman emperors early on: Julius Caesar was assassinated; Caligula/Gaius was also stabbed to death; Claudius was poisoned; Nero committed suicide by stabbing himself in the throat; Domitian was assassinated with a dagger. See the documentation in ibid., 949.

8. A number of authors considered Domitian to be a second Nero (Juvenal 4.37–38; Martial 11.33; Pliny, *Pan.* 53; Tertullian, *Apol.* 5; *Pall.* 4). My configuration of Revelation 17:9–11 assumes two things: (1) With many scholars, I do not count the three individuals who made bid for the throne between Nero's death (AD 68)

The "ten horns" are unnamed individuals soon to be appointed as client (puppet) kings under Rome's thumb (vv. 12 – 13). They will join forces with the Roman emperor to fight against the Lamb, but they will be destroyed (v. 14). There may be irony in the choice of title applied to the Lamb — "King of kings" — because the Parthian rulers described themselves with that term (Plutarch, *Pomp.* 38.2; Dio Cassius 37.6.1 – 3).[9] Yet they will be no match for the Lamb, the real King of Kings.[10] "Lord of lords" may allude to Daniel (Dan. 4:37 LXX);[11] if so, that title would also convey irony, because therein Nebuchadnezzar, king of Babylon, called Daniel's God "Lord of lords." Thus, for John, Jesus is "Lord of lords," not the Roman emperor of New Babylon.

Verse 14b is a touché: the followers of the Beast are not predestined to salvation, but the followers of the Lamb are.

Verses 15 – 17 seem to offer a different version of the intent of the ten horns than what is found in verses 12 – 14. There the ten client kings are aligned with the Beast to fight the Lamb, while here in verses 15 – 17 they seem to turn on the Beast, probably an allusion to the Nero Redivivus legend of Nero leading Parthians against Rome. Behind this civil war and the implosion of the Roman Empire is the hand of God. Thus the harlot on the Beast will rule only for a little while longer (v. 18).

---

and Vespasian's enthronement (AD 69), namely, Galba (June AD 68 – January 69), Otho (AD 69), and Vitellius (AD 69). (2) I begin counting the Caesars with Augustus (27 BC – AD 14), not Julius Caesar (101 – 44 BC). In the first century, some writers did begin their count with Julius Caesar (Suetonius, *Lives of the Caesars*; Dio Chrysostom, *Or.* 34.7; Josephus, *Ant.* 18.32), while others began with Augustus (Suetonius, *Laud.* 41; Tacitus, *Ann.*) as the first Caesar.

9. The references come from Aune, *Revelation 17 – 22*, 954.

10. There does seem to be tension between vv. 13 – 14 and vv. 15 – 17 relative to the ten horns/client kings. Thus: The kings join the beast in fighting the Lamb (vv. 13 – 14). The kings fight against the beast, which is instigated by the Lamb/God (vv. 15 – 17). This tension is perhaps solved if Revelation 17 were written in two stages: The time of Nero, when he was expected to lead the Parthian armies to overthrow Rome (vv. 15 – 17), and the time of Domitian, when the Parthian threat no longer loomed large thanks to the peace pact Domitian established with Parthia (vv. 13 – 14). See David E. Aune, *Revelation 6 – 16*, WBC 52B (Nashville: Thomas Nelson, 1998), 891 – 904, for discussion.

11. So G. F. Beale, *The Book of Revelation: A Commentary on the Greek Text*, NIGTC (Grand Rapids: Eerdmans, and Carlisle: Paternoster, 1999), 881 – 82.

REVIEW QUESTIONS

1. Why is the imagery of a harlot applied to ancient Rome (Rev. 17:1 – 3)?

2. How should we explain the relationship between the harlot and the Beast (Rev. 17:3b – 6)?

3. Who are the seven heads of Revelation 17:9 – 11?

4. Who are the "ten horns" (Rev. 17:12 – 17)?

KEY TERMS

Babylon the Great

harlot/Beast

Parthians

seven hills of Rome

ten horns

CHAPTER 54

The Fall of Babylon/Rome

REVELATION 18

Objectives

After reading this chapter, you should be able to:

- Discuss the three reasons for Babylon's fall.
- Discuss why the people of God should separate themselves from Rome.
- Identify the three groups who lament the fall of Rome.

INTRODUCTION

With Revelation 18 we reach the full extent of the pouring out of the bowl judgments upon Babylon/Rome. While, for John, Rome's destruction is soon, the seer's actual depiction of it is especially based on Jeremiah 50–51 (LXX 27–28) and the description there of the fall of ancient Babylon. Even though the fall of Babylon/Rome had not yet occurred, John speaks of it in the past tense because its fate is certain.

> With Revelation 18, we reach the full extent of the pouring out of the bowl judgments upon Babylon/Rome. Even though the fall of Babylon/Rome had not yet occurred, John speaks of it in the past tense because its fate is certain.

For summary purposes, we may divide Revelation 18 into four parts: prelude to the fall of Babylon (vv. 1–3), separation before the fall of Babylon (vv. 4–8), lament over the fall of Babylon (vv. 9–20), and finale of the fall of Babylon (vv. 21–24).

I. PRELUDE TO THE FALL OF BABYLON/ROME (18:1–3)

An angel with extraordinary authority descended from heaven, illuminating the earth by his splendor (v. 1). The angel cried out with a loud voice, announcing the fall of Babylon/Rome as if it had already happened (see v. 2a; cf. 21:9). In verses 2b–3, the angel cites three reasons for Babylon/Rome's fall: it had become a den of demons (cf. 17:3, Babylon in the "desert"), it was filled with immorality, and it was irresponsibly opulent and luxurious. The imperial cult no doubt fostered the first two accusations, while the third accusation—Rome's excessive wealth—was well-known in the first and second centuries (see Aelius Aristides, *Oratio* 26, AD 155).

II. SEPARATION BEFORE THE FALL OF BABYLON (18:4–8)

Then John heard another voice from heaven—probably God Himself—warning Christians to depart from Rome before divine judgment fell upon it (v. 4). The command is at least figurative: Christians in the Johannine community (and beyond) should be careful to disassociate themselves from any form of Rome's sins, including immorality, luxury, and obviously, any signs of worshiping the Beast (v. 5). But it may be that John intends the warning literally—Christians living in Rome should depart from the city before it falls. If so, then one might detect in this a similar directive to the one to Jewish Christians to leave Jerusalem before it fell in AD 70 (cf., i.e., Rev. 7, 12, 14).

The nature of God's judgment upon Rome is that of the covenantal curses, the divine cup of wrath (vv. 5–6), which will consist of pestilence, sorrow, famine, and other destruction (vv. 7–8). All this is in return for Rome's glorifying herself (implied—through the imperial cult) and playing the spiritual harlot (v. 7).

Rome and Italy.

III. LAMENT OVER THE FALL OF BABYLON (18:9–19)

Three groups of people are singled out by John as those who lament the fall of Babylon/Rome. First are the client kings/Rome's puppet governments (vv. 9–10). Second, the merchants of the world that traded with Rome grieve over the screeching halt brought to Rome's economy by the wrath of God. Some twenty-eight items of merchandise are listed in verses 11–17 (cf. a similar indictment against Rome's economy in *Sib. Oracles* 3.350–68). Third, the sea captains lament the fall of Rome as they watch from Ostia, Rome's port city (vv. 18–19). In contrast, the saints in heaven rejoice over God's punishment of Babylon/Rome because she shed the blood of God's people and dishonored his name (v. 20; cf. v. 24).

IV. THE FINALE OF THE FALL OF BABYLON (18:21–24)

Like the grand finale of a fireworks show, the seventh bowl judgment witnesses the complete destruction of Babylon/Rome. An angel throws a giant millstone into the sea, which disappears forever, thus symbolizing Rome's fate. Rome will come crashing down in a moment. No longer will the sound of music come from that city (v. 22a; cf. *Sib. Oracles* 8:113–19 [ca. AD 175]). All other traces of civilization will be gone from Rome: industry (v. 22b), family, even light itself (v. 23). All of this is because Rome persecuted God's people (v. 24).

> The angel cites three reasons for Babylon/Rome's fall: it had become a den of demons, it was filled with immorality, and it was irresponsibly opulent and luxurious.

Todd Bolen/www.BiblePlaces.com

Ancient Ostia.

A coin from the reign of Nero depicting a galley ship from Alexandria, Egypt.

CONCLUSION

Revelation 17–18 flesh out the seventh bowl judgment, which itself is the culmination point of the seal and trumpet judgments. Did Rome conquer Jerusalem and take its people captive? Then in a divine turning of the tables, God will defeat Rome, according to Revelation 17–18.

Although John did not see the day of the fall of Rome, Christians a couple of centuries later did, when Rome surrendered its sword to the cross of Christianity in AD 313. Mighty Rome fell to the Lamb that was slain!

REVIEW QUESTIONS

1. For what three reasons will Babylon/Rome be destroyed by God (Rev. 18:1–3)?

2. Why should the people of God separate themselves from Rome (Rev. 18:4–8)?

3. What three groups lament the fall of Rome (Rev. 18:9–19)?

KEY TERMS

Jeremiah 50–51

laments over Rome

Ostia

reasons for Babylon's fall

CHAPTER 55

The Parousia of Christ

REVELATION 19

Objectives

After reading this chapter, you should be able to:

- Summarize the four hallelujah hymns in Revelation 19:1–6.
- Discuss the messianic banquet and the bride of the Lamb (Rev. 19:7–10).
- Discuss whether the parousia has already occurred.

INTRODUCTION

The parousia of Christ, the second coming of Jesus, the return of the Lord—these are powerful synonymous descriptors for Revelation 19. Or are they? Perhaps the parousia that John has in mind refers not to a future fall of Rome but to the past fall of Jerusalem in AD 70. We will sort out this issue and others as we move through this magnificent chapter.

Before doing so, however, I want to call attention to the fact that Revelation 19:1–10 is a text that alludes to two very different cities: Babylon, the harlot (Rev. 17–18), and the New Jerusalem, the bride of Christ (Rev. 21–22). Indeed, the two fates of Babylon and the New Jerusalem are juxtaposed in Revelation 19:1–10:

vv. 1–5: the destruction of Babylon

vv. 6–10: the deliverance of the bride of Christ

Keep these two antithetical destinies in mind as we move through the remainder of Revelation. But now let's turn our attention to a survey of Revelation 19, which divides into two parts: the hallelujahs (vv. 1–10) and the parousia of Christ (vv. 11–21).

> The parousia of Christ, the second coming of Jesus, the return of the Lord—these are powerful synonymous descriptors for Revelation 19. Or are they?

I. THE HALLELUJAHS (19:1–10)

As mentioned above, two themes dominate these verses: the destruction of Babylon and the deliverance of the bride of Christ, the New Jerusalem.

A. The Destruction of Babylon/Rome (vv. 1–5)

After the fall of Babylon, John hears the heavenly hosts sing hallelujah to God for inflicting punishment on Babylon/Rome. Indeed, the word *hallelujah* (which means "praise Yahweh") occurs four times in verses 1–6 (vv. 1, 3, 4, 6). Two of the hallelujahs introduce judgment doxologies in the aftermath of the fall of Babylon (vv. 1, 3), while the other two hallelujahs introduce deliverance doxologies concerning the bride of Christ.

The first hallelujah introduces a hymn to God, ascribing to him victory ("salvation and glory and power") over wicked Babylon (v. 1b). God's righteousness has just been manifested in stupendous victory in two ways: the wickedness of the great whore Babylon/Rome is ended (v. 2a), and the deaths of the servants of the Lord are finally avenged (v. 2b).

The second hallelujah is a shortened version—a chorus if you will—of the first: the smoke of Babylon's fall ascends forever. That is, its destruction is eternal (v. 3).

Todd Bolen/www.BiblePlaces.com

This young woman in marble shows the elaborate hairstyles popular among aristocratic women of the late first century. The author of Revelation denounces Rome in the symbol of a vain and luxurious woman (Rev. 17:1–5).

The third hallelujah begins to take on a positive note by focusing on the arrival of God's kingdom—the heavenly hosts, including the twenty-four elders and the four cherubim, fall prostrate before God and worship him (v. 4). An invitation is then given to all the saints of God to join in the heavenly worship (v. 5).

B. The Deliverance of the Bride of Christ (vv. 6–10)

The fourth hallelujah is uttered again by the heavenly hosts in view of the arrival of the kingdom of God (vv. 6–10). For John, the full manifestation of that kingdom on earth was so certain that he could pronounce it as present (v. 6). The divine judgments recorded in Revelation 6–18 will have accomplished their purpose of preparing the earth for the descent of God's kingdom by purging the world of all evil.

In verses 7–10, John specifies the subjects of God's kingly rule—the righteous bride of Christ. Comments are then made concerning three aspects of these people of God: their wedding to the Lamb, their clothing, and wedding feast.

1. The people of God—those martyred and those alive at the return of Christ (see vv. 11–21)—are called the "wife" of the Lamb. In other words, the second coming of Christ constitutes the wedding day of the church to Jesus the Messiah (v. 7a; cf. v. 9). The metaphors of Christ as the bridegroom and the people of God as the bride were widespread in early Christianity (Matt. 9:15b//Mark 2:20//Luke 5:35; Matt. 25:1–13; 2 Cor. 11:2; Eph. 5:25–32; Rev. 19:7; 21:2, 9; 22:17; *2 Clem.* 14:2; Tertullian, *Marc.* 5–18; Augustine, *Serm.* 40.6; et al.). The "bride of Christ" figure of speech is the Christian adaptation of the Old Testament concept of the marriage of Yahweh, or Messiah, to Israel (Isa. 49:18; 50:1; 54:1–6; 62:5; Jer. 3:20; Ezek. 16:8–14; Hos. 2:19–20; et al.; cf. the allegorical reading of the Song of Songs by the first century AD).

2. The wedding clothing, the trousseau, with which the church adorns itself is righteousness (vv. 7b–8; 21:2; cf. Isa. 61:10; 2 Cor. 11:2; Eph. 5:22–33). This is in stark contrast to the wickedness of Babylon/Rome (18:12, 16). Such righteous acts stem from the believer's faithfulness to Christ even when pressured to the point of death to receive the mark of the Beast—that is, to submit to the worship of Caesar.

3. The people of God/bride of Christ will celebrate the wedding feast of the Lamb at the parousia (v. 9).

This is the fourth of seven beatitudes, or makarisms, in Revelation (the others are found in 1:3; 14:13; 16:15; 20:6; 22:7, 14). This blessing is pronounced over those who are invited to participate in the messianic banquet. This banquet seems to combine the hope of an end-time meal for the righteous provided by God (Isa. 25:1–8; Matt. 8:11//Luke 13:29; cf. Matt. 26:29//Mark 14:25//Luke 22:18)

> The divine judgments recorded in Revelation 6–18 will have accomplished their purpose of preparing the earth for the descent of God's kingdom by purging the world of all evil.

> The people of God/bride of Christ will celebrate the wedding feast of the Lamb at the parousia.

Jewish wedding feast. The bride and groom are like king and queen under a decorated canopy at their wedding feast.

and the eschatological nourishment to be given by the Messiah (Luke 22:28–30; *1 Enoch* 62:14; *3 Enoch* 48a:10; cf. Rev. 2:7; 22:14).

John's response to these hallelujahs to God for his saving acts was to (inappropriately) worship the angel, the interpreter of the vision (v. 10a). The angel rightly rebuked John for doing so, reminding him that he (the angel) was a fellow servant with the saints, whose task was the same as theirs — to testify concerning Jesus, empowered by the Holy Spirit of prophecy (cf. Rev. 22:8b–9).

II. THE PAROUSIA OF CHRIST (19:11–21)

Before summarizing this section, I will first interact with the key interpretive issue regarding these verses.

A. The Interpretive Issue of Revelation 19:11–21

The key hermeneutical decision that must be made about Revelation 19:11–21 concerns the nature of the parousia of Christ. Does it refer to Christ's coming in judgment on Jerusalem in AD 70 at the hands of the Romans, as many preterists think? Or does the parousia refer to Christ's future second coming to destroy his enemies (Rome and beyond)?

1. Many preterists read Revelation 19:11–21 as referring to Christ's coming in judgment on Jerusalem in AD 70. In other words, there will be no future second coming of Christ. This view is based on the assumption that Babylon in Revelation 17–18 was past Jerusalem, not future Rome. Rome was the Beast that turned on and destroyed Jerusalem the harlot because she joined Rome in persecuting Christians in Asia Minor.[1]

---

1. See Kenneth L. Gentry Jr. in *Four Views on the Book of Revelation*, ed. C. Marvin Pate (Grand Rapids: Zondervan, 1998), 80–81.

2. However, while there is an element of truth to the strictly preterist view here, the preterist-futurist view of the parousia of Christ spelled out in Revelation 19:11–21 (that the second coming of Christ still lies in the future) seems to be the correct interpretation of that passage, for four reasons.

   a. We observed earlier that New Babylon in Revelation 17–18 undoubtedly is Rome, not Jerusalem.

   b. We saw from the three sets of judgments in Revelation 6–16 that the already–not yet pattern therein presupposes the fall of Jerusalem in the past has been the backdrop to the fall of Rome in the future. Thus the seal judgments (Rev. 6–7) reapply the Olivet Discourse (which was largely fulfilled at the fall of Jerusalem in AD 70) to a future fall of Rome. The trumpet judgments (Rev. 8–9) and the bowl judgments (Rev. 15–16) assume Jerusalem's fall to ancient Babylon to be the backdrop for an imminent fall of Rome to the new Medo-Persians — the Parthians.

   c. We saw from Revelation 16:12–16 that John probably believed that Rome and Parthia will clash near Jerusalem (at Armageddon) in their bid to rule the world. In particular, Rome will be unsuccessful in its attempt to conquer Jerusalem, a theme anticipated in ancient Judaism (cf. Rev. 19:11–17; 20:7–10 with Pss. 46; 48:1–8; 76:1–9; Isa. 17:12–14; 29:1–8; Ezek. 38–39 [the battle of Gog and Magog]; Joel 3:1–17; Zech. 12:1–9; *1 Enoch* 56:5–8; 100:1–6; *4 Ezra* 13:5–11, 29–38; *Sib. Oracles* 3.657–701; 1QM 11:16–17).[2]

A historic commercial crossroad and the site of important battles in Israel's history, the plain of Esdraelon is sometimes identified as the scene of the vast conflict pictured in Revelation 16 and 19. The Mount of Megiddo (Armageddon) overlooks the plain of Esdraelon.

© Dr. James C. Martin (bibleworldseminars@gmail.com).

   d. Revelation 19:11–21 matches descriptions from elsewhere in the New Testament that refer to the second coming of Christ in glory at the end of history (Matt. 24:30–31//Mark 13:26//Luke 21:27–28; 2 Thess. 2:8; Titus 2:13–14; Jude 14–15).

Only with great difficulty can these texts be explained in terms other than the traditional understanding of the parousia, and they concur with Revelation 19:11–21.[3]

---

2. Revelation 11 may presume the same scenario of the deliverance and restoration of Israel; see ibid., 169–70.

3. Though some have tried to do so; see Kenneth L. Gentry Jr., *Before Jerusalem Fell: Dating the Book of Revelation* (Powder Springs, Ga.: American Vision, 1998), 133–45; Gary DeMar, *Last Days Madness: Obsession of the Modern Church* (Powder Springs, Ga.: American Vision, 1999), 263–65; David Chilton, *The Days of Vengeance: An Exposition of the Book of Revelation* (Fort Worth, Tex.: Dominion, 1987), 5–75.

B. A Survey of Revelation 19:11–21

Revelation 19:11–21 divides into two parts: the return of Christ (vv. 11–16) and the carnage that falls on the enemies of Christ (vv. 17–21).

1. The Return of Christ (vv. 11–16)

John's vision of the parousia of Christ resumes with the opening again of heaven in verse 11 (cf. 4:1). What is revealed to the author is the future descent to earth of Christ on a white stallion (v. 11), which is a parody of the Antichrist (see Rev. 6:2), the Roman emperor. Christ is faithful and true (cf. 3:14), with reference to his word and actions. Truly, the war Christ rages is a just war (v. 11). Christ's eyes are like a brilliant flame (cf. 1:14; 2:18), which, along with the dazzling diadems on his head, bespeak his authority over human existence, including Caesar (v. 12; see 12:3). The name that no one knows (v. 12) is inscribed on Christ's thigh and may only be known by the saints as "the King of kings and Lord of lords" (cf. "Word of God," v. 13; and v. 12 [see also v. 16; 17:14]). Indeed, the sword that proceeds from Christ's mouth (v. 15) is the Word of God (v. 13).

> Revelation 19:11–21 matches descriptions from elsewhere in the New Testament that refer to the second coming of Christ in glory at the end of history.

Christ's robe is stained with blood (v. 13), an allusion to his sacrificial death and also to his conquest of his enemies (cf. Ex. 15; Deut. 33; Judg. 5; Isa. 26:16–27:6; 59:15–20; 63:1–6; Hab. 3; Zech. 14:1–21).

The heavenly armies that followed Christ are no doubt comprised of the 144,000, the martyred saints, and the angelic hosts. They, like Christ their leader, ride on white horses and are clothed with white linen — righteousness (v. 14). Ironically, the actual involvement of the heavenly army in the eschatological holy war is not mentioned.

> Christ's robe is stained with blood (v. 13), an allusion to his sacrificial death and also to his conquest of his enemies.

Jesus is the Davidic Messiah. His sword smites the nations (Isa. 11:3–4), and he rules them with a rod of iron (Ps. 2:9). His judgment upon his enemies is compared to the divine wrath of the winepress (recall 14:17–20; cf. Isa. 63:1–6). Here Christ is portrayed in similar terms as Yahweh the Warrior who destroys Israel's enemies in the Old Testament (see again Isa. 63:1–6; cf. Ex. 15:3–4).

2. The Carnage of the Enemies of Christ (vv. 17–21)

An inclusio centering on the theme of birds eating the flesh of Christ's enemies frames verses 17–21. The paragraph is a gross parody of the wedding feast of the Lamb (v. 9). An angel issues an invitation to the birds of the skies to eat the flesh of the dead enemies of Christ: kings, generals, the powerful, the cavalry, free and slave, small and great—all opposed to God (vv. 17–18). Revelation 19:17–18 parallels the defeat and destruction of Gog and Magog recorded in Ezekiel 39:17–18.

The beast, the fallen prophet, and the kings of the earth and their armies are captured, and their imposition of Caesar worship is ended with their demise in the lake of fire (vv. 19–21; cf. 17:14; 20:7–10). "Lake of fire" refers to the torment of eternal hell (see

20:10, 14–15[3x]; 21:8). It seems to be John's usage of an Egyptian concept of punishment (*The Book of the Dead*), though it must be said that Judaism knew of the idea of streams of fire falling from heaven as divine judgment (*Pss. Sol.* 15:6–7; *Sib. Oracles* 2.196–205, 286; 3.54, 84–85; 7.120–21; 8:243). That metaphor could also be applied to the underworld (see Isa. 66:24; *1 Enoch* 10:6, 13; Matt. 5:22; 13:42, 50; 18:9; 25:41; Mark 9:43, 48).[4] *Second Enoch* 10:2 pulls the above two traditions together, which portray the underworld as the site for a river of fire.

CONCLUSION

Revelation 19 is unique in the New Testament in its depiction of the actual proceedings to unfold at the parousia of Christ. Jesus, the Divine Warrior, will return to repay Rome for its unjust treatment of him and his followers. Moreover, did the Roman general celebrate his victory over Jerusalem in a triumphant parade in Rome (see the Arch of Titus)? So will Christ at his return celebrate his triumph over Rome.

> An inclusio centering on the theme of birds eating the flesh of Christ's enemies frames verses 17–21. The paragraph is a gross parody of the wedding feast of the Lamb (v. 9).

Interestingly, the messianic armies that accompany Jesus at his second coming do not engage in conflict with the enemies of God. That task is accomplished by Christ alone. This whole scene raises a powerful question of John's readers: will they bow before Christ the sacrificed Lamb now, or will they wait to bow before Jesus the Lion of the tribe of Judah later? The first response leads to mercy; the last response leads to unending torment.

---

4. References come from David E. Aune, *Revelation 17–22*, WBC 52C (Nashville: Thomas Nelson, 1998), 1066.

Arch of Titus in Rome.

REVIEW QUESTIONS

1. Please summarize the four hallelujah hymns in Revelation 19:1 – 6.

2. What is the Old Testament background of the concept that the church is the bride of Christ (Rev. 19:6 – 10)?

3. What is the wedding clothing of the bride of Christ a symbol of?

4. What is the messianic banquet (Rev. 19:9 – 10)?

5. What reasons suggest the parousia of Christ is still a future event and not to be equated with the fall of Jerusalem in AD 70?

6. Please explain the titles/descriptions of Christ at his return (Rev. 19:11 – 16).

7. What is the carnage of Christ's enemies a parody of (Rev. 19:17 – 21)?

KEY TERMS

Babylon	fall of Jerusalem in AD 70	parousia
beatitude	Gog and Magog	second coming of Christ
bride of Christ	hallelujah choruses	Yahweh the Warrior
Davidic Messiah	judgment doxologies	triumphant procession of the Roman general
deliverance doxologies	King of kings and Lord of lords	

CHAPTER 56

The Millennium

REVELATION 20

Objectives

After reading this chapter, you should be able to:

- Explain the three schools of interpretation of Revelation 20.
- Identify who reigns with Christ during the millennium.
- Identify Gog and Magog.

INTRODUCTION

Three schools of thought have competed for the interpretation of Revelation 20 and the millennial kingdom described therein. *Amillennialists* argue that the kingdom of God portrayed in Revelation 20 is spiritual in nature and is to be viewed figuratively: God's kingdom is intimately associated with the church, which between the first and second comings of Christ accomplishes God's will on earth. And the church does this despite the opposition it encounters in the midst of the Great Tribulation. For this school of thought, the binding of Satan in Revelation 20 for a short period of time corresponds to the present rule of Christ through the church until the parousia (vv. 1–4), which began at the cross/resurrection (John 12:31–33). The reference to the first resurrection is an allusion to Christians' conversion, at which time they began to reign with Christ (cf. Eph. 2:1–7; Col. 3:1–4). The reference to the battle of Gog and Magog anticipates the second coming of Christ, who at that time will finally defeat Satan and then establish the eternal state (Rev. 21–22). So in this configuration there will be no temporary, one-thousand-year reign of Jesus on earth between his parousia and the eternal state. The kingdom of God is here and now. Hence the name—"a [no] millennium."

Postmillennialists also argue that the kingdom of God is presently being manifested through the church of Christ, which will so effectively preach the gospel that the very structures of society will be transformed into righteous institutions. This will be the millennium and may or may not last for a thousand years. After the reign of the church over the world, Christ will return (at the end of the millennium) to establish the eternal state (Rev. 21–22). Hence the name—"post [after] the millennium": Christ will return after the millennium. Other postmillennialists argue that Christ returned in judgment on Jerusalem in AD 70, and at that point his kingdom began to rule through the church. This state of affairs will continue until the eternal state is ushered in.

Late Roman iron house key.

Premillennialists argue that Christ will return at the end of the Great Tribulation and establish his literal one-thousand-year reign in Jerusalem. Christians will reign with him, representing his kingdom throughout the earth. This will be a time of unprecedented peace, because Satan will be bound during this time. After the thousand years, Satan will be released for a little time for the purpose of stirring up the nations to overthrow Christ's rule. But the enemies of God will finally be defeated by Christ, and then the eternal state will begin (Rev. 21–22). Thus Christ will return "pre" (before) the millennium to establish his temporary kingdom. This chapter will argue that the premillennial view is the most natural reading of Revelation 20.

The eschatological drama of Revelation 20 unfolds in four acts: the temporary binding of Satan (vv. 1–3), the enthronement of the martyrs (vv. 4–6), the release of Satan and the end-time holy war (vv. 7–10), the eternal judgment at the great white throne (vv. 11–15).

I. THE TEMPORARY BINDING OF SATAN (20:1–3)

An angel descended from heaven with a key to the Abyss (the bottomless pit below the surface of the earth reserved for Satan and his demons) and a chain. The use of chains to bind Satan and his hosts is an apocalyptic motif (*2 Bar.* 56:13; *1 Enoch* 54:3–5; *Sib. Oracles* 2.289; 2 Peter 2:4; Jude 6) and may derive from earlier Greek traditions that record the binding of the Titans in Tartarus (Hesiod, *Theog.* 718; Hyginos, *Fabulae* 15c).[1] Satan's aliases are used — "dragon," "serpent," "devil," "Satan" (cf. v. 2 with Rev. 12:3, 4, 7, 9, 13, 16, 17; 13:2, 4). As Aune notes, the binding of Satan and casting him into the Abyss is essentially an exorcism (see 2 Peter 2:4; Jude 6; *2 Bar.* 56:13; *1 Enoch* 10:4, 11–12; 13:1; 14:5; 18:16; 21:3–6; *Jub.* 5:6; 10:7–11).[2] The "Abyss," or bottomless pit, seems to refer to a temporary subterranean place of incarceration for fallen angels at the present time (2 Peter 2:4; Jude 6) and for Satan at the end of time (Rev. 20:1–3), analogous to the Greek idea of Tartarus. The temporary Abyss will itself eventually be thrown into the eternal lake of fire (Rev. 20:7–15). While this scene could be a dramatization of Christ's defeat of Satan at the cross, the mention in verse 3 that Satan would not be able to deceive the nations for a thousand years more likely is understood by John as a literal event to occur in the near future, for obviously it had not happened by John's day. *Chilia* is the Greek word for a thousand years and also appears to be understood by John as literal. Christ will return (Rev. 19:11–21) and cast Satan into the Abyss for one thousand years. This will provide unprecedented peace and harmony on earth for that period of time, that is, the millennium (the Latin translation of chilia). After that temporary period, Satan will be released (implied, by God) for the purpose of staging one last, brief stand for evil (v. 3).[3]

> Christ will return (Rev. 19:11–21) and cast Satan into the Abyss for one thousand years. This will provide unprecedented peace and harmony on earth for that period of time, that is, the millennium.

II. THE ENTHRONEMENT OF THE MARTYRS (20:4–6)

There is much debate over the identification of the "thrones on which were seated those who had been given authority to judge" that John sees, with three possibilities emerging: heavenly thrones seating angels (cf. Dan. 7:9–10); thrones seating martyrs who are singled out for special privilege by reigning with Christ while the rest of humanity (Christians included) await the general resurrection at the end of the millennium (cf. Dan. 7:22a); and thrones seating all the saints who will reign with Christ during the millennium.

Two reasons might indicate that it is the martyred Christians that John sees as enthroned in the future millennial reign with Christ. First, grammatically, undoubtedly the antecedent of "they" who came to life (v. 4b) is the martyrs of the Great Tribulation (v. 4a). Contextually, the description of the martyrs in verse 4 matches the description of the martyrs of the Neronian persecution referred to in Revelation 6:9. Still, however, elsewhere in Revelation John expects that all Christians will reign with Christ (Rev. 1:6; 2:26–28; 3:12, 21; 5:10).

---

1. See David E. Aune's references in his *Revelation 17–22*, WBC 52C (Nashville: Thomas Nelson, 1998), 1081.

2. Ibid., 1082–83.

3. John may derive his concept of one thousand years from Psalm 90:4, where a day is said to equal a thousand years in God's timetable (cf. 2 Peter 3:8). In other Jewish works advocating a temporary messianic kingdom, the time of that period varies: according to *1 Enoch* 91:12–17, a week; according to *4 Ezra* 7:26–30, four hundred years; according to *2 Apocalypse of Baruch* 73:1–2, the time is not specified.

With the preceding two reasons in mind, verse 4 should tentatively be understood to say that John believed Christians who are martyred because they do not worship Caesar (Nero and Domitian, Nero Redivivus) and receive his mark will be raised bodily at the second coming of Christ for the purpose of reigning with him in his one-thousand-year millennial kingdom.[4] Thus those martyred by Rome will be vindicated before Rome at the parousia.[5]

The rest of the dead—Christians and non-Christians alike—apparently will not be resurrected until after the one-thousand-year millennial reign of Christ on earth (v. 5a). The martyrs are especially blessed because they participate in the first resurrection at the return of Christ, which ensures that they will not face the second death—that is, eternal judgment (vv. 5b–6).

Verses 7–10 tell of the dramatic release of Satan and the end-time holy war.

III. THE RELEASE OF SATAN AND THE END-TIME HOLY WAR (20:7–10)

Verses 7–10 tell of the dramatic release of Satan and the end-time holy war. The paragraph raises three questions:

1. Who are Gog and Magog (vv. 7–8a)? "Gog and Magog" allude to Ezekiel 38–39 and the prophet's prophecy therein that a hostile nation from the north (Ezek. 38:6, 15–39:2) will attack peaceful Israel in the latter days (38:8–16), but that enemy nation will be destroyed by God (38:17–23; 39:1–6). Interpreters have understood 20:7–10 in several different ways: (a) Gog and Magog are a *demonic* army. (b) Gog and Magog represent the rest of the dead who are resurrected and judged. (c) The destruction narrated in 19:17–21 does not include *all* the inhabitants of the earth, so the forces led by Gog and Magog are the *rest*. (d) The use of mythical metaphoric language in 20:7–10 means that one need not necessarily follow the logic of the narrative.[6] The third view is to be preferred. Beyond that, the careful interpreter will not say.[7]

2. If view c above is correct, then it would help provide an answer to a second question raised by this text: Where did the nations come from that Satan deceived (v. 8b)? On that reading, Gog and Magog would be "leftovers" from the battle of Armageddon (Rev. 19:17–21). Perhaps, then (and this is pure speculation), those nations will propagate people during the millennial kingdom. The innumerable number also

---

4. The idea that only the martyrs rule with Christ in the millennial kingdom is a wrinkle in the premillennial view.

5. Recall Psalm 90:4 as the possible source of the one-thousand-year time period.

6. So Aune, *Revelation 17–22*, 1098.

7. There has always been speculation about the identity of Gog and Magog. In Old Testament times, Gyges, the king of Media, was thought to be a good candidate for such an enemy. In the intertestamental period, Gog and Magog were equated with Antiochus Epiphanes. In post–New Testament times, the rabbis equated Gog and Magog with the Gentile nations that will invade Israel at the end of time. Since then the Monguls, Turks, Russia, and numerous others have been identified as Gog and Magog. But obviously all of these views cannot be correct. It seems far more preferable, therefore, to refrain from trying to pinpoint the identification of Gog and Magog, but rather to let their identification unfold in time.

reminds one of the attack on Jerusalem by the nations in the end time and God's defeat of them (Pss. 46; 48; 76; Ezek. 38–39; cf. *4 Ezra* 13:5).

3. What is "the city he loves" (v. 9)? Most likely the beloved city is Jerusalem. The "camp of God's people" would then be the messianic army gathered outside the city's walls ready to defend the Holy City, or the encampment of God could be the beloved city itself. When Satan and the nations surround the Holy City, God will utterly destroy them.

Marie-Lan Nguyen/Wikimedia Commons

A statue of the underworld god Hades.

It is interesting that John does not record any actual fighting on the part of the people of God in their stand against Gog and Magog. It is unclear here whether John thought the people of God would or would not join in that fight; if the latter, then the battle will be the Lord's alone. God sends his fire to destroy the nations. He then will cast the Devil, the Beast, and the False Prophet (the Roman imperial cult) into the eternal lake of fire (vv. 9b–10).

IV. THE ETERNAL JUDGMENT AT THE GREAT WHITE THRONE (20:11–15)

After the put-down of the revolt of Satan, Gog and Magog, the throne of God appeared to John. God's throne is huge and white (cf. v. 11 with 1 Kings 6:23–28; Isa. 6:1; *4 Ezra* 8:21). All the dead appeared before that throne (vv. 12–13). The phrase "and books were opened" alludes to Daniel 7:10, probably with reference to two books: one for the deeds of the righteous and one for the deeds of the wicked (cf. Ps. 56:8; Isa. 65:6; Jer. 22:30; Dan. 7:10; Mal. 3:16; *Jub.* 30:22; 36:10; *Asc. Isa.* 9:22; *Leviticus Rabba* 26; et al.). The other book is the Book of Life (cf. vv. 12–13 with Rev. 3:5; 13:8; 17:8; 20:15; 21:27). The deeds of the righteous proceed from their persevering in their faith in Jesus. The deeds of the unrighteous do not (vv. 13–15). The wicked, along with death and hades, will be cast into the eternal lake of fire (v. 15). This is the second death (cf. 2:11; 20:6, 14; 21:8).

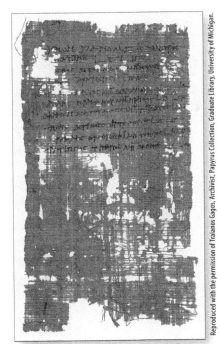

Reproduced with the permission of Traianos Gagos, Archivist, Papyrus Collection, Graduate Library, University of Michigan.

A first-century AD papyrus census list from Egypt.

CONCLUSION

I have interpreted Revelation along the lines of premillennialism: that John expects Christ to return and set up his one-thousand-year reign on earth, probably in Jerusalem. But such a view need not exclude the present, spiritual reality of the kingdom of God in the hearts of Christians. This is an aspect that all schools of interpretation of Revelation can agree upon. What is left for the Christian to do, therefore, is to pray with Jesus, "Thy kingdom come; Thy will be done on earth as it is in heaven."

REVIEW QUESTIONS

1. Define the differing views of the amillennialist, postmillennialist, and premillennialist in terms of their interpretations of Revelation 20.

2. According to premillennialists, why will there be peace on earth during the millennium (Rev. 20:1 – 3)?

3. Who are the ones who will rule with Christ during the millennium (Rev. 20:4 – 6)?

4. Who are Gog and Magog? How does that relate to Revelation 20:7 – 10?

KEY TERMS

amillennialism

binding of Satan

Book of Life

chilia/millennium

Gog and Magog

hades/Tartarus/bottom-less pit

lake of fire

martyrs

physical/spiritual resurrection

postmillennialism

premillennialism

temporary messianic kingdom

CHAPTER 57

The New Jerusalem

REVELATION 21–22

Objectives

After reading this chapter, you should be able to:

- List some connections between Revelation 21–22 and Genesis 1–3.

- Discuss the meaning of "the new heaven and new earth."

- Identify three key features that John draws attention to in his vision of the New Jerusalem.

INTRODUCTION

We come now to the final two chapters of Revelation and to the conclusion of the Johannine writings as a whole. Revelation 21–22 go together, for they are devoted to the theme of the New Jerusalem. John's beatific vision of the New Jerusalem is breathtaking. The celestial city's splendor, purity, and brilliance fulfill humanity's hope for utopia and perfection. Only the New Jerusalem's appearance at the very end of history can remove humankind's guilt, allay their fears, right the wrongs, and banish sickness and sorrow.

> Only the New Jerusalem's appearance at the very end of history can remove humankind's guilt, allay their fears, right the wrongs, and banish sickness and sorrow.

I propose to treat these two chapters by noting their twofold background, after which I will summarize the text itself.

The Twofold Background of Revelation 21–22

Two key backgrounds inform Revelation 21–22: primeval and covenantal.

The Primeval Background

Revelation 21–22 correlates with Genesis 1–3 to form the *Urzeit-Enzeit* pattern. That is, Revelation 21–22 — *Endzeit* (end of times) — restores what was lost in Genesis 1–3 — *Urzeit* (beginning of time). I will highlight some of those parallels below as I survey Revelation 21–22, but here I simply list them in chart form on the next page.[1]

> Revelation 21–22 correlates with Genesis 1–3 to form the *Urzeit-Endzeit* pattern.

The Covenantal Background

Interpreters of Revelation have long recognized that the words, "for I will be their God and they will be my people" (cf. 21:3, 7) comprise the covenant formula — the divine adoption of Old Testament Israel as the people of God (2 Sam. 7:14; 1 Chron. 17:13; 22:10; 28:6; Pss. 2:7; 89:26–27 [MT 27–28]; Jer. 3:19; 31:9; cf. 4QFlor. 1:10–11; cf., e.g., 2 Cor. 6:18 in the New Testament). In effect, Revelation 21–22 portrays the church as partaker of the new covenant.

Survey of Revelation 21–22

We may conveniently outline these two chapters as follows:

    I. Introduction to the vision of the New Jerusalem (21:1–8).

    II. Content of the vision of the New Jerusalem (21:9–22:9).

    III. Conclusion to the vision of Revelation (22:10–21).

---

1. The chart comes from J. Scott Duvall, J. Daniel Hays, E. Randolph Richards, W. Dennis Tucker, and Preben Vang, *The Story of Israel: A Biblical Theology*, ed. C. Marvin Pate (Downers Grove, Ill.: InterVarsity, 2004), 271–72.

Genesis 1–3	Revelation 21–22 (cf. Rev. 19)	
Sinful people scattered	God's people unite to sing his praises	19:6–7
"Marriage" of Adam and Eve	Marriage of Last Adam and his bride, the church	19:7; 21:2, 9
God abandoned by sinful people	God's people (New Jerusalem, bride of Christ) made ready for God; marriage of Lamb	19:7–8; 21:2, 9–21
Exclusion from bounty of Eden	Invitation to marriage supper of Lamb	19:9
Satan introduces sin into world	Satan and sin are judged	19:11–21; 20:7–10
Serpent deceives humanity	Ancient serpent is bound "to keep him from deceiving the nations"	20:2–3
God gives humans dominion over the earth	God's people will reign with him forever	20:4, 6; 22:5
People rebel against the true God, resulting in physical and spiritual death	God's people risk death to worship the true God and thus experience life	20:4–6
Sinful people sent away from life	God's people have their names written in the Book of Life	20:4–6, 15; 21:6, 27
Death enters the world	Death is put to death	20:14; 21:4
God creates first heaven and earth, eventually cursed by sin	God creates a new heaven and earth where sin is nowhere to be found	21:1
Water symbolizes unordered chaos	There is no longer any sea	21:1
Sin brings pain and tears	God comforts his people and removes crying and pain	21:4
Sinful humanity cursed with wandering (exile)	God's people given a permanent home	21:3
Community forfeited	Genuine community experienced	21:3, 7
Sinful people banished from presence of God	God lives among his people	21:3, 7, 22; 22:4
Creation begins to grow old and die	All things are made new	21:5
Water used to destroy wicked humanity	God quenches thirst with water from spring of life	21:6; 22:1
"In the beginning, God …"	"I am the Alpha and the Omega, the beginning and the end."	21:6
Sinful humanity suffers wandering exile in the land	God gives his children an inheritance	21:7
Sin enters the world	Sin banished from God's city	21:8, 27; 22:15
Sinful humanity separated from presence of holy God	God's people experience God's holiness (cubed city = Holy of Holies)	21:15–21
God creates light and separates it from darkness	No more night or natural light; God himself is the source of light	21:23; 22:5
Languages of sinful humanity confused	God's people are a multicultural people	21:24, 26; 22:2
Sinful people sent away from garden	New heaven and earth includes a garden	22:2
Sinful people forbidden to eat from Tree of Life	God's people may eat freely from Tree of Life	22:2, 14
Sin results in spiritual sickness	God heals the nations	22:2
Sinful people cursed	Curse removed from redeemed humanity and they become a blessing	22:3
Sinful people refuse to serve and obey God	God's people serve him	22:3
Sinful people ashamed in God's presence	God's people will "see his face"	22:4

I. INTRODUCTION TO THE VISION OF THE NEW JERUSALEM (21:1–8)

Just as John was carried away in a prophetic trance to see the Great Harlot in the desert (Rev. 17:3), so John is now carried away in a prophetic trance to see the New Jerusalem descending from heaven (Rev. 21:10). The introduction to that vision is provided in Revelation 21:1–8,[2] which contains a number of significant images.

A. New Heaven and New Earth (v. 1)

Just as God created the heaven and earth (Gen. 1), so he now creates a new heaven and a new earth (Rev. 21:1). And, in doing so, he removes any trace of sin. The new heaven and new earth are based on the promise of Isaiah 65:17 (cf. 66:22). A number of other passages in early Jewish apocalyptic literature refer to the re-creation or transformation of an eternal heaven or an eternal earth or both (though the ambiguity of some texts often makes it difficult to distinguish between creation and transformation): (1) *creation of a new heaven and/or earth* (2 Peter 3:13; *1 Enoch* 72:1; 91:16; *Jub.* 1:29; 4:26; *Sib. Oracles* 5.212; *Bib. Ant.* 3:10; *Apoc. Elijah* 5:38 [dependent on Rev. 21:2]; see 2 Cor. 5:17; Gal. 6:15) and (2) *transformation or renewal of heaven and/or earth* (Matt. 19:28; Rom. 8:21; *2 Bar.* 32:6; 44:12 ["new world"]; 49:3; 57:2; *1 Enoch* 45:4–5; *4 Ezra* 7:30–31, 75; *Jub.* 1:29; *Bib. Ant.* 32:17; *Tg. Yer.* 23:23).

It seems that Revelation 21:1 presumes the first of these conceptions of the new heaven and new earth. The mention that there is no sea in the new creation (v. 1) would have allayed the fears of John's audience, for the sea terrified the ancients (note Gen. 1:2; Gen. 6–9). Moreover, in the Old Testament the sea often symbolized the opponents of God (Pss. 29:3; 32:6; 46:3; 74:13; 77:16; Isa. 27:1; Jer. 6:23; Dan. 7:2–3; cf. Rev. 13:1–8).

> Just as John was carried away in a prophetic trance to see the Great Harlot in the desert (Rev. 17:3), so John is now carried away in a prophetic trance to see the New Jerusalem descending from heaven (Rev. 21:10).

B. The Holy City, New Jerusalem (vv. 2, 7)

The heavenly New Jerusalem is called "holy" (v. 2) because it is composed of those who did not bow before Caesar but rather kept the stipulation of the new covenant: faith in Jesus Christ. Just as ancient Israel was the wife of Yahweh by virtue of his covenant with her, so the church is the bride of Christ by virtue of his new covenant with her (see v. 3), and she has conquered the Beast by being faithful to Christ (v. 7). As such, she is the heavenly counterpart to Babylon the harlot (Rev. 17–18).

C. The Dwelling of God (vv. 3–5a; 6b–7)

As noted earlier, the words "they will be [God's] people and God himself will be with them and be their God" (v. 3) is the covenant formula.

---

2. It may be, as Aune suggests, that Revelation 21:3–4 was once followed immediately by Revelation 22:3–5, and 21:5–22:2 was later inserted into that section. David E. Aune, *Revelation 17–22*, WBC 52C (Nashville: Thomas Nelson, 1998), 1149.

And the great blessing of that covenant is the privilege of being the dwelling place of God (Ex. 29:45; Lev. 26:11–12; Ezek. 37:27; Zech. 2:11–13; *Tg. Ezek.* 37:26–27; 43:7; et al.). The dwelling of God among his people—the church—is the supreme blessing of the new covenant. Revelation 21:1–5 taps into that theme.

D. Curses Removed (vv. 4b, 8)

The flip side of God dwelling with his people is that the curses of the covenant have been removed. Suffering, pain, death, and tears will be no more in the New Jerusalem (v. 4b).

Those who worship the Beast, however, will experience the curses of the covenant because they broke the laws of God (v. 8): (1) *murder* (Ex. 20:13; Deut. 5:17; Matt. 5:21; 15:19; 19:18//Mark 10:19//Luke 18:20; Mark 7:21; Rom. 1:29; 13:9; James 2:11; 1 Peter 4:15; Rev. 9:21; 21:8; 22:15; *Barn.* 20:1; *Did.* 2:2); (2) *sexual immorality* (Ex. 20:14//Deut. 5:18; Matt. 5:27; 15:19; 19:18//Mark 10:19//Luke 18:20; Mark 7:21–22; Rom. 13:9; 1 Cor. 5:9–10; 2 Cor. 12:21; Gal. 5:19; Eph. 5:5; Col. 3:5; 1 Tim. 1:10; James 2:11; *Barn.* 20:1; *Did.* 2:2); (3) *sorcerers or sorcery* (absent from Decalogue; Rev. 9:21; 21:8; 22:15; Gal. 5:20; *Barn.* 20:1; *Did.* 2:2; 3:4); (4) *idolaters or idolatry* (Ex. 20:4–6//Deut. 5:8–10; 1 Cor. 5:10; 6:9; Gal. 5:20; Eph. 5:5; 1 Peter 4:3; Rev. 9:20; 21:8; 22:15; *Barn.* 20:1; *Did.* 5:1; Aristides, *Apol.* 15:2 [Syrian text]; Clement of Alexandria, *Paed.* 3.89.1; Tertullian, *Scorp.* 2:2); and (5) *liars* (Ex. 20:16//Deut. 5:20; Matt. 15:19; 19:18//Mark 10:19//Luke 18:20; 1 Tim. 1:9–10; Rev. 21:8; 22:15; *Barn.* 20:2, "lovers of falsehood"; *Did.* 3:5).[3] Those who show their cowardice and unbelief by receiving the mark of the Beast will earn for themselves the full measure of the curses of the covenant (v. 8).

E. God and Christ (vv. 5–6)

The God of the new creation/new covenant is referred to as the one "sitting on the throne" (cf. Rev. 21:5 with Isa. 6:1; 1QH 13:11–12). Christ, the Alpha and the Omega (Rev. 1:8; 21:6; 22:13); the Beginning and the End (cf. 22:13), is placed on par with God by John. Through Christ's death and resurrection, atonement for sin is completed (cf. v. 6 with 16:17; John 19:28).

F. Witness: God Himself (v. 5)

There can be no higher authority to appeal to for credibility of this message to John besides God himself, and that is who is appealed to in verse 5 (cf. Rev. 1:11, 19; 21:5). God is ultimately the one who guarantees the reliability of John's vision.

The words "they will be [God's] people and God himself will be with them and be their God" (v. 3) is the covenant formula.

The flip side of God dwelling with his people is that the curses of the covenant have been removed. Suffering, pain, death, and tears will be no more in the New Jerusalem.

---

3. Ibid., 1131

II. CONTENT OF THE VISION OF THE NEW JERUSALEM (21:9–22:9)

John's vision of the New Jerusalem consists of external (vv. 9–21) and internal descriptions of the city (21:22–22:9). The descriptions are breathtaking; words fail to capture their beauty.

A. External Description of the City (21:9–21)

One of the seven angels pouring out the bowl judgments transported John in a prophetic trance to a high mountain to see the church, the bride of the Lamb, also called the Holy City, Jerusalem. It was descending from heaven (vv. 9–11a; 11QTemple; cf. *4 Ezra* 13:35–36; *Bar.* 4:2–7). Several features of the heavenly city attracted John's attention.

1. The city was radiant with the glory of God, like clear jasper (cf. v. 11b with 4:3).
2. The walls of the city were wide and high (v. 12a) and also of jasper (v. 18a). This no doubt recalled old Jerusalem with its forty-foot-high walls, portions of which stand to this day.
3. Twelve gates provided entrance into the heavenly Jerusalem, each guarded by an angel (v. 12a), with the names of the twelve tribes of Israel inscribed on each gate (vv. 12b–13). Three gates faced the east, three faced the north, three faced the south, and three faced the west (v. 13). This suggests that John believed that the promised restoration of Israel was now fulfilled by the church.
4. The wall of the city had twelve foundation stones, and upon them were inscribed the names of the twelve apostles of the Lamb (v. 14; cf. 1 Kings 5:17; 7:10; Eph. 2:20). Each foundation consisted of a precious stone. What John may be saying here is that the twelve foundation stones compare with the twelve stones on the breastplate of the high priest (Ex. 28:16–21; 39:9–14). Indeed, on each stone was engraved the name of one of the twelve tribes of Israel. This connection between the twelve apostles/stones and the twelve gates/tribes of Israel indicates that John viewed the church to be the true successor to Israel, the people of God.

The Golden Gate is located on the eastern side of Jerusalem's wall. The gate's structure is from the seventh century, which means it predates the Turkish wall that we know today. Remains of an even older gate dating to the time of the Second Temple were found.

Twelve precious stones. These are the twelve stones used in the breastplate of the high priest.

Z. Radovan/www.BibleLandPictures.com

The Golden Gate.

The gate divided into two gates, both blocked today with bricks. The northern gate is called the Gate of Grace, and the southern gate is called the Gate of Mercy.

The Christian tradition marks the Golden Gate as the gate through which Christ entered Jerusalem, and that is why the gate is also named the Golden Gate. That tradition also tells that this gate is where the Byzantine emperor Heracles entered Jerusalem after freeing it from the Persians during the seventh century (a short while before the city was taken by Muslims).

Jewish tradition says that the Golden Gate is the gate through which the Messiah will enter Jerusalem, bringing the Jewish nation to redemption. The emperor Suleiman, who heard this tradition, decided to prevent the arrival of the Messiah by blocking the gates with bricks and by building a Muslim cemetery in front of the gate (the Messiah is a cohen, or priest, so he cannot enter a cemetery).

Today the gate's structure houses a Muslim prayer and study hall. Entrance to the gate is from the Temple Mount only.

> The wall of the city had twelve foundation stones, and upon them were inscribed the names of the twelve apostles of the Lamb.

5. The city itself was made of gold (vv. 18, 21). The golden color may have reminded John of the yellow sandstone out of which old Jerusalem was constructed. Apocalyptic Judaism expected the eschatological Jerusalem to be built out of gold (Tobit 13:16–17; 11QTemple 36:11; 39:3; 41:15).

6. The New Jerusalem was an enormous cube measuring some 1,500 miles in each direction (cf. Ezek. 40–48; 11QTemple). The implication is that it will be big enough to house converted humanity.

B. Internal Description of the City (21:22–22:9)

John uses several negatives in the internal description of the New Jerusalem.

> The New Jerusalem was an enormous cube measuring some 1,500 miles in each direction.

1. It will have no temple, because God and the Lamb are the temple (v. 22). The absence of a future temple in the eschatological Jerusalem was apparently a polemic of early Christianity against the old temple in Jerusalem (cf. John 4:21, 23–24; Acts 6:13; 7:47–51; Heb. 9:1–14; cf. Matt. 21:12–13//Mark 11:15–19// Luke 19:45–48; cf. 1QS 8). The idea that God is the temple comes perhaps from Isaiah 8:14, while the idea that Jesus is the temple is rooted in John 2:18–22.

2. There will be no need for the sun or moon in the heavenly Jerusalem because the glory of God and the lamp of the Lamb will illumine it (v. 23; 22:5; cf. Isa. 60:19–20; *Leviticus Rabba* 24:2). By this light the nations will walk in the New Jerusalem, and because of the perpetual illumination, there will be no need to close the gates at night (vv. 24–26). Verses 24–26 paraphrase Isaiah 60:3–5, 11 and envision the conversion of the nations to God and Christ at the end of time (cf. Tobit 13:8, 11; *1 Enoch* 90:30, 37–38; *Pss. Sol.* 17:32–35; *Sib. Oracles* 3:16ff; 5.492–502; 'Abod. Zar. 3b; T. Ash. 7:3; T. Benj. 9:2; T. Jud. 25:5; T. Levi 2:11; 4:4; 8:14; 14:4; 18:9; T. Naph. 8:3; Ep. Arist. 702–31).

3. There will be no impurity of any kind in the New Jerusalem (v. 27). The mark of the Beast will be gone; only the name of God on the forehead of the righteous will be present (Rev. 22:4).

Left: The Wailing Wall, the west wall of the Temple Mount, is said to be what was left of Solomon's original temple after its destruction. *Right:* Jewish men praying at the Western/Wailing Wall.

4. Related to this, the curse of the Garden of Eden will be removed from the Holy City (cf. Rev. 22:3 with Gen. 3:14–19). Replacing Adam's curse will be the river of God (cf. Rev. 22:1 with Gen. 2:10–14; Ezek. 47:1–12) and the Tree of Life (cf. Rev. 22:2 with Gen. 3:22–24; Ezek. 47:12; *1 Enoch* 25:4–6; 1QH 8:5–7); the latter provides for the healing of the nations (cf. Rev. 22:3 with Ezek 47:12). The righteous will worship and see God and reign with him (Rev. 22:4).

> John uses several negatives in the internal description of the New Jerusalem.

The angel confirmed the truthfulness of the vision granted to John (Rev. 22:6a), and John, as a prophet, was now responsible to share this vision of Revelation with others (v. 6b). The vision would motivate John's readers to obey the Lord until Jesus returned (v. 7). John was so overwhelmed at the angel's message that he began to worship him. But the angel quickly rebuked John for doing so, reminding him that he (the angel) was a fellow servant of God along with John's prophetic community. Rather, John should worship only God (vv. 8b–9).

III. CONCLUSION TO THE VISION OF REVELATION (22:10–21)

We conclude John's Revelation by making five points concerning Revelation 22:10–21.

First, there is a prophecy of the imminent appearing of Christ (vv. 10, 12, 20). It is interesting that whereas Daniel was told to seal up his book of prophecy because the end of history was far away (Dan. 12:4), by contrast John is told not to seal up his book of prophecy because the parousia of Jesus and the end of history are near.

Second, there are contrasting destinies of two groups of people: the righteous and the wicked. To the former belong the covenant blessings, but to the latter belong the covenant curses. We simply note these contrasts in the chart below:

	Blessing of the Covenant on the Righteous	Curses of the Covenant on the Wicked
v. 11	Does right and is holy	Does wrong and is vile
vv. 14–15	The blessing (v. 14 is the seventh covenant blessing in Revelation): have tree of life and enter the holy city	The curse, outside of the holy city: dogs (unclean), practice magic; immorality; murder; idolatry; falsehood

Third, there is an exalted testimony to Christ. He is equal to God (Alpha and Omega, First and Last, Beginning and End, v. 13), and he is the Messiah (the Davidic Root/Branch—cp. v. 16 with Isa. 11:1, 10) and the Davidic Star (cp. v. 16 with Num. 24:17).

Fourth, there is the opportunity given to all to drink of the water of life (v. 17).

Fifth, there is the solemnity of the covenant (vv. 18–19). These verses draw on Deuteronomy 4:2; 12:32 in that Old Testament book of the covenant. Ancient Israel was to obey the stipulations of the covenant and not add to or subtract from them. So for John, Christians are to obey the stipulations of Revelation—God's book of the covenant—regarding the command to obey Christ. Nothing should be added to or subtracted from that.

With these comments in mind, John utters a benediction: "The grace of the Lord Jesus be with God's people. Amen."

REVIEW QUESTIONS

1. List some of the connections between Revelation 21–22 and Genesis 1–3.

2. How does the description of the New Jerusalem (Rev. 21:9–22:9) contrast with the portrait of Babylon the prostitute (Rev. 17–18)?

3. What are the two possibilities for understanding the new heaven and new earth?

4. What Old Testament laws do the followers of the Beast break (Rev. 21:4, 8)?

5. What three features of the New Jerusalem interested John (Rev. 21:9–12)?

6. What will be missing from the New Jerusalem, according to Revelation 21:22–22:9?

KEY TERMS

covenantal background of Revelation 21–22

dwelling of God

Great Harlot

jasper

new heaven and new earth

New Jerusalem

primeval background of Revelation 21–22

twelve foundation stones

twelve gates

walls of Jerusalem and New Jerusalem

Conclusion

I have argued throughout this work that the apostle John, the Beloved Disciple, wrote all three "books" associated with his name: the fourth gospel, the letters, and Revelation. I now summarize his message in those writings.

The fourth gospel addressed two historical periods—the period of the historical Jesus in Palestine in the early 30s and the period of the churches of John in the 80–90s in Asia Minor. For both times the Beloved Disciple made his case that Jesus is the Son of God and that believing in him is the only way to salvation (John 20:30–31). John shows this to have been the case for the historical Jesus and his Palestinian audience in the 30s. In John 1 our author attributes a number of exalted titles to Jesus, from Messiah to Son of Man to Son of God. It is no surprise, then, that John 2–11 presents Jesus as the culmination point of the story of Israel, fulfilling the latter's feasts and sacrifices, and offering the true restoration of Israel—one characterized by the new birth into the spiritual kingdom of God. And the seven "I am's" and the seven sign miracles only reinforce that claim, placing Jesus on par with none other than God himself. John 12–21, however, records the surprising response of Israel to Jesus: led by the Jewish leadership, Israel rejected their Messiah; indeed, Israel had their Messiah crucified. But God raised Jesus from the dead to demonstrate that he was precisely who he claimed to be—the Christ, the Son of God. Those who receive him become the true children of God. In John's day in the 80–90s, the Jewish rejection of Jesus persisted in the form of the synagogue's expulsion of Jewish Christians from their assemblies.

By the time of the writings of the letters of John to his churches in Asia Minor in the 90s, some in his congregations had gone overboard with the message of the fourth gospel, claiming that Jesus was only God and not human. But, for John, such a docetic perspective set in motion a spiritual domino effect: to deny Jesus' humanity was to deny the incarnation; to deny the incarnation was to deny the atonement; and to deny the atonement was to deny Christian ethics. Hence John's emphasis in his letters on Jesus' humanity (1 John 1:1–4; 2:22; 4:1–6; 2 John 7), the efficacy of Jesus' atonement (1 John 2:1–2; 5:6–12), and the importance of living in the light (1 John 1:5–3:10) and in love (1 John 3:11–5:12) for the Christian ethic.

By the writing of Revelation in the mid-90s during the reign of Caesar Domitian, a new threat faced the Johannine churches in Asia Minor: should they cave in to the pressure to worship the Roman emperor? The apostle John thundered forth, "No!" Christians must worship only Christ. This Christ is the risen Lord who controls the church and indeed the whole cosmos (Rev. 1). He, not Caesar, is the one the Christians in the seven churches of Asia Minor should follow (Rev. 2–3). In reality, it is Jesus who is the Lord over all, though presently veiled from the world's watching eye (Rev. 4–5). But even now Jesus is sending his judgments upon the earth in retaliation for destroying Jerusalem and for persecuting the church. These judgments will culminate in the overthrow of Rome and any future Antichrist system that might survive beyond the first century (Rev. 6–18). The parousia of Jesus is imminent, which should embolden Christians to be true to the gospel (Rev. 19). At that time Jesus will return to set up his literal one-thousand-year reign on earth where his saints (the martyrs?) will rule with him (Rev. 20). And, after that, comes the grand finale of the new heaven and the new earth, which will restore Paradise (Rev. 21–22).

From Lamb of Calvary to the conquering Lion-Lamb of history, Jesus is Messiah of Israel, Savior of the world, and Lord of the universe. This is the message of the apostle John, Beloved Disciple, to all who will receive it.

Glossary

Abomination of Desolation	The desecration of the Jerusalem temple in 167 BC by the Syrian king Antiochus Epiphanes. It is applied to the Antichrist in the book of Revelation.
already – not yet	A phrase popularized by Oscar Cullmann to indicate that the age to come dawned with the first coming of Christ but will not be complete until the second coming of Christ.
amillennialism	A view of Revelation 20 that takes the millennium to be a figurative description of the present kingdom of God manifested in the church.
Ancient of Days	A title of God in Daniel 7 that is applied to Jesus Christ in Revelation 1.
Antichrist	The archenemy of Christ who is to appear at the end of history, which may be prefigured in the Roman Caesar in the first century.
Antiochus Epiphanes	The ancient Syrian ruler who desecrated the Jerusalem temple in 167 BC.
Apocalypse	The Greek title of Revelation.
apocalyptic literature	Ancient Jewish and Christian literature that deals with end-time events such as the kingdom of God, the signs of the times, the Antichrist, the advent of the Messiah. Such a genre is the substructure of the entire New Testament and fits in with the already – not yet aspects of the age to come.
apostasy	End-time turning away from God by some of the people of God. The New Testament views such an expectation as happening in the form of the Jewish rejection of Jesus as the Messiah. Revelation especially warns believers not to reject the Messiah by worshiping Caesar.
Armageddon	The "Mountain of Megiddo," with reference in Revelation to the end-time battle to be fought between Christ and Antichrist.

Babylon the Great	Probably a symbolic allusion to ancient Rome, which was expected to be defeated by Christ at his return. But it could refer to any anti-God world system.
Balaamites	A cryptic name for those in the Johannine churches who followed after the Roman Caesar.
Beast, the	The Antichrist, or the Roman Emperor, as spelled out in Revelation, which draws on imagery from Daniel 2, 7, 9.
Beast from the Earth	The false prophet of the Antichrist, which in Revelation may have originally been equated with the local priests in Asia Minor whose responsibility it was to secure the worship of Caesar.
Beast from the Sea	A figure presented in Revelation 13 and thereafter as the Antichrist, who may have been equated with the Roman magistrate sent from Rome across the sea to enforce the worship of Caesar on the mainline of Asia Minor.
Beloved Disciple	A term used by many scholars in the past and present to identify the apostle John, the author of the Johannine corpus.
Birth Pangs of the Messiah	Another name for the Messianic Woes or the Great Tribulation, because ancient Judaism believed that the persecution of the people of God would culminate in the birth of the Messiah. The Johannine literature applies this term to the suffering of Jesus and his followers.
Bisellium	A two-seat throne upon which two deities sat, as attested to in ancient Roman literature and art. In Revelation 4–5, God and Jesus are portrayed as being seated on such a throne because the two are equal in status.
Book of Glory	John 12–21.
Book of Signs	John 1–11.
born again/born from above	According to Jesus in John 3, the only way to enter the kingdom of God.
bowl judgments	The last and the greatest of the sevenfold divine judgments poured out on earth in the end-times; described in Revelation 15–18.
Bread of Life Discourse(s)	The discourse in John 6 in which Christ equated himself with the Bread of Life/Manna from Heaven.
Caesar worship	The demand by Roman Emperor Domitian in the first century that he be worshiped, which is the most likely background of the book of Revelation.

Caiaphas	The official high priest at the trial of Jesus.
Cerinthus	A contemporary of the apostle John who denied the humanity of Christ, arguing that deity came upon the man Jesus at birth but left him at the cross.
Christ/Messiah	The Greek and Hebrew words for God's anointed one, especially Jesus Christ.
classical dispensationalism	A rather recent theological development (ca. 1800s) that separates the return of Christ into a secret rapture of the church before the Tribulation period on earth and a visible second coming of Christ to earth after the Tribulation period. This view also holds to a literal reading of Revelation 20: the millennium will be a 1,000-year rule of Christ on earth, beginning with his second coming.
consistent eschatology	The view of Albert Schweitzer that Jesus preached the soon arrival of the kingdom of God but that it did not arrive after all during Jesus' lifetime. Thus the kingdom of God/Age to Come is still forthcoming.
Curse of the *Minim*	The curse that resulted in the expulsion of Johannine Christians, who were called heretics ("minim"), from the synagogues in Asia Minor.
Cyrus	The Persian king who graciously decreed in 539 BC that the Jews could return to their homeland and rebuild their temple.
Davidic Messiah	The Jewish expectation that their Messiah would be a descendant of King David and would come at the end of history to deliver Israel from her enemies. The New Testament presents Jesus as such a person, but tempers it with the notion that he is also the Suffering Servant.
Dead Sea Scrolls	An amazing treasure of texts both biblical and nonbiblical discovered in 1947 in the caves adjacent to the Dead Sea and near the excavations at Qumran. These texts help to confirm the Old Testament text and shed significant light on the thought world of the New Testament, especially the apocalyptic mindset of first-century Palestine.
***Dea Roma* coin**	A Roman coin minted in the late first century that depicts ancient Rome as situated on seven hills and protected by the goddess Roma. This coin may be a part of the background of Revelation 17.
delay of the Parousia	The growing realization in the first century that Jesus' second coming may be delayed for some time.

Devil	One of the terms for Satan used in the Johannine writings.
Diotrephes	The villain referred to in 3 John who may have rejected the apostle John's emissaries after siding with John's docetic opponents.
docetic	Greek word meaning "appear," with reference to the opponents of the apostle John in 1, 2, 3 John because they argued that Jesus only appeared to be human.
Domitian	The Roman emperor (AD 81–96) who demanded to be worshiped and who persecuted the Christians of Revelation who did not do so.
Egyptian plagues	The ten Egyptian plagues, which form the backdrop of the trumpet judgments of Revelation 8–9 and the bowl judgments of Revelation 15–18.
elect lady	A term in John 2 that is probably an allusion to one of John's churches.
eschatology	The end-time; a term similar to "apocalypticism" and dealing with the signs of the times to be fulfilled before the return of Christ.
eternal life	In Johannine literature, the life of the age to come/kingdom of God that is a present possession of the believer.
False Prophet	The associate of the Beast/Antichrist in the book of Revelation.
farewell speech	An ancient genre that consists of speeches containing the last thoughts of a famous Jewish leader. It is the genre of the Upper Room Discourse of Jesus in John 13–18.
Feast of Dedication	The feast that Jews celebrate in commemoration of the taking back from Antiochus Epiphanes of the Jerusalem temple and its cleansing by Judas Maccabees in 164 BC. It is called Hannakuh by Jews and is celebrated in December.
Feast of Passover	The feast that Jews celebrate in March-April in commemoration of their deliverance from ancient Egypt.
Feast of Tabernacles	The feast that Jews celebrate in September in commemoration of their wilderness wanderings.
fellowship	A blessing emphasized in the epistles of John that belongs to those who believe that Jesus is both God and human.
forgiveness of sins	Another blessing in the epistles of John that belongs to the true believer.

four horsemen of the Apocalypse	The first four seal judgments of Revelation 6.
four living creatures	Heavenly creatures (perhaps angels) who worship God nonstop, according to Revelation 4–5.
Gaius	A faithful follower of Jesus Christ who welcomed the apostle John's emissaries, according to 3 John.
garden of Gethsemane	The garden on the Mount of Olives where Jesus went to pray the night before his arrest and trial.
gematria	Ancient cryptic readings of names based on their numerical value, the most famous of which is 666 (see Rev. 13).
Gnosticism	A late first-century to second-century aberration of the Gospel that was based on the Platonic disparagement of the body. Gnostics argued that such knowledge was the real message of Jesus and those who embraced such a message were delivered from evil. But Gnosticism posed a serious threat to the Incarnation and therefore the epistles of John refute it.
Gog and Magog	Titles for the enemies of God to be defeated at the end of the millennium.
Gospel	Both the genre of the four Gospels and the good news of those Gospels proclaimed to followers of Jesus.
Gospel of Thomas, The	A third-fourth century Gnostic rereading of the New Testament discovered in 1948 in connection with the Gnostic texts that comprise the Nag Hammadi collection; named after the town in Southern Egypt in which they were unearthed. Some New Testament scholars today believe that The Gospel of Thomas should be accorded the same honor as the canonical four Gospels, but most scholars rightly disagree.
harlot/beast	A possible allusion in Revelation 17 to the Roman empire to be judged by Christ at his return.
Heavenly Son of Man	A title first occurring in Daniel 7 and applied to Jesus in the Gospels. It was Jesus' favorite title for himself.
hilasmos	A Greek word for "atonement" or "propitiation" that appears in the New Testament only in 1 John (twice).
historicist	A view of Revelation popular among the Protestant Reformers that the fulfillment of the events of Revelation occurs in history rather than in the future.
historic premillennialism	A view of Revelation going back at least to the church fathers that taught that the church would go through

the Tribulation period before the second coming of Christ to establish his 1,000-year reign on earth.

hospitality In the epistles of John, favor that is to be shown to true believers and not to John's docetic opponents.

house-church The settings for the epistles of John.

hypostatic union The teaching of the church fathers that Jesus Christ is fully God and fully human.

I am (*egō eimi*) One of Jesus' self-references in the gospel of John that places him on a par with God.

I am statements Seven statements in the gospel of John characterizing Christ.

idealist A view of Revelation that avoids locating the events of Revelation in history but rather sees them as symbolic of the battle between God and evil throughout history.

Incarnation The truth that Jesus Christ is both God and human.

Jesus' Olivet Discourse Jesus' predictions about the end-times as recorded in Matthew 24/Mark 13/Luke 21, part of which seem to have been fulfilled at the fall of Jerusalem to the Romans in AD 70 and which foreshadow Christ's second coming.

Jewish Revolt A rebellion against the Jews' Roman oppressors in AD 66. The Roman legions eventually defeated Israel by AD 73.

Jezebel The Old Testament Canaanite pagan queen of Israel, whose name is applied in Revelation 2–3 to those professing Christians who led their brothers astray from Christ.

Johannine literature The Fourth Gospel, the epistles of John, and Revelation; works associated with the apostle John.

Johannine school The theory that the writings associated with the apostle John were produced not by him alone but also by his followers.

Josephus A first-century Jewish historian who defected to the Roman side of the Jewish Revolt. He was a witness to the fall of Jerusalem to the Romans and later became a court historian to Rome.

King of kings and Lord of lords A title for the Parthian kings that is applied to Jesus Christ in Revelation.

koinōnia A Greek word that means "fellowship" with reference to one's relationship with God through Christ, a major concept in the epistles of John.

Lake of Fire	The final abode of the Beast, False Prophet, Satan, and all their followers, according to Revelation 20.
Lazarus	The friend whom Jesus raised from the dead (John 11), precipitating the Jewish leadership's decision to kill Jesus.
lion-lamb	The imagery Revelation 5 uses to portray Jesus as both the Davidic Messiah and the Suffering Servant. Thus, Jesus' death was his moment of victory.
Logos	A famous first-century word that reminded Greek audiences of the divine reason that permeates every person and that reminded Jewish audiences of God's spoken word that brought creation into being. John 1 applies these nuances to Jesus, God's pre-existent Word.
Maccabees	Led by Judas Maccabeus, a clan of brothers who were Jewish freedom fighters resisting Antiochus Epiphanes in their efforts to liberate Israel from that tyrant.
mark of the beast	666; the number of the mark of the Beast in Revelation; the Antichrist. It perhaps referred to Caesar Nero.
Mary Magdalene	The woman who was the first witness of the resurrected Jesus (John 20).
Medo-Persians	Led by Cyrus, the people groups who defeated Babylonia in 539 BC. Cyrus then allowed the captive Jews to return home to Israel.
merkabah	The Hebrew name for the divine throne that Jewish mystics longed to see. The apostle John experienced the throne of God in the book of Revelation.
mid-tribulation rapture	The view of Revelation that Jesus will return halfway through the Tribulation period to rapture his church to heaven.
Nero	A terrible first-century Roman Caesar who persecuted Christians, perhaps including Paul and Peter. Many interpreters of Revelation view Nero as the Beast described therein.
Nero Redivivus	The belief in the late first century that Nero would come back from the dead and lead a Parthian army to retaliate against Rome.
new covenant	According to the four Gospels, a concept initiated by Jesus' institution of the Lord's Supper, namely, the time longed for by the Old Testament prophets as the day

	when Israel would finally obey God from the heart, and fulfilled in the death and resurrection of Christ.
new heaven and new earth	The vision in Revelation 21–22 of the Garden of Eden as being restored in the events following the return of Christ; that is to say, the new heaven and earth.
New Jerusalem	Another image for the eternal state and the new heaven and new earth in Revelation 21–22.
Nicodemus	The Pharisee who confronted Jesus at night (John 3) and was told that he must be born again to see the kingdom of God. Nicodemus became a follower of Jesus Christ and later went public with his faith, according to the gospel of John.
Nicolaitans	Like Jezebel, a term referring to the opponents of John in Revelation 2–3 who advocated that Christians could compromise with Caesar.
overcomers	The key description of Christians in Revelation who are faithful to Christ in the face of persecution.
Pantokrator	Greek for "all powerful," a title used of Caesar but applied to Jesus Christ in the book of Revelation.
Papias	A disciple of the apostle John.
Paraclete	An allusion to the Holy Spirit in the gospel of John.
Parousia	A Greek term referring to the second coming of Christ.
Parthians	The people who lived east of the Euphrates and whom Rome was never able to conquer. Romans feared that Nero would lead the Parthian cavalries from across the Euphrates to invade the Roman Empire. This may be the background of the fourth seal jugdment in Revelation 6.
Pella	The Transjordan area that Jewish Christians fled to just before Jerusalem fell to the Romans in AD 70. This may be the background to Revelation 7 and 14.
Pharisees	The major opponents of Jesus signaled out in the Fourth Gospel. The Pharisees increased the laws of Moses into the thousands and in doing so enslaved Israel with the traditions of men.
Philo	A Jewish philosopher-theologian in the first century who tried to harmonize the thinking of Judaism and Hellenism. John 1's use of logos may be partially rooted in Philo's terminology.
Pilate	The infamous governor of Judea who condemned Jesus to die even though he pronounced Jesus three times to be innocent, according to the gospel of John.

Platonic dualism	The view propounded by the Greek philosopher Plato (ca. 350 BC) of the soul and body being in opposition, as with the real world of the ideas being in contrast to the shadowy world of the copies. Such thinking forms the backdrop of Gnosticism.
postmillennialism	The view of Revelation 20 that says that the church will bring the kingdom of God/millennium to earth through the preaching of the Gospel before the second coming of Christ takes place.
post-tribulation rapture	The view that the church will go through the Tribulation and not be raptured from the earth before it. Thus the rapture is the second coming of Christ.
premillennialism	The view of Revelation 20 that says that Christ will return to earth to establish his literal 1,000-year reign after the Tribulation period.
presbyter	A title of dignity applied to the apostle of John in the epistles of John and in early Christian literature.
preterist	A Latin term that means "past." With regard to Revelation, the preterist view understands that most, if not all, of the predicted events in the last book of the Bible were fulfilled in the first century.
pre-tribulation rapture	The view that propounds that the church will be raptured from the earth before the beginning of the Tribulation period (so 1 Thess. 4:13–18 and Rev. 4).
pre-wrath rapture	Similar to the mid-tribulation view of Revelation, a view that holds that the church will be raptured from the earth approximately halfway through the Tribulation period.
prophetic oracle	An Old Testament literary genre that may be a part of the background of the letters to the seven churches in Revelation 2–3.
realized eschatology	The view, popularized by C. H. Dodd, that the kingdom of God/Age to Come fully came at the first coming of Christ without remainder.
Revelation of Jesus Christ, The	The English title of the Apocalypse as well as its content.
Roman triumphant processional	A victorious Roman general who was honored at this celebration, which consisted of a parade in Rome honoring the Roman general but humiliating the defeated army. This custom is probably a part of the imagery of Revelation 19 and the return of Christ.

Samaritans	A mixture of Jews and Assyrians that populated northern Israel after its fall to the Assyrians in 722 BC. Samaritans and Jews thereafter did not get along. In a surprising and gracious move, Jesus reached out to a Samaritan woman in John 4.
Sanhedrin	The political ruling body over Israel during Jesus' day. It comprised 71 members, including the high priest. Jesus appeared before this body at his trial, and it unjustly condemned him to death.
Satan's throne	An allusion to Pergamum in Revelation 2, the capital seat of the Roman Empire in Asia Minor.
seal judgments	The first set of seven judgments (Rev. 6) poured out on the earth by God. The first four of these are called the "Four Horsemen of the Apocalypse."
secessionists	John's docetic opponents who betrayed the Gospel by departing from his churches in Asia Minor.
second coming of Christ	A term understood by most interpreters to refer to Christ's return at the end of history to establish his kingdom on earth. Preterists, however, hold that the return of Christ took place at the fall of Jerusalem to the Romans in AD 70 as an expression of divine judgment on Israel for rejecting Jesus as their Messiah.
Septuagint	The Greek translation of the Hebrew Old Testament, occurring somewhere around 250 BC.
Seven Sealed Scroll	The divine book Jesus opens as he unleashes God's judgments on the earth recorded in Revelation 6–18.
sign miracle	The seven sign/miracles, described in John 1–11, that reveal Jesus to be the Messiah, the Son of God.
signs of the times	The end-time events that precede the return of Christ, including apostasy, the rise of the Antichrist, cosmic disturbances, and unprecedented persecution of the people of God.
sin unto death	Most likely, the sin of Docetism opposed by John in his epistles.
Son of God	A favorite title for Jesus in the gospel of John, emphasizing both Jesus' equality with God and his subordination (but not inferiority) to him.
Son of Man	Jesus' favorite title for himself, which draws on Daniel 7. It conveys the conviction that Jesus is the Messiah but without implying that he was a political Messiah.

story of Israel	The Old Testament story of Israel's sin, exile, and restoration. The New Testament presents Jesus as Israel's ultimate hope for being restored to God, but not to be confused with establishing a new theocracy in Israel.
synagogue of Satan	A polemical label for those Jews who expelled Johannine Christians from the synagogues in ancient Asia Minor.
Synoptic Gospels	A term referring to Matthew, Mark, and Luke, three gospels that are considerably different from John in their presentations of Jesus.
Tatian's *Diatessaron*	An early "harmony of the Gospels," produced about AD 170. Hence the name diatessaron — "through four."
temporary messianic kingdom	The idea in *4 Ezra, 2 Baruch,* and perhaps Revelation 20 that there would be a temporary kingdom set up on earth by the Messiah that would afterward give way to the eternal kingdom of God.
ten horns	Possibly a reference to the ten client-kings of the Roman Caesar in the first century as referred to in Revelation.
text criticism	The science of collecting, comparing, and contrasting ancient manuscripts of the Bible to determine the original reading. Today we do not have the autographs (the original manuscripts) of the Bible, but rather thousands of copies from which scholars provide today's various translations.
triclinium	A three-sided table that was common to dine upon in the first century. Jesus probably ate his last Passover at such a table.
trumpet judgments	The second set of seven divine end-time judgments poured out upon the earth (see Rev. 8–9) and portrayed against the imagery of the Old Testament Egyptian plagues.
twelfth "benediction"	A statement designed by the first-century synagogues to weed out Jewish Christians from their number.
Zerubbabel's temple	The Jewish temple restored in 519 BC after its fall to the Babylonians in 586/7 BC. This temple began Second Temple Judaism and was magnificently refurbished by Herod the Great but destroyed by the Romans in AD 70.

Scripture Index

Apocryphal Books

General Index

Abraham, 39, 84, 107, 111-12, 153, 413
Acts of the Apostles, 23, 35
Adam and Eve, 285, 505
Adultery, 98, 106, 480
Affirmations, John the Baptist's, 53, 57
Agape, 265
Age to come, 28-29, 40, 72, 139, 144, 168, 169, 174, 214, 244, 251, 266, 272-73, 278, 314, 316, 337, 352, 515, 517, 518, 523
Alexander the Great ("the King"), 24, 35, 36, 458
Alexandria, 16, 26, 488
Alexandrian school, 345, 374
Allegory, 158, 159, 160, 345, 491
Allison, Dale C., 169
Alpha and Omega, 359, 505, 507, 511
Already–not yet, 29, 87, 286, 348, 352, 357, 493, 515
Amillennialism, 345, 346, 348, 357, 362, 498, 515
Ancient of Days, 356, 361, 515
Ancient wonders of the world, 369, 432
Andrew, 20, 54, 58, 91, 138
Angelic hosts, 35, 494
Angel of the prophecy, 433
Angelology, 351
Angels, 39, 55, 59, 60, 191, 212, 356, 390
    fallen, 351, 425, 429, 450, 499
    interpreters of the vision, 481, 486, 492, 511
    patron, 362
    seven for judgment, 473-77, 508
    See also Archangels; Colossus of Rhodes; Angels of the seven churches
Angels of the seven churches, 361, 366, 368, 369, 373, 376, 378, 382, 383, 384, 386, 391n, 395, 396, 408, 417, 418, 423, 432, 433, 434, 435, 469, 476, 480, 481, 487, 494, 498, 519
Annas, 180, 183, 184, 186, 193, 195, 196, 219
Anomia, 284
Anthropology, 350, 351
Antichrist, 29, 41, 232, 244, 256, 272, 276-78, 285, 296-97, 339, 418, 438, 441, 456, 457n, 458n, 462, 494, 515, 516, 524

    as beast, 460, 515, 518, 521
    in contrast to Jesus, 277, 283-84, 297
    as white horse, 403-4
    world system, 351, 514
Antioch, 102, 236
Antiochus II, 385
Antiochus III, 382
Antiochus IV (Epiphanes), 123, 443, 450n, 459, 500n, 515, 518, 521
Antiphonal hymn, 444
Anti-Semitism, 33, 196
Aorist tense. *See* Verbs
Apocalypse, 169, 170, 336-39, 341, 343, 348-51, 356-60, 362, 405, 407, 432, 448, 477, 515, 519. *See also* Four horsemen
Apocalypticism, Jewish, 25, 139-40, 150, 161, 390n
Apocalyptic Lamb, 57, 393, 466
Apocalyptic literature, 28, 34, 140, 148, 173, 184, 336-38, 360n, 361, 393n, 407, 466, 506, 515
Apocrypha, 107, 320
Apollo, 370, 371, 377, 386, 428, 448, 458
Apollonius, 226
Apostasy, 29, 140, 159, 161, 168, 169, 245, 276, 277, 316, 378, 387, 515, 524
Apostles, 19, 20, 35-36, 155, 176, 211, 221, 249, 271, 291, 416, 444
    false, 371
    the twelve, 18, 21, 22, 396, 508
Archangels, 422, 448, 450
Ark of the Covenant, 259, 260, 444, 468
Armageddon, 401, 473, 475, 476, 493, 500, 515
Arrian, 35
Ascent to heaven, John's, 360, 390-91
Asia Minor, 31, 34, 234, 236, 237, 359, 405, 448, 457, 459, 492, 513, 516, 517, 524, 525
    imperial cult in, 459n, 460, 461
    seven churches of, 339, 342, 349, 351, 357, 361, 366-78
Athanasius, 23, 228
Atonement, 67, 234, 240, 259, 283, 292, 297, 298, 303, 329, 330, 507, 513, 519

mandatory, 145
See also Day of Atonement
Augustine, 16, 345, 491
Augustus, 34, 35, 65n, 194n, 340, 341, 369, 370, 374,
    382, 392, 404, 457, 459, 474n, 480, 482n
Aune, D. E., 366, 391, 416n, 427, 458n, 461, 468n,
    473n, 499, 506n
Authenticity, 212, 302, 304-5, 356
Authorship, John's, 17-23, 27, 166n, 226, 227-30. *See
    also* Canonicity

Babylon, 65, 78, 102n, 226n, 320, 340, 341, 342, 425,
    427, 442, 516
    fall of, 352, 401, 429, 468, 486-88, 490
    the harlot, 490, 506
    New, 426, 427, 429, 477, 480-82, 486-88, 493
    and New Jerusalem, 490
    Rome called, 341, 352, 442, 467n, 468, 473n, 480-
        82, 486-88, 491, 492, 493
Babylonian exiles, 50, 57, 78
Balaamites, 371, 375, 376, 377, 516
Baptism, 41, 56, 73, 75, 78, 203, 279, 309, 412, 413;
    Jesus', 38, 202, 204, 236, 248, 249, 298, 308,
    309
Barabbas, 192
Basar, 34
Basilides, 236, 237
Beagley, Alan J., 406, 407
Beale, G. F., 367, 369
Beast, the, 276, 342, 350, 400, 401, 423, 426, 434,
    435, 443-44, 452, 458, 467, 468, 472, 473-75,
    477, 480, 482, 486, 492, 494, 501, 506, 516,
    518, 519, 521
    and Caesar, 349, 393, 480
    Nero as, 342n, 403, 442, 443, 456, 458, 459, 481
    Domitian as, 459
    See also Mark of the Beast
Beasts, two (land and sea), 448, 456-62, 467, 475, 516
Beatitudes, 486n, 491
Begetting, divine, 282
Belief, 16, 22, 40, 50, 68, 131, 241, 243, 284, 304,
    308, 310, 314-16, 391n, 406, 414, 439, 521
Beloved Disciple, 17, 18, 21, 22n, 146, 180, 201, 204,
    214, 218, 219, 220, 238, 308, 309, 513, 514, 516
Benediction, 331, 512, 525
Benediction, Twelfth, 31, 33, 116, 367, 525
Benedictions, Eighteen, 31, 32, 33, 116, 413, 422

Bethany, 128, 129, 130, 181
Bethesda, 84
Bethlehem, 57, 59, 102, 103
Betrayal, 136, 142, 146, 150, 159, 180, 181
Bible, Hebrew, 17, 24
Biographies, historical, 36
Birth. *See* Rebirth, spiritual
Bishops, 234, 235, 236, 271, 326, 338, 373
Black horse of famine, 405
Blasphemy, 86, 112, 124, 167, 191, 193, 195, 458, 459,
    475, 480
Blessing of the Covenant, 507, 511
Blindness, 114, 116, 254; spiritual, 114, 117, 118
Blood, 201, 202, 212, 237, 255, 259, 308-9, 310, 339, 401,
    407, 423, 425, 441, 42, 469, 475, 481, 487, 494
    of the Lamb, 448, 469
    and water, 200, 202-3, 230, 234, 238, 308, 441, 474
Boismard, M. E., 47
Book of Glory, 37, 136n, 240, 516
Book of Life, 31, 383, 392, 459, 501, 505
Book of Signs, 37, 136, 140, 240, 516
Book of the Covenant, 394, 432-33, 435, 512
Borgen, Peder, 92
Borgen, Raymond, 42, 142, 144n, 154, 220, 221, 229n,
Bowl judgments, 400, 407n, 422-23, 426, 432-33, 434,
    439, 444, 448, 467, 472-77, 480, 486, 487, 493,
    508, 516, 518
Branches. *See* Vine and branches
Bread, 93, 94, 145, 260
    and fishes, 91
    unleavened, 66, 67, 146
Bread of Life, 42, 89, 92-94, 95, 107, 516
Bride of Christ, 41, 352, 480, 490, 491, 505, 506
Brotherly love, 285n, 290
Brown, Dan, 211
Brown, Raymond, 42, 142, 144n, 154, 220, 221, 229n,
    230n, 240n, 242, 257, 286n, 308, 310
Burge, Gary M., 175n, 190n, 194n, 194n, 212n, 237n,
    240n, 270, 271, 290
Burridge, Richard, 36

Caesar
    cult of, 31, 234, 342n, 349, 451, 480
    emperor, 194, 196, 234, 341, 350, 358, 359, 362,
        374n, 450, 457, 474n, 481, 522, 525
    worship of. *See* Emperor worship
    See also Augustus; Julius Caesar; Tiberius
Caiaphas, 65, 132, 183-86, 189, 193, 195, 517

Galba, 340, 341, 404, 457, 482n
Galilee, 58, 63, 78, 81, 98, 104, 121, 193, 475-76
Galilee, Sea of, 90, 91, 201, 208n, 218-19
Gardener, 158, 159, 212
Garden of Eden, 511, 522
Gemara, 30n
Gematria, 340, 462, 519
Genre, literary, 34-36, 142, 143, 226, 227, 240-41,
    337n, 339, 356, 366-69, 392n, 515, 518, 519, 523
Gentiles, 55, 65, 73, 81, 102, 104, 122-23, 132, 138,
    180, 200, 375n, 413-15, 416, 440, 452, 500n
Gentry, Kenneth L., 343, 417, 469
Gethsemane, 106, 146, 180, 181, 519
Gihon Spring, 103, 115
Glorification, 39, 112, 139; of Jesus, 37, 74, 86, 110,
    146-47, 174, 212, 213
Gnosis, 23, 25, 26, 264, 316
Gnosticism, 16, 23, 24, 25, 26, 28, 40, 42, 46n, 47, 50,
    152, 174, 202, 204, 216, 234, 235, 236-37, 239,
    240, 243, 298, 316, 349, 377, 519, 523
Gnostic writings, 25, 28, 211, 519
God
    bond with Jesus, 251
    characteristics outlined in Revelation, 350
    covenant promise, 174, 202, 392
    dwelling of, 60, 150, 506-7
    is a trinity, 48, 151, 244, 298, 350, 351, 358, 394n
    is light, 37, 242, 243, 254-55, 266, 290, 291, 405
    is love, 159, 176, 242, 243, 291, 302
    judgment upon Rome, 407, 467, 468, 486
    justice of, 350, 416
    kingdom of. *See* Kingdom of God
    knowledge of, 26, 122, 153, 168, 169
    light of, 37, 266
    love for the world, 74, 265, 302-3, 304, 329
    love of, 265, 292, 302-3, 304, 329
    name of, 50, 174-75, 182, 271, 293, 314, 359, 487,
        510
    promise to Abraham, 413
    and righteousness, 175, 266, 282, 284, 285, 350,
        490
    seal of, 412, 413n
    testimony about Christ, 75, 87, 243, 303, 308-10,
        359, 441, 443, 452, 511
    throne of, 257, 350, 390-96, 450, 473, 501, 521
    as true and holy, 39, 175, 243, 316, 377, 384, 396
    union with, 176, 244, 303, 316

wrath of, 175, 402, 414, 415, 426, 444, 468, 469,
    472-77, 486, 487, 494
Gog and Magog, 473, 493, 494, 498, 500-501, 519
Golden Gate, 508-9
Golgotha, 200, 208
Good Shepherd, 93, 98, 120, 122, 123, 220
Gospel of John
    and anti-Semitism, 33, 191n
    authorship of, 17-23, 27, 58n, 166n, 218n
    canonicity, 17, 23-24, 107, 211
    Christology, 33, 39-40, 244
    compared with Synoptic gospels, 17, 18, 21, 23, 33, 38,
        39, 58n, 60, 65, 68, 78n, 92, 95, 108, 121, 124n,
        142, 146n, 161, 180, 191, 192, 195, 200, 208, 231
    compared with epistles, 231-34, 240, 290, 314, 338,
        348
    conceptual background, 19, 23, 24-30, 40, 47
    dualism, 16, 25, 26, 33, 42, 73
    ecclesiology, 11, 39, 41, 350, 352
    epilogue, 37, 218-21, 238, 314n
    eschatology. *See* Eschatology
    group authorship of, 21-23, 28
    historical setting, 17, 30-34, 218-221
    introduction to, 16–42
    as literary genre, 34-36
    manuscript evidence for, 17-21, 37-38, 106-7
    meaning of, 16-17
    nontraditional views of authorship, 21–23
    prologue, 16, 27, 37, 39, 42, 46-51, 314
    purpose of, 30-34, 36, 37, 46-47, 214
    second conclusion of, 218, 220-21
    seven signs/miracles in, 62, 214
    soteriology, 39, 40-41
    structure of, 17, 36-37, 290
Gospels, as historical biographies, 36
Grain judgment, 468-69
Great Tribulation, 41, 161, 169, 244, 347, 352, 360,
    362, 385, 400, 412-16, 418, 450n, 467, 473, 498,
    499, 516
Great white throne, 498
Greek manuscripts, 17, 37-38, 106, 117n, 226, 227,
    243, 248, 291n, 309n, 336, 339, 343, 524
Grief, 129-30, 143, 209
Guilds, 374, 375, 376, 377, 378, 461-62
Guilt, 117n, 161, 162, 190, 193, 256, 257, 504
Guilt offering, 145
Guthrie, Donald, 21

his mission, 73, 74, 80, 101, 102, 138, 156n

hostility from Jewish leadership, 86, 98

"I am the resurrection," 93, 128, 130

interrogated by Caiaphas, 195

and John the Baptist, 47, 48, 49, 50, 54, 57, 58, 72, 74-75, 78, 87, 125, 248, 309, 310

as judge, 107, 108, 378, 466, 519

as King of Israel, 40, 59, 137, 214

last discourse, 142, 144, 145, 146, 154, 155, 166-70

and Lazarus, 21, 62, 128-32, 136-37, 150, 231n

as Light of the World, 93, 107, 114

Lion-Lamb, 350, 396, 462, 477, 514, 521

and Mary Magdalene, 208, 211, 212-13

as Messiah, 30, 33, 40, 49, 50, 57, 58-59, 60, 68n, 73, 75, 81, 101-2, 103, 123, 124, 137, 138, 139, 204, 251, 350, 491, 494, 511, 513-14, 515, 516, 517, 521, 524

ministry of, 30, 33, 38, 50, 54, 57, 58, 65n, 68, 75, 78, 98, 122, 123, 125, 136, 139, 140, 214, 248

moment of exaltation, 74

as new temple, 50, 66, 103

and Nicodemus, 72–74, 80, 104, 180, 203-4, 522

origin and nature, 101-2, 107, 108, 188

as Passover Lamb, 142, 194, 201-2, 204, 393

before Pilate, 180, 188-96, 205, 236

plan to kill him, 128, 131-32

post-resurrection appearances, 37, 155, 168-69, 208, 209, 211-14, 218-21

prayer for future disciples, 174, 176

prayer to be glorified, 174

predicts his soon departure, 150, 152-54

predicts Judas' betrayal, 142, 146

as prophet, 80, 104, 116, 118, 214

public ministry, 36, 54, 62, 65, 78, 98, 123, 125, 136, 140

rejection by Israel, 33, 46, 49, 87, 138, 140, 181, 192, 193, 195, 204, 234, 240, 272

rejection by the world, 49, 162, 176n

return to the Father, 37, 102, 146, 147, 168, 212-13

sacrificial love, 145

as subordinate to his Father, 39, 86, 156n

as suffering Messiah, 138, 139, 204

as Suffering Servant, 57, 139, 140, 202, 204, 350, 517, 521

in Sychar, 79

as teacher, 58, 72, 100, 101, 212

tomb of, 131, 208, 209, 210, 211, 212

trial of, 35, 108, 124n, 167, 180, 184, 185, 188-96, 205

triumph over Satan, 139, 167, 170, 244, 259

true faith in, 50, 68, 110, 314

as true light, 48, 49, 231

as True Shepherd, 120, 121-22

walks on water, 38, 90, 92

washes disciples' feet, 38, 145-46, 159

as wisdom, 47, 48, 49

witness to, 40, 48, 49, 54, 56-60

as the Word, 40, 42, 46, 47, 48, 49-50, 231n, 238, 248, 339, 466

See also Antichrist: in contrast to; Atonement; Crucifixion; Discourses; Incarnation; Lamb of God; Miracles; Resurrection; Second Coming; Son of God; Son of Man

Jewish authorities and leaders, 73, 85, 98, 102, 103-4, 107, 116, 117n, 121-23, 125, 129, 131-32, 137, 146, 152, 167, 180-83, 189, 190-96, 200, 202

Jewish Christians, 31, 32, 116, 234, 237, 344, 349, 373, 384, 402, 406, 412, 413, 414, 416-17, 418, 449, 450, 452, 467, 486, 513, 522, 525

Jewish feasts. *See* Feast

Jewish remnant, 78, 412, 413, 414n, 440, 441, 442, 448, 467

Jewish Revolt, 30-31, 63, 123, 278, 402, 403, 405, 406, 439, 443, 451, 452, 466, 520; Second, 476

Jewish writings, 29, 73, 337, 341, 342, 361, 390n, 426, 466n, 469, 499n, 506, 515

Jews

demand Jesus' death, 189-91, 193

Diaspora, 102, 122n

and interrogation of Jesus, 180, 183, 184, 186, 195, 196

salvation of, 138, 303, 393

sects, 32

unbelieving, 111, 125, 369

Jezebel, 371, 377-78, 520, 522

Jezreel, 475-76

Joel, 422, 424, 427, 469

Johannine Christians, 30, 237, 265, 278, 282n, 297, 314, 316, 321, 322, 486, 517, 525

Johannine churches. *See* Church: Johannine

Johannine community: *See* Community: Johannine

Johannine literature, 21, 23n, 27, 29, 50, 58n, 170, 237, 255, 283, 292n, 296, 303, 316, 339, 504, 516, 518, 520

Lazarus, 21, 62, 128-32, 136-37, 150, 231n
Left Behind fiction series, 346
Letter writing, ancient, 226–27
Leviathan, 450, 459n
Levites, 56, 102n
Liars/lying, 111, 255, 257, 264, 265, 298, 507
Libation bowls, 474, 476
"Lifted up" sayings, 74
Light ceremony, 107, 108
Light of the World, 93, 107-8, 114
Lindsey, Hal, 346
Lion of Judah, 393
Little scroll, 432-35
Living water, 78, 79, 80, 103
Loaves and fishes, 91, 93
Locusts, 401, 422, 423, 424, 427-29
Logos, 26–27, 46, 248, 265, 521, 522
Lord of the Sabbath, 85
Love
    command to, 230, 290, 291-92, 296, 302, 304-5,
        321, 323, 329, 330
    God's (divine), 39, 49, 74, 123, 159, 161, 176, 240,
        242, 243, 256, 265, 302-4, 305, 329
    in motion, 302-5
    one another, 37, 41, 147, 155, 161, 176, 229-30, 240,
        242, 244, 265-66, 291-93, 303, 304n, 323
    origin of, 302, 303
    revelation of, 302-3
    sacrificial, 145, 358

Makarisms, 491
Malatesta, Edward, 159
Malherbe, Abraham J., 327
Mandaean texts, 26
Manna, 39, 91, 92, 93, 94, 260, 375-76, 377, 516
Mark of the Beast, 351, 413n, 456, 461, 462, 491, 507,
        510, 521
Martha (Lazarus' sister), 128, 129-31, 136
Martyn, Louis, 30–33
Martyrs/martyrdom, 18, 221, 236, 350, 373, 401, 406-
        7, 413, 416, 418, 422, 441, 442, 444, 451, 467,
        473-74, 481, 491, 494, 498, 499-500, 514
Mary (Jesus' mother), 180, 204, 236, 298, 450n, 452
Mary (Lazarus' sister), 128, 129-30, 136
Mary Magdalene, 201, 208, 211, 212-13, 521
Mary of Clopas, 201
Medo-Persian Empire, 427, 429, 458, 473, 493, 521

Memoirs, 36
Menorah, 260, 361, 372, 440-41. *See also* Lampstands
Merkabah, 153n, 390-91
Messiah. *See* Jesus: as Messiah
Messianic age, 62, 63-64
Messianic banquet, 491
Messianic expectation, 55, 57, 91, 103, 517
Messianic woes, 29, 41, 139, 140, 161, 168, 169, 244,
        347-48, 360, 393n, 400, 406, 408n, 422, 449,
        516
Metaphors, 72, 122, 150, 158, 169, 352, 427, 468-69,
        480, 481, 491, 495, 500
Methodius, 338
Michael (angel), 448, 450
Midtribulationists, 413, 414n, 415
Millennium, 344, 345, 347, 348, 352, 414, 415, 498-
        99, 515, 517, 519, 523
Miracles, 37, 38, 39, 48, 62-64, 68, 72, 81, 84-85, 87,
        91, 92, 94, 102, 115-16, 118, 124, 128, 130, 131,
        132, 136, 153, 154, 214, 236, 357, 494–95
Mishnah, 30, 62, 85, 191n
Monotheism, 39, 48, 86, 156n, 174, 243, 350, 361n,
        461
Moses, 28, 48, 49, 55, 87, 93, 117, 424, 425, 426, 472,
        473
    and Elijah, 438, 440-41, 443
    contrasted with Christ, 50-51, 74, 80, 91, 103
    Farewell Discourse, 143, 144n
    law of, 30n, 39, 47, 117n, 153, 160, 441, 522
    as prophet, 56, 58
Mother and child, 448-50
Motifs, 25, 106, 360n, 390, 391n, 426, 433, 461, 499
Mountain, burning, 425-26
Mount of Olives, 65n, 106, 128, 137, 181, 519
Müller, U. B., 366
Multitude, 38, 62, 68, 90-91, 95; innumerable, 412,
        413, 418
Muratorian Fragment, 19, 338
Murder, 111, 192, 285, 403, 507, 511

Nathanael, 54, 58-59, 60, 62, 218
Natural birth, 73
Nature miracles, 128n
Nauck, Wolfgang, 254
Nazareth, 59, 62, 102, 182
Nero, 277, 339-44, 367, 370, 403-5, 429, 458, 488; as
        Beast, 344, 452, 458, 481, 521

Neronian persecution. *See* Persecution
Nero Redivivus, 342, 403-4, 428, 457n, 458, 459-60, 462, 475, 480, 481-82, 500, 521, 522
New Babylon. *See* Babylon
New birth, 75, 285, 513
New Commandment, 146, 147, 229, 266
New covenant, 40, 41, 49, 50, 51, 73, 90, 94, 147, 152-52, 155, 159, 160, 161, 170, 174, 202, 214, 245, 251, 255, 257, 260, 265, 266, 314, 315, 322, 332, 347n, 349, 352, 378, 384, 387, 393, 504, 506-7, 521
New creation, 29, 41, 54, 506, 507
New exodus, 56, 90, 91, 92, 475
New Jerusalem, 29, 352, 391, 490, 504-12, 522
New Passover, 90–92
New Temple. *See* Temple
New Testament, 16, 21, 22, 23, 24, 34, 37, 40, 46, 49, 63, 73, 115, 139, 150, 192, 211, 228, 254, 278, 296, 343, 413, 517
    compared with ancient letter writing, 226-27, 303, 357, 515, 519
    distinction of gospel of John in, 21, 24, 39, 41, 156n, 231, 283, 296, 321, 328, 330, 357, 412, 493, 495, 519
    scholarship, 25, 30, 33, 35, 35, 36, 237n
Nicodemus, 72–74, 80, 104, 180, 203-4, 522
Nicolaitans, 371, 375, 376, 377, 522
Nobleman's son, 62, 81, 84n
Number 666, 340-42, 456, 462, 519, 521

Obedience, 87, 139, 147, 153, 154, 158, 174, 265, 266, 293, 323, 346, 358, 393
Old Testament, 47n, 66, 86, 94, 104, 125, 138, 145, 183, 195n, 205, 237
    background to New Testament, 18, 33, 34, 35, 39, 56, 59, 66, 73, 79, 87, 93, 103, 117, 122, 137n, 143, 158, 159, 161, 175, 180, 193, 201-2, 204-5, 211, 243, 251, 255, 256
    about end times, 104, 138, 169, 278
Olivet Discourse. *See* Discourses
Olive trees, 405, 440, 441
144,000, the, 401, 412-18, 466-69, 494. *See also* Multitude: innumerable
One who is and was, 475
Opistograph, 392
Oracle
    judgment, 366-67

prophetic, 359, 362n, 366-67, 369, 371, 373-74, 376-77, 378, 382-83, 384-85, 386, 403n, 416, 523
true, 372, 374, 377, 378, 383, 385, 386
"woe," 426
Origen, 16, 19, 24, 338, 345
Osborne, Grant, 342, 350, 351, 424
Otho, 340, 341, 404, 457, 482n

Paidia, 270-71, 276
Pain, 159, 169, 209, 428, 475, 505, 507
Painter, John, 327
Pale horse of death, 401, 406
Palestinian Judaism. *See* Judaism
Palm Sunday, 137-38
Papias, 20, 21, 228, 230, 338, 522
Parables, 16, 38, 80, 120-21, 158
Paraclete, 22n, 40, 143, 154-55, 156, 166, 202, 213, 229, 257, 309, 522
Paradox, 128-29, 393, 418, 428
Parousia, 60, 152, 155, 168, 176, 220, 232, 244, 276, 279, 282, 283, 286, 321-22, 341, 347-48, 351, 352, 357, 359, 362, 400, 475, 489-95, 498, 500, 511, 514, 517, 522
Parthians, 341, 403-5, 422, 424, 427-29, 458n, 473, 475-76, 481, 482, 493, 520, 521
Paschal lamb. *See* Lamb
Passion narrative, 38, 39, 57, 180, 231
Passion of Christ, 41, 107, 146, 153, 179-85
Passover, 18, 38, 39, 57, 64-65, 66, 68, 72, 78, 84, 90, 91, 92, 132, 136, 142, 145, 147, 181, 188, 189-90, 192, 194, 518, 525
Passover Lamb. *See* Lamb
Patmos, 238, 336, 337, 339, 359-60
Patron angels, 362
Patron deity, 375, 377, 432, 461
Paul, 22, 39, 277, 286, 296, 329, 406, 441, 443-44, 457, 521
    and Peter, 441, 443-44, 457, 521
    writings of, 23, 107, 226, 227, 231, 338n, 358, 386n
Peace, 28, 40, 74, 143, 156, 213, 239, 321, 331, 358, 401, 404, 474n, 482n, 498
Pella, 416-17, 418, 440, 441, 449, 450, 451-52, 522
Pentateuchal citation, 93
Pentecost, 65, 66, 152, 155, 169
    "Johannine," 213
    See also Feast

People of God, 41, 111, 132, 140, 169, 202, 257, 272, 277, 297, 340-41, 348, 377, 384, 393, 395, 396, 406, 456, 459n, 475, 491, 501, 508, 515

Pergamum, 361, 368, 374-77, 382, 524

Persecution, 33, 42, 140, 144, 156, 161, 162, 163, 166, 168, 175, 176, 221, 236, 337n, 340, 342, 343-44, 349, 351, 402, 403, 406-7, 439, 456, 457, 467, 477, 487, 492, 513, 516, 518, 522, 524
  faithful despite, 357, 374
  Neronian, 407, 416, 417-18, 441-42, 443-44, 452, 457, 459, 481, 499
  by Trajan, 460

Pestilence, 402, 486

Peter (apostle), 18, 20, 23, 37, 54, 58, 81, 146, 166n, 181, 182-83, 218, 219, 221, 320
  confession of, 58n, 95, 130
  denies Jesus, 147, 183-84, 186, 219
  and John, 146, 208, 211-12, 219, 220, 221, 228, 406
  and Paul, 441, 443-44, 457, 521
  rehabilitation of, 219-20, 221

Pharisees, 31, 32, 55, 56, 72, 78, 85, 102, 103-4, 108, 114, 115-18, 120, 121, 123-25, 131-32, 138, 191n, 522

Philadelphia, 361, 368, 384-85

Philemon, 23

Philip, 20, 54, 58, 91, 138, 153

Philo, 22, 26-27, 192, 522

Pilate. *See* Pontius Pilate

Pisteuete, 150, 214

Plagues, Egyptian, 413, 422-23, 424-29, 441, 472-73, 474-75, 477, 518, 525

Plato/Platonic, 25, 26, 35, 152, 234, 243, 519, 523

Pleroma, 236, 237

Plummer, Alfred, 309

Plutarch, 35, 36, 218n, 482

Pneumatics, 296

Pneumatology, 39, 40, 243, 244, 350, 351

Polycarp, 19, 20, 228, 234, 235, 330, 373

Pontius Pilate, 132, 200, 202, 203, 204, 236, 522; trial of Jesus, 180, 188-96, 205

Postmillennialism, 344, 345, 498, 523

Posttribulationists, 412, 415, 416

Praetorium, 188, 189

Prayer, 131, 143, 144, 180, 226, 279, 290, 315, 331, 390, 396, 407n, 422, 461n, 474
  answered, 154, 161, 293, 314
  Jesus' farewell, 174-77

In Jesus' name, 293

Predestination, 175

Premillennialism, 346, 347-48, 349, 357, 362, 498, 500n, 501, 519, 523

Prerogatives, divine, 86-87

Presbyter, 228, 229, 239, 271, 320, 322, 323, 326, 328, 329, 330, 331, 523

Preterism, 343-44, 345, 348, 357, 359, 362, 417n, 438, 441, 456, 492-93

Pretribulation rapture, 347, 414, 523

Pride, 110, 273, 369, 414, 523

Priests, 55, 56, 103, 107, 132, 190n, 352, 384, 393, 395-96, 441, 456, 467, 508, 509, 516, 517
  chief, 102, 132
  imperial, 460, 461, 462
  Jesus as, 170, 201, 361
  priest kings, 191
  See also Caiaphas; High priest

Productivity, spiritual, 159

Prologue
  to epistles, 314
  to Revelation, 356, 367, 368, 371, 374, 376, 378, 383, 384, 386
  See also Gospel of John

Prophecy, 433, 441, 468

Prophetic literature, 35, 40

Prophetic oracle, 359, 366-67, 369, 373, 376, 378, 383, 384, 386, 403n, 416, 523

Prophetic salvation, 367

Prophetic trance, 506, 508

Prophets
  Old Testament, 17, 33, 35, 39, 40, 56, 58, 66, 67, 80, 93, 94, 116, 138, 338, 342, 367, 408, 441, 521
  See also False prophets; Jesus: as prophet

Prostitute imagery, 480. *See also* Harlot

Protestant Reformation, 343, 345, 439

Protoevangelium, 452

Punishment, 55, 132, 191, 408, 418, 487, 490, 495

Purity, 283-84, 416n, 504, 510; ritual, 56, 189, 190

Pythagorean school, 22

Rabbinic Judaism. *See* Judaism

Rabbinic literature. 25, 30, 32, 55n, 73, 79, 85, 107, 137

Rabbis, 22, 49, 58, 72, 73, 85, 101, 115, 125, 129

Rapture, 347, 390, 412, 414-15, 517, 521, 523

temporary binding of, 489-99
See also Devil
Savior of the World, 303, 391, 514
Schürer, Emil, 116
Scofield Bible, The, 346
Scroll, 18, 19, 28, 170, 357, 401
    little, 432-35
    seven-sealed, 391, 392-94, 524
    See also Dead Sea Scrolls
Sealing, 413
Seal judgments, 400, 402-8, 412, 416, 422, 429, 473,
    493, 519, 524
Seal of God, 412, 428
Sea of Galilee, 90, 91, 201, 208n, 218-19
Sea of Tiberias, 208n, 218
Secessionists, Docetic, 22, 202, 232, 234, 238-39, 240,
    241, 242, 243, 244, 251, 255-56, 257, 260, 264-
    66, 272-73, 276-79, 284, 285, 291-93, 297, 302-
    5, 308, 314, 315-16, 322, 326-28, 330-31, 524
Second coming, 29, 41, 42, 60, 152, 168, 232, 244,
    276, 279, 341, 342, 346, 348, 356, 359, 466,
    469, 490, 491, 492-93, 495, 498, 508, 515, 517,
    520, 522, 523, 524
Second death, 500, 501
Second John (writings), 249, 251
    format of, 239, 320, 323
    relationship with 3 John, 239, 241
Second Temple Judaism, 57n, 139, 143, 153n, 226n,
    422, 525
Sectarian perspective, 22, 33
Seraphim, 395
Serpent, 429, 449, 450, 452, 499, 505
Seven ancient wonders of the world, 432
Seven churches of Asia Minor, 338, 342, 347, 351, 356,
    357-58, 359, 361, 362, 366-78, 387, 396n, 513, 523
Seven hills of Rome, 450, 480, 517
Seven kings, 340, 351
Seven lampstands, 361, 362, 371
Seven letters, 366-67, 369
Seven-sealed scroll, 392-94
Seven signs, 62, 128, 130, 214
Seven spirits, 358, 383
Seven stars, 361, 362, 371
Seventh seal, 400, 412, 422
Seven trumpets, 422, 423
Shea, W. H., 367
Shema, 174

Shepherds, 27, 120-21, 122, 169, 202, 370. *See also*
    Jesus: as Good Shepherd
Shroud, 211
Shroud of Turin, 203, 212
Sibling rivalry, 291, 347
Sickness, 39, 114, 128, 377, 504, 505
Sign miracles, 16, 62, 64, 81, 84, 115, 128, 130, 132,
    136n, 513, 524
Signs of the times, 29, 161, 276, 279, 402, 404, 515,
    518, 524
Siloam, 103, 106, 114, 115
Simon of Cyrene, 180, 200, 202-3, 204, 205, 237
Simon Peter, 219. *See also* Peter (apostle)
Sin offering, 145
Sin unto death, 314-15, 524
Skull place, 200
Smoke, 474, 490
Smyrna, 234, 342, 361, 368, 372-74, 382, 384
Socrates, 26, 35
Song of Songs, 491
Song of the Lamb, 474
Son of God, 16, 30, 33, 34, 37, 40, 48, 59, 123, 124,
    130, 167, 175, 214, 232, 234, 237, 240, 251, 297,
    298, 303, 308, 309, 310, 314, 321
Son of Man, 25, 40, 42, 59-60, 62, 74, 110, 117, 139,
    214, 513, 519, 524; heavenly, 356, 361
Sons of darkness, 29, 139, 245
Sons of light, 29, 139, 245
Sorcery, 507
Sorrow, 161, 169, 486, 504
Soteriology, 39, 40-41, 243
Spirit, 24, 41, 42, 48, 57, 73, 80, 103, 104, 166-70,
    176n, 205, 242, 265, 278, 285, 290, 296, 297
    arrival of, 170
    contrasted with flesh, 73, 234
    future coming of, 154, 155, 156, 162
    See also Holy Spirit
Spiritual birth, 73, 285, 513
Spiritual blindness, 117–18, 266, 386
Spiritual darkness, 72, 118, 255, 266, 298, 339, 401, 475
Spiritualist view, 344
Spiritual life, 93, 130, 291, 315
Spiritual union, 176, 244, 303, 316
Stars
    seven, 361, 362, 371, 383, 396n
    twelve, 401, 402, 423, 425, 426, 449
Stoicism, 22, 25, 26-27, 43, 47n

Stolen body theory, 209
Substitutionary death, 244
Suffering, 28, 60, 139, 146, 169, 183, 257, 330, 360, 377, 406, 450, 516
Suffering Servant, 57, 139, 140, 202, 204, 350, 393, 517, 521
Supernatural world, 337n, 429, 448
Supreme sign miracle, 128n
Swoon theory, 209
Sychar, 79
Synagogue, 34, 55, 81, 93, 184, 382, 383, 525
    debate, 234
    expulsion from, 30-33, 34, 116-17, 163, 234, 237, 349, 373, 384, 513, 517
    "of Satan," 342, 373, 384, 525
Syncretism, 371, 376, 383, 386
Synoptic Gospels
    cleansing of the temple, 38, 68
    disciples, 58n, 180
    Jesus in Gethsemane, 146n, 180
    Jesus on trial, 108, 124n, 191, 195
    Jesus' parables, 121
    Jesus' passion, 180
    Jesus walking on water, 92
    John the Baptist in prison, 78
    Last Supper, 18, 21, 38, 142
    Olivet Discourse, 161, 168n, 402-8
    Passover, 65, 142
    Peter's confession, 95
    resurrection, 208
    seal judgment, 402-8
    Simon of Cyrene, 180, 200
    Son of Man, 60

Tabernacle, 50, 67, 258, 259, 266, 474
Tabernacles feast. *See* Feast
Talmud, 30n, 161, 190
Tatian, 24, 525
Teknia, 147, 257, 270, 271, 276, 279, 282n, 330n
Teleioō, 265
Temple
    cleansing of, 38, 62, 64-68
    eschatological, 103, 150, 153, 438, 439n, 441, 475
    feasts, 377
    figurative vs. literal, 439-40
    heavenly, 390n, 391, 392, 418, 423, 439n, 468, 469, 474

Herod's, 100, 109, 112n, 438, 525
    inner court, 65, 443
    Jesus at, 101, 102, 108, 114, 123, 184
    Jewish, 39, 50, 55, 78, 84, 104, 107, 110, 123, 132, 142, 150, 185, 189, 190, 226n, 266, 278, 457
    New, 50, 66, 103, 178, 440
    outer court, 443n
    pagan/imperial, 369, 371, 373, 374-76, 377, 382, 385-86, 424, 461
    police, 102, 103-4, 181, 184, 186, 189, 196
    See also Second Temple Judaism
Tertullian, 19, 24, 230, 338
The Baptist. *See* John the Baptist
Theodicy, 350
Theology
    covenant, 159
    Deuteronomic, 160
    of John, 17, 39-42, 180, 226, 243-45
    of Revelation, 336, 350-52
    Samaritan, 80
Theophilus of Antioch, 19
Theurgy, 461
Third John (writings), 22, 228-29, 230, 231, 235, 237, 239, 243, 519
    format and genre, 226-27, 240, 328
    relationship with 2 John, 239, 241, 326, 327
This age, 28-29, 139, 244, 337
Thomas, 20, 152-53, 166n, 208, 213, 218
Three Fathers, 110
Throne
    of God, 350, 360, 390n, 395, 396
    heavenly, 391, 392, 499
    satanic, 351, 374
Thunder, 396, 432, 476-77
Thyatira, 361, 368, 377-78, 382
Tiberius, 65n, 194, 384, 457, 480
Tiber River, 480
Tree of Life, 372, 505, 511
Tribulation period, 41, 161, 169, 244, 347-48, 349, 412, 413-14, 415, 441, 452, 453, 467, 516, 517. *See also* Great Tribulation
Trinity
    divine, 48, 155, 162n, 244, 298, 350, 351, 358, 394n
    evil, 475
True faith, 50, 68, 72, 110, 277, 314
True God, 152, 174, 243, 316, 375, 377, 505
True Israel, 33, 158, 352, 361, 426, 449, 450n, 451

True light, 48, 49, 231
True One, 316, 384
True oracle. *See* Oracle
True worship, 78, 79–80, 443
Trumpet judgments, 400, 401, 407n, 416, 422-27, 429,
    432, 433, 434, 438, 444, 473-77, 488, 493, 518,
    525
Truth, 72, 73, 101, 108, 111n, 156, 167, 235, 242, 244,
    248, 254-56, 264, 265, 266, 277, 279, 290, 292,
    293n, 315, 328, 329, 331, 339, 520
    about Jesus, 40, 48, 86, 93, 94n, 152, 168, 189, 191,
        236, 250, 321, 323, 350
    and love, 321-22, 326-27, 329
    Spirit and, 80, 242
    Spirit of, 296, 297
    walk in, 321-22, 330
Twelfth benediction, 31, 33, 116, 367, 525
Twelve tribes of Israel, 352, 412, 413, 416n, 418, 449,
    467, 508
Twenty-four elders, 391, 395-96, 418, 491
Twofold theme, 166–67
Two spirits, 29, 296, 297

Unbelieving Jews, 98, 125, 369
Underworld, 370, 495, 501
Unfaithful, 426, 434, 480
Unity (union), spiritual, 40, 41, 124, 176-77, 221, 244,
    303, 316
Universalism, 49
Unrighteousness, 256, 501
Upper Room Discourse. *See* Discourses
Urzeit-Endzeit pattern, 504

Valentinus, 23, 236-37
Vast throng, 395, 396
Verbs, 36, 48, 49, 115n, 150, 162n, 194n, 218n, 249,
    250, 254n
    aorist tense, 124n, 147n, 214, 248, 249, 302n, 308,
        362n
    perfect tense, 270, 271
    present tense, 162, 249, 254n, 286n, 308, 315
    present participle, 176n
    present subjunctive, 214
    preterist tense, 378–379, 383, 393, 395, 398, 472,
        474, 490, 530
    sensory, 248, 249
    subjunctive, 279, 292n, 304

Vespasian, 63, 340, 341, 403n, 405, 417, 457, 480, 481
Vesuvius, Mount, 407, 422, 424, 425-26, 429
Victorinus, 341
Vine and branches, 158-61
Vitellius, 132, 340, 341, 404, 457, 482n
Von Wahlde, Urban C., 231-32

War, Holy. *See* Holy War
War Scroll, 170
Water. *See* Blood and water; Living Water; Jesus: walks
    on
Water-drawing ceremony, 102, 107
Water of life, 42, 511
Wedding (at Cana), 54, 62, 78
Westcott, B. F., 18, 19, 240
White horse of Antichrist, 401, 403-4
Wicked, the, 29, 55, 139, 481n, 501, 511
"Wicked Priest," 132
Wine, 160n, 201, 342, 370, 374, 405, 461; changing
    water into, 62-64, 84n
Winepress judgment, 466, 468-69, 494
Wisdom, 22, 26, 37, 236, 370, 394; Jesus as, 47, 48, 49
Wisdom texts, 46, 47, 94
Witnesses, 20, 153, 184, 196, 211, 438-42, 443-44
    eyewitnesses, 20, 339, 403n, 426
    of Jesus, 48, 58, 84, 87, 108, 249, 310
"Woe" oracle, 426
Woman
    adulterous, 98, 106-7
    with child, 448
    protection of, 451-52
    at the well, 78–80
Wonders of the world, ancient, 466
Word, the, 40, 42, 47, 48, 231n, 238, 248, 309n
Word became flesh, 42, 46, 47, 229, 231n, 232
Word of life, 20, 229, 248
World, 34, 39, 42, 46, 48, 49, 57, 80, 108, 122, 138,
    143, 152, 155, 158, 161, 162, 163, 167, 169, 170,
    177, 188, 205, 213, 221, 236, 240, 244, 272-73
    ancient, 24, 31, 102n, 366, 369, 377, 391, 392, 413
    correlated phrases about, 175-76
    Greek, 22, 24
    Jewish, 22, 181
    Mediterranean, 24
    modern, 25
    "not of this world," 188, 191, 193
    separation from, 316

Dictionary of Biblical Prophecy and End Times

J. Daniel Hays, J. Scott Duvall, and C. Marvin Pate

All you ever wanted to know about biblical prophecy from A to Z, the *Dictionary of Biblical Prophecy and End Times* is a comprehensive reference tool. It is written for those who truly desire to understand prophecy and the end times. Starting with "Abomination of Desolation" and continuing through hundreds of articles until "Zionism," this book provides helpful and interesting discussions of the entire range of biblical prophecy, all at your fingertips.

This exhaustive work contains articles on a broad sweep of topics relevant to the study of biblical prophecy and eschatology. The articles are based on solid scholarship, yet are clear and accessible to the lay reader, illuminating even the most complicated issues. The authors balance their presentation by laying out differing positions along with each position's strengths and weaknesses. They do not push any specific theological or interpretive agenda, but have a firm commitment to seeking to understand the Scriptures. This is a valuable tool you will refer to time and again.

Available in stores and online!